Research Handbook on
Rights Law

RESEARCH HANDBOOKS IN INTERNATIONAL LAW

This highly original series offers a unique appraisal of the state of the art of research and thinking in international law. Taking a thematic approach, each volume, edited by a prominent expert, covers a specific aspect of international law or examines the international legal dimension of a particular strand of the law. A wide range of sub-disciplines in the spheres of both public and private law are considered; from international environmental law to international criminal law, from international economic law to the law of international organisations, and from international commercial law to international human rights law. The *Research Handbooks* comprise carefully commissioned chapters from leading academics as well as those with an emerging reputation. Taking a genuinely international approach to the law, and addressing current and sometimes controversial legal issues, as well as affording a clear substantive analysis of the law, these *Handbooks* are designed to inform as well as to contribute to current debates.

Equally useful as reference tools or introductions to specific topics, issues and debates, the *Handbooks* will be used by academic researchers, post-graduate students, practising lawyers and lawyers in policy circles.

Titles in this series include:

Research Handbook in International Economic Law
*Edited by Andrew T. Guzman and Alan O. Sykes*

Research Handbook on International Human Rights Law
*Edited by Sarah Joseph and Adam McBeth*

Handbook of Research on International Consumer Law
*Edited by Geraint Howells, Iain Ramsay and Thomas Wilhelmsson with David Kraft*

# Research Handbook on International Human Rights Law

*Edited by*

Sarah Joseph

*Professor of Law and Director, Castan Centre for Human Rights Law, Monash University, Australia*

Adam McBeth

*Senior Lecturer and Deputy Director, Castan Centre for Human Rights Law, Monash University, Australia*

RESEARCH HANDBOOKS IN INTERNATIONAL LAW

**Edward Elgar**
Cheltenham, UK • Northampton, MA, USA

© The Editors and Contributors Severally 2010

All rights reserved. No part of this publication may be reproduced, stored in a retrieval system or transmitted in any form or by any means, electronic, mechanical or photocopying, recording, or otherwise without the prior permission of the publisher.

Published by
Edward Elgar Publishing Limited
The Lypiatts
15 Lansdown Road
Cheltenham
Glos GL50 2JA
UK

Edward Elgar Publishing, Inc.
William Pratt House
9 Dewey Court
Northampton
Massachusetts 01060
USA

A catalogue record for this book is available from the British Library

Library of Congress Control Number: 2009937758

ISBN 978 1 84720 368 7 (cased)

Typeset by Cambrian Typesetters, Camberley, Surrey
Printed and bound by MPG Books Group, UK

# Contents

| | | |
|---|---|---|
| *List of contributors* | | vii |
| *Preface* | | xiii |
| 1 | The United Nations and human rights<br>*Sarah Joseph and Joanna Kyriakakis* | 1 |
| 2 | Economic, social and cultural rights: an examination of state obligations<br>*Manisuli Ssenyonjo* | 36 |
| 3 | Extraterritoriality: universal human rights without universal obligations?<br>*Sigrun I Skogly* | 71 |
| 4 | Non-state actors and international human rights law<br>*Robert McCorquodale* | 97 |
| 5 | NGOs and human rights: channels of power<br>*Peter J Spiro* | 115 |
| 6 | Human rights in economic globalisation<br>*Adam McBeth* | 139 |
| 7 | Human rights and development<br>*Stephen P Marks* | 167 |
| 8 | Gender and international human rights law: the intersectionality agenda<br>*Anastasia Vakulenko* | 196 |
| 9 | Refugees and displaced persons: the refugee definition and 'humanitarian' protection<br>*Susan Kneebone* | 215 |
| 10 | International criminal law<br>*Elies van Sliedregt and Desislava Stoitchkova* | 241 |
| 11 | The four pillars of transitional justice: a gender-sensitive analysis<br>*Ronli Sifris* | 272 |
| 12 | The International Court of Justice and human rights<br>*Sandesh Sivakumaran* | 299 |
| 13 | The Council of Europe and the protection of human rights: a system in need of reform<br>*Virginia Mantouvalou and Panayotis Voyatzis* | 326 |

| | | |
|---|---|---|
| 14 | The Inter-American human rights system: selected examples of its supervisory work<br>*Diego Rodríguez-Pinzón and Claudia Martin* | 353 |
| 15 | African human rights law in theory and practice<br>*Magnus Killander* | 388 |
| 16 | The political economy and culture of human rights in East Asia<br>*Michael C Davis* | 414 |
| 17 | Islam and the realization of human rights in the Muslim world<br>*Mashood A Baderin* | 440 |
| 18 | Religion, belief and international human rights in the twenty-first century<br>*Peter Cumper* | 467 |
| 19 | DRIP feed: the slow reconstruction of self-determination for Indigenous peoples<br>*Melissa Castan* | 492 |
| 20 | Counter-terrorism and human rights<br>*Alex Conte* | 512 |
| 21 | Human rights education: a slogan in search of a definition<br>*Paula Gerber* | 541 |

*Index* 567

# Contributors

**Mashood A Baderin** is currently Professor of Law and Head of the School of Law at the School of Oriental and African Studies (SOAS), University of London. He researches in the areas of Islamic Law; International Law; International and Comparative Human Rights Law; Human Rights and Islamic Law, with particular interest in the interaction between International Law, Human Rights Law and Islamic law in Muslim States. Amongst his publications are *International Human Rights and Islamic Law* (OUP, 2003 and 2005), *International Law and Islamic Law* (Ashgate, 2008) and articles in leading international academic journals. He is a founding co-editor of the *Muslim World Journal of Human Rights*.

**Melissa Castan** is a Senior Lecturer and Deputy Director for the Castan Centre for Human Rights Law. Her teaching and research interests are domestic and international Indigenous legal issues, constitutional law, international human rights law and legal education. She has various publications on Indigenous rights under international law, and recently authored *Constitutional Law* (Pearson Education, 2008). She is co-author of *The International Covenant on Civil and Political Rights: Cases, Commentary and Materials* (OUP, 2004) and *Federal Constitutional Law: A Contemporary View* (Lawbook, 2006). She is currently running a major research project on capacity building for native title bodies with the Australian government.

**Alex Conte** is a consultant on security and human rights (www.alexconte.com) who has worked within government and international organisations, in private legal practice, and as a professor of international law. A member of the advisory panel of experts to the United Nations Special Rapporteur on the Promotion and Protection of Human Rights and Fundamental Freedoms while Countering Terrorism, Dr Conte is also a fellow to the International Policy Institute on Counter-Terrorism. He is the Series Editor of the Ashgate International Law Series, and was the founding General Editor of the *New Zealand Yearbook of International Law*.

**Peter Cumper** is a Senior Lecturer in the School of Law in the University of Leicester, where he teaches Constitutional and Administrative Law, Human Rights Law, and Law and Religion. He has published in a number of journals in the UK and overseas, and is the joint editor of *Minority Rights in the 'New' Europe* (Kluwer, 1999).

**Michael C Davis** is a Professor of Law at the Chinese University of Hong Kong. He has served as the J. Landis Martin Visiting Professor of Law at Northwestern University Law School (2005–2006), the Robert and Marion Short Visiting Professor of Law at Notre Dame Law School (2004–2005) and as the Schell Senior Fellow in Human Rights at the Yale Law School (1994–1995). He has also served as the Chair of the Human Rights Research Committee of the International Political Science Association and Chair of the Pacific Rim Interest Group of the American Society of International Law. His books include *Constitutional Confrontation in Hong Kong* (Macmillan Press, 1990), *Human Rights and Chinese Values* (OUP, 1995), and *International Intervention in the Post-Cold War World: Moral Responsibility and Power Politics* (M.E. Sharpe, 2004). He holds degrees from Ohio State University, the University of California and Yale Law School.

**Paula Gerber** has been a lawyer for over 20 years. She spent five years working as a solicitor in London, and five years as an attorney in Los Angeles before returning to Australia where she became a partner in a leading Melbourne law firm. Paula is now a Senior Lecturer in Law at Monash University and a Deputy Director of the Castan Centre for Human Rights Law. Dr Gerber is an internationally recognised expert on human rights education. She is the author of the book *From Convention to Classroom: The Long Road to Human Rights Education* (VDM Publishing, 2008), as well as numerous articles and book chapters about educating for human rights.

**Sarah Joseph** is Professor of Human Rights Law and Director of the Castan Centre for Human Rights Law in the Faculty of Law at Monash University. She has published many books and articles on human rights, on topics such as the International Covenant on Civil and Political Rights, corporations and human rights, trade and human rights, terrorism and human rights, torture, and self determination. She is also an expert on Australian constitutional law. She has been the recipient of Australian government funded grants for human rights research. She has taught human rights in many different contexts nationally and internationally, including undergraduate, postgraduate, and at professional training seminars.

**Magnus Killander** is a doctoral candidate and research co-ordinator at the Centre for Human Rights, Faculty of Law, South Africa. He has a law degree from the University of Lund, Sweden, and a European Masters Degree in Human Rights and Democratisation. Mr Killander is co-editor of the *African Human Rights Law Reports*, associate editor of *International Law in Domestic Courts (ILDC)* and editor of the Africa component of *International Human Rights Law (IHRL)*. ILDC and IHRL form part of the *Oxford Reports on International Law*, an online service published by Oxford University Press.

The research of Mr Killander has been published in inter alia *African Human Rights Law Journal*, *Human Rights Quarterly* and the *Max Planck Encyclopedia of Public International Law*.

**Susan Kneebone** is a Professor of Law and a Deputy Director of the Castan Centre for Human Rights Law at the Faculty of Law, Monash University. Susan teaches forced migration and human rights, international refugee law and practice, and citizenship and migration law. She has organised several conferences and workshops on these issues, made submission to public enquiries and frequently handles media enquiries. She is the author of many articles on these issues and editor of several books, as well as the recipient of several research grants from the Australian government.

**Joanna Kyriakakis** is a Lecturer at the Faculty of Law, Monash University. Joanna received Arts/First Class Honours Law degrees from Flinders University in 2001 and a Doctor of Juridical Science degree from Monash University in 2009. She has published a number of articles on the subject of corporations and public international law appearing in the *Journal of International Criminal Justice*, *Criminal Law Forum*, and the *Monash University Law Review*. Joanna has worked as a Legal Officer with the South Australian Crown Solicitor's Office and as a Solicitor in both private and community legal practice, specialising in criminal, family and administrative law. Her current research focus is international criminal law, comparative criminal law and international human rights law.

**Virginia Mantouvalou** is Lecturer in Law and Deputy Director of the Centre for European Law and Integration at the University of Leicester. She holds a PhD and an LLM in Human Rights from the London School of Economics, and an LLB from the University of Athens.

**Stephen P Marks**, Docteur d'État, Dipl. IHEI, is the François-Xavier Bagnoud Professor of Health and Human Rights and Director of the Program on Human Rights in Development at the Harvard School of Public Health. He also teaches in the Faculty of Arts and Sciences at Harvard University. He is currently chair of the UN High Level Task Force on the Implementation of the Right to Development of the Human Rights Council.

**Claudia Martin** is a Professorial Lecturer in Residence and Co-Director of the Academy on Human Rights and Humanitarian Law at American University Washington College of Law. She holds a law degree from the University of Buenos Aires, an LLM from American University Washington College of Law, and also completed graduate studies in international relations at a program sponsored by the Ministry of Foreign Affairs of Argentina and the Government of Italy. She teaches and specialises in international law, international and comparative human rights law and Inter-American human rights law. She serves on several international boards, including the Editorial Board of Oxford Reports on International Law in Domestic Courts, Oxford University Press and Amsterdam Center for International Law. Professor Martin is also a contributor on Inter-American Human Rights Law for several specialised human rights publications.

**Adam McBeth** is a Deputy Director of the Castan Centre for Human Rights Law and a senior lecturer in the Faculty of Law at Monash University, where he specialises in international law and human rights subjects. Adam has been part of a team delivering human rights training courses to government and civil society representatives from Australia, Indonesia and Iraq. He is the author of *International Economic Actors and Human Rights* (Routledge, 2009).

**Robert McCorquodale** is the Director of the British Institute of International and Comparative Law in London. He is also Professor of International Law and Human Rights, and former Head of the School of Law, at the University of Nottingham. Previously he was a Fellow and Lecturer in Law at St. John's College, University of Cambridge and at the Australian National University in Canberra. Before embarking on an academic career, he worked as a qualified lawyer in commercial litigation with leading law firms in Sydney and London. Robert's research and teaching interests are in the areas of public international law and human rights law. He has published widely on these areas, and has provided advice to governments, corporations, international organisations, non-governmental organisations and peoples concerning international law and human rights issues, including advising on the drafting of new constitutions and conducting human rights training courses.

**Diego Rodríguez-Pinzón** is Professorial Lecturer in Residence and Co-Director of the Academy on Human Rights and Humanitarian Law at American University, Washington College of Law. He teaches courses in the fields of international law and human rights law. He is currently Ad Hoc Judge in the Inter-American Court on Human Rights of the Organization of American States. He has published extensively in the field of human rights law. As correspondent for the British periodical *Butterworths Human Rights Cases*, Professor Rodríguez-Pinzón covers the Americas; he also reports on the Inter-American system for the *Netherlands Quarterly of Human Rights*.

**Ronli Sifris** received her BA/ LLB (Hons) from Monash University in 2003 where she graduated first in her class and her LLM in International Legal Studies from New York University in 2006 as a Hauser Scholar. She was admitted to practice in Victoria in 2005 and New York in 2008. Ronli has worked as a consultant with the International Center for Transitional Justice in

New York and is currently completing a PhD at Monash University. She has published numerous articles addressing various aspects of international law.

**Sandesh Sivakumaran** is a lecturer at the School of Law and member of the Human Rights Law Centre, University of Nottingham. He has worked at the International Court of Justice, the International Criminal Tribunal for the former Yugoslavia and the Special Court for Sierra Leone. He is a member of the International Law Association Committee on International Human Rights Law.

**Sigrun I Skogly** is Professor of Human Rights Law at Lancaster University Law School, UK and Visiting Professor at Buskerud University College, Norway. She is the author of a number of articles on human rights obligations, economic, social, and cultural rights, and the relationship between human rights and poverty. Her current research concerns states' extraterritorial human rights obligations. She is the author of *The Human Rights Obligations of the World Bank and the International Monetary Fund* (Cavendish, 2001), *Beyond National Borders: States' Human Rights Obligations in International Cooperation* (Intersentia, 2006), and co-editor with Mark Gibney of *Universal Human Rights and Extraterritorial Obligations* (forthcoming 2010).

**Peter J Spiro** is Charles Weiner Professor of Law at Temple University Law School. He has written widely on the role of non-state actors in international affairs, the constitutional law of US foreign relations, and citizenship practice. He is the author of *Beyond Citizenship: American Identity after Globalization* (OUP, 2008).

**Manisuli Ssenyonjo** is a Senior Lecturer in Law at Brunel University, London, where he teaches and researches in areas of Public International Law and Human Rights Law. He has published widely on these areas, and has provided advice to governments, corporations, international organisations, and non-governmental organisations concerning human rights issues, including conducting human rights training courses. His recent publications include several articles published in international journals including the *Nordic Journal of International Law*, *Netherlands International Law Review*, *International Journal of Constitutional Law*, *Chinese Journal of International Law*, *Netherlands Quarterly of Human Rights*, *African Journal of International an Comparative Law*, *Human Rights Law Review*, *International Journal of Law, Policy and the Family*, *The International Journal of Human Rights*, and *International Criminal Law Review*. He is the author of several book chapters and a recent monograph on *Economic, Social and Cultural Rights in International Law* (Hart Publishing, 2009).

**Desislava Stoitchkova** is doctoral researcher and lecturer of international criminal law at Utrecht University, the Netherlands. Her research is currently focused on the topic of direct corporate criminal responsibility in the context of the International Criminal Court (ICC). She is also involved in human rights training projects with magistrates and non-governmental organisations both in the Netherlands and abroad. Previously she was a researcher at the Netherlands Institute of Human Rights (2004–2006) and clerked at the ICC in 2003.

**Anastasia Vakulenko** is a lecturer in law at the University of Birmingham. Having obtained her LLM and PhD degrees at the University of Nottingham, she previously lectured at the University of Dundee. Her research interests are in the area of human rights law, examined through the prism of feminist and critical theory, as well as religion and secularism studies.

**Elies van Sliedregt** is Professor of Criminal Law and Procedure at VU University Amsterdam. She is a member of the editorial board of the *Leiden Journal of International Law* and is President of the International Criminal Law Network, based in the Hague. She sits as a part-time judge in the extradition chamber of the District Court in Amsterdam and is a member of The Young Academy of The Royal Netherlands Academy of Arts and Sciences. Her research interests lie in the field of international, European and comparative criminal law.

**Panayotis Voyatzis** is a Lawyer at the European Court of Human Rights. He holds a PhD and an LLM in Public Law and Human Rights from the University Paris I (Panthéon-Sorbonne), and an LLB from the University of Athens.

# Preface

The compilation and editing of a research handbook on international human rights law is a daunting task, given the vast breadth of the subject matter and, alas, the sheer number of different human rights issues arising around the globe. We can assure readers that we know that many important topics have been missed – it is simply impossible to encapsulate them all in a single book. However, we are also confident that the chapters presented herein provide a first-rate grounding for scholars seeking to wrap their heads around most of the major topics within the discipline. The chapters are designed to be both accessible to the novice human rights scholar and yet of great interest to the seasoned human rights researcher.

This handbook brings together the work of 25 leading human rights scholars from all over the world. As the various chapters overlap in theme, it was not possible to organise the book into separate parts: rather we have chosen to organise the book into a logical order, though the chapters can of course be read in any order. The book begins with some chapters outlining general issues regarding human rights, such as the history of norm generation, institution building and enforcement at the global level (Chapter 1 – Sarah Joseph and Joanna Kyriakakis) and the state of play regarding economic, social and cultural rights (Chapter 2 – Manisuli Ssenyonjo). The book then moves to examine jurisdictional issues, such as human rights and extraterritoriality (Chapter 3 – Sigrun Skogly), and human rights in the non-state sphere (Chapter 4 – Robert McCorquodale). Chapter 5 (Peter Spiro) logically follows Chapter 4, outlining the crucial role of non-government organisations in enforcing and promoting human rights norms. The next six chapters cover overlaps between human rights law and, respectively, international economic law (Chapter 6 – Adam McBeth), development law (Chapter 7 – Stephen Marks), feminist theory (Chapter 8 – Anastasia Vakulenko), international refugee law (Chapter 9 – Susan Kneebone), international criminal law (Chapter 10 – Elies van Sliedregt and Desislava Stoitchkova), and transitional justice (Chapter 11 – Ronli Sifris). The following chapters then take a more institutional approach, focusing on the role of the International Court of Justice in the protection of human rights (Chapter 12 – Sandesh Sivakumaran), the protection of human rights within the European system (Chapter 13 – Virginia Mantouvalou and Panayotis Voyatzis), protection of human rights within the Inter-American system (Chapter 14 – Diego Rodríguez-Pinzón and Claudia Martin), and protection of human rights within the African Union

(Chapter 15 – Magnus Killander). Continuing the regional theme, Chapter 16 (Michael Davis) analyses human rights initiatives in Asia, while Chapter 17 (Mashood Baderin) captures human rights perspectives from the Muslim world. Chapter 18 (Peter Cumper) connects to Chapter 17, in examining human rights and religious rights. Like Chapter 18, the final three chapters examine human rights in relation to specific issues: namely Indigenous rights (Chapter 19 – Melissa Castan), terrorism (Chapter 20 – Alex Conte), and human rights education (Chapter 21 – Paula Gerber).

We must thank our authors for their excellent contributions and cooperation in the preparation of this volume. In particular, we must thank Cameron Miles and Sarah Mauriks for their invaluable research assistance. We must thank all of the crew at Edward Elgar for their support, assistance and patience. Sarah must thank her family, especially her parents, and friends for their support. Adam wishes to thank his wife, Belinda, and his parents. We must both thank our colleagues at the Castan Centre for Human Rights Law, as well as the Monash Law Faculty.

# 1. The United Nations and human rights
## *Sarah Joseph and Joanna Kyriakakis*

## 1 Introduction

After the Second World War, the United Nations ('UN') brought human rights firmly into the sphere of international law in its own constituent document, the UN Charter,[1] in 1945.[2] The purposes of the UN included, in Article 1(3), the promotion and encouragement of human rights and fundamental freedoms. Under Articles 55 and 56, Member States are committed to 'joint and separate action' to create 'conditions of stability and well-being' across the world, including the promotion of 'universal respect for, and observance of, human rights and fundamental freedoms for all without distinction as to race, sex, language, or religion'. Thus, from 1945, it was clear that human rights could no longer be characterised as a domestic issue, hidden by the veil of State sovereignty.

Since 1945, the UN has been instrumental in the process of standard-setting, that is, creating treaties and other documents that set out universally recognised human rights. Most famously of course, it adopted the *Universal Declaration on Human Rights* ('UDHR') in 1948,[3] following up (though years later) with a series of treaties protecting various human rights.

The UN has also created various internal institutions to monitor and supervise the implementation of human rights. There are political bodies, established under the rubric of the UN Charter, such as the Human Rights Council and its predecessor, the Commission on Human Rights. There are treaty bodies, established under the core UN human rights treaties, which monitor the implementation and interpretation of their particular treaties.

State sovereignty, however, continues to play a crucial role in relation to the enforcement of human rights, long regarded as the 'Achilles heel' of the global human rights system. Enforcement mechanisms are generally quite

---

[1] Charter of the United Nations, 1 UNTS XVI, 24 October 1945 ('UN Charter').

[2] Human rights were largely unprotected by international law prior to the Second World War, with exceptions arising, for example, in the context of international humanitarian law and the rights of aliens.

[3] GA Res 217(111) of 10 December 1948, UN Doc A/810 at 71 (1948) ('UDHR').

weak, with only the UN Security Council empowered to mandate sanctions that go beyond mere condemnation by the international community. While international human rights law has developed to the point where States can no longer legitimately claim that human rights are solely a domestic matter, there are significant limits to the international community's ability to respond to recalcitrant States that persist in human rights abuses. Enforcement machinery has not kept pace with standard-setting.

In this chapter, we will analyse three elements of the UN's role in international human rights law: standard-setting, the main UN human rights institutions, and the vexed question of enforcement.

## 2 Standard-setting

The UN endorsed a list of recognised human rights in the UDHR. No State, either in 1948 or upon joining the UN, has ever denounced the UDHR.[4] The UDHR itself was reaffirmed in the *Vienna Declaration and Programme of Action*,[5] adopted after the World Conference on Human Rights in 1993, and remains the cornerstone expression of global human rights values. The UDHR was not adopted as a legally binding instrument. It is arguable however that its norms have come to be crystallised as customary international law by the present day.[6] Furthermore, it is arguable that the UDHR defines 'human rights' for the purposes of the human rights provisions of the UN Charter, such as Articles 1(3), 55 and 56, which are recognised as peremptory international norms.[7]

The standard-setting activities of the UN, which had got off to such a quick start with the UDHR being adopted within a few years of the institution's creation, became bogged down with Cold War politics. No new standards were adopted until 1965, with the adoption of the *International Convention on the Elimination of all Forms of Racial Discrimination* ('CERD').[8] Between

---

[4] Eight States abstained when the General Assembly adopted the UDHR: Byelorussia, Czechoslovakia, Poland, the Ukraine, the USSR, Yugoslavia, Saudi Arabia, and South Africa.

[5] UN Doc A/CONF.157/23 (1993), 25 June 1993, endorsed by GA Res 48/121 of 14 February 1994, [2].

[6] See, eg, Louis B Sohn, 'The new international law: protection of the rights of individuals rather than States' (1982) 32 *American University Law Review* 1, 15–17. On the other hand, it is perhaps arguable that, while some UDHR rights may satisfy the tests of customary international law (State practice and *opinio juris*), such as the right to be free from torture, it is optimistic to ascribe such a status to the full slate of UDHR rights.

[7] Ibid, 16. See also Chapter 12, p. 316.

[8] Opened for signature 7 March 1966, 660 UNTS 195 (entered into force 4 January 1969).

1948 and 1965, however, an important circumstance was the influx of newly decolonised nations into the UN, bringing a new perspective to the human rights debate. The strong influence of this group within the UN is evident in the *Declaration on the Granting of Independence to Colonial Countries and Peoples* of 1960,[9] which acknowledged the evils of colonialism and the importance of the right of self-determination, and the strong condemnation of apartheid in General Assembly Resolution 1761 of 1962.[10] It is not surprising that CERD, the first human rights treaty adopted by the UN, focused on an issue with which developing States were most concerned.

In 1966, most of the norms in the UDHR[11] were enshrined in two legal documents, the *International Covenant on Economic, Social and Cultural Rights* ('ICESCR')[12] and the *International Covenant on Civil and Political Rights* ('ICCPR').[13] The three documents are often collectively called 'The International Bill of Rights'. The splitting of the UDHR rights into two sets of rights was driven by a number of issues, including perceived differences between the respective categories of rights[14] and Cold War divisions: the Eastern bloc tended to champion ICESCR rights, while Western States were seen as the major proponents of ICCPR rights.[15] An Optional Protocol to the ICCPR was also adopted in 1966, providing for a right of individual petition in respect of violations of the ICCPR against States that ratify that Protocol.

Another lull in standard-setting was followed in 1979 by the adoption of the *Convention on the Elimination of All Forms of Discrimination against Women* ('CEDAW'),[16] the *Convention against Torture and other Cruel, Inhuman and Degrading Treatment or Punishment* ('CAT')[17] in 1984, the *Convention on*

---

[9] GA Res 1514 (XV) of 14 December 1960, UN Doc A/4684 (1960).

[10] GA Res 1761 (XVII) of 6 November 1962.

[11] Certain discrete rights are excluded, such as the right to seek and enjoy asylum (Article 14) and the right to property (Article 17).

[12] Opened for signature 16 December 1966, 993 UNTS 3 (entered into force 3 January 1976).

[13] Opened for signature 16 December 1966, 999 UNTS 171 (entered into force 23 March 1976).

[14] See also Chapter 2.

[15] Sarah Joseph, Jenny Schultz and Melissa Castan, *The International Covenant on Civil and Political Rights* (2nd ed, Oxford University Press, Oxford, 2004) 7. For an analysis of the decision to draft two separate covenants see UN Secretary-General, *Annotations to the Text of the Draft International Covenants on Human Rights*, UN Doc A/2929 (1955) 7–8. The decision itself was confirmed in GA Res 543 (VI) of 5 February 1952.

[16] Adopted by GA Res 34/180 of 18 December 1979. Opened for signature 18 December 1979, 1249 UNTS 13 (entered into force 3 September 1981).

[17] Adopted by GA Res 39/46 of 10 December 1984. Opened for signature 10 December 1984, 1465 UNTS 85 (entered into force 26 June 1987).

the *Rights of the Child* ('CRC')[18] in 1989 and the *International Convention on the Protection of the Rights of All Migrant Workers and Members of their Families* ('MWC')[19] in 1990. The *Declaration on the Right to Development* ('DRD')[20] was adopted in 1986, the culmination of years of lobbying by developing States. However, its passage to recognition in a legally binding treaty has stalled since. A similar fate has befallen the *Declaration on the Elimination of Intolerance based on Religion or Belief*,[21] which was adopted in 1981.

The 1990s and the early part of the 2000s saw the adoption of a number of optional protocols, some of which added substantive rights to their respective parent treaties,[22] while others provided for new procedural mechanisms.[23]

In 2006, the UN adopted the *Convention on the Rights of Persons with Disabilities* ('Disabilities Convention')[24] and the *International Convention for the Protection of All Persons from Enforced Disappearance* ('Disappearances Convention').[25] In 2007, in another nod to the recognition of new generations of rights, the General Assembly adopted the *Declaration on the Rights of Indigenous Peoples* ('DRIP').[26]

Most recently, the UN adopted an Optional Protocol to ICESCR in 2008,[27]

---

[18] Adopted by GA Res 44/25 of 20 November 1989. Opened for signature 20 November 1989, 1577 UNTS 3 (entered into force 2 September 1990).

[19] Adopted by GA Res 45/158 of 18 December 1990. Opened for signature 18 December 1990 (entered into force 1 July 2003).

[20] GA Res 41/128 of 4 December 1986: see, generally, Chapter 7.

[21] GA Res 36/55 of 25 November 1981: see also Chapter 18.

[22] See, eg, Optional Protocol to the *Convention on the Rights of the Child on the Involvement of Children in Armed Conflict*, adopted by GA Res 54/263 of 25 May 2000, opened for signature 25 May 2000 (entered into force 12 February 2002); Optional Protocol to the *Convention on the Rights of the Child on the Sale of Children, Child Prostitution and Child Pornography*, adopted by GA Res 54/263 of 25 May 2000, opened for signature 25 May 2000 (entered into force 18 January 2002); Second Optional Protocol to the ICCPR, aiming at the abolition of the death penalty, adopted by GA Res 44/128 of 15 December 1989, opened for signature 15 December 1989, 1642 UNTS 414 (entered into force 11 July 1991).

[23] See, eg, Optional Protocol to the CEDAW, adopted by GA Res 54/4 of 6 October 1999, opened for signature 10 December 1999 (entered into force 22 December 2000); Optional Protocol to the CAT, adopted by GA Res 57/199 of 18 December 2002, opened for signature 4 February 2003 (entered into force 22 June 2006).

[24] Adopted by GA Res 61/106 of 13 December 2006. Opened for signature 30 March 2007 (entered into force 3 May 2008).

[25] Adopted by GA Res 61/177 of 20 December 2006. Opened for signature 6 February 2007 (not yet in force).

[26] GA Res 61/295 of 13 September 2007: see also Chapter 19.

[27] Adopted by GA Res A/RES/63/117 of 10 December 2008, opened for signature 24 September 2009.

which will allow for individual petitions regarding alleged violations of ICESCR once ten States ratify it. The adoption of this Protocol finally kills off a long-standing supposition that economic, social and cultural rights are not justiciable – an unfortunate assumption that has hampered their development.[28]

The UN has been active over its history in recognising and adopting human rights standards. It has branched out into new areas of human rights, though it has cautiously failed to enshrine many of them into legal form, as can be seen with the DRD and the 25-year battle to recognise distinct indigenous rights in the non-binding DRIP. The International Bill of Rights remains the core of the UN human rights system, with the other treaties, and most other declarations, tending to expand upon distinct rights within the UDHR and the Covenants, or to provide more detailed protection for distinct classes of human rights victims.

## 3   UN human rights institutions

The UN human rights institutions are generally either 'Charter bodies' or 'treaty bodies'. Charter bodies are established by the Charter itself, or by bodies which are themselves created by the Charter. Treaty bodies are created by the respective UN human rights treaties, referred to above. The main Charter bodies are the political UN human rights institutions, as they are made up of the representatives of governments, while the treaty bodies are the quasi-judicial arm of UN human rights supervision, composed of human rights experts acting in their individual capacity. Both types of bodies are supported by the Office of the High Commissioner for Human Rights.

*Charter bodies*

The General Assembly is a principal organ of the UN,[29] comprising all members of the UN[30] with equal voting status.[31] In relation to human rights the General Assembly has considerable authority. The General Assembly is entitled to 'initiate studies and make recommendations ... assisting in the realization of human rights and fundamental freedoms'.[32] Further, all other UN human rights bodies report back to the General Assembly, including the Security Council through its annual report. The General Assembly can make recommendations for action either through resolutions or through declarations. While both are non-binding in nature, they can have a significant effect, for example, on the structures of the various UN human rights bodies and

---

[28] See also Chapter 2.
[29] UN Charter, Article 8.
[30] UN Charter, Article 9.
[31] UN Charter, Article 18.
[32] UN Charter, Article 13.

through their moral force, representing as such the majority State opinion on an issue.[33] Unanimous or consensus resolutions can also constitute strong evidence of the existence of a customary norm.[34]

Another principal organ under the Charter is the Economic and Social Council ('ECOSOC'). ECOSOC consists of 54 members, each with equal voting status,[35] elected by the General Assembly to serve three-year terms.[36] Like the General Assembly, ECOSOC has a reasonably wide mandate in relation to human rights. It is authorised by Article 62 of the UN Charter to 'make or initiate studies and reports with respect to international, economic, cultural, educational, health and related matters' and may 'make recommendations for the purpose of promoting respect for, and observance of, human rights and fundamental freedoms'. ECOSOC receives and transmits to the General Assembly the reports of the treaty bodies and also coordinates a wide variety of UN programmes.[37]

ECOSOC effectively delegated its human rights functions to the Commission on Human Rights ('CHR') in 1946 in accordance with Article 68 of the UN Charter.[38] The CHR became the engine room of UN human rights activity. For example, the CHR drafted most of the UN human rights documents prior to its dissolution in 2006.[39] In that year, it was replaced by the Human Rights Council, which is now the main Charter body dealing with human rights.

### A  The Commission on Human Rights

In its final form, the Commission on Human Rights had 53 members, elected by ECOSOC to serve three-year renewable terms in their capacity as representatives of their governments. Over its 60 years the CHR made significant contributions to the establishment of an increasingly robust international human rights legal framework. Through its standard-setting and norm development it produced the bulk of international human rights law, outlined above,

---

[33] Rhona K M Smith, *Textbook on International Human Rights* (Oxford University Press, Oxford, 3rd ed, 2007) 53.
[34] See, eg, Anthony Aust, *Handbook of International Law* (Cambridge University Press, Cambridge/New York, 2005) 7; Andrew T Guzman, 'Saving Customary International Law' (2005) 27 *Michigan Journal of International Law* 115, 154–5.
[35] UN Charter, Article 67.
[36] UN Charter, Article 61.
[37] Smith, above n 33, 56.
[38] ECOSOC resolution 5[1], 16 February 1946.
[39] CEDAW is an exception; it was developed and drafted by another subsidiary committee of ECOSOC, the Commission on the Status of Women.

that now governs the conduct of States.[40] It also developed complaints mechanisms and a system of special procedures to garner reports on thematic human rights issues or the human rights situations in particular States. It was credited as the most accessible UN body for non-government organisations ('NGOs') to provide input on human rights issues.[41] The CHR was assisted in its functions by the Sub-Commission on the Promotion and Protection of Human Rights, a 'think tank' composed of 26 human rights experts serving in their individual capacities.[42]

The CHR did not initially envisage its role as incorporating enforcement. Until 1967, the CHR, by its own initiative, was not entitled to take any action in response to complaints concerning human rights.[43] However, the increasing number of newly decolonised nations in the UN by the mid-1960s agitated for measures to be taken by the CHR against apartheid in South Africa and ongoing colonialism. In response, the CHR overturned the limitation on its enforcement powers and developed a number of different procedures to deal with alleged violations of human rights. Although initially focused on racial and colonial policies, over time these procedures were applied to the broad spectrum of human rights issues.[44]

The first procedure adopted was the 1235 procedure for public debate focusing on violations in particular States.[45] The procedure evolved so that it eventually involved two aspects. First, public debate during the CHR's annual session allowed the public identification and discussion of country-specific situations involving human rights abuses, which could result in the shaming of the scrutinised State, offers of technical assistance or resolutions critical of the

---

[40] Of course, the Commission did not adopt the treaties which post-date its existence, such as the Disabilities Convention.

[41] International Service for Human Rights, *A New Chapter for Human Rights: A Handbook on Issues of Transition from the Commission on Human Rights to the Human Rights Council* (International Service for Human Rights and Friedrich Ebert Stiftung, Geneva, June 2006) 10.

[42] The Sub-Commission on Prevention of Discrimination and Protection of Minorities, formed in 1947, was renamed the Sub-Commission on the Promotion and Protection of Human Rights in 1999.

[43] ECOSOC resolution 75(V) of 5 August 1947, approving a Statement adopted by the Commission in its first session.

[44] For an outline of the various techniques for responding to human rights violations and their development see Henry J Steiner, Philip Alston and Ryan Goodman, *International Human Rights in Context: Law, Politics, Morals* (3rd ed, Oxford University Press, Oxford, 2008) 746–91.

[45] The procedure takes its name from the original ECOSOC resolution establishing it: ECOSOC resolution 1235 (XLII) of 6 June 1967.

performance of the State in question.⁴⁶ Second, the CHR could appoint a Special Rapporteur with a mandate to investigate and report on the human rights situation in a specific country following on from matters raised during the public debate, or request the UN Secretary-General to appoint a Special Representative with a similar function.⁴⁷ This second aspect derived from the 1235 procedure became known as one of the 'special procedures' of the CHR (subsequently transferred to the Human Rights Council), together with a similar procedure focusing on thematic, rather than country-specific, situations.

The thematic procedures, also derived from the 1235 procedure, involved the appointment of experts to investigate and report on all aspects, including violations, of human rights relevant to a specific theme. Current thematic mandates under the Human Rights Council include the working groups on enforced or involuntary disappearances, the right to food, and the situation of human rights and fundamental freedoms of indigenous persons.⁴⁸

Country-specific mandates became one of the most controversial functions of the CHR and have only been adopted in relation to a small proportion of situations identified in the CHR's public debates. However, the country and thematic special procedures have also been 'celebrated as one of the major achievements of the Commission', particularly as a means of highlighting the existence or development of urgent human rights situations.⁴⁹

Another technique developed by the CHR to deal with alleged human rights violations was the 1503 procedure.⁵⁰ As it developed, the 1503 procedure established a means by which the CHR, through its Sub-Commission and a specialised Working Group, could consider confidentially the complaints received from any person or group who was a victim or had knowledge of human rights violations in order to determine whether the complaint revealed a 'consistent pattern of gross and reliably attested violations of human rights

---

⁴⁶ Steiner, Alston and Goodman, above n 44, 760–61.
⁴⁷ Ibid.
⁴⁸ For a complete list, and details, of current thematic special procedure mandate holders, see Special Procedures assumed by the Human Rights Council, *Thematic Mandates* (20 November 2008) Office of the United Nations High Commissioner for Human Rights <http://www2.ohchr.org/english/bodies/chr/special/themes.htm> accessed at 12 December 2008.
⁴⁹ Jeroen Gutter, 'Special Procedures and the Human Rights Council: Achievements and Challenges Ahead' (2007) 7(1) *Human Rights Law Review* 93, 105.
⁵⁰ The procedure takes its name from the original ECOSOC resolution establishing it: ECOSOC resolution 1503 (XLVIII) of 27 May 1970. For an outline of the main steps in the evolution of the 1503 procedure see Maria Francisca Ize-Charrin, '1503: A Serious Procedure' in Gudmundur Alfredsson et al (eds), *International Human Rights Monitoring Mechanisms: Essays in Honour of Jakob Th. Moller* (Martinus Nijhoff Publishers, The Hague, 2001) 293–310.

and fundamental freedoms'.[51] If such a pattern was identified the CHR could work confidentially with the State in question in relation to the complaint.

The value of the 1503 procedure was its scope, which allowed consideration of complaints from individuals against any country regardless of whether it was a party to particular human rights treaties. One of the major problems of the mechanism was the degree of secrecy around the progress of a complaint and inefficiencies in the processing of complaints.[52]

Despite its successes, the CHR came increasingly to be seen as unable to properly fulfil its functions due to 'its declining credibility and professionalism'.[53] A number of key problems were widely recognised. Cynical manipulation of the CHR's mechanisms by Member States in order to avoid scrutiny and possible public censure or to score political points against other States,[54] the increasing 'politicisation' of the CHR and in particular the selectivity reflected in the choice of States singled out for country-specific measures,[55] and a number of high-profile elections to the CHR of States with particularly poor human rights records[56] all fuelled the view that the CHR needed to be radically reformed in order to preserve the integrity of the UN system.

### B  The Human Rights Council

The Human Rights Council ('Council') came into existence on 15 March

---

[51]  ECOSOC resolution 1503 (XLVIII), above n 50, [1].

[52]  Claire Callejon, 'Developments at the Human Rights Council in 2007: A Reflection of its Ambivalence' (2008) 8 (2) *Human Rights Law Review* 323, 333–4.

[53]  Secretary-General Kofi Annan, *In Larger Freedom: Toward Development, Security and Human Rights for All,* [182], UN Doc A/59/2005 (21 March 2005). See also High Panel on Threats, Challenges and Changes, *A More Secure World: Our Shared Responsibility,* [283], UN Doc A/59/565 (2 December 2004).

[54]  Annan, above n 53, [182]; High Panel, above n 53, [283]; Nazila Ghanea, 'From UN Commission on Human Rights to UN Human Rights Council: One Step Forwards or Two Steps Sideways?' (2006) 55 *International and Comparative Law Quarterly* 695, 697–8.

[55]  See, eg, Ved P Nanda, 'The Protection of Human Rights under International Law: Will the UN Human Rights Council and the Emerging Norm "Responsibility to Protect" Make a Difference?' (2007) 35 *Denver Journal of International Law and Policy* 353, 357–64; Patrizia Scannella and Peter Splinter, 'The United Nations Human Rights Council: A Promise to be Fulfilled' (2007) 7(1) *Human Rights Law Review* 41, 45.

[56]  For example, the defeat in May 2001 of the United States in its bid for re-election to the CHR, together with the concurrent membership of the Sudan and its re-election in May 2004, was significant in contributing to the controversy surrounding membership: see Philip Alston, 'Reconceiving the UN Human Rights Regime: Challenges Confronting the New UN Human Rights Council' (2006) 7 *Melbourne Journal of International Law* 185, 191–3.

2006[57] to replace the CHR as the key political human rights body in the UN, with a general mandate to address human rights issues. Like the CHR before it, the Council is responsible for promoting the protection of human rights, fostering international cooperation on human rights, providing capacity-building assistance to States to help them to meet their human rights obligations, and responding to specific violations of human rights.

In the context of the negative dynamics that had come to characterise the CHR and the open hostility shown by some States to the more condemnatory aspects of the CHR's work, concern arose that the opportunity presented by the reform process might be exploited by States in order to clip the wings of the CHR and to potentially dilute some of its more controversial powers, particular those regarding the special procedures. Ultimately, the status quo has largely been retained. The new Council is not substantially different in composition to its predecessor and has retained all of the same general mechanisms available to the CHR – special procedures, a complaints mechanism, significant NGO access and an independent advisory body – as well as obtaining a new mechanism: universal periodic review.[58] There have, however, been some changes to the mechanisms retained, some of which tend to strengthen and others to weaken human rights protection.

*(i) Composition, status and meetings of the Council* The question of membership came to dominate the reform debates as a principal factor in the negative dynamics that had come to characterise the former CHR.[59] Ultimately, from the 53-member CHR, the size of the Council has been reduced to 47 Member States. This satisfies neither proposals to reduce the Council's size more dramatically to foster more focused debates,[60] nor proposals for universal membership to avoid the risk of further politicisation,[61] nor the more radi-

---

[57] The Human Rights Council was established by resolution of the General Assembly: *Resolution on the Human Rights Council,* GA Res 60/251, UN GAOR, 6th sess, 72nd plen mtg, UN Doc A/RES/60/251 (2006) ('GA Res 60/251'). The Human Rights Commission was abolished, taking effect 1 June 2006, by resolution of the Economic and Social Council: *Implementation of GA Res 60/251,* ESC Res 2/2006, UN ESCOR, 62nd sess, UN Doc E/RES/62/2 (2006). For an outline of the reform process see Callejon, above n 52.
[58] The retention of a system of special procedures, expert advice and a complaints procedure was confirmed by GA Resolution 60/251, [6].
[59] Alston, above n 46, 188–98; Ghanea, above n 54, 699.
[60] For example, Secretary-General Kofi Annan, *Human Rights Council: Explanatory Note of the Secretary General,* [13], UN Doc A/59/2005/Add. 1 (23 May 2005).
[61] See, eg, High Panel, above n 53, [285].

cal option of composing the Council of non-State actors to remove the political nature of the body altogether.[62]

As had been the case with the CHR, membership is predicated on the equitable geographical distribution of Member States across regional groups. The geographical distribution of seats on the Council among regional groups is: 13 African States, 13 Asian States, 6 Eastern European States, 8 Latin American and Caribbean States, and 7 Western Europe and other States.[63] The redistribution of the more limited member positions has resulted in a weakening in numbers of those States that traditionally supported country-specific resolutions.[64]

The Council has a higher status in the UN as a direct subsidiary to the General Assembly,[65] whereas the CHR was a working sub-commission of the ECOSOC, a welcome escalation in the profile of human rights in the UN machinery. There is in fact the potential for the Council to be raised to a principal body of the UN, of equal status with the General Assembly and ECOSOC.[66] The Council also has greater time and flexibility around its meetings. Unlike the CHR, which only met for one annual six-week session, the Council is a standing body that meets for at least three sessions per year, each of several weeks' duration, with the possibility of convening special sessions when needed.[67]

In addition, a number of new features were introduced in an attempt to discourage States with particularly poor human rights records from nominating for, being elected to, or remaining members of the Council. Unlike the CHR, all Council members are elected individually by the majority of members of the General Assembly through a secret ballot. States are supposed to take account of the candidate's human rights record in electing members. As the General Assembly elects each member, regional groups have an incentive to nominate more candidates than positions available, which ensures that a genuine vote takes place. Regional groups run the risk of losing a Council seat if they nominate the same number of States as positions, as one or more

---

[62] Balakrishnan Rajagopal, 'Lipstick on a Caterpillar? Assessing the New UN Human Rights Council Through Historic Reflection' (2007) 13 *Buffalo Human Rights Law Review* 7, at 15.

[63] GA Resolution 60/251 [7].

[64] Marc Bossuyt, 'The New Human Rights Council: A First Appraisal' (2006) 24(4) *Netherlands Quarterly of Human Rights* 551, 552.

[65] GA Res 60/251 [1].

[66] The status of the Council is to be reviewed by March 2011: GA Res A/RES/60/251 [1].

[67] Special sessions can be convened at the request of a Council member with the support of one-third of the membership of the Council: GA Res 60/251, [10]. At the time of writing, twelve special sessions had been convened.

of those States may fail to garner majority approval from the General Assembly. Nevertheless, it is troubling that ony 20 States ran for 18 Council positions in May 2009. Members may only serve two consecutive three-year terms before having a mandatory break, and members can be suspended by a two-thirds majority of the General Assembly for committing systematic and gross violations of human rights. [68]

It is not obvious how great an impact these changes will have on improving the working culture of the Council and its credibility. In the first round of Council elections, some of the worst State violators of human rights did not seek election, but the resulting composition of the Council was not substantially different from that of the CHR.[69] Promisingly, in the second round of elections Belarus was rejected in favour of Bosnia-Herzegovina, because of its poorer human rights record.[70] On the other hand, the passing over of Timor-Leste in favour of Pakistan and South Korea in the third round of elections in May 2008 may raise questions as to whether the need for a majority vote will disadvantage smaller nations.[71]

*(ii) Early assessment of the substantive work of the Council* The Council has successfully adopted important new human rights conventions, as outlined above, such as the Disabilities Convention and the Optional Protocol to ICESCR. It also finally adopted the DRIP, after the long impasse over that instrument.

Despite these successes, the Council's earliest substantive business has given rise to concern that the negative dynamics of the CHR will be reproduced in the Council. The CHR came to be plagued by claims of double standards and declining credibility due to the repeated singling out of Israel and its human rights violations in the Occupied Palestinian Territory for country-specific measures, while resolutions on other equally grave country situations were often blocked.[72] In a similar fashion, of the twelve special sessions convened by the Council to date, six have focused on the conduct of Israel,[73]

---

[68] GA Res 60/251, [7–9].
[69] Alston, above n 46, 202; Francoise J Hampson, 'An Overview of the Reform of the UN Human Rights Machinery' (2007) 7 (1) *Human Rights Law Review* 7, 14–15.
[70] Nanda, above n 55, 362.
[71] See, eg, Hadar Harris, 'The Politics of Depoliticization: International Perspectives on the Human Rights Council' (2006) 13(3) *Human Rights Brief* 8.
[72] According to UN Watch, 30 per cent of all of the Commission's resolutions condemning human rights violations by specific States were against Israel, having risen to almost 50 per cent in its final years: Nanda, above n 55, 358.
[73] On the human rights situation in the Occupied Palestinian Territory: 1st special session, July 2006; 3rd special session, November 2006; 6th special session, January 2008; 9th special session, January 2009; and 12th special session, October 2009. On the grave situation of human rights in Lebanon caused by Israeli military

with resolutions adopted showing a one-sided focus on Israel's violations to the exclusion of other players relevant to the conflict, in a manner typical of the CHR. More promisingly, the Council has also convened special sessions in relation to the human rights situations in Myanmar,[74] Darfur,[75] the Democratic Republic of the Congo[76] and Sri Lanka.[77] The outcomes in regard to the latter three situations were, however, arguably weak and too deferential to the state concerned. The seventh special session focused on 'the negative impact on the realization of the right to food of the worsening of the world food crisis',[78] confirming the importance and increasing recognition of economic, social and cultural rights in the work of the Council.

Another contentious development in the early substantive work of the Council is the emergence of 'defamation of religion', and in particular defamation of Islam, as an issue of priority following the Danish cartoon controversy.[79] From its first session in June 2006, the Council has shown a particular preoccupation with this issue, adopting a resolution on 'Combating Defamation of Religions',[80] mandating reports from the Special Rapporteur on Racism and the United Nations High Commissioner[81] on the issue, as well as amending the mandate of the Special Rapporteur on Freedom of Expression to include reporting on 'instances where the abuse of the right of freedom of expression constitutes an act of racial and religious discrimination'.[82] Voting on this issue has exposed two clear blocs within the Council: the Organisation of the Islamic Conference and the African Group, on the one hand, and the Western Europe and Other Group ('WEOG') on the other, largely around the question of whether defamation of religion is properly a discrete human rights

---

operations: 2nd special session, August 2006. Furthermore, the only country situation which is the subject of a standing item on the Council's ordinary agenda is the 'human rights situation in Palestine and other occupied Arab territories'.

[74] 5th special session, October 2007.
[75] 4th special session, December 2006.
[76] 8th special session, November 2008.
[77] 11th special session, May 2009.
[78] 7th special session, May 2008.
[79] Callejon, above n 52, 341–2; John Cerone, 'Inappropriate Renderings: The Danger of Reductionist Resolutions' (2008) 33 *Brooklyn Journal of International Law* 357, 373–8.
[80] *Combating Defamation of Religions,* HRC Res 4/9, 4th session, UN Doc A/HRC/4/123 (30 March 2007). See also *Combating Defamation of Religions,* HRC Res 7/19, 27 March 2008.
[81] *Combating Defamation of Religions,* HRC Res 4/9, 4th session, UN Doc A/HRC/4/123 (30 March 2007) at [12] and [13].
[82] *Mandate of the Special Rapporteur on the Promotion and Protection of the Right to Freedom of Opinion and Expression,* HRC Res 7/36, 7th sess, 42nd mtg, UN Doc A/HRC/7/78 (28 March 2008), [4(d)].

issue at all.[83] The language of resolution 4/9 in 2007 clouded this question, appearing to correlate 'defamation of religion' with violations of human rights, and introducing a hitherto foreign principle to human rights law: the concept of 'respect for religion and beliefs' as a ground to limit the right to freedom of expression.[84] As John Cerone points out, this latter principle, if adopted as an international normative notion, would appear to license blasphemy laws that significantly limit comment about religions, despite no further link to a violation of another's human rights.[85]

*(iii) The Advisory Committee* The Advisory Committee has replaced the Sub-Commission and, like its predecessor, is responsible for undertaking studies and providing research-based advice to assist the Council in its work. To do so, it is composed of independent experts selected for that purpose.[86] However, following rationalisation of the Sub-Commission, the Advisory Committee has been restricted in a number of ways that may impact negatively on the Council's potential to progressively develop human rights norms.

A collegial standing body, the Advisory Committee comprises 18 members. This is in contrast to its predecessor's 26 members and despite the Sub-Commission's recommendation that, if replaced, its numbers should not be decreased[87] to ensure the geographical, gender and disciplinary representation necessary to fulfil its functions and for the equitable distribution of its work.[88] However, the selection process for members of the Advisory Committee has been somewhat improved through the introduction of technical and objective requirements for appointment relating to qualifications, expertise and established competence in the field of international human rights law and availability to fulfil the functions of the mandate.[89]

Most troublingly, the Advisory Committee has no power of initiative and can therefore only undertake studies and make recommendations at the request

---

[83] Callejon, above n 52, 342; Cerone, above n 79, 373.
[84] HRC Res 4/9 (2007) [10]. It must be noted that this aspect of the resolution was watered down in the follow-up resolution a year later: HRC Res 7/19, [12].
[85] Cerone, above n 79, 375.
[86] For the framework of the Advisory Committee, see *Institution-Building of the United Nations Human Rights Council,* HRC Res 5/1, 5th sess, UN Doc A/HRC/RES/5/1 (2007), [65–84].
[87] *Implementation by the Sub-Commission of Human Rights Council Decision 2006/102,* Sub-Commission on the Promotion and Protection of Human Rights Decision 2006/112, 58th sess, 23rd mtg, UN Doc A/HRC/Sub.1/58/Dec.2006/112 (25 August 2006), [27].
[88] Hampson, above n 69, 23.
[89] Human Rights Council decision 6/102 of 27 September 2007.

of the Council.[90] This was not the case with the Sub-Commission. Indeed, one of the Council's first substantive tasks was to adopt the Disabilities Convention and the Disappearances Convention, both of which were developed by, and *at the initiative of*, the Sub-Commission.[91] Without a power of initiative, the Advisory Committee will not have the same opportunity to deliver similar results in the future.[92] Like the Sub-Commission before it, the Advisory Committee should serve as an important counter-balance to the political machinations that necessarily take place in the Council as a political body composed of State representatives. It therefore needs to be a robust and independent expert advisory body, with powers to initiate studies and make recommendations with or without the Council first identifying and reaching consensus on a need. As experts acting without political motives, the Advisory Committee is better placed than the Council to identify gaps in human rights law and spearhead developments beyond the more narrow limits created by the dynamics of member State interests. If 'depoliticisation' of the Council is the yardstick for measuring the success of the reforms, restrictions placed on the size and especially the powers of the Advisory Committee are counter-productive.

*(iv) Special procedures in the Council* There were real fears that the system of special procedures would not survive the reform process given their effectiveness in publicly denouncing the human rights violations of States. This fear was driven by the 'negative reform agenda' of the 'Like-Minded Group' of States seeking to limit the independence and working methods of the special procedures.[93] While special procedures have been maintained in much the same form as under the Commission, the negative reform agenda has had some success. Special procedure mandate holders now have a code of conduct[94] and an Internal Advisory Procedure has been established to consider

---

[90] *Institution-Building of the United Nations Human Rights Council*, HRC Res 5/1, 5th sess, UN Doc A/HRC/RES/5/1 (2007), [75]. It has also been stripped of its powers to adopt decisions or resolutions: at [77]. However, this had also been the case for the Sub-Commission for a number of years.

[91] Hampson, above n 69, 21.

[92] Hampson, above n 69, 21–2.

[93] Gutter, above n 49, 104–5; International Service for Human Rights, above n 41, 40–41; Alston, above n 46, 204–6. Such States included Algeria, China, Cuba, Egypt, Indonesia, Iran, Libya, Malaysia, Pakistan, the Philippines, Saudi Arabia and Sudan.

[94] *Code of Conduct for Special Procedure Mandate-holders of the Human Rights Council*, HRC Res 5/2 (18 June 2007) available online at <http://www2.ohchr.org/english/bodies/chr/special/docs/CodeofConduct_EN.pdf> at 20 October 2008.

their practices and working methods on an ongoing basis.[95] Both of these initiatives are likely to limit the independence of mandate holders and have the effect of suggesting that it is the behaviour of mandate holders, and not of States, which requires regulation.[96] In addition, country mandates have been reduced from three-year to one-year terms.[97] As a result of the Council's review of all existing special procedure mandates, the country mandates for Cuba, Belarus and the Democratic Republic of the Congo have been discontinued, while the mandate for Sudan was extended for only six months, creating a concerning precedent to further restrict the length of country mandates.[98] The initiation of new country mandates is likely to remain difficult and controversial.[99]

*(v) Complaint procedure* The Council has retained the 1503 procedure with some improvements. Complainants are now entitled to more regular updates regarding the progress of their complaint,[100] and a time limit has been placed on the processing of a complaint.[101] Complainants are also now entitled to request that their identity not be transmitted to the State concerned,[102] addressing a gap in the former complaint procedure. The system is otherwise largely identical to its predecessor, representing a lost opportunity to strengthen the procedure's utility for victims[103] and to introduce better harmonisation with other Council mechanisms, such as the special procedures and the new Universal Periodic Review.[104]

*(vi) Universal Periodic Review ('UPR')* The principal new mechanism of the Council is its process of UPR. This procedure involves the periodic review

---

[95] *Internal Advisory Procedure to Review Practices and Working Methods* (adopted at the 15th Annual Meeting of Special Procedures) (25 June 2008) available online at <http://www2.ohchr.org/english/bodies/chr/special/annual_meetings/docs/InternalAdvisoryProcedure.doc> at 20 October 2008.

[96] Meghna Abraham, *Building the New Human Rights Council: Outcome and Analysis of the Institution-building Year* (Friedrich Ebert Stiftung, Occasional paper, August 2007) 44.

[97] *Institution-Building of the United Nations Human Rights Council*, HRC Res 5/1, 5th sess, UN Doc A/HRC/RES/5/1 (2007), [60]. Thematic mandates are still three years in length.

[98] *Situation of Human Rights in Sudan*, HRC Res 9/17, 9th sess, 23rd mtg, UN Doc A/HRC/9/L.11 (24 September 2008) [15].

[99] Abraham, above n 96, 44.

[100] *Institution-Building of the United Nations Human Rights Council*, HRC Res 5/1, 5th sess, UN Doc A/HRC/RES/5/1 (2007) [106–107].

[101] Ibid [105].

[102] Ibid [108].

[103] Callejon, above n 52, 333.

[104] Abraham, above n 96, 22.

of the human rights performance of all UN Member States in four-year cycles,[105] which means that 48 States are reviewed every year.[106] The review is conducted by a UPR Working Group comprising the 47 members of the Council but sitting in three special sessions of two weeks each, with each review facilitated by groups of three States, referred to as 'troikas' and chosen randomly, who act as rapporteurs.[107] Non-Member States may participate in the interactive dialogue that takes place with the State under review. The records of States are assessed against the Charter of the United Nations, the UDHR, the human rights instruments to which the reviewed State is a party, any voluntary pledges and commitments, and applicable international humanitarian law.[108] The review involves consideration of information prepared by the State concerned, information provided by the Office of the High Commissioner for Human Rights compiled from the reports of treaty bodies, special procedures, and other relevant official UN materials, and a summary of other 'credible and reliable information provided by other relevant stakeholders', also compiled by the Office of the High Commissioner for Human Rights.[109] This latter document allows for the input of specialist NGOs and human rights experts.

The institution-building documents regarding the UPR reflect a view that the UPR process is to be primarily cooperative, non-confrontational and non-politicised,[110] and this is reflected in the language adopted in the conclusions and recommendations set out in the final reports so far delivered by the UPR Working Group.[111] Importantly, however, the possibility of criticism is retained as the Council can address 'cases of persistent non-cooperation' with the UPR after 'exhausting all efforts to encourage a State to cooperate',[112] and the outcome of the UPR need not involve State consent and might include follow-up steps if deemed necessary.

The UPR is a welcome addition to the mechanisms available to the Council given that it ensures that all States, regardless of size or political status, will

---

[105] *Institution-Building of the United Nations Human Rights Council*, HRC Res 5/1, 5th sess, UN Doc A/HRC/RES/5/1 (2007) [14].

[106] For access to all relevant documents and details on the Universal Periodic Review process, see <http://www.upr-info.org/> accessed 12 December 2008.

[107] *Institution-Building of the United Nations Human Rights Council*, HRC Res 5/1, 5th sess, UN Doc A/HRC/RES/5/1 (2007), [14 and 18].

[108] Ibid [1–3].

[109] Ibid [15].

[110] Ibid [3].

[111] Final reports are available by country at <http://www.upr-info.org/> accessed 12 December 2008.

[112] *Institution-Building of the United Nations Human Rights Council*, HRC Res 5/1, 5th sess, UN Doc A/HRC/RES/5/1 (2007) [38].

be assessed against their human rights obligations. It is particularly welcome in that it has not come at the loss of mechanisms that enable the Council to publicly criticise non-cooperative or rights-violating States, for example through country-specific special procedures and resolutions. The UPR may in fact work to strengthen these mechanisms, as States may agree to allow special procedure mandate holders access to their territories, for example, as a part of their voluntary undertakings following review.[113] It is premature, as at November 2009, less than half way through the first round of UPR, to comprehensively assess the worthiness of this new procedure.

*(vii) Conclusion on the Human Rights Council* If reform of the CHR is assessed, as Francois Hampson suggests, against the principle that it should 'do no harm' to the level of protection of human rights achieved by the CHR,[114] then the preservation of a Council largely similar to its predecessor is an achievement. If, on the other hand, the yardstick is whether human rights protection has been improved overall by the reforms or whether the cost of the reform was warranted, then the outcome is not as clear. The relatively limited changes resulting from the reform process may not lead to the radical change in culture that had been hoped for. Early signs suggest that the practice of bloc voting is persisting, and that country mandates, already partially curtailed, will continue to be challenged by the many States hostile to the vision of a confrontational, as well as cooperative, Council. As the key innovation, the UPR will play a significant role in promoting the reputation of the Council.

On 12 December 2008, at a commemorative session of the Council to honour the 60th anniversary of the UDHR, Secretary-General Ban Ki Moon pleaded with UN Members to 'rise above partisan posturing and regional divides', and reminded them that they all shared 'a responsibility to make the Council succeed'.[115] These comments indicate that the Secretary General does not consider that the Council's early years can be termed a success.

*The Office of the High Commissioner for Human Rights*
The Office of the High Commissioner for Human Rights ('OHCHR') is an umbrella organisation for the coordination and achievement of the human

---

[113] See, for example, *Report of the Working Group on the Universal Periodic Review: Bahrain,* UN Doc A/HRC/8/19 of 22 May 2008 [11 and 61(3)].
[114] Hampson, above n 69, 27.
[115] UN press release, 'Remarks of the UN Secretary-General to the Commemorative Session of the Human Rights Council on the Sixtieth Anniversary of the Universal Declaration of Human Rights', 12 December 2008, at <http://www.unhchr.ch/huricane/huricane.nsf/view01/56C98BCD69A2D501C125751D0054CBF7?opendocument> (14 December 2008).

rights efforts of the UN system as a whole. Proposals for the establishment of a body of its kind date back to as early as 1947 but it was not until December 1993 that the OHCHR was finally established.[116] Julie Mertus describes the establishment of the Office as embodying enormous expectations regarding a new era in the achievement of human rights, where the gap between the growth of global human rights norms and their enforcement would be addressed.[117]

The OHCHR comprises an Executive Office and six functional branches.[118] The role of the OHCHR can be conceived in terms of its internal aspects, in relation to the UN system itself, and its external aspects, concerning its interaction with other bodies. In relation to supporting the human rights performance of the UN, the mandate of the OHCHR includes coordinating the UN's education and public information programmes, coordinating human rights promotion and protection activities throughout the UN system, and strengthening and streamlining UN machinery in the field of human rights. More broadly, the OHCHR is also charged with providing advisory services and technical and financial assistance to requesting States and regional organisations for the purpose of supporting their human rights programmes and actions, engaging in dialogue with governments and generally taking an active role in removing obstacles to the realisation of human rights and in preventing the continuation of human rights violations.[119]

A key activity of the OHCHR is its role in providing technical assistance to national institutions and regional organisations aimed at the implementation of international human rights standards. Examples of the practical help provided by the OHCHR include training judicial officials in the administration of justice, advising national parliaments in constitutional and legislative reform and training government officials in preparing State treaty reports and national human rights plans of action.[120] Increasingly important is the OHCHR's field presence in conflict and post-conflict States, the first large-scale example of

---

[116] GA Res 48/141 of 20 December 1993.
[117] Julie A Mertus, *The United Nations and Human Rights: A Guide for a New Era* (Routledge, Oxford, 2005) 8–13.
[118] These are the Administrative Branch; the External Relations Branch; the Research and Right to Development Branch; the Treaties and Commission Branch; the Capacity Building and Field Operations Branch; and the Special Procedures Branch: see Mertus, above n 117, at 15. See also Bertrand Ramcharan, *A UN High Commissioner in Defence of Human Rights* (Martin Nijhoff Publishers, Leiden, 2005) Chapter VI.
[119] The mandate of the OHCHR is set out in paragraph 4 of GA Res 48/141 of 20 December 1993.
[120] See Mertus, above n 117, 17–18.

which was in Rwanda in the aftermath of the 1994 genocide,[121] and its involvement in supporting the establishment and standards of national human rights institutions.[122]

The High Commissioner may engage in public comment regarding specific human rights crises and the extent to which he or she does so reflects the strategic approach of the individual High Commissioner in question. Mary Robinson, former President of Ireland and the second individual to hold the post of High Commissioner, was noted for her public condemnation of human rights abuses by States during her tenure, for example in relation to the behaviour of Russian soldiers in Chechnya and abuses in the US detention centre in Guantanamo Bay in Cuba.[123] Both Russia and the US subsequently opposed her candidacy for an extended term.[124] Mary Robinson's term was also notable for her engagement with the corporate sector regarding its role in the advancement of human rights.[125]

With the establishment of the new Human Rights Council, the OHCHR's tasks have grown. In supporting the work of the Council, the OHCHR is responsible for, among other things, maintaining the list of possible candidates to become special procedure mandate holders and compiling materials forming the basis of assessments under the UPR process. The OHCHR also provides expertise and assistance to the treaty bodies.

*Treaty bodies*

The treaty bodies are established under the respective UN human rights treaties. For example, the Human Rights Committee ('HRC') is established under Article 28 of the ICCPR to fulfil various roles with regard to that treaty. The exception is the Committee on Economic, Social and Cultural Rights, which was established by a resolution of ECOSOC,[126] rather than the ICESCR itself.

The treaty bodies are made up of independent human rights experts, unlike the government representatives that populate the Charter bodies. A prospective Committee member is nominated by a State party to the relevant treaty

---

[121] Mertus, above n 117, 19–27; Bertrand G Ramcharan, *Human Rights and Human Security* (Kluwer Law International, The Hague, 2002) 131–2.

[122] This was highlighted as a task of priority in the report of Secretary-General Kofi Annan, *Strengthening the United Nations: An Agenda for Further Change,* General Assembly UN Doc A/57/387 of 9 September 2002 at 12, cited in Mertus, above n 117, 27–8.

[123] Mertus, above n 117, 39–40.

[124] Mertus, above n 117, 40.

[125] Bertrand G Ramcharan, *Human Rights and Human Security* (Kluwer Law International, The Hague, 2002) 136–40.

[126] ECOSOC Resolution 1985/17 of 28 May 1985.

and is elected by the States parties to serve a four-year term, renewable upon re-election.[127] As with most UN bodies, a fair geographic spread should be reflected in the countries of origin of the members.

The treaty bodies are part-time bodies, and are not paid for their work, though their expenses are paid. The HRC, for example, sits for three sessions a year, with each session being three weeks long, preceded by working group meetings of a subset of the HRC for one week. The part-time nature of the bodies is problematic, as it has led to backlogs in their work.

The decisions of the treaty bodies are not legally binding. However, their interpretations of their respective treaties have strong persuasive force, as they represent authoritative interpretations of legally binding documents.[128] The treaty bodies act as the quasi-judicial arm of the UN human rights machinery.

The treaty bodies have a range of functions, though their functions are not identical to each other. All treaty bodies monitor their respective treaties by way of reporting processes, and all are able to issue general comments. Some treaty bodies are empowered to receive and decide upon individual and inter-state complaints.

*(i) Reporting function*  A State party to a treaty must submit an initial report on its record of implementation of the relevant treaty, followed by periodic reports. The periodicity of reports varies under the different treaties. Under the Covenants, for example, the periodicity is roughly five years. Exceptionally, a treaty body may call for an emergency report to receive information on perceived crisis situations. The CERD Committee uses this procedure most frequently under its Urgent Action procedure.[129]

State reports are examined by the treaty body in a dialogue with representatives of the relevant State. The dialogue is not limited to the content of the

---

[127] CERD, Article 8; HRC: ICCPR, Article 32; Committee on Social, Cultural and Economic Rights: Economic and Social Council Resolution 1985/17 of 28 May 1985, [(c)]; CEDAW, Article 17; CAT, Article 17; CRC, Article 43; Committee on Migrant Workers: MWC, Article 72; Committee on the Rights of Persons with Disabilities, Article 34.

[128] See, eg, Human Rights Committee, *The Obligations of States Parties under the Optional Protocol to the International Covenant on Civil and Political Rights*, General Comment 33, UN Doc CCPR/C/GC/33 (5 November 2008) [11–15].

[129] Since their adoption in 1993, the CERD Committee has taken action under its Early Warning and Urgent Action procedures in relation to more than 20 States parties: <http://www2.ohchr.org/english/bodies/cerd/early-warning.htm> accessed at 15 December 2008. For an outline of the development, and examples of the application, of these procedures, see Theo van Boven, 'Prevention, Early-warning and Urgent Procedures: A New Approach by the Committee on the Elimination of Racial Discrimination' in Erik Denters and Nico Schrijver (eds), *Reflections on International Law from the Low Countries* (Kluwer Law International, The Hague, 1998) 165–82.

report, as treaty body members often receive information from NGOs regarding human rights concerns that are omitted from a report or which are 'spun' in a pro-government way. At the conclusion of the dialogue, the treaty body will adopt Concluding Observations on a State, which are like a report card on the State's record of implementation of the treaty. The Concluding Observations will contain comments on positive developments, as well as matters of concern, and recommendations for future action. Those recommendations are followed up by a specially appointed treaty body member, and should form the foundation of the State's next report and dialogue.[130]

The reporting process allows treaty bodies to gain an overall picture of a State's record of implementing a particular treaty, compared with the more specific and particularised situations they address under complaints processes, discussed below.

However, the reporting process has been beset by problems. States are often late with their reports, and/or may submit extremely inadequate reports which simply whitewash serious human rights issues. It must be noted that proper reporting is a resource-intensive activity, which can make it difficult for States which lack relevant technical expertise and resources, especially given the proliferation of treaty bodies and reporting requirements. In any case, the treaty bodies lack the time to address reports in a timely manner. Finally, many States have failed to abide by the recommendations of the treaty bodies.

Due to these issues, the reporting process has undergone renovations, particularly in the last decade, designed to streamline the process and to increase effectiveness. For example, treaty bodies now follow up on the implementation of Concluding Observations within a year, and publicly report on a State's progress, or lack thereof. The treaty bodies are also now prepared to examine the record of a State in the absence of a report in the case of chronic failure to abide by reporting obligations.[131] In recent years there have been reforms to the reporting process. Reports under the revised reporting procedure now involve two documents: a 'core document', which has been expanded beyond background information to include information relating to substantive treaty provisions congruent across a number of treaties; and a 'treaty-specific' document dealing, as its name implies, with information specific to a State's obligations under a particular treaty.[132] These reforms are

---

[130] Concluding Observations may be found on a number of websites, including www.bayefsky.com and the SIM documentation site at the University of Utrecht: http://sim.law.uu.nl/SIM/Dochome.nsf?Open.
[131] Joseph, Schultz and Castan, above n 15, 20.
[132] *Compilation of Guidelines on the Form and Content of Reports to be Submitted by States Parties to the International Human Rights Treaties*, UN Doc HRI/GEN/2/Rev.5 (29 May 2008).

designed to harmonise reporting procedures and reduce the reporting burden on States.

*(ii) General Comments*  All treaty bodies may issue General Comments, which address matters of relevance to all States parties to a particular treaty. Most General Comments contain expanded interpretations of particular rights in a relevant treaty,[133] though a General Comment can address any issue of relevance to the implementation of a particular treaty.[134] General Comments are extremely useful jurisprudential tools.

*(iii) Complaints processes*  Interstate complaints processes and individual complaints mechanisms exist under some of the treaties, as shown in Table 1.1 below. Those mechanisms marked with an asterisk are not yet in force.

Given the likely tit-for-tat response of a respondent State to an interstate complaint, it is not surprising that there never has been an interstate complaint in the UN treaty system.

The respective individual complaints mechanisms, on the other hand, have been widely utilised, particularly under the Optional Protocol to the ICCPR. These mechanisms are always optional. If a State does choose to take part, for example by ratifying the Optional Protocol to the ICCPR, an individual (or a

*Table 1.1  Complaints processes*

| Treaty | Interstate complaints | Individual complaints |
| --- | --- | --- |
| ICCPR | Yes (Article 41) | Yes (Optional Protocol) |
| ICESCR | No | Yes (Optional Protocol)* |
| CERD | Yes (Article 11) | Yes (Article 14) |
| CEDAW | No | Yes (Optional Protocol) |
| CAT | Yes (Article 21) | Yes (Article 22) |
| CRC | No | No |
| MWC | Yes (Article 76)* | Yes (Article 77)* |
| Disabilities Convention | No | Yes (Optional Protocol) |
| Disappearances Convention | Yes (Article 32)* | Yes (Article 31)* |

[133]  The General Comments of the treaty bodies may be found via <http://www2.ohchr.org/english/bodies/treaty/comments.htm> (21 December 2008)

[134]  For example, treaty bodies have issued General Comments on reporting guidelines, reservations to treaties, denunciations of treaties, derogations, and guidance on domestic means of implementing a treaty.

group of individuals) may submit a complaint to the relevant treaty body regarding an alleged violation of his or her rights under the relevant treaty. It does not cost anything to have one's complaint considered by a treaty body.[135] The entire procedure is conducted in writing,[136] with submissions from the complainant and the State. The deliberations of the treaty bodies regarding these complaints are conducted in closed session.[137]

A complaint must satisfy certain criteria before it will be deemed admissible.[138] There are jurisdictional criteria. First, the complaint must concern an alleged violation of the rights of a person, rather than be a complaint in the abstract about an unsatisfactory human rights situation.[139] Secondly, the complaint must relate to events that take place after the date at which the individual complaints procedure becomes active for a State.[140] Thirdly, the complaint must relate to a matter within the State's territory or jurisdiction.[141] There are also procedural criteria. First, a person cannot simultaneously submit a complaint to another comparable complaints procedure, such as an individual complaints procedure under a regional human rights treaty.[142] Secondly, a person must exhaust all available effective domestic remedies before a treaty body will address his or her complaint.[143] Finally, there are substantive admissibility criteria. The complaint must prima facie relate to an alleged violation of the provisions of the relevant treaty, rather than a violation of human rights per se (or no apparent violation of any human right). There also must be sufficient evidence to sustain a consideration of the merits of the complaint.

If a case is found to be admissible, the treaty body will proceed to consider the merits of the case.[144] Ultimately, the treaty body will issue its views on a

---

[135] Of course, it may cost to obtain legal assistance to assist one in drafting the complaint. It is not compulsory to have one's complaint submitted by a qualified lawyer.

[136] The Rules of the CAT and CERD Committees provide for the possibility of giving oral evidence, but this has never happened: see (2002) CAT/C/3/Rev 4, Rule 111; UN Doc CERD/C/35/Rev.3 (1 January 1989), Rule 94(5).

[137] See, eg, *Rules of Procedure of the Human Rights Committee,* UN Doc CCRP/C/3/Rev.8 (22 September 2005), Rule 102.

[138] Not all complaints will be considered by the full Committee. For example, a Special Rapporteur for New Communications in the HRC can dismiss a complaint if it is blatantly inadmissible without registering it: see 'How to complain about Human Rights Treaty violations: CCPR', at http://www.bayefsky.com/complain/10_ccpr.php.

[139] See, eg, Joseph, Schultz and Castan, above n 15, Chapter 3.
[140] Ibid Chapter 2.
[141] Ibid Chapter 4.
[142] Ibid Chapter 5.
[143] Ibid Chapter 6.
[144] The treaty bodies normally consider the admissibility and move on to the merits directly if the case is admissible. However, in complex cases, the two stages may be split. See, eg, ibid, above n 15, 25.

case, and decide on available evidence whether a violation (or violations) has arisen, or whether no violation has taken place. If a violation is found, remedial measures will be recommended to the State. The treaty body will then follow up on whether a State has in fact adopted those remedial measures, or whether the State has failed to satisfactorily address the violation.

Occasionally, a treaty body will issue a request for interim measures to a State, in situations where a complainant may be in danger of irreparable damage to his or her rights. For example, such measures may be requested in respect of a prisoner on death row who is complaining about the fairness of her trial which resulted in the death sentence: obviously the execution of the person while a treaty body is considering the complaint would make it impossible to vindicate that person's rights if a violation is ultimately found. The treaty bodies have been particularly affronted when States fail to abide by requests for interim measures.[145]

The individual complaints processes serve the valuable function of providing an international avenue for the vindication of an individual's rights, in the absence of an effective domestic remedy. The quality of some of the decisions may be questioned, with the reasoning on occasion being quite sparse, compared with, for example, the decisions of the regional courts in Europe and the Americas.[146] On the other hand, some decisions contain excellent and groundbreaking reasoning.[147] The process itself is reasonably functional, with most merits decisions now being rendered within a few years of submission. The worst aspect of the process is probably the record of State compliance, discussed below in the context of human rights enforcement. However, even in the absence of consistent State compliance, the views are enormously important as global jurisprudential resources. That is, a decision with regard to State X on a particular issue can impact on later decisions on that same issue in regard to other States, whether at the international, regional or domestic level, regardless of the response of State X.

---

[145] See, eg, *Piandong et al v Philippines* UN Doc CCPR/C/70/D/869 (1999) and *Ahani v Canada* UN Doc CCPR/C/80/D/1051 (2002). See also General Comment 33, above n 128, [19].

[146] See, for an example of a poor decision in the opinion of the authors, in that the CERD Committee did not clarify if or how a violation arose, *Hagan v Australia* UN Doc CERD/C/62/D/26 (2002).

[147] Examples of such cases, in the opinion of the authors, include *Broeks v Netherlands* UN Doc CCPR/C/29/D/172 (1984), *A v Australia* UN Doc CCPR/C/59/D/560 (1993), and *Guengueng v Senegal* UN Doc CAT/C/36/D/181 (2001).

*(iv) Miscellaneous processes* Some of the treaties also contain other miscellaneous processes to assist in the implementation of State treaty obligations. Article 29 of CEDAW, Article 30 of CAT and Article 92 of the MWC create mechanisms for the resolution of inter-State disputes concerning the interpretation or application of those treaties. Under Article 20 of CAT and Articles 8–10 of the Optional Protocol to CEDAW, the CAT and CEDAW Committees are empowered to initiate and conduct inquiries and report urgently where they receive reliable information regarding grave or systematic violations by a State party. While the procedure is confidential, the relevant Committee may decide to include an account of its proceedings in its annual report. The consent of the relevant State party is not required for either the CEDAW or CAT Committees to proceed with an inquiry, though State parties may opt out of either inquiry procedure by making a declaration that they do not recognise the relevant competency of the Committee(s). Finally, the Optional Protocol to CAT provides for the establishment of complementary international and national procedures for regular visits to places of detention, in order to prevent the practice of torture and other ill-treatment in such places.

## 4 Global enforcement of human rights

### A 'Naming and shaming'

None of the human rights institutions discussed above are able to make legally binding decisions, unlike, for example, the regional human rights courts. Their powers of 'enforcement' lie in the process of naming and shaming a State that is engaged in human rights abuses. States are named in the public reports of the treaty bodies, and some 'shame' is attached to their adverse findings.[148] States are exposed to more pronounced shame in country resolutions by their peers in the political bodies such as the former CHR and the Council, or in reports to those bodies from Special Rapporteurs.

No government enjoys being the subject of such shaming processes, and even the most powerful States will lobby to avoid such consequences. For example, China lobbied fiercely (and successfully) for many years to avoid a country resolution against it in the CHR.[149] It would not have lobbied so hard

---

[148] See General Comment 33, above n 128, [17].

[149] China was successful in leading 11 'no action' motions on draft country resolutions against it in the CHR between 1900 and 2005. This included in 2004 a no action motion carried by a vote of 28–16–9: Office of the United Nations High Commissioner for Human Rights, *Results of Recorded Votes on Proposals, 60th Session of the Commission on Human Rights* (2004) <http://www.unhchr.ch/html/menu2/2/60chr/results.htm> (29 January 2009). For results on earlier China resolutions, see Michael J Dennis, 'The Fifty-sixth Session of the UN Commission on Human Rights' (2001) 95 *American Journal of International Law* 213, 219.

if condemnation was meaningless.[150] Beyond embarrassment, shaming can have real consequences for a government. The shaming of a government can galvanise and lend credibility to domestic opposition groups. Shaming can prompt further pressure from other States, public protests, the media, and NGOs.[151] In extreme cases, allies of a shamed government can find themselves the target of secondary pressure to 'do something' about the shamed State, placing extreme strain on the relevant alliance. Certain non-State actors, such as corporations that invest in a delinquent State, might be pressured to remove their investments, or to not invest in the first place.[152] While shaming may not, in many circumstances, lead to immediate changes in behaviour by target States, it can have a long-term corrosive effect on a delinquent government, playing a role in a government's change in behaviour or ultimate demise.[153] Finally, shaming can prompt individual States, or groups of States, or even the international community as a whole, to threaten or adopt stronger measures against a State. These stronger measures are, however, not without problems, and are discussed below.

Nevertheless, shaming is a weak sanction. Most obviously, it has been conspicuously unsuccessful in motivating prompt changes in behaviour by delinquent States. Certainly, the effects of shame can be blunted in the States governed by the most incorrigible human rights violators. Shaming has less capacity to galvanise local opposition if that opposition is totally suppressed and the media censored, as for example in Myanmar. Indeed, there is little empirical evidence on the effects of shaming. A recent empirical study concluded that shaming may prompt governments to enact legislation to 'officially' grant greater political rights, but that it may also prompt, at least in the short run, an increase in the perpetration of more 'unofficial' acts of political terror.[154] The study made no conclusions on the longer-term effects of persistent shaming.[155]

---

[150] See, eg, Sandeep Gopalan, 'Alternative sanctions and social norms in international law: the case of Abu Ghraib' [2007] *Michigan State Law Review* 785, 789.

[151] See also Chapter 5. Of course, shaming by UN bodies can also be prompted by shaming originating from such entities.

[152] See James H Lebovic and Erik Voeten, 'The politics of shame: the condemnation of country human rights practices in the UNCHR' (2006) 50 *International Studies Quarterly* 861, 868–9.

[153] The peaceful demise of the Pinochet military government in Chile in 1989 may have been prompted in part by the constant shaming of Chile by human rights organisations, including the CHR. See, eg, Darren D Hawkins, *International Human Rights and Authoritarian Rule in Chile* (University of Nebraska Press, Lincoln, Nebraska, 2002).

[154] See Emilie M Hafner-Burton, 'Sticks and Stones: Naming and Shaming the Human Rights Enforcement Problem' (2008) 62 *International Organization* 689.

[155] For a comprehensive theoretical study of the process of 'acculturation' of

A further problem is that the application of the sanction of shame by the UN political bodies, such as the former CHR and the Human Rights Council, is inconsistent and biased: political alliances and hostilities play an unfortunately prominent role in the selection of targets for condemnation. Indeed, the mechanism of shaming is under some threat within the Council, with a number of States eager to lessen the number of country resolutions and special procedures. As noted above, Israel has received a disproportionate amount of criticism from the UN political bodies due to the number of States that are openly hostile to that country for reasons that extend beyond the realm of human rights.[156] On the other hand, China was able to lobby to avoid the passage of a country resolution in the CHR; its human rights record suggests that it did not deserve to be able to do so. Indeed, it is perhaps the *lack of condemnation* by the political bodies, which results in the de facto exoneration of States that is of more concern than the instances of condemnation. Even if the latter may often be motivated, or partially motivated, by political point scoring, the situations condemned normally involve serious human rights abuses.[157]

### B Diplomatic and economic sanctions

While shaming is the most common form of international enforcement of human rights, the most serious human rights situations can prompt stronger unilateral and multilateral sanctions. Stronger sanctions may involve the cessation of diplomatic relations between a State and the target State. A State may be expelled or suspended from a particular organisation, such as the UN[158] or the Commonwealth group of nations.[159] Such actions are not prob-

---

States, including by way of the process of shaming, see Ryan Goodman and Derek Jinks, 'How to Influence States: Socialization and International Human Rights Law' (2004) 54 *Duke Law Journal* 621.

[156] Lebovic and Voeten, above n 152, describe Israel's treatment by the Commission as 'politically unique' at 879.

[157] While noting that 'hypocrisy [thrived] on the commission', Lebovic and Voeten, above n 152, nevertheless conclude that political partisanship played a lesser role in CHR country resolutions in the post-Cold War period than realist theorists might expect: 'evidence demonstrates compellingly that the commission went after the worst offenders and that this effect dominated all others' (884).

[158] A State may only be expelled by decision of the Security Council for persistent violations of Charter principles: UN Charter, Article 6. No State has ever been expelled. A draft resolution to expel South Africa was submitted by Iraq, Kenya, Mauritania and Cameroon in 1974: *Relationship between the UN and South Africa*, UN Doc S/11543. The resolution was defeated by the vetoes of the US, France and the UK: UN SCOR, 1808th meeting, 30 October 1974.

[159] Although a State cannot be expelled from the Commonwealth of Nations, it can be suspended from membership. Examples include the suspension of Zimbabwe in 2002 over electoral concerns; Fiji in 2006 over concerns regarding its military coup; and Pakistan in 2007 for failing to lift emergency rule.

lem-free. The cessation of diplomatic relations diminishes the influence that a sanctioning State (or States) has over the target State. If most States take this option, a State may be effectively isolated, such as North Korea, which might reduce the likelihood of it responding to calls for behaviour change from other States.[160] On the other hand, the application of human rights conditions for membership in certain organisations, especially those with great material benefits like the European Union ('EU'), might constitute a powerful incentive for reform in applicant States.[161]

Moving up in the scale of consequence, economic sanctions may be imposed unilaterally, or by groups of States, in response to another State's human rights abuses.[162] For example, the US and the EU have imposed economic sanctions on Myanmar in response to its appalling human rights record.[163] Multilateral economic sanctions, especially those mandated by the Security Council, are of course more effective in squeezing the economy of a State, as they deprive the State of alternative trading partners. However, economic sanctions are deeply problematic from a human rights point of view, as they can lead to grave suffering on the part of innocent target populations if a recalcitrant government refuses to cave in to the demands of the sanctioners.[164]

Concerns regarding effects on innocent parties have led to 'smart sanctions', which are designed to harm culpable leaders rather than innocent populations, in the form of asset freezes, travel bans, and bans on strategic commodities such as arms. However, one study of sanctions imposed between 1990 and 2001 indicates that smart sanctions are not as effective as comprehensive sanctions at achieving their aim;[165] nor are such sanctions free of

---

[160] See Goodman and Jinks, above n 155, 669.

[161] For example, it has been argued that the promise of material benefits by the EU can be effective in prompting democratic developments in applicant States, provided the costs to the target government are not too great: Frank Schimmelfennig, Stefan Engert and Heiko Knobel, 'Costs, Commitment and Compliance: The Impact of EU Democratic Conditionality on Latvia, Slovakia and Turkey' (2003) 41(3) *Journal of Common Market Studies* 495–518.

[162] Generally, economic sanctions, in the form of a refusal to trade with a particular State, are legal in general international law, though they are illegal under certain international law treaties outside the human rights arena, such as World Trade Organization agreements. See Carlos Manuel Vázquez, 'Trade sanctions and human rights – past, present, and future' (2003) 6 *Journal of International Economic Law* 797.

[163] See Michael Ewing-Chow, 'First do no harm: Trade sanctions and human rights' (2007) 5 *Northwestern Journal of International Human Rights* 153.

[164] See Committee on Economic, Social and Cultural Rights, 'The relationship between economic sanctions and respect for economic, social and cultural rights', General Comment 8: E/C.12/1997/8, 12 December 1997. See also John Mueller and Karl Mueller, 'Sanctions of Mass Destruction' (1999) 78(3) *Foreign Affairs* 43.

[165] See David Cortright and George A Lopez, 'Introduction: Assessing Smart

social consequences.[166] Indeed, the overall success rate of sanctions regimes is low.[167] On the other hand, economic sanctions probably played a large role in the eventual conformity of South Africa and Serbia-Montenegro with international demands regarding human rights.[168]

C  Military force

The most extreme sanction is of course the use of military force to, for example, replace a delinquent government. Military intervention for the purposes of stopping human rights abuses is labelled 'humanitarian intervention'. The Security Council is able to authorise the use of military force under Chapter VII of the UN Charter in order to respond to threats to international peace and security.[169] Large-scale human rights abuses have triggered such action against Iraq in 1991 (regarding the establishment of a safe haven for Kurds), Somalia in 1992–93, and Haiti in 1994.[170] The Security Council has also authorised humanitarian intervention by regional organisations, such as that of the Economic Community of West African States ('ECOWAS') in Liberia in 1990 and Sierra Leone in 1998.[171]

---

Sanctions', in David Cortright and George A Lopez (eds) *Smart Sanctions: Targeting Economic Statecraft* (Rowman and Littlefield Publishers, New York, 2002) 8.

[166]  Ibid 6.

[167]  See Peter Wallensteen, 'A century of economic sanctions: a field revisited', Uppsala Peace Research Paper No 1, Department of Peace and Conflict Research, Uppsala University, Sweden, 2000, available at <http://www.pcr.uu.se/pcr_doc/uprp/UPRP_No_1.pdf> (14 December 2008). See also Gary Hufbauer et al, *Economic Sanctions Reconsidered: History and Current Policy* (Institute for International Economics, 2nd ed, 1990).

[168]  On South Africa, see Ewing-Chow, above n 163, 174–6. On Serbia, see Charles J Kacsur, 'Economic Sanctions Targeting Yugoslavia: An Effective National Security Strategy Component', *Storming Media*, 22 January 2003.

[169]  UN Charter, Articles 39 and 42.

[170]  See generally Ruth Gordon, 'Intervention by the United Nations: Iraq, Somalia and Haiti' (1996) 31 *Texas International Law Journal* 43. Whilst many other armed operations have been authorised, they have involved peacekeeping missions, conducted with the consent of the recognised government of the territory in question.

[171]  See generally Thomas M Franck, *Recourse to Force: State Action against Threats and Armed Attacks* (Cambridge University Press, Cambridge, 2002) 155–62. According to Article 53 of the Charter, regional organisations must not take enforcement action without Council authorisation. In both cases however the military operations initiated by ECOWAS were retrospectively approved in the form of 'commending' resolutions by the Council (Liberia: Presidential Statement of the United Nations Security Council, S/22133 of 22 January 1991; Security Council resolution S/RES/788 of 19 November 1992. Sierra Leone: Security Council resolution S/RES/1270 of 22 October 1999) and the subsequent deployment of UN observer missions operating in partnership with the regional interventions. Franck, 155–62, has argued that the response of the Security Council to the ECOWAS interventions

There are numerous problems in relying on the Security Council to authorise force to overthrow the most tyrannical governments. Most obviously, political will may be lacking amongst Security Council members, or one of the five permanent members (US, UK, France, Russia and China) may exercise its power to veto such a resolution. As with the Human Rights Council, political considerations inevitably influence the Security Council.[172] The persistence of Security Council inaction on numerous occasions, even in the face of extreme human rights abuses, such as ongoing genocide in the Sudan[173] and humanitarian catastrophe in Zimbabwe,[174] has led to calls for the legalisation of unilateral humanitarian intervention, that is military force against governments responsible for gross and persistent human rights abuses without Security Council authorisation. Such intervention has indeed occurred, for example by India in Bangladesh in 1971, Tanzania in Uganda in 1979,

---

demonstrated the reticent UN system's increasing propensity to let regional organizations use force, even absent specific prior Security Council authorization, when that seemed the only way to respond to impending humanitarian disasters'.

[172] Ironically, given Israeli grievances against the General Assembly and the HRC, Palestinians complain about bias towards Israel in the Security Council, given Israel's close relationship with the US. Israel has never been subjected to a Chapter VII measure of the Security Council, though numerous Chapter VI resolutions (dealing with the pacific resolution of disputes) have been passed. See 'Iraq, Israel, and the United Nations' (10 October 2002) *The Economist*.

[173] While the Security Council has passed numerous resolutions since 2004 aimed at ending the violence in the Sudan and bringing the perpetrators to justice, these have been criticised as largely ineffectual, in part due to China's use of its position in the Security Council to weaken their content: see Russell P McAleavey, 'Pressuring Sudan: The Prospect of an Oil-for-Food Program for Darfur' (2008) 31 *Fordham International Law Journal* 1058, 1058–9, 1066–8. Most recently, the Security Council authorised an African Union/United Nations Hybrid operation in Darfur ('UNAMID') under Chapter VII of the Charter to, among other things, protect civilians and humanitarian operations: Security Council resolutions S/RES/1769 of 31 July 2007 (establishing UNAMID) and S/RES/1828 of 31 July 2008 (extending the mandate of UNAMID until 31 July 2009). UNAMID is prospectively the largest UN peacekeeping operation in history, however its capacities to meet its objectives are being hampered by, for example, delays in the deployment of troops and other resources from contributor States: *Darfur–UNAMID–Background* (2008) <http://www.un.org/Depts/ dpko/missions/unamid/background.html> at 30 January 2009.

[174] For example, on 11 July 2008 a US draft resolution in the Security Council aimed at imposing targeted sanctions against Zimbabwe was vetoed by China and Russia: 'Russia, China Veto UN Sanctions on Mugabe' *ABC News*, 12 July 2008 available at <http://www.abc.net.au/news/stories/2008/07/12/2301839.htm> at 29 January 2009. The draft proposal did not include the use of force, but rather the imposition of an arms embargo on the country and travel bans and financial freezes on key members of the government: UN Doc S/2008/447 of 11 July 2008.

Vietnam in Cambodia in 1978,[175] and NATO in order to stop ethnic cleansing in Kosovo in 1999.

However, the orthodox position is that the use of military force is illegal unless conducted for the purposes of proportionate self-defence (including collective self-defence) or authorised by the Security Council: unilateral military force by one State or a coalition of States is otherwise not legal without the consent of the target State,[176] even if exercised for humanitarian purposes.[177] However, a significant minority of international lawyers argue that unilateral humanitarian intervention is legal in certain circumstances. We will not engage in this debate here,[178] though we remind readers that the advocacy of the legality of humanitarian intervention equates with the advocacy of the legality of more instances of international warfare.[179]

In 2005, the General Assembly confirmed at the World Summit that each State has a responsibility to protect its population from grave human rights abuses, notably genocide, war crimes, ethnic cleansing and crimes against humanity. This responsibility devolved to 'the international community', notably the Security Council, if the relevant State was unwilling or unable to fulfil that duty.[180] The General Assembly did not, however, confirm any duty, or right, of unilateral humanitarian intervention if the Security Council should fail to act. An early General Assembly resolution, the 'Uniting for Peace

---

[175] See Byron F Burmester, 'On Humanitarian Intervention: The New World Order and Wars to Preserve Human Rights' (1994) *Utah Law Review* 269, 285–95. The classification of an intervention as 'humanitarian', however, can be problematic. For example, Vietnam's intervention was possibly opportunistic and imperialistic, rather than motivated by a desire to prevent the Khmer Rouge genocide.

[176] Military force is exercised with a target State's consent in, for example, the case of the deployment of peacekeeping missions.

[177] See UN Charter, Articles 2(4) and 2(7).

[178] The majority of international law scholars argue against the legality of unilateral humanitarian intervention. For examples against see Ian Brownlie, *Principles of Public International Law* (6th ed, Oxford University Press, Oxford, 2003) 710–12; Antonio Cassese, 'Ex Iniuria Ius Oritur: Are We Moving Towards International Legitimation of Forcible Humanitarian Countermeasures in the World Community?' (1999) 10(1) *European Journal of International Law* 23–30; Bruno Simma, 'NATO, the UN and the Use of Force: Legal Aspects' (1999) 10(1) *European Journal of International Law* 1–40. For examples in favour see Martha Brenfors and Malene Maxe Peterson, 'The Legality of Unilateral Humanitarian Intervention – A Defence' (2000) 69 *Nordic Journal of International Law* 449–99; Christopher Greenwood, 'International Law and the NATO Intervention in Kosovo' (2000) 49 (4) *International and Comparative Law Quarterly* 926–34.

[179] See generally Burmester, above n 175.

[180] General Assembly, *2005 World Summit Outcome*, UN Doc. A/60/L.1, 20 September 2005 [139].

Resolution',[181] arguably provides a basis for a positive vote of two-thirds of the General Assembly to authorise actions to maintain international peace and security if the Security Council is stymied by a veto.[182] The 'duty to protect' in the 2005 World Summit provides further support for the argument that the General Assembly can step up to the plate if the Security Council manifestly fails to do so. The question of unilateral intervention in the absence of Security Council action is not explicitly addressed by the World Summit document. Perhaps it is arguable that a manifest failure by the target State and the international community to fulfil their responsibility to protect means that a State or group of States may respond outside the UN framework to redress that dereliction of duty.[183] Even if such a window for unilateral humanitarian intervention can be identified, unilateral action would only be justified in the cases of the most extreme human rights abuses, and only after reasonable attempts at utilising peaceful and multilateral avenues of resolution had failed.[184]

### D  Costs of enforcement

It is clear that the enforcement of international human rights law is problematic, and perhaps inevitably so. The 'costs of enforcement' against a delinquent State are high, while the benefits for an enforcing State are 'low by traditional State interest calculations', such as the protection of reciprocal interests.[185] Existing forms of enforcement can be, depending on the situation, weak, inconsistently applied, or counter-productive in terms of producing more harm than good. The consequences of punishing a State in international human rights law are much less predictable and rational than, for example, the dynamics of punishing an individual under a State's domestic law. The punishment of a State inevitably involves the punishment of innocents within the State, probably the very human rights victims that the relevant sanction is

---

[181]  Resolution A/RES/377(V), 3 November 1950.

[182]  The legality of the use of force authorised by the General Assembly under this procedure and not the Security Council is a matter of debate. However, such an authorisation, endorsed by two-thirds of the world community, would have 'powerful moral and political support': International Commission on Intervention and State Sovereignty (ICISS), 'The Responsibility to Protect' (2001), available via <www.iciss.ca/pdf/Commission-Report.pdf> [6.7]; see also [6.29. 6.30] at 3 March 2009. It must be noted that it is politically very difficult to gain a 2/3 majority vote in a case where the Security Council is gridlocked: see ICISS, [6.30].

[183]  Alicia L Bannon, 'The Responsibility to Protect: the UN World Summit and the Question of Unilateralism', (2006) 115 *Yale Law Journal* 1157, 1162. See also ICISS, [6.28].

[184]  Ibid 1163–5.

[185]  Harold Hongju Koh, 'Internalization through Socialization', (2005) 54 *Duke Law Journal* 975, 977.

aimed at protecting. Target populations may also respond in unpredictable ways, for example, with a nationalistic backlash rather than with a desire that their government alter its ways.[186] These observations are not meant to defend the current weaknesses in international human rights enforcement so much as to explain that alternatives are (also) deeply problematic.

*E   International criminal law*
The advent, since the 1990s, of international criminal courts is a promising development in our view, as they are designed as forums for the prosecution and punishment of the worst abusers of human rights, without the side effect of punishing the abusers' fellow country-people.[187] The prosecutorial policy of the International Criminal Court is to focus on those most responsible for gross violations of human rights such as key military and civilian leaders involved in orchestrating and carrying out international crimes. This serves to balance the systemic nature of egregious human rights abuses and the principle under international criminal law of individual criminal responsibility. In a remarkably bold act, the Court issued an indictment in 2009 against the serving Sudanese President, Omar Al-Bashir, on seven counts of war crimes and crimes against humanity, the first of its kind against an acting head of State. On the one hand the indictment marks a significant turning point in the challenge of impunity of heads of State and other high-ranking political players. On the other hand, the African Union has opposed the indictment because of concerns regarding its prospective impact on the peace process in Darfur.[188] Whether or not true, this indicates that the indictment of individuals of political significance will also generate allegations of a collateral negative impact on innocent people.[189]

## 5   Conclusion
Sixty years on from the adoption of the UDHR, the UN can perhaps be given a pass mark with regard to its human rights record, but not a high grade. Its greatest achievements lie in standard-setting, and in the general (if not always

---

[186]   Note, for example, the pro-China rallies held across the world in response to attacks on the Olympic flame in the lead-up to the Beijing Olympics of 2008. See also Anna di Robilant, 'Genealogies of Soft Law', (2006) 54 *American Journal of Comparative Law* 499, 508.

[187]   See also Chapter 10.

[188]   'African Union Against Indicting Bashir' *Los Angeles Times*, (31 January 2009) <http://www.latimes.com/news/nationworld/world/la-fg-sudan31-2009 jan31.0.5070523.story> at 31 January 2009.

[189]   Of course, international criminal law is beset with its own problems, such as cumbersome processes and resource limitations.

unanimous) acceptance that human rights are not a sovereign matter but a matter of genuine international obligation. Another achievement is the increasing mainstreaming of human rights into international and national institutions, for example through the work of the OHCHR. Its political institutions have a mixed record, with successes entailed in the establishment of the special procedures and failures entailed in the undue focus on political point-scoring ahead of human rights enforcement. The treaty bodies have generated impressive and important human rights jurisprudence, but the record of State compliance with their recommendations is not so impressive. As noted above, human rights enforcement often fails to alter the behaviour of human rights abusers, but the solution to this problem is not obvious.

Thus, the main success has been in the normative arena, that is standard-setting by way of the creation of treaties, and the interpretations thereof from specialist human rights bodies. It is hoped that the new millennium will usher in a focus on making existing global norms and UN human rights institutions more effective and credible.

## 2. Economic, social and cultural rights: an examination of state obligations
*Manisuli Ssenyonjo*

### 1 Introduction

Economic, Social and Cultural Rights ('ESC rights') are protected in several international human rights treaties, the most comprehensive of which is the *International Covenant on Economic, Social and Cultural Rights* ('ICESCR' or the 'Covenant').[1] On 10 December 2008 the United Nations ('UN') General Assembly adopted the Optional Protocol to the ICESCR,[2] which provides the Committee on Economic, Social and Cultural Rights ('CESCR'), an expert body which monitors the implementation of ESC rights under the ICESCR, with three new roles: (i) to receive and consider individual and group communications claiming 'a violation of any of the economic, social and cultural rights set forth in the Covenant'; (ii) to receive and consider inter-State communications to the effect that a State party claims that another State party is 'not fulfilling its obligations under the Covenant'; and (iii) to conduct an inquiry in cases where the Committee receives reliable information indicating 'grave or systematic violations' by a State party of any ESC rights set forth in the ICESCR.[3]

The Optional Protocol will come into force after ratification by the required number of ten States in accordance with Article 18 of the Optional Protocol. This will usher in a new era of accountability for violations of ESC rights in international law and dispel claims that ESC rights under the ICESCR were not intended to be justiciable.[4] This means that, more than ever before, it is

---

[1] Opened for signature 16 December 1966, 993 UNTS 3 (entered into force 3 January 1976).

[2] See the *Optional Protocol to the International Covenant on Economic, Social and Cultural Rights*, GA Res A/RES/63/117 (10 December 2008). For a discussion of the Optional Protocol see L Chenwi, 'Correcting the Historical Asymmetry between Rights: The Optional Protocol to the International Covenant on Economic, Social and Cultural Rights (2009) 9 *African Human Rights Law Journal* 23 and Tara J Melish, 'Introductory Note to the Optional Protocol to the International Covenant on Economic, Social and Cultural Rights' (2009) 48 *International Legal Materials* 256.

[3] Articles 1, 2, 10, and 11 ICESCR Protocol.

[4] See M Dennis and D Stewart, 'Justiciability of Economic, Social and Cultural

pertinent to examine the nature and scope of State obligations under the ICESCR for which States could be held accountable under the Optional Protocol, in light of the current state of international law, in order to provide a clear understanding of the obligations contained in the Covenant.

ESC rights include the rights to work and to just and favourable conditions of work; to rest and leisure; to form and join trade unions and to strike; to social security; to protection of the family, mothers and children; to an adequate standard of living, including adequate food, clothing and housing; to the highest attainable standard of physical and mental health; to education and to participate in cultural life and enjoy the benefits of scientific progress.[5] The effective respect, protection, and fulfilment of these rights is an important – and under-explored – component of international human rights. This is despite the fact that the *Universal Declaration of Human Rights* ('UDHR')[6] recognised two sets of human rights: civil and political rights, as well as ESC rights. In transforming the provisions of the UDHR into legally binding obligations, the UN adopted two separate but interdependent covenants: the *International Covenant on Civil and Political Rights* ('ICCPR')[7] and the ICESCR. As of March 2009, there were 160 States parties to the ICESCR compared with 164 States parties to the ICCPR. The two covenants, along with the UDHR, constitute the core of the international human rights law.

This chapter examines three aspects of ESC rights divided into three sections – namely general State obligations (Section 2); extraterritorial application of ESC rights (Section 3); and non-derogability of ESC rights (Section 4) – with a particular focus on the ICESCR because the Covenant deals with this category of rights more comprehensively than other existing human rights instruments. The chapter specifically deals with the following questions. First, what are the obligations of States parties to the ICESCR under Article 2(1) ICESCR? Secondly, are States parties' human rights obligations arising under the ICESCR limited to individuals and groups within a State's territory, or can a State be liable for the acts and omissions of its agents which produce negative effects on the progressive enjoyment of ESC rights or are undertaken beyond national territory (for example, to those individuals and groups who are not within the State's territory but who are subject to a State's jurisdiction)? Thirdly, does the ICESCR apply fully in the time of armed conflict, war

---

Rights: Should There be an International Complaints Mechanism to Adjudicate the Rights to Food, Water, Housing and Health?' (2004) 98 *American Journal of International Law* 462.

[5] Articles 6–15 ICESCR.
[6] GA Res 217A (III), UN Doc A/810, 71 (1948).
[7] Opened for signature 16 December 1966, 999 UNTS 171 (entered into force 23 March 1976).

or other public emergency? Apart from the first issue, which has been included to provide a general overview to the Covenant, the other issues have been selected because, despite their significance, they are not specifically addressed in the Covenant and few studies have explored them in relation to ESC rights.

This chapter aims to demonstrate that the ICESCR lays down clear human rights legal obligations for States parties, noting that, while the Covenant provides for 'progressive realisation' and acknowledges the constraints due to the limits of 'available resources', it also imposes various obligations which are of immediate effect (for example, the obligation to take steps, and to eliminate discrimination in the enjoyment of ESC rights). It notes that the increase in domestic case law on ESC rights clearly indicates that violations of ESC rights are justiciable, and States should ensure their justiciability in practice at a national level. At the international level, the adoption of an Optional Protocol to the ICESCR by the General Assembly on 10 December 2008 providing for individual and group communications, inter-State communications and an inquiry procedure in cases of grave or systematic violations of any ESC rights was long overdue.[8]

Further, this chapter argues that every State party to the ICESCR can be found to be in violation of its obligations under the ICESCR for actions taken by it extraterritorially, in relation to anyone within the power, effective control or authority of that State, as well as within an area over which that State exercises effective overall control.

Finally, this chapter notes that the absence of a clause allowing derogation in times of public emergency in the ICESCR indicates that the Covenant generally continues to apply in time of armed conflict, war or other public emergency, and, at the least, States cannot derogate from the Covenant's minimum core obligations.

A clarification of the above aspects may provide an incentive for States to take their human rights obligations under the Covenant more seriously. It may also help to develop the necessary political will among states parties to the ICESCR required for the signature and ratification by States of the Optional Protocol to strengthen an international legal framework of accountability for violations of ESC rights, whether within or outside a State's borders and regardless of whether it is during peacetime or in time of armed conflict, war or other public emergency. Such a development would strengthen the international legal protection of ESC rights and assist States in complying with their international human rights legal obligations.

---

[8] See ICESCR Protocol.

## 2 State human rights obligations under Article 2(1) ICESCR

In this section, specific human rights obligations of States parties to the ICESCR arising from Article 2(1) ICESCR are examined since these directly inform all of the substantive rights protected in Articles 6 to 15 ICESCR. Article 2(1) ICESCR is fundamental to the Covenant since it is the general legal 'obligation' provision.[9] Under Article 2(1) ICESCR:

> Each State Party to the present Covenant undertakes to take steps, individually and through international assistance and co-operation, especially economic and technical, to the maximum of its available resources, with a view to achieving progressively the full realisation of the rights recognised in the present Covenant by all appropriate means, including particularly the adoption of legislative measures.

It is noteworthy that, although some States have made reservations and declarations to the Covenant, none has ever made a reservation or declaration in respect of Article 2(1) ICESCR.[10] It has to be borne in mind that since the Covenant is an international treaty, the human rights obligations undertaken by States under it, and consequently by the international community, must be performed in good faith (*pacta sunt servanda*).[11] Moreover, the Covenant as a human rights treaty must generally be 'interpreted in good faith in accordance with the ordinary meaning to be given to the terms of the treaty in their context and in light of its object and purpose'.[12] Interpretation can be supplemented by recourse to the preparatory work (*travaux préparatoires*) of the Covenant to confirm the meaning of the treaty provisions or to determine it where the ordinary meaning leaves the meaning 'ambiguous or obscure' or 'manifestly absurd or unreasonable'.[13]

---

[9] M Craven, *The International Covenant on Economic, Social and Cultural Rights: A Perspective on its Development* (Clarendon Press, Oxford, 1995) 106–52.

[10] See http://www2.ohchr.org/english/bodies/ratification/3.htm#reservations at 5 December 2008. For a discussion see M Ssenyonjo, 'State Reservations to the ICESCR: A Critique of Selected Reservations' (2008) 26 *Netherlands Quarterly of Human Rights* 315.

[11] *Vienna Convention on the Law of Treaties*, opened for signature 23 May 1969, 1155 UNTS 331 (entered into force 27 January 1980) ('VCLT'). Article 26 VCLT provides: 'Every treaty in force is binding upon the parties to the treaty and must be performed by them in good faith.' See also 'Report of the ILC to the General Assembly' [1966] II *Year Book of the International Law Commission* 175, 211.

[12] Article 31 VCLT; *Golder v United Kingdom* [1975] 18 Eur Ct HR (ser A) 14.

[13] Article 32 VCLT. For a discussion of treaty interpretation, see A Aust, *Modern Treaty Law and Practice* (Cambridge University Press, Cambridge, 2nd ed, 2007) 230–55. The ICJ recognised these principles as embodying customary international law ('CIL') in *Territorial Dispute (Libyan Arab Jamahariya/Chad)* [1994] ICJ Rep [41].

Thus, in interpreting human rights obligations arising from human rights treaties, including the ICESCR, it is useful to look to the 'ordinary meaning' by referring to the text. This must be done in the 'context' of a treaty, which includes the treaty's text, including its preamble and annexes.[14] The Covenant's preamble and many other human rights instruments reiterate the indivisibility of ESC rights and civil and political rights.[15] Treaty terms (of the Covenant) must be interpreted in the light of the Covenant's 'object and purpose', which like that of other human rights instruments is the 'effective protection of human rights' of individuals and groups. Effectiveness demands that treaty provisions be given full effect and that treaty monitoring bodies (in the context of the Covenant, the CESCR) adopt an 'evolutionary' view of human rights instruments as expanding in scope over time.[16] It is in this context that Article 2(1) ICESCR is examined below.

It has been observed that '[r]elative to Article 2 of the ICCPR, Article 2 of the ICESCR is weak with respect to implementation'.[17] Hence Craven expressed the position as follows:

> Article 2(1) itself is somewhat confused and unsatisfactory provision. The combination of convoluted phraseology and numerous qualifying sub-clauses seems to defy any real sense of obligation. Indeed it has been read by some as giving States an almost total freedom of choice and action as to how the rights should be implemented.[18]

---

[14] Article 31(2) VCLR.

[15] Preamble [4] ICESCR recognises that, 'in accordance with the Universal Declaration of Human Rights, the ideal of free human beings enjoying freedom from fear and want can only be achieved if conditions are created whereby everyone may enjoy his economic, social and cultural rights, as well as his civil and political rights'.

[16] By way of analogy, the Inter-American Court of Human Rights ('IACtHR') has stated in *The Right to Information on Consular Assistance in the Framework of the Guarantees of Due Process of Law*, Advisory Opinion No OC-16/99, 16 (ser A) (1 October 1999) [114]: 'Both this Court, in the Advisory Opinion on the *Interpretation of the American Declaration of the Rights and Duties of Man*, Advisory Opinion No OC-10/89, 10 (ser A) (14 July 1989) [43], and the European Court of Human Rights, in *Tyrer v United Kingdom* [1978] 26 (ser A) 15, [31]; *Marckx v Belgium* [1979] 31 (ser A) 19 [41]; *Loizidou v Turkey (Preliminary Objections)* [1995] 310 (ser A) 26, [71], among others, have held that human rights treaties are living instruments whose interpretation must consider the changes over time and present-day conditions.'

[17] H Steiner and P Alston, *International Human Rights in Context: Law, Politics, Morals – Text and Materials* (Oxford University Press, Oxford, 2nd ed, 2000) 275. For analysis of Article 2(1) ICCPR, see D Harris, 'The *International Covenant on Civil and Political Rights* and the United Kingdom: An Introduction' in D Harris and S Joseph (eds) *The International Covenant on Civil and Political Rights and United Kingdom Law* (Clarendon Press, Oxford, 1995) 1–8; M Nowak, *UN Covenant on Civil and Political Rights: CCPR Commentary* (N P Engel, Kehl, 2nd ed, 2005) 37–42.

[18] M Craven, 'The Justiciability of Economic, Social and Cultural Rights' in

The language of Article 2(1) ICESCR is clearly wide and full of caveats and any assessment of whether a State has complied with or infringed its general obligation to 'take steps to the maximum of its available resources, with a view to achieving progressively the full realisation of the rights recognised in the Covenant' of a particular individual is a complex matter.[19] For example, in the context of individual and collective communications such difficulty arises when deciding whether a particular State's resources were such that it should have provided a petitioner with a doctor/hospital treatment (in the context of the right to health)[20] or with a teacher/school (in the context of the right to education).

However, the nature and scope of the States parties' obligations under the Covenant, including the provisions of Article 2(1) ICESCR above, and the nature and scope of violations of ESC rights and appropriate responses and remedies have been examined by groups of experts in international law who adopted the *Limburg Principles on the Implementation of the ICESCR*[21] in 1986 and the *Maastricht Guidelines on Violations of Economic Social and Cultural Rights*[22] in 1997. Although the Limburg Principles and Maastricht Guidelines are not legally binding *per se*, they may arguably provide 'a subsidiary means' for the interpretation of the Covenant as 'teachings of the most highly qualified publicists of the various nations' under Article 38(1)(d) of the *Statute of the International Court of Justice*. Moreover the participants who adopted the Limburg Principles believed that they 'reflect[ed] the present state of international law, with the exception of certain recommendations indicated by the use of the verb "should" instead of "shall"'.[23] The participants who adopted the Maastricht Guidelines considered them to 'reflect the evolution of international law since 1986'.[24]

---

R Burchill, D Harris and A Owers (eds) *Economic, Social and Cultural Rights: Their Implementation in United Kingdom Law* (University of Nottingham Human Rights Law Centre, Nottingham, 1999) 1, 5 (footnotes omitted).

[19] D Harris, 'Comments' in F Coomans and F Van Hoof (eds) *The Right to Complain about Economic, Social and Cultural Rights* (SIM Special No 18, Utrecht, 1995) 103.

[20] Ibid.

[21] UN Doc E/CN.4/1987/17, Annex (1987) ('Limburg Principles'). The 29 participants who adopted the Limburg Principles came from various States and international organisations.

[22] (1998) 20 *Human Rights Quarterly* 691 ('Maastricht Guidelines'). The Maastricht Guidelines were adopted by a group of more than thirty experts. For a commentary on these guidelines see E Dankwa, C Flinterman and S Leckie, 'Commentary to the Maastricht Guidelines on Violations of Economic, Social and Cultural Rights' (1998) 20 *Human Rights Quarterly* 705.

[23] Limburg Principles, above n 21, Introduction [4].

[24] Maastricht Guidelines, above n 22, Introduction.

The CESCR has also, in numerous General Comments and Statements, spelt out the content of State obligations and individual/group rights under the Covenant. By May 2009, the Committee had adopted 20 General Comments, 13 of which related to substantive rights while 7 dealt with other aspects of the Covenant.[25] In addition the Committee had issued 16 Statements on several key issues relevant to ESC rights including, for example, poverty, globalisation, intellectual property and the world food crisis.[26] While General Comments and Statements are not legally binding, they can have a persuasive effect, setting out interpretive positions around which State practice may unite. No State has ever raised any formal objections to the General Comments or Statements, apparently suggesting wide acceptance of the Committee's Comments and Statements by States.

Having established the framework within which the Covenant should be interpreted, it is now useful to establish what human rights obligations arise from Article 2(1) ICESCR, taking into account the Covenant's object and purpose, the ordinary meaning, the preparatory work and relevant practice.[27] Adopting this approach, the following obligations arise from Article 2(1) ICESCR.

*A  Obligation to 'take steps . . . by all appropriate means'*

Under Article 2(1) ICESCR, States[28] undertake to 'take steps . . . by all appropriate means, including particularly the adoption of legislative measures' towards the full realisation of the rights guaranteed under the Covenant. The scope of this obligation was clarified by the CESCR in 1990 in General Comment 3 on the nature of States parties' obligations.[29] The Committee noted in [1] and [2] of General Comment 3 that Article 2 ICESCR imposes on the State 'obligations of conduct and obligations of result' and that, while the Covenant provides for progressive realisation and acknowledges the

---

[25]  CESCR General Comments are available online: http://www2.ohchr.org/english/bodies/cescr/comments.htm at 5 December 2008.

[26]  Statements of the Committee are available online: http://www2.ohchr.org/english/bodies/cescr/statements.htm at 5 December 2008.

[27]  Articles 31 and 32 VCLT.

[28]  The obligations of the Covenant in general and Article 2 ICESCR in particular are binding on every State party as a whole. All branches of government (executive, legislative and judicial), and other public or governmental authorities, at whatever level – national, regional or local – are in a position to engage the responsibility of the State party. The Human Rights Committee ('HRC') has taken a similar view with respect to the ICCPR. See HRC, *General Comment 31[80]: Nature of the General Legal Obligation on States Parties to the Covenant*, UN Doc. CCPR/C/21/Rev.1/Add.13 (26 May 2004) [4].

[29]  UN Doc E/1991/23 (1991) Annex III, 86.

constraints due to the limits of available resources, it also imposes various obligations which are of immediate effect. One of these is the 'undertaking to guarantee' that relevant rights 'will be exercised without discrimination'; and the other is the undertaking in Article 2(1) ICESCR 'to take steps'.

General Comment 3 indicates that Article 2(1) imposes an 'obligation of conduct'[30] (that is, action – active or passive – to follow, or abstain from, a given conduct to realise the enjoyment of a particular right) to begin to take steps *immediately* in a manner which constantly and consistently advances towards the full realisation of ESC rights. The obligation to 'take steps' is not qualified or limited by other considerations.[31] A failure to comply with this obligation cannot be justified by reference to social, cultural or economic considerations within the State.[32]

In addition, Article 2(1) ICESCR obliges a State to continue taking steps consistently, without any deliberate regressive action.[33] The steps taken should be geared towards achieving the principal 'obligation of result'[34] (to achieve specific targets/standards), which is to achieve 'progressively the full realisation of the rights guaranteed' in the Covenant.[35] In respect of the right to primary education, for example, the obligation of conduct could involve the adoption and implementation of a plan of action to ensure that children are going to primary schools. The obligation of result requires that children are learning to read and write.

Significantly, steps towards the goal of full realisation 'must be taken within reasonably short time after the Covenant's entry into force for the States concerned' and such steps must be 'deliberate, concrete and targeted'

---

[30] Maastricht Guidelines, above n 22, [7]. The obligation of conduct requires action reasonably calculated to realise the enjoyment of a particular right. In the case of the right to health, for example, the obligation of conduct could involve the adoption and implementation of a plan of action to reduce maternal mortality.

[31] CESCR, *General Comment 3: The nature of States parties obligations (Art 2(1))*, UN Doc E/1991/23 (14 December 1990) [2]; Limburg Principles, above n 21, [16], [21].

[32] CESCR, *Concluding Observations: Iraq*, UN Doc E/1998/22 (20 June 1998) [253], [281].

[33] See also Inter-American Commission on Human Rights ('IACmHR'), *Second Report on the Situation of Human Rights in Peru*, IACmHR Doc OEA/Ser.L/V/II.106/Doc. 59 rev (2 June 2000) Ch VI, [11].

[34] Maastricht Guidelines, above n 22, [7]: The obligation of result requires States to achieve specific targets to satisfy a detailed substantive standard. With respect to the right to health, for example, the obligation of result requires the reduction of maternal mortality to levels agreed at the 1994 Cairo International Conference on Population and Development and the 1995 Beijing Fourth World Conference on Women.

[35] General Comment 3, above n 31, [9].

towards the full realisation of the Covenant rights.[36] Some steps that States parties are required to take are of *immediate* nature, especially in the case of negative obligations that largely require non-interference, with limited direct resource implications. As shown below, the prohibition of discrimination falls within this category.[37] Other steps may be taken over a period of time, being *progressive* in nature, especially those requiring largely positive obligations that may have significant direct resource implications.[38] This distinction is significant in determining State compliance/non-compliance or unwillingness or inability to comply with the Covenant obligations, as non-compliance or violation of an obligation can only arise if compliance is due at a particular point in time.

In general terms, States are required to adopt two types of measures: legislative and non-legislative measures. Legislative measures include not only the adoption of new legislation but also the duty to reform, amend and repeal legislation manifestly inconsistent with the Covenant.[39] While the Covenant does not formally oblige States to incorporate its provisions in domestic law,[40] the Committee has stated:

> [I]n many instances legislation is highly desirable and in some cases may even be indispensable. For example, it may be difficult to combat discrimination effectively in the absence of a sound legislative foundation for the necessary measures. In fields such as health, the protection of children and mothers, and education, as well as in respect of the matters dealt with in Articles 6 to 9, legislation may also be an indispensable element for many purposes.[41]

Unsurprisingly, in 2005 the Committee, in General Comment 16 on the equal right of men and women to the enjoyment of all ESC rights, stated that:

---

[36] CESCR, *General Comment 13: The right to education (Art 13)*, UN Doc E/C.12/1999/10 (8 December 1999) [43]; *General Comment 14: The right to the highest attainable standard of health (Art 12)*, UN Doc E/C.12/2000/4 (11 August 2000) [30].

[37] See below nn 57–8 and accompanying text. See also UN Commission on Human Rights, *The right to education*, UN Doc E/CN.4/Res/2002/23 (22 April 2002) [4(b)].

[38] For example, the progressive introduction of free secondary and higher education: see Articles 13(2)(b) and (c) ICESCR.

[39] See, for example, CESCR, *Concluding Observations: Cyprus*, UN Doc E/C.12/1/Add.28 (4 December 1998) [26].

[40] CESCR, *General Comment 9: The domestic application of the Covenant*, UN Doc E/C.12/1998/2 (3 December 1998) [8].

[41] General Comment 3, above n 31, [3].

Failure to adopt, implement, and monitor effects of laws, policies and programmes to eliminate de jure and de facto discrimination with respect to each of the rights enumerated in Articles 6 to 15 of the Covenant constitutes a *violation of those rights*.[42]

There is no doubt that legislative measures are indispensable in the protection of all human rights including ESC rights,[43] since a sound legislative foundation provides a firm basis to protect such rights and enforce them in the case of violations. Legislation is particularly essential to combat *de jure* discrimination such as that against women, minorities, children and persons with disabilities.[44] It is in this regard that the Committee on the Elimination of Discrimination against Women ('CEDAW Committee') has urged States with discriminatory laws against women to accelerate the law review process and to work effectively with Parliament in ensuring that all discriminatory legislation is amended or repealed.[45]

While legislation is essential, it is not enough *per se* for the realisation of ESC rights. Therefore, in addition to legislation, other 'appropriate means', such as the provision of judicial or other effective remedies, administrative, financial, educational or informational campaigns and social measures, must be undertaken to achieve the intended result. This calls for putting in place appropriate means of redress, or remedies to any aggrieved individual or group, and appropriate means of ensuring accountability of States and non-State actors.[46] This entails making ESC rights justiciable at a national level.

## B  Progressive realisation

As noted above, the steps taken should be geared towards the obligation of result which is 'achieving progressively the full realisation' of the Covenant

---

[42] CESCR, *General Comment 16: The equal right of men and women to the enjoyment of all economic, social and cultural rights (Art 3)*, UN Doc. E/C.12/2005/3 (11 August 2005) [41] (emphasis added).

[43] See General Comment 3, above n 31, [3]; General Comment 14, above n 36, [56]: 'States should consider adopting a framework law to operationalise their right to health national strategy.'

[44] See, for example, CESCR, *Concluding Observations: Iraq*, UN Doc E/C.12/1/Add.17 (12 December 1997) [13], [14]; CESCR, *Concluding Observations: Morocco*, UN Doc E/C.12/1/Add.55 (1 December 2000) [34], [45] and [47]; CESCR, *General Comment 5: Persons with disabilities*, UN Doc E/1995/22 (9 December 1994) [16].

[45] CEDAW Committee, *Concluding Observations: Tanzania*, UN Doc CEDAW//C/TZA/CO/6 (18 July 2008) [16], [17] and [55]; CEDAW Committee, *Concluding Observations: Nigeria*, UN Doc CEDAW/C/NGA/CO/6 (18 July 2008) [13], [14] and [44].

[46] General Comment 9, above n 40, [2]. See also Chapter 4.

rights. The appropriateness of the steps taken should therefore be examined by reference to the standard of 'progressive realisation'. But what is meant by 'progressive' realisation? Does the word 'progressive' enable the obligations of States parties 'to be postponed to an indefinite time in the distant future' as argued by Hungary during the preparatory work on the Covenant?[47]

According to its ordinary meaning, the term 'progressive' means 'moving forward'[48] or 'advancing by successive stages'[49] in a manner that is 'continuous, increasing, growing, developing, ongoing, intensifying, accelerating, escalating, gradual, step by step'.[50] Thus, States parties are obliged to improve continuously the conditions of ESC rights, and generally to abstain from taking regressive measures. This notion of progressive realisation of ESC rights over a period of time 'constitutes a recognition of the fact that full realisation of all [ESC rights] will generally not be able to be achieved in a short period of time . . . reflecting the realities of the real world and the difficulties involved for any country in ensuring full realisation of [ESC rights]'.[51]

This obligation contrasts with the immediate obligation imposed by Article 2(1) ICCPR that obliges States to 'respect and ensure' the substantive rights under the ICCPR. Despite this, the 'reality is that the full realisation of civil and political rights is heavily dependent both on the availability of resources and the development of the necessary societal structures'.[52] As a result States are required to take positive measures for the realisation of civil and political rights.[53] For example, the right to a fair trial as protected by Article 14(1)

---

[47] UN Doc A/2910/Add.6 (1955) [9].
[48] H W Fowler (ed) *The Concise Oxford Dictionary of Current English* (Oxford University Press, Oxford, 1990) 954.
[49] E M Kirkpatrick (ed) *Chambers Family Dictionary* (Chambers, Edinburgh, 1981) 613.
[50] P Hanks (ed), *The New Oxford Thesaurus of English* (Oxford University Press, Oxford, 2000), 754.
[51] General Comment 3, above n 31, [9]. Under the *Convention on the Rights of the Child*, opened for signature 18 December 1979, 1249 UNTS 13 (entered into force 3 September 1981) ('CRC'), which includes ESC rights and corresponding State obligations, there is no reference to the qualifying clause 'progressive realisation'. Thus, its obligations arise immediately, although implementation is qualified by the phrase 'within their means'.
[52] P Alston and G Quinn, 'The Nature and Scope of States Parties' Obligations under the *International Covenant on Economic, Social and Cultural Rights*' (1987) 9 *Human Rights Quarterly*, 156, 172. See also H Steiner, 'International Protection of Human Rights' in M D Evans (ed) *International Law* (Oxford University Press, Oxford, 2003) 757.
[53] See A Mowbray, *The Development of Positive Obligations under the European Convention on Human Rights by the European Court of Human Rights* (Hart Publishing, Oxford, 2004).

ICCPR and Article 6 of the *European Convention on Human Rights* ('ECHR')[54] encompasses the right of access to a court in cases of determination of criminal charges and rights and obligations in a suit at law,[55] and the provision of free legal aid if this is 'indispensable for an effective access to court', for example for individuals who do not have sufficient means to pay for it.[56] Accordingly fair trial necessitates the provision of independent and accessible organs of justice.

Since the obligation upon States under Article 2(1) ICESCR is the progressive achievement of ESC rights, it might be argued that to demand their immediate implementation is not required by the ICESCR. Two responses are essential here. First, some rights under the ICESCR give rise to obligations of immediate effect. One example is the right to be free from discrimination in the enjoyment of all ESC rights. The Committee has stated:

> The prohibition against discrimination enshrined in Article 2(2) of the Covenant is subject to neither progressive realisation nor the availability of resources; it applies fully and immediately to all aspects of education and encompasses all internationally prohibited grounds of discrimination.[57]

Thus, a State cannot argue that it is providing primary education or primary health care to boys immediately but will extend it to girls progressively. Similarly, the argument that a State is paying women less than men for work of equal value until resources are available would not be acceptable since the right of women to an equal salary for equal work should be implemented immediately.[58]

Another example is that every substantive ICESCR right has a minimum core content which gives rise to minimum core entitlements to individuals and groups and corresponding minimum core State obligations of immediate effect.[59] On the latter, the CESCR has found that, with regard to every substantive ICESCR right, there is:

---

[54] *Convention for the Protection of Human Rights and Fundamental Freedoms*, opened for signature 4 November 1950, 213 UNTS 222 (entered into force 3 September1953).

[55] HRC, *General Comment 32: Right to Equality before Courts and Tribunals and to a Fair Trial (Art 14)*, UN Doc CCPR/C/GC/32 (23 August 2007) [9]; *Golder v United Kingdom* [1975] 18 Eur Ct HR (ser A) 14, [34], [35].

[56] *Airey v Ireland* (1979) 32 (ser A) [26]; General Comment 3, above n 31, [10].

[57] General Comment 13, above n 36, [31]. See also UN Commission on Human Rights, above n 37, [4(b)].

[58] See Article 7(a)(i) ICESCR.

[59] For a discussion of minimum core obligations, see generally A Chapman and S Russell (eds) *Core Obligations: Building a Framework for Economic, Social and Cultural Rights* (Intersentia, Antwerp, 2002).

[A] minimum core obligation to ensure the satisfaction of, at the very least, minimum essential levels of each of the rights is incumbent upon every State party. Thus, for example, a State party in which any significant number of individuals is deprived of essential foodstuffs, of essential primary health care, of basic shelter and housing, or of the most basic forms of education is, prima facie, failing to discharge its obligations under the Covenant.[60]

The Committee has identified minimum core obligations in several General Comments,[61] and held that a State party cannot, under any circumstances whatsoever, justify its non-compliance with these core obligations, which are 'non-derogable'.[62] Otherwise the ICESCR would be largely deprived of its *raison d'être*.

Second, the CESCR has explained that Article 2 ICESCR 'imposes an obligation to move as expeditiously and effectively as possible' towards the Covenant's goal of full realisation of the substantive rights under the Covenant.[63] However the Committee has not specified how 'expeditiously and effectively' a State should act in achieving the full realisation of all ESC rights. Nonetheless, the Committee has established in several General Comments[64] that the full realisation of ESC rights, like other human rights, imposes three types or levels of multi-layered State obligations: the obliga-

---

[60] General Comment 3, above n 31, [10].

[61] See for example CESCR, *General Comment No 11: Plans of Action for primary education (Art 14)*, UN Doc E/C.12/1999/4 (10 May 1999) [17]; General Comment 13, above n 36, [57]; General Comment 14, above n 36, [43]; *General Comment 15: The right to water (Arts 11 and 12)*, UN Doc E/C.12/2002/11 (20 January 2003) [37]; *General Comment 17: The right of everyone to benefit from the protection of the moral and material interests resulting from any scientific, literary or artistic production of which he or she is the author (Art 15(1)(c))*, UN Doc E/C.12/GC/17 (12 January 2006) [39]; *General Comment 18: The right to work (Art 6)*, UN Doc E/C.12/GC/18 (6 February 2006) [31]; and *General Comment 19: The right to social security*, UN Doc E/C.12/GC/19 (4 February 2008) [59].

[62] General Comment 14, above n 36, [47]; General Comment 15, above n 61, [40]. See also CESCR, *Poverty and the International Covenant on Economic, Social and Cultural Rights*, UN Doc. E/C.12/2001/10 (10 May 2001) [18].

[63] See, for example, General Comment 3, above n 31, [9]; General Comment 13, above n 36, [44]; *General Comment 14*, above n 36, [31]; and General Comment 15, above n 61, [18]; Limburg Principles, above n 21, 21. See also CESCR, *Statement on Poverty and the ICESCR*, UN Doc E/C.12/2001/10 (4 May 2001) [18].

[64] See, for example, General Comment 19, above n 61, [43]; General Comment 18, above n 61, [22]; General Comment 17, above n 61, [28]; General Comment 16, above n 42, [18]–[21]; General Comment 15, above n 61, [20]–[29]; General Comment 14, above n 36, [33]; General Comment 13, above n 36, [46]. The General Comments of all UN human rights treaty bodies are compiled in UN Doc HRI/GEN/1/Rev.7 (12 May 2004) http://www.unhchr.ch/tbs/doc.nsf/0/ca12c3a4ea8d6c53c1256d500056e56f?Opendocument at 5 December 2008.

tions to *respect, protect* and *fulfil*.⁶⁵ This approach has also been applied by regional human rights supervisory bodies such as the African Commission on Human and Peoples' Rights in some of its decisions,⁶⁶ and provides a useful analytical framework to understanding State obligations.

In order to comply with the obligation to achieve ESC rights 'progressively', States parties are required to monitor the realisation of ESC rights and to devise appropriate strategies and clearly defined programmes (including indicators, carefully chosen yardsticks, national benchmarks or targets for measuring elements of the right) for their implementation.⁶⁷ A human rights approach to government actions must begin with a proper understanding of the actual situation in respect of each right, accurate identification of the most vulnerable groups, and the formulation of appropriate laws, programmes and policies.⁶⁸

The CESCR should also be in a position to measure consistently and scrutinise progress made by States by reference to good quantitative and qualitative data, indicators/benchmarks (in respect of the rights recognised under the Covenant)⁶⁹ developed, *inter alia*, by the relevant UN specialised agencies such as the International Labour Organisation ('ILO'); the Food and Agriculture Organization of the United Nations ('FAO'); the United Nations Educational, Scientific and Cultural Organization ('UNESCO'); and the

---

⁶⁵ This analysis follows Eide's taxonomy, whereby State obligations for all human rights can be seen as involving obligations to 'respect, protect and fulfil' the rights in question. See A Eide, *The Right to Adequate Food as a Human Right*, UN Doc E/CN.4/Sub.2/1987/23 (7 July 1987) [66]; A Eide, 'Economic and Social Rights', in J Symonides (ed) *Human Rights: Concepts and Standards*, (UNESCO Publishing, Aldershot, 2000) 109.

⁶⁶ See, for example, *The Social and Economic Rights Action Center and the Center for Economic and Social Rights/Nigeria*, Communication No 155/96 [2001] African Human Rights Law Reports 60, [44].

⁶⁷ General Comment 14, above n 36, [57], [58]; P Alston, 'Out of the Abyss: The Challenges Confronting the New UN Committee on Economic, Social and Cultural Rights' (1987) 9 *Human Rights Quarterly* 332, 357–8; Maastricht Guidelines, above n 22, [8]. For example, in the 2002 World Summit on Sustainable Development Plan of Implementation, States made a commitment to halve, by the year 2015, the proportion of people who are unable to reach or to afford safe drinking water (as outlined in the Millennium Declaration) and the proportion of people who do not have access to basic sanitation.

⁶⁸ CESCR, *Concluding Observations*: *Republic of Korea*, UN Doc E/C.12/1/Add.59 (21 May 2001) [34].

⁶⁹ See P Hunt, *State Obligations, Indicators, Benchmarks and the Right to Education*, UN Doc E/C.12/1998/11 (16 June 1998); A Chapman, *Indicators and Standards for Monitoring Economic, Social and Cultural Rights* (UNDP, 2000), http://hdr.undp.org/docs/events/global_forum/2000/chapman.pdf at 5 December 2008.

World Health Organization ('WHO').[70] For example, in assessing the realisation of the right to health, the WHO provides possible sources of data. These include: (1) Service Availability Mapping ('SAM'), which is a free, on-line service that includes only government-released data; (2) WHO country fact sheets; (3) the WHO database, which includes census data, vital registration and population studies; and (4) relevant WHO reports. For instance, the core goals of a good functioning health system as set out in *World Health Report 2000* may provide a useful handful of generic indicators against which all States should be monitored under the right to health (good health, responsiveness and fair financial contribution).[71] Since national averages reveal little about the real situation of specific (vulnerable and disadvantaged) groups and communities, much of this data, to be meaningful, must be disaggregated into relevant categories, including gender, race, ethnicity, religion, socio-economic group and urban/rural divisions.[72] Unfortunately, few States parties have either the requisite data or the willingness to share such detailed data with a UN supervisory body or with NGOs.[73]

In determining progressive realisation, the Committee applies a strong presumption against 'any deliberately retrogressive measures'.[74] Unless otherwise justified 'after the most careful consideration of all alternatives' and 'by reference to the totality of the rights provided for in the Covenant in the context of the full use of the State party's maximum available resources',[75] the adoption of measures (legislation or policy) that cause a clear deterioration or setback in the protection of rights hitherto afforded violates the ICESCR.[76] For example, unless justified in accordance with the above criteria, 'the re-introduction of fees at the tertiary level of education . . . constitutes a deliber-

---

[70] Useful information on these agencies is available on the website of the UN Economic and Social Council at http://www.un.org/docs/ecosoc/unagencies.html at 5 December 2008.

[71] See WHO, *The World Health Report 2000 – Health Systems: Improving Performance* (World Health Organization, Geneva, 2000). For a discussion of health indicators see http://www.who.int/hhr/activities/indicators/en/index.html at 5 December 2008.

[72] See *Guidelines on Treaty-Specific Documents to be Submitted by States Parties Under Articles 16 and 17 of the International Covenant on Economic, Social and Cultural Rights*, UN Doc E/C.12/2008/2 (24 March 2009), [3(g)].

[73] See, for example, CESCR, *Concluding Observations: Republic of Moldova*, UN Doc E/C.12/1/Add.91 (28 November 2003) [18]: 'The Committee is concerned about the absence of adequate statistical data on social benefits since 1997 in the State party's report.'

[74] General Comment 3, above n 31, [9].

[75] General Comment 13, above n 36, [45]; General Comment 14, above n 36, [32]; General Comment 15, above n 61, [19].

[76] Maastricht Guidelines, above n 22, [14(e)].

ately retrogressive step',[77] especially where adequate arrangements are not made for students from poorer segments of the population or lower socio-economic groups.[78]

## C Obligation to utilise 'maximum available resources'

The steps that a State party is obliged to take under Article 2(1) ICESCR to progressively realise the enumerated rights must be 'to the maximum of its available resources'.[79] Chapman noted that evaluating progressive realisation within the context of resource availability 'considerably complicates the methodological requirements' for monitoring.[80] There are two practical difficulties in applying this requirement to measure State compliance with the full use of maximum available resources. The first is in determining what resources are 'available' to a particular State to give effect to the substantive rights under the Covenant. The second difficulty is to determine whether a State has used such available resources to the 'maximum'. It has been suggested that the word 'available' leaves too much 'wiggle room for the State',[81] making it difficult to define the content of the progressive obligation and to establish when a breach of this obligation arises.[82] Nonetheless, it is clear that the Covenant does not make an absurd demand – a State is not required to take steps beyond what its available resources permit. The implication is that more would be expected from high-income States than low-income States, particularly the least developed States.[83] This means that both

---

[77] CESCR, *Concluding Observations: Mauritius*, UN Doc E/C.12/1994/8 (31 May 1994) [16].
[78] See, for example, General Comment 13, above n 36, [14], [20] and [45]; CESCR, *Concluding Observations: United Kingdom*, UN Doc E/C.12/1/Add.79 (5 June 2002) [22], [41].
[79] See General Comment 3, above n 31, [9]; General Comment 13, above n 36, [44]; General Comment 14, above n 36, [31]; Limburg Principles, above n 21, [21].
[80] A Chapman, 'A "Violations Approach" for Monitoring the International Covenant on Economic, Social and Cultural Rights' (1996) 18 *Human Rights Quarterly* 23, 31; A Chapman and S Russell, 'Introduction' in A Chapman and S Russell (eds) *Core Obligations: Building a Framework for Economic, Social and Cultural Rights* (Intersentia, Antwerp, 2002) 1, 5.
[81] See R Robertson, 'Measuring State Compliance with the Obligation to Devote the "Maximum Available Resources" to Realising Economic, Social and Cultural Rights' (1994) 16 *Human Rights Quarterly* 693, 694.
[82] S Joseph, J Schultz and M Castan, *The International Covenant on Civil and Political Rights: Cases, Materials and Commentary* (Oxford University Press, Oxford, 2000) 7.
[83] In 2004 the UN identified 50 States as the 'Least Developed Countries' ('LDCs'): http://www.un.org/special-rep/ohrlls/ldc/list.htm at 5 December 2008; UNCTAD, *The Least Developed Countries Report 2004* (United Nations, New York and Geneva, 2004) 318.

the content of the obligation and the rate at which it is achieved are subject to the maximum use of available resources.

The availability of resources refers not only to those which are controlled by or filtered through the State or other public bodies, but also to the social resources which can be mobilised by the widest possible participation in development, as necessary for the realisation by every human being of ESC rights.[84] In this respect 'available resources' refer to resources available within the society as a whole, 'from the private sector as well as the public. It is the State's responsibility to mobilise these resources, not to provide them all directly from its own coffers.'[85] As shown below, available resources also include those available through international cooperation and assistance.

States should demonstrate that the available resources are used equitably and effectively targeted to subsistence requirements and essential services.[86] To this end, the Committee requires States to combat corruption that negatively impacts on the availability of resources.[87] At the same time States should demonstrate that they are developing societal resources to fulfil ESC rights.[88] In this respect, it is important to note that although States generally have a 'margin of discretion'[89] to decide how to allocate the available resources, 'due priority' must be given to the realisation of human rights including ESC rights.[90] Thus, it is important for the State to make appropriate choices in the allocation of the available resources in ways which ensure that the most vulnerable are given priority.[91] All domestic resources must be

---

[84] See Eide, above n 65, stating in part: '1. The human being is a central subject of development and should be the active participant and beneficiary of the right to development. 2. All human beings have a responsibility for development, individually and collectively.'

[85] Chapman and Russell, above n 80, 11.

[86] Limburg Principles, above n 21, [23], [27] and [28].

[87] See, for example, CESCR, *Concluding Observations: Nigeria*, UN Doc E/1999/22 (1999) [97] and [119]; *Concluding Observations: Mexico*, UN Doc E/2000/22 (1999) [381], [394].

[88] Limburg Principles, above n 21, [24].

[89] General Comment 14, above n 36, [53]; General Comment 15, above n 61, [45]; General Comment 16, above n 42, [32]. See also CESCR, below n 97, [11] stating that 'in accordance with the practice of judicial and other quasi-judicial human rights treaty bodies, the Committee always respects the margin of appreciation of States to take steps and adopt measures most suited to their specific circumstances'.

[90] Limburg Principles, above n 21, [28]. See also CRC, *Concluding Observations: Rwanda*, UN Doc CRC/C/15/Add.236 (4 June 2004) [18].

[91] See A Eide, 'The Use of Indicators in the Practice of the Committee on Economic, Social and Cultural Rights' in A Eide, C Krause and A Rosas (eds) *Economic, Social and Cultural Rights: A Textbook* (Martinus Nijhoff Publishers, Dordrecht, 2nd ed, 2001), 545, 549.

considered for use by the State because human rights generally deserve priority over all other considerations.[92]

In determining State compliance with the obligation to utilise the 'maximum available resources', the CESCR has developed in its Concluding Observations some useful indicators. One indicator is to consider the percentage of the national budget allocated to specific rights under the Covenant (such as health, education, housing, and social security) relative to areas outside the Covenant (such as military expenditure or debt-servicing). Many resource problems revolve around the misallocation of available resources: for example, to purchase expensive weapons systems rather than to invest in primary education or primary or preventive health services.[93] In 2001, for example, with respect to Senegal, the CESCR stated:

> The Committee [was] concerned that funds allocated by the State party for basic social services... fall far short of the minimum social expenditure required to cover such services. In this regard the Committee note[d] with regret that more is spent by the State party on the military and on servicing its debt than on basic social services.[94]

It is, accordingly, imperative to consider the priority or rate of resource allocation to military expenditure in comparison to the expenditure on ESC rights.[95] A reordering of priorities may alleviate some of the resource burden of any State. Another indicator that may be applied is to consider the resources spent by a particular State in the implementation of a specific Covenant right and that which is spent by other States at the same level of development.

It is striking to note that if the Optional Protocol to the Covenant enters into force, it would be possible for the Committee to receive and consider communications submitted by or on behalf of individuals or groups of individuals under the jurisdiction of a State party, claiming to be victims of a violation of

---

[92] Robertson, above n 81, 700.

[93] See, for example, CESCR, *Concluding Observations: Philippines*, UN Doc E/C.12/1995/7 (7 June 1995) [21] stating that 'in terms of the availability of resources, the Committee notes with concern that a greater proportion of the national budget is devoted to military spending than to housing, agriculture and health combined'.

[94] CESCR, *Concluding Observations: Senegal*, UN Doc E/C.12/1/Add.62 (24 September 2001), para. [23].

[95] Eide rightly argued that 'The "expenditure of death" should be turned into "expenditure of life" (public action to combat poverty)': see A Eide, 'Economic, Social and Cultural Rights as Human Rights' in A Eide, C Krause and A Rosas (eds) *Economic, Social and Cultural Rights: A Textbook* (Martinus Nijhoff Publishers, Dordrecht, 2nd ed, 2001) 9, 28.

any of the ESC rights set forth in the Covenant, against States parties to the Optional Protocol.[96] If a communication was brought against a State party to the ICESCR and its Optional Protocol, and the State used 'resource constraints' as an explanation for any retrogressive steps taken, the Committee has indicated that it would consider such information on a country-by-country basis in the light of objective criteria such as:

(a) the country's level of development;
(b) the severity of the alleged breach, in particular whether the situation concerned the enjoyment of the minimum core content of the Covenant;
(c) the country's current economic situation, in particular whether the country was undergoing a period of economic recession;
(d) the existence of other serious claims on the State party's limited resources; for example, resulting from a recent natural disaster or from recent internal or international armed conflict;
(e) whether the State party had sought to identify low-cost options; and
(f) whether the State party had sought cooperation and assistance or rejected offers of resources from the international community for the purposes of implementing the provisions of the Covenant without sufficient reason.[97]

The obligation to take steps to the maximum of a State's 'available resources' means that in making any assessment as to whether a State is in breach of its obligations to fulfil the rights recognised under the Covenant of a particular individual or group, an assessment must be made as to whether the steps taken were 'adequate' or 'reasonable' by taking into account, *inter alia*, the following considerations:

(a) the extent to which the measures taken were deliberate, concrete and targeted towards the fulfilment of economic, social and cultural rights;
(b) whether the State party exercised its discretion in a non-discriminatory and non-arbitrary manner;
(c) whether the State party's decision (not) to allocate available resources is in accordance with international human rights standards;
(d) where several policy options are available, whether the State party adopts the option that least restricts Covenant rights;
(e) the time frame in which the steps were taken;
(f) whether the steps had taken into account the precarious situation of disadvantaged and marginalised individuals or groups and, whether they were non-discriminatory, and whether they prioritized grave situations or situations of risk.[98]

---

[96] Articles 1 and 2 ICESCR Protocol.
[97] CESCR, *Statement: An Evaluation of the Obligation to Take Steps to the 'Maximum of Available Resources' Under an Optional Protocol to the Covenant*, UN Doc E/C.12/2007/1 (10 May 2007) [10].
[98] Ibid [8].

In the context of an Optional Protocol communication, where the Committee considers that a State party has not taken reasonable or adequate steps, the Committee could make recommendations, *inter alia*, along four principal lines:

(a) recommending remedial action, such as compensation, to the victim, as appropriate;
(b) calling upon the State party to remedy the circumstances leading to a violation. In doing so, the Committee might suggest goals and parameters to assist the State party in identifying appropriate measures. These parameters could include suggesting overall priorities to ensure that resource allocation conformed with the State party's obligations under the Covenant; provision for the disadvantaged and marginalised individuals and groups; protection against grave threats to the enjoyment of economic, social and cultural rights; and respect for non-discrimination in the adoption and implementation of measures;
(c) suggesting, on a case-by-case basis, a range of measures to assist the State party in implementing the recommendations, with particular emphasis on low-cost measures. The State party would nonetheless still have the option of adopting its own alternative measures;
(d) recommending a follow-up mechanism to ensure ongoing accountability of the State party; for example, by including a requirement that in its next periodic report the State party explain the steps taken to redress the violation.[99]

From the above, it is clear that the obligation to use 'maximum available resources' is capable of being subjected to judicial or quasi-judicial scrutiny and as such it is not a bar to justiciability. Domestic courts have dealt with cases that aim at the protection of ESC rights. In South Africa, for example, the *Constitution of the Republic of South Africa*, which guarantees numerous ESC rights, the justiciability of ESC rights has been demonstrated through constitutional case law.[100] For example, the case of *Minister of Health v Treatment Action Campaign* concerned State provision of Nevirapine, an antiretroviral drug used to prevent mother-to-child transmission of the HIV.[101] Applying the concepts of progressive realisation and resource availability, the South African Constitutional Court declared that:

> Sections 27(1) and (2) of the Constitution require the government to devise and implement within its available resources a comprehensive and co-ordinated programme to realise progressively the rights of pregnant women and their newborn children to have access to health services to combat mother-to-child transmission of HIV.[102]

---

[99] Ibid [13]. See also Article 9 ICESCR Protocol.
[100] For a discussion see D M Davis, 'Socioeconomic Rights: Do They Deliver the Goods?' (2008) 6 *International Journal of Constitutional Law* 687.
[101] (CCT 8/02) [2002] ZACC 15.
[102] (CCT 8/02) [2002] ZACC 15, 135. Section 27 reads: '(1) Everyone has the

The programme to be realised progressively within available resources had to include reasonable measures for counselling and testing pregnant women for HIV, counselling HIV-positive pregnant women on the options open to them to reduce the risk of mother-to-child transmission of HIV, and making appropriate treatment available to them for such purposes.[103]

Therefore, although the 'availability of resources' is an important qualifier to the realisation of ESC rights, it does not alter the immediacy of the obligation to 'take reasonable legislative and other measures' to achieve the 'progressive realisation' of these rights. Similarly resource constraints alone should not justify inaction and not a bar to judicial review. Where the available resources are demonstrably inadequate, the obligation remains for a State to ensure the widest possible enjoyment of ESC rights under the prevailing circumstances. It follows therefore that even in times of severe resource constraints the State must protect the most disadvantaged and marginalised members or groups of society by adopting relatively low-cost targeted programmes.

## 3 Extraterritorial application and international assistance and cooperation

This section considers whether States parties' human rights obligations arising under the ICESCR are limited to individuals and groups within a State's territory or whether a State can be liable for the acts and omissions of its agents which produce effects on ESC rights or are undertaken beyond national territory (that is, affecting individuals or groups who are not within the State's territory but who are subject to a State's jurisdiction).[104] Although the ICESCR refers to 'international assistance and cooperation', it does not make any explicit reference to territory or jurisdiction, in contrast to the ICCPR.[105]

---

right to have access to (a) health care services, including reproductive health care; (b) sufficient food and water; and (c) social security, including, if they are unable to support themselves and their dependants, appropriate social assistance. (2) The state must take reasonable legislative and other measures, within its available resources, to achieve the progressive realisation of each of these rights. (3) No one may be refused emergency medical treatment.'

[103] (CCT 8/02) [2002] ZACC 15, 135.

[104] For a detailed discussion of the term 'jurisdiction' in public international law see generally M Shaw, *International Law* (Cambridge University Press, Cambridge, 6th ed, 2008) 645–96; I Brownlie, *Principles of Public International Law* (Oxford University Press, Oxford, 7th ed, 2008) 299–321; V Lowe, 'Jurisdiction' in M Evans (ed), *International Law* (Oxford University Press, Oxford, 2nd ed, 2006) 335; and M Akehurst, 'Jurisdiction in International Law' 46 *British Year Book of International Law* (1972–1973) 145.

[105] Article 2(1) ICCPR provides: '1. Each State Party to the present Covenant undertakes to respect and to ensure to all individuals *within its territory* and *subject to its jurisdiction* the rights recognised in the present Covenant' (emphasis added).

The International Court of Justice ('ICJ') has acknowledged some space, albeit in a restrictive way, for the extraterritorial application of the ICESCR. In its Advisory Opinion of 9 July 2004, *Legal Consequences of the Construction of a Wall in the Occupied Palestinian Territory*, the ICJ held:

> The International Covenant on Economic, Social and Cultural Rights contains no provision on its scope of application. This may be explicable by the fact that this Covenant guarantees rights which are essentially territorial. However, it is not to be excluded that it applies both to territories over which a State party has sovereignty and to those over which that State exercises territorial jurisdiction. Thus Article 14 makes provision for transitional measures in the case of any State which 'at the time of becoming a Party, has not been able to secure in its metropolitan territory or other territories under its jurisdiction compulsory primary education, free of charge'.[106]

This position was confirmed by the ICJ in its decision in *Democratic Republic of Congo v Uganda*, where the ICJ stated that 'international human rights instruments are applicable in respect of acts done by a state in the exercise of its jurisdiction outside its own territory, particularly in occupied territories.'[107] Thus, human rights treaties extend State obligations to those within their territory and jurisdiction, the latter term not being limited by a State's territorial boundaries. State responsibility can for example be incurred by acts or omissions by a State's authorities which produce effects outside their territories.[108] This means that a State party to the ICESCR must respect, protect and fulfil ESC rights laid down in the Covenant to anyone within the power or effective control of that State, even if not situated within the territory of the State party.

The extraterritorial application of the ICESCR is reflected in a number of General Comments of the CESCR that interpret State obligations as extending to individuals under its jurisdiction. General Comment 1 indicates that States parties to the ICESCR have to monitor the actual situation with respect to each of the rights on a regular basis and thus be aware of the extent to which the various rights are, or are not, being enjoyed by 'all individuals *within its territory*

---

[106] *Legal Consequences of the Construction of a Wall in the Occupied Palestinian Territory* [2004] ICJ Reports 4, [112] (*'The Wall'*). For a discussion of this Advisory Opinion see S R S Bedi, *The Development of Human Rights Law by the Judges of the International Court of Justice* (Hart Publishing, Oxford, 2007) 337–51.

[107] *Armed Activities on the Territory of the Congo (Democratic Republic of the Congo v. Uganda) (Merits)* (2006) 45 ILM 271, [217].

[108] See the European Court of Human Rights (ECtHR), *Drozd and Janousek v France and Spain* (1992) 14 EHRR 745, [91]; *Loizidou v Turkey (Preliminary Objections)* (1995) 20 EHRR 99, [52] (confirmed in *Cyprus v Turkey* (2002) 35 EHRR 30, [76]–[81]).

or *under its jurisdiction*.[109] For example, in its Concluding Observations of 1998 on Israel, the CESCR confirmed that 'the State's obligations under the Covenant apply to all territories and populations under its effective control';[110] and that 'the Covenant applies to all areas where Israel maintains geographical, functional or personal jurisdiction'.[111] Therefore, State obligations with respect to the Covenant apply to individuals and groups within a State's territory and to those individuals who are subject to a State's jurisdiction. Thus, under the Optional Protocol adopted by the General Assembly in December 2008, '[c]ommunications may be submitted by or on behalf of individuals or groups of individuals, *under the jurisdiction* of a State Party'.[112] This anticipates that a State can be found to be in violation of its obligations under the ICESCR for actions taken by it extraterritorially, in relation to anyone within the power, effective control or authority of that State, as well as within an area over which that State exercises effective overall control.[113]

The extraterritorial application of the ICESCR is further supported by the reference to 'international assistance and cooperation' in the Covenant. The ICESCR refers to international assistance and cooperation, or similar formulations, in five articles.[114] International assistance and cooperation can be understood as entailing obligations to respect, protect and fulfil at an international level. The obligation to *respect* requires States to refrain from interfering directly or indirectly with the progressive realisation of ESC rights in other States[115] and not to impose on another State measures that might be foreseen to work against the progressive realisation of ESC rights. This means that States must refrain from causing harm to ESC rights extraterritorially, for

---

[109] CESCR, *General Comment 1: Reporting by States Parties*, UN Doc E/1989/22, Annex III, 87 (24 February 1989) [3] (emphasis added). See also CESCR, *General Comment 8: The Relationship between Economic Sanctions and respect for Economic, Social and Cultural Rights*, UN Doc E/C.12/1997/8 (12 December 1997) [10]; General Comment 14, above n 36, [12(b)]; General Comment 15, above n 61, [12(c)].

[110] CESCR, *Concluding Observations: Israel*, UN Doc E/C.12/1/Add.27 (4 December 1998) [8]. See also CESCR, *Concluding Observations: Israel*, UN Doc E/C.12/1/Add.90 (23 May 2003) [15], [31].

[111] CESCR, *Concluding Observations: Israel*, UN Doc E/C.12/1/Add.27 (4 December 1998) [6].

[112] Article 2(1) ICESCR Protocol (emphasis added).

[113] See generally R McCorquodale and P Simons, 'Responsibility Beyond Borders: State Responsibility for Extraterritorial Violations by Corporations of International Human Rights Law' (2007) 7 *The Modern Law Review* 598.

[114] See Articles 2(1), 11, 15, 22, and 23 ICESCR. See also Articles 1, 55, and 56 of the *Charter of the United Nations*; Articles 22 and 28 UDHR; Articles 4, 7(2), 11(2), 17(b), 21(e), 22(2), 23(4), 24(4), 27(4), 28(3), 34 and 35 CRC.

[115] General Comment 19, above n 61, [53].

example by not supporting armed conflicts in other States in violation of international law and by not providing assistance to corporations to violate ESC rights in other States. This is consistent with international law providing a general duty on a State not to act in such a way as to cause harm outside its territory.[116]

In addition the obligation to *protect* requires States parties to prevent third parties, including individuals, groups, corporations and other entities within a State's jurisdiction, as well as agents acting under their authority, from interfering in any way with the enjoyment of ESC rights in other States. This is part of international cooperation and assistance and the State's obligation to exercise due diligence not to violate human rights in other States and not to permit non-State actors within the State's jurisdiction to violate human rights in other States. While there is some debate over precisely when a State should protect human rights in other States, international law permits a State to exercise extraterritorial jurisdiction provided there is a recognised basis, for example, where the actor or victim is a national, where the acts have substantial adverse effects on the State, or where specific international crimes are involved.[117] Although the Committee has not consistently inquired into the issue of extraterritorial jurisdiction, it has been raised in the course of examining some State reports. For example, in 1999 one Committee Member asked 'whether Germany exercised extraterritorial jurisdiction over German nationals who committed crimes against children abroad'.[118]

The extra territorial obligation includes, *inter alia*, adopting the necessary and effective legislative and other measures to restrain third parties within a State's jurisdiction from any activities that might be foreseen to cause harm to the progressive realisation of ESC rights in other States. For example, with respect to the right to social security the Committee stated:

> States parties should extraterritorially protect the right to social security by preventing their own citizens and national entities from violating this right in other countries. Where States parties can take steps to influence third parties (non-State actors) within their jurisdiction to respect the right, through legal or political means, such steps should be taken in accordance with the Charter of the United Nations and applicable international law.[119]

---

[116] See, for example, *The Rainbow Warrior (New Zealand v France)* (1990) 82 ILR 449.

[117] See J Ruggie, *Business and Human Rights: Mapping international Standards of Responsibility and Accountability for Corporate Acts*, UN Doc A/HRC/4/35 (19 February 2007) [15].

[118] See CESCR, *Summary Record of the 49th Meeting: Germany*, UN Doc E/C.12/2001/SR.49 (30 August 2001) [48].

[119] General Comment 19, above n 61, [54]. See also General Comment 15, above n 61, [33].

In principle a similar duty to protect ESC rights extraterritorially should apply to all substantive rights. Extraterritorial protection of ESC rights offers an important means to strengthen the protection and enforcement of ESC rights especially where host States lack the ability to effectively regulate non-State actors and monitor their compliance yet home States are able to do so.

The obligation to *fulfil* may entail the provision of international technical, economic or other forms of assistance to realise ESC rights in other States in need of such assistance. This is a key feature of the ICESCR. What is uncertain is the extent to which States and other actors are legally obliged to furnish assistance for the realisation of ESC rights in other States.

International assistance and cooperation may be regarded as one element of the more extensive right to development which was affirmed in the *Declaration on the Right to Development*[120] and the *Vienna Declaration and Programme of Action*.[121] More recently, 191 States recognised explicitly in the Millennium Declaration the link between the realisation of the right to development and poverty reduction, and committed themselves to make 'the right to development a reality for everyone' and to free 'the entire human race from want'.[122]

In general, while most developed States give assistance to developing States,[123] developed States have consistently denied the existence of any clear legal obligation to transfer resources to the developing States.[124] It has further been argued that 'although there is clearly an obligation to cooperate internationally, it is not clear whether this means that wealthy States Parties are obliged to provide aid to assist in the realisation of the rights in other countries'.[125] In debates surrounding the drafting of an Optional Protocol to the ICESCR the representatives of the United Kingdom, the Czech Republic,

---

[120] GA Res 41/128, UN GAOR, 41st sess, 97th plen mtg, UN Doc A/Res/41/128 (4 December 1986).

[121] UN Doc A/CONF.157/23 (12 July 1993) [9], [12] and [34].

[122] UNHCHR, *Draft Guidelines: A Human Rights Approach to Poverty Reduction Strategies* (2002) UNHCHR, http://www.unhchr.ch/pdf/povertyfinal.pdf at 5 December 2008, [215].

[123] P Heller, P Gupta and S Gupta, *Challenges in Expanding Development Assistance,* (IMF, Washington DC, 2002) IMF, http://www.imf.org/external/pubs/ft/pdp/2002/pdp05.pdf at 5 December 2008. For the designation of a State as 'developed' or 'developing' see United Nations, Standard Country or Area Codes for Statistical Use (2008) United Nations Statistics Division, http://unstats.un.org/unsd/methods/m49/m49regin.htm at 5 December 2008.

[124] Alston and Quinn, above n 52, 186–91.

[125] M Craven, 'The International Covenant on Economic, Social and Cultural Rights' in R Hanski and M Suksi (eds) *An Introduction to the International Protection of Human Rights: A Text Book*, (Abo Akademi University, Abo, 2nd ed, 1999) 101–23.

Canada, France and Portugal believed that international cooperation and assistance was an 'important moral obligation' but 'not a legal entitlement', and did not interpret the Covenant to impose a legal obligation to provide development assistance or give a legal right to receive such aid.[126] It is not surprising, then, that the final text of the Optional Protocol as adopted by the General Assembly in December 2008 contained a weaker provision on 'international assistance and cooperation' in its Article 14 by referring only to the 'need for technical advice or assistance' in Article 14(1) and establishing a trust fund with a view to 'providing expert and technical assistance to State Parties' without prejudice to the obligations of each State party to fulfil its obligations under the Covenant in Articles 14(3) and (4) of the Protocol. Significantly, the Optional Protocol did not exclude other possible forms of international cooperation and assistance.

However, if there is no legal obligation underpinning the human rights responsibility of international assistance and cooperation, inescapably all international assistance and cooperation fundamentally rests upon charity.[127] Is such a position tenable and acceptable in the twenty-first century? Increasingly human rights scholars have argued for a legal obligation to underpin international assistance and cooperation.[128] The Committee's approach also seems to suggest that the economically developed States parties to the Covenant are under an obligation to assist developing States parties to realise the core obligations of ESC rights. Thus, the CESCR has stressed that 'it is particularly incumbent on all those who can assist, to help developing countries respect this international minimum threshold.'[129]

For example, after identifying core obligations in relation to the right to water, the Committee emphasised that 'it is particularly incumbent on States parties, and other actors in a position to assist, to *provide* international assistance and cooperation, especially economic and technical which enables developing countries to fulfil their core obligations'.[130] In the course of examination of State reports, the Committee has inquired into the percentage of

---

[126] See *Report of the Open-ended Working Group to Consider Options Regarding the Elaboration of an Optional Protocol to the International Covenant on Economic, Social and Cultural Rights on its Second Session*, UN Doc E/CN.4/2005/52 (10 February 2005) [76].

[127] See Paul Hunt, *Report of the Special Rapporteur on the Right of Everyone to the Enjoyment of the Highest Attainable Standard of Physical and Mental Health: Addendum: Missions to the World Bank and the International Monetary Fund in Washington DC and Uganda*, UN Doc A/HRC/7/11/Add.2 (5 March 2008) [133].

[128] Ibid.

[129] CESCR, *Poverty and the International Covenant on Economic, Social and Cultural Rights*, above n 62, [17].

[130] General Comment 15, above n 61, [38] (emphasis added).

Gross Domestic/National Product ('GDP/GNP') that developed reporting States dedicate to international cooperation[131] and overseas development assistance ('ODA').[132] The UN-recommended target/benchmark of 0.7 per cent GDP[133] was reiterated along with other targets in the Monterrey Consensus, arising from the 2002 International Conference on Financing for Development.[134] However, by 2000 only five States had reached or exceeded the target of 0.7 per cent of GDP in ODA.[135] Most developed States (particularly the Group of Eight industrialised States) were far below the level of 0.7 per cent with an average of 0.22 per cent.[136] For example in 2008–2009 Australia devote 0.32 per cent only of its gross national income (GNI) to ODA.[137] In 2007, the only countries to reach or exceed the United Nations target of 0.7 per cent of their gross national income ('GNI') were Denmark, Luxembourg, the Netherlands, Norway and Sweden.[138] The average for all member countries of the Development Assistance Committee ('DAC') of the Organisation for Economic Co-operation and Development ('OECD') was just 0.09 per cent.[139]

Despite this State practice, the CESCR commonly 'recommends' and 'encourages' developed States parties 'to increase ODA as a percentage of GNP to a level approaching the 0.7% goal established by the United

---

[131] See, for example, CESCR, *Summary Record: Ireland*, UN Doc E/C.12/1999/SR.14 (7 May 1999) [38].

[132] See, for example, CESCR, *Summary Records: Japan*, UN Doc E/C.12/2001/SR.42 (18 September 2001) [10]; *Summary Records: Germany*, UN Doc. E/C.12/2001/SR.49 (30 August 2001) [37].

[133] This was originally proposed by the Pearson Commission in 1968 and adopted in 1970. See GA Res 2226, 25 UN GAOR Supp (No 28) [43], UN Doc A/8028 (1970); K Tomasevski, *Development Aid and Human Rights Revisited* (Pinter, London, 1993) 32. This target was reaffirmed in the *Copenhagen Declaration on Social Development*, UN Doc A/CONF.166/9 (14 March 1995) Commitment 9 [1].

[134] *Monterrey Consensus of the International Conference on Financing for Development*, UN Doc A/CONF.198/11 (22 August 2002).

[135] These States are Denmark (1.06 per cent); the Netherlands (0.82); Sweden (0.81); Norway (0.8) and Luxembourg (0.7): see OECD Press release (20 April 2001).

[136] Examples are: Belgium (0.36 per cent); Switzerland (0.34); France (0.33); Finland and the UK (0.31); Ireland (0.3); Japan, Germany and Australia (0.27); New Zealand and Portugal (0.26); Canada and Austria (0.25); Spain (0.24); Greece (0.19); Italy (0.13) and the United States (0.1): ibid. See also UN Wire, 'World Bank Head Blasts Rich Nations For Record on Aid' (5 May 2004).

[137] (CESCR), Concluding Observations: Australia UN Doc E/C.12/AU/CO/4 (22 May 2009 [12]).

[138] See the MDG Gap Task Force Report 2008, *Millennium Development Goal 8: Delivering on the Global Partnership for Achieving the Millennium Development Goals* (United Nations, New York, 2008) vii.

[139] Ibid.

Nations'.[140] States have been criticised where the levels devoted to international assistance and cooperation fall below this target,[141] and urged to 'review ... budget allocation to international cooperation'[142] with a view 'to ensure' that State contribution to international development cooperation increases 'as quickly as possible, to the United Nations target of 0.7 per cent GNP'.[143] Other States that have donated more than this target have been commended.[144] Given a large and growing gap between developed and developing States, and the fact that half the world – nearly three billion people – live on less than two dollars a day,[145] economically developed States can play a key role in enhancing the enjoyment of ESC rights by granting further assistance, especially technical or economic, to developing States targeted to ESC rights. The large investment requirements of developing States imply that a successful transition to increased reliance on domestic resources and private capital inflows will require more,rather than less, official development assistance.[146] Interestingly, the European Union ('EU') member States have made commitments to increase their ODA over a period of time. The targets were stated as

---

[140] See, for example, CESCR, *Concluding Observations: Belgium*, UN Doc E/C.12/1/Add.54 (1 December 2000) [16], [30]; *Concluding Observations: Finland* UN Doc E/C.12/1/Add.52 (1 December 2000) [13], [23]; *Concluding Observations: Ireland* UN Doc E/C.12/1/Add.77 (5 June 2002) [38]; *Concluding Observations: Spain*, UN Doc E/C.12/1/Add.99 (7 June 2004) [27]. In May 2008 the CESCR recommended that France 'increase its official development assistance to 0.7 per cent of its GDP, as agreed by the Heads of State and Government at the International Conference on Financing for Development, held in Monterrey (Mexico) on 18–22 March 2002'. See CESCR, *Concluding Observations: France*, UN Doc. E/C.12/FRA/CO/3 (16 May 2008) [32]. See also Committee on the Rights of the Child, *General Comment 5, General Measures of Implementation for the Convention on the Rights of the Child*, UN Doc CRC/GC/2003/5 (3 October 2003) [61].
[141] See, for example, CESCR, *Spain*, above n 140, [10], [27]; *France*, above n 140, [12].
[142] CESCR, *Belgium*, above n 140, [30].
[143] CESCR, *Ireland*, above n 140, [38].
[144] See, for example, CESCR, *Concluding Observations: Denmark*, UN Doc E/C.12/1/Add.34 (14 May 1999) [11], commended for devoting 1 per cent of GDP to international assistance and cooperation. See also CESCR, *Concluding Observations: Luxembourg*, UN Doc E/C.12/1/Add.86 (23 May 2003) [6].
[145] UNDP, *The Human Development Report 2007/2008* (Palgrave Macmillan, New York, 2007) 25, http://hdr.undp.org/en/reports/global/hdr2007-2008/chapters/ at 6 December 2008. The report notes that 'There are still around 1 billion people living at the margins of survival on less than US$1 a day, with 2.6 billion – 40 percent of the world's population – living on less than US$2 a day.'
[146] See UNCTAD, 'The Challenge of Financing Development in LDCs' (Paper presented at the 3rd United Nations Conference on the Least Developed Countries, Brussels, 14–20 May 2001), http://r0.unctad.org/conference/e-press_kit/financing.pdf at 6 December 2008.

follows: (i) 0.33 per cent by 2006 according to the EU Barcelona commitment; and (ii) 0.51 per cent by 2010 and 0.7 per cent by 2015 according to the May 2005 EU Council agreement.[147] While this progressive commitment to increase ODA is a step in the right direction, it should be noted that international assistance and cooperation including economic aid entails procedural fairness. Thus, donor States have a responsibility not to withdraw critical aid without first giving the recipient State reasonable notice and opportunity to make alternative arrangements.[148]

In order to monitor the use of transferred resources, the Committee has sought to establish whether resources transferred are used to promote respect for the ICESCR and whether such resources are contingent upon the human rights record of the receiving country.[149] The Committee has also asked whether States have formulated a policy on the objective of allocating 0.7 per cent of GDP to ODA.[150]

While the Committee can investigate all such issues, it is questionable whether the Committee can find a particular developed State to be in violation of Article 2(1) ICESCR for the failure to devote 0.7 per cent of its GDP to international assistance. Similarly, it is inconceivable that the Committee can direct or identify a specific developed State to assist a particular developing State party since the criteria for doing so are not yet clearly drawn and seem to be difficult to justify. For example there is no legal basis for directing Canada to assist Mali. Nonetheless, it is important to note that international assistance and cooperation should not be understood as encompassing only financial and technical assistance: it also includes a responsibility to work actively towards equitable multilateral trading, investment and financial systems that are conducive to the realisation of human rights and the elimination of poverty.[151] This may entail genuine special and preferential treatment of developing States so as to provide such States with better access to developed States' markets.[152]

---

[147] See (2003) 7 *OECD Journal on Development* 38.
[148] See Hunt, above n 127, [29].
[149] See, for example, CESCR, *Summary Records: Ireland*, UN Doc E/C.12/1999/SR.14 (2 February 2000) [38]; *Summary Records: Germany*, UN Doc E/C.12/2001/SR.48 (31 August 2001) [19] and *Summay Records: Finland*, UN Doc E/C.12/2000/SR.61 (21 November 2000) [48].
[150] See CESCR, *Summary Records: Finland*, UN Doc. E/C.12/2007/SR.11 (15 May 2007) [11].
[151] Paul Hunt, *Report of the Special Rapporteur: The right of everyone to the enjoyment of the highest attainable standard of physical and mental health: Addendum: Mission to the WTO*, UN Doc. E/CN.4/2004/49/Add.1 (8 March 2004) [28].
[152] UNHCHR, *Analytical study of the High Commissioner for Human Rights on*

This equitable system is yet to be realised. In 2006, for example, Joseph Stiglitz, former Chief Economist of the World Bank, noted that:

> We see an unfair global trade regime that impedes development and an unsustainable global financial system in which poor countries repeatedly find themselves with unmanageable debt burdens. Money should flow from the rich to poor countries, but increasingly, it goes in the opposite direction.[153]

Therefore ODA alone without an equitable multilateral trading system would not lead to meaningful realisation of ESC rights in poorer developing States. As Oxfam International estimated in 2002, an increase of 5 per cent in the share of world trade by low-income States 'would generate more than $350 billion – seven times as much as they receive in aid'.[154]

It should be recalled that the object and purpose of the Covenant, as a human rights treaty, requires that its provisions be interpreted so as to make its safeguards practical and effective. Effectiveness requires that the human rights obligation to 'respect, protect and fulfil' extends beyond a State's borders to include individuals and groups subject to a State's jurisdiction in other States.[155] Although 'from the standpoint of public international law, the jurisdictional competence of a State is primarily territorial',[156] a State's human rights obligations, as noted above, are not territorially limited. Human rights obligations may extend beyond a State's borders to areas where a State exercises power, authority or effective control over individuals, or where a State exercises effective control of an area of territory within another State.[157] States are legally responsible for policies that violate human rights beyond their own

---

*the fundamental principle of non-discrimination in the context of globalization*, UN Doc E/CN.4/2004/40 (15 January 2004) [40]. For a summary of issues relating to the participation of developing countries in the multilateral trading system see S Lester and B Mercurio, *World Trade Law: Text, Materials and Commentary* (Hart Publishing, Oxford, 2008) 779–817; M Matsushita, T J Schoenbaum and P C Mavroidis, *The World Trade Organization: Law, Practice and Policy* (Oxford University Press, Oxford, 2nd ed. 2006) 763–84. See also Chapters 6 and 7.

[153] J Stiglitz, 'We Have Become Rich Countries of Poor People' *Financial Times*, London (7 September 2006).

[154] Oxfam, *Rigged Rules and Double Standards: Trade, Globalisation and the Fight against Poverty* (Oxfam, Oxford, 2002) 48. For a further discussion of the intricacies of foreign aid see generally R C Riddle, *Does Foreign Aid Really Work?* (Oxford University Press, Oxford, 2008).

[155] See CESCR, *Concluding Observations: Cameroon*, UN Doc E/C.12/1/Add.40 (8 December 1999) [38].

[156] *Bankovic v Belgium and Others*, Application No 52207 (Unreported, European Court of Human Rights, Trial Chamber, 12 December 2001) [59].

[157] See McCorquodale and Simons, above n 113, 624.

borders, and for policies that indirectly support violations of ESC rights by third parties. It follows, then, that States may, under certain circumstances, be required to respect, protect and fulfil ESC rights in other States.

## 4 Non-derogability of ESC rights

Does the ICESCR apply fully in time of armed conflict, war or other public emergency? It is crucial to note that unlike some other human rights treaties, there are no clauses in the UN treaties protecting ESC rights allowing for or prohibiting derogations in a state of emergency, for example in the situation of a failed state, armed conflict or institutional collapse post-conflict.[158] The absence of specific derogation clauses from a treaty is not *per se* determinative of whether derogations are permitted or prohibited. In the case of the ICESCR this may be taken to mean either that derogations to ESC rights are not permissible (since they are not provided for[159] and would seem inherently less compelling given the nature of ESC rights) or that they may be permissible for non-core obligations where the situation appears to be sufficiently grave to warrant derogation (since they are not explicitly prohibited). The *travaux préparatoires* of the ICESCR do not reveal any specific discussion on the issue of whether or not a derogation clause was considered necessary, or even appropriate.[160] Thus the possible reasons for its omission are open to speculation. It is possible that this could have been as a result of a combination of factors including: (i) the nature of the rights protected in the Covenant; (ii) the existence of a general limitations clause in Article 4 ICESCR; and (iii) the general obligation contained in Article 2(1) ICESCR being 'more flexible and accommodating'.[161]

In General Comment 3, the Committee confirmed that States parties have a core obligation to ensure the satisfaction of minimum essential levels of each of the rights enunciated in the Covenant, such as essential health care, basic shelter and housing, water and sanitation, foodstuffs, and the most basic forms of education. Accordingly, the CESCR has taken the view that core obligations arising from the rights recognised in the Covenant are non-derogable. In General Comment 14 on the highest attainable standard of health, the CESCR

---

[158] Such derogation clauses may be found in, for example, Article 4(1) ICCPR, Article 17 ECHR, and the *American Convention on Human Rights*, opened for signature 1969, 1144 UNTS 123 (entered into force 18 July 1978) Article 27.

[159] In *Media Rights Agenda v Nigeria* [2000] African Human Rights Law Reports 262, the African Commission stated that the lack of any derogation clause in the African Charter means that 'limitations on the rights and freedoms . . . cannot be justified by emergencies or special circumstances'.

[160] Alston and Quinn, above n 52, 217.

[161] Ibid. See also Craven, above n 9, 27.

stated: '[i]t should be stressed, however, that a State party cannot, under any circumstances whatsoever, justify its non-compliance with the core obligations set out in paragraph 43 above, which are non-derogable'.[162] In General Comment 15, on the right to water, the CESCR stated that a 'State party cannot justify its non-compliance with the core obligations set out ... which are non-derogable'.[163]

It can thus be argued that, without a clause providing for derogation in the ICESCR, core obligations arising from ESC rights cannot be derogated from in an emergency, including a situation of military occupation. In *The Wall*,[164] the ICJ asserted the applicability of the ICESCR in Occupied Palestinian Territory. It cited Concluding Observations of the CESCR and also stated that:

> [T]erritories occupied by Israel have for over 37 years been subject to its territorial jurisdiction as the occupying Power. In the exercise of the powers available to it on this basis, *Israel is bound by the provisions of the International Covenant on Economic, Social and Cultural Rights*. Furthermore, it is under an obligation not to raise any obstacle to the exercise of such rights in those fields where competence has been transferred to Palestinian authorities.[165]

The ICJ also stated that, save through the effect of provisions for derogation, 'the protection offered by human rights conventions does not cease in case of armed conflict'.[166]

Similarly the UN General Assembly confirmed in 1970 the applicability of human rights norms in times of armed conflict, stating that '(f)undamental human rights, as accepted in international law and laid down in international instruments, continue to apply fully in situations of armed conflict'.[167] In principle this position applies to ESC rights as protected by the ICESCR. Some of the General Comments of the CESCR have confirmed this position. For example in General Comment 15, on the right to water, the committee noted that 'during armed conflicts, emergency situations and natural disasters, the right to water embraces those obligations by which States parties are bound under international humanitarian law'.[168] This includes protection of

---

[162] General Comment 14, above n 36, [47].
[163] General Comment 15, above n 61, [40].
[164] [2004] ICJ Reports 136.
[165] [2004] ICJ Reports 136, [112] (emphasis added).
[166] [2004] ICJ Reports 136, [106].
[167] See *Basic Principles for the Protection of Civilian Populations in Armed Conflicts*, UN Gen Res 2675 (xxv) UN Doc A/Res/2675 (xxv) (9 December 1970) [1].
[168] General Comment 15, above n 61, [22]. For the interrelationship of human rights law and humanitarian law, the Committee noted the conclusions of the

objects indispensable for the survival of the civilian population, including drinking water installations and supplies and irrigation works, protection of the natural environment against widespread, long-term and severe damage and ensuring that civilians, internees and prisoners have access to adequate water.[169]

Thus, the absence of a clause allowing derogation in times of public emergency in the ICESCR indicates that the Covenant generally continues to apply,[170] and, as a minimum, States cannot derogate from the Covenant's core obligations. In the words of the CESCR, 'because core obligations are non-derogable, they continue to exist in situations of conflict, emergency and natural disaster'.[171] Does this mean that States can derogate from non-core obligations under the ICESCR provided they comply with the general rules of derogation? The Committee's use of the word 'non-derogable' in relation to core obligations might be interpreted as implying that other duties are indeed derogable. However, it is vital to note that the statement of the Committee was not a general reference to derogations under the Covenant but a specific example of the non-derogable nature of core obligations. It cannot therefore be taken as being conclusive on the question of whether or not States can derogate from non-core aspects of ESC rights. Given the nature of the rights protected in the Covenant, the existence of a general limitations clause in Article 4 ICESCR, and the fact that States are not required to do more than what the maximum available resources permit, derogations from the ICESCR in situations of conflict, war, emergency and natural disaster would be unnecessary.

## 5 Conclusion

This chapter has considered State obligations with respect to ESC rights under the ICESCR. It has noted that States parties to the ICESCR are obliged to 'take steps by all appropriate means' to achieve 'progressively' the full realisation

---

International Court of Justice in *Legality of the Threat or Use of Nuclear Weapons (Request by the General Assembly)* [1996] ICJ Reports 226, [25].

[169] [1996] ICJ Reports 226, [25], citing *Protocol Additional to the Geneva Conventions of 12 August 1949, and Relating to the Protection of Victims of International Armed Conflicts (Protocol I)*, 1125 UNTS 3 (entered into force 7 December 1978) Articles 54 and 56; *Protocol Additional to the Geneva Conventions of 12 August 1949, and Relating to the Protection of Victims of Non-International Armed Conflicts (Protocol II)*, 1125 UNTS 609 (entered into force 7 December 1978) Article 54; *Geneva Convention relative to the Treatment of Prisoners of War*, 75 UNTS 135 (entered into force 21 October 1950).

[170] See E Mottershaw, 'Economic, Social and Cultural Rights in Armed Conflict: International Human Rights Law and International Humanitarian Law' (2008) 12 *International Journal of Human Rights* 449.

[171] CESCR, *Statement on Poverty and the ICESCR*, above n 62, [18].

of ESC rights. As noted above, the goal of full realisation entails the obligation to respect, protect and fulfil ESC rights. The 'appropriate means' required to achieve this goal include the adoption of legislative measures to protect ESC rights in national law, as well as the adoption of non-legislative measures including the provision of judicial or administrative remedies for violations of ESC rights.[172]

Although some States have claimed that a greater part of the ICESCR consists of statements of 'principles' and 'objectives', rather than justiciable legal obligations,[173] the CESCR has affirmed 'the principle of the interdependence and indivisibility of all human rights, and that all economic, social and cultural rights are justiciable'.[174] The adoption of the Optional Protocol to the ICESCR by the General Assembly in December 2008 is, therefore, a welcome development that was long overdue. It is hoped that this adoption will bring ESC rights onto the same footing and give them the same emphasis as civil and political rights in terms of enforcement at an international level. Indeed, there is nothing in the ICESCR to indicate that the rights recognised therein are merely 'principles' and 'objectives'. On the contrary, it is clear from Article 2(1) ICESCR that, although the rights protected in the Covenant have to be realised 'progressively', some rights under the Covenant such as freedom from discrimination in the enjoyment of all ESC rights and core obligations give rise to obligations of immediate effect. As noted above, in any case, the CESCR has explained that Article 2 ICESCR 'imposes an obligation to move as expeditiously and effectively as possible' towards the Covenant's goal of full realisation of the substantive rights under the Covenant.[175]

It has also been established that States have to use the 'maximum available resources' to realise ESC rights and that this includes resources made available

---

[172] See CESCR, *Concluding Observations: Kenya*, UN Doc E/C.12/1993/6 (3 June 1993) [10], the Committee noted 'with concern that the rights recognised by Kenya as a State party to the International Covenant on Economic, Social and Cultural Rights are neither contained in the constitution of Kenya nor in a separate bill of rights; nor do the provisions of the Covenant seem to have been incorporated into the municipal law of Kenya. Neither does there exist any institution or national machinery with responsibility for overseeing the implementation of human rights in the country.'

[173] See for example, *Third Periodic Report of the United Kingdom of Great Britain and Northern Ireland*, UN Doc E/1994/104/Add.11 (17 June 1996) [9].

[174] CESCR, *Concluding Observations: United Kingdom of Great Britain and Northern Ireland – Dependent Territories*, UN Doc E/C.12/1/Add.79, (5 June 2002) [24]. For a collection of cases on ESC rights, see ESCR-Net, *Caselaw Database: A Database of Economic, Social and Cultural Rights Related Jurisprudence, Cases and Other Decisions*, available at http://www.escr-net.org/caselaw/ at 5 December 2008.

[175] See General Comment 3, above n 31, 9; General Comment 13, above n 36, [44]; General Comment 14, above n 36, [31]; and General Comment 15, above n 61, [18]; Limburg Principles above n 21, [21].

through international assistance and cooperation. As argued above, international assistance and cooperation encompasses more than financial and technical assistance; it must also be understood as entailing the responsibility of States to work actively towards equitable multilateral trading, investment and financial systems that are conducive to the realisation of ESC rights. This may entail genuine special and preferential treatment of developing States so as to provide such States with fairer and better access to developed States' markets.[176]

The chapter has also argued that the human rights obligations of States under the ICESCR may extend to anyone within the power, effective control or authority of a State, as well as within an area over which that State exercises effective overall control. In this respect, human rights obligations with respect to ESC rights, though essentially territorial, are not necessarily territorially limited. There is a possibility of extraterritorial application, for example where a State is an occupying power or where a State directly or indirectly causes harm to ESC rights extraterritorially.

Finally, it has been shown that the absence of a clause allowing derogation in times of public emergency in the ICESCR indicates that the Covenant's human rights obligations, particularly its core obligations, are non-derogable; they continue to exist in situations of conflict, emergency and natural disaster.

---

[176] See also Chapters 6 and 7.

# 3. Extraterritoriality: universal human rights without universal obligations?

*Sigrun I Skogly*

## 1 Introduction

In international human rights discourse, the concept of universalism has been key since the adoption of the *Charter of the United Nations* (*'UN Charter'*) in 1945, and the labelling of the 1948 Declaration as the *Universal Declaration of Human Rights* ('UDHR')[1] signifies the importance of this concept. Added to this, the strong position of the non-discrimination provisions in the UN Charter, the UDHR and all subsequent human rights treaties and declarations is further evidence of the primacy of universal and non-discriminatory enjoyment of human rights. This was also confirmed by the International Court of Justice ('ICJ') in its determination that the practice of *apartheid* was a flagrant violation of the purposes and principles of the UN Charter.[2]

Yet, in the development of human rights law and its implementation through national and international bodies, the concept of universalism has been rather one-sided: it concerns human rights enjoyment, but not human rights obligations. While all individuals everywhere are considered to have the same rights based on international law, the obligation-holders (normally states) do not have the same obligations with regard to individuals everywhere. According to common perceptions of human rights obligations, whether a state can in any way be held responsible for human rights violations depends not only on the state's actions, but also on where those actions took place, and/or the nationality of the victims of the violations.

However, this way of looking at obligations has in recent times been questioned by a number of actors in the international human rights community. Academics,[3]

---

[1]   GA Res 217A (III), UN Doc A/810, 71 (1948).
[2]   *Legal Consequences for States of the Continued Presence of South Africa in Namibia (South-West Africa) Notwithstanding Security Council Resolution 276 (1970)* [1971] ICJ Reports 16, [131] ('Namibia Opinion').
[3]   F Coomans and M T Kamminga, *Extraterritorial Application of Human Rights Treaties* (Intersentia, Antwerp, 2004); M Gibney, 'Genocide and State Responsibility' (2007) 7 *Human Rights Law Review* 760; M Gibney, E Roxstrom and T Einarsen 'The NATO Bombing Case (*Bankovic v Belgium et al*): One Step Forward or Two Steps Back?' (2005) 23 *Boston University Journal of International Law* 55;

policymakers,[4] non-governmental organisations ('NGOs'),[5] and international institutions (as discussed below) have begun to question the logic of this approach, and indeed the legal justifications for it. A significant number of international court cases have also in recent years debated the reach of international human rights obligations. Thus, the altered approach is to address whether states have obligations in regard to the human rights effects on individuals in other states as a result of actions and omissions in their international cooperation or foreign policy.

There are different reasons for this shift in attention concerning these obligations. One of the more obvious reasons is the phenomenon of 'globalisation', understood in a broad sense. The increased international interaction among states, between states and international institutions, and between states and private entities, such as multinational corporations ('MNCs'), may have posi-

---

Mark Gibney, Katarine Thomasevski and Jens Vedsted-Hansen, 'Transnational State Responsibility for Violations of Human Rights' (1999) 12 *Harvard International Law Journal* 267; Menno T Kamminga, *Inter-state Accountability for Violations of Human Rights* (University of Pennsylvania Press, Philadelphia, 1992); R Lawson, 'The Concept of Jurisdiction and Extraterritorial Acts of State' in G Kreijen (ed) *State, Sovereignty, and International Governance* (Oxford University Press, Oxford, 2002) 281; S Narula, 'The Right to Food: Holding Global Actors Accountable Under International Law' (2006) 44 *Columbia Journal of Transnational Law* 691; M Sepulveda, 'Obligations of "International Assistance and Cooperation" in an Optional Protocol to the International Covenant on Economic, Social and Cultural Rights' (2006) 24 *Netherlands Quarterly of Human Rights* 271; Sigrun I Skogly, *Beyond National Borders: States' Human Rights Obligations in International Cooperation* (Intersentia, Antwerp, 2006); Ralph Wilde, 'Legal "Black Hole"? Extraterritorial State Action and International Treaty Law on Civil and Political Rights' (2005) 26 *Michigan Journal of International Law* 739; Ralph Wilde, 'Casting Light on the "Legal Black Hole": Some Political Issues at Stake' [2006] *European Human Rights Law Review* 552; Judith Bueno de Mesquita, *International Covenant on Economic, Social and Cultural Rights: Obligations of International Assistance and Cooperation* (University of Essex, Colchester, 2002).

[4] This is, *inter alia*, the position taken by the Norwegian government in its white paper of 1999, *Human dignity in focus (Menneskeverd i sentrum)*, where it states that '[t]he government will clearly give priority to work towards improved compliance with human rights obligations at home as well as abroad'; and 'Norwegian development assistance shall contribute to enhance the ability of recipient countries to meet their human rights obligations'. Norwegian Government, Foreign Office, *White Paper to the Norwegian Parliament: Human Dignity in Focus*, Parliamentary Paper No 21 (1999/2000) Section 2, 12, 48 (translated by author).

[5] See, for example, FIAN Belgium, *Compliance of Belgium with its Obligations under the International Covenant on Economic, Social and Cultural Rights* (FIAN Belgium, Brussels, 2007); 3Dthree, *US and EU Cotton Production and Export Policies and Their Impact on West and Central Africa: Coming to Grips with International Human Rights Obligations* (2004) 3Dthree, http://www.3dthree.org/en/page.php?IDpage=27 at 12 January 2009.

tive or negative effects on the human rights situation outside the control of the territorial state. The more far-reaching international regulation of financial matters and trade, combined with an emphasis on certain economic models, compliance with which is imperative for international assistance, has resulted in nation states being less able to control events within their own borders and direct development in ways that they themselves choose.

This increased interaction and interdependence of states in the international community has resulted in a debate that questions whether states have obligations that go beyond their national borders and include human rights problems caused by the actions or omissions of one state in the territory of another state. The question raised is whether the foreign state fails to comply with legal obligations if its actions or omissions result in human rights violations abroad. This debate concerns questions that have been addressed through the use of different terms: extraterritorial obligations, transnational obligations, international obligations, and global obligations, to mention the most common. While these terms do not necessarily signify exactly the same phenomenon,[6] the main aim of this discussion is to address the problem that may occur if one state acts in a manner whereby its actions undermine human rights for individuals in another country. For the purpose of this chapter, I will use the term 'extraterritorial obligations'.[7]

## 2 The content of extraterritorial obligations

Before discussing the legal foundation for, and current obstacles to the implementation of, extraterritorial obligations, it is necessary to dwell briefly on what the content of such obligations are. It was alluded to in the introduction that the understanding of what human rights obligations are has become more sophisticated and nuanced in the past two decades. While human rights obligations were initially thought to be mainly negative (to refrain from interfering with individuals' human rights enjoyment), both the language in the various human rights treaties and the jurisprudence from human rights courts and committees have confirmed that such an approach is too limited. Indeed, it is now generally accepted that human rights obligations are of both a negative and a positive nature, in that states are obliged not only to refrain from violating rights but also to take steps to ensure human rights enjoyment. This is the case for economic, social and cultural rights as well as civil and political

---

[6] For a discussion on the various terms used in these discussions see Mark Gibney, *Terminology* (Paper delivered at the University of Tilburg, 24–6 January 2008).

[7] For a discussion as to why I have chosen to use this term in my work on the issue, see Skogly, above n 3, 5.

rights.[8] Furthermore, based on works by Henry Shue[9] and Asbjørn Eide,[10] a common understanding of three levels of obligations has emerged: the obligations to *respect,* to *protect,* and to *fulfil.*[11] These levels of obligations have been explained in the *Maastricht Guidelines*:

> The obligation to respect requires States to refrain from interfering with the enjoyment of economic, social and cultural rights. Thus, the right to housing is violated if the State engages in arbitrary forced evictions. The obligation to protect requires States to prevent violations of such rights by third parties. Thus, the failure to ensure that private employers comply with basic labour standards may amount to a violation of the right to work or the right to just and favourable conditions of work. The obligation to fulfil requires States to take appropriate legislative, administrative, budgetary, judicial and other measures towards the full realization of such rights. Thus, the failure of States to provide essential primary health care to those in need may amount to a violation.[12]

According to the UN Committee on Economic, Social and Cultural Rights, the same levels apply to extraterritorial (international) obligations.[13] The obligation to respect implies that a state has to respect the human rights of individuals in another country when entering into cooperation with, or carrying out foreign policy (including military activity) that impacts on, these individuals. The obligation to protect refers to the activities of private parties, and therefore entails that states have an obligation to ensure that private parties (including private businesses) over which they assert (jurisdictional or other)

---

[8] *Maastricht Guidelines*, Guideline 6. The *Maastricht Guidelines on Violations of Economic, Social and Cultural Rights* ('*Maastricht Guidelines*') were adopted by a group of experts that met in Maastricht on 22–6 January 1997. The Guidelines are reprinted at (1998) 20 *Human Rights Quarterly* 691; see also http://www1.umn.eduhumanrts/instree/Maastrichtguidelines.html at 12 January 2009.

[9] H Shue, *Basic Rights: Subsistence, Affluence and US Foreign Policy* (Princeton University Press, Princeton, 2nd ed, 1996) 52.

[10] Asbjørn Eide, *The Right to Adequate Food as a Human Right: Special Rapporteur's Report on the Right to Adequate Food*, UN Doc E/CN.4/Sub.2/1987/23 (7 July 1987).

[11] In a follow-up study on the right to adequate food, Eide proposes two separate elements of the fulfil part of obligations: to promote and to facilitate. See Asbjórn Eide, *The Right to Adequate Food and to be Free From Hunger: Updated Study on the Right to Food*, UN Doc E/CN.4/Sub.2/1999/12 (28 June 1999).

[12] *Maastricht Guidelines*, Guideline 6. Please note that the focus here is on violations of economic, social and cultural rights. However, the sentence preceding the quoted part above confirms that these levels are also relevant for civil and political rights.

[13] The UN Committee on Economic, Social and Cultural Rights refers to extraterritorial obligations as 'international obligations'.

control do not violate the rights of individuals in other states.[14] Finally, the obligation to fulfil requires states to take such measures that are necessary for the full realisation of rights in other states.

This final point is by far the most controversial element of extraterritorial obligations. Without going into the details of the debates concerning this level of extraterritorial obligation,[15] and the problems that it may raise in terms of sovereignty of the home state of individuals facing human rights problems, as well as the practical problems of resources available for full realisation of all human rights in foreign states, it should be noted that the special rapporteur on the Right to Food, Jean Ziegler, introduced the concept of 'support fulfilment' of rights in other states. He explained this terminology in the following manner:

> It underlines that the principal obligation to guarantee the right to food is incumbent on the national Government, but other States, if they have available resources, have a complementary obligation to help the national State, when it does not have the resources to realize the right to food of its population.[16]

## 3 Legal foundation for extraterritorial human rights obligations

While states' extraterritorial human rights obligations often have been ignored, this does not imply that they are non-existent, nor that there are no legal foundations for such obligations. Indeed, extraterritorial human rights obligations have their grounding in international human rights law, and this has been confirmed by international courts and committees. It should be noted that the jurisprudence in this area is not conclusive, and that different approaches have been taken by different international institutions, and that

---

[14] In *General Comment 15* on the right to water, the UN Committee on Economic, Social and Cultural Rights ('ECOSOC') confirms that 'international obligations' includes that '[s]teps should be taken by States parties to prevent their own citizens and companies from violating the right to water of individuals and communities in other countries': ECOSOC, *General Comment 15: The Right to Water*, UN Doc E/C.12/2002/1 (20 January 2002) [33]. Likewise, in *General Comment 14* on the right to the highest attainable standard of health, the same Committee confirms that '[t]o comply with their international obligations in relation to Article 12, States parties have to respect the enjoyment of the right to health in other countries, and to prevent third parties from violating the right in other countries, if they are able to influence these third parties by way of legal or political means, in accordance with the *Charter of the United Nations* and applicable international law': ECOSOC, *General Comment 14: The Right to the Highest Attainable Standard of Health*, UN Doc E/C.12/2000/4 (11 August 2000) [39].

[15] For a more in-depth discussion of these issues, see Skogly, above n 3, Ch 3.

[16] Jean Ziegler, *The Right to Food: Report of the Special Rapporteur on the Right to Food*, UN Doc E/CN.4/2005/47 (24 January 2005) [47].

even the same institution may not appear to be consistent in its application of extraterritorial obligations. This thesis will be discussed below.

A  *The Charter of the United Nations*
Little attention has been given to the possibility that the *UN Charter* provides for more than domestic human rights obligations. Commonly, the *UN Charter* is criticised for not being specific enough in terms of human rights and the corresponding obligations. However, there may be more in the *UN Charter* than has been recognised.

Article 1 of the *UN Charter* establishes the purposes of the organisation, and as a member of the UN each individual state is bound by the *UN Charter*, and has obligations to assist in fulfilling these purposes. The fundamental principle of universal and international protection of human rights is provided in Article 1(3). It is that the

> purpose of the United Nations [is to] achieve *international co-operation* in solving international problems of an economic, social, cultural or humanitarian character, and in *promoting and encouraging respect for human rights and for fundamental freedoms for all*. (emphasis added)

The inclusion of the statement that the organisation's purpose is, *inter alia*, to 'achieve international co-operation' in relationship to the substantive content of the rest of the paragraph is not insignificant in relation to the question of extraterritorial human rights obligations. If international cooperation is to be achieved, the members of the UN will have an obligation to contribute to this cooperation which is aimed at addressing problems of an economic, social, humanitarian and human rights character. If member states of the United Nations claim that human rights obligations are uniquely territorial, this disregards the principle of international cooperation in Article 1.

Further, Articles 55 and 56 provide that the United Nations shall promote '*universal* respect for, and observance of human rights and fundamental freedoms for all',[17] and that this shall be done through 'joint and separate action in co-operation with the Organization'.[18] These articles are commonly referred to in UN documents when the international promotion of human rights is discussed. However, until recently there has been little interpretation of the obligations that stem from these two provisions.[19]

---

[17] *UN Charter*, Article 55(c) (emphasis added).
[18] *UN Charter*, Article 56.
[19] Margot E Salomon, *Global Responsibility for Human Rights: World Poverty and the Development of International Law* (Oxford University Press, Oxford, 2007) 67–71.

In an elaboration of the legislative history and interpretation of Article 56, it is explained that the text is a compromise between a wording suggested by Australia and the views of the United States in the drafting process.[20] Australia had proposed that 'all members of the UN should pledge to take action, on both national and international levels, for the purpose of securing for all peoples, including their own, such goals as improved labour standards'[21] and thus suggested a formulation in which the pledge would mean that the 'members would both co-operate internationally and act within their own countries to pursue the economic and social objectives of the Organization, in their own way and without interference in their domestic affairs by the Organization'.[22] This was opposed by the US, as it claimed that all that could be included in the Charter was to provide for 'collective action and thus it could not oblige a nation to take separate action because that would constitute an infringement upon the internal affairs of the member states'.[23] Thus, the interpretation of the Article has tended to accept a compromise between the two positions, whereby the

> rather limited obligatory function of Article 56 is ... the result of the wording of Article 55, to which it refers. The latter only describes purposes (and not substantive obligations) to be achieved by means of co-operation. To this extent, Article 56 can thus only create substantive obligations (as opposed to procedural obligations) in so far as Article 55 contains a corresponding basis in that respect.[24]

However, Simma holds that Article 55(c) contains substantive obligations in regard to human rights,[25] and it can thus be held that Articles 55 and 56 in conjunction establish obligations to take action to promote respect for human rights. According to this interpretation, there is a firm obligation for states to act individually as well as collectively to promote respect for human rights.

It is, however, interesting to note that the opposition by the United States did not concern the international obligations, but rather that the UN Charter could not prescribe what states should do domestically. As domestic human rights obligations have now gained virtually universal acceptance, it is rather paradoxical that the international (or extraterritorial) obligations have become the controversial ones.

---

[20] Bruno Simma (ed) *The Charter of the United Nations – A Commentary* (Oxford University Press, Oxford, 1994) 793.
[21] Ibid.
[22] Ibid.
[23] Discussion UNCIO X, Doc 699 II/3/30 and Doc 747 II/3/46, 139–40: cited in Simma, above n 20.
[24] Simma, above n 20, 794.
[25] Ibid.

The meaning of 'jointly' as used in Article 56 is not quite clear though. In Simma's commentary on the *UN Charter*, the meaning of the term 'joint' is not substantially discussed.[26] However, 'jointly' could imply action through the United Nations, as a way to practically carry out the organisation's mandate, in recognition that the organisation may not be able to fulfil its purposes without joint commitment from the membership. However, the interpretation that this would be the entire meaning of 'joint action' in Article 56 seems too narrow. The article provides that this joint action shall take place 'in cooperation with the organisation.' If it was intended to imply a narrow obligation to promote respect for human rights through the work of the United Nations, one would have expected the wording to reflect this, for instance by saying 'joint and separate action through the United Nations'. But this wording was not chosen. Rather, a wider formulation is used, and the understanding of 'joint' therefore implies an obligation to act jointly to promote respect for human rights, and also an obligation to cooperate with the United Nations in this regard.[27] This joint action has a clear extraterritorial element to it: only one of the states acting 'jointly' may at any given time address the promotion of the respect for human rights domestically – all the other states involved in the joint action will logically be addressing respect for human rights in another state.

Furthermore, Article 56 does not only call for joint action, but indeed also 'separate' action in cooperation with the United Nations. These words, seen in conjunction with the provision in Article 55(c), which calls for *universal* respect for human rights, further strengthens arguments for human rights obligations beyond national borders for individual states. As the article uses the term 'universal' rather than 'domestic', it is submitted that this wording has extraterritorial implications, and that it adds to the Charter's non-discrimination principle, in that states shall promote respect for human rights not only of their own populations, but indeed universally as well.

In addition to the *UN Charter*, the various specific human rights treaties are the main sources of human rights obligations. Some of these treaties have provisions which give a specific content to extraterritorial obligations, while others have been interpreted to contain such obligations without specific mention in the treaty text.[28]

---

[26] The seminal work edited by Simma covers 1400 pages. However, only three pages are devoted to Article 56. Very little scholarly work on this article is found elsewhere.
[27] Simma, above n 20, 948.
[28] For a deeper analysis on the sources of extraterritorial obligations, see Skogly, above n 3; and Coomans and Kamminga, above n 3.

There are three international human rights treaties that are specifically important based on their own provisions for the discussions on extraterritorial obligations. These are the *International Covenant on Economic, Social and Cultural Rights* ('ICESCR'),[29] the *Convention on the Rights of the Child* ('CRC'),[30] and the recent *Convention on the Rights of Persons with Disabilities* ('CRPD').[31]

B   *The International Covenant on Economic, Social and Cultural Rights*

The ICESCR is particularly interesting in any discussion on extraterritorial human rights obligations.[32] Not only does Article 2(1) ICESCR refer specifically to the states parties' obligations to take steps 'individually and through international assistance and co-operation'[33] for the realisation of the rights guaranteed, but it also omits the reference to 'jurisdiction' or 'territory' which is common in other human rights instruments.[34] This being so, the understanding of the content of the extraterritorial obligations stemming from this provision in Article 2(1) ICESCR has not been significantly developed.[35] The

---

[29]  Opened for signature 19 December 1966, 999 UNTS 3 (entered into force 3 January 1976).

[30]  Opened for signature 20 November 1989, 1577 UNTS 3 (entered into force 2 September 1990).

[31]  Opened for signature 30 March 2007, 993 UNTS 3 (entered into force 3 May 2008).

[32]  In this chapter, I will only address Article 2(1) ICESCR. I have addressed the significance of other articles of the ICESCR in other publications: see generally Sigrun I Skogly, 'The obligation of international assistance and co-operation in the *International Covenant on Economic, Social and Cultural Rights*' in B Morten (ed) *Human Rights and Criminal Justice for the Downtrodden: Essays in Honour of Asbjorn Eide* (Kluwer Law International, Dordrecht, 2003) 403; and Skogly, above n 3, 83–98.

[33]  Article 2(1) of the *International Covenant on Civil and Political Rights*, opened for signature 16 December 1966, 999 UNTS 171 (entered into force 23 March 1976) reads: '[e]ach State Party to the present Covenant undertakes to take steps, individually and through international assistance and co-operation, especially economic and technical, to the maximum of its available resources, with a view to achieving progressively the full realization of the rights recognized in the present Covenant by all appropriate means, including particularly the adoption of legislative measures.'

[34]  For the text of these instruments, see below p. 91.

[35]  In *General Comment No 3: The nature of States parties obligations (Art 2(1))*, UN Doc E/1991/23 (14 December 1990) ('*General Comment No 3*') the Committee referred to this passage as indicating that 'available resources' included those available through international assistance (at [13]), and, read in conjunction with Articles 55 and 56 of the *UN Charter*, that 'international cooperation for development and thus for the realization of economic, social and cultural rights is an obligation of all States. It is particularly incumbent upon those States which are in a position to assist others in this

Committee on Economic, Social and Cultural Rights has in later years, however, begun to include explicit and implicit references to this provision in its General Comments and in questioning of and concluding observations to states' reports.[36]

A review of some of the drafting history of Article 2(1) ICESCR sheds light on the debates that took place in the 1950s and '60s. As has been documented elsewhere,[37] there was some discussion over the inclusion of the passage 'international assistance and co-operation' in the Article. The discussions in the Commission on Human Rights and in the General Assembly's Third Committee were, however, not conclusive as to the drafting parties' intentions. What did seem rather clear, though, was that international cooperation and assistance was seen as necessary if the Covenant's rights were to be realised. What was more discussed was the nature of this cooperation, and whether the added provision of 'especially economic and technical' was too limited.[38] International assistance and cooperation was included as one of the means of realisation of the rights in the original (and subsequent) general obligation provision of the Covenant. However, more than 40 years later, it has proven to be one of the more controversial aspects of the document.

## C  The Convention on the Rights of the Child
As is the case for the ICESCR, the CRC incorporates specific obligations of international assistance and cooperation in regard to economic, social and cultural rights. Article 4 states that:

---

regard' (at [14]); The *Limburg Principles*, [29]–[34], deal with this passage in Article 2(1), but use rather general terms, such as 'international co-operation and assistance shall' give priority to 'the realization of all human rights'; and that it should contribute to the establishment of a social and international order conducive to human rights. There is no clear indication as to the content of obligations for states. The *Limburg Principles on the Implementation of Economic, Social and Cultural Rights* were adopted by a group of distinguished experts in international law, convened by the International Commission of Jurists, the Faculty of Law of the University of Limburg and the Urban Morgan Institute for Human Rights, University of Cincinnati, which met in Maastricht on 2–6 June 1986. These principles can *inter alia* be accessed through the International Human Rights Obligations Network ('IntHRON') at: http://www.lancs.ac.uk/fss/organisations/humanrights/inthron/index.php at 12 January 2009.

[36] For a detailed analysis of the way in which the Committee on Economic, Social and Cultural Rights has approached this issue, see Magdalena Sepulveda, 'Obligations of "International Assistance and Cooperation" in an Optional Protocol to the International Covenant on Economic, Social and Cultural Rights' (2006) 24 *Netherlands Quarterly of Human Rights* 271.

[37] Skogly, above n 32, 403–20.

[38] General Assembly, 17th Session, 3rd Committee, 1204th meeting, *UN Official Records*, [49]. For further discussions on this, see Skogly, above n 32, 407–12.

> States Parties shall undertake all appropriate legislative, administrative, and other measures for the implementation of the rights recognized in the present Convention. With regard to economic, social and cultural rights, States Parties shall undertake such measures to the maximum extent of their available resources and, where needed, within the framework of *international cooperation* (emphasis added).

During the drafting of this article, there were a number of issues debated, including the reference to 'available resources'.[39] However, what is noticeable in this context is that 'international co-operation' was already included in the first draft of the convention text presented by Poland in January 1980, and it was readily accepted, and not considered controversial, as evidenced by the lack of debate about it.[40]

Contrary to the position of the Committee on Economic, Social and Cultural Rights, the Committee on the Rights of the Child has not dealt with the concept of international cooperation as part of the treaty obligations in any detail. The only aspect of international cooperation that is included in the Committee's General Comments[41] relates to the seeking of international assistance, and does not include recognition of extraterritorial obligations.[42]

### D  The Convention on the Rights of Persons with Disabilities

A recent addition to international human rights law was made with the adoption and entry into force of the CRPD. There are two articles that specifically address international cooperation: Article 4 CRPD 'General Obligations' and Article 32 CRPD 'International Cooperation'. Article 4 (2) CRPD provides that:

> With regard to economic, social and cultural rights, each State Party undertakes to take measures to the maximum of its available resources and, where needed, within the framework of international cooperation, with a view to achieving progressively the full realization of these rights, without prejudice to those obligations contained in the present Convention that are immediately applicable according to international law.

In contrast to Article 2(1) ICESCR, the Article only refers to 'international cooperation' rather than 'international assistance and cooperation'. As international assistance (technical, financial, humanitarian) is now commonly seen

---

[39] Skogly, above n 3, 103.
[40] Skogly, above n 3, 104.
[41] Committee on the Rights of the Child, *General Comment No 5: General Measures of Implementation of the Convention on the Rights of the Child*, UN Doc CRC/GC/2003/5 (3 October 2003).
[42] Skogly, above n 3, 159–60.

to be part of international cooperation,[43] this difference is unlikely to imply a more narrow sphere for the extraterritorial obligations.

The second article that deals with international cooperation, Article 32 CRPD, emphasises 'the importance of international cooperation and its promotion, in support of national efforts for the realization of the purpose and objectives of the present Convention'. This refers to the same concept as Ziegler labelled 'obligation to support fulfilment'.[44] It then goes on to call for international development programmes that are inclusive and accessible to persons with disabilities,[45] and for measures to facilitate and support capacity building,[46] to facilitate research cooperation;[47] and to provide technical assistance and technology transfer.[48]

The Article ends with: 'The Provisions of this article are without prejudice to the obligations of each State Party to fulfil its obligations under the present Convention'.[49] This final sentence is of particular interest, as it addresses some of the concerns opponents to extraterritorial obligations have voiced, namely that states (and particularly poorer states) will feel relieved of their treaty obligations, as they can advocate that they need external funding to implement the rights in the treaties. This provision emphasises the primary obligation for the territorial state to comply with its obligations and carry out its implementation.

### E   Other human rights treaties

It is noticeable that the specific treaties discussed so far all address economic, social and cultural rights in relation to extraterritorial obligations. One could then easily conclude that any extraterritorial human rights obligations are confined to that part of international human rights law. However, such an interpretation would not reflect the current understanding of international human rights treaties. Indeed, the ICJ, the UN Human Rights Committee (which monitors the implementation of the *International Covenant on Civil and Political Rights*), the European Court of Human Rights, and the Inter-American Commission on Human Rights have all confirmed that international human rights treaties protecting civil and political rights contain obligations for the states parties that go beyond the national territory. This is in spite of the clauses in some of these treaties

---

[43] For further discussions on this, see Salomon, above n 19, 98–109.
[44] See Ziegler, above n 16 and accompanying text.
[45] Article 32(1)(a) CRPD.
[46] Article 32(1)(b) CRPD.
[47] Article 32(1)(c) CRPD.
[48] Article 32(1)(d) CRPD.
[49] Article 32(2) CRPD.

providing that the states parties are to protect and ensure the rights within their territory and/or their jurisdiction.[50]

In the Namibia Opinion, the ICJ found that South Africa, having established a system of *apartheid* in the neighbouring state, was in breach of its international obligations under the *UN Charter*. Therefore, the fact that South Africa acted outside of its own territory was of no consequence; the Court still found that South Africa was in breach of its obligations.[51]

Furthermore, in the advisory opinion on the *Legal Consequences of the Construction of a Wall in the Occupied Palestinian Territory*, the ICJ considered the relevance of obligations stemming from human rights treaties that Israel has ratified. In regard to the ICCPR, the Court held that it was applicable 'in respect of acts done by a State in the exercise of its jurisdiction outside its own territory'.[52] Likewise, in respect of the ICESCR, the Court held that

> The territories occupied by Israel have for over 37 years been subject to its territorial jurisdiction as the Occupying Power. In the exercise of the powers available to it on this basis, Israel is bound by the provisions of the ICESCR.[53]

Similarly, in *Lopez Burgos v Uruguay*, the UN Human Rights Committee held that

> [I]t would be unconscionable to so interpret the responsibility under Article 2 of the [ICCPR] as to permit a State party to perpetrate violations of the Covenant on the territory of another State, which violations it could not perpetrate on its own territory.[54]

Adding his individual opinion to this case, Committee Member Tomuschat held that

> Never was it envisaged [...] to grant States parties unfettered discretionary power to carry out wilful and deliberate attacks against the freedom and personal integrity of their citizens living abroad.[55]

While this case concerned the abduction and arrest of a Uruguayan citizen living abroad by members of the Uruguayan security forces, and the question

---

[50] For text, see below p. 91.
[51] See above n 2 and accompanying text.
[52] *Legal Consequences of the Construction of a Wall in the Occupied Palestinian Territory*, ICJ Advisory Opinion (9 July 2004) [111] (*'The Wall'*).
[53] *The Wall* [112].
[54] *Lopez Burgos v Uruguay*, Communication No 052/1979, UN Doc CCPR/C/OP/1 (29 July 1981) [12.3] (*'Lopez Burgos'*).
[55] *Lopez Burgos* 184.

before the Committee became whether a state had the same obligations towards its citizens abroad as at home,[56] it is probably reasonable to suggest that Tomuschat's opinion could also be applied to foreigners abroad and that states should not have 'unfettered discretionary power to carry out wilful and deliberate attacks against the freedom and personal integrity' of individuals in other states. This understanding is supported by another passage in his statement, where he holds that the 'words "within its territory" . . . was intended to take care of objective difficulties which might impede the implementation of the Covenant in specific situations'.[57]

This view is confirmed by both the Committee against Torture ('CAT') and the Human Rights Committee in their deliberations and conclusions regarding the United States' reports concerning *inter alia* the conditions at Guantanamo Bay. CAT, in its concluding observations in 2006

> reiterates its previously expressed view that 'territory under [the State party's] jurisdiction' includes all areas under the *de facto* effective control of the State party, by whichever military or civil authorities such control is exercised. The Committee considers that the State party's view that those provisions are geographically limited to its own de jure territory to be regrettable.[58]

Likewise, the Human Rights Committee has noted

> with concern the restrictive interpretation made by the State party of its obligations under the Covenant, as a result in particular of: (a) its position that the Covenant does not apply with respect to individuals under its jurisdiction but outside its territory, nor in time of war, despite the contrary opinions and established jurisprudence of the Committee and the International Court of Justice; . . . The State party should in particular: (a) acknowledge the applicability of the Covenant with respect to individuals under its jurisdiction but outside its territory.[59]

---

[56] In this respect, the case is similar to that heard by the European Court of Human Rights in *Öcalan v. Turkey*, where Mr. Öcalan, a Turkish citizen, was arrested by Turkish authorities at the international airport in Nairobi, Kenya, and brought back to Turkey. The Court considered that 'directly after being handed over to the Turkish officials, the applicant was effectively under Turkish authority and therefore within the "jurisdiction" of that State for the purposes of Article 1 of the Convention, even though in this instance Turkey exercised its authority outside its territory': *Öcalan v Turkey*, Application No 46221/99 (Unreported, European Court of Human Rights, Trial Chamber, 12 May 2005) [91].

[57] *Lopez Burgos* 184ff.

[58] UN CAT, *Conclusions and recommendations: United States of America*, UN Doc CAT/C/USA/CO/2 (25 July 2006) [15].

[59] UN Human Rights Committee, *Concluding Observations: United States of America*, UN Doc CCPR/C/USA/CO/3/Rev.1 (18 December 2006) [10].

The European Court of Human Rights has also found that actions by a High Contracting Party beyond its territory may be in breach of that State's obligations. In *Loizidou v Turkey*,[60] which concerned the ability of a Greek-Cypriot to access her property in Northern Cyprus after the Turkish occupation of that part of the island, the Turkish government argued that the case could not be admissible as it concerned an area outside the territory of Turkey. However, the European Court clearly stated that a state's responsibility for its own acts can reach outside the territorial jurisdiction of that state. The Court held that the

> responsibility of Contracting Parties can be involved because of acts of their authorities, whether performed within or outside national boundaries, which produce effects outside their own territory.[61]

The Inter-American Commission on Human Rights ('IACHR') has taken a similar view in cases involving transnational human rights obligations. In *Armando Alejandre Jr and Others v Cuba*[62] the petitioners complained to the IACHR about the deaths of four individuals caused by the shooting down of two civilian aircrafts by a Cuban military MiG-29. The civilian aircrafts were in international territory when they were shot down. The IACHR held Cuba responsible for violating the victims' right to life and to a fair trial and stated the following with regard to the extraterritorial nature of the acts:

> The fact that the events took place outside Cuban jurisdiction, does not limit the Commission's competence *ratione loci,* because, as previously stated, when agents of a state, whether military or civilian, exercise power and authority over persons outside national territory, the state's obligation to respect human rights continues – in this case the rights enshrined in the American Declaration. The Commission finds conclusive evidence that agents of the Cuban State, although outside their territory, placed the civilian pilots of the 'Brothers to the Rescue' organization under their authority. Consequently, the Commission is competent *ratione loci* to apply the American Convention extraterritorially to the Cuban State in connection with the events that took place in international airspace on February 24, 1996.[63]

In this case, the IACHR recognised that Cuba was acting outside its territorial jurisdiction, but that in certain circumstances it is not only consistent with, but also required by, the applicable rules to hold a state accountable for acts outside its territory.[64]

---

[60] *Loizidou v Turkey* (1995) 310 Eur Court HR (ser A) 7 (*'Loizidou'*).
[61] *Loizidou* [62].
[62] *Armando Alejandre Jr and Others v Cuba*, Inter-American Commission of Human Rights, Report No 86/99, Case No 11.589 (29 September 1999).
[63] *Armando Alejandre Jr and Others v Cuba* [25].
[64] *Armando Alejandre Jr and Others v Cuba* [23].

This recital of cases by international courts and opinions by monitoring Committees should not be taken as an indication that extraterritorial obligations in relation to human rights are necessarily always accepted, and that they are not seen as controversial by many institutions and human rights lawyers. Indeed, the European Court of Human Rights has stated that only 'in exceptional circumstances' can obligations go beyond the territory of the state.[65] Furthermore, the ICJ has gone to great lengths to avoid apportioning responsibility to states whose conduct contributes to human rights violations in third countries.[66] This reality calls for an assessment of the obstacles to full recognition of extraterritorial obligations.

## 4 Obstacles to the recognition of extraterritorial obligations

There are a number of obstacles to the development of a consensus regarding the content of states' obligations for their involvement in human rights violations in other states. Some are obstacles in (the interpretation of) the law and others are of a more political nature.

### A State responsibility

According to the International Law Commission's *Articles on Responsibility for Internationally Wrongful Acts* (*'ILC Articles'*),[67] if a state commits an act or omits to carry out prescribed conduct and this act or omission represents a breach of an international obligation, the state has committed an internationally wrongful act for which it is responsible.[68] The *ILC Articles* also set out the legal consequences for such unlawful acts.[69] This is a reflection of the reciprocal character of international law as between states. However, state responsibility is not commonly invoked in situations where the actions of one state breach or threaten the human rights of individuals in another state.

---

[65] *Bankovic and Ors v Belgium and Ors* (2000) 123 ILR 94, [71], [80] (*'Bankovic'*).

[66] This thesis is evident both in *Nicaragua v United States of America* [1986] ICJ Reports 14 (*'Nicaragua'*) and the *Case Concerning the Application of the Convention on the Prevention and Punishment of the Crime of Genocide* [2007] ICJ Reports, http://www.icj-cij.org/docket/index.php?p1=3&p2=3&k=f4&case=91&code=bhy&p3=4 at 12 January 2009 (*'Genocide'*). For a critical appraisal of these cases and the implication for state responsibility for breaches of extraterritorial obligations, see Mark Gibney, 'Genocide and State Responsibility' (2007) 7 *Human Rights Law Review* 760.

[67] Adopted by the International Law Commission in 2001: see http://untreaty.un.org/ilc/texts/instruments/english/draft%20articles/9_6_2001.pdf at 12 January 2009.

[68] *ILC Articles* Articles 1 and 2.

[69] *ILC Articles* Part II.

Inter-state complaint procedures exist in some of the regional human rights systems,[70] and in some of the international conventions adopted through the United Nations system.[71] These procedures, while sparingly used, are somewhat different from the regular application of state responsibility, as they are procedures specifically provided for in certain treaties, and are not reactions to breaches of normal reciprocal international law obligations independent of specific treaty-based procedures. Yet, the inter-state complaint procedures underscore the argument that international human rights treaties operate according to the general principles contained in the Law of Treaties. It is the reciprocal obligations undertaken by ratifying the treaty that are essential, not the nationality of the individual whose rights have been violated. In order to complain about the treatment of its own citizens abroad, a state need not rely on human rights treaties to seek redress, as customary international law principles regarding diplomatic protection cover that issue.[72]

Therefore, when entering into international human rights treaties, states not only guarantee that they will treat their inhabitants according to the standards provided in the treaties, but also that they are obligated to do so in their relationship to the other states that have ratified the same treaties. In essence, there is no relinquishment of the reciprocal nature of international treaties. To illustrate, states A and B are in a human rights treaty relationship with each other and the treaty prohibits torture. State A tortures its prisoners. The acts of torture violate the rights of the prisoners, but they also breach its treaty obligation in

---

[70] See Article 33 of the *Convention for the Protection of Human Rights and Fundamental Freedoms*, opened for signature 4 November 1950, 213 UNTS 262 (entered into force 3 September 1953) ('ECHR') as amended by Protocol 11; the *American Convention on Human Rights*, opened for signature 22 November 1969, 1144 UNTS 123 (entered into force 18 July 1978) provides for a similar procedure in Article 44; see also the *African Charter on Human and Peoples' Rights*, opened for signature 27 June 1981, 21 ILM 58 (entered into force 21 October 1986), Article 47. None of these procedures has been significantly used.

[71] Inter-state complaints procedures are available under the ICCPR; the *Convention Against Torture and Other Cruel, Inhuman or Degrading Treatment or Punishment*, opened for signature 10 December 1984, 1465 UNTS 85 (entered into force 26 June 1987); the *Convention on the Elimination of All Forms of Racial Discrimination*, opened for signature 21 December 1965, 660 UNTS 195 (entered into force 4 January 1969); and the *Convention on the Protection of All Rights of Migrant Workers and their Families*, opened for signature 18 December 1990, 30 ILM 1517 (entered into force 1 July 2003). As of November 2007, no such complaints have been filed in the UN system.

[72] This issue relates to the discussion about minimum standards of treatment of citizens of another state, an issue that goes beyond the scope of this chapter. For a discussion on this, see Antonio Cassese, *International Law* (Oxford University Press, Oxford, 2nd ed, 2005) 120.

relationship to state B. This conception concerns the traditional international obligations, breaches of which give rise to state responsibility as defined in Articles 1 and 2 of the *ILC Articles*.

The scenario used in this example reflects the domestic operation of human rights law, as the violations are committed by state A in regard to its own citizens or residents. However, the lack of application of state responsibility becomes increasingly more relevant in extraterritorial human rights relations. What if state A acts in a manner that violates the rights of state B's residents, while they are within the territory of state B? This example illustrates a lack of 'reverse diplomatic protection'. According to principles of customary international law, diplomatic protection may be afforded by one state if another state infringes upon the first state's citizens while they are in the territory of the second state.[73] The principle works on the basis that a violation of the rights of a citizen of one state by another state is considered a wrongful act against the citizen's home state.[74] However, if one state violates the rights of a citizen of another state while that citizen is in his/her home state, the principle of diplomatic protection does not seem to apply, or at least is not being used.[75]

The problem faced in these situations is that while we have a definition as to what triggers state responsibility, namely a wrongful act on the part of a state, we have very little guidance as to what constitutes a wrongful act by states in extraterritorial relations, and in particular in human rights cases. There is little international jurisprudence in this field, and what is available is not necessarily consistent. As has been mentioned above, the ICJ has heard some relevant cases, in particular the *Nicaragua* case and the *Genocide* case, and so have regional courts and commissions (in particular the European Court of Human Rights and the IACHR) and international criminal tribunals (in particular the International Criminal Tribunal for the Former Yugoslavia ('ICTY')). What is common for these cases is that the courts, commissions and tribunals go to great lengths to determine, on the basis of the evidence available, the exact detail of control that one state may have had over the events in another state, events that have led to (often highly significant) human rights violations.

In the *Nicaragua* case the ICJ considered, *inter alia*, whether the significant support by the United States to the *contras* in Honduras triggered responsibility for the actions taken by them when operating in Nicaragua. The Court held that

---

[73] Vaughan Lowe, *International Law* (Oxford University Press, Oxford, 2007) 132.
[74] Ibid.
[75] We have, however, seen that if a person has his/her human rights violated by their home state while residing in another state, extraterritorial applications of human rights treaties have been accepted. See, for instance, *Burgos Lopez*.

[E]vidence available to the Court indicates that various forms of assistance provided to the *contras* by the United States have been crucial to the pursuit of their activities, but it is insufficient to demonstrate their *complete dependence* on the United States aid.[76] ... The Court has taken the view ... that United States participation, even if preponderant or decisive, in the financing, organizing, training, supplying and equipping of the *contras*, the selection of its military or paramilitary targets, and the planning of the whole of its operation, is still insufficient in itself ... for the purpose of attributing to the United States the acts committed by the *contras* in the course of their military or paramilitary operations.[77] ... For this conduct to give rise to legal responsibility of the United States, it would in principle have to be proved that the State had *effective control* of the military and paramilitary operations in the course of which the alleged violations were committed.[78]

Furthermore, in the more recent *Genocide* case, the Court built on the concept of 'effective control' from the *Nicaragua* case, and used Article 8 of the *ILC Articles*, when determining whether Serbia and Montenegro ('FRY') could be considered to have responsibility for the genocide that had taken place in Bosnia and Herzegovina.[79] Article 8 holds that

The conduct of a person or a group of persons shall be considered an act of a State under international law if the person or group of persons is in fact acting on the instructions of, or under the direction or control of that State in carrying out the conduct.

The question in this case was whether the Bosnian Serbs during the genocide had been under the 'direction or control of' the government of the FRY. According to the applicants, up to 90 per cent of the material needs of the self-proclaimed 'Republic Srpska' (the Bosnian Serbs) had been provided by Serbia; a substantial portion of the Bosnian Serb paramilitary forces were being salaried by Serbia; and the economies of the Republic of Srpska and Serbia were almost completely integrated.[80] This claim was not challenged by the Court,[81] as it confirmed that

[T]he Respondent was thus making its considerable military and financial support available to the Republic Srpska, and had it withdrawn that support, this would have greatly constrained the options that were available to the Republic Srpska authorities.[82]

---

[76] *Nicaragua* [110] (emphasis added).
[77] *Nicaragua* [115].
[78] *Nicaragua* [115] (emphasis added).
[79] *Genocide* [399].
[80] *Genocide* [239], [240].
[81] Gibney, above n 66, 764.
[82] *Genocide* [240].

Yet, the Court did not find that the FRY was legally responsible, because it

> is not established beyond any doubt in the argument between the Parties whether the authorities of the FRY supplied – and continued to supply – the [Bosnian Serb forces] who decided upon and carried out those acts of genocide with their aid and assistance, at a time when those authorities were clearly aware that genocide was about to take place or was under way.[83]

What these two cases decided by the ICJ illustrate is that the Court applies an extremely high threshold for responsibility. In applying the concept of 'effective control' over, or whether a non-territorial state 'directed or controlled', the impugned actions, the ICJ seems to conclude that unless the foreign state has complete control over actions in a given situation, no legal responsibility can be attributed.

The ICJ's decisions demonstrate that, contrary to domestic legal systems, the international legal system does not utilise the concept of complicity by states in actions that lead to human rights violations in another state.[84] This is at least the way in which the ICJ approaches serious human rights violations. The *ILC Articles* contain the possibility of complicity through the notion of 'aid or assistance' to another state for its commission of an internationally wrongful act.[85] However, the ICJ has interpreted this 'aid and assistance' to be so significant that it represents 'effective control' over the situation, which more or less deprives the concept of complicity of any real meaning.

As with domestic criminal cases, violations of international human rights law are often complex occurrences where more than one actor may be involved. In such circumstances, a concept of complicity ('aiding and abetting') ought to be developed, to ensure that states may be held internationally responsible for their own actions or omissions.[86]

### B  Jurisdictional obstacles

As was mentioned above, some human rights treaties contain provisions that

---

[83] *Genocide* [422].

[84] It should be noted that complicity is provided for in international criminal law, but that concept refers to acts committed by individuals rather than states. The complicity by individuals as a foundation for criminal responsibility is provided for in the *Rome Statute of the International Criminal Court*, opened for signature 17 June 1998, 2187 UNTS 90 (entered into force 1 July 2002) Article 25.

[85] *ILC Articles* Articles 16–18.

[86] The concept of complicity of non-state actors (such as multinational corporations) in human rights violations is addressed in Andrew Clapham, *Human Rights Obligations of Non-State Actors* (Oxford University Press, Oxford, 2006); Andrew Clapham and Scott Jerbi, 'Categories of Corporate Complicity' (2001) 24 *Hastings International and Comparative Law Review* 339.

provide that the rights guaranteed by the treaty shall be respected, protected and/or ensured within the jurisdiction and/or territory of the ratifying state. This has resulted in a perceived geographical limitation which may be interpreted as granting these states impunity in terms of human rights conduct outside their own territory, or the territory covered by the relevant treaty.

Article 2(1) ICCPR provides:

> Each State Party to the present Covenant undertakes to respect and to ensure to all individuals *within its territory and subject to its jurisdiction* the rights recognized in the present Covenant, without distinction of any kind, such as race, colour, sex, language, religion, political or other opinion, national or social origin, property, birth or other status. (emphasis added)

Article 1 ECHR states:

> The High Contracting Parties shall secure to everyone *within their jurisdiction* the rights and freedoms defined in Section I of this Convention. (emphasis added)

Finally, Article 1 of the *American Convention on Human Rights* states:

> The States Parties to this Convention undertake to respect the rights and freedoms recognized herein and to ensure to all persons *subject to their jurisdiction* the free and full exercise of those rights and freedoms, without any discrimination for reasons of race, color, sex, language, religion, political or other opinion, national or social origin, economic status, birth, or any other social condition. (emphasis added)

The *African Charter on Human and Peoples Rights* does not contain any specific jurisdictional or territorial limitation.[87]

The European Court of Human Rights has found that Article 1 contains a concept of 'European legal space' (*'espace juridique'*) in the *Bankovic* case.[88] This case, which concerned the responsibility of 17 NATO states parties under the ECHR for the death and injury caused by the bombing of the television tower in Belgrade in 1999, was found by the Court to be inadmissible, mainly because the alleged human rights violations were not found to fall within the jurisdiction of the Court, as the events took place outside the geographical area of the Convention, and the states in question did not have 'effective control'

---

[87] Article 1 reads: '[t]he Member States of the Organization of African Unity parties to the present Charter shall recognize the rights, duties and freedoms enshrined in this Chapter and shall undertake to adopt legislative or other measures to give effect to them.'
[88] See *Bankovic*. For a critique of this case and the concept of a 'legal space' for human rights enjoyment, see Gibney et al, above n 3, 55; Wilde, above n 3 (2005).

over the victims of the bombings.[89] The Court dismissed the applicants' argument by holding that it was

> tantamount to arguing that anyone adversely affected by an act imputable to a Contracting State, wherever in the world that act may have been committed or its consequences felt, is thereby brought within the jurisdiction of that State for the purpose of Article 1 of the Convention.
> 
> The Court is inclined to agree with the Governments' submission that the text of Article 1 does not accommodate such an approach to 'jurisdiction'. Admittedly, the applicants accept that jurisdiction, and any consequent State Convention responsibility, would be limited in the circumstances to the commission and consequences of that particular act. However, the Court is of the view that the wording of Article 1 does not provide any support for the applicants' suggestion that the positive obligation in Article 1 to secure 'the rights and freedoms defined in Section I of this Convention' can be divided and tailored in accordance with the particular circumstances of the extra-territorial act in question.[90]

This position by the European Court of Human Rights raises a number of questions, including the issue as to whether states have impunity to commit human rights violations as long as they take place geographically outside the territorial reach of a regional human rights instrument. This understanding of jurisdiction is very limited.

Article 2(1) ICCPR has a slightly different wording from that of Article 1 ECHR, in that it uses the terms 'within its territory and subject to its jurisdiction', while the ECHR only uses the provision 'within their jurisdiction'. On the face of it, the ICCPR's obligation article seems more limited than that of the ECHR. However, in the *travaux préparatoires* of the ICCPR, it is explained that the UN Human Rights Commission chose to include the words 'within its territory' because it might not be possible for a state to protect the rights of persons subject to its jurisdiction when they are outside its territory.[91] On the other hand, the Commission decided that a state should not be relieved of its obligations under the ICCPR to persons who remained within its jurisdiction merely because they were not within its territory.[92] Thus, this understanding represents a more practical than legal distinction, in that the drafters recognised that it would be difficult for a state to ensure the enjoyment of human rights in another state, but when such human rights enjoyment is threatened or influenced by acts from another state, that other state was not relieved of its obligations.

---

[89] *Bankovic* [76].
[90] *Bankovic* [75].
[91] See M J Bossuyt, *Guide to the Travaux Préparatoires of the International Covenant on Civil and Political Rights* (Martinus Nijhoff Publishers, Dordrecht, 1989) 54, referring to UN Docs E/CN.4/SR.138 and E/CN.4/SR.329.
[92] See ibid 53, referring to UN Doc E/CN.4/SR 194.

Therefore, it seems that there is confusion as to what this 'jurisdictional' limitation actually refers to in the ICCPR and the ECHR. On one level one might question whether there is confusion between the concept of 'jurisdiction' and 'state responsibility'. As Higgins clarifies, 'the law of jurisdiction is about *entitlements to act,* the law of state responsibility is about *obligations incurred when a state does act*.'[93] Therefore, the violation of the human rights of individuals by a state outside its jurisdiction would imply that the state has committed an internationally wrongful act, and should not be able to do so with impunity. This possibility of state action outside its jurisdiction becomes more sinister when assessed in light of recent developments where, for instance, the United States (with the assistance of other states) has deliberately chosen to remove individuals from its territory (and therefore arguably from its jurisdiction) in order to deprive these individuals of their rights.[94] The distinction between jurisdiction as related to a geographic area (territory),[95] and jurisdiction as related to the effect and control a state has over the individual, becomes essential. If the protection from human rights treaties is dependent upon states acting within their jurisdiction, the danger is that extra-jurisdictional acts can be carried out without responsibility being triggered.

## C  States' concern about human rights developments

The two obstacles discussed above concern the perceived legal hindrances in this debate. There are also political obstacles to be overcome. States' approaches to international human rights differ, and the international human rights climate changes over time. Currently, developments within international human rights law seem to be under stress, in that states are increasingly resentful towards this legal regime which they see as limiting their freedom of

---

[93]  R Higgins, *Problems and Process: International Law and How we Use it* (Clarendon Press, Oxford, 1994) 146 (emphasis original).

[94]  This is arguably the position for individuals brought to Guantanomo Bay, and those subjected to extraordinary rendition in recent years. For comments on these practices see Leila Zerrougui, Leandro Despouy, Manfred Nowak, Asma Jahangir and Paul Hunt, *Situation of detainees at Guantanamo Bay*, UN Doc E/CN.4/2006/120 (27 February 2006); Amy Bergquist and David Weissbrodt, 'Extraordinary Rendition: A Human Rights Analysis' (2006) 19 *Harvard Human Rights Journal* 123; Dick Marty, *Alleged Secret Detentions and Unlawful Inter-state Transfers Involving Council of Europe Member States*, Council of Europe, Parliamentary Assembly, AS/Jur (2006) 16 Part II Assembly, Parliamentary Resolution 1507 (2006). While the United States has argued that persons it detains outside its territory do not enjoy the protection of US or international human rights law, this has been refuted by the UN Human Rights Committee. See *Concluding Observations*, UN Doc CCPR/C/USA/CO/3/Rev.1 (18 December 2006) [10]–[21].

[95]  Bankovic [76].

manoeuvre.[96] Indeed, the approach by the 17 NATO member states in the *Bankovic* case, which indicated that they did not consider themselves bound by international human rights law outside Europe, underscores the change from a universal focus in human rights protection. It should be recognised that the Court, even if finding the case inadmissible, did not say that these countries could carry out human rights violations with impunity outside their territory. But by the Court holding it did not have jurisdiction to hear the case, the *de facto* result was that there were no Court procedures available for the individuals in that case, where they had been adversely affected by the actions of foreign states. The decision in *Bankovic* can be interpreted as being based on a procedural limitation of the European Convention on Human Rights, but the result is impunity from legal redress for states.[97] This demonstrates how far reality is from the ideals of universalism of human rights. If states are able to carry out with impunity acts against individuals in another state that they are not able to carry out against their own population, because of a narrow understanding of jurisdiction, the notion of universalism (and non-discrimination) does not carry much weight.

It should be added to this discussion that the jurisprudence of the various courts and UN Committees is not necessarily coherent in these cases, as has been shown above. The ICJ, the regional courts and the UN Committees have decided cases in which extraterritorial obligations of states have been recognised, as well as rejected. While states may be more hesitant in affording human rights respect and protection to individuals in other states, this is clearly an area where the law is developing, and the views of international accountability structures may differ.

## 5 Current approach in the international human rights community

States are wary about further extending the human rights protection that they are obliged to respect and protect. Particularly in a world where there is greater interaction among states, international organisations and multinational private

---

[96] See, for example, the comments of the (now former) Prime Minister of the UK, Tony Blair, when he in 2005 'served notice that he was ready to renounce parts of the European Convention on Human Rights if British and European judges continued to block deportation of Islamic extremists in the wake of the London bombings': George Jones, 'Blair to curb human rights in war on terror', *The Telegraph* (London), 7 August 2005.

[97] Lorna McGregor, 'Torture and State Immunity: Deflecting Impunity, Distorting Sovereignty' (2007) 18 *European Journal of International Law* 906. Writing on torture, McGregor holds that '[p]rocedural rules cannot be used to evade substantive obligations, as this would defeat the core basis for *jus cogens* norms such as the prohibition of torture, by facilitating unlawful derogation'.

actors, many states will see further human rights protection as limiting their options, and will resent it. The events of 11 September 2001 and the following 'war on terror' have not helped the international human rights project. In this climate, extraterritorial obligations have not received much support from states. Indeed, the portrayal of these obligations as extensions of obligations, or new obligations, indicates the reluctance of states to take these obligations seriously. However, it has been demonstrated above that these obligations are not new; they are contained in the various human rights instruments starting with the *UN Charter*, and confirmed in international treaties as recently as 2006, with the adoption of CRPD.

This recognition, and the recognition that the way in which individuals are now often more dependent upon actions of foreign actors (including states) than their own government for their human rights enjoyment, has led actors in the international human rights community to take these questions far more seriously. The UN Committee on Economic, Social and Cultural Rights has emphasised the need for states to take the effect of their development assistance and their actions through international financial institutions (such as the World Bank and the IMF) into account.[98] Furthermore, they have also emphasised the need for poorer states to seek international assistance in situations where their domestic resources are insufficient to comply with their legal obligations in relationship to economic, social and cultural rights.[99] Likewise, the Human Rights Committee has confirmed that the obligations under the ICCPR also extend beyond the territory of the state, for instance in situations where individuals are 'within the power or effective control of the forces of a State Party acting outside its territory, regardless of the circumstances in which such power or effective control was obtained, such as forces constituting a national contingent of a State Party assigned to an international peace-keeping or peace-enforcement operation.'[100] The similar approach to extraterritorial obligations taken by the Inter-American Commission on Human Rights was discussed above.[101]

As well as in UN and regional human rights bodies, attention to extraterritorial human rights obligations is increasing in academic circles. There is now a growing body of literature on extraterritorial obligations. This attention has been matched by interest from the non-governmental human rights organisations, and several of these are now actively involved in documenting

---

[98] See Sepulveda, above n 36 and accompanying text.
[99] *General Comment No 3*, above n 35, [13], [14].
[100] UN Human Rights Committee, *General Comment No 31: The nature of the general legal obligation imposed on States parties*, UN Doc. CCPR/C/21/Rev.1/Add.13 (26 May 2004) [10].
[101] See above n 62 and accompanying text.

negative human rights effects as a result of foreign states' activities,[102] as well as taking part in conceptual and analytical developments in this field.

## 6 Concluding remarks

There is a *de facto* difference between the proposed universal enjoyment of human rights and the accepted universal obligations of human rights. The proposition here is obviously that if we are advocating universal enjoyment of human rights, it does not make sense to limit the protection of human rights to national borders. This chapter has demonstrated that there are significant legal foundations for extraterritorial obligations in current international human rights law. The drafters of human rights treaties from the 1940s onwards have been aware of the need for international cooperation in the implementation and the promotion of human rights, and this logically extends to the responsibility of states for their own behaviour that has adverse effects on individuals' human rights enjoyment in foreign states.

There remain, however, obstacles to overcome to attain general recognition for these obligations. These obstacles are of both a legal and a political nature. States are reluctant to accept what they conceive of as an extension of their human rights obligations. This political obstacle is probably the most important one to address, as with an improved political climate, the (perceived) legal obstacles would be easier to address. It is also necessary to develop an understanding of what extraterritorial obligations imply. Some confusion about their extent exists, and further work on the content of the obligations and their limitations still needs to be carried out. For instance, the obligation to provide assistance, and how much, remains controversial. Furthermore, the relationship between the national and the foreign states' obligations may need further clarification. Nevertheless, if states take responsibility for the effect of their actions, whether committed at home or abroad, rather than trying to escape responsibility, this will be a big step forward. Too much effort has been put into trying to evade responsibility, or to develop legal loopholes to do so, rather than to respond to the underlying philosophy of human rights: that we are born free and equal in dignity and rights.[103]

---

[102] A project on 'Universal Human Rights in Practice', aimed at documenting the human rights effect of extraterrestrial activities undertaken by states and developing further principles on the extraterritorial obligations for violations of economic, social and cultural rights, is currently being undertaken by a group of approximately 30 NGOs and academics. For further information, please visit http://www.lancs.ac.uk/fss/organisations/humanrights/inthron/projects.htm at 21 January 2009.

[103] Article 1 UDHR.

# 4. Non-state actors and international human rights law
*Robert McCorquodale**

## 1 Introduction

Non-state actors cannot breach international human rights law. Actions by any organization, group or individual that is not a state, irrespective of the severe impact that those actions may have on the human rights of others, cannot cause a violation of international human rights law. This disturbing situation arises because international human rights law has been created to place the legal obligations on states, and states alone. This chapter will examine the reason for this legal position and demonstrate the attempts taken, especially by the international human rights treaty monitoring bodies, to deal with the actions of non-state actors that violate human rights. It will also offer ways forward, both conceptually and practically, to ensure the greater protection of human rights, no matter who is the perpetrator of the violation.

## 2 Non-state actors

There have been many definitions offered for those participants in the international legal system which are not states. Some of these definitions have focused on a particular context, such as internal armed conflict or trade, with the European Union defining non-state actors as those in the private sector, economic and social partners (including trade union organizations) and civil society 'in all its forms according to national characteristics'.[1] A broader-based definition includes all organizations:

- Largely or entirely autonomous from central government funding and control: emanating from civil society, or from the market economy, or from political impulses beyond state control and direction;

---

\* The author is grateful for the research work of Fiona Adolu, Ningthi Mangsatabam and Deirdre Sheahan.
[1] *Partnership Agreement Between the Members of the African, Caribbean and Pacific Group of States and the European Community and its Member States*, opened for signature 23 June 2000, 2000 OJ (L 317) 3 (entered into force 1 April 2003) Art 6 ('*Cotonou Agreement*').

- Operating as or participating in networks which extend across the boundaries of two or more states – thus engaging in 'transnational' relations, linking political systems, economies, societies;
- Acting in ways which affect political outcomes, either within one or more states or within international institutions – either purposefully or semi-purposefully, either as their primary objective or as one aspect of their activities.[2]

This definition, by dealing with the cross-border aspect of activities, places non-state actors within an international context. However, it is limited in that it excludes both individuals[3] and international (inter-state) organizations,[4] which can each have significant impacts on human rights. It is also too broad in that, although international law generally requires actors to participate on the international plane, a violation of human rights does not need to be transnational for international human rights law to operate.[5]

Therefore, for the purposes of this chapter, 'non-state actors' includes all individuals, groups and organizations (whether or not composed of states), when acting within or beyond territorial boundaries; in other words, it includes all actors other than states.[6] This definition is deliberately wide to indicate the diversity of actors which can have an impact on human rights. Yet it remains problematic in that it defines these actors by what they are not, that is *non*-state actors. As Philip Alston notes, this is a definition that has been 'intentionally adopted in order to reinforce the assumption that the state is not only the central actor, but also the indispensible and pivotal one around which all other entities revolve'.[7] This state-centred focus is a general difficulty in interna-

---

[2] D Josselin and W Wallace (eds) *Non-State Actors in World Politics* (Palgrave Macmillan, Basingstoke, 2001), as quoted in P Alston (ed) *Non-State Actors and Human Rights* (Oxford University Press, Oxford, 2005) 15–16.

[3] See R McCorquodale, 'The Individual in the International Legal System' in M Evans (ed) *International Law* (Oxford University Press, Oxford, 2nd ed, 2006) 307 and A Orakhelashvili, 'The Position of the Individual in International Law' (2001) 31 *California Western International Law Journal* 241.

[4] See, for example, K Klabbers (ed) *International Organizations* (Ashgate, Aldershot, 2005) and J Alvarez, *International Organizations as Law-Maker* (Oxford University Press, Oxford, 2005).

[5] See, for example, the *Vienna Declaration and Programme of Action on Human Rights*, UN Doc A/CONF.157/23 (12 July 1993) [4]: 'the promotion and protection of human rights is a legitimate concern of the international community'.

[6] See also the definition in M-E O'Connell, 'Enhancing the Status of Non-State Actors through a Global War on Terror' (2005) 43 *Columbia Journal of International Law* 425: '[n]on-state actors, therefore, are those actors on the international plane that are not members of the United Nations. Inter-governmental organizations, non-governmental organizations ('NGOs') and individuals – natural and juridical – can all be classified as non-state actors.'

[7] P Alston 'The "Not-a-Cat" Syndrome: Can the International Human Rights

tional law.⁸ Despite this difficulty, the term 'non-state actor' will be used throughout this chapter because it is the term generally used throughout the international legal system.

## 3  Non-state actors' activity

Non-state actors are a major presence in the daily lives of most people. Indeed, for many people around the world their local community leaders, social and religious hierarchy, and employers, as well as those who might bring protection and/or violence, will impact on them significantly, with the state being a distant presence.⁹ These actors can and do act in ways that impact on the human rights of others. These actors include, in particular, armed opposition groups and terrorists, corporations, international organizations, and individuals. While the purpose of this chapter is not to provide a series of detailed case studies, a few examples of actions by non-state actors that impact on human rights will be provided here, and there is significant additional material in other chapters in this volume.¹⁰

Almost all states face terrorist or armed opposition groups, with the vast majority of armed conflicts today being internal, some of which have been very long-term.¹¹ Many European, South American, African and Asian states are familiar with violence from these groups, often daily, and the events of 11 September 2001 in the United States highlighted that this violence is not contained within territorial borders.¹² The activity of corporations, especially transnational corporations ('TNCs'), is also felt in most states, with some negative impacts felt in many states, such as the use of child labour and the effect on standards of living through environmental damage.¹³ There is

---

Regime Accommodate Non-State Actors?' in P Alston (ed) *Non-State Actors and Human Rights* (Oxford University Press, Oxford, 2005) 3, 3.

⁸ See the excellent discussion in I Butler, *Unravelling Sovereignty: Human Rights Actors and the Structure of International Law* (Intersentia, Mortsel, 2007).

⁹ See, for example, World Bank, *Voices of the Poor* (World Bank/Poverty Net, Washington DC, 2000).

¹⁰ See, for example, the chapters on NGOs (Chapter 5) and Human Rights and Globalisation (Chapter 6). This chapter will aim not to deal directly with the same issues as in those chapters.

¹¹ See, for example, the discussion on the activities of paramilitaries in Colombia in Centre for Humanitarian Dialogue ('CHD'), *Humanitarian Engagement with Armed Groups: The Colombian Paramilitaries* (CHD, Geneva, 2003).

¹² For a prescient discussion, see A Cassese, 'Terrorism is also Disrupting some Crucial Legal Categories of International Law' (2001) 12 *European Journal of International Law* 993, and see also F Hoffmann, 'Human Rights and Terrorism' (2004) 26 *Human Rights Quarterly* 932.

¹³ See, for example, R Sharma, 'Crime without Punishment: International Criminal Jurisdiction, Corporate Accountability and the Failure of Legal Imagination'

increasing evidence of the negative impact on human rights of the activities and policies of international organizations, such as the World Bank, the International Monetary Fund and the World Trade Organization,[14] and even those United Nations agencies that are meant to uphold human rights.[15] Individuals, community leaders, groups and non-governmental organizations can all impact on the human rights of others, as the former President of the Czech Republic, Vaclav Havel, has noted:

> The exercise of power is determined by thousands of interactions between the world of the powerful and that of the powerless, all the more so because these worlds are never divided by a sharp line: everyone has a small part of himself in both.[16]

The reality of the world today is that there are a wide variety of activities by non-state actors that affect, sometimes very severely, human rights. These activities are violations of human rights. Yet they are not violations of international human rights *law* by the non-state actor due to the structure of that law.

## 4 International human rights law

International human rights law, for all its diversity and size, places direct legal obligations only on states. Under all human rights treaties and customary international law, the state is solely responsible for any violation of human rights protected by international law.[17] For example, Article 2(2) of the *International Covenant on Civil and Political Rights*[18] ('ICCPR') provides:

---

(2004) 147 *Criminal Lawyer*, and R McCorquodale, 'Human Rights and Global Business' in S Bottomley and D Kinley (eds) *Commercial Law and Human Rights* (Ashgate, Aldershot, 2004) 89. Note that TNCs can be involved in armed conflict: see 'Banana Company "Armed Guerrillas"', *The Times* (London), 16 November 2007, 50, in relation to the activities of the US company Chiquita in Colombia.

[14] See, for example, M Darrow, *Between Light and Shadow: The World Bank, the International Monetary Fund and International Human Rights* (Oxford University Press, Oxford, 2003) and J Harrison, *The Human Rights Impact of the World Trade Organization* (Hart, Oxford, 2007).

[15] See, for example, G Verdirame, 'Human Rights and Refugees: The Case of Kenya', (1999) 12 *Journal of Refugee Studies* 54; C Wickremasinge and G Verdirame, 'Responsibility and Liability for Violations of Human Rights in the Course of UN Field Operations' in C Scott (ed) *Torture as Tort* (Hart, Oxford, 2001) 465.

[16] V Havel, *Disturbing the Peace* (Faber, London, 1990) 182.

[17] Issues with regard to international criminal law and international humanitarian law, which may give rise to direct obligations on non-state actors, are beyond the scope of this chapter. See, regarding international criminal law, Chapter 10.

[18] Opened for signature 16 December 1966, 999 UNTS 171 (entered into force 23 March 1976).

> Where not already provided for by existing legislative or other measures, each State Party to the present Covenant undertakes to take the necessary steps, in accordance with its constitutional processes and with the provisions of the present Covenant, to adopt such legislative or other measures as may be necessary to give effect to the rights recognized in the present Covenant.

Thus the legal obligations under the treaty to ensure the rights are protected are obligations placed on the state.

In some treaties, the roles of non-state actors are acknowledged; for example, under the *Convention on the Rights of the Child*,[19] it is provided:

> Article 2(2): States Parties shall take all appropriate measures to ensure that the child is protected against all forms of discrimination or punishment on the basis of the status, activities, expressed opinions, or beliefs of the child's parents, legal guardians, or family members.

> Article 3(2): States Parties undertake to ensure the child such protection and care as is necessary for his or her well-being, taking into account the rights and duties of his or her parents, legal guardians, or other individuals legally responsible for him or her, and, to this end, shall take all appropriate legislative and administrative measures.

In all cases, though, the state itself remains under the sole legal obligation to respect, protect and fulfil the human rights under the treaty.[20]

Further, the actions for which a state is responsible under international law are normally limited to actions by state officials:

> The conduct of an organ of the State shall be considered as an act of that State under international law, whether that organ belongs to the constituent, legislative, executive, judicial or other power, whether its functions are of an international or an internal character and whether it holds a superior or a subordinate position in the organization of the State.[21]

---

[19] Opened for signature 20 November 1989, 1577 UNTS 3 (entered into force 2 September 1990).

[20] See, for example, the analysis by the UN Committee on Economic, Social and Cultural Rights, *General Comment No 13 on the Right to Education*, UN Doc E/C.12/1999/10 (8 December 1999) [46], where the Committee states: 'The right to education, like all human rights, imposes three types or levels of obligations on states parties: the obligations to respect, protect and fulfil. In turn, the obligation to fulfil incorporates both an obligation to facilitate and an obligation to provide.'

[21] International Law Commission, 'Articles on the Responsibility of States for Internationally Wrongful Acts: Article 6' in *Report of the International Law Commission on the Work of its 53nd session*, UN Doc A/56/10(SUPP) (21 August 2001) ('ILC Articles'). Not all the ILC Articles can be considered to be customary international law, though most of them, including those relevant to this chapter, have

Public or state officials would usually include, for example, members of the state's executive, legislature, judiciary, armed forces, police and security services. A state is responsible for the actions of these officials even where those actions are committed outside the scope of the officials' apparent authority if they 'acted, at least apparently, as authorized officials or organs, or that, in so acting, they ... used powers or measures appropriate to their official character'.[22] It is generally accepted that these rules of state responsibility are applicable to international human rights law.[23] Certainly, the human rights treaty bodies have applied the general rules of state responsibility to key aspects of human rights matters before them, both explicitly[24] and, more often, implicitly.[25]

In contrast, the acts of non-state actors are not generally attributable to the state.[26] However, the International Law Commission identified four key situ-

---

been adopted by international tribunals as reflective of customary international law: see H Duffy, 'Towards Global Responsibility for Human Rights Protection: A Sketch of International Developments' (2006) 15 *Interights Bulletin* 104. Note that the rules set out in the Articles are considered by the ILC to be secondary rules of international law: see J Crawford, *The International Law Commission's Articles on State Responsibility: Introduction, Text and Commentaries* (Cambridge University Press, Cambridge, 2002) 74 ('ILC Commentaries').

[22] *France v Mexico (Caire Claim)* (1929) 5 Reports of International Arbitral Awards 516.

[23] See ILC Commentaries, above n 21, 76 and its references to human rights cases, for example, 135–40 and 145–6. See also B Simma and D Pulkowski, 'Of Planets and the Universe: Self-contained Regimes in International Law' (2006) 17 *European Journal of International Law* 488, 525. There is some criticism of this position: see A Clapham, *Human Rights Obligations of Non-State Actors* (Oxford University Press, Oxford, 2006) 318, and C Jochnick, 'Confronting the Impunity of Non-State Actors: New Fields for the Promotion of Human Rights' (1999) 21 *Human Rights Quarterly* 56, 59.

[24] For example, the Inter-American Court of Human Rights held in *Awas Tingni v Nicaragua*, Judgment of August 31, 2001, Inter-Am Ct HR, (Ser C) No 79 (2001) [154]: '[a]ccording to the rules of law pertaining to the international responsibility of the State and applicable under International Human Rights Law, actions or omissions by any public authority, whatever its hierarchic position, are chargeable to the State which is responsible under the terms set forth in the American Convention [on Human Rights]'. See also *Behrami and Behrami v France* and *Saramati v France, Germany and Norway*, Application No 71412/01; 78166/01 (Unreported, European Court of Human Rights, Grand Chamber, 31 May 2001) [122].

[25] R Lawson 'Out of Control. State Responsibility and Human Rights: Will the ILC's Definition of the "Act of State" Meet the Challenges of the 21st Century?' in M Castermans, F van Hoof and J Smith (eds) *The Role of the Nation-State in the 21st Century* (Kluwer Law International, The Hague, 1998) 91, 115: 'the European Court of Human Rights has consistently applied the principles articulated in the ILC Draft Articles on State Responsibility, without, however, referring expressly to the Draft Articles'.

[26] ILC Commentaries, above n 21, 91, 121.

ations in which the acts of private or non-state actors can be attributed to the state, for which the state will incur international responsibility where there is a breach of an international obligation (such as an obligation under a human rights treaty).[27] First, a state would be responsible for the acts of a person or entity where the latter was exercising elements of governmental activity.[28] Second, a state would be responsible for the acts of a person or entity that was acting under the instructions or direction or control of the state.[29] Third, a state may incur international responsibility for the acts of a person or entity where the state adopts or acknowledges the act as its own.[30] Fourth, a state may also incur international responsibility where it is complicit in the activity of the non-state actor or fails to exercise due diligence to prevent the effects of the actions of non-state actors.[31]

In each instance, the actions of non-state actors are attributed to the state and so the action becomes a state action, for which the state is responsible, and it is not then a non-state action. Non-state actors are treated as if their own actions could not violate human rights or it is pretended that states can and do control all their activities. As a consequence, what appears to have been created by international human rights law is a silence in relation to the non-state actors themselves, so that a great number of human rights violations are excluded from the direct protection of international human rights law. International human rights law seems not to hear the voices of those who are being violated by non-state actors. It legalizes silences. After all,

> All systems of knowledge depend on deeming certain issues as irrelevant or of little significance. In this sense, the silences of international law may be as important as its positive rules and structures.[32]

---

[27] For a fuller discussion see R McCorquodale and P Simons, 'Responsibility beyond Borders: State Responsibility for Extraterritorial Violations by Corporations of International Human Rights Law' (2007) 70 *Modern Law Review* 598.

[28] Article 5 ILC Articles.

[29] ILC Commentaries, above n 21, 91 and 121. Interestingly, non-state actors such as corporations may wish their actions to be attributable to the state in order to avoid national legal claims, and yet at the same time claim that they are private entities.

[30] See Article 11 ILC Articles.

[31] See *Case Concerning United States Diplomatic and Consular Staff in Teheran (United States of America v Iran)* [1980] ICJ Rep 3, [57], [69]–[71]: 'a receiving state is not responsible, as such, for the acts of private individuals in seizing an embassy, but it will be responsible if it fails to take all necessary steps to protect the embassy from seizure, or to regain control over it'.

[32] H Charlesworth, C Chinkin and S Wright, 'Feminist Methods in International Law' (1999) 93 *American Journal of International Law* 379, 381. See also R McCorquodale, 'Overlegalizing Silences: Human Rights and Non-State Actors' (2002) *Proceedings of the American Society of International Law Annual Conference* 394.

## 5 Development of international human rights law

Despite the apparent limitations of international human rights law, the international human rights treaty monitoring bodies have been aware that non-state actors do violate human rights. They have tried to open up possibilities of ensuring that the activities of non-state actors that violate human rights are seen as a breach of international human rights law.

One key development occurred in the Inter-American human rights system, where the Inter-American Court of Human Rights considered the general obligation on states to exercise due diligence to prevent violations of human rights against all those within the state. In *Vélásquez Rodriguez v Honduras*[33] the Court held that the international responsibility of a state may arise

> not because of the act itself, but because of a lack of due diligence to prevent the violation or to respond to it as required by [the human rights treaty] . . . [the] state is obligated to investigate every situation involving a violation of rights under the [*American Convention on Human Rights*]. If the state apparatus acts in such a way that the violation goes unpunished and the victim's full enjoyment of such rights is not restored as soon as possible, the state has failed to comply with its duty to ensure the free and full exercise of those rights to persons within its jurisdiction. *The same is true when the state allows private persons or groups to act freely and with impunity to the detriment of the rights recognized in the Convention.*[34]

Similarly, the European Court of Human Rights has held in several cases that the failure of the state's security forces to protect civilians during internal armed conflict, and the inadequacy of subsequent investigations by the state, amounted to a breach by the state of its obligations under the *European Convention on Human Rights* ('ECHR').[35] The Court has gone further to decide that the failure by the state to provide adequate protection for a boy who was caned by his stepfather violated the ECHR.[36] While the state did not have control over the caning, it was held that it did have control over its national law and therefore it had an obligation to ensure that the child would

---

[33] *Vélásquez Rodriguez v Honduras* (1989) 28 ILM 294 ('*Rodriguez*'). An earlier instance was the views of the United Nations Human Rights Committee in *Herrera Rubio v Colombia*, Application No 161/1983, UN Doc CCPR/C/OP/2 (2 November 1987), where it was not clear whether the victims had been murdered or disappeared by state or non-state officials.

[34] *Rodriguez*, [172], [176] (emphasis added).

[35] *Convention for the Protection of Human Rights and Fundamental Freedoms*, opened for signature 4 November 1950, 213 UNTS 222 (entered into force 3 September 1953). In terms of case law, see *Ergi v Turkey* (1998) 32 European Human Rights Reports 388; and *Timurtas v Turkey*, Application No 23531/94 (Unreported, European Court of Human Rights, Trial Chamber, 13 June 2000).

[36] *A v UK* (1999) 27 European Human Rights Reports 611.

be protected by the law from the actions of the stepfather.[37] As the national law allowed for 'reasonable chastisement', which had resulted in the stepfather being found not guilty under UK law, the state had failed to protect the child and so was in breach of its international human rights obligations.

The legal foundation for this series of decisions is that the state has an international obligation to take measures domestically to ensure compliance with its human rights obligations *by all persons* within the state's jurisdiction. Indeed, all the major universal and regional human rights treaties place an obligation on state parties to adopt legislation or other measures to 'ensure' or 'realize' the rights in the human rights treaty, whether immediately or progressively.[38] As all states are party to at least one of the major treaties, this obligation can be considered to apply to all states.[39] So a state is considered to have an obligation to protect (or to exercise due diligence), so as to prevent human rights violations by all persons within its jurisdiction.[40] This obligation of due diligence is a positive obligation on a state, demanding considerable state resources, to undertake fact-finding, criminal investigation and, perhaps, prosecution in a transparent, 'accessible and effective manner',[41] and to provide redress.[42]

---

[37]  A Smith, 'To Smack or Not to Smack? A review of *A v United Kingdom* in an International and European context and its potential impact on physical parental chastisement' (1999) 1 *Web Journal of Current Legal Issues*, http://webjcli.ncl.ac.uk at 23 November 2008.

[38]  See, for example, *International Covenant on Economic, Social and Cultural Rights*, opened for signature 16 December 1966, 999 UNTS 3 (entered into force 3 January 1976) ('ICESCR') Article 2; Article 2 ICCPR.

[39]  The issue of reservations is not considered here because no state has argued that it has no obligation to adopt any measures to comply with its international human rights treaty obligations: see J P Gardiner (ed), *Human Rights as General Norms and a State's Right to Opt Out* (British Institute of International and Comparative Law, London, 1997).

[40]  See generally A Clapham, *Human Rights in the Private Sphere* (Clarendon Press, Oxford, 1993), A Clapham, 'Revisiting *Human Rights in the Private Sphere*: Using the ECHR to Protect the Right of Access to the Civil Court' in C Scott C (ed) *Torture as Tort* (Hart, Oxford, 2001) 513 and also A Clapham, *Human Rights Obligations of Non-State Actors* (Oxford University Press, Oxford, 2006).

[41]  See *Jordan v UK*, Application No 24746/94 (Unreported, European Court of Human Rights, Trial Chamber, 4 May 2001) [143], where the European Court of Human Rights considered that the conduct of the investigation, the coroner's inquest, the delay, the lack of legal aid for the victim's family and the lack of public scrutiny of the reasons of the Director of Public Prosecutions not to prosecute were a violation of Article 2 ECHR. See also *Halimi-Nedzibi v Austria* (1994) 1 International Human Rights Reports 190, [13.5].

[42]  See *Z v UK*, Application No 29392/95 (Unreported, European Court of Human Rights, Trial Chamber, 10 May 2001) 109 and *Keenan v UK*, Application No

The United Nations Human Rights Committee ('HRC') has expressed the obligations on the state in this way:

> The article 2, paragraph 1, obligations are binding on States [Parties] and do not, as such, have direct horizontal effect as a matter of international law. The Covenant cannot be viewed as a substitute for domestic criminal or civil law. However the positive obligations on States Parties to ensure Covenant rights will only be fully discharged if individuals are protected by the State, not just against violations of Covenant rights by its agents, but also against acts committed by private persons or entities that would impair the enjoyment of Covenant rights in so far as they are amenable to application between private persons or entities. There may be circumstances in which a failure to ensure Covenant rights as required by article 2 would give rise to violations by States Parties of those rights, as a result of States Parties' permitting or failing to take appropriate measures or to exercise due diligence to prevent, punish, investigate or redress the harm caused by such acts by private persons or entities. States are reminded of the interrelationship between the positive obligations imposed under article 2 and the need to provide effective remedies in the event of breach under article 2, paragraph 3.[43]

Accordingly, states have been found by the human rights treaty monitoring bodies to be in breach of such obligations in situations, for example, where employees of corporations have been dismissed or victimized for joining a trade union,[44] where the activities of corporations have polluted both air and land,[45] including in Africa,[46] and where the state has failed to protect indigenous peoples' land from harm caused by corporate activities or from corporate

---

27229/95 (Unreported, European Court of Human Rights, Trial Chamber, 3 April 2001). See also N Rhot-Arriaza, 'State Responsibility to Investigate and Prosecute Grave Human Rights Violations in International Law' (1990) 78 *California Law Review* 449.

[43] HRC, *General Comment 31: Nature of the General Legal Obligation Imposed on States Parties to the Covenant*, UN Doc CCPR/C/21/Rev.1/Add.13 (29 March 2004) [8]. The HRC does endorse the notion of due diligence in this Comment and it also notes that some articles of the ICCPR address more directly the positive obligations of states in relation to the activities of non-state actors (for example, Article 7 ICCPR). See, for example, HRC, *General Comment 20: Article 7 (Prohibition of Torture, or Other Cruel, Inhuman or Degrading Treatment or Punishment)*, UN Doc HRI/GEN/1/Rev (10 March 1992) [4].

[44] *Young, James and Webster v UK* (1982) 4 European Human Rights Reports 38.

[45] See, for example, *Lopez Ostra v Spain* (1994) 20 European Human Rights Reports 277; *Guerra v Italy* (1998) 26 European Human Rights Reports 357.

[46] See *Social and Economic Rights Action Centre and the Centre for Economic and Social Rights v Nigeria*, Communication No 155/96 (Unreported, African Commission on Human and Peoples' Rights, 27 October, 2001) [59]: '[Nigeria is in violation] of local people's rights to ... health ... and life [by] breaching its duty to protect the Ogoni people from damaging acts of oil companies.'

development.[47] This has extended to criticism of states in regard to actions by them in relation to the activities of international organizations of which they are members.[48] In all of these cases, the state was in breach of its obligations under the relevant human rights treaty because its acts or omissions enabled the non-state actor to act as it did. The state may also be in breach of its obligations when it acquiesces in violations of human rights by non-state actors, such as where the state has a policy of non-action on domestic violence or dowry killings. For example,

> Perhaps the greatest cause of violence against women is government inaction with regard to crimes of violence against women . . . a permissive attitude, a tolerance of perpetrators of violence against women, especially when this . . . is expressed in the home.[49]

Such an approach opens up the possibility of women in the 'private' sphere receiving international human rights protection. It significantly extends the obligations of states to protect people from human rights violations by non-state actors.[50]

These actions by non-state actors for which a state has been found to be in breach of its international human rights legal obligations do not arise because the actions of non-state actors are being attributed to the state. Rather, this responsibility arises owing to the state's obligation to exercise due diligence to protect the human rights of all persons in a state. Therefore, even where a state (or a state official) is not directly responsible for the actual violation of international human rights law, the state can still be held responsible for a lack of positive action in responding to, or preventing, the violation of human rights by a non-state actor. This is the position even where such violations were committed by non-state actors over which the state has no direct

---

[47] See *Yanomami Community v Brazil*, Resolution No 12/85 (Unreported, Inter-American Commission on Human Rights, 5 March 1985); *The Mayagna (Sumo) Awas Tingni Community v Nicaragua*, Judgment of 31 August 2001, Inter-Am Ct HR, (Ser C) No 79 (2001) and *Hopu and Bessert v France*, Communication No 549/1993, UN Doc CCPR/C/60/D/549/1993/Rev.1 (29 December 1997).

[48] Committee on Economic Social and Cultural Rights, *General Comment 4: The Right to Adequate Housing (Art 11(1))*, UN Doc E/1992/23 (13 December 1991) [19]. See also M Ssenyonjo, 'Non-State Actors and Economic, Social and Cultural Rights' in M Baderin and R McCorquodale (eds) *Economic, Social and Cultural Rights in Action* (Oxford University Press, Oxford, 2007) 109.

[49] Radhika Coomaraswamy, *Preliminary Report submitted by the Special Rapporteur on Violence against Women*, UN Doc E/CN.4/1995/42 (22 November 1994) [72].

[50] For a fuller discussion, see R McCorquodale and R La Forgia, 'Taking off the Blindfolds: Torture and Non-State Actors' (2001) 1 *Human Rights Law Review* 169.

control.⁵¹ This is a considerable development in international human rights law in terms of the scope of a state's obligations beyond its own direct actions by state organs and officials.

Nevertheless, not all of these developments fit easily with the drafting of some human rights treaties and can lead to convoluted reasoning. For example, in *Elmi v Australia*⁵² before the United Nations Committee Against Torture, the actions feared by the victim were actions by one or more of the armed groups that controlled various regions of Somalia, in the complete absence of a Somali government. The *Convention Against Torture and other Cruel, Inhuman or Degrading Treatment or Punishment*⁵³ ('CAT') makes absolutely clear in Article 1 CAT that for the action to be torture (and so, in this case, to prevent the victim from being sent back to Somalia) there had to be some involvement in the impugned action of 'a public official or other person acting in an official capacity'.⁵⁴ On the facts it was evident that no Somali public official could be involved in any torture of Elmi, as there was no Somali government, and thus there could be no violation of international human rights law under the terms of Article 1 CAT. Yet, the Committee Against Torture held that:

> [D]e facto, those [armed groups] exercise certain prerogatives that are comparable to those normally exercised by legitimate governments. Accordingly, the members of those [armed groups] can fall, for the purposes of the application of the Convention, within the phrase 'public officials or other persons acting in an official capacity'.⁵⁵

Hence, the actions by these non-state actors in Somalia were considered to be sufficiently 'state-like' to amount to torture under Article 1 CAT. This was despite the fact that those actors were clearly not the state, at no stage indicated that they thought that they were the state or were public officials, and were effectively acting against the existence of a 'state'. However, for the

---

⁵¹ See also Committee on the Elimination of Discrimination Against Women ('CEDAW'), *General Recommendation 19: Violence against Women* (11th session, 1992). http://www.un.org/womenwatch/daw/cedaw/recommendations/recomm.htm#recom19 at 23 November 2008. This obligation to exercise due diligence applies even where a state does not exercise effective control over part of its territory: see *Ilascu v Moldova and Russia*, Application No 48787/99 (Unreported, European Court of Human Rights, Trial Chamber, 8 July 2004).

⁵² *Sadiq Shek Elmi v Australia* (2000) 7 *International Human Rights Reports* 603 (2000) ('*Sadiq Shek Elmi*') [6.5]. The author argued the case for the complainant.

⁵³ Opened for signature 10 December 1984, 1465 UNTS 85 (entered into force 26 June 1987).

⁵⁴ Art 1 CAT.

⁵⁵ *Sadiq Shek Elmi*, [6.5].

purpose of attributing responsibility to a state under international human rights law, they were given imaginary 'official capacity'. The Committee Against Torture has since limited the scope of the application by considering that the mere existence of a Somali government, even if not permanently sited within the territory of Somalia, was sufficient to prevent the attribution of armed groups' activities to the state.[56]

Therefore it can be seen that the international human rights treaty monitoring bodies have made strong, dynamic and important advances in extending the obligations on states to protect those within their jurisdiction from actions by non-state actors. This has created very significant increased protections for all people, with the identity of the perpetrator of the human rights violation not needing to be a state or a state official for a breach of international human rights law to be found. However, in order to interpret the human rights treaties in this way, these bodies are sometimes using a form of legalized imagination to deal with the actions of non-state actors that violate human rights. In all instances it has been the state itself that has been found to violate international human rights legal obligations and not the non-state actor who was the real violator. There remain no direct legal obligations on non-state actors for violations of human rights under international human rights law. Therefore, non-state actors remain hidden from the direct light of international human rights law. This position has largely reflected a particular and limited conceptual approach to human rights, as will be seen in the next section.

## 6   Concepts of human rights

The development of international human rights law since 1945 has been largely built upon two foundations. One was the creation of the United Nations, with one of its purposes being to uphold human rights,[57] and one of its early actions was to agree to the *Universal Declaration of Human Rights* ('UDHR') to carry out this purpose, in 1948.[58] All subsequent global human rights treaties affirm their connection with the UDHR.[59] The other foundation was the philosophical basis for the protection of human rights. For example,

---

[56]   *HMHI v Australia*, Committee Against Torture, Communication No 177/2001, UN Doc A/57/44 (1 May 2002).
[57]   *Charter of the United Nations* Art 1.
[58]   *Universal Declaration of Human Rights*, GA Res 217A (III), UN Doc A/810, 71 (1948) Preamble.
[59]   See, for example, the preambles to the ICESCR, ICCPR, *International Convention on the Elimination of All Forms of Racial Discrimination*, opened for signature 7 March 1966, 660 UNTS 195 (entered into force 4 January 1969), *Convention on the Elimination of all forms of Discrimination against Women*, opened for signature 18 December 1979, 1249 UNTS 13 (entered into force 3 September 1981), and the *Convention on the Rights of the Child*.

the ICCPR notes that the 'equal and inalienable rights of all members of the human family . . . *derive* from the inherent dignity of the human person'[60] and the *African Charter of Human and Peoples' Rights* ('ACHPR') provides that: 'fundamental human rights stem from the *attributes* of human beings.'[61] These treaties acknowledge that the philosophical foundation of human rights pre-exists the formulation of human rights law in the treaties and that human rights are not created by law.[62] As Jerome Shestack observed:

> How we understand the meaning of human rights will influence our judgments on such issues as which rights are regarded as absolute, which are universal, which should be given priority, which can be overruled by other interests, which call for international pressures, which can demand programs for implementation, and which will be fought for.[63]

There is a considerable debate about the nature and philosophical foundations of human rights, which will not be canvassed here.[64] Rather, the focus here is how a particular aspect of the concept of human rights has been adopted by international human rights law. Human rights, as developed by international human rights law, have been conceived as being only those within the relationship between the individual and the state. They have been conceived in terms of binary opposition between the individual and the state, with the individual being 'rights-bearing' solely in relation to the state.[65] Accordingly, the individual (or, occasionally, the group) has rights against the state – and only the state – and the individual's identity is defined by the state's obligations.

---

[60] Preamble ICCPR (emphasis added).
[61] Opened for signature 27 June 1981, 21 ILM 58 (entered into force 21 October 1986) preamble (emphasis added).
[62] The formulation of human rights concepts into the legal language of treaties can change those concepts, as compromises, exceptions and restrictions are made to the rights: see the discussion in T Campbell, 'Introduction: Realizing Human Rights' in T Campbell, D Goldberg, S McLean and T Mullen (eds) *Human Rights: From Rhetoric to Reality* (Blackwell, Oxford and New York, 1986) 1.
[63] J Shestack, 'The Jurisprudence of Human Rights' in T Meron (ed) *Human Rights in International Law: Legal and Policy Issues* (Clarendon Press, Oxford, 1984) 70.
[64] For a selection of writing in this area, see P Alston (ed) *Human Rights Law* (Ashgate, Aldershot, 1996) and R McCorquodale, *Human Rights* (Ashgate, Aldershot, 2003).
[65] D Otto, 'Rethinking Universals: Opening Transformative Possibilities in International Human Rights Law' (1997) 18 *Australian Year Book of International Law* 1.

This is a very limited and constrictive view of the concept of human rights. A number of scholars have noted how this construct of the state and the individual is created in the form of an ideal of the European or Western centralized model of the state and of an autonomous self-interested individual, even though the model has limited utility elsewhere.[66] Dianne Otto has shown how this construction erases alternative experiences, particularly of those having communitarian traditions and of women, and reinforces that some actions are 'private' and so not within the coverage of international human rights law.[67] This limited focus of human rights has created a legal institutional framework that privileges some experiences and forces claimants to fit within certain restrictive legal parameters.[68] One other consequence, as Philip Allott has astutely pointed out, is that:

> Human rights [have been] quickly appropriated by governments, embodied in treaties, made part of the stuff of primitive international relations, swept up into the maw of an international bureaucracy. The reality of the idea of human rights has been degraded. From being a source of ultimate anxiety for usurping holders of public social power, they were turned into bureaucratic small-change.[69]

What is lost in this narrow conception of human rights adopted by international human rights law is the broader concept of human rights being about empowering humans.[70] Human rights are about protecting individuals (and groups) from oppressive power primarily in the context of the communities within which they live. As Patricia Williams' notes:

---

[66] See, for example, M Foucault, 'Two Lectures' in C Gordon (ed) *Power/Knowledge* (Pantheon, New York, 1980) 78, N Tsagourias, *Jurisprudence of International Law: The Humanitarian Dimension* (Manchester University Press, Manchester, 2000) and L Henkin, *International Law: Politics and Values* (Nijhoff, Leiden, 1995).

[67] Otto, above n 65.

[68] See, for example, P Cheah, 'Posit(ion)ing Human Rights in the Current Global Conjuncture' (1997) 9 *Public Culture: Society for Transnational Studies* 233, 256. The issue as to whether non-human non-state actors, such as corporations, have human rights is beyond the scope of this chapter; though see, for example, M Addo (ed) *Human Rights Standards and the Responsibility of Transnational Corporations* (Kluwer, The Hague, 1999).

[69] P Allott, *Eunomia* (Oxford University Press, Oxford, 1988) 288.

[70] See, for example, J Finnis, *Natural Law and Natural Rights* (Clarendon Press, Oxford, 1980) 205, who considers that 'the modern vocabulary and grammar of rights is a many-faceted instrument for reporting and asserting the requirements or other implications of a relationship of justice *from the point of view of the person(s) who benefit(s)* from that relationship. It provides a way of talking about "what is just" from a special angle: the viewpoint of the "other(s)" to whom something . . . is owed or due, and who would be wronged if denied that something' (emphasis original).

> [F]or the historically disempowered, the conferring of rights is symbolic of all the denied aspects of their humanity: rights imply a respect that places one in referential range of self and others, that elevates one's status from human body to social being ... 'Rights' feels new in the mouths of most black [and other oppressed] people. It is still deliciously empowering to say. It is the magic wand of inclusion and exclusion, of power and no power. The concept of rights, both positive and negative, is the maker of citizenship, our relation to others.[71]

As indicated in this quotation, human rights are founded on our relationship to others. Those 'others' can be political institutions, and yet they are also social and cultural communities, and economic and other structures that are encountered in our daily lives.

Oppressive power can come from any source. It does not have to be political power; it can be economic, social, cultural or any other type of power. However, international human rights law has adopted a concept of human rights that focuses on only one source of power: the state. It has thus limited the possibilities of extending direct legal obligations on other – non-state – sources of power.

## 7 Ways forward

It is possible for international human rights law to take a broader conceptual approach and a more realistic view of human rights violations by non-state actors. There have been indications that international law can develop to take account of the actions of non-state actors. For example, in regard to actions by terrorists that violate, *inter alia*, human rights, the Security Council

> Declare[d] that acts, methods, and practices of terrorism are contrary to the purposes and principles of the United Nations and that knowingly financing, planning and inciting terrorist acts are also contrary to the purposes and principles of the United Nations.[72]

This statement does not expressly link the terrorist activities to state obligations. Rather, it indicates that terrorist activities *of themselves* are a breach of international law. As the Resolution does not refer to crimes against humanity or other acknowledged areas of individual responsibility under international law, it must be asserting that terrorist actions *per se* give rise to individual obligations.[73] So certain actions by non-state actors (being terrorist actions)

---

[71] P Williams, *The Alchemy of Race and Rights* (Harvard University Press, Boston, 1991) 164.

[72] *Mandatory Action to Fight Terrorism*, SC Res 1373, UN SCOR, 56th sess, 4385th mtg, UN Doc S/Res/1317 (2001) (28 September 2001) [5].

[73] Whilst Security Council Resolutions do not automatically constitute international law, they can indicate the direction in which international law may be headed:

are in breach of international law and, it must be assumed, give rise to, *inter alia*, international human rights obligations by those non-state actors. In addition, the development of the emerging concept of a 'responsibility to protect', by which states have a responsibility to act where there are violations of international humanitarian law,[74] may include situations where non-state actors are the cause of the violations.[75]

States can make non-state actors directly responsible for human rights violations, in the same way as they have chosen to do in relation to international criminal law.[76] This change could be by way of an Optional Protocol to the existing treaties, though this is likely to be resisted by many states and non-state actors, not least due to the effective economic and persuasive powers of some of these non-state actors in relation to the state.[77] Some non-state actors may be prepared to accept this; for example, such action could give armed opposition groups some international credibility as long as they accepted some international legal responsibility.[78] In the meantime states could explore the

---

M Koskenniemi, 'The Place of Law in Collective Security' (1996) 17 *Michigan Journal of International Law* 455 and M Byers, *Custom, Power and the Power of Rules: International Relations and Customary International Law* (Cambridge University Press, Cambridge, 1999) 40–43.

[74] International Commission on Intervention and State Responsibility, *The Responsibility to Protect* (2001) ICISS, http://www.iciss.ca/pdf/Commission-Report.pdf at 23 November 2008.

[75] See S von Schorlemer, *The Responsibility to Protect as an Element of Peace* (Policy Paper 28, SEF, 2007).

[76] For example, under the *Rome Statute of the International Criminal Court*, opened for signature 17 July 1998, 2187 UNTS 90 (entered into force 1 July 2002) Art 75, victims can be heard and receive compensation for violations of human rights by a non-state actor.

[77] See M Ssenyonjo, 'Non-State Actors and Economic, Social and Cultural Rights' in M Baderin and R McCorquodale (eds) *Economic, Social and Cultural Rights in Action* (Oxford University Press, Oxford, 2007), who notes that 'states where protection of human rights against violations by [non-state actors] is most needed are often those least able to enforce them against [non-state actors] such as international financial institutions and TNCs – the main driving agents of the global economy, exercising control over global trade, investment and technology transfers – who possess much desired investment capital or technology'. It is doubtful that legally binding international human rights obligations for corporations will be developed, let alone implemented, in the near future. See for example, the views of John Ruggie, the United Nations Special Representative of the Secretary-General on the Issue of Human Rights and Transnational Corporations and Other Business Enterprises: J. Ruggie, 'Business and Human Rights: The Evolving International Agenda' (2007) 101 *American Journal of International Law* 819 and in his Report to the Human Rights Council: UN Doc A/HRC/8/5, 7 April 2008.

[78] See, for example, International Council on Human Rights, *Ends and Means: Human Rights Approaches to Armed Groups* (ICHR, Geneva, 2000).

possibilities of making non-state actors jointly responsible for any of their activities that violate human rights, in the same way as joint liability operates in some areas of national law.[79] In that case, it would be necessary to ensure that the state retained primary responsibility for international human rights law, so that it remains directly responsible to all persons within its jurisdiction.

Such developments would be consistent with a better understanding of the international legal system in which the participants are not only states. Non-state actors do participate in the creation, development and enforcement of international law,[80] and therefore should have obligations under international law for their actions that breach international law. This should also strengthen the legitimacy and effectiveness of international law.[81] After all, consistent with the discussion of the broader concept of human rights above: 'there is no closed list of duties which correspond to the right ... A change of circumstances may lead to the creation of new duties based on the old right.'[82]

It is possible to imagine and create an international human rights legal system where non-state actors have direct obligations for violations of human rights. This requires a move towards a more dynamic and victim-orientated approach, where international human rights law becomes an effective limitation on oppressive power, no matter what its source. These developments should also strengthen the effectiveness of international human rights law in relation to creating direct obligations on non-state actors for their violations of human rights. It will then allow the 'voices of the suffering' to be heard much more clearly.[83]

---

[79] See, for example, A-E Yamin, 'The Future in the Mirror: Incorporating Strategies for the Defense and Promotion of Economic, Social and Cultural Rights into the Mainstream Human Rights Agenda' (2005) 27 *Human Rights Quarterly* 1200; A Clapham, *Human Rights in the Private Sphere* (Oxford University Press, Oxford, 1993); and D Friedmann and D Barak-Erez (eds) *Human Rights in Private Law* (Hart, Oxford, 2001). The TNC Norms, above n 77, provide for primary and secondary responsibility of states and corporations respectively.

[80] For a fuller discussion see R McCorquodale, 'An Inclusive International Legal System' (2004) 17 *Leiden Journal of International Law* 477.

[81] See A-K Lindblom, *Non-Governmental Organisations in International Law* (Cambridge University Press, Cambridge, 2005); J Klabbers, '(I Can Get No) Recognition: Subjects Doctrine and the Emergence of Non-State Actors' in M Koskenniemi, J Petman and J Klabbers, *Nordic Cosmopolitanism* (Nijhoff, Leiden, 2003); F Gaer, 'Implementing International Human Rights Norms: UN Human Rights Treaty Bodies and NGOs' (2003) 2 *Journal of Human Rights* 339; and J Mertus, 'Considering Non-State Actors in the New Millennium' (2000) 32 *NYU Journal of International Law and Politics* 537.

[82] J Raz, 'Legal Rights' (1984) 4 *Oxford Journal of Legal Studies* 1.

[83] U Baxi, 'Voices of Suffering, Fragmented Universality and the Future of Human Rights' in B Weston and S Marks (eds) *The Future of International Human Rights* (Transnational Publishing, New York, 1999).

# 5. NGOs and human rights: channels of power
*Peter J Spiro*

## 1 Introduction

Non-governmental organizations ('NGOs') present a formidable theoretical challenge to traditional conceptions of international law and international relations. In the Westphalian model, states alone have enjoyed international legal personality. To the extent that other actors must be processed by international law, it has been only in relation to the state. NGOs and other non-state actors were historically framed as dependent entities, insofar as they were addressed at all.[1]

That was an understandable tendency, as a matter of both empirics and theory. Although the history is now being rewritten in light of their rising contemporary prominence, NGOs were of secondary importance in international relations on the ground during the modern period. As a matter of theory, to concede independent power to NGOs would have undermined the logic of the state-based system. In the one sense, NGOs could be ignored; in the other, they had to be ignored.

That is no longer an option. Since the end of the Cold War and the dawn of globalization, no analysis of international relations can credibly bracket the role of NGOs. Non-state actors have emerged as important players on the international scene. Across issue areas, NGOs exercise influence on international processes. The role is perhaps most prominent in the context of human rights, in terms of both the density and the prominence of NGO activity.

The role of NGOs remains under-theorized. A burgeoning social science literature relating to NGOs has emerged in recent years. However, this work tends to be narrow in scope, confronting discrete elements of NGO activity. This is unsurprising, given the novelty of much of the activity and the need for descriptive accounts in a range of contexts. To the extent that theorists have attempted to situate NGOs in international process, it has been relative to the state. This approach fails to recognize the consequentiality of NGO activity not directly implicating state action.

This chapter attempts to systematize NGO activity relating to human rights. It first describes why human rights supply fertile ground for the study of

---

[1] See also Chapter 4.

NGOs. As human rights obligations cannot be described in terms of reciprocal state interest, non-state actors are a probable causal agent in the entrenchment of human rights regimes. The chapter confronts NGOs as agents of material power. It then offers a typology of human rights NGOs, distinguishing generalist from identity-oriented human rights NGOs and domestic from transnational. It is not clear, however, that these distinctions are meaningful.

The chapter then describes four primary pathways for the exercise of NGO power: through and against states, international organizations, corporations, and other NGOs. Only by situating NGO power relative to state and non-state entities does the breadth and novelty of the NGO role in today's global decision-making come into full relief. Given the fact of that broad power, the chapter ends by addressing the question of NGO accountability, concluding that institutionalization of NGO power holds the most promise for appropriately constraining its exercise.

Much of the commentary on non-governmental organizations is at least implicitly celebratory (though some of it, to be sure, is openly hostile).[2] This chapter attempts to avoid this tendency of first-generation analyses. The exercise of power is always subject to the risk of abuse, in which respect the exercise of power by NGOs is no different than any other. At the same time, NGOs are clearly a durable element of the international scene, and any conception of the new global order must account for them as an agent of democracy and legitimacy.

## 2 NGOs on the testing ground of human rights

Human rights NGOs are sometimes tagged as 'the conscience of the world'.[3] This is clearly not true as a categorical matter. NGOs are no longer uniformly progressive. As international decision-making becomes more important, any constituency seeking to advance an agenda will constitute a non-governmental vehicle for doing so. NGO politics will become increasingly variable.

Perhaps in the realm of human rights more than others, the 'conscience' label is understandable. NGOs have largely pressed for the expansion of rights, and they have often framed their efforts in moral terms. Framing NGO

---

[2] Compare Jackie Smith, *Social Movements for Global Democracy* (Johns Hopkins University Press, Baltimore, 2008) iv ('taking sides in favor of pro-democracy' social movements and NGOs) with Kate O'Beirne, 'Agendas All Their Own: The Perils of NGOs', *National Review* (New York), 26 January 2004.

[3] Peter Willetts (ed) *'The Conscience of the World': The Influence of Non-Governmental Organizations on the UN System* (The Brookings Institution, Washington DC, 1996); Antonio Cassese, *Human Rights in a Changing World* (Cambridge University Press, Cambridge, 1990) 173 (NGOs as the 'mouthpiece of world conscience').

activity in normative terms also implies that ideas are causal. That may be true, and it may be more true of NGO activity relating to human rights than in other areas, to the extent that economic interests are less readily implicated. But NGO power on human rights issues also has material aspects, in the sense that NGOs enjoy international power. NGOs can inflict material harm on target actors. That is, actors who do not conform with NGO preferences on human rights issues can be made to pay for their non-conformance; this points to the possibility that NGOs are influential not because they are right or because they are persuasive, but rather because they have power in a more conventional sense.

Once one understands the possibility of this more conventional power, human rights present a particularly fertile ground on which to unpack the role of NGOs. State compliance with human rights norms is difficult to explain from the perspective of state interests. Unlike in other areas (including comparatively new global issues such as environmental protection and anti-terrorism policies), states have no clear motivation to prefer that other states treat their own nationals in a rights-respecting fashion. There are no reciprocal interests involved, nor is there any gain from cooperation. This is why human rights pose a challenge to rational actor models of international relations; game theory cannot explain why human rights norms would have any traction.

Assuming that international law relating to human rights constrains state behaviour,[4] then, there has to be a causal agent outside the universe of states. It is a control test for the impact of non-state actors. Unlike other areas, there is little danger that outcomes are over-determined, in the sense of an alternative explanation not involving non-state influence. Left to their own devices, states would have no incentive to establish and comply with human rights norms otherwise inconsistent with their interests. If states are complying with human rights, then non-state actors surely supply part of the explanation of why that is the case.

This suggestion of NGO power is offered as a matter of institutional logic by way of confirming intuition from recent gains in the global protection of human rights. Others are now establishing the proposition in a more systematic empirical fashion. This empirical research is producing interesting counterintuitive twists on how human rights norms are established on the ground.

---

[4] Rational choice theorists often argue that, in fact, human rights norms are inconsequential, which eliminates the challenge to their models; see, for example Jack L Goldsmith and Eric A Posner, *The Limits of International Law* (Oxford University Press, Oxford, 2006) 119–26.

For instance, one study concludes that accession to human rights conventions is negatively correlated with compliance with human rights norms.[5] But the more conventional wisdom would seem well founded. International human rights standards have at some level clearly become more robust in recent decades. NGO participation is just as clearly part of the story.

Not that the story of human rights is a new one. Some human rights have been long established, for example, the international norm against slavery. NGO participation also dates back to early human rights successes. NGOs were central to the adoption of anti-slavery rules.[6] As NGOs have become more prominent in the contemporary human rights context, historians and international law scholars have reached back to detail the earlier influence they have exercised, which may have been forgotten under the statist constraints of the Cold War.[7] These histories highlight continuities at the same time that the breadth and channels of NGO power are being transformed.

## 3 Human rights NGOs: a proto-typology

The term 'non-governmental organization' is by now notoriously unwieldy at the same time that it is firmly entrenched in common parlance and therefore unavoidable. By way of the negative definition, the category cuts a wide swathe. It is generally understood not to include for-profit entities. That still leaves a range of entities. This chapter considers groups that are politically activist as a matter of institutional identity. This subset cannot be exactly drawn. At its core, it comprises groups that focus on human rights law development and enforcement, with Amnesty International and Human Rights Watch as archetypes. But it also includes such humanitarian NGOs as Oxfam, CARE and Médecins sans Frontières, which, while oriented to service delivery, pursue parallel political activities.[8] The category aims beyond the category of expert groups and epistemic communities. These groups often have political agendas, however. Many thus are also subject to the analysis offered here.

Activist rights NGOs can be further divided into two major subcategories: those that represent identity groups (for example, organizations advancing the

---

[5] Oona Hathaway, 'Do Human Rights Treaties Make a Difference?' (2002) 111 *Yale Law Journal* 1935.

[6] Margret E Keck and Kathryn Sikkink, *Activists Beyond Borders: Advocacy Networks in International Politics* (Cornell University Press, Ithaca, 1998) 41–51.

[7] Steve Charnovitz, 'Nongovernmental Organizations and International Law' (2006) 100 *American Journal of International Law* 348; William Korey, *NGOs and the Universal Declaration of Human Rights* (St Martin's Press, New York, 1998).

[8] Menno T Kamminga, 'The Evolving Status of NGOs in International Law: A Threat to the Inter-State System?' in P Alston (ed) *Non-State Actors and Human Rights* (Oxford University Press, Oxford, 2005) 93, 96.

rights of gays, women, indigenous peoples, the disabled, and scores of other communities) and those which advocate human rights more generally (Amnesty International and Human Rights Watch as examples). Only the latter might purport to embody the conscience of humankind, to the extent that they do not discriminate, or at least purport not to discriminate, in favour of one group or another. Identity-oriented NGOs have more or less clear constituencies whose interests they privilege in undertaking political action.

The distinction is not necessarily salient to the understanding of human rights NGOs. Even the generalist organizations represent sympathetic constituencies, at the same time that they purport to advance universalist values. That is, even generalist NGOs work to advance the preferences of supporters. Though the organization would no doubt reject the proposition, Human Rights Watch will act consistently with the preferences of its major donors if it wants to thrive as an institution.[9] Amnesty International is itself organized as a membership organization, with national sections allocated proportional representation in an international council whose decisions are undertaken on a majoritarian basis.[10] In either case, the organization must pick and choose among possible agenda items. In this respect, all NGOs are interest groups; 'much like other political actors', as Paul Wapner observes, NGOs 'are self-interested entities engaged in advancing their own agendas'.[11] This has been a key point in highlighting the Northern orientation of such groups as Amnesty International and Human Rights Watch, and the extent to which they have pressed an agenda dominated by liberal political rights, de-emphasizing economic and social ones.[12]

Some analyses distinguish transnational and national NGOs. This distinction may also be artificial. Constructivist accounts of NGO participation in

---

[9] See Joseph Carens, 'The Problem of Doing Good in a World That Isn't: Reflections on the Ethical Challenges Facing INGOs' in D A Bell and J-M Coicaud (eds) *Ethics in Action: The Ethical Challenges of International Human Rights Nongovernmental Organizations* (Cambridge University Press, Cambridge, 2007) 257, 258–62 (defending this proposition from a moral perspective).

[10] See *Statute of Amnesty International* (2007) [16], [23].

[11] Paul Wapner, 'The State or Else! Statism's Resilience in NGO Studies' (2007) 9 *International Studies Review* 85, 86.

[12] Makau Mutua, 'Human Rights International NGOs: A Critical Evaluation' in C E Welch Jr (ed) *NGOs and Human Rights: Promise and Performance* (University of Pennsylvania Press, Philadephia, 2001) 151, 156; Kenneth Roth, 'Defending Economic, Social and Cultural Rights: Practical Issues Faced by an International Human Rights Organization' in Bell and Coicaud, above n 9. Both Amnesty International and Human Rights Watch have expanded their brief in recent years to include economic and social rights, although political and civil rights still appear dominant in both organizations.

international relations show how even the most local NGOs can work through transnational channels.[13] The United Nations no longer makes a hard distinction for accreditation purposes.[14] National NGOs may have more limited institutional entry points than transnational NGOs (especially in the channels of international organizations), but this may be just another way of saying that national NGOs will be on average less powerful than transnational ones. There does not appear to be an intrinsic difference between national and transnational NGOs. The categorization merely reifies the former importance of boundaries in a way that NGO activity is otherwise transcending. In either case, again, NGOs will seek to advance discrete interests, whether on behalf of national or transnational constituencies.

A distinction might be usefully made between activist and service NGOs. Service NGOs have constituency relationships (donors on the one hand, aid recipients on the other). Service NGOs are primarily in the business of transferring goods and services. They do not aim to establish or enforce rights, or they do so only incidentally to their primary mission of delivery. Service NGOs supply public and other goods otherwise provided by governments (they are often funded by governments as contractors). The distinction is imperfect, as large humanitarian groups increasingly press a parallel political agenda. To the extent that service NGOs are oriented to the international law-making and enforcement process, the models sketched here may apply.

Finally, so-called epistemic communities may be oriented to law-changing activities. Experts aspire to policy-making salience. The notion, however, that expert groups are neutral or objective has been debunked.[15] Expert human rights groups, including legal ones such as the International Commission of Jurists, are in the business of advancing agendas, if under cover of objective (or even transcendant) principles. They are amenable to description as interest groups, albeit ones empowered with something more than represented

---

[13] Keck and Sikkink, above n 6.

[14] See ECOSOC, Resolution on the *Consultative relationship between the United Nations and non-governmental organizations*, UN Doc E/1996/31 (25 July 1996), which governs NGO accreditation and provides for the recognition of national-level NGOs on the same basis as international NGOs so long as they can demonstrate that 'their programme of work is of direct relevance to the aims and purposes of the United Nations'.

[15] See, for example, Nicholas Guilhot, *The Democracy Makers: Human Rights and International Order* (Columbia University Press, New York, 2005) 166–85; Mutua, above n 12, 155–7. Expert subjectivity is possibly more prevalent in the context of human rights than in other contexts, insofar as it is more difficult to frame rights in objective scientific terms. Rights are more susceptible to characterization as culturally embedded, whereas the discourse of climate change, for example, lends itself to an appearance at least of scientific exactitude.

constituencies. Expert groups can thus be included in the category of activist NGOs for the purposes of this analysis.

This chapter thus addresses the place of NGOs that work to influence international human rights norms. The category is broad and indistinct. A more elaborated actor typology is probably unhelpful in addressing the channels of their influence. These channels do not appear correlated to organizational form. This may reflect the fact that such channels are only crudely institutionalized. Unlike in more mature political systems, new global decision-making processes have yet to sort organizational identities. In the meantime, any group with power will be able to use it. Nonetheless, there are emerging patterns in how this power is deployed. These patterns are usefully modelled by way of locating NGO power in international human rights law-making.

## 4  Levers and targets of influence

The web of NGO influence is complex. Most treatments of the NGO role in global governance focus on a single channel of activity. This section attempts a broader overview of NGO activity relating to international human rights.

In advancing agendas, NGOs have levers and targets of influence. That is, in some contexts they aim to influence an actor to influence other actors in turn (levers). In other contexts, they may seek to influence an actor with respect to its own conduct (targets). NGOs interact with states, international organizations, corporations, and other NGOs in both respects.

### A  NGO–state interaction

International human rights NGOs continue primarily to affect state conduct, either as levers or targets. States remain the most institutionally powerful international actor. Enlisting state allies as levers against other actors will typically pose the most effective channel for advancing NGO interests. Because states remain the most salient actor for purposes of international human rights norms, they are also most often the ultimate target of NGO activity.

As levers, states are brought to bear as agents against other states and other actors. This process plays out familiarly in the sphere of domestic politics. A domestic human rights NGO lobbies its own government to press a human rights agenda with other states and in international organizations through the channels of interstate relations. The domestic NGO works with the standard tools of domestic politics, including money and votes, as well as offering expertise in the way of conventional lobbyists. NGOs in effect enlist their governments as agents against other states and other actors. The strategy allows NGOs to enlist traditional state power.

Once states are enlisted, the remaining sequence looks much like international relations in its traditional mode: states pressing their interests on other states through the exercise of diplomatic and economic power backed (at least in extreme cases) by military force. This account fits comfortably within theoretical accounts of international relations, the logic of two-level games and Liberal international relations theory: domestic politics helps explain international outcomes.[16] Under these approaches, NGOs are consequential insofar as they partially constitute home-state interests.

The story gets more complex where NGOs act outside the confines of domestic politics. It is now often the case that NGOs from one state work to influence other states with respect to the conduct of a third state, or even of their home state. For instance, the US-based Human Rights Watch lobbies the government of the United Kingdom with respect to its position regarding, for example, Myanmar, or with respect to post-9/11 anti-terror policies in the United States itself.

This channel is more difficult to explain in terms of conventional power politics, insofar as the source of NGO power outside domestic politics is not obvious. Two explanations are possible. First, it may be that NGO power is founded not on the ordinary currency of politics (votes and money) but rather on the power of ideas. This is a core tenet of the Constructivist school of international relations theory.[17] NGOs advance ideas that become important to states' identities as such. NGOs facilitate the internalization of the ideas they help to shape. Along similar lines, NGOs are positioned to offer expertise, which may help advance agendas in particular cases. Of course, there will be many cases in which NGO and state agendas coincide, so that neither persuasion nor discipline is necessary, and in which NGOs serve state interests as much as the other way around. One observer explains the Ottawa Process resulting in the *Convention on the Prohibition of the Use, Stockpiling, Production and Transfer of Anti-Personnel Mines and on their Destruction*[18] in those terms, insofar as some states understood their interests to coincide with NGO agendas against the 'political hegemony of the United States'. As others noted, the undertaking presented a context in which 'small and medium-sized states [could], in partnership with global civil society, overcome great power opposition; the US does not always have to lead the new post-Cold War environment'.[19]

---

[16] See, for example, Andrew Moravcsik, 'Taking Preferences Seriously: A Liberal Theory of International Politics' (1997) 51 *International Organization* 513.

[17] See, for example, Martha Finnemore and Kathryn Sikkink, 'International Norm Dynamics and Political Change' (1998) 52 *International Organization* 887.

[18] Opened for signature 3 December 1997, 36 ILM 1507 (entered into force 1 March 1999) ('Landmines Treaty').

[19] Kenneth Anderson, 'The Ottawa Convention Banning Landmines, the Role of International Non-Governmental Organizations, and the Idea of International Civil Society' (2000) 11 *European Journal of International Law* 91, 107–8; Maxwell A

Alternatively (or additionally), NGOs are able to exert influence on states because they are in a position to mobilize powerful agents against them even outside ordinary politics. For instance, the British government is aware that, in securing action from the UK against a third state, Human Rights Watch can mobilize sympathetic constituencies in the UK with respect to the third-country policy at issue, or (for that matter) with respect to unrelated policies of the UK. With respect to the latter, Human Rights Watch can also mobilize other agents (including other states) to act against the UK.

In other words, states can be both levers and targets. States will typically be the ultimate target of NGO activity in the realm of human rights. Most human rights norms apply primarily and even exclusively to state actors. As targets, states have reason to accommodate NGO demands because NGOs can deploy powerful agents against them, including other states and corporate and other non-governmental entities. In other words, NGOs can make states pay for non-conforming practices. This is the price of 'shaming' strategies on the part of NGOs.

That does not by any means translate into unlimited powers for NGOs. Cost–benefit calculations on the part of target-state regimes may point to rebuffing NGO advances. Many NGOs are weak and have minimal leverage. Target-state governments will reject NGO demands where relenting to them risks regime collapse: for example the military government in Myanmar defies NGO demands because acceptance might well result in its being forced from power. As political actors, NGOs have to pick their battles and marshal their capital. Sympathetic constituencies and other agents can be mobilized on a selective basis only. But to the extent that NGOs enjoy and effectively deploy their political power, there will be cause for target states to respond.

*B NGO–international organization interaction*
As the protection of human rights becomes more institutionalized at the global level, international organizations ('IOs') have become correspondingly more important to the advancement of human rights. NGOs work various channels to use IOs as levers against target actors. In some contexts, IOs are themselves the target of NGO activity.

The category of IOs itself represents a broad institutional range, including the United Nations and its component parts (including treaty bodies), regional organizations, ad hoc world conferences, and international tribunals. Some of these institutions are engaged in standard-setting, others in applying standards in particular cases. NGOs engage with the full spectrum of IOs. Activity can

---

Cameron, Brian W Tomlin and Robert J Lawson, 'To Walk Without Fear' in M A Cameron, B W Tomlin and R J Lawson (eds) *To Walk Without Fear: The Global Movement to Ban Landmines* (Oxford University Press, Toronto, 1998) 1, 13.

be undertaken on a direct basis or indirectly through state agents. In many IO contexts, states remain the ultimate decison-makers, and to that extent NGO influence will ultimately be indirect.

Standard-setting supplies an efficient mechanism for advancing the international human rights agenda, in the same way that affecting legislation will be efficient for advancing domestic agendas. NGOs undertake to influence standard-setting through all of the many vehicles by which international law is made.

Building momentum towards and crafting the language of human rights conventions presents a key opportunity for NGOs to influence the making of hard law. As a historical matter, NGOs were central players in the framing of anti-slavery treaties in the early 19th century. Korey documents NGO influence in the drafting of the *Universal Declaration of Human Rights*,[20] the *International Covenant on Civil and Political Rights*,[21] and other foundational human rights regimes.[22] More recently, NGOs played a critical role in the conclusion of the Landmines Treaty and of the *Rome Statute of the International Criminal Court*.[23] As one commentator has written, '[i]t is no exaggeration to conclude that some of the most important international legal instruments of recent years would not have seen the light without the input of NGOs.'[24]

NGOs have formal status in many standing international institutions. More than 2500 NGOs have 'consultative status' with the UN Economic and Social Council ('ECOSOC') pursuant to Article 71 of the *Charter of the United Nations*.[25] The latest procedural elaboration of Article 71, ECOSOC Resolution 1996/31,[26] affords NGOs rights of participation, including the capacity to make statements and submissions and to request that items be included on the ECOSOC agenda. As Wapner observes, '[s]ince NGO participation in the UN burgeoned in the 1990s, accredited NGOs have left their signatures, as it were, on almost all significant UN policymaking'.[27] The inter-

---

[20] GA Res 217A, UN Doc A/810, 71 (1948).
[21] Opened for signature 16 December 1966, 999 UNTS 171 (entered into force 23 March 1976).
[22] Korey, above n 7.
[23] Opened for signature 17 June 1998, 2187 UNTS 90 (entered into force 1 July 2002).
[24] Kamminga, above n 8, 101.
[25] See generally Dianne Otto, 'Nongovernmental Organizations in the United Nations System: The Emerging Role of the International Civil Society' (1996) 18 *Human Rights Quarterly* 107.
[26] See ECOSOC, above n 14.
[27] Paul Wapner, 'Civil Society' in T G Weiss and S Daws (eds) *The Oxford Handbook on the United Nations* (Oxford University Press, Oxford, 2007) 258.

agency body UNAIDS includes five NGO representatives as full members of its Programme Coordinating Board. NGOs were able to initiate so-called 1503 procedures before the United Nations Commission on Human Rights. Although the jury is still out on the efficacy of its successor body, the United National Human Rights Council, NGOs are given a formal role in the Universal Periodic Review of all member-state human rights practices. The major world conferences of the 1990s extended formal participation rights to NGOs. At the 1993 World Conference on Human Rights in Vienna, NGOs were permitted to participate in meetings of the conference, and their statements were issued as official documents, although NGOs were pointedly excluded from the main drafting committee.[28] At the 1996 Second United Nations Conference on Human Settlements (Habitat II), which addressed sustainable urban development, NGOs were permitted to table amendments to conference texts.[29]

NGOs are influential in multilateral treaty negotiations.[30] Human rights regimes do not typically extend formal roles to NGOs in their implementation through the channel of treaty committees or otherwise. Exceptions are the *Convention on the Rights of the Child*,[31] which recognizes NGOs in Article 45 as a source of 'expert advice', and the *Convention on the Protection of the Rights of All Migrant Workers and Members of their Families*,[32] which allows for written submissions from NGOs under Article 74(4). Through practice and committee procedure, however, NGOs are playing an increasingly important role in the elaboration of the treaty regimes.[33] NGOs assist UN working

---

[28] See Anne Marie Clark, Elisabeth J Friedman and Kathryn Hochstetler, 'The Sovereign Limits of Global Civil Society: A Comparison of NGO Participation in UN World Conferences on the Environment, Human Rights and Women' (1998) 51 *World Politics* 1.

[29] See Peter Willetts, 'From "Consultative Arrangements" to "Partnership": The Changing Status of NGOs in Diplomacy at the UN' (2000) 6 *Global Governance* 191, 194–6.

[30] Christine Chinkin, 'The Role of Non-Governmental Organizations in Standard Setting, Monitoring and Implementation of Human Rights' in J J Norton, M Andreas and M Footer (eds) *The Changing World of International Law in the Twenty-First Century: A Tribute to the Late Kenneth R Simmons* (Kluwer International, The Hague, 1998) 51.

[31] Opened for signature 20 November 1989, 1577 UNTS 3 (entered into force 2 September 1990).

[32] Opened for signature 18 December 1990, 30 ILM 1517 (entered into force 1 July 2003).

[33] Anna-Karin Lindblom, *Non-Governmental Organisations in International Law* (Cambridge University Press, Cambridge, 2005) 395–406. For example, NGOs commonly submit shadow reports pursuant to the treaty body reporting systems. See, for example, *Civil and Political Rights: Major NGO Report on Australia to UN Human*

groups and special rapporteurs on an informal basis. In these contexts, NGOs interact with secretariats and other entities acting in their IO capacity. NGO participation has also advanced in regional institutions. For example, NGOs are routine amicus participants in proceedings before the African Commission on Human and Peoples' Rights, the European Court of Human Rights and the Inter-American Court of Human Rights.[34]

NGOs also impact IO decision-making indirectly through state actors. States can be influenced, as described above, through domestic or transnational political interaction. That was an important element of the landmines negotiations; the success of an NGO network (working as the International Campaign to Ban Landmines) in persuading Canada to support their efforts was a watershed on the way to securing the convention.[35] It is routinely the case (indeed it serves as a primary channel of influence) that NGOs will secure the support of states to advance agendas in intergovernmental fora. Particular to the IO context is the practice of including NGO representatives on state delegations. Although this may be more exceptional than in some other fields in which technical expertise is valued and NGO–government cooperation is common (international environmental protection, for example), NGO representatives have participated on government delegations in IO proceedings involving women's and other group rights, as well as in the Rome conference negotiations leading to the establishment of the International Criminal Court.[36] Participation on government delegations is indirect insofar as it works through governmental filters. It does, nonetheless, bring NGO representatives to the intergovernmental table.

Treaty and other legal regimes contribute to the advancement of a human rights norm or set of norms by giving target state actors a focal point for conforming their practices to a standard. Once a convention is in place, NGOs and their allies can work to secure accession by states.[37] Their participation in a variety of ways, both direct and indirect, in working groups, with special

---

*Rights Committee* (2008) Human Rights Law Reform Commission, http://www.hrlrc.org.au/html/s01_home/home.asp at 8 January 2009.

[34] Steve Charnovitz, above n 7, 354; Dinah Shelton, 'The Participation of International Nongovernmental Organizations in International Judicial Proceedings' (1994) 88 *American Journal of International Law* 611.

[35] Motoko Mekata, 'Building Partnerships Toward a Common Goal: Experiences of the International Campaign to Ban Landmines' in A M Florini (ed) *The Third Force: The Rise of Transnational Civil Society* (Carnegie Endowment, Washington DC, 2000) 143, 156–8.

[36] Kamminga, above n 8, 94; Benjamin N Schiff, *Building the International Criminal Court* (Cambridge University Press, Cambridge, 2008) 146–52.

[37] Note, for example, the Coalition for the International Criminal Court, which campaigns for accession to the Rome Statute: see www.iccnow.org at 9 January 2009.

rapporteurs, and in the treaty committees presents opportunities to press the development of conventional norms.

NGOs also contribute to the development of norms of customary international law, often coupled with treaty regimes to the end of instant custom (where treaty obligations are asserted to bind non-party states). The fears of some conservative activists notwithstanding, NGOs cannot independently erect human rights norms on a clean slate. They can, however, build on existing norms and on treaty regimes to establish rights coverage. This occurs in the context of interpretation and application, in something like a common law process. NGOs are positioned to press novel but not discontinuous conceptions of human rights norms. Those conceptions will be accepted by states and other actors in some cases.[38]

The establishment and expansion of legal regimes enable NGOs to engage in monitoring and other follow-up activities. NGOs measure state conduct against legal metrics, which they have had a hand in making, and then seek to mobilize agents against target states to secure compliant behaviour. This is a core NGO strategy. NGO positions are legitimated with agents insofar as they reflect legal norms. Human Rights Watch executive director Kenneth Roth has observed that human rights NGOs have 'no choice but to rest on a positive-law justification for [their] work', and that the dominant shaming methodology requires NGOs 'to show persuasively that a particular state of affairs amounts to a violation of human rights standards'.[39] In this sense, international law is a use of IOs as a lever, at least insofar as international organizations make international law. For target states, the use of legal norms is shorthand for establishing the bona fides of NGO positions.

As with states (and as through states), NGOs can also spend the currency of ideas in securing IO action. Expertise is particularly valuable in the IO context. As monitors, NGOs supply IOs with information that would otherwise be hard for them to come by, given limited resources and the inherent conflicts of interest that may incline states to under-resource IO fact-finding. IO human rights secretariats are often staffed with former NGO officials, and are thus all the more receptive to NGO arguments. IOs find themselves in a competitive institutional environment, and NGOs can offer legitimacy by delivering the approval of powerful constituencies. To the extent that IO action is driven by states, moreover, NGOs are in a position to influence IO decision-making through political power.

---

[38] See Anne Marie Clark, *Diplomacy of Conscience: Amnesty International and Changing Human Rights Norms* (Princeton University Press, Princeton, 2001) Ch 6, on the NGO role in norm emergence.

[39] Roth, above n 12, 170, 172.

NGOs primarily seek to influence IOs as levers, that is, as a means to the end of conforming behaviour on the part of target actors. There are also contexts in which IO conduct itself implicates human rights norms, as with respect to peacekeeping operations.[40] NGOs are also bringing human rights law to bear on the policymaking apparatus of international economic organizations, such as the World Trade Organization, the International Monetary Fund, and the World Bank.[41] Where IOs are targets, they can be influenced indirectly and directly as where they are pursued as levers. The calculus of legitimacy is particularly powerful in this context to the extent that IO operations are fledgling and institutionally fragile.

### C  NGO–corporate interaction

NGO interaction with corporate actors has witnessed important developments since the advent of globalization. In the past, the NGO–corporate dynamic was largely filtered through state intermediaries, with states as levers to secure corporate conformities. Reflecting the rise of non-state actors generally, that paradigm has changed in recent years. NGOs interact directly with corporations as both levers and targets, in many cases without state or IO intermediation.

As levers, corporations are an important resource for advancing NGO interests. Corporations are politically powerful. In the realm of domestic politics they are a key source of campaign money. In transnational politics, corporations also have the power of siting decisions. That is, corporate decisions to invest, or not to invest, in one jurisdiction or another can present a make-or-break difference to local economic prosperity. This power has increased with the enhanced mobility of capital. To the extent that corporate decision-making takes human rights factors into account, NGOs can leverage their power against states.

Increasingly, corporate actors are also the target of NGO activity. Although states have traditionally been the sole object of international human rights regimes, transnational corporate actors are being held accountable to international human rights law with respect to core human rights relating to physical injury and liberty from restraint.[42] With respect to labour rights, constraining

---

[40] For instance, with respect to the question of whether United Nations forces are subject to the humanitarian law rules of the Geneva Conventions. See August Reinisch, 'The Changing International Legal Framework for Dealing with Non-State Actors' in Alston, above n 8.

[41] At the World Bank, for instance, NGOs are allowed to bring complaints on behalf of affected communities before an Inspection Panel. See Daniel D Bradlow, 'Private Complainants and International Organizations: A Comparative Study of the Independent Inspection Mechanisms in International Financial Institutions' (2005) 36 *Georgetown Journal of International Law* 403.

[42] See, for example, Steven R Ratner, 'Corporations and Human Rights: A Theory of Legal Responsibility' (2001) 111 *Yale Law Journal* 443.

corporate conduct is the ultimate aim of rights initiatives, in which context corporations are the natural target of rights proponents. And in some cases corporations will find themselves in the crosshairs as both levers and targets. Where a corporation has operations within a state engaged in serious human rights violations, NGOs will seek to constrain the conduct of both the state and the corporation itself, using the corporation as a channel for achieving both ends. Recent examples include NGO targeting of corporations doing business in Myanmar and the Sudan.

NGOs are able to influence corporate behaviour as both levers and targets to the extent they command consumer constituencies. In highly competitive and brand-sensitive business contexts, NGO activity can have a non-trivial impact on corporate bottom lines. Corporations understand the potential of NGO 'naming and shaming' campaigns. That gives NGOs leverage over corporate behaviour, whether they are seeking to have corporations press their influence with states or to have corporations conform their own conduct to human rights norms. As corporations recognize the potential of NGO power, it is unnecessary for NGOs to deploy it in all, or even many, cases. In other words, they may exercise power over corporations well short of a boycott call.

The result has been an increasingly elaborated superstructure arising from the interaction of repeat players. Interaction between NGOs and corporations in recent years has become more cooperative, not unlike interaction between regulators and regulated entities in the traditional public sphere. As corporations seek certainty, they have been amenable to negotiating 'voluntary' regimes, increasingly refined, with NGO counterparts.[43] These undertakings serve corporate interests insofar as they provide guidance on what sort of conduct will be insulated from punitive NGO responses. They serve NGO interests because they directly advance the rights agenda where national regulation may be failing (in the face of mobile capital) and supranational regulation remains institutionally immature.

These regimes, typically denominated as codes of conduct or as working 'principles' of one description or another, are beginning to look more like law. They are detailed and – for the big brand-name companies, at least – voluntary in name only. The *Voluntary Principles on Security and Human Rights*,[44] for example, brings together such corporations as ExxonMobil, Freeport McMoRan and Rio Tinto with Amnesty International, Human Rights Watch and Oxfam on questions relating to extractive industry participation in host

---

[43] Sean D Murphy, 'Taking Multinational Codes of Conduct to the Next Level' (2005) 43 *Columbia Journal of Transnational Law* 389.
[44] See http://www.voluntaryprinciples.org/principles/index.php at 9 January 2009.

country security regimes. The Fair Labor Association sets out a detailed code of conduct relating to clothing manufacturing in the developing world, implicating such issues as child labour, hours of work, and health and safety.[45] Participants include H&M, Nike, and Nordstrom, as well as manufacturers producing garments under licence from American universities.

Most of the codes are not backed by governmental or intergovernmental enforcement, but they can be (at least in theory) effectively monitored by non-governmental agents. To the extent that monitoring is effective, NGOs can punish violations through shaming. The Fair Labor Association's code of conduct, for example, includes a third-party complaint system under which individuals can allege code violations by corporate participants. Although these regimes do not constitute formal legal regimes, they have the capacity to secure corporate conformity with human rights and other international norms.

At a more general level, as agents of sympathetic constituencies, NGOs have surely played an important role in the movement towards corporate social responsibility. Leaving specified codes of conduct aside, transnational corporations have been sensitized to taking account of human rights and other social values. Corporate social responsibility creates an environment in which such values (again, at least in theory) condition all corporate decision-making. It becomes unnecessary to apply outside pressure in every case (from either governments or NGOs) as the values become internalized to corporate and shareholder culture.

These arrangements and values remain unstable. Corporate social responsibility runs the risk of veering towards whitewash (or 'greenwash', in the context of environmental protection), with corporations using image enhancement as a cloak for business as usual on the ground. Similarly, NGOs may not have the resources to effectively monitor codes of conduct and vague 'principles' regimes, in which case corporate interests get the benefit of looking virtuous without having to pay the price in terms of constrained decision-making.[46]

The upshot could be the migration of such regimes to more broadly institutionalized settings at the supranational level, either in IOs or in private standard-setting venues such as the International Organization for Standardization ('ISO') or umbrella accounting rule-making bodies. There is also the possibility of innovating hybrid regimes which include governmental

---

[45] See http://www.fairlabor.org/about_us_code_conduct_e1.html at 9 January 2009.

[46] For a critique of the Fair Labor Association along these lines, for example, see Mark Barenberg, 'Corporate Social Responsibility and Labor Rights in US-Based Corporations' in M Feher (ed) *Nongovernmental Politics* (Zone Books, New York, 2007) 223.

and non-governmental actors in non-pyramidal structures. The Kimberley Process[47] relating to conflict diamonds and the UN Global Compact[48] supply examples. In that event, NGOs would mobilize to enlist state and IO actors, as described above, to discipline corporate conduct.

## D  NGO–NGO interaction

NGOs also act on each other in a range of contexts. Much of this interaction is cooperatively undertaken in the establishment of networks in which NGO interests coincide and coordinated action serves mutual interests. This activity has been widely documented.[49] Less studied are potentially adverse relationships in which NGOs seek to advance their agendas by influencing and constraining other NGOs, both as levers and as targets.

To the extent that NGOs have power which can be applied against other actors (as in the interactions described above), NGOs may find it useful to enlist other NGOs by way of securing objectives against target actors. The mandates and priorities of particular NGOs will necessarily be limited. To shift or broaden a powerful NGO's brief may advance the interests of another NGO or a network of NGOs.

As a powerful human rights NGO, Amnesty International is prominently the object of such activity. Amnesty was founded with the strictly bounded mission to work for the release of political prisoners.[50] It took many years for it to broaden this mandate to, for instance, condemn the apartheid regime in South Africa. More recently, it was pressed to take up persecution on account of sexual orientation as a matter of official organization policy. There is now an effort to have it work on behalf of abortion rights.[51] Amnesty's support for such particular causes can powerfully leverage the efforts of relevant identity-oriented NGOs and the constituencies they represent. Insofar as Amnesty frames its work in terms of norms, and insofar as Amnesty is now in a position to facilitate their recognition, its enlistment marks a greater advance for

---

[47] *The role of diamonds in fuelling conflict: breaking the link between the illicit transaction of rough diamonds and armed conflict as a contribution to prevention and settlement of conflicts*, GA Res 55/56, UN GAOR, 55th sess, 79th plen mtg, UN Doc A/Res/55/56 (1 December 2000).

[48] See http://www.unglobalcompact.org/ at 9 January 2009.

[49] See, for example, Sanjeev Khagram, James V Riker and Kathryn Sikkin (eds) *Restructuring World Politics: Transnational Social Movements, Networks, and Norms* (University of Minnesota Press, Minneapolis, 2002).

[50] Korey, above n 7, 166.

[51] See Mutua, above n 12, 156; Stephen Hopgood, *Keepers of the Flame: Understanding Amnesty International* (Cornell University Press, New York, 2006) 158–9.

entrenching any given right than does the support of all but the most powerful states.[52]

For the same reason, Southern NGOs have pressed Amnesty and other prominent Northern human rights NGOs to broaden their missions to press economic and social rights in addition to political ones. These efforts have enjoyed only mixed success to date, and have provoked sometime bitter exchanges on an NGO–NGO basis (what would be considered fratricidal to those outside the NGO community).[53] The tension demonstrates the power dynamics of NGO–NGO interaction. Southern NGOs have few material resources to mobilize against their Northern counterparts. By contrast, NGOs pressing sexual orientation and abortion rights have various tools for enlisting the support of other NGOs, including access to money and powerful media. That is not to say that NGOs from the North have been blind to Southern concerns; some have become vigorous advocates for economic and social rights,[54] and the acknowledgment of distinctive developing world interests has emerged as an important point of legitimation. But '[b]y habit or established practice, NGOs' reports stress the nature and number of violations, rather than explore the socioeconomic and other factors that underlie them'.[55] Southern NGO perceptions that their perspectives are given shorter shrift in the mix of global human rights advocacy further demonstrate the fact that all NGOs are political in one way or another.[56]

NGOs may also work to influence other NGOs as targets. This activity is along the lines of NGO efforts to influence corporate conduct; corporations share with NGOs the central characteristic of being non-governmental. NGOs may become targets where they act beyond the ultimately representative functions of political activism. Religions supply an example among non-state

---

[52] For a case study in a national NGO seeking – and failing to secure – Amnesty's support, see Clifford Bob, *The Marketing of Rebellion* (Cambridge University Press, Cambridge, 2005) 72–6 (describing efforts by Ken Saro-Wiwa on behalf of Nigeria's Ogoni in the early 1990s).

[53] For an example, see the exchange between Human Rights Watch director Kenneth Roth and University of Delhi professor Neera Chandhoke in Roth, above n 12.

[54] Oxfam International is an example of such an NGO: see Duncan Green, *From Poverty to Power* (Oxfam, London, 2008).

[55] Henry J Steiner, *Diverse Partners: Non-Governmental Organizations in the Human Rights Movement* (Harvard Law School Human Rights Program, Cambridge, 1991) 19. See also Hopgood, above n 51, 161–75 on Amnesty's difficulties in assimilating Southern concerns into its organizational culture.

[56] See, for example, Balakrishnan Rajagopal, *International Law From Below: Development, Social Movements, and Third World Resistance* (Cambridge University Press, Cambridge, 2003) 261; Mutua, above n 12. See also Christine Chinkin, 'Human Rights and the Politics of Representation' in M Byers (ed) *The Role of Law in International Politics* (Oxford University Press, Oxford, 2000) 131, 144.

actors (they may or may not be categorized as NGOs, but share the basic characteristics of being both non-governmental and non-profit). Women's rights NGOs, for example, have pressed the Catholic Church on issues relating to reproductive freedom.[57] Relief NGOs may also be monitored for adherence to best practices for humanitarian operations, as for instance in the wake of the 2005 Asian tsunami. Relief and human rights groups have clashed over strategies in crisis areas, leading not just to competing lobbying efforts with government and IO officials but also to attempts to influence each other's agendas.[58] A group of NGOs including Amnesty, Save the Children, Oxfam, and World Vision have signed up to an 'Accountability Charter' to guide management, fundraising, and advocacy practices.[59] On much the same model as interaction with other actors, NGOs can impact other NGOs by steering the support of interested publics.[60]

This sort of NGO–NGO interaction gives the lie to monolithic conceptions of the NGO community. NGOs will often find themselves using each other to advance particularistic ends, and they may find themselves in conflict where interests diverge.

## 5 Enhancing NGO accountability

Perhaps the best evidence of NGO power is the increasing number of calls to enhance the accountability of NGOs.[61] Accountability is a concern only in the presence of power. One does not fret for the accountability of weak actors. Because NGOs have power, accountability questions are appropriately raised. Power without accountability predictably results in abuses of power. Objections to addressing accountability concerns, which include a denial that power is being exercised or, if it is, that it advances objective or natural positions should, be viewed with suspicion. Religions offer an obvious cautionary tale in this respect, which as a historical matter, at least, have engaged in a broad range of injustice in the name of a higher, unaccountable power.

---

[57] See Laura Lambert, 'The Church and Condom Sense' (2006) Planned Parenthood, http://www.plannedparenthood.org/issues-action/international/articles/condom-sense-6466.htm at 9 January 2009.
[58] See David Rieff, 'Good vs Good' *Los Angeles Times* (Los Angeles), 24 June 2007 (describing efforts by Doctors Without Borders to effect leadership changes in the Save Darfur coalition).
[59] See http://www.ingoaccountabilitycharter.org/ at 9 January 2009.
[60] See Bob, above n 52.
[61] See, for example, Kenneth Anderson and David Rieff, 'Global Civil Society: A Skeptical View' in M Kaldor, H Anheier and M Glacias (eds) *Global Civil Society 2004/5* (SAGE, London, 2004) 26. See also, for example, Lisa Jordan and Peter van Tuijl (eds) *NGO Accountability: Politics, Principles and Innovations* (Earthscan, London, 2006).

NGOs might welcome the accountability inquiry. To the extent it is satisfied, it will legitimate power more transparently exercised. The response, at least in part, to the accountability objections should be the institutionalization of NGO power. The accountability objection is fairly posed but it is exaggerated and likely to fade. Part of the answer is found by reversing the power relationships described above. As the density of NGO interactions with other actors increases, accountability mechanisms will evolve organically, at least insofar as other actors themselves retain power. The most serious remaining challenge is on what terms NGO power is institutionalized in the context of international organizations. Accountability values point towards an expanded formal role for NGOs, but state resistance is substantial. The location of the new nodes of global decision-making may hang in the balance.

First to frame the problem: to the extent that they are unaccountable, NGOs may be able to play the role of policy potentates. That is, NGO leaders will be able to wield influence to advance their own preferences, along the lines described above, without constraint. Accountability has two dimensions, internal and external.[62] Internal accountability is absent where organizational leaderships can act without regard for the preferences of organizational members or other followers. External accountability, by contrast, is to process and to institutional arrangements. External accountability is absent where actors are able to depart without penalty from the terms of process bargains.

Internal accountability is an agency problem. It is a challenge in all organizational contexts. In the context of states, it is not always the case that state leaders will represent the preferences of their constituents in matters involving human rights. On the contrary, the agency problem is compounded in the human rights context because human rights norms will (for the most part) apply to constrain the action of state leaders as such. In other words, state actors suffer systematic conflicts of interest with respect to representing the human rights preferences of their citizens. Internal accountability concerns are not unique to NGOs.

As a general matter, however, NGOs are not amenable to the standard mechanism by which state leaders may in theory be held accountable, namely through democratic elections. Some NGOs (such as Amnesty) are member-governed with refined mechanisms for having member preferences reflected in organization policies, but most NGO leaderships are not on so tight a leash. The resulting concern is mitigated by the highly competitive and unstable nature of NGO power. In contrast to the agency relationship between state

---

[62] Peter J Spiro, 'Accounting for NGOs' (2002) 3 *Chicago Journal of International Law* 161; Ruth Grant and Robert O Keohane, 'Accountability and Abuses of Power in World Politics' (2005) 99 *American Political Science Review* 1.

officials and citizens, if NGO leaders persistently press agendas that are out of step with their membership and other sympathetic constituencies, supporters can migrate to other organizations with relatively low transaction costs; it does not take much to change NGO allegiances. This holds true for rank-and-file supporters (members or not) as well as funders (perhaps more so for the latter, insofar as funders will have incentives to monitor organizational activity more closely). NGO leaderships may be unelected, but they stray from their base at their peril.

External accountability presents a more complex dynamic. The concern here is that NGOs will play the role of spoiler in international decision-making; that is, that they will try to have their cake and eat it, too. NGOs may destabilize international processes if they are in a position both to exercise influence and to undermine results where they are unable to secure assent to their positions. It is an accountability problem where a powerful actor can interfere with decision-making (assuming that decision-making enjoys some satisfactory level of legitimacy among other actors).

This problem too may be mitigated by the competitive nature of NGO power and the fact that NGOs, by way of entrenching their power, have incentives as repeat players to respect the results of bargains in the making of which they participate. Other institutional players have their own powers to wield against irresponsible NGOs. This situation is the reverse of the dynamic described above. States and corporations have goodies to offer NGOs that can be withheld. These goodies include money, although many NGOs will not accept government or (less often) corporate funding, or only under restrictive conditions, for risk of co-option. The incentives also include partnerships, information, and cooperation. If an NGO can show to its members and funders that it has secured governmental or corporate agreement to a certain course of conduct conforming to the NGO's agenda, that is a deliverable reaping future gains. A corporation or state that feels burnt by an NGO is unlikely to make the same mistake twice. The target entity will re-engage only if it has some certainty that bargains made will be respected.

This dynamic requires direct participation as responsible agents on the part of NGOs in regime formation and maintenance. The distinction is between lobbyist and principal. Where NGOs act as mere lobbyists, attempting to influence other actors who shoulder ultimate decision-making responsibility, they have no ownership of resulting bargains, and are free to support or reject them. Where, by contrast, NGOs themselves share decision-making authority, they shoulder responsibilities to the process itself. The proposition can be conceived in stakeholder terms. For accountability purposes, the nature of participation (and not the fact of influence by itself) is key.

Corporate codes of conduct are a case in point. In some of these regimes NGOs participate with corporations (and sometimes governments) on the basis of formal equality. They negotiate the code terms directly, not through an agent. They are also transparently associated with the result, in the sense that organizational participation and assent is openly acknowledged and formalized. With some codes of conduct (that of the Fair Labor Association, for example), NGOs have a status analogous to treaty partner. As such, they have invested in the persistence of the regime and cannot walk away from particular elements of the deal. As part of the bargain under which other parties undertake to adjust their behaviour, NGOs have themselves agreed to live by the terms of the deal. The result is a form of accountability, in the sense that the exercise of NGO power is constrained by the process itself.

Nonetheless, NGOs may be vulnerable to co-option (and even corruption) in privately ordered regimes. To the extent that NGOs buy into such regimes, at the margins at least they may have incentives to accept non-conforming conduct, or to undertake monitoring at less than optimal levels. As NGOs identify themselves as partners of targeted actors (especially corporations) more than adversaries, leaders may develop relationships that cut against strict enforcement. Monitoring by and competition from non-participating NGOs should counteract such tendencies in serious cases. There is a danger, however, of market failure as power consolidates in a small number of NGOs, to the point where challenges to their primacy by other NGOs become difficult. It would take more to overcome the co-option of Amnesty or Human Rights Watch than that of other, less powerful human rights NGOs. The more powerful some groups become, the greater the danger of unaccountable activity.

Part of the answer to this danger may lie with the further institutionalization of NGO participation in public international institutions. NGO participation in international organizations is not yet so advanced as with codes of conduct. NGOs are plainly influencing IO decision-making. NGOs are also accumulating formal roles in the formulation and maintenance of IO regimes. But there is great resistance to elevating NGOs to a status even remotely equating them with states.[63] That is evidenced on many fronts. ECOSOC consultative arrangements, treaty regimes, and ad hoc conference procedures include boilerplate provisions excluding NGOs from negotiating and voting roles.[64] In the World Trade Organization, acceptance of NGO submissions by the organization's dispute resolution arm set off a firestorm of criticism among states-party.[65]

---

[63] Otto, above n 25.
[64] Willetts, above n 29.
[65] See Steve Charnovitz, 'Opening the WTO to Nongovernmental Interests' (2000) 24 *Fordham International Law Journal* 173, 183–90.

Resistance on the part of states has been coupled with hesitation on the part of NGOs, which have sought formal participation rights on a tactical basis only.[66] It is also interesting that prominent, sympathetic commentators on the rise of NGOs are careful to stop short of calling for participation on the basis of formal equality.[67] That counterintuitive posture bolsters the institutional logics of accountability. NGOs fear that explicit constraints attached to institutional recognition may be used by states to censor their activities. The 1996 ECOSOC resolution governing consultative status, for instance, incorporated an eligibility requirement that NGOs 'have a representative structure and possess appropriate mechanism of accountability to [their] members'.[68] For powerful NGOs that already have significant influence through informal channels, institutional recognition may pose a net negative, in what might be called the inclusion paradox. However, assuming that recognition criteria such as those included in the ECOSOC resolution are not abused,[69] NGO resistance here is self-interested rather than principled. Furthermore, even in the absence of substantive recognition criteria, the extension of formal authorities and responsibilities to NGOs in the establishment and maintenance of international regimes would render them more accountable to those institutions.

Finally, the shift would elevate transparency values. States and IOs sometimes act at the behest of NGOs. The phenomenon is well documented in the context of international environmental protection, where NGOs have in effect borrowed state delegation nameplates to further their agendas at the bargaining table without any filter.[70] But human rights NGOs also shop (and launder) their claims through other institutional channels. The World Health Organization's request to the International Court of Justice for an advisory opinion on the legality of nuclear weapons was decried by some as an NGO-engineered case, for example, in circumvention of rules barring non-state participation in ICJ proceedings.[71]

Hence the virtue of greater IO participation rights for NGOs, as a general matter but also specifically with respect to human rights norms. The modalities

---

[66] Phillip Alston, 'The "Not-a-Cat" Syndrome: Can the International Human Rights Regime Accommodate Non-State Actors?' in P Alston (ed) *Non-State Actors and Human Rights* (Oxford University Press, Oxford, 2005) 1, 5.
[67] Lindblom, above n 33, 35; Charnovitz, above n 7; Willetts, above n 29, 206.
[68] ECOSOC, above n 14.
[69] There have been a small handful of controversial cases involving the denial of consultative status: see Otto, above n 25, 113–16.
[70] See Kal Raustiala, 'State, NGOs and International Environmental Institutions' (1997) 41 *International Studies Quarterly* 719.
[71] This was so, even though the WHO request was denied, and the ICJ acted only on a subsequent request by the UN General Assembly: see Chinkin, above n 56, 138.

here may be complex and institutionally variable. Selecting participants from among potentially infinite eligible NGOs presents a notable challenge. In some contexts that challenge appears to have been overcome, for instance, by composing 'liaison' committees between non-state and governmental forums at the world summits on women, population and development, human rights, and other subjects. The International Labour Organization, in which employers and unions are directly represented along with states, demonstrates the efficacy of formal non-state participation. Intermediate possibilities include advisory committees, as already innovated by the World Bank and the OECD. In judicial-type tribunals, standing to bring suit and to participate in *amicus curiae* capacities presents a logical end-point. Here the domestic models translate more easily, as gate-keeping is easily undertaken by judicial authorities.

## 6 Conclusion

Of the many tacks this chapter could have taken (for the subject is now vast), it has looked to establish a typology of NGO activity in the realm of international human rights. NGOs are now firmly enmeshed in the web of global decision-making. Their salience transcends mere influence. NGOs no longer channel their power only through states. They have a transnational autonomy which is giving rise to international legal personality.

This account has been largely descriptive and focused on modalities. It has also addressed tenable concerns that NGO power is undisciplined. But none of this is to lose sight of the importance of NGO participation (in whatever mode) to the making and protection of international human rights. NGOs have been crucial to the human rights revolution. Their participation has become a premise to norm legitimacy. Indeed, NGOs are playing an important part in addressing concerns regarding the accountability of the international legal system as a whole.

# 6. Human rights in economic globalisation
*Adam McBeth*

## 1 Introduction

In Chapter 4 of this volume, Robert McCorquodale gives an overview of the evolving position of international human rights law in terms of the responsibilities of entities other than states. McCorquodale highlights the problems of a system that was conceived on the assumption that states can and do control the activities of entities operating within their respective territories, and which therefore freely ignores the actions of non-state actors in seeking to ensure the protection and promotion of human rights and to prevent and punish human rights violations.

Nowhere is the fallacy of that assumption more apparent than in the context of economic globalisation. In today's globalised economy, there are many different types of entity that are capable of operating across borders and transcend the regulatory capacity of any one state. Many of those entities, such as multinational corporations, international financial institutions and development banks, engage in activities that can have profound effects, both positive and negative, on human rights.

Corporations, for example, have an obvious and direct potential to impact labour rights, both positively and negatively, through the way in which they treat their workers, including the provision or denial of reasonable rates of pay, reasonable conditions of work, a safe and healthy workplace, non-discrimination, freedom of association and the right to organise. They can also have profound effects on the human rights of the communities in which they operate, for instance in the way land and water is acquired, by causing serious pollution which can affect the rights to water, health and possibly life, or in the excessive use of security to protect an enterprise or to silence opponents.

International economic institutions commonly contend that the overall prosperity brought about by their operations makes a positive impact on the enjoyment of human rights, both directly and by providing the means for states to take action for the realisation of economic, social and cultural rights in particular. On the other hand, development institutions have been criticised for supporting large-scale infrastructure projects that evict the local people without appropriate safeguards, violating their right to housing and affecting their livelihoods, which in different cases could affect the right to work, the right to adequate food and water, the right to health and many other rights. The economic policies demanded by international financial institutions such as the International Monetary Fund ('IMF') have been blamed for reductions in social security, public sector employment and state-subsidised services, leading to regression in the enjoyment of human rights supported by those services, including rights to health, education, work, access to water and so on.

The manner in which international trade rules have been negotiated and applied within the World Trade Organization ('WTO') has similarly been blamed for the neglect of human rights goals in deference to market forces, particularly in relation to access to essential services and affordable medicines, while standing accused of imposing barriers to the economic development of the world's poorest people.

In all of these cases, the impact on the enjoyment of human rights for the individuals affected is undeniable, whether or not there was any state involvement. As Skogly notes, 'for the victims of human rights violations, the effects are the same whoever is responsible for atrocities'.[1] Everyone – government, institution, individual and corporation alike – is therefore capable of infringing human rights, if not necessarily violating international human rights *law* as it currently stands.[2] However, if none of those entities are beholden to a given state, there is an obvious problem in relying on a state-based system for human rights accountability.

For these reasons, there has been an increasing call in recent years for international human rights law to recognise direct legal obligations on the part of non-state actors in the economic arena with regard to their impact on human rights. The appropriate response to that call is not as straightforward as it might first appear, because the various international economic actors to which these arguments are commonly applied serve very different purposes in the international economic and legal systems and take a number of distinctly different legal forms. The legal basis for an imposition of direct human rights obligations, the nature of those obligations and the manner in which they could be effectively enforced will therefore be quite different from one type of actor to another.

The aim of this chapter is to give an overview of the relevance of human rights principles to the operations of different categories of international economic actors. For that purpose, two very different types of economic actor have been chosen. Private multinational enterprises are examined as actors

---

[1] Sigrun Skogly, *The Human Rights Obligations of the World Bank and the International Monetary Fund* (Cavendish Publishing, London, 2001) 51.

[2] See Chapter 4 of this volume for a discussion of the traditional treatment of non-state actors under international human rights law and the methods some of the enforcement bodies have used to address the realities of infringements committed by non-state actors within a state-centric system.

that affect human rights directly and do not have any public institutional status, but are nevertheless capable of transcending the jurisdiction of any given state in many cases. At the opposite end of the public–private spectrum, the WTO is examined as a regulatory institution, a body that regulates and enforces international trade, potentially affecting the human rights of millions of people without interacting with the 'victims' in a direct sense. As an institution, the WTO has a personality and a life of its own on the international plane, while at the same time being composed of member states and being therefore the product of collective state action, without being within the legal control of any one state.

In between these two extremes of the spectrum lie many other international economic actors that have a concrete effect on human rights in various ways but are not beholden to any state that can be held responsible for their actions. Among them are the public international financial institutions, such as the World Bank and the IMF, and regional development banks. While space precludes a discussion of such actors in this chapter, the case studies of multinational enterprises and the WTO should illustrate the need for a broader conception and application of human rights duties beyond the responsibilities of states alone, which is applicable with some adaptation to other kinds of international actors.

Before turning to the discussion of each category of actor, the following section considers the phenomenon of the fragmentation of international law. That issue is crucial for the topic of this chapter, because it determines the relationship between international human rights law and other areas of international law that more directly govern international economic activity. Having found that international human rights standards are indeed relevant to the economic arena, the next section then turns to the question of whether entities other than states have the capacity to bear human rights obligations. The case studies of multinational enterprises and the WTO are then examined in turn. The chapter concludes with an observation that a purely state-based system for the protection of human rights is clearly inadequate in the context of economic globalisation, while warning that theoretical avenues for incorporating human rights standards in economic activity are meaningless without the practical co-operation of states.

## 2 Human rights, international economic law and the phenomenon of fragmentation

Leaving aside for the moment the question of whether international human rights law can have any application to non-state actors, it is worth considering briefly the relationship between the principles of human rights law and those of the various strains of international economic law that characterise the realms in which many of the international economic actors operate.

The WTO, through the agreements that are negotiated, enforced and litigated under its auspices, effectively oversees its own corner of international law. The day-to-day operations of the international financial institutions are conducted under the policies and processes established under the Articles of Agreement or other constitutional documents of the respective institutions, which set the general parameters of decision-making within the institutions. Insofar as international law touches the operations of multinational enterprises, it is likely to be in the realm of investment agreements and arbitration.

The existence and increasing specialisation of each of these – and many other – sub-fields of international law creates an environment in which the risk of isolation from, and potentially conflict with, other areas of international law is increasingly serious. The International Law Commission formed a study group to report on this phenomenon of the fragmentation of international law, which described the problem in the following way:

> What once appeared to be governed by 'general international law' has become the field of operation for such specialist systems as 'trade law', 'human rights law', 'environmental law', 'law of the sea', 'European law' and even such exotic and highly specialized knowledges as 'investment law' or 'international refugee law' ... each possessing their own principles and institutions. The problem, as lawyers have seen it, is that such specialized law-making and institution-building tends to take place with relative ignorance of legislative and institutional activities in the adjoining fields and of the general principles and practices of international law. The result is conflicts between rules or rule-systems, deviating institutional practices and, possibly, the loss of an overall perspective on the law.[3]

None of these specialised fields can be completely isolated from general international law.[4] A regime established by a treaty or a series of treaties, with its

---

[3] *Fragmentation of International Law: Difficulties Arising from the Diversification and Expansion of International Law: Report of the Study Group of the International Law Commission*, finalised by Martti Koskenniemi, UN Doc A/CN.4/L.682 (13 April 2006) [8].

[4] It is theoretically possible for groups of states to contract out of specific substantive rules of international law, other than norms of *jus cogens*, by establishing a self-contained legal regime. However it is not possible to contract out of the system of international law, which provides the principles to determine the relationship between the purportedly self-contained regime and the outside world, including the basis for the legitimacy of the self-contained regime itself in the doctrine of *pacta sunt servanda*. See Joost Pauwelyn, *Conflict of Norms in Public International Law: How WTO Law Relates to Other Rules of International Law* (Cambridge University Press, Cambridge, 2003) 37. However, the International Law Commission's study group on the question of fragmentation has confirmed that '[n]one of the treaty-regimes in existence today is self-contained in the sense that the application of general international law would be generally excluded': Koskenniemi, above n 3, [172].

own judicial organs for interpreting and applying the treaties – as exists with the WTO and also with regional human rights regimes – still operates within the broader scheme of general international law. At a minimum, general international law provides the rules for how those treaties should be interpreted and how they relate to other treaties and international norms, as well as filling the gaps that are not addressed in the treaty regime. The WTO's dispute settlement organs have confirmed that, 'to the extent there is no conflict or inconsistency, or an expression in a covered WTO agreement that implies differently ... the customary rules of international law apply to the WTO treaties and to the process of treaty formation under the WTO'.[5]

The WTO Appellate Body used similar reasoning to determine that the phrase 'conservation of exhaustible natural resources' 'must be read by a treaty interpreter in the light of contemporary concerns of the community of nations about the protection and conservation of the environment', and therefore extended to the conservation of sea turtles.[6]

As such, when treaties in the economic sphere are interpreted and applied, one should be conscious of the central position accorded to human rights in the international system. The existence of treaty and customary human rights obligations for states (leaving aside for the moment the possibility of human rights obligations for non-state actors) must therefore be borne in mind in construing economic treaties between states or agreements between a state and a non-state actor. The various WTO treaties, host state investment agreements and the Articles of Association of the international financial institutions all belong in that category. In applying such instruments, one must assume, without clear evidence to the contrary, that the states that are parties to them did not intend to repudiate or contradict their commitments to human rights in other fora. Among the institutions charged with implementing the will of their member states, an implied duty not to violate such human rights commitments – effectively a duty to do no harm – is a reasonable implication in these circumstances.

---

[5] *Korea – Measures Affecting Government Procurement*, WTO Doc WT/DS163/R (19 June 2000) (Report of the Panel) [7.96].
[6] *United States – Import Prohibition of Certain Shrimp and Shrimp Products*, WTO Doc WT/DS58/AB/R (12 October 1998) (Report of the Appellate Body) ('*United States – Shrimp*') [129–31]. The provision in question, Article XX(g) of the *General Agreement on Tariffs and Trade 1994* ('GATT'), permits member states to take measures 'relating to the conservation of exhaustible natural resources if such measures are made effective in conjunction with restrictions on domestic production or consumption' that would otherwise be inconsistent with WTO rules.

## 3 The position of human rights in international law

The centrality of human rights to the broader system of international law is evident in the *Charter of the United Nations* ('*UN Charter*'). The four purposes of the UN listed in Article 1 of the *UN Charter* are directed towards human rights, international peace and security and international co-operation, forming a vision for the international system that has the protection and fulfilment of human rights at its core. One of those purposes is:

> To achieve international co-operation in solving international problems of an economic, social, cultural, or humanitarian character, and in promoting and encouraging respect for human rights and for fundamental freedoms for all without distinction as to race, sex, language or religion.[7]

The Charter further provides that the UN and its member states in co-operation should promote:

(a) higher standards of living, full employment, and conditions of economic and social progress and development;
(b) solutions of international economic, social, health, and related problems; and international cultural and educational co-operation; and
(c) universal respect for, and observance of, human rights and fundamental freedoms for all without distinction as to race, sex, language, or religion.[8]

Aside from these broad statements of purpose and intention, the *UN Charter* does not contain much detail of the content of member states' obligations with regard to human rights. The drafting history of the *UN Charter* suggests that the broad references to human rights were intended to cloak human rights principles with the authority of the Charter, leaving the content of a comprehensive human rights instrument to be concluded separately under the auspices of the new organisation.[9] Some commentators, most notably Louis Sohn, have argued that the *Universal Declaration of Human Rights*[10] fills that role.[11]

---

[7] *UN Charter* Article 1(3).
[8] Ibid., Article 55.
[9] Bruno Simma, Hermann Mosler, Albrecht Randelzhofer, Christian Tomuschat and Rüdiger Wolfrum (eds), *The Charter of the United Nations: A Commentary* (Oxford University Press, Oxford, 2nd ed, 2002) 35, 44. Simma et al note that the inclusion of human rights references in the Preamble and Article 1(3) of the final text, which is referred to as a 'mini human rights charter', was a compromise between states that advocated the inclusion of a human rights charter within the Preamble or the text of the *UN Charter* and those that objected.
[10] UN Res 217A (III) UN Doc A/810, 71 (1948) ('UDHR').
[11] Louis Sohn, 'The Human Rights Law of the Charter' (1977) 12 *Texas International Law Journal* 129.

Given that the provisions of the *UN Charter* will prevail over any inconsistent international obligation by virtue of article 103,[12] treaties in the international economic arena should be construed in a manner consistent with the human rights aims of the *UN Charter*. Policies and operational decisions made pursuant to such treaties should likewise be cognisant of the human rights goals of the international community and their foundational role in international law. If it is accepted that the UDHR – and potentially the subsequent instruments that elaborate on elements of the UDHR, such as the *Convention on the Elimination of All Forms of Racial Discrimination*[13] – constitutes an authoritative elaboration of the human rights provisions of the *UN Charter*, a case can be made that the obligations for states set out in those instruments must prevail over any inconsistent obligations. A minimum consequence of such an approach would be an implied duty to refrain from any action in the economic sphere – or any other sphere for that matter – which causes a state to default on its human rights obligations, on the ground that the proper interpretation of the applicable legal framework of treaties, implementing legislation and institutional policies should be consistent with the relevant state's pre-eminent obligations to respect, protect and fulfil human rights within its jurisdiction.

For those human rights norms that constitute norms of *jus cogens*, such as the prohibitions on genocide and the slave trade, the same result is achieved without the need to resort to the *UN Charter*. Other treaties and subordinate instruments are void to the extent that they contravene a norm of *jus cogens*,[14] and therefore must be construed in conformity with such norms. Beyond a certain minimum core of norms, there is disagreement as to which human rights norms constitute norms of *jus cogens* and no conclusive source of

---

[12] For affirmation that a provision of the UN Charter prevails over all international legal obligations other than a norm of *jus cogens*, see *Application of the Convention on the Prevention and Punishment of the Crime of Genocide (Bosnia and Herzegovina v Yugoslavia (Serbia and Montenegro)) (Order of 13 September 1993)* [1993] ICJ Rep 407, [100] (Separate Opinion of Judge Lauterpacht); endorsed by Koskenniemi, above n 3, [360].

[13] *International Convention on the Elimination of All Forms of Racial Discrimination*, opened for signature 7 March 1966, 660 UNTS 195 (entered into force 4 January 1969) ('CERD'). Sohn has argued that the CERD and other instruments that elaborate upon the UDHR, which in turn elaborates upon the human rights obligations in the UN Charter, retain the hierarchical primacy of the Charter provisions they interpret: Sohn, above n 11, 133; Louis Sohn, 'The New International Law: Protection of the Rights of Individuals Rather than States' (1982) 32 *American University Law Review* 1, 15–16.

[14] *Vienna Convention on the Law of Treaties*, opened for signature 23 May 1969, 1155 UNTS 331 (entered into force 27 January 1980) Article 53.

authority on that question, other than jurisprudence of international courts on a case-by-case basis. Shelton has pointed to authority from the European Court of Justice suggesting that the entire body of human rights law constitutes *jus cogens*,[15] while others are far more cautious, warning that casting the *jus cogens* net too broadly might 'weaken the credibility of all rights'.[16]

Whatever list one chooses for the rights that attract the hierarchical status of the *UN Charter* or norms of *jus cogens*, it is clear that the intention of the international community to guarantee protection of human rights as a fundamental purpose of the international legal system cannot be disregarded in deference to specialisation or fragmentation. Of course, none of this necessarily creates direct legal obligations for non-state actors. Rather, these principles play a role in defining the international legal framework within which non-state economic actors operate. To the extent that such a framework constrains the actions that non-state actors are lawfully able to take, the practical effect may be a de facto duty for actors within that framework to respect (and perhaps to protect or fulfil) human rights in the course of those operations, even if international human rights law places no formal obligations on those actors directly.

## 4 Capacity of international economic actors to bear human rights obligations

While the primary subjects of international law are states, it is beyond doubt that entities other than states are capable of enjoying rights and bearing obligations directly under international law, without invoking the protection or responsibility of a state. Thus, individuals in some circumstances can assert an international wrong directly in an international forum without relying on their home state to take action on their behalf, for example under several human rights treaties, and they can be held directly responsible for violating rules of international law, as in international criminal law. Corporations also have the capacity to assert rights in certain international fora, such as arbitration under the *North American Free Trade Agreement*[17] and the *Convention on the Settlement of Investment Disputes*.[18] It is also universally accepted that inter-

---

[15] Dinah Shelton, 'Normative Hierarchy in International Law' (2006) 100 *American Journal of International Law* 291, 311, citing *Kadi v Council of the European Union* [2005] ECR II-3649, especially [228–31].

[16] Theodor Meron, *The Humanization of International Law* (Martinus Nijhoff, Leiden, 2006) 207.

[17] *North American Free Trade Agreement*, opened for signature 8 December 1992, 32 ILM 605 (entered into force 1 January 1994).

[18] *Convention on the Settlement of Investment Disputes between States and Nationals of Other States*, opened for signature 18 March 1965, 575 UNTS 159 (entered into force 14 October 1966).

national organisations have international legal personality.[19] However, that is not to say that the capacity of these non-state actors to assert rights or bear obligations under international law is co-extensive with that of states.

In one of the earliest judgments of the International Court of Justice ('ICJ'), the advisory opinion in *Reparations for Injuries Suffered in the Service of the United Nations*,[20] the court was asked to advise whether the United Nations could be considered a legal person separate from its member states for the purposes of bringing a claim against a non-member state for injuries it inflicted on UN personnel. En route to concluding that the UN is an international legal person, the court emphasised the flexible nature of international personality and the exercise of rights and imposition of obligations under international law:

> The subjects of law in any legal system are not necessarily identical in their nature or in the extent of their rights, and their nature depends on the needs of the community. Throughout its history, the development of international law has been influenced by the requirements of international life, and the progressive increase in the collective activities of States has already given rise to instances of action upon the international plane by certain entities which are not States.[21]

Similar reasoning was applied by the ICJ in the later advisory opinion on the *Legality of Nuclear Weapons*,[22] in which the court confirmed that the World Health Organization ('WHO') had international legal personality, but held that the capacity of the WHO was not unlimited in the manner of a state's capacity, and did not extend to a capacity to request an advisory opinion on the topic of the use of armed force and nuclear weapons.

Therefore, if an entity is capable of acting on the international plane – as international organisations and private multinational enterprises clearly are – it may be considered to have international legal personality, although the extent of that capacity will be determined by the 'needs of the international community', and will not be the same for every kind of entity. If international economic actors are to have direct obligations under international human rights law, those obligations should be adapted to the operations of the relevant entity. Deciding that corporations ought to bear direct human rights obligations, for example, therefore need not equate to a requirement that corporations devote

---

[19] Meron, above n 16, 315.
[20] *Reparations for Injuries Suffered in the Service of the United Nations (Advisory Opinion)* [1949] ICJ Rep 174 ('*Reparations for Injuries*').
[21] Ibid., 178–9.
[22] *Legality of the Use by a State of Nuclear Weapons in Armed Conflict (World Health Organization) (Advisory opinion)* [1996] ICJ Rep 66.

the maximum of their available resources to the progressive fulfilment of economic, social and cultural rights, as states are obliged to do.[23] It would be quite possible to limit the obligations of such actors to the scope of their usual operations, taking direct responsibility for any human rights violations occurring in the course of those operations. A duty conceived in those terms need not supplant the primary duty of the state as the guarantor of human rights, but could ensure that reliance on the state's duty to protect human rights from violations by non-state actors is not the only option. Indeed, as McCorquodale's chapter makes clear, when dealing with entities that are beyond the jurisdictional control of any given state, reliance solely on the state's duty to protect is no option at all.

While it is therefore possible for international economic actors to have direct human rights obligations under international law, and possible for those obligations to be limited and adapted appropriately to the roles played by the respective actors on the international plane, it is first necessary in a state-centric system of international law to identify an intention on the part of the community of states to impose such obligations. Such an intention could be explicit, as in a treaty imposing direct obligations such as the direct liability of individuals for international crimes under the *Rome Statute of the International Criminal Court*,[24] or it could be implied from state practice and the *opinio juris* of states to give rise to a norm of customary international law, as was the basis for individual and organisational criminal liability before the international criminal tribunals at Nuremberg and Tokyo.

It is this intention to create obligations for non-state actors that McCorquodale in this volume argues is currently missing. For the protection of human rights in the economic arena to be effective and enforceable, explicit recognition from states – perhaps in the form of a declaration of the General Assembly – that existing standards impose duties of some sort on economic actors would be extremely useful, while a treaty setting out the specific obligations would be more useful still. In the absence of such explicit state recognition, exercises to reconcile human rights with international economic activity, such as those described below in relation to multinational enterprises and the application of trade rules respectively, will continue to be necessary but continue to be inadequate in their outcomes.

---

[23] *International Covenant on Economic, Social and Cultural Rights*, opened for signature 16 December 1966, 993 UNTS 3 (entered into force 3 January 1976) ('ICESCR') Article 2(1).

[24] Opened for signature 17 June 1998, 2187 UNTS 90 (entered into force 1 July 2002).

## 5 Private actors: multinational enterprises

It is beyond doubt that the operations of corporations can have profound effects on human rights. To the extent that they bring foreign investment, employment and economic growth, the prosperity that corporations bring to communities in which they operate can have significant positive effects on the realisation of human rights by bringing a higher standard of living and providing the means for improved levels of health care, education and other social services. Improvements in infrastructure are also common when multinational enterprises establish a presence in an underdeveloped area, which can sometimes boost the realisation of human rights through access to clean water, sanitation and electricity.

The potential for harm is also beyond doubt and well documented. Direct human rights violations committed by corporations include killing, serious violence and torture of project opponents or unionists and the procurement of forced labour carried out by corporate security forces.[25] Complicity of corporations in the actions of state authorities in such atrocities has also been well documented.[26] Corporate activities can infringe the rights to life and health through harmful products or widespread environmental damage, potentially poisoning thousands of people for decades when air or water is seriously contaminated.[27] Labour rights, particularly relating to conditions of work and freedom of association, have an obvious connection to corporate operations, given the direct connection between a corporation and its employees, and have been the subject of a number of high-profile campaigns against multinational enterprises, particularly in the clothing, textiles and footwear industries.[28]

---

[25] See for example the allegations of killings of union activists in Colombia at a Coca-Cola bottler in *Sinaltrainal v Coca-Cola* 256 F Supp 2d 1345 (SD Fla 2003) and at mining facilities in *Estate of Rodriguez v Drummond* 256 F Supp 2d 1250 (ND Al 2003).

[26] See for example the allegations of murder, torture and forced labour by the Myanmar military on an oil pipeline controlled by Unocal and Total in *Doe v Unocal* 395 F 3d 932 (9th Cir 2002), and the allegations of murder of protesters on a Chevron oil platform by Nigerian security forces in *Bowoto v Chevron*, No C 99-020506SI, 2007 WL 2455752 (ND Cal 2007). Note however that the defendant corporations in *Bowoto* were found not to be liable in a jury trial in December 2008: 2009 WL 593872 (ND Cal 2009).

[27] See for example the 1984 explosion at the Union Carbide gas plant in Bhopal, described in *In Re Union Carbide Corp Gas Plant Disaster at Bhopal* 634 F Supp 842 (SDNY 1987), and mass pollution of land and water by BHP in Ok Tedi, Papua New Guinea, in *Dagi v BHP* [1995] 1 VR 428.

[28] See for example the Clean Clothes Campaign at http://www.cleanclothes.org/companies.htm at 18 December 2008. See also the campaign against Nike, culminating in the case of *Kasky v Nike*, 123 SCt 2554 (2003) (Supreme Court of the United States) 24 Cal 4th 939 (2002) (Supreme Court of California).

150  *Research handbook on international human rights law*

That list is of course not exhaustive. Given the enormous power and influence that many corporations have over the lives of individuals, and in some cases over governments, the potential ways for them to impact human rights are virtually limitless.[29]

*A   Corporations and international law*
Corporations have traditionally been regulated by municipal law and largely ignored by international law, as their activities have historically been confined within the regulatory reach of the home state. However, many modern multinational enterprises are beyond the regulatory power of any one state. The state in which it is incorporated or domiciled – the home state – will have a certain degree of regulatory power over the enterprise, but will face jurisdictional obstacles in trying to exercise that power in relation to human rights abuses suffered in the territory of another state. Conversely, the latter state – the host state – will have jurisdiction over the events occurring on its territory, but its practical enforcement power is limited over an enterprise based in a foreign country, particularly if the local operations are conducted through a separately incorporated subsidiary. Furthermore, when the host state is itself complicit in the human rights abuses, as is the case in many of the examples listed above, relying on the host state's responsibility alone will result in impunity for the perpetrators, including a foreign-based enterprise that may have facilitated or benefited from the abuses.

For these reasons, the fact that many multinational enterprises now operate on a truly international plane, rather than merely being based in one country with foreign operations, has caused human rights advocates to investigate the direct application of international human rights law to corporations. Work began on a draft *Code of Conduct on Transnational Corporations* in the United Nations in 1974,[30] but was abandoned by 1994.[31] In the meantime, various instruments such as the Organisation for Economic Co-operation and Development's *Guidelines for Multinational Enterprises*,[32] the ILO's

---

[29]   For examples of how each of the rights enumerated in international human rights instruments can be affected by corporate activity, see Castan Centre for Human Rights Law, International Business Leaders Forum and Office of the United Nations High Commissioner for Human Rights, *Human Rights Translated: A Business Reference Guide* (2008) Monash University http://www.law.monash.edu.au/castancentre/publications/human-rights-translated.html at 5 January 2009.

[30]   *Draft United Nations Code of Conduct on Transnational Corporations*, UN Doc E/1990/94 (1990 draft); UN Doc E/1983/17/Rev.1, Annex II (1983 draft); 23 ILM 626.

[31]   Sean Murphy, 'Taking Multinational Corporate Codes of Conduct to the Next Level' (2005) 43 *Columbia Journal of Transnational Law* 389, 405.

[32]   *OECD Guidelines for Multinational Enterprises* (2000 revision), adopted

*Tripartite Declaration of Principles concerning Multinational Enterprises and Social Policy*[33] and the *UN Global Compact*[34] all urged corporations to abide by international human rights standards. However, those instruments did not elaborate on what standards applied to corporations or how their implementation differed from the duties imposed on states. Crucially, they also lacked any coercive enforcement mechanism, preferring either self-implementation or mediation.

The UN Sub-Commission on the Promotion and Protection of Human Rights attempted to fill that void in producing its *Norms on the Responsibilities of Transnational Corporations and Other Business Enterprises with Regard to Human Rights*, completed in 2003.[35] The UN Norms purported to restate existing human rights responsibilities in a form that was relevant to corporations, drawing them from a multitude of existing international instruments. As an instrument, the UN Norms carry no independent legal authority, given that their status is merely a document compiled by a sub-commission of the former Commission on Human Rights. However, at a minimum, the Norms constitute a useful reference point for the types of human rights responsibilities for corporations that can be said to derive from general international law. The primary responsibility of the state for the realisation of human rights was retained in the UN Norms, including the obligation to ensure that corporations respect human rights.[36] However, a concurrent obligation was recognised on the part of transnational corporations, 'within their respective spheres of activity and influence', to respect and secure human rights.[37]

The UN Norms therefore represented a new approach in relation to the application of international human rights law to corporations. They asserted

---

27 June 2001 ('*OECD Guidelines*'). The OECD Guidelines are part of the OECD *Declaration on International Investment and Multinational Enterprises*, OECD Doc DAFFE/IME/WPG(2000)15/FINAL.

[33] International Labour Organization, *Tripartite Declaration of Principles concerning Multinational Enterprises and Social Policy* (2000) LXXXIII OB, Ser A (November 1977) (Governing Body of the International Labour Office), amended November 2000.

[34] *United Nations Global Compact* (2000) (amended June 2004) http://www.globalcompact.org at 5 January 2009.

[35] United Nations Sub-Commission on the Promotion and Protection of Human Rights, *Norms on the Responsibilities of Transnational Corporations and Other Business Enterprises with Regard to Human Rights*, UN Doc E/CN.4/Sub.2/2003/12/Rev.2 (26 August 2003) ('UN Norms'). The Norms were adopted by the Sub-Commission on the Promotion and Protection of Human Rights by Resolution 2003/16, UN Doc E/CN.4/Sub.2/2003/L.11 (13 August 2003) 52.

[36] Ibid [1].

[37] Ibid.

that human rights law already demanded compliance with human rights standards by non-state entities, but that no enforcement mechanism currently existed outside of reliance on the state's responsibility to protect human rights within its jurisdiction. The UN Norms therefore commenced two parallel projects: the clarification of the content of human rights responsibilities for corporations and the development of new methods for the enforcement of those responsibilities.

In 2005, the Commission on Human Rights (which was replaced by the Human Rights Council in 2006) referred the issue of corporations and human rights to a Special Representative of the Secretary-General, John Ruggie.[38] The mandate, originally for two years, has since been extended to 2011, making six years in total.[39] The Special Representative thus took the baton from the Sub-Commission in continuing the projects of clarifying corporate obligations and developing enforcement methods, even though he took a markedly different tack.

## B  Existing international obligations?

Ruggie's initial report in 2006 was scathing of the UN Norms for their contention that international human rights law already placed obligations on corporations:

> What the Norms have done, in fact, is to take existing State-based human rights instruments and simply assert that many of their provisions are now binding on corporations as well. But that assertion itself has little authoritative basis in international law – hard, soft or otherwise.[40]

However, by his 2008 report, Ruggie had come around to the prospect that corporations had a duty to respect human rights in parallel with the state's duty to protect human rights within its jurisdiction.[41] That position has been

---

[38] Commission on Human Rights, *Human Rights and Transnational Corporations and Other Business Enterprises*, UN Doc E/CN.4/2005/L.20/Add.17 (20 April 2005).

[39] Human Rights Council, *Mandate of the Special Representative of the Secretary-General on the issue of human rights and transnational corporations and other business enterprises*, UN Doc A/HRC/RES/8/7 (18 June 2008).

[40] John Ruggie, *Interim Report of the Special Representative of the Secretary-General on the Issue of Human Rights and Transnational Corporations and Other Business Enterprises*, UN Doc E/CN.4/2006/97 (22 February 2006) [60].

[41] John Ruggie, *Protect, Respect and Remedy: A Framework for Business and Human Rights: Report of the Special Representative of the Secretary-General on the Issue of Human Rights and Transnational Corporations and Other Business Enterprises*, UN Doc A/HRC/8/5 (7 April 2008) [23–4], [51], [55].

endorsed by prominent business groups.[42] The 2008 resolution of the Human Rights Council that extended Ruggie's mandate included a paragraph in its preamble, '[e]mphasizing that transnational corporations and other business enterprises have a responsibility to protect human rights',[43] treating that proposition as accepted fact. There thus appears to be some coalescence around the idea of an independent duty to respect human rights from quarters that were recently sceptical of such a concept. However, neither Ruggie's 2008 report nor any of the statements or resolutions endorsing his framework elaborate on the legal source of the corporate duty to respect human rights or its content and scope. Those issues are among the priorities nominated for the next three years of the mandate.[44]

With both the UN Norms and the Special Representative embracing a formula wherein the primary human rights duty remained with states, including a duty to protect human rights within their respective jurisdictions in the context of business activity, but with a concurrent duty on the part of corporations directly to respect human rights within their own operations, the key point of difference came down to the scope of the business duty. The UN Norms did not stop at a duty to respect human rights – essentially an obligation to refrain from doing harm to the realisation of human rights. Instead, the Norms advocated an obligation 'to promote, secure the fulfilment of, respect, ensure respect of, and protect human rights recognized in international as well as national law', within the corporation's sphere of activity and influence.[45]

A legal obligation – as opposed to a moral one – to devote resources towards the positive improvement of human rights, which is implied by a duty to promote or fulfil human rights, is difficult to justify on the part of a corporation. The different social role of a corporation or another private actor compared with that of a state makes it inappropriate to have the same expectations of state and non-state actors in terms of the realisation of human rights. However, a duty to respect human rights within an enterprise's everyday activities, not requiring any expansion in the enterprise's role, is more difficult to argue against.[46]

---

[42] International Organisation of Employers, International Chamber of Commerce, and Business and Industry Advisory Council to the OECD, *Joint Initial Views of the IOE, ICC and BIAC to the Eighth Session of the Human Rights Council on the Third Report of the Special Representative of the UN Secretary-General on Business and Human Rights* (2008) Business and Human Rights Resource Center, http://www.reports-and-materials.org/Letter-IOE-ICC-BIAC-re-Ruggie-report-May-2008.pdf at 9 January 2009.
[43] Human Rights Council, above n 39, Preamble [5].
[44] Ibid Preamble [4(b)].
[45] UN Norms, above n 35, [1].
[46] The scope of this chapter does not allow for a thorough discussion of this

The emerging consensus therefore seems to favour a direct duty on multinational enterprises – and possibly other non-state actors – to respect human rights, which is complementary to the state's primary obligation to respect, protect and promote human rights within its territory and jurisdiction. However, the legal source of such a duty has yet to be satisfactorily identified and its practical scope is yet to be precisely defined.

Furthermore, even if there were a direct obligation of a universally agreed character and scope upon multinational enterprises to respect human rights, there is no existing avenue for such an obligation to be enforced. Among those who do not accept that there is an existing obligation, there is considerable agreement about the necessity for some mechanism for safeguarding human rights in the context of transnational business beyond what currently exists.

### C Concluding remarks on multinational enterprises

There is no doubt that corporations have the ability to cause violations of individuals' human rights in the course of their business operations. Nor is there any doubt that the state-based enforcement system, relying on states' obligations to protect human rights within their jurisdictions, is inadequate to prevent, monitor and punish such violations in the case of businesses that operate on a truly international scale.

Private actors are clearly capable of bearing obligations under international law. It may be that direct human rights obligations can already be implied under international law, or it may be that action such as a new treaty is required to make such obligations explicit and legally binding. Either way, action is clearly required to provide an avenue for individuals to enforce their rights and for an enterprise to be held accountable in situations where state-based systems are inadequate. Exploration of enforcement options comprises the third prong of the Special Representative's 'protect, respect and remedy' framework outlined in his 2008 report.[47] The challenge is now to build a system for the protection of human rights in the context of transnational business that transcends state borders as effectively as the business it seeks to monitor.

## 6 Trade rules: the World Trade Organization

Criticisms of the WTO and its impact on human rights can generally be grouped into three categories. First, some agreements negotiated and enforced

---

issue. For a more detailed discussion by this author on the reasoning behind different levels of obligations for different non-state actors, see Adam McBeth, 'Every Organ of Society: The Responsibility of Non-State Actors for the Realization of Human Rights' (2008) 30 *Hamline Journal of Public Law and Policy* 33.

[47] Ruggie, above n 41.

by the WTO are alleged to form a barrier to the realisation of human rights, perhaps worsening the situation or at least preventing it from improving. One of the most prominent examples of this category of criticism is the effect of the *Agreement on Trade-Related Aspects of Intellectual Property Rights*[48] on human rights related to access to essential medicines.

The second category of criticism focuses on the perceived failure of the WTO to seize opportunities to contribute positively to the realisation of human rights. Criticisms in this category invoke a sin of omission, pointing to appropriate measures that could have been taken to advance human rights. Often the comparison is drawn with other interests that are secured and advanced in various areas of international trade law, while human rights are not. The general exceptions to the GATT and some of the other WTO agreements are often criticised under this category.

The final category involves the way WTO instrumentalities interpret legal provisions within the WTO system. There are a number of instances where an agreement could be interpreted in a way that is conducive to human rights or takes international human rights norms into account, but where a different interpretation is ultimately preferred. Criticisms of this kind arise principally in relation to the WTO dispute settlement mechanisms.

Each of these different categories of criticism will be briefly examined in turn with a view to understanding the potential impact of WTO activity on human rights and the changes that an approach consistent with human rights principles might require.

## A  Trade agreements as a barrier to human rights: TRIPS and the right to health

When the WTO was formed at the conclusion of the Uruguay Round of trade negotiations in 1994, all of the member states of the new organisation signed up to a range of agreements annexed to the *Marrakesh Agreement Establishing the World Trade Organization*.[49] Most of those agreements, such as the GATT, the *General Agreement on Trade in Services*[50] and the *Agreement on Technical Barriers to Trade*,[51] were directed towards liberalising trade in goods and

---

[48] *Agreement on Trade-Related Aspects of Intellectual Property Rights*, Annex 1C to the *Marrakesh Agreement,* below n 49 ('TRIPS').
[49] *Marrakesh Agreement Establishing the World Trade Organization*, opened for signature 15 April 1994, 1867 UNTS 3 (entered into force 1 January 1995) ('*Marrakesh Agreement*').
[50] *General Agreement on Trade in Services,* Annex 1B to the *Marrakesh Agreement,* ibid ('GATS').
[51] *Agreement on Technical Barriers to Trade,* Annex 1A to the *Marrakesh Agreement,* above n 49.

services, imposing strict limits on the types of regulatory barriers states can impose on trade. TRIPS had the opposite objective: it mandated a regulatory barrier in the form of member states' recognition of intellectual property rights, such as patents, thus prohibiting free trade in protected goods by anyone other than the right-holder. TRIPS is therefore the result of a conscious decision to subordinate the principle of unfettered free trade to the protection of a particular interest, namely intellectual property rights.

The protection of intellectual property through measures such as patents, which grant a monopoly to the patent holder for the exploitation of an invention for a specified period,[52] in recognition of the research and development that the inventor has invested and to encourage such innovation in the future, is not in itself antithetical to human rights. Indeed, both the UDHR and the ICESCR recognise the right of authors and inventors to 'the protection of the moral and material interests' resulting from their works and inventions.[53] Those interests are clearly balanced in human rights law by the right of 'everyone to enjoy the benefits of scientific progress and its applications'.[54]

The potential clash between human rights and the protection of intellectual property arises when access to the protected product is essential for the realisation of human rights. A stark example is the availability of patented drugs to populations with epidemic disease and no capacity to pay monopoly-inflated prices. The right to health includes an obligation on states to prevent, treat and control diseases and to make medical treatment available,[55] while the right to life includes an obligation to take measures to prevent death through disease, particularly epidemics.[56] Those obligations have been held to include an obligation to secure access to essential drugs.[57] Monopoly protection of pharmaceutical products in the form of patents makes them more expensive than they would be if they faced competition from other producers, who would not

---

[52] The minimum patent monopoly period mandated by TRIPS is 20 years: Article 33 TRIPS.
[53] This wording is adopted in both Article 27(2) UDHR and Article 15(1)(c) ICESCR.
[54] Article 27(1) UDHR; Article 15(1)(b) ICESCR.
[55] Article 12(2) ICESCR.
[56] Human Rights Committee, *General Comment 6: The Right to Life* (30 April 1982) OHCHR, http://www.unhchr.ch/tbs/doc.nsf/0/84ab9690ccd81fc7c12563ed0046fae3 at 5 January 2009, [5].
[57] Committee on Economic, Social and Cultural Rights, *General Comment 14: The right to the highest attainable standard of health*, UN Doc E/C.12/2000/4 (2000) [17]; World Health Organization, *WHO Policy Perspectives on Medicines – Globalization, TRIPS and Access to Pharmaceuticals* (2001) WHO, http://whqlibdoc.who.int/hq/2001/WHO_EDM_2001.2.pdf at 5 January 2009, 5.

*Human rights in economic globalisation* 157

need to recoup the research and development costs of the original inventor. Accordingly, enforcing patent protection for essential medicines creates a barrier for access to those medicines, particularly for people in poor countries who cannot afford patent-inflated prices and whose governments cannot afford to provide free or heavily subsidised medicines on a large scale. The treatment of HIV/AIDS epidemics in poor regions, especially sub-Saharan Africa, is a pertinent example. The realisation of the right to health is thus inhibited by trade rules that mandate patent protection.

The solution to this dilemma included in TRIPS as it was originally drafted was to allow compulsory licences. Governments were thereby entitled to grant a licence to other suppliers to exploit the patent without the consent of the patent holder,[58] albeit with payment of royalties to the patent holder.[59] A number of conditions were imposed on compulsory licences under TRIPS, including a requirement to negotiate with the patent holder in good faith before a compulsory licence could be issued in the event that no agreement was reached,[60] and the stipulation that the compulsory licence be 'predominantly for the supply of the domestic market'.[61] The barrier to access to essential medicines posed by patent protection was thereby significantly reduced for countries with a manufacturing base capable of supplying the domestic market, provided that a generic manufacturer could be found and provided that there existed sufficient political will to defy the wishes of the patent holder, which was typically a large and financially powerful multinational pharmaceutical corporation with significant leverage in the form of foreign investment.[62]

Compulsory licences under those conditions, however, were of benefit to only a handful of developing countries. The countries with the greatest need

---

[58] Article 31 TRIPS.
[59] Article 31(h) TRIPS.
[60] Article 31(b) TRIPS.
[61] Article 31(f) TRIPS.
[62] On this point, note that pharmaceutical companies and their home states have periodically threatened litigation and trade sanctions to pressure other states not to make use of compulsory licences: Naomi Bass, 'Implications of the TRIPS Agreement for Developing Countries: Pharmaceutical Laws in Brazil and South Africa in the 21st Century' (2002) 34 *George Washington International Law Review* 191, 219; Kara Bombach, 'Can South Africa Fight AIDS? Reconciling the South African Medicines and Related Substances Act with the TRIPS Agreement' (2001) 19 *Boston University International Law Journal* 273, 274; Patrick Marc, 'Compulsory Licensing and the South African Medicine Act of 1997: Violation or Compliance of the Trade Related Aspects of Intellectual Property Rights Agreement?' (2001) 21 *New York Law School Journal of International and Comparative Law* 109, 110, 123; Judy Rein, 'International Governance Through Trade Agreements: Patent Protection for Essential Medicines' (2001) 21 *Northwestern Journal of International Law and Business* 379, 402.

for access to affordable medicines typically do not have the resources or infrastructure for domestic manufacture of generic versions of patented drugs.[63] Consequently, TRIPS was subjected to significant criticism for its effect on access to essential medicines in the countries in most desperate need, especially in relation to HIV/AIDS, malaria and tuberculosis. So great was the criticism that the Fourth Ministerial Conference of the WTO in Doha in 2001 took the unprecedented step of addressing it in a separate Ministerial Declaration: the *Declaration on TRIPS and Public Health*.[64]

While not using the nomenclature of human rights, the Doha TRIPS Declaration directly addressed the potential clash between TRIPS and the realisation of the right to health, stating:

> We agree that the TRIPS Agreement does not and should not prevent Members from taking measures to protect public health. Accordingly, while reiterating our commitment to the TRIPS Agreement, we affirm that the Agreement can and should be interpreted and implemented in a manner supportive of WTO Members' right to protect public health and, in particular, to promote access to medicines for all. In this connection, we reaffirm the right of WTO Members to use, to the full, the provisions in the TRIPS Agreement, which provide flexibility for this purpose.

The interpretation of international trade law to achieve legitimate non-trade purposes, such as the realisation of the right to health, was thereby endorsed by the Ministerial Conference of the WTO. However the problem of countries unable to manufacture their own drugs – a problem created by the text of TRIPS – could not be resolved with mere interpretation of existing 'flexibility'.

In counterargument to those advocating wide exceptions to patent monopolies for essential medicines, pharmaceutical companies argued that patent protection was positive for the right to health, because without the incentive of patent monopolies, research and development expenditure could not be recouped and new drugs would not be invented.[65] At a minimum, the compa-

---

[63] World Health Organization Commission on Macroeconomics and Health, *Investing in Health for Economic Development* (2001) WHO, http://whqlibdoc.who.int/publications/2001/924154550X.pdf at 5 January 2009, 90.

[64] *Declaration on the TRIPS Agreement and Public Health*, Doha, WTO Doc WT/MIN(01)/DEC/2 (14 November 2001) (Fourth Ministerial Conference of the WTO).

[65] For discussion and analysis of such claims, see: Pedro Roffe, Christoph Spennemann and Johanna von Braun, 'From Paris to Doha: The World Trade Organization Doha Declaration on the Agreement on Trade-Related Aspects of Intellectual Property Rights and Public Health' in P Roffe, G Tansey and D Vivas-Eugui (eds) *Negotiating Health. Intellectual Property and Access to Medicines* (Earthscan, London, 2005) 9; Sarah Joseph, 'Pharmaceutical Corporations and Access to Drugs: The "Fourth Wave" of Corporate Human Rights Scrutiny' (2003) 25 *Human Rights Quarterly* 425, 435.

nies insisted on maintaining patent monopolies in developed countries if poor countries were to be permitted to import drugs manufactured under a compulsory licence. The maintenance of a two-tiered system, with monopoly protection in developed countries but cheap generic imports permitted for certain least developed countries, would open the possibility of diversion of the cheap generic drugs back to more lucrative developed markets, thereby undermining both access to drugs in the poor country and patent protection in relation to the developed country.

The various practical difficulties of such a scheme led to protracted negotiation within the WTO.[66] An interim decision was reached in 2003,[67] with a permanent amendment to the text of TRIPS currently awaiting acceptance by the required number of WTO members.[68] The agreed system includes several onerous conditions, such as strict notification conditions, distinctive colouring, shaping and packaging of the generic drugs to prevent surreptitious re-exportation, as well as requiring royalty payments to the patent holder at the exporting country's end. Although lauded as a breakthrough at the time, the scheme has had only one notification from a prospective importing country – Rwanda – in its first four years of operation to September 2009.[69]

In practical terms, the WTO's solution to the problem of access to essential medicines has achieved very little in comparison with the magnitude of the problem. However, the case is illustrative of three significant issues in relation

---

[66] For a detailed discussion of the negotiations and the various solutions posited, see Adam McBeth, 'When Nobody Comes to the Party: Why Have No States Used the WTO Scheme for Compulsory Licensing of Essential Medicines?' (2006) 3 *New Zealand Yearbook of International Law* 69, Part IV.

[67] *Implementation of Para 6 of the Doha Declaration on the TRIPS Agreement and Public Health*, WTO Doc WT/L/540 (1 September 2003) (Decision of the General Council).

[68] *Protocol Amending the TRIPS Agreement*, annexed to *Amendment of the TRIPS Agreement*, WTO Doc WT/L/641 (8 December 2005) (Decision of the General Council). The protocol inserts a new Article 31 *bis* and adds an annex to TRIPS substantially reflecting the system agreed by the General Council in 2003. The deadline for acceptance of the protocol by two-thirds of WTO members, which is necessary for the amendment to take effect, was extended to 31 December 2009: *Amendment of the TRIPS Agreement – Extension of the Period for the Acceptance by Members of the Protocol Amending the TRIPS Agreement*, WTO Doc WT/L/711 (21 December 2007) (Decision of the General Council).

[69] Rwanda, *Notification under paragraph 2(A) of the decision of 30 August 2003 on the implementation of paragraph 6 of the Doha Declaration on the TRIPS Agreement and Public Health*, WTO Doc IP/N/9/RWA/1 (19 July 2007). Canada has made a notification as a prospective manufacturer and exporter to match Rwanda's notification: WTO Doc IP/N/CAN/1 (5 October 2007). The notifications involved a three-drug cocktail for combating HIV/AIDS known as TriAvir.

to the interaction of human rights and economic globalisation. First, it proves that international trade rules can impede the realisation of human rights in a concrete way. Secondly, even though the amendments implemented to date have had little practical effect, the case is evidence that trade rules can be modified, both in their legal interpretation and by amending the text of the instruments themselves, to achieve an outcome that is more consistent with human rights.[70] In this case, proof of an insurmountable barrier posed by TRIPS was accompanied by enormous social and political pressure to achieve change. To be sure, the changes were fairly minimal and significant practical hurdles were left intact. Nevertheless, this case demonstrates that legal change is possible. Finally, this case is evidence of the limited impact that formal legal tinkering can have on entrenched social problems. In the absence of financial incentives for generic manufacturers and political will from exporting and importing governments, removing the legal prohibition has not been sufficient to facilitate action.[71]

## B  Failure to protect human rights: import restrictions and the 'general exceptions'

The principal objective of trade liberalisation under the GATT, and later under the WTO, has been to ensure transparency of barriers to trade by expressing such barriers as tariffs, to reduce the level of such tariffs over time, and to abolish all other impediments to free trade. Accordingly, WTO member states are prima facie prohibited from imposing any measures, other than tariffs within the agreed parameters, on foreign goods that would impede their importation or discriminate against goods from a particular country.[72] That general prohibition covers domestic rules including tax treatment, quotas, content requirements, product standards and anything else that affects the treatment of goods within an economy.

---

[70] Another example of such an outcome is the waiver of GATT rules granted by the General Council in 2003 to permit states to take measures to curtail the trade in 'conflict diamonds' pursuant to the Kimberley Process, commonly known as the Kimberley Waiver: see http://www.wto.org/english/news_e/news03_e/goods_council_26fev03_e.htm at 5 January 2009.

[71] For a discussion of the difficulties faced by Médecins Sans Frontières in trying to facilitate the export of generic drugs under the WTO scheme, see Ann Silversides, 'Canada's Pioneering Law to get Cheap AIDS Drugs to Poor Nations Falls on Face', *The Ottawa Citizen* (Ottawa), 14 August 2006.

[72] The Most Favoured Nation principle, expressed in Article I GATT, operates to prohibit discrimination against imports compared with imports from different countries, while the National Treatment principle, expressed in Article III GATT, prohibits discrimination between local and imported goods.

A number of specific exceptions to that general position are enunciated in the GATT, recognising that state regulation to achieve a legitimate domestic policy goal will sometimes necessarily impact trade. These include exceptions that have some potential relevance for human rights policies, including measures necessary to protect public morals[73] and measures necessary to protect human, animal or plant life or health.[74] Most of the exceptions to the non-discrimination principles, however, relate to sensitive economic interests and have no obvious application in a human rights context.

The criticism of this aspect of trade law from a human rights perspective is not that the rules cause active human rights infringements, but rather that positive measures to protect human rights are not permitted if they would impact upon trade. A domestic law that sought to ban goods made with slave labour or child labour, for example, would almost certainly violate WTO rules. Such a law would discriminate between physically identical products according to the manner in which they were produced, rather than the inherent characteristics of the products themselves. A country that was affected by such a ban would be able to challenge it as unjustifiable discrimination. As none of the exceptions cover labour rights, at least under the interpretation currently prevailing, the human rights interest would be subordinated to the principle of non-discrimination in trade.[75]

It should be noted that this scenario is not a direct clash between states' human rights obligations and their trade obligations, since it cannot be said that states currently have an obligation to take measures to prevent human rights violations or improve labour standards outside their own territory or jurisdiction. While states are not obliged to take such proactive measures,[76] the fact that they are prohibited from doing so is problematic, particularly insofar as a state's aim is not to be complicit in human rights abuses by importing products made under those conditions. Under the prevailing interpretation, therefore, states are not necessarily prevented from fulfilling their obligations under international human rights law in this respect, but they could be

---

[73] Article XX(a) GATT.
[74] Article XX(b) GATT.
[75] Following *obiter dicta* in the Appellate Body's reasoning in *United States – Shrimp*, it appears that measures that discriminate between products on the basis of their process and production methods, rather than their physical or functional characteristics, in order to achieve a policy goal permitted in the general exceptions, will be acceptable provided that the measure does not constitute arbitrary or unjustifiable discrimination.
[76] However, see Chapter 3 of this volume for a discussion of the prospect for states to be held to extraterritorial human rights obligations.

prevented from taking non-mandatory measures for the international protection of human rights.

Measures designed to protect the human rights of a country's own people are a different story. Bans on harmful products to protect the life and health of consumers – which are of course human rights issues, even though they are rarely labelled as such – are quite common. Some of these have been challenged as inconsistent with WTO rules, such as bans by the European Union on products containing asbestos[77] and on meat produced with the use of growth hormones[78] and its moratorium on genetically modified organisms.[79] While the asbestos ban was held to be a reasonable measure to protect human life and health, the bans on meat hormones and genetically modified organisms were held to violate WTO law, largely because of an absence of conclusive scientific evidence showing that the measures were necessary.

In cases such as these, the WTO rules and their prevailing interpretation operate to impose limits on measures a state may take to protect human life and health within its own borders by banning or limiting the import of harmful and potentially harmful products. The more serious threat that such an approach poses to human rights is one of perception rather than a direct legal clash. As long as there is a perception that WTO rules might be invoked to challenge measures taken to improve the realisation of human rights, the financial and diplomatic cost involved in such a dispute acts as a disincentive for states to take bold human rights measures that might have a trade impact. Where human rights and trade priorities are inconsistent, the current perception is that the human rights priorities will often be the ones to yield.

*C  Interpretation: dispute settlement*
The manner in which WTO dispute settlement organs – the dispute panels and the Appellate Body – interpret and apply WTO law and broader international law has also been the subject of criticism from a human rights perspective.

It was noted in the previous section that exceptions to general trade rules, such as the exception for the protection of human life or health, tend to be

---

[77] *European Communities – Measures Affecting Asbestos and Asbestos-Containing Products*, WTO Doc WT/DS135/AB/R (5 April 2001) (Report of the Appellate Body).
[78] *European Communities – Measures Concerning Meat and Meat Products (Hormones)*, WTO Doc WT/DS48/AB/R (13 February 1998) (Report of the Appellate Body).
[79] *European Communities – Measures Affecting the Approval and Marketing of Biotech Products*, WT/DS291/R, WT/DS292/R and WT/DS293/R (29 September 2006) (Report of the Panel).

fairly restrictively applied within the WTO system. The members of WTO panels and the Appellate Body are trade and economic experts; they are not experts in human rights (or the environment for that matter), nor should they be. However, conscious of the fact that WTO agreements form part of the body of public international law and should be interpreted in a manner consistent with other international obligations, including human rights obligations, the neglect of human rights issues in WTO jurisprudence to date is troubling.

There is clear scope for human rights law to be invoked in relation to exceptions for the protection of human life and health, given their obvious overlap with the rights to life and health. However, no state has yet framed a WTO argument in those terms. Howse has suggested that the exception allowing measures to protect public morals could be used as a more encompassing human rights provision. He has argued:

> In the modern world, the very idea of public morality has become inseparable from the concern for human personhood, dignity, and capacity reflected in fundamental rights. A conception of public morals or morality that excluded notions of fundamental rights would simply be contrary to the ordinary contemporary meaning of the concept.[80]

According to Howse, any measure taken by a state for the genuine protection or promotion of human rights, and thus the protection of human dignity, is necessarily a measure to protect public morals which is a legitimate exception to the trade rules prohibiting discrimination. Indeed, Howse argues that the vast body of international human rights law could provide transparent parameters for a public morals exception that is otherwise extremely broad and nebulous.[81] The public morals exception, however, has only once been invoked in a WTO dispute, and that case made no connection to international human rights law.[82]

Therein lies the problem. The links between human rights standards and trade rules identified by academic commentators are worth little if states are not prepared to raise them in the context of a WTO dispute, and even less if states are scared off implementing human rights measures in the first place for

---

[80] Robert Howse, 'Back to Court After *Shrimp/Turtle*? Almost but not Quite Yet: India's Short Lived Challenge to Labor and Environmental Exceptions in the European Union's Generalized System of Preferences' (2003) 18 *American University International Law Review* 1333, 1368.

[81] Robert Howse, 'The World Trade Organization and the Protection of Workers' Rights' (1999) 3 *Journal of Small and Emerging Business Law* 131, 169.

[82] *United States – Measures Affecting the Cross-Border Supply of Gambling and Betting Services*, WTO Doc WT/DS285/AB/R (7 April 2005) (Report of the Appellate Body).

fear of violating WTO rules. The major obstacle to greater complementarity of human rights and trade law is therefore the attitude of governments rather than the content of the law itself.

If the wishes of human rights advocates were to be granted and the WTO bodies began to interpret trade law by reference to international human rights law, a further potential problem would emerge in that human rights law could be adjudicated upon by trade experts. It is no more desirable for trade experts to determine the development of human rights jurisprudence than it would be for human rights experts to rule on the technicalities of trade law, the law of the sea or any other aspect of international law. The WTO dispute bodies have the capacity to seek expert opinions and advice from any source they deem appropriate.[83] The various human rights treaty monitoring bodies, the Office of the High Commissioner for Human Rights and the ILO are among the obvious candidates for such a request on a human rights issue, although no such opinion has ever been sought, primarily because a WTO dispute has yet to be framed with reference to human rights law, in contrast to a willingness to incorporate international environmental law.[84] The WTO should not become a *de facto* forum for the enforcement of human rights law, but at the same time its enforcement of trade law should not be allowed to be an impediment to the implementation of human rights. States should be prepared to invoke human rights arguments and WTO bodies should be prepared to take those arguments into account, with guidance from appropriate expert bodies, in recognition of the holistic nature of international law and the coexistence of the two subfields within the same system.

## 7 Conclusion

There is widespread agreement that an international human rights system that places obligations solely on states is inadequate to protect human rights in the course of international economic activity. At the more conservative end of the spectrum, Ruggie identifies an absence of supervision and enforcement, which he refers to as 'governance gaps':

> The root cause of the business and human rights predicament today lies in the governance gaps created by globalization – between the scope and impact of economic forces and actors, and the capacity of societies to manage their adverse consequences. These governance gaps provide the permissive environment for wrongful acts by companies of all kinds without adequate sanctioning or reparation.

---

[83] *Understanding on the Rules and Procedures Governing the Settlement of Disputes*, Annex 2 to the *Marrakesh Agreement*, above n 49.
[84] See, for example, *United States – Shrimp*.

How to narrow and ultimately bridge the gaps in relation to human rights is our fundamental challenge.[85]

At the other end of the spectrum, Pogge regards the entire international economic system, including the institutions and actors considered in this chapter, to be moribund in terms of its failure to protect human rights and its tolerance and perpetuation of poverty and suffering:

> Given that the present global institutional order is foreseeably associated with such massive incidence of poverty, its (uncompensated) imposition manifests an ongoing human rights violation – arguably the largest such violation ever committed in human history ... The continuing imposition of this global order, essentially unmodified, constitutes a massive violation of the human right to basic necessities – a violation for which the governments and electorates of the more powerful countries bear primary responsibility.[86]

Whichever stance one takes in terms of the magnitude of the problem and the extent to which the existing order can accommodate satisfactory reform, the inescapable conclusion is that there is a fundamental mismatch between a system of international human rights law that looks only to states for enforcement and accountability and the reality of international economic activity, which is largely conducted at a supra-national level. Whether the actions in question are the result of collective state action, as in the formulation of trade rules in the WTO, institutional action, as in the actions of international financial institutions or the jurisprudence of the WTO's judicial organs, or the actions of private actors such as multinational enterprises, they are clearly outside the theoretical responsibility and practical capacity of any one state. Globalisation in the economic arena has outpaced international human rights law, which remains wedded to state-based lines of accountability.

The two examples of economic globalisation focused on in this chapter – multinational enterprises and the WTO – illustrate two very different areas where significant systemic obstacles to the realisation of human rights have been identified and where some change to accommodate human rights is beginning to take place, albeit at a glacial pace. This chapter has considered interpretations of existing law that would oblige economic institutions to take human rights into account, as well as proposals for the imposition of direct obligations on actors such as multinational enterprises. It has demonstrated

---

[85] Ruggie, above n 41, [3].
[86] Thomas Pogge, 'Severe Poverty as a Human Rights Violation' in T Pogge (ed) *Freedom from Poverty as a Human Right: Who Owes What to the Very Poor?* (Oxford University Press, Oxford, 2007) 11, 52–3.

that possible avenues exist for the application of human rights standards in the course of international economic activity, recognising the holistic nature of international law, of which human rights law is an integral part.

However, the theoretical possibility for international economic actors having regard to human rights standards is meaningless if not implemented in practice. For multinational enterprises, that means recognition by states that such enterprises do or should have human rights duties, as well as the creation of practical mechanisms to implement and enforce those duties. For the WTO, it means consciousness on the part of member states and WTO organs of the impact that particular trade rules can have on human rights and a willingness of states to persevere with positive human rights measures rather than bowing to a restrictive interpretation of trade rules. For other international economic actors not examined in this chapter, the necessary steps for practical implementation will differ, but the principles remain the same: reliance on a state-based system for the protection of human rights is inadequate in the context of economic globalisation, but, in order for human rights standards to be applied to other entities, states and the entities themselves must take those responsibilities seriously and integrate them into the everyday work of the economic entities in question.

# 7. Human rights and development
*Stephen P Marks*

## 1 The relationship between human rights and development in international law

The international law of human rights and the international law of development are fairly circumscribed, as other chapters in this work clearly point out. International norms and institutions govern each of these fields, although with overlapping domains and ambiguous conceptual linkages. Human rights law draws upon and has its own standards relating to such issues as protection of refugees, victims of armed conflict, workers, children, and the like, and therefore covers a wide range of situations in which the human person is in need of the protection of the law from harm and abuse, as part of a broader endeavour to promote human welfare.[1]

The law of development is less well defined but includes such topics as international finance, aid, trade, investments, anti-corruption, and lending. The treaties and other standard-setting instruments considered part of international development law in one way or another contribute to national and international efforts to protect vested interests, while often introducing a discourse about raising the populations of developing countries out of poverty and establishing a rules-based international political economy conducive to human welfare.[2]

How should these two strategies of human welfare be distinguished? Reduced to their most basic purposes, international human rights law promotes the flourishing of the human person while international development law promotes wealth creation and growth. Some approaches to development – often called 'classical' or 'neoliberal' and preceded by the word ' economic' – treat wealth creation as an end in itself, whereas others, usually using the

---

[1] 'Welfare' is used here in the economic sense of health, education and resources adequate for a life worth living rather than the political meaning of government 'handout' to those unable or unwilling to provide for themselves. This use is virtually synonymous with well-being.

[2] A classical work in this field is F.V. Garcia-Amador, *The Emerging International Law of Development: A New Dimension of International Economic Law* (Oceana Publications, New York, 1990). For a systematic critique of the pretensions of international development law, see Balakrishnan Rajagopal, *International Law from Below: Development, Social Movements and Third World Resistance* (Cambridge University Press, Cambridge, 2003).

language of 'human development', consider wealth creation as a means to improving human welfare or well-being. Growth-based models of development are those that consider development as the increase of goods and services for consumers, of infrastructure, social capital and industry for productive capacity, of market efficiency for maximising utility, and of trade and investment for comparative advantages in the global economy. The welfare models refer to approaches to development that focus on the human person as the end rather than a means of development, on sustainability in order to meet the needs of future as well as present generations, and on expanding choices through increased capabilities. The welfare model corresponds to a large extent with the concept of 'human development', defined by the United Nations Development Programme ('UNDP') in its *Human Development Report* as 'creating an environment in which people can develop their full potential and lead productive, creative lives in accord with their needs and interests'.[3]

This chapter focuses on the legal dimensions of the relationship between international human rights law, on the one hand, and both of these approaches to development, on the other. I will define the scope of human rights in development as a sub-branch of international human rights law dealing with the legal norms and processes through which internationally recognised human rights are applied in the context of national and international policies, programmes and projects relating to economic and social development.

The application of human rights in development is based on the general proposition that the theory and practice of development may be enriched by the introduction of normative dimensions of a human rights framework and that development and human rights are mutually reinforcing strategies for the improvement of human well-being. However, there remains considerable uncertainty regarding the content and practical value of human rights in development practice and the mutually reinforcing character is highly contested.

There are several approaches to human rights in development, ranging from the basic concern for specific duties under human rights treaties within specific sectors of development (such as health or education) to more systematic efforts to link human rights norms to the entire process of development, through the concept, identified in the early 1970s, of the 'right to development' and subsequently further elucidated in both non-binding and binding legal instruments. Although I will begin with the right to development, the topic is broader and is best identified as 'human rights in development', a terminology adopted by the Office of the High Commissioner for Human Rights. The meaningful application of human rights concepts to the process of

---

[3] UNDP, *Human Development Report 2001* (Oxford University Press, New York, 2001) 9.

development requires linking the essentially legal and political approach of the former to the essentially economic and social context of the latter.

This chapter will examine successively the legal basis of the right to development, human rights law as applied to aid and poverty reduction strategies, and the tensions between human rights law and the legal regimes of international trade and investment. In other words, we begin with the full integration of human rights into development through the claim that development itself is a human right, then examine the emerging law and practice of the phased introduction of human rights means and methods into development practice, and end with the claim that human rights and development are separate spheres that intersect only in minor ways.

## 2  The legal basis of the right to development

The right to development has been defined in the 1986 *Declaration on the Right to Development*[4] and in the writings of many scholars, including the UN Independent Expert on the Right to Development. Briefly expressed, it is a right to a process as well as to progressive outcomes aiming at the full realisation of all human rights in the context of equitable growth and 'sustained action ... to promote more rapid development ... [and] effective international cooperation ... in providing [developing] countries with appropriate means and facilities to foster their comprehensive development', in the words of the DRD.

The right to development and human rights in development are related in the sense that the implementation of the right to development requires that governments and development partners apply human rights in their development policies and practices in an integrated way, along with the other requirements stipulated in or implied by the DRD. Thus the right to development includes but is not coterminous with a human rights approach to development insofar as this approach – to be discussed in the next section – may be applied in a single sector of the economy or in a localised development project, whereas the right to development calls for human rights to be systematically integrated into all sectors of development in the context of international efforts to facilitate such development.

The greatest challenge of any definition of the right to development or of a human rights approach to development is to make it operational in practice. Describing the component elements of the right to development does not specify the steps required to implement it. At the current stage of experience with the right to development, this right cannot be implemented with the same rigour as other human right norms, nor can appropriate measures of accountability and

---

[4]  GA Res 41/128 Annex 41, UN GAOR Supp No 53, 186, UN Doc A/41/53 (4 December 1986) ('DRD').

remedial action be put in place to respond to instances of failure to implement this right. However, it can be reasonably argued that taking this right seriously means that states, civil society and international institutions should treat it with a sufficient degree of rigour by identifying and applying appropriate measures of accountability. Otherwise, the right to development will remain primarily rhetorical.

### A  Legal status of the right to development

Governments have taken widely varying positions regarding the legal status of the right to development, ranging from the outright rejection of the claim that it is a human right at all to the position that it is a core right that should be legally binding and central to all efforts to promote and protect human rights. The intermediate view considers the right to development to be grounded in international law but the extent to which it constrains states legally is in the process of evolution. Indeed, official statements of governments since the mid-1970s, especially in their support for the DRD and for the right to development in the 1993 *Declaration of the Vienna Conference on Human Rights*,[5] and other resolutions of the General Assembly and summits, attach legal significance to this human right. The DRD, like other declarations adopted by the General Assembly, creates an enhanced expectation that governments will move from political commitment to legal obligations. The DRD, therefore, is a legitimate reference by which to hold governments at least politically accountable as an international norm crystallises into law.

The political support for this transformation has been reiterated at several UN summits, which tend to make one allusion to the right to development, often as a reluctant political compromise, and then deal with the key issues of the event without any further reference to the right to development. For example, world leaders agreed in September 2000 at the United Nations Millennium Summit on a set of goals and targets for combating poverty, hunger, disease, illiteracy, environmental degradation, and discrimination against women, which eventually became the Millennium Development Goals ('MDGs'). The Summit Declaration included the commitment 'to making the right to development a reality for everyone and to freeing the entire human race from want' but made no further mention of it.[6]

The *Human Development Report 2003* of the UNDP, which was devoted to the MDGs, affirmed that the MDGs contribute to the right to development.[7] In

---

[5]   UN Doc A/CONF.157/23 (12 July 1993) [72] ('*Vienna Declaration*').
[6]   *United Nations Millennium Declaration*, GA Res 55/2, UN GAOR, 55th sess, 8th plen mtg, UN Doc A/Res/55/2 (8 September 2000) [11].
[7]   UNDP, *Human Development Report 2003* (2003) UNDP, http://hdr.undp.org/en/reports/global/hdr2003/ at 14 January 2009.

particular, the report not only affirmed that 'achieving the Goals will advance human rights'[8] but also recognised 'that the targets expressed in the Goals are not just development aspirations but also claimable rights'.[9] The analysis uses the language of obligations:

> Viewing the Goals in this way means that taking action to achieve them is an obligation, not a form of charity. This approach creates a framework for holding various actors accountable, including governments, citizens, corporations, and international organizations. Human rights carry counterpart obligations on the part of others – not just to refrain from violating them, but also to protect and promote their realization.[10]

Finally, the report affirms that '[t]he Millennium Development Goals more explicitly define what all countries agree can be demanded – benchmarks against which such commitments must be measured'.[11]

It is understandable that the political climate in which the right to development emerged continues to place this right more in the realm of rhetoric than as the normative basis for setting priorities and for allocating resources. Taking the right to development seriously requires that development partners put in place bilateral facilities or country-specific arrangements.[12] Such arrangements offer an alternative to human rights conditionality in that they institutionalise the responsibility of developing countries to fulfil the obligations which they have freely accepted to apply human rights-consistent development policies. Equally important is the responsibility of donor countries and institutions to support the right to development through international co-operation, including debt relief, better conditions of trade and increased development assistance. The appeal of the right to development lies in its perceived potential for transforming international economic relations, especially between the developed and developing countries, on the basis of equity, partnership and shared responsibilities rather than creating confrontation. A moral commitment to such goals is easier to achieve than a legal commitment.

---

[8] Ibid 28.
[9] Ibid.
[10] Ibid.
[11] Ibid.
[12] For example, see the 'development compacts' proposed by the UN Independent Expert on the Right to Development: see generally, for example, Arjun Sengupta, *Study in the Current State of Progress of the Implementation of the Right to Development*, UN Doc E/CN.4/1999/WG.18/2 (27 July 1999); *The Right to Development*, UN Doc E/CN.4/2000/WG.18/CRP.1 (11 September 2000); *Third report of the independent expert on the right to development*, E/CN.4/2001/WG.18 (2 January 2001).

### B   Legal commitment to the right to development

To the extent that the human right to development reaffirms rights that are already contained in legally binding instruments, such as the two international Covenants on human rights,[13] it builds on and integrates binding norms. Taken as a composite right, the right to development involves 'perfect obligations' of its component rights and, therefore, the duty-bearers may be identified and claims of non-conforming action may be legally adjudicated.

However, to the extent that the right to development establishes the obligation to integrate those components into a coherent development policy, it corresponds more to the notion of 'imperfect obligation', the realisation of which requires complex sets of actions and allocation of resources to develop and apply indeterminate policies at national and international levels. Governments have a moral obligation to establish such policies to ensure that development is advanced in a way that systematically integrates the five principles of equity, non-discrimination, participation, transparency and accountability. In this sense, it is an aspirational right to which governments may be politically committed but for which there are not yet legal remedies. The imperfect obligation to realise the right to development should be progressively translated into more specific obligations if the political posturing that has so far characterised this right can be replaced by specific policies and programmes with measurable outcomes. The current role of the Open-Ended Working Group on the Right to Development and its high-level task force offer an opportunity to move in that direction.[14]

While the political discourse shows divergent approaches to the duties implied by the DRD, the legal basis for asserting that states do have such obligations derives not from the legal nature of the DRD, which is a resolution expressing views of member states in an instrument that did not purport to create legally binding rights and obligations, but rather, on the legal obligation to act jointly and separately for the realisation of human rights and 'economic and social progress and development', as stipulated in the *Charter of the United Nations* at Articles 55 and 56. For the states parties to the ICESCR, the core legal argument is contained in Article 2 of that treaty. It is in the logic of the right to development that the full realisation of 'all rights' cannot be

---

[13]   *International Covenant on Economic, Social and Cultural Rights*, opened for signature 19 December 1966, 999 UNTS 3 (entered into force 3 January 1976) ('ICESCR'); *International Covenant on Civil and Political Rights*, opened for signature 16 December 1966, 999 UNTS 171 (entered into force 23 March 1976) ('ICCPR').

[14]   The Working Group on the Right to Development was established by the UN Commission on Human Rights in 1998 by Commission on Human Rights resolution 1998/7. See generally http://www2.ohchr.org/english/issues/development/groups/index.htm at 14 January 2009.

successful if pursued piecemeal, but can only be achieved through a policy that is deliberately designed to achieve all the rights, progressively and in accordance with available resources. In that sense, the ICESCR creates legal obligations to do essentially what the right to development calls for. These are the legal obligations of each of the 160 states parties (as of October 2009) not only to alter its internal policy but also to act through international co-operation toward the same end. Specifically, the duty, in Article 2(1) ICESCR, 'to take steps, individually and through international assistance and co-operation' provides a legal basis for the reciprocal obligations mentioned above. The putative extension of this duty to co-operate with the right to development is expressed in Article 4(2) DRD: '[a]s a complement to the efforts of developing countries [to promote more rapid development], effective international co-operation is essential in providing these countries with appropriate means and facilities to foster their comprehensive development.'

The obligation to co-operate as a legal obligation can have a restrictive and an extensive interpretation. According to the restrictive interpretation, an affluent state could argue that its legal obligation to engage in 'effective international co-operation' in the realisation of the right to development is fulfilled by three elements of its foreign policy. The first is its policy of foreign aid; the second is its participation in development institutions like the UNDP and the Organisation for Economic Co-operation and Development ('OECD'), as well as in international financial institutions, like the World Bank and the regional development banks; and the third is its role in deliberations about development issues at the General Assembly, the Economic and Social Council ('ECOSOC'), and international conferences and summits. Beyond that general involvement in the process of international co-operation, according to this restrictive interpretation, it has no other legal (or moral) obligations. Thus, under the restrictive interpretation, a country that provides aid at any level, even far below the 0.7 per cent of GDP target prescribed in the MDGs; that participates in development institutions, even without doing much to promote innovative development policies; and that joins in deliberations on development at the UN, regardless of how it votes, would have no further obligations under the right to development. It has 'co-operated' in development and could argue that the reference to be 'effective' in Article 4 (2) DRD is too vague to require more. This narrow approach does not give sufficient attention to the politically significant pronouncements of high-level conferences and the legally significant interpretations of expert bodies, which suggest a more extensive interpretation.

Such an extensive interpretation of the legal obligation to co-operate in development would add substance to the vague obligation to co-operate through the incorporation by reference of the most significant documents relating to the specifics of co-operation. According to this interpretation, the content of the obligation to co-operate would be provided by such documents as the General Comments drafted by the human rights treaty bodies, the declarations and programmes of action of the international conferences and summits, resolutions that purport to contribute to the progressive development of international law, and opinions expressed by leading experts and institutions. The declarations and programmes of action of international conferences and summits are not directly linked to a binding legal instrument in the way the General Comments are. Such declarations, and the General Assembly resolutions that endorse them, do nevertheless provide a considerable degree of guidance as to the specifics of the general legal obligation of international co-operation contained in the *Charter of the United Nations* and the ICESCR. Thus, a broader interpretation extends the responsibility of countries and other entities – including non-state actors – to the creation, in the words of Article 3(1) DRD, 'of national and international conditions favourable to the realization of the right to development' and, therefore, to structural transformation of the international political economy. The commitment of the international community to meeting the MDGs and the recent assessments of the human rights dimensions of the MDGs may be invoked in this context, notwithstanding the low probability that all the MDG targets will be reached by 2015.

The process of globalisation and the trend favouring free markets and free trade is rightfully seen by many as exacerbating the disparities and injustices of unequal development and weakening human rights protections. It is equally true that free movement of ideas, peoples, goods, images, technology, capital and labour offers enormous opportunities for the equitable growth and poverty alleviation that are essential to the realisation of the right to development. The predatory trends and negative impact of globalisation should be seen as the result of the failure of states to create 'national and international conditions favourable to the realization of the right to development' and 'to formulate appropriate national development policies', as required by Article 2(3) DRD. Thus, the right to development perspective offers a normative toolkit for assessing processes of globalisation through the lenses and principles of international distributive justice.

This duty, expressed in the non-binding DRD, is reinforced by the legally binding obligation on member states of the United Nations to act jointly and separately for the realisation of human rights and for states parties to the ICESCR to contribute through international co-operation to the realisation of economic, social and cultural rights, including through foreign aid, and to reflect this concern in their voice and vote in international financial institutions and development agencies. Although the same obligation of international co-operation is not present in the ICCPR, the preambles of both Covenants refer to the need to create 'conditions ... whereby everyone may enjoy his civil and political rights, as well as his economic, social and cultural rights' and the *Universal Declaration of Human Rights*[15] refers, in Article 28, to the right to a social and international order in which all rights can be fully realised. These universally accepted standards reinforce the idea of an obligation to co-operate internationally for the realisation of the right to development. The reference in Article 3(1) DRD to responsibility of states for the creation of 'international conditions favourable to the realization of the right to development' applies primarily to affluent countries, which have 'the duty to take steps, individually and collectively, to formulate international development policies with a view to facilitating the full realization of the right to development'. Accordingly, donor countries – acting through their development programmes or through the international institutions to which they belong – have a duty to facilitate the efforts of developing countries to advance the right to development by relaxing constraints on productive resources, and by supporting institutional development.

Another relevant interpretative document is the *Maastricht Guidelines*,[16] which include the following regarding the obligations of states parties to the ICESCR:

> The obligations of States to protect economic, social, and cultural rights extend also to their participation in international organizations, where they act collectively. It is particularly important for States to use their influence to ensure that violations do not result from the programmes and policies of the organizations of which they are members.[17]

The ICESCR, accordingly, requires that states act in international agencies and lending institutions, as well as during Security Council consideration of sanctions, in a way that does not cause economic, social or cultural rights to suffer in any other country. It is, therefore, possible to speak of 'obligations', even of legal obligations, falling on those states that have ratified the ICESCR. These obligations do not fall only on developed countries but also apply to developing countries, which have a legal obligation to pursue development policies based on meaningful participation, equitable sharing, and full realisation of human rights, all of which are explicitly contained in the DRD. Thus the DRD articulates in terms acceptable to virtually every country a set of obligations that derive their legal force from existing treaty obligations. Whether this particular articulation of duties, including international co-operation aimed at

---

[15] GA Res 217A (III), UN Doc A/810, 71 (1948).
[16] 'Maastricht Guidelines on Violations of Economic, Social and Cultural Rights' (1998) 20 *Human Rights Quarterly* 691 ('*Maastricht Guidelines*'). The *Maastricht Guidelines* were adopted by a group of more than thirty experts. They are not legally binding.
[17] *Maastricht Guidelines* Guideline 19.

176   *Research handbook on international human rights law*

the full realisation of the DRD, will acquire a legally binding character through a new treaty or the emergence of a customary norm is uncertain.

In 2004, the UN Commission on Human Rights established a high-level task force on the implementation of the right to development, within the framework of the Working Group on the Right to Development (which had been established in 1998), and gave it a mandate at its first session to consider 'obstacles and challenges to the implementation of the MDGs in relation to the right to development' and to identify specifically social impact assessments and best practices in the implementation of the right to development.[18] At its second session, in 2005, the mandate of the task force was 'to consider Millennium Development Goal 8, on global partnership for development, and to suggest criteria for its periodic evaluation with the aim of improving the effectiveness of global partnerships with regard to the realization of the right to development'. The task force completed this mandate at its November 2005 session and its report[19] was approved by the Working Group by consensus in February 2006.[20] The task force's mandate has focused since then on applying the 15 criteria it developed to selected partnerships 'with a view to operationalizing and progressively developing these criteria, and thus contributing to mainstreaming the right to development in the policies and operational activities of relevant actors at the national, regional and international levels, including multilateral financial, trade, and development institutions'.[21]

---

[18]   Commission on Human Rights resolution 2004/7 of 13 April 2004, approved by the Economic and Social Council in its decision 2004/249. See also *Report of the High-Level Task Force on the Implementation of the Right to Development (Geneva, 13–17 December 2004)*, UN Doc E/CN.4/2005/WG.18/2 (24 January 2005) [3]. The first session was extensively analysed by Margot E Salomon, 'Towards a Just Institutional Order: A Commentary on the First Session of the UN Task Force on the Right to Development' (2003) 23 *Netherlands Quarterly of Human Rights* 409.

[19]   *Report of the High-Level Task Force on the Implementation of the Right to Development on Its Second Meeting (Geneva, 14–18 November 2005)*, UN Doc E/CN.4/2005/WG.18/TF/3 (8 December 2005).

[20]   *Report of the Working Group on the Right to Development on Its Seventh Session (Geneva, 9–13 January 2006)*, UN Doc E/CN.4/2006/26 (22 February 2006) [35].

[21]   Ibid [77]. See also OHCHR, *Report of the High-level Task Force on the Implementation of the Right to Development on its First Meeting*, UN Doc E/CN.4/2005/WG.18/2 (24 Jan. 2005); OHCHR, *Report of the High-level Task Force on the Implementation of the Right to Development on its Second Meeting*, UN Doc E/CN.4/2005/WG.18/TF/3 (8 Dec. 2005); OHCHR, *Report of the High-level Task Force on the Implementation of the Right to Development on its Third Meeting*, UN Doc A/HRC/4/WG.2/TF/2 (13 Feb. 2007); OHCHR, *Report of the High-level Task Force on the Implementation of the Right to Development on its Fourth Session*, UN Doc. A/HRC/8/WG.2/TF/2 (31 Jan. 2008); OHCHR, *Report of the High-level Task Force on the Implementation of the Right to Development on its Fifth Session* (Geneva, 1–9 April 2009), UN Doc. A/HRC/12/WG.2/TF/2 (17 June 2009).

*Human rights and development* 177

C *Toward a convention on the right to development?*

The general trend in international human rights law-making has been from study to declaration to convention to optional protocol with a complaint procedure. In the case of the right to development, the path-breaking study by the UN Division of Human Rights of 1979 provided the first stage;[22] the DRD provided the second in 1986. The Non-Aligned Movement ('NAM') countries have pushed for a convention, especially in resolutions adopted at the summit level of the heads of state, for example in Havana in September 2006.[23]

In spite of this strong political support for a convention from NAM, a convention would not create obligations either for institutions essential to the realisation of the right to development, such as the World Trade Organization ('WTO'), the World Bank, the International Monetary Fund ('IMF') or the OECD, or for the equally important private sector. It is unlikely that donor countries would support a convention since there are other vehicles of international law for the cancellation of bilateral debt, or more favourable terms of trade, or enhanced aid. It is difficult to conceive of an international convention on the right to development containing the full range of obligations implied by this right; a comprehensive convention seems unlikely and would have to be quite unwieldy. Existing negotiating frameworks, such as those in the OECD, the WTO, the international financial institutions, the International Labour Organization ('ILO'), the UN Conference on Trade and Development ('UNCTAD') and others are more likely to appeal to the broad range of states involved than a new politically motivated convention.

However, the Human Rights Council has agreed to have the Working Group use the RTD criteria being developed by the high-level taskforce to elaborate 'a comprehensive and coherent set of standards for the implementation of the right to development', which could take the form of 'guidelines on the implementation of the right to development, and evolve into a basis for consideration of an international legal standard of a binding nature, through a collaborative process of engagement.'[24] In addition, legal scholars have examined the pros and cons

---

[22] Secretary-General, *The International Dimensions of the Right to Development as a Human Right in Relation with other Human Rights based on International Cooperation, including the Right to Peace taking into account the Fundamental Human Needs*, UN Doc E/CN.4/1334 (2 January 1979).

[23] *Final Document, 14th Summit Conference of Heads of State or Government of the Non-Aligned Movement, Havana, Cuba, 11–16 September 2006*, NAM Doc NAM 2006/Doc.1/Rev.3, (16 September 2006) [235.10]. Reaffirmed by XV Summit of Heads of State and Government of the Non-Aligned Movement, Sharm el Sheikh, Egypt, 11–16 July 2009, *Final Document*, NAM2009/FD/Doc. 1, 16 July 2009 [421.13].

[24] *The Right to Development*, HRC res 9/4, 9th session, UN Doc A/HRC/RES/9/3, at [2(c)] and [2(d)]. Reiterated in HRC res 12/23, 12th session, UN Doc A/HRC/RES/12/23 (2 October 2009).

178   *Research handbook on international human rights law*

of a convention and proposed numerous alternative approaches to using binding obligations under international law to advance the right to development.[25]

## 3   Human rights law as applied to aid and poverty reduction strategies
The second dimension of the intersection of human rights and development in international law is the idea of 'human rights in development' – or the 'human rights-based approach to development', by which is meant the application of legal obligations and other commitments concerning human rights that states have accepted to their development policies and practices. The recent trend of governments and international institutions to develop, clarify and apply their own definitions and policies in this area represents a new and promising trend in development discourse, leading in some cases to new models for development interventions and programmes by national and international actors. As discussed in the previous section, the right to development requires better conditions for development and systematic integration of human rights into development policy at the national and international levels. This section deals with a less burdensome and therefore less controversial interpretation of the place and function of human rights in development, namely, development policies and practices that selectively imbed a human rights dimension. The most salient of these are: (a) adaptation of national policies and practices in co-operation with the UN system and bilateral donors, (b) poverty reduction strategies, and (c) the MDGs.

### A   Obligations of states regarding their national policies and practices in co-operation with the UN system and bilateral donors
The primary responsibility for the realisation of human rights and development rests with the state, although other states and civil society are also instrumental in achieving national goals in relation to both. The state is legally bound by its international human rights obligations and politically bound by its commitment to internationally agreed development goals ('IADGs'), including the MDGs, adopted at the global summits and conferences. The cumulative effect is that the state has an obligation to impose duties in the context of development on its agents to respect human rights in the development process, to protect people from violations of these rights by third parties (non-state actors, including business enterprises), and to take steps to promote, facilitate and provide for human rights to the limits of its capacity, including by drawing on external support and assistance.

---

[25]   Stephen P Marks (ed) *Implementing the Right to Development: The Role of International Law* (Friedrich Ebert Stiftung and Harvard School of Public Health Program on Human Rights in Development, Geneva, Switzerland, 2008).

Therefore, the essence of human rights in development is to draw on the combined IADGs and human rights treaty obligations and to devise coherent and integrated policies and practices. Perhaps the most frequently used term to link human rights and development policy has been the so-called 'rights-based' approach to development, affirming that development should be pursued in a 'human rights way' or that human rights must 'be integrated into sustainable human development'. The 'rights way to development' is the shorthand expression for 'the human rights approach to development assistance', as articulated in the mid-1990s by André Frankovits of the Human Rights Council of Australia.[26] The essential definition of this approach is:

> [T]hat a body of international human rights law is the only agreed international framework which offers a coherent body of principles and practical meaning for development cooperation, [which] provides a comprehensive guide for appropriate official development assistance, for the manner in which it should be delivered, for the priorities that it should address, for the obligations of both donor and recipient governments and for the way that official development assistance is evaluated.[27]

The Office of the High Commissioner for Human Rights uses the expression 'rights-based approach to development', which it defines as the integration of 'the norms, standards and principles of the international human rights system into the plans, policies and processes of development'.[28] Such an approach incorporates into development the express linkage to rights, accountability, empowerment, participation, non-discrimination and attention to vulnerable groups.[29]

In his report on *Strengthening of the United Nations: An Agenda for Further Change*, the UN Secretary-General called human rights 'a bedrock requirement for the realization of the Charter's vision of a just and peaceful world'[30] and listed, among 36 actions, 'Action 2' on joint UN efforts at the country level, which formed the basis for the Action 2 Plan of Action, adopted

---

[26] The Human Rights Council of Australia ('HRCA'), *The Rights Way to Development: A Human Rights Approach to Development Assistance* (HRCA, Sydney, 1995). The same organisation has produced a manual on the subject. See André Frankovits and Patrick Earle, *The Rights Way to Development: Manual For a Human Rights Approach to Development Assistance* (HRCA, Sydney, Australia).
[27] Ibid.
[28] Office of the High Commissioner for Human Rights ('OHCHR'), *Human Rights in Development* (2002) OCHCHR, http://www.unhchr.ch/development/approaches-04.html at 14 January 2009.
[29] Ibid.
[30] See Kofi Annan, *Strengthening of the United Nations: An Agenda for Further Change*, UN Doc A/57/387 (9 September 2002) [45].

by 21 heads of UN departments and agencies.[31] The Action 2 interagency Task Force, consisting of the Office of the High Commissioner for Human Rights ('OHCHR'), UNDP, the UN Population Fund ('UNFPA'), the UN Children's Fund ('UNICEF') and the UN Development Fund for Women ('UNIFEM'), has pursued the clarification and training of staff in this approach, including an Action 2 Global Programme and a common learning package.[32] The Programme became fully operational in 2006.[33] It is 'a global programme designed to strengthen the capacity of UN country teams to support the efforts of Member States, at their request, in strengthening their national human rights promotion and protection systems'.[34] This programme integrates human rights throughout humanitarian, development and peace-keeping work in the UN system.

In 2003 representatives from across the UN system met in Stamford, Connecticut, USA, and defined a *UN Common Understanding on a Human Rights Based Approach*.[35] This document has become a standard reference for translating normative human rights commitments of Member States into development co-operation policies and projects of UN agencies, funds and programmes. The core definitions of the Common Understanding of a human rights based approach to development co-operation and development programming by UN agencies are:

1. All programmes of development cooperation, policies and technical assistance should further the realization of human rights as laid down in the Universal Declaration of Human Rights and other international human rights instruments.
2. Human rights standards contained in, and principles derived from, the Universal Declaration of Human Rights and other international human rights instruments guide all development cooperation and programming in all sectors and in all phases of the programming process.

---

[31] See http://www.un.org/events/action2/ at 14 January 2009.

[32] In 2007, the Working Group on Training, in collaboration with the UN System Staff College, issued the *UN Common Learning Package on Human Rights-Based Approach* (2007) UNDG, http://www.undg.org/index.cfm?P=531 at 14 January 2009.

[33] See United Nations, *Action 2 Global Programme 2006 Annual Report* (United Nations, New York, 2007).

[34] *Action 2: Summary of Action* (2002) UN, http://www.un.org/events/action2/summary.html at 14 December 2009.

[35] *The Human Rights Based Approach to Development Cooperation: Towards a Common Understanding Among UN Agencies*, Inter-Agency Workshop on a Human Rights Based Approach in the Context of UN Reform, Stamford, 5–7 May 2003. See http://www.unescobkk.org/fileadmin/user_upload/appeal/human_rights/UN_Common_understanding_RBA.pdf at 14 January 2009.

3. Development cooperation contributes to the development of the capacities of 'duty-bearers' to meet their obligations and/or of 'rights-holders' to claim their rights.[36]

UNICEF contributed to the translation of the ideas of rights-based development into development practice through its *Human Rights-Based Approach to Programming* ('HRBAP').[37] UNDP, for its part, adopted a policy of integrating human rights with human development in January 1998.[38] According to the Director of the Bureau for Development Policy, '[s]ince 1998, human rights have emerged as a key area of the organisation's development activities, something reflected in the decisions of the UNDP Executive Board when adopting the UNDP Strategic Plan'.[39] Since adopting that policy, it has devoted an issue of its *Human Development Report* to human rights,[40] trained staff at headquarters and in the field, created the Human Rights Strengthening Programme ('HURIST') to fund activities based on the 1998 policy,[41] and issued 'practice notes' on UNDP's commitment to the integration of human rights with human development,[42] and it currently supports human rights initiatives in more than 100 countries. Significantly, the *Practice Note on Human Rights in UNDP* calls human rights the business of every staff member, and guides the work of country teams who are expected to develop 'a comprehensive and coherent process towards genuine human rights-based programme development in all policies and programmes supported and implemented by UNDP'.[43]

---

[36] Ibid.

[37] See, for example, Urban Jonsson, *Human Rights Approach to Development Programming* (2003) UNICEF/FAO, http://www.fao.org/righttofood/KC/downloads/vl/en/details/212953.htm at 14 January 2009 (manuscript revised 9 October 2004).

[38] See UNDP, *Integrating human rights with sustainable human development* (1998) UNDP, http://www.undp.org/governance/docs/HR_Pub_policy5.htm at 14 January 2009.

[39] Olav Kjorven in UNDP, *Human Rights for Development News Brief*, vol. 1, January 2009 (Democratic Governance Group, Bureau for Development Policy, United Nations Development Programme, New York, 2009), p. 2. Available at http://www.undp.org/governance/.

[40] UNDP, *Human Development Report 2000* (Oxford University Press, New York, 2000).

[41] See http://www.undp.org/governance/programmes/hurist.htm at 14 January 2009.

[42] UNDP, *Practice Note on Poverty Reduction and Human Rights* (2003) UNDP, http://www.undp.org/governance/sl-justice.htm at 14 January 2009; *Practice Note on Human Rights in UNDP* (2005) UNDP, http://www.undp.org/governance/sl-justice.htm at 14 January 2009.

[43] UNDP, above n 42 (2005).

Parallel to multilateral institutions building on government human rights obligations to implement human rights in development, bilateral development agencies, responding to parliamentary statutory authority, have integrated human rights features in their development partnerships. International assistance and co-operation, primarily through official development assistance ('ODA'), is a significant source for financing development, reaching $107.1 billion in 2005 but declining to $103.7 billion in 2007, due mainly to the decline in debt relief grants, and increasing to $119.8 billion in 2008.[44] In 2005 developed countries committed to increasing aid to $130 billion in 2010 although it is doubtful they will meet these commitments.[45] Since 1990, the goal for developed countries is to devote 0.7 per cent of their gross national income ('GNI' – the value of all income earned by residents of an economy whether it is earned within or outside of the national borders) to ODA. However, only Denmark, Luxembourg, the Netherlands, Norway and Sweden had reached or exceeded this target by 2007, the combined figure for the developed countries as a group in 2007 being 0.28 per cent.[46]

The donor countries have been embracing human rights-based approaches to ODA for several decades. A recent study by the OECD on the approaches of its member states drew the lesson that 'human rights offer a coherent normative framework which can guide development assistance'.[47] The advantages identified by OECD relate to adaptability to different political and cultural environments, the potential for operationalising human rights principles, relevance to good governance and meaningful participation, poverty reduction and aid effectiveness.[48] Extensive analysis and elaborate policy

---

[44] United Nations, *The Millennium Development Goals Report 2008* (UN, New York, 2008) 44; United Nations, *The Millennium Development Goals Report 2009* (UN, New York, 2009) 48.

[45] World Bank, *Global Monitoring Report 2007: Millennium Development Goals: Confronting the Challenges of Gender Equality and Fragile States* (The World Bank, Washington, DC, 2007) 15.

[46] Id. at 45. See also UNDP, *Human Development Report 2007/2008* (2008) UNDP, http://hdr.undp.org/en/reports/global/hdr2007-2008/ at 14 January 2009, 289–93, Table 17 (OECD-DAC country expenditures on aid), Table 18 (Flows of aid, private capital and debt).

[47] Organisation for Economic Co-operation and Development ('OECD'), *Integrating Human Rights into Development: Donor Approaches, Experiences and Challenges* (OECD, Paris, 2006) 58.

[48] Ibid 58–68. See also Andrew Frankovits and Patrick Earle, *Report of the Donor Workshop: Working Together: The Human Rights-based Approach to Development Cooperation* (2000) CIDA, http://www.acdi-cida.gc.ca/CIDAWEB/acdi-cida.nsf/En/REN-218124433-NUP at 14 January 2009; Laure-Hélène Piron and Tammie O'Neil, *Integrating Human Rights into Development: A synthesis of donor approaches and experiences* (2005) ODI, http://www.odi.org.uk/rights/Publications/humanrights_into_development.pdf at 14 January 2009.

papers have been drawn up by the major European and Canadian funding agencies, incorporating a human rights approach, most notably by the UK Department for International Development and the Swedish International Development Agency.[49] The United States, for its part, announced at the International Conference on the Financing for Development in Monterrey, Mexico, in March 2002, the doubling of ODA by $5 billion by the 2006 financial year, through a newly created Millennium Challenge Account ('MCA'). Human rights (defined as 'civil liberties' and 'political freedoms') are among the criteria assessed before funding is approved.[50] However, the MCA has failed to meet the goals set,[51] and has been criticised for pushing a neoliberal agenda[52] and devoting little attention to human rights.[53]

To complete the picture of human rights based approaches to development, mention must also be made of the policies and practices of non-governmental organisations. Several major development NGOs, such as Oxfam, CARE, Save the Children and Médecins Sans Frontières ('MSF'), have similarly embraced a human rights framework for their operations.[54] The growing trend among scholars, development NGOs and international institutions to use the human rights based approach to development both integrates concepts that already had currency in development and adds a dimension with which development practitioners were less familiar. The familiar components of this approach include accountability and transparency in the context of good governance, and equity and pro-poor policies in the definition of objectives. The less familiar component is the explicit reference to government obligations deriving from international human rights law and procedures.

---

[49] See below n 76.

[50] See http://www.mcc.gov/mcc/selection/indicators/index.shtml at 19 October 2009. It should be noted that the Obama Administration added the State Department Human Rights reports as supplemental information and requested a 63% increase in funding for FY2010.

[51] The President proposed only $3 billion for the MCA in 2006 and 2007 and Congress allocated only $2 billion in 2007 and the MCA has greatly underspent the allocation. See W Dugger, 'US Agency's Slow Pace Endangers Foreign Aid', *New York Times* (New York), 12 December 2007.

[52] Susanne Soederberg, 'American empire and "excluded states": the Millennium Challenge Account and the shift to pre-emptive development' (2004) 25 *Third World Quarterly* 279.

[53] See Stephen Marks, 'The Human Right to Development: Between Rhetoric and Reality' (2004) 17 *Harvard Human Rights Journal* 156.

[54] On this subject, see Paul J Nelson and Ellen Dorsay, 'At the Nexus of Human Rights and Development: New Methods and Strategies of Global NGOs' (2003) 31 *World Development* 2013; Hans-Otto Sano, 'Development and Human Rights: The Necessary, but Partial Integration of Human Rights and Human Development' (2000) 22 *Human Rights Quarterly* 734.

From the standpoint of human rights, ODA presents three controversial issues: the donor's control over the character of the aid, the legitimacy of conditionality, and the value of directing aid towards human rights purposes. The sensitivity of these issues is reflected in the 2005 Paris Declaration on Aid Effectiveness.[55] The Paris Declaration seeks to reform the delivery of aid by scaling up and 'to increase the impact of aid . . . in reducing poverty and inequality, increasing growth, building capacity and accelerating the achievement of the MDGs'.[56] It outlines the five overarching principles of ownership, alignment, harmonisation, managing for development results and mutual accountability, with agreed indicators, targets, timetables and processes to monitor the implementation up to 2010. Each of these has been examined critically from the human rights perspective in a paper commissioned from the Overseas Development Institute by the OECD and arguing for using human rights to broaden the scope and content of the Paris Declaration's 56 commitments and indicators on mutual accountability.[57] Although the focus on aid delivery mechanisms in the Paris Declaration has merit, it reflects a technocratic approach to development that neglects the human rights commitments both of donors and recipients of aid and a reluctance on the part of donors to be seen as imposing human rights conditions on aid, which is often greatly resented by the recipients.

The deficiencies of the Paris Declaration from the human rights perspective were further elucidated at a workshop on *Development Effectiveness in Practice* convened in April 2007 by the government of Ireland,[58] the main message of which was that gender equality, human rights and environmental sustainability should be 'fundamental cornerstones for achieving good development results' and used in the implementation of the Paris Declaration. This effort did result in a reference to the need to address 'in a more systematic and coherent way' those three issues in the Accra Agenda for Action, adopted by the Third High Level Forum on Aid Effectiveness on 4 September 2008, but this outcome and the follow-up are very limited.[59]

---

[55] (2005) OECD, http://www.oecd.org/dataoecd/11/41/34428351.pdf at 14 January 2009 (*'Paris Declaration'*). The *Paris Declaration* was adopted on 2 March 2005 by Ministers or senior officials of some 85 developed and developing countries and heads of 20 bilateral and multilateral development agencies.

[56] *Paris Declaration* [2].

[57] Marta Foresti, David Booth and Tammie O'Neil, *Aid effectiveness and human rights: strengthening the implementation of the Paris Declaration* (London: Overseas Development Institute, October 2006).

[58] The workshop, organised jointly by the DAC Networks on Environment and Development, Governance and Gender Equality and the Working Party on Aid Effectiveness, was held in Dublin on 26–27 April 2007. See www.oecd.org/dac/effectiveness/inpractice at 15 January 2009.

[59] Third High Level Forum on Aid Effectiveness, Accra Agenda for Action, available at http://www.oecd.org/dataoecd/58/16/41202012.pdf.

## B Poverty reduction strategies ('PRS')

In 1993, the World Conference on Human Rights declared,

> The existence of widespread extreme poverty inhibits the full and effective enjoyment of human rights; its immediate alleviation and eventual elimination must remain a high priority for the international community.[60]

> [E]xtreme poverty and social exclusion constitute a violation of human dignity and ... urgent steps are necessary to achieve better knowledge of extreme poverty and its causes, including those related to the problem of development, in order to promote the human rights of the poorest, and to put an end to extreme poverty and social exclusion and to promote the enjoyment of the fruits of social progress. It is essential for States to foster participation by the poorest people in the decision-making process by the community in which they live, the promotion of human rights and efforts to combat extreme poverty.[61]

Development is largely concerned with the elimination of mass poverty, which in 2005 affected 2.56 billion people living on less than $2.00 per day (2.096 billion excluding China) according to the World Bank; those living in extreme poverty (less than US$1.25 per day) were estimated at 1.38 billion (1.176 billion excluding China).[62] The slight decline since 1981 is much greater when expressed as a percent of the world population: in 1981, 69.2 per cent of the population of the developing world were living on less than US$2.00 per day (58.6 excluding China), declining to 47.0 per cent (50.3 excluding China) in 2005, while those living on less than US$1.25 per day were 51.8 per cent (39.8 excluding China) in 1981 and only 25.2 (28.2 excluding China) in 2005.[63]

The focus of the World Bank and the IMF has been on the Poverty Reduction Strategy process to reduce the debt of Heavily Indebted Poor Countries ('HIPC') that have submitted Poverty Reduction Strategy Papers ('PRSPs'). Launched in September 1999, PRSPs should be prepared by the government through a *country-driven* process, including broad participation

---

[60] *Vienna Declaration* [14].
[61] *Vienna Declaration* [25].
[62] Shaohua Chen and Martin Ravaillion, *The Developing World is Poorer Than We Thought, But no Less Successful in the Fight Against Poverty*, Washington DC: Development Research Group, World Bank, tables 5 [41]. For a critique of the methods used by the World Bank, see Stephan Klasen, 'Levels and Trends in Absolute Poverty in the World: What we know and what we don't', Courant Research Centre, 'Poverty, Equity and Growth in Developing and Transition Countries: Statistical Methods and Empirical Analysis', Discussion Papers No. 11, Georg-August-Universität Göttingen, August 2009.
[63] Ibid., table 4 [41]. See also World Bank, *2008 World Development Indicators* (World Bank, Washington DC, 2008).

that promotes *country ownership* [and] link the use of debt relief under the enhanced ... HIPC initiative to public actions to reduce poverty'.[64]

How have the institutions responsible for international human rights promotion and protection engaged with the poverty reduction agenda? In a Concept Note, the High Commissioner for Human Rights drew the World Bank's attention to the following:

> In linking a Poverty Reduction Strategy to a universal normative framework and State obligations emanating from the human rights instruments, the goals of the Poverty Reduction Strategy could be sustained with enhanced accountability of the relevant stake-holders. The universal nature of human rights, their mobilization potential and their emphasis on legal obligations to respect, protect and promote human rights, while encouraging national ownership and people's empowerment makes the human rights framework a useful tool to strengthen the accountability and equity dimensions of the Poverty Reduction Strategies.[65]

The issue had already been raised by the Commission on Human Rights, which in 1990 requested its Sub-Commission to consider the relationship between human rights and poverty[66] and the Sub-Commission appointed a Special Rapporteur on human rights and extreme poverty, whose report was published in 1996.[67] The High Commissioner hosted an expert seminar in February 2001 to consider a declaration on human rights and poverty, leading the Commission to request the Sub-Commission to consider 'guiding principles on the implementation of existing human rights norms and standards in the context of the fight against extreme poverty'.[68]

In a related development and in direct response to a request from the Chair of the Committee on Economic, Social and Cultural Rights, the High Commissioner commissioned in 2001 guidelines for the integration of human rights into poverty reduction strategies from professors Paul Hunt, Manfred

---

[64] Jeni Klugman (ed.), *A Sourcebook for Poverty Reduction Strategies*, Washington DC: The World Bank, 2002 [2] (emphasis in original).

[65] United Nations Office of the High Commissioner for Human Rights, *Comments on the Concept Note Joint World Bank and IMF Report on Poverty Reduction Strategy Papers – Progress in Implementation 2005 PRS Review* (2005) World Bank, http://siteresources.worldbank.org/INTPRS1/Resources/PRSP-Review/un_ohchr.pdf at 14 January 2009.

[66] Commission on Human Rights, *Human Rights and Extreme Poverty*, UN Doc E/CN.4/Res/1990/15 (23 February 1990) [5].

[67] Leandro Despouy, *The Realization of Economic, Social and Cultural Rights: Final report on human rights and extreme poverty, submitted by the Special Rapporteur*, UN Doc E/CN.4/Sub.2/1996/13 (28 June 1996).

[68] Commission on Human Rights, *Human Rights and Extreme Poverty*, UN Doc E/CN/4/Res/2001/31 (23 April 2001).

Nowak and Siddiq Osmani. The authors consulted with national officials, civil society and international development agencies, including the World Bank, and produced a 60-page document setting out basic principles of a human rights approach to: (a) formulating a poverty reduction strategy; (b) determining the content of a poverty reduction strategy; and (c) guiding the *monitoring* and *accountability* aspects of poverty reduction strategies, with a special section on accountability.[69]

In 1998 the Commission appointed an Independent Expert on the subject of human rights and extreme poverty[70] and between 1999 and 2008 the three successive Independent Experts have issued ten annual reports[71] and reports of visits to nine different countries: Portugal (October 1998), Bulgaria, Yemen (November 1998), Bolivia (May 2001), Benin (August 2001), the Dominican Republic (December 2002), Yemen (October 2003), Sudan (November 2004), the United States of America (October 2005) and Ecuador (November 2008).[72]

## C Millennium Development Goals

The MDGs define the priorities for the international community and guide much of the technical co-operation and assistance provided by bilateral and multilateral donors.[73] They are a set of eight goals with 18 numerical targets and over 40 quantifiable indicators. The MDGs are:

---

[69] Paul Hunt, Manfred Nowak and Siddiq Osmani, *Draft Guidelines: A Human Rights Approach to Poverty Reduction Strategies* (OHCHR, Geneva, 2002) (emphasis added). See also Paul Hunt, Manfred Nowak and Siddiq Osmani, *Human Rights and Poverty Reduction Strategies – Human Rights and Poverty Reduction – A Conceptual Framework* (OHCHR, Geneva, 2003).

[70] UN Doc E/CN.4/Res/1998/25 (17 April 1998).

[71] See UN Doc E/CN.4/1999/48 (29 January 1999); UN Doc E/CN.4/2000/52 (25 February 2000); UN Doc E/CN.4/2001/54 (16 February 2001); UN Doc E/CN.4/2002/55 (15 March 2002); UN Doc E/CN.4/2003/52 (20 January 2003); UN Doc E/CN.4/2004/43 (29 April 2004); UN Doc E/CN.4/2005/49 (11 February 2005); UN Doc E/CN.4/2006/43 (2 March 2006); UN Doc A/HRC/5/3 (11 June 2007); UN Doc A/HRC/7/15 (28 February 2008); UN Doc A/HRC/11/9 (27 March 2009).

[72] See respectively UN Doc E/CN.4/1999/48 (29 January 1999); UN Doc E/CN.4/2002/55 (15 March 2002); UN Doc E/CN.4/2003/52/Add.1 (16 January 2003); UN Doc E/CN.4/2004/43/Add.1 (8 January 2004); UN Doc E/CN.4/2004/43 (29 April 2004); UN Doc E/CN.4/2006/43/Add.1 (27 March 2006); A/HRC.11.9/Add. 1 (19 May 2009).

[73] The MDGs build on the commitments of the heads of 189 countries, meeting in New York in September 2000, to adopt a United Nations *Millennium Declaration*: see G A Res 55/2, UN GAOR, 55th sess, 8th plen mtg, UN Doc A/Res/55/2 (8 September 2000).

- Eradicate extreme poverty and hunger
- Achieve universal primary education
- Promote gender equality and empower women
- Reduce child mortality
- Improve maternal health
- Combat HIV/AIDS, malaria, and other diseases
- Ensure environmental sustainability
- Develop a global partnership for development.

While economists may be best equipped to define and analyse poverty in terms of market forces, income distribution, utility, budgeting, and access to resources, concepts of good governance, the rule of law and human rights have become widely accepted as part of sustainable human development and poverty reduction, and consequently of the MDGs. The High Commissioner for Human Rights has focused attention on the relationship between MDGs and human rights by disseminating to governments charts on the intersection of human rights and MDGs and has published a fairly exhaustive analysis of how human rights can contribute to MDGs,[74] as have the UNDP[75] and national development agencies.[76]

Philip Alston has characterised the relation between human rights and the MDGs as 'ships passing in the night' and takes the argument for mainstreaming human rights in the MDGs a step further by noting that these goals 'have

---

[74] OHCHR, *Claiming the MDGs: A Human Rights Approach* (United Nations, New York/Geneva, 2008).

[75] UNDP published a primer, *Human Rights and the Millennium Development Goals: Making the Link* (Oslo Governance Centre, Oslo, 2007) as a follow-up to a 2006 UN E-Discussion 'How to Effectively Link MDGs and Human Rights in Development?' (see http://www.undg.org/archive_docs/8073-e-Discussion_MDGs_ and_HR_-_Final_Summary.doc at 15 January 2009) and a Working Group Meeting 'Human Rights and the MDGs – Theoretical and Practical Implications', as well as the deliberations of the Working Group Meeting 'Human Rights and the MDGs – Theoretical and Practical Implications' (see http://www.undg.org/archive_docs/8991-Linking_Human_Rights_and_the_Millennium_Development_Goals__theoretical_and_Practical_Implications.doc at 15 January 2009).

[76] See, for example, the Swedish International Development Agency (http://www.sida.se/English/About-us/Organization/Policy/ at 20 October 2009); the UK's DFID (http://www.dfid.gov.uk/Global-Issues/How-we-fight-Poverty/Human-Rights/Human-rights-and-justice/; http://www.dfid.gov.uk/mdg at 20 October 2009); the US MCA (http://www.mcc.gov/mcc/bm.doc/mcc-report/fy09-criteriaandmethodology.pdf at 20 October 2009); Canada's CIDA (Canadian International Development Agency Sustainable Development Strategy 2007–2009, Action 4, 2006, available at http://www.cida.gc.ca/sds); Denmark's DANIDA (http://www.danidadevforum.um.dk/en/menu/MonitoringAndIndicators/MDGAndPRSPAlignment/ at 20 October 2009).

been endorsed in an endless array of policy documents adopted not only at the international level but in the policies and programmes of the national governments to whom they are of the greatest relevance'.[77] In assessing whether the MDGs involve obligations under customary international law, Alston applies the two tests for a human rights claim having that character: '(i) the right is indispensable to a meaningful notion of human dignity (upon which human rights are based); and (ii) the satisfaction of the right is demonstrably within the reach of the government in question assuming reasonable support from the international community' – and concludes that 'many of the MDGs have the virtue of satisfying these criteria without giving rise to great controversy' and therefore 'that at least some of the MDGs reflect norms of customary international law'.[78]

Alston has reservations regarding MDG 8 (global partnership for development) because, with respect to that goal, 'developed country governments would be expected to resist strongly any suggestion that there are specific obligations enshrined in customary international law'.[79] He points out that the persistent rejection by developed countries of a more general legal duty to provide aid 'and the failure of even the most generous of donors to locate their assistance within the context of such an obligation, would present a major obstacle to any analysis seeking to demonstrate that such an obligation has already become part of customary law'.[80] Further, he considers that '[a]t some point, the reiteration of such commitments [to mobilize resources to ensure that countries committed to the MDGs have the additional resources necessary] . . . will provide a strong argument that some such obligation has crystallized into customary law'.[81]

As described above, the way the UN system, NGOs, and bilateral donors approach aid programmes and policies, the rethinking of poverty reduction strategies, and the realigning of MDGs have accommodated to a considerable degree a human rights approach. The same cannot be said for the international legal regimes of trade and investment.

---

[77] Philip Alston, 'Ships Passing in the Night: The Current State of the Human Rights and Development Debate Seen Through the Lens of the Millennium Development Goals' (2005) 27 *Human Rights Quarterly* 774. This article is based on a paper prepared by Alston as a contribution to the work of the Millennium Project Task Force on Poverty and Economic Development entitled *A Human Rights Perspective on the Millennium Development Goals* (2003) HuRiLINK, http://www.hurilink.org/tools/HRsPerspectives_on_the_MDGs—Alston.pdf at 15 January 2009.
[78] Ibid.
[79] Ibid 775.
[80] Ibid 777.
[81] Ibid 778.

## 4 The tensions between human rights law and the legal regimes of international trade and investment

The third dimension of human rights in development is the most visible feature of globalisation, namely international trade and investment. Regarding the relationship between trade, development and finance, it is widely acknowledged that least developed countries, landlocked developing countries and small, vulnerable countries, particularly in Africa, do not benefit from the global trading system and need greater access to markets in developed countries, as well as to financial assistance to remove supply-side constraints (lack of capacity to produce a surplus of exportable goods of sufficient quantity and reliable quality).

Similarly, in the realm of international law, the tension that characterises the relationship between international human rights law and the legal regimes of trade and investment is based on perceived teleological incompatibility. The essential aims of international trade are to make goods and services available at low prices for consumers of the importing country, to improve trade balances for the exporting country, and to increase the gross national product for the trading partners. The related aims of foreign direct investment are to maximise profits for multinational corporations investing abroad and to provide jobs for workers and revenue and related advantages in the country of investment. These are the interests pursued by those who negotiate legal arrangements for trade and investment. Vast numbers of legal relationships are involved at all levels of these operations, which are often characterised by asymmetrical power relations giving advantages to rich countries and powerful corporations and causing resources to flow to investors and national treasuries (or to private bank accounts where corruption occurs). These ends are best pursued by means of free markets and free trade, which are not the preferred means of human rights and are often perceived to have negative impacts on human rights.

The related issues of trade and investment each pose serious problems and give rise to much controversy regarding the applicable norms of international law.

### A  International trade

At a ministerial meeting of the WTO held in Doha in November 2001, the 'Doha Round' of trade negotiations was launched, the purpose of which was 'to ensure that developing countries, and especially the least developed among them, secure a share in the growth of world trade commensurate with the needs of their economic development'.[82] The negotiations collapsed in July

---

[82]  UN Doc A/C.2/56/7 annex (14 November 2001) [2].

2008 and it was unclear at the time of writing whether they would resume. The WTO has been criticised not only for failing to meet the development needs of less-developed countries, but also for reinforcing the tendency of government representatives from the finance sector to disregard the human rights obligations better known in other departments of government. A considerable body of scholarship has emerged in the last decade on the failure of the international trade system to engage productively with the international human rights regime.[83]

Several human rights concerns regarding the international trade regime are discussed in the chapter by Adam McBeth in this volume.[84] Another is respect for international labour standards. Many argue that the trade liberalisation driven by WTO rules might generate a 'race to the bottom', whereby states compete with each other for foreign investment by lowering regulatory costs, such as labour standards: WTO rules restrict the ability of states to protect their workforces from such transnational regulatory competition. Formally the trade ministers meeting in Singapore in 1996 renewed their 'commitment to the observance of internationally recognized core labour standards' and acknowledged the ILO as the competent body to set and deal with these standards, and affirmed their 'support for its work in promoting them'.[85] However, they added:

---

[83] On WTO and human rights generally, see Padideh Ala'i, 'A Human Rights Critique of the WTO: Some Preliminary Observations' (2002) 33 *George Washington International Law Review* 537; Arthur E Appleton, 'The World Trade Organization: Implications for Human Rights and Democracy' (2000) 29 *Thesaurus Acroasium* 415; Jagdish Bhagwati, 'Trade Linkage and Human Rights' in J Bhagwati and M Hirs (eds) *The Uruguay Round and Beyond: Essays in Honor of Arthur Dunkel* (Springer, Heidelberg/New York, 1998) 241; Sarah H Cleveland, 'Human Rights Sanctions and the World Trade Organization', in F Francioni (ed) *Environment, Human Rights and International Trade* (Hart Publishing, Oxford, 2001) 199; Marjorie Cohn, 'The World Trade Organization: Elevating Property Interests Above Human Rights' (2001) 29 *Georgia Journal of International and Comparative Law* 247; T Flory and N Ligneul, 'Commerce international, droits de l'homme, mondialisation: les droits de l'homme et l'Organisation mondiale du commerce', in *Commerce mondial et protection des droits de l'homme: les droits de l'homme à l'épreuve de la globalisation des échanges économiques* (Bruylant, Brussels, 2001) 179; Hoe Lim, 'Trade and Human Rights: What's At Issue?' (2001) 53 *Journal of World Trade* 275; Ernst-Ulrich Petersmann, 'From "Negative" to "Positive" Integration in the WTO: Time for "Mainstreaming Human Rights" into WTO Law' (2000) 37 *Common Market Law Review* 1363; Asih H Qureshi, 'International Trade and Human Rights from the Perspective of the WTO', in F Weiss, E Denters and P de Waart (eds) *International Economic Law with a Human Face* (Kluwer Law International, The Hague, 1998) 159.

[84] See Chapter 6 at pp. 154–64.

[85] *Singapore Ministerial Declaration*, WTO Doc WT/MIN(96)/DEC (18 December 1996) [4].

> We believe that economic growth and development fostered by increased trade and further trade liberalization contribute to the promotion of these standards. We reject the use of labour standards for protectionist purposes, and agree that the comparative advantage of countries, particularly low-wage developing countries, must in no way be put into question.[86]

Even though the Singapore meeting agreed that the ILO and WTO secretariats would continue to collaborate, as the ILO candidly recognised, 'it is not easy for them to agree, and the question of international enforcement is a minefield'.[87]

Whether protecting workers' rights against the race to the bottom, or any of the myriad other problems resulting from free market and trade liberalisation, the basic argument from the human rights perspective is that governments should respect their human rights obligations when they negotiate membership in and participation in the treaties adopted under the auspices of organisations like the WTO.

The Committee on Economic, Social and Cultural Rights threw down the gauntlet at the time of the Seattle Third Ministerial meeting of the WTO in 1999 when it stated that the process of global governance reform

> must be driven by a concern for the individual and not by purely macroeconomic considerations alone. Human rights norms must shape the process of international economic policy formulation so that the benefits for human development of the evolving international trading regime will be shared equitably by all, in particular the most vulnerable sectors.[88]

Significantly, it sought to convince the ministerial gathering that

> trade liberalization must be understood as a means, not an end. The end which trade liberalization should serve is the objective of human well-being to which the international human rights instruments give legal expression.[89]

It also urged WTO members to ensure that

---

[86] Ibid.

[87] WTO/ILO, *Labour standards: consensus, coherence and controversy* (2008) WTO, http://www.wto.org/English/thewto_e/whatis_e/tif_e/bey5_e.htm at 15 January 2009.

[88] CESCR, *Statement of the UN Committee on Economic, Social and Cultural Rights to the Third Ministerial Conference of the World Trade Organization (Seattle, 30 November to 3 December 1999)*, UN Doc. E/C.12/1999/9 (26 November 1999) [5].

[89] Ibid [6].

their international human rights obligations are considered as a matter of priority in their negotiations which will be an important testing ground for the commitment of States to the full range of their international obligations'.[90]

This claim was echoed in a resolution by the Sub-Commission requesting 'all Governments and economic policy forums to take international human rights obligations and principles fully into account in international economic policy formulation'.[91]

The Secretary-General expressed the essence of the link between trade and human rights in the following terms:

> There is an unavoidable link between the international trading regime and the enjoyment of human rights. Economic growth through free trade can increase the resources available for the realization of human rights. However, economic growth does not automatically lead to greater promotion and protection of human rights. From a human rights perspective, questions are raised: does economic growth entail more equitable distribution of income, more and better jobs, rising wages, more gender equality and greater inclusiveness? From a human rights perspective, the challenge posed is how to channel economic growth equitably to ensure the implementation of the right to development and fair and equal promotion of human well-being.[92]

### B   Foreign direct investment

In 2006, global flows of foreign direct investment ('FDI') reached a new all-time peak, with FDI inflows to developed countries more than double the total amount of inflows from developed to developing countries.[93] The total number of transnational corporations ('TNCs') is estimated by UNCTAD as representing 78,000 parent companies with over 780,000 foreign affiliates. This activity represents 10 per cent of global GDP and one-third of world exports.[94]

These commercial non-state actors have been the object of efforts to establish guidelines for decades, beginning with the OECD *Guidelines for Multinational Enterprises* of 1976 and the ILO *Tripartite Declaration of*

---

[90]   Ibid [7].

[91]   Sub-Commission on the Prevention of Discrimination and Protection of Minorities, *Trade Liberalisation and Its Impact on Human Rights*, UN Doc E/CN.4/Sub.2/RES/1999/9 (26 August 1999).

[92]   Kofi Annan, *Globalization and its impact on the full enjoyment of all human rights, Preliminary report of the Secretary-General*, UN Doc A/55/342 (31 August 2000) [13].

[93]   Ban Ki-Moon, *Annual ministerial review: implementing the internationally agreed goals and commitments in regard to sustainable development*, UN Doc E/2008/12 (21 April 2008) [62].

[94]   Ibid xvi.

*Principles concerning Multinational Enterprises and Social Policy Reform* of 1977. Other milestones in introducing human rights considerations into the practices of TNCs include the Global Compact, a voluntary and self-regulatory mechanism, launched by UN Secretary-General Kofi Annan in 2000, by which the corporations commit to nine core human rights, labour rights and environmental principles; and the Norms on the responsibilities of transnational corporations and other business enterprises with regard to human rights,[95] which were adopted by the Sub-Commission in 2003.[96]

In 2005, the Commission created the position of Special Representative on the issue of human rights and transnational corporations and other business enterprises,[97] to which John Ruggie was appointed. His report of 2008 outlines the three core principles of the state's duty to protect, the corporate responsibility to respect, and the need for more effective access to remedies.[98] A more detailed discussion of the relationship between human rights and multinational corporations is provided in the chapter by Adam McBeth in this volume.[99] The application of international law to relations between business and human rights in the context of globalisation is only partially covered by the work of the Special Representative. The field is evolving through lawsuits against corporations, revision of company policies incorporating human rights, proxy resolutions at meetings of shareholders, consideration of new standards by international organisations, and other ways of harmonising the international law of human rights with that of international business transactions.[100]

## 5   Conclusion

The relationship between human rights and development is relatively straightforward at the theoretical level since both deal with advancing human well-being, with the first focusing on normative constraints on power relations to ensure dignity and the elimination of repressive and oppressive practices,

---

[95] UN Doc E/CN.4/Sub.2/2003/12/Rev.2 (26 August 2003).
[96] However, the Commission decided that the Norms had 'no legal standing, and that the Sub-Commission should not perform any monitoring function'. Commission on Human Rights Decision 2004/16 (20 April 2004).
[97] Human rights and transnational corporations and other business enterprises, Commission on Human Rights Resolution 2005/59, adopted on 20 April 2005. The decision to create the position was endorsed by the Economic and Social Council in its decision 2006/273, adopted on 25 July 2005.
[98] *Protect, Respect and Remedy: A Framework for Business and Human Rights*, UN Doc A/HRC/8/5, 7 April 2008.
[99] See Chapter 6.
[100] The Business & Human Rights Resource Centre provides access to a vast amount of information and analysis on all aspects of the subject. See http://www.business-humanrights.org/Home.

while the latter focuses on the material conditions and distributional arrangements that allow people to benefit from economic processes. The difficulty comes with the current state of international law governing this relationship. This chapter has outlined three dimensions of the international law of human rights and development, each of which provides a different approach with differing degrees of political acceptability.

The law governing the right to development, as we have seen, is fraught with political posturing but provides the most systematic legal definition of human rights in development by making development itself a human right and governments – of both developed and developing countries – the bearers of obligations to enhance prospects for equitable development while fully integrating human rights into the process.

The law relating to development assistance and poverty reduction strategies is far less controversial, insofar as most governments and bilateral and multilateral development agencies have acknowledged the value of introducing human rights into the related strategies and programmes and have translated this awareness into specific modes of doing development in a human rights way.

The field of international trade and investment offers a stark contrast to the general consensus on human rights in development due to the fundamental divergence in objectives and purposes. Indeed, the law governing trade and investment has evolved over the centuries to increase the comparative economic advantages of transactions by powerful economic interests. Efforts to draw the attention of governments seeking those advantages to constraints based on human rights obligations are met with reactions ranging from benign neglect to open hostility.

Each of these three dimensions of the international law of human rights and development will evolve with the changes in the international political economy and is likely to be transformed in the coming decades by new market forces, especially in the energy sector, and by the emerging economic powers of India, Brazil, and above all China, but also by responses to the financial crisis and growing disparities and inequalities, as well as by the wave of rising expectations generated by the refining and clarifying of human welfare through the law and practice of human rights.

# 8. Gender and international human rights law: the intersectionality agenda
*Anastasia Vakulenko**

## 1 Introduction

The Fourth World Conference on Women, held in Beijing in 1995, was a true turning point for feminism. It was then that the concerted feminist effort to challenge the historic male bias of international human rights law finally led to formal recognition, giving birth to the global human rights strategy of gender mainstreaming. The importance of this strategy, which essentially means incorporating a gender perspective into all human rights action,[1] was subsequently restated in numerous UN resolutions,[2] as well as in the work of the UN General Assembly and Security Council.[3] At least nominally, gender was accepted by the mainstream.

Productive feminist engagement with international human rights law did not stop there, however. Since then, feminism has consistently targeted the very category of gender as it provides the basis for gender mainstreaming policies. It has done so by bringing the idea of *intersectionality* to the fore of its engagement with international human rights discourse. Intersectionality is about exploring how gender interacts with 'multiple social forces, such as

---

\* The author thanks the anonymous reviewer for her helpful comments and the editors for their wonderful editorial support.

[1] The United Nations ('UN') Economic and Social Council ('ECOSOC') defines gender mainstreaming as 'the process of assessing the implications for women and men of any planned action, including legislation, policies and programmes, in all areas and at all levels, and as a strategy for making women's as well as men's concerns and experiences an integral dimension of the design, implementation, monitoring and evaluation of policies and programmes in all political, economic and social spheres so that women and men benefit equally and inequality is not perpetuated. The ultimate goal is to achieve gender equality.' See *Report of the Economic and Social Council for the year 1997*, UN GAOR Official Records, 52nd Session Supplementary No 3, UN Doc A/52/3/Rev.1 (1999) Ch IV, [4].

[2] The most recent is *Mainstreaming a gender perspective into all policies and programmes in the United Nations system*, UN Doc E/Res/2006/36 (27 July 2006).

[3] For more information, see the website of the UN Commission on the Status of Women: http://www.un.org/womenwatch/daw/csw/ at 9 December 2008.

race, class ... age, sexuality, and culture'.[4] It means that our experiences of gender are shaped by all those things, thus complicating simplistic, singular understandings of the nature of women's disadvantage.

Indeed, it is now impossible to speak of gender and international human rights law without taking notice of the intersectionality agenda. What is more, intersectionality is one area in which feminist theory has had a remarkable influence over feminist activism and practice, refuting the criticism, often levelled at feminism, of retreating into theorising instead of making a difference in the real world.

This chapter explores the ascendancy of intersectionality in both feminism and international human rights law, assessing successes as well as stalemates in this process. It also considers the role that internal feminist critique might play in moving intersectionality, both a theoretical concept and an international human rights agenda, beyond its present limitations.

## 2 How intersectionality evolved

Within the last couple of decades, intersectionality has truly pervaded feminist theory and activism. It has even been asserted that 'intersectionality is the most important theoretical contribution that women's studies, in conjunction with related fields, has made so far'.[5] It has permeated the international human rights arena. How has this come to be?

The idea of intersectionality is both complex and simple. The academic definition is 'signifying the complex, irreducible, varied, and variable effects which ensue when multiple axes of differentiation – economic, political, cultural, psychic, subjective and experiential – intersect in historically specific contexts'.[6] Essentially, this means that it is impossible to experience 'pure' gender or gender discrimination. Rather, one's experience as a woman is always formed in the context of one's broader belonging in the world.

This seemingly obvious fact had nonetheless for a long time proved elusive for mainstream, white middle-class feminism – as captured by the 19th century political locution 'Ain't I a Woman?' This famous phrase is attributed to Sojourner Truth, an enslaved, illiterate black woman who campaigned for both the abolition of slavery and women's rights. In her famous speech at the 1851 Women's Rights Convention in Akron, Ohio, she challenged dominant white, upper-class constructions of womanhood prevalent at that time: '[t]hat man over there says that women need to be helped into carriages, and lifted

---

[4] M Deckha, 'Is Culture Taboo? Feminism, Intersectionality, and Culture Talk in Law' (2004) 16 *Canadian Journal of Women and the Law* 14, 16.
[5] L McCall, 'The Complexity of Intersectionality' (2005) 30 *Signs* 1771, 1771.
[6] A Brah and A Phoenix, 'Ain't I a Woman? Revisiting Intersectionality' (2004) 5 *Journal of International Women's Studies* 75, 76.

over ditches, and to have the best place everywhere. Nobody helps me any best place. And ain't I a woman?'[7] As Avtar Brah and Ann Phoenix observe, this 'deconstructs every single major truth-claim about gender in a patriarchal slave social formation',[8] and as such mirrors black feminist voices more than a century later.[9]

Although Sojourner Truth's rhetoric is a powerful antecedent of intersectionality feminism, the concept of intersectionality as we know it today was more closely mirrored in feminist discourse in the 1970s and was gradually accepted by mainstream feminism during the 1980s and 1990s. One of the first to pioneer the study of intersectionality was a black lesbian feminist organisation from Boston, the Combahee River Collective. In 1977, they issued a statement in which they affirmed their commitment to 'struggling against racial, sexual, heterosexual and class oppression' and 'the development of integrated analysis and practice based upon the fact that the major systems of oppression are interlocking'.[10] In the early 1980s, the writings of Adrienne Rich[11] and Marilyn Frye[12] exposed the heteronormative foundations of mainstream feminist theory. More generally, Denise Riley famously wrote about the impossibility of being exhausted by the category 'woman'.[13]

In its earlier stages, intersectionality was associated with mostly US black and Latina feminist critiques of mainstream feminist theory and law which were seen as imposing the essentialist standard of the white (middle-class, heterosexual) woman.[14] In Britain, the project of 'black British feminism'

---

[7] No formal record of Sojourner Truth's speech exists. This quotation is from the version recounted by the president of the Convention, Frances Gage, in 1863, as cited in ibid 77.

[8] Ibid 77.

[9] On Sojourner Truth, see also D Haraway, *'Ecce Homo*, Ain't (Ar'n't) I a Woman, and Inappropriate/d Others: The Human in a Post-Humanist Landscape' in J Butler and J W Scott (eds) *Feminists Theorize the Political* (Routledge, New York, 1992) 86.

[10] Combahee River Collective, 'A Black Feminist Statement' in L Nicholson (ed) *The Second Wave: A Reader in Feminist Theory* (Routledge, New York, 1997).

[11] A Rich, 'Compulsory Heterosexuality and Lesbian Existence' (1980) 5 *Signs* 631.

[12] M Frye, *The Politics of Reality: Essays in Feminist Theory* (The Crossing Press, Trumansburg, 1983).

[13] D Riley, *'Am I That Name?' Feminism and the Category of Women in History* (University of Minnesota Press, Minneapolis, 1988).

[14] G Anzaldúa, *La Frontera/Borderlands: The New Mestiza* (Aunt Lute Books, San Francisco, 1987); P H Collins, *Fighting Words: Black Women and the Search for Justice* (University of Minnesota Press, Minneapolis, 1998); P H Collins, 'Some Group Matters: Intersectionality, Situated Standpoints, and Black Feminist Thought' in L Richardson, V Taylor and N Whittier (eds) *Feminist Frontiers* (McGraw-Hill, Boston,

combined the efforts of women of African, Caribbean and South-Asian origin whose political coalition was intended to challenge racism within both wider society and white feminism.[15] According to Brah and Phoenix, much of the early black British feminism grew out of local women's organisations, which eventually formed a national organisation called the Organisation of Women of Asian and African Descent in 1978.[16] These early developments were crucial for challenging the essentialism embedded in the first and second-wave feminist movements on both sides of the Atlantic, which were traditionally dominated by white middle-class heterosexual women.[17] As Rebecca Johnson points out, the rise of intersectionality is mired in 'the past that gave it birth', that is, feminism's persistent grappling with the issues of essentialism and identity.[18]

---

2004) 66; K W Crenshaw, 'Demarginalizing the Intersection of Race and Sex: A Black Feminist Critique of Antidiscrimination Doctrine, Feminist Theory and Antiracist Politics' (1989) 129 *University of Chicago Legal Forum* 139; K W Crenshaw, 'Mapping the Margins: Intersectionality, Identity, Politics, and Violence against Women of Color' (1991) 43 *Stanford Law Review* 1241; A Y Davis, 'Racism, Birth Control, and Reproductive Rights' in M G Fried (ed) *From Abortion to Reproductive Freedom: Transforming a Movement* (South End Press, Boston, 1990) 15; T Grillo, 'Anti-Essentialism and Intersectionality: Tools to Dismantle the Master's House' (1995) 10 *Berkeley Women's Law Journal* 16; A P Harris, 'Race and Essentialism in Feminist Legal Theory' (1990) 42 *Stanford Law Review* 581; B Hooks, *Feminist Theory: From Margin to Center* (South End Press, Cambridge, 1984); M Kline, 'Race, Racism and Feminist Legal Theory' (1989) 12 *Harvard Women's Law Journal* 115; M J Matsuda, 'Beside My Sister, Facing the Enemy: Legal Theory out of Coalition' (1991) 43 *Stanford Law Review* 1183; C T Mohanty, 'Under Western Eyes: Feminist Scholarship and Colonial Discourses' (1988) 30 *Feminist Review* 61; E V Spelman, *Inessential Woman: Problems of Exclusion in Feminist Thought* (Beacon Press, Boston, 1988).

[15] See the summary in Brah and Phoenix, above n 6. See also A Brah, *Cartographies of Diaspora, Contesting Identities* (Routledge, London, 1996); S Grewal, J Kay, L Landor, G Lewis and P Parmar (eds) *Charting the Journey* (Sheba, London, 1988); and H S Mirza (ed) *Black British Feminism* (Routledge, London, 1997).

[16] Brah and Phoenix, above n 6, 78, list these organisations' main concerns as follows: 'wages and conditions of work, immigration law, fascist violence, reproductive rights, and domestic violence.'

[17] See, for example, K-K Bhavnani (ed) *Feminism and 'Race'* (Oxford University Press, Oxford, 2001); H Carby, 'White Women Listen! Black Feminism and Boundaries of Sisterhood' in P Gilroy (ed) *The Empire Strikes Back* (Hutchinson, London, 1982) 212; B Smith, *Home Girls: A Black Feminist Anthology* (Kitchen Table/Women of Color Press, New York, 1983).

[18] R Johnson, 'Gender, Race, Class and Sexual Orientation: Theorizing the Intersections' in G MacDonald, R L Osborne and C C Smith (eds) *Feminism, Law, Inclusion: Intersectionality in Action* (Sumach Press, Toronto, 2005) 21, 33.

The seminal work of the American feminist scholar, Kimberlé Crenshaw introduced intersectionality into feminist legal scholarship.[19] Crenshaw argued that the focus on traditional identity categories (such as race and gender) in anti-discrimination law and doctrine works to exclude those who are at the categories' intersections, notably black women. According to her, intersectionality aims:

> [T]o bring together the different aspects of an otherwise divided sensibility, arguing that racial and sexual subordination are mutually reinforcing, that black women are commonly marginalized by a politics of race alone or a politics of gender alone, and that a political response to each form of subordination must at the same time be a political response to both.[20]

Intersectionality has also burgeoned in fields of feminist knowledge other than law and human rights. Indeed, it has been asserted that 'there has been a veritable explosion of output of scholarship on this theme recently'.[21] In 2006, the *European Journal of Women's Studies* published a special issue (13 (3)) devoted to intersectionality, with articles cutting across various academic disciplines. Jessica Ringrose suggests that intersectionality has also influenced broader disciplines beyond women's studies, 'from psychology to European politics, and around specialist areas of research such as health, counseling and sexuality'.[22] Noticeably, intersectionality is becoming a dominant framework in education research.[23] Intersectionality has also been theorised as a research methodology, including for empirical work.[24] Leslie McCall has argued that

---

[19] Crenshaw, above n 14 (1989).
[20] Crenshaw above n 14 (1991), 1283.
[21] J Ringrose, 'Troubling Agency and "Choice": A Psychoanalytical Analysis of Students' Negotiations of Black Feminist "Intersectionality" Discourses in Women's Studies' (1997) 30 *Women's Studies International Forum* 264, 264, referring to Brah and Phoenix, above n 6; A Phoenix and P Pattynama, 'Editorial: Intersectionality' (2006) 13 *European Journal of Women's Studies* 187; N Yuval-Davis, 'Intersectionality and Feminist Politics' (2006) 13 *European Journal of Women's Studies* 193.
[22] Ringrose, above n 21, citing A Bredström, 'Intersectionality: A Challenge for Feminist HIV/AIDS Research?' (2006) 13 *European Journal of Women's Studies* 229; E Burman, 'From Difference to Intersectionality: Challenges and Resources' (2003) 6 *European Journal of Psychotherapy, Counselling and Health* 293; M Verloo, 'Multiple Inequalities, Intersectionality and the European Union' (2006) 13 *European Journal of Women's Studies* 211.
[23] Ringrose, above n 21, 265.
[24] A Ludvig, 'Difference between Women? Intersecting Voices in a Female Narrative' (2006) 13 *European Journal of Women's Studies* 245; McCall, above n 5; B Prins, 'Narrative Accounts of Origins: A Blind Spot in the Intersectional Approach?' (2006) 13 *European Journal of Women's Studies* 277.

intersectionality remains a valuable statistical tool for studying existing inequalities, despite the considerable theoretical disagreement about the categories along which such inequalities are constituted.[25]

## 3 The global ascendancy of intersectionality

Crenshaw's work has been so influential that intersectionality now features noticeably in legal doctrine, practice and feminist legal activism across the globe. The Beijing Platform for Action called on governments to:

> intensify efforts to ensure equal enjoyment of all human rights and fundamental freedoms for all women and girls who face multiple barriers to their empowerment and advancement because of such factors as their race, age, language, ethnicity, culture, religion, or disability, or because they are indigenous people.[26]

Since then, intersectionality has acquired considerable conceptual purchase in international human rights law and activism. In 2000, the UN Human Rights Committee ('HRC') issued its *General Comment 28 on Equality of Rights between Men and Women*, in which it stated:

> Discrimination against women is often intertwined with discrimination on other grounds such as race, colour, language, religion, political or other opinion, national or social origin, property, birth or other status. States parties should address the ways in which any instances of discrimination on other grounds affect women in a particular way, and include information on the measures taken to counter these effects.[27]

Thanks to the persistent activist lobbying of intersectionality as 'a springboard for a social justice action agenda',[28] as well as respective academic work,[29] gender has firmly made its way into the UN law and practice dealing with racial discrimination. In 2000, the UN Committee on the Elimination of

---

[25] McCall, above n 5.

[26] *Report of the Fourth World Conference on Women*, UN Doc A/Conf. 177/20 (17 October 1995) Annex I, [32].

[27] HRC, *General Comment 28: Equality of Rights between Men and Women (Article 3)*, UN Doc CCPR/C/21/Rev.1/Add.10 (29 March 2000) [30].

[28] Association for Women's Rights in Development ('AWID'), 'Intersectionality: A Tool for Gender and Economic Justice' (2004) 9 *Women's Rights and Economic Change* 2.

[29] See, for example, L A Crooms, 'Indivisible Rights and Intersectional Identities or, "What Do Women's Human Rights Have to Do with the Race Convention?"' (1997) 40 *Howard Law Journal* 619; C Romany, 'Themes for a Conversation on Race and Gender in International Human Rights Law' in A Y Davis and A K Wing (eds) *Global Critical Race Feminism: An International Reader* (New York University Press, New York, 2000) 53.

202  *Research handbook on international human rights law*

Racial Discrimination ('CERD') issued *General Recommendation XXV* on *Gender Related Dimensions of Racial Discrimination*, in which it for the first time admitted that '[t]here are circumstances in which racial discrimination only or primarily affects women, or affects women in a different way, or to a different degree than men'.[30] The Recommendation lists sexual violence against women members of particular communities committed in detention or armed conflict, coerced sterilisation of indigenous women and abuse of women workers in the informal sector or domestic workers employed abroad as forms of racial discrimination directed specifically at women. It also acknowledges specific consequences of racial discrimination suffered by women, such as pregnancy and ostracism resulting from racially motivated rape. Gender bias in the legal system and discrimination against women in the private sphere of life are named as factors preventing women's access to remedies for racial discrimination.[31]

In line with the Recommendation's assurance that 'the Committee will endeavour in its work to take into account gender factors or issues which may be interlinked with racial discrimination',[32] the CERD has more recently demonstrated its awareness of how grounds such as descent intertwine with gender, producing unique forms of discrimination.[33] In another general recommendation, the disadvantaged situation of Roma girls and women in the fields of education and health has been acknowledged.[34] In the area of protection of non-citizens, the Committee has also 'endeavour[ed] . . . to take into account gender factors or issues which may be interlinked with racial discrimination'.[35] It has acknowledged the different standards of treatment of female non-citizen spouses of citizens and the abuse faced by the children and spouses of non-citizen workers.[36] CERD *General Recommendation XXX on Discrimination against Non-Citizens* also prompts states parties to address

---

[30] UN Committee on the Elimination of Racial Discrimination ('CERD'), *General Recommendation XXV, Gender Related Dimensions of Racial Discrimination*, UN Doc A/55/18 (20 March 2000) Annex V, 152, [1].

[31] Ibid [2].

[32] Ibid [3].

[33] For example CERD, *General Recommendation XXIX on Article 1, Paragraph 1 of the Convention (Descent)*, UN Doc HRI/GEN/1/Rev.6XXIX (1 November 2002) [1(k)]: 'Take into account, in all programmes and projects planned and implemented and in measures adopted, the situation of women members of the communities, as victims of multiple discrimination, sexual exploitation and forced prostitution.'

[34] CERD, *General Recommendation XXVII: Discrimination Against Roma*, UN Doc A/55/18 (20 March 2000) Annex V, 154, [22], [34].

[35] CERD, above n 30, [3].

[36] CERD, *General Recommendation XXX: Discrimination Against Non-Citizens*, UN Doc CERD/C/64/Misc.11/Rev.3 (1 October 2002) [8].

specific problems faced by non-citizen domestic workers, such as debt bondage, passport retention, illegal confinement, rape and physical assault.[37]

Intersectionality issues featured prominently at the 2001 World Conference against Racism, Xenophobia and Related Intolerance ('WCAR'), which was held in Durban, South Africa. The final text of the Declaration adopted at Durban refers to the 'differentiated manner' in which 'racism, racial discrimination, xenophobia and related intolerance reveal themselves . . . for women and girls' and recognises 'the need to integrate a gender perspective into relevant policies, strategies and programmes of action against racism, racial discrimination, xenophobia and related intolerance in order to address multiple forms of discrimination'.[38] This was so largely thanks to the feminist NGOs that had consistently advanced this agenda in the international arena.[39] Their work was informed by that of feminist scholars; Crenshaw even delivered a background paper at the Expert Group Meeting on Gender and Race held by the UN Division for the Advancement of Women in Zagreb, Croatia, prior to the 2001 World Conference.[40]

The Center for Women's Global Leadership ('CWGL') was particularly instrumental in centring the intersectionality agenda on Durban, proclaiming it 'an occasion to renew our commitment to looking at the intersection of racism, sexism and other oppressions in a rights based context . . . as we must keep the effects of multiple oppressions central in all our work'.[41] CWGL pioneered 'the expansion of existing methodologies and the design of new methodologies that address intersectional discrimination [which] not only surface the diversity of women's experiences but also seek to address discrimination that occurs when

---

[37] Ibid [34].
[38] WCAR, *Declaration* (2001) OHCHR, www.unhchr.ch/pdf/Durban.pdf at 9 December 2008, [69].
[39] See S George, *Why Intersectionality Works* (2001) Women In Action, http://www.isiswomen.org/pub/wia/wiawcar/intersectionality.htm at 9 September 2008; AWID, above n 28; R Raj (ed) *Women at the Intersection: Indivisible Rights, Identities, and Oppression* (Center for Women's Global Leadership, Rutgers, 2002); and J Riley, 'GAD and Intersectionality in the Region: Forging the Future' (Working Paper No 8, Melbourne University Private Working Paper Series: Gender and Development Dialogue, 2003).
[40] United Nations, *Gender and Racial Discrimination: Report of the Expert Group Meeting: 21–4 November 2000, Zagreb, Croatia* (2000) UN, http://www.un.org/womenwatch/daw/csw/genrac/report.htm. See also Women's International Coalition for Economic Justice ('WICEJ'), *How Women Are Using the United Nations World Conference Against Racism, Racial Discrimination and Related Intolerance, Durban 2001* (2003).
[41] Center for Women's Global Leadership, *A Women's Human Rights Approach to the World Conference Against Racism* (2001) CWGL, http://www.cwgl.rutgers.edu/globalcenter/policy/gcpospaper.html at 9 December 2008.

multiple identities intersect'.[42] As a result of CWGL's and other women's groups' lobbying at various preparatory meetings prior to the WCAR, the special session of the UN Commission on the Status of Women ('CSW') in March 2001 called upon governments and the international community to:

> [D]evelop methodologies to identify the ways in which various forms of discrimination converge and affect women and girls and conduct studies on how racism, racial discrimination, xenophobia and related intolerance are reflected in laws, policies, institutions and practices and how this has contributed to the vulnerability, victimization, marginalization and exclusion of women and the girl child.[43]

A Working Group on Women and Human Rights, which operated at the CSW session, advanced disaggregated data collection, contextual analysis, intersectional review of policies and design and implementation of intersectionality policy initiatives as the four elements of a methodology to address intersectional discrimination.

*Disaggregated data collection* is intended to describe women's realities more accurately and to determine what factors (such as race, ethnicity, descent) contribute to women's discrimination. The idea is that data disaggregated by various identity categories:

> [W]ill make it possible to identify the magnitude of impact of particular problems and policies on particular groups of women. For example, in order to evaluate the problem of the feminization of poverty it is important to identify the extent of the impact of poverty on different groups of women.[44]

Nira Yuval-Davis notes that the need for this was highlighted in several WCAR forums, including by the then UN High Commissioner for Human Rights, Mary Robinson.[45]

*Contextual analysis* is intended to identify the root causes and context of the problems that women face as a result of convoluted identities. Such contextual realities could include:

---

[42] Ibid.
[43] UN Commission on the Status of Women, *Draft Agreed Conclusions on Gender and All Forms of Discrimination, in particular Racism, Racial Discrimination, Xenophobia and Related Intolerance* (2001) UNCSW, http://www.un.org/womenwatch/daw/csw/draftacrace.htm at 9 December 2008, [40].
[44] Working Group on Women and Women's Rights ('WGWWR'), *Background Briefing on Intersectionality* (2001) WGWWR, http://www.cwgl.rutgers.edu/globalcenter/policy/bkgdbrfintersec.html at 9 December 2008.
[45] Yuval-Davis, above n 21, 204.

> [T]he legacy of slavery or colonialism or ancient animosities, as well as religious and cultural factors. For example, disaggregated data may reveal the extent of rape of ethnic women during a situation of war, but an analysis of the context reveals a history of inter-ethnic struggle for economic power that created a climate of acceptance among the majority group for the rape of minority women.[46]

*Intersectional review of policies and systems of implementation* is intended as a tool to evaluate policy initiatives and implementation systems for their usefulness and efficacy for different women.

> For example, does a policy initiate [sic] addressing racial discrimination and economic opportunity for one group of women create further tensions with other racial or ethnic women creating a competition and hierarchy of minorities that serves to perpetuate the domination of a majority group. Or on the other hand, do the implementation procedures for national machinery include a variety of strategies that are sensitive to the different situations of subordination of women within different groups.[47]

*Design and implementation of intersectional policy initiatives* are intended to develop new strategies to combat identified patterns of discrimination.

> National machineries and the UN systems can take concrete steps and implement plans of action based on the data to support such work; governments need to enable data collection, analysis and the allocation of adequate resources for this task. In addition to the implementation there must be mechanisms for effective review of such implementation.[48]

This practical and detailed methodology has been applauded as 'impressive and a step forward'.[49] At present, UN human rights committees and special rapporteurs explicitly use intersectionality as a framework when dealing with gender issues. The important 2002 UN *Resolution on the Integration of the Human Rights of Women and the Gender Perspective* 'recognizes the importance of examining the intersection of multiple forms of discrimination, including their root causes from a gender perspective, and their impact on the advancement of women and the enjoyment by women of their human rights'.[50] The concept of intersectionality is particularly salient in the work of the current Special Rapporteur on violence against women, Professor Yakin

---

[46] WGWWR, above n 44.
[47] Ibid.
[48] Ibid.
[49] Yuval-Davis, above n 21, 205.
[50] UN Commission on Human Rights, *Resolution on the Integration of the Human Rights of Women and the Gender Perspective*, UN Doc E/CN.4/2002/L.59 (16 April 2002).

Ertürk.[51] Prosecution of crimes of sexualised violence at times of war and genocide is another area aided by intersectional approaches.[52] In this way, intersectionality, which originally emerged as a theory at the margins of academic feminism, has now been widely accepted in international feminist activism and human rights discourse.

## 4  Problems with intersectionality

Despite these evident successes, intersectionality is not devoid of problems. It can be surmised that the term 'intersectionality' in feminist discourse has at least two dimensions: (1) a concern with subjectivity, referring to a particular paradigm based in individual identity categories; and (2) the interplay of different power relations and/or systems of oppression in society. Arguably, these two dimensions have tended to serve as quite separate analytical categories in feminist theory and practice, prompting Nira Yuval-Davis to assert, with reference to the 2000 Zagreb meeting, that 'the analytical attempts to explain intersectionality ... are confusing'.[53]

Overall, the first meaning (referring to a combination of different identity characteristics of an individual) has featured more saliently. For example, McCall asserts that the word intersectionality 'immediately suggests a particular theoretical paradigm based in *identity categories*'.[54] Although many scholars believe that intersectionality 'emphasizes that different dimensions of social life cannot be separated out into discrete and pure strands',[55] it is arguable that the concept's application has tended to rely on overlapping, if not cumulative, *identities*.[56] Crenshaw's own metaphor to explain intersectionality is that of crossroads:

---

[51]  Recent examples include Yakin Ertürk, *Towards an Effective Implementation of International Norms to End Violence Against Women: Report of the Special Rapporteur on Violence Against Women, Its Causes and Consequences*, UN Doc E/CN.4/2004/66 (26 December 2003); Yakin Ertürk, *Intersections of Violence Against Women and HIV/AIDS: Report of the Special Rapporteur on Violence Against Women, Its Causes and Consequences*, UN Doc E/CN.4/2005/72 (17 January 2005); Yakin Ertürk, *Indicators on Violence against Women and State Response: Report of the Special Rapporteur on Violence Against Women, Its Causes and Consequences*, UN Doc A/HRC/7/6 (29 January 2008).

[52]  See, for example, D Buss, 'Sexual Violence, Ethnicity, and Intersectionality in International Criminal Law' in E Grabham, D Cooper, J Krishnadas and D Herman (eds) *Intersectionality and Beyond: Law, Power and the Politics of Location* (Routledge Cavendish, London, 2008) 105.

[53]  Yuval-Davis, above n 21, 196.

[54]  McCall, above n 5, 1771 (emphasis added).

[55]  Brah and Phoenix, above n 6, 76.

[56]  See, for example, W Brown, 'The Impossibility of Women's Studies' (1997) 9 *Differences* 79, 86; McCall, above n 5, 1771.

> Intersectionality is what occurs when a woman from a minority group ... tries to navigate the main crossing in the city ... The main highway is 'racism road'. One cross street can be Colonialism, then Patriarchy Street ... She has to deal not only with one form of oppression but with all forms, those named as road signs, which link together to make a double, a triple, multiple, a many layered blanket of oppression.[57]

Accordingly, an individual is treated as a composition of (discrete) identity elements, such as gender, race, sexuality, religion, class and so on. This is problematic precisely because it seems to defeat the very point of intersectionality – that one strand of identity (gender) cannot exist in isolation from others.

This conundrum is already inherent in the CSW's much-praised four-step methodology. Yuval-Davis notes that disaggregated data collection would by definition rely on the fiction of 'unambiguous and mutually exclusive categories'.[58] Furthermore, the strategy of disaggregated data collection might be at odds with the fundamental premise of the indivisibility of human rights. To be fair, though, this is a dilemma pertaining to human rights doctrine itself. According to CWGL:

> The human rights system is based on the idea that human rights are indivisible and interrelated. But the treaties and mechanisms set up to defend and promote human rights tend to be linear – that is, they treat different aspects of abuse and discrimination (race, sex, age, migrant status, and so forth) separately.[59]

The second usage of 'intersectionality', prevalent in feminist theory as well as activism, is concerned with 'large-scale, historically constructed and hierarchical power systems'.[60] This usage refers to the interaction of what has been described as 'systems of hostility and depreciation'[61] or the 'interlocking

---

[57] K W Crenshaw, 'Mapping the Margins: Intersectionality, Identity Politics and Violence Against Women of Color' (1994) Harvard School of Public Health, http://www.wcsap.org/Events/Workshop07/mapping-margins.pdf at 9 December 2008.
[58] Yuval-Davis, above n 21, 205.
[59] CWGL, above n 41.
[60] B T Dill, S M Nettles and L Weber, 'What Do We Mean by Intersections?' (Spring 2001) *Connections: Newsletter of Consortium for Research on Race, Gender, and Ethnicity* 4.
[61] L McWhorter, 'Sex, Race, and Biopower: A Foucauldian Genealogy' (2004) 19 *Hypatia* 38, 55. See also N Zack (ed) *Race/Sex: Their Sameness, Difference, and Interplay* (Routledge, New York, 2007); H Zia, 'Where Race and Gender Meet: Racism, Hate Crime and Pornography' in E Disch (ed) *Reconstructing Gender: A Multicultural Ontology* (Mayfield, Mountain View, 1997) 504.

systems of domination',[62] roughly corresponding to the identity constituents described above. In other words, the second usage conceptualises gender, race, sexuality and so on in terms of systemic forces that shape societies rather than as traits featured by individuals. However, this second meaning of intersectionality has tended to be less prominent and has even been more adequately addressed under different covers. It has been observed that human rights activists who deal with what might be termed intersectional issues may eschew the concept in their work, as they may believe that they already address the complexity of social inequality by other means.[63]

As far as theory goes, there is an abundance of literature that theorises the complexity of contemporary modalities of power – the aspect that proponents of intersectionality tend to pay insufficient attention to. For example, the rich literature on governmentality, which explores ways in which late modern subjects are constituted through discourses of power, does not at all use the term 'intersectionality' (and arguably does not need to). For example, Davina Cooper has advanced the concept of 'organising principles' as a better theoretical alternative. She describes organising principles as (1) operating not just between subjects, but as organisational processes, social practices and norms; (2) not linear, but asymmetrical and contradictory; and (3) not simply imposed from 'above', but part of the constitution of a community and individual practices.[64]

Furthermore, Iris Marion Young proposed conceptualising gender as seriality, drawing on Jean-Paul Sartre's idea of series.[65] Seriality implies an understanding of gender as:

[A] particular form of the social positioning of lived bodies in relation to one another within historically and socially specific institutions and processes that have

---

[62] S H Razack, 'Speaking for Ourselves: Feminist Jurisprudence and Minority Women' (1991) 4 *Canadian Journal of Women and the Law* 400, 454.
[63] See, for example, E Grabham, 'Intersectionality: Traumatic Impressions' in E Grabham, D Cooper, J Krishnadas and D Herman (eds) *Intersectionality and Beyond: Law, Power and the Politics of Location* (Routledge Cavendish, London, 2008) 183. On the practical co-operation of various interest groups, see S Goldberg, 'Intersectionality in Theory and Practice' in E Grabham, D Cooper, J Krishnadas and D. Herman (eds) *Intersectionality and Beyond: Law, Power and the Politics of Location* (Routledge Cavendish, London, 2008) 124.
[64] D Cooper, '"And You Can't Find Me Nowhere": Relocating Identity and Structure within Equality Jurisprudence' (2000) 27 *Journal of Law and Society* 249.
[65] I M Young, *Intersecting Voices: Dilemmas of Gender, Political Philosophy and Policy* (Princeton University Press, Princeton, 1997), drawing on J-P Sartre, *Critique de la raison dialectique: Théorie des ensembles pratiques* (Gallimard, Paris, 1960).

material effects on the environment in which people act and reproduce relations of power and privilege among them.[66]

This means a passive grouping of individuals according to structural relations 'in ways too impersonal to ground identity',[67] insofar as it makes strategic or political sense. In this scheme, gender remains a useful category of analysis insofar as it continues to serve as a major organising principle of society. Likewise, it remains a useful basis for political affinities insofar as people's lives continue to be influenced by gender-related disadvantage. In this way, a 'gender identity' only makes sense if its conditionality and political purposefulness are acknowledged.

Due to its insufficient emphasis on the broader, structural dimensions, intersectionality has been criticised for fragmenting both subjectivity and the forces that shape it. Prominent critical and feminist theorists such as Judith Butler and Wendy Brown have insisted that it is misleading to think of gender in isolation from race, or of race as free of all inflection of gender or sexuality.[68] Various streams of subjectivity literature have highlighted the pointlessness of constructing the individual as an atomistic, detached, 'relentlessly self-interested'[69] entity. For Félix Guattari for example, 'the fundamentally pluralist, multi-centred, and heterogeneous character of contemporary subjectivity' means that 'an individual is *already* a "collective" of heterogeneous components'.[70] Feminist authors as diverse as Iris Marion Young, Toril Moi and Wendy Brown all agree, albeit in very different registers, that structural influences are always subsumed and internalised in the individual before individual identity components can be meaningfully articulated.[71] In addition, Brown has emphasised that the social powers constituting identity are not simply different powers, but different *kinds* of power, as gender, sexuality, race, religion and so on are not equivalent problematics.[72]

---

[66] I M Young, 'Lived Body vs Gender: Reflections on Social Structure and Subjectivity' (2002) XV *Ratio (new series)* 410, 422.
[67] Ibid.
[68] See V Bell, 'On Speech, Race and Melancholia: An Interview with Judith Butler' (1999) 16 *Theory, Culture and Society* 163; Brown, above n 56; W Brown, 'Suffering Rights as Paradoxes' (2000) 7 *Constellations* 230; J Butler, *Bodies That Matter: On the Discursive Limits of 'Sex'* (Routledge, London, 1993).
[69] W Brown, *States of Injury: Power and Freedom in Late Modernity* (Princeton University Press, Princeton, 1995) 25.
[70] F Guattari, 'Remaking of Social Practices' in G Genosko (ed) *The Guattari Reader* (Blackwell, Oxford, 1996) 266 (emphasis added).
[71] Young, above nn 65–6; T Moi, *What Is a Woman? And Other Essays* (Oxford University Press, Oxford, 1999); Brown, above n 69; Brown, above n 56; Brown, above n 68.
[72] Brown, above n 56. See also W Brown, *Regulating Aversion: Tolerance in the Age of Identity and Empire* (Princeton University Press, Princeton, 2006).

In light of these insights, the concept of intersectionality appears to be flawed as it more often than not tends to presume that 'intersections' exist prior to the subject and are more or less co-extensive. This is so despite numerous reiterations by feminist activists that the intersectional disadvantage is not simply cumulative. Indeed, 'the metaphor of the intersection appears too static to respond to such complexities'.[73] According to Davina Cooper, the 'ontological fallacy' of intersectionality is that it assumes that 'the axes have an existence apart from the ways in which they combine'.[74]

Most recent feminist theorising has asserted that intersectionality has reached the limits of its potential for feminism, with its value being confined to simply highlighting complex experiences before the law.[75] Although this function itself may be a sound political strategy, intersectionality is, according to Joanne Conaghan, *rather limited in its theory-producing power. In particular, while it acts as an aid to the excavation of inequality experiences at a local level, it tells us little about the wider context in which such experiences are produced, mediated and expressed*'.[76]

Furthermore, drawing analysis on the very categories that produce and sustain 'intersectional' subjects can promote 'entrenching rather than loosening identities' attachments to their current constitutive injuries'.[77] According to Emily Grabham, whose analysis draws on Brown's critique of identity,[78] 'focusing on the "intersections" between categories merely leads to the

---

[73] Grabham, above n 63, 185.
[74] She further explains: 'Models that emerge as rough approximations, developed by humans in an effort to try to understand the social, become reified as phenomena with an independent and prior existence. Discrete axes of gender, class, race and age do not exist independently on some distant plane prior to their convergence in the form of distinct social permutations. Rather, identifying axes of class, gender, race and age occur in the course of making sense of social life.' D Cooper, *Challenging Diversity: Rethinking Equality and the Value of Difference* (Cambridge University Press, Cambridge, 2004), 48.
[75] J Conaghan, 'Intersectionality and the Feminist Project in Law' in E Grabham, D Cooper, J Krishnadas and D Herman (eds) *Intersectionality and Beyond: Law, Power and the Politics of Location* (Routledge Cavendish, London, 2008) 21.
[76] Ibid 29 (emphasis added). Cf Rebecca Johnson's argument that '[t]he point of intersectional analysis is to see whether or not the experiences of those located at the intersections can provide insights crucial to the construction of better theories': Johnson, above n 18, 29.
[77] Brown, above n 69, 134. Cf Johnson's argument that intersectionality should be seen as not merely about victimisation, but highlighting unique strategies of resistance: Johnson, above n 18, 29. Johnson draws on Mann, who argues that 'we should think of ourselves as conflicted actors rather than as fragmented selves': P S Mann, *Micro-Politics: Agency in a Post-Feminist Era* (University of Minnesota Press, Minneapolis, 1994) 4.
[78] Brown, above n 69.

production of "more" categories, thereby supporting the law's propensity to classify'.[79] Intersectionality thus is very prone to falling back into the trap of binarism, replicating and multiplying 'the taxonomy of the norm and its deviations', of which '[identity] categories are merely sub-sets'.[80]

This replication is most apparent in intersectional discrimination claims. The phenomenon of 'intersectional discrimination' has received considerable attention in doctrinal legal scholarship, where 'intersectional' tends to be used more or less interchangeably with adjectives such as 'double', 'compound', 'additive', 'cumulative' and 'multiple'.[81] Sarah Hannett explains that '"multiple discrimination" can occur in at least two ways: where the grounds of discrimination are additive [or double] in nature, and/or where the discrimination is based on an indivisible combination of two or more social characteristics'.[82] In this scheme, 'additive discrimination' denotes situations where an individual suffers cumulatively from (different) discriminatory practices to which the two or more different groups he or she belongs to are susceptible, with statistics being key in determining such discrimination.

Grabham is right to point out that such claims 'do not interrogate social positions as effects of power'.[83] On another occasion, she recounts her own experience as a lawyer of preparing a discrimination claim on behalf of a trans lesbian woman who had experienced harassment at work: having to squeeze the case into 'one or more of the following grounds: sex, sexual orientation and/or gender reassignment'[84] reified rather than challenged these categories. The utterly fragmentary nature of discrimination law meant that it was impossible to even accurately translate what had happened or how the individual herself felt about it into a legally intelligible picture.[85]

---

[79] Grabham, above n 63, 186.

[80] R Sandland, 'Feminist Theory and Law: Beyond the Possibilities of the Present?' in J Richardson and R Sandland (eds) *Feminist Perspectives on Law and Theory* (Cavendish, London, 2001) 89, 114.

[81] See M Eaton, 'Patently Confused: Complex Inequality and *Canada v Mossop*' (1994) 1 *Review of Constitutional Studies* 203; S Hannett, 'Equality at the Intersections: The Legislative and Judicial Failure to Tackle Multiple Discrimination' (2003) 23 *Oxford Journal of Legal Studies* 65; and E W Shoben, 'Compound Discrimination: The Interaction of Race and Sex in Employment Discrimination' (1980) 55 *New York University Law Review* 793.

[82] Hannett, above n 81, 68.

[83] Grabham, above n 63, 192.

[84] E Grabham, 'Taxonomy of Inequality: Lawyers, Maps and the Challenge of Hybridity' (2006) 15 *Social and Legal Studies* 5, 15.

[85] 'M herself could not identify one sole "discriminatory ground" that accounted for the way she had been treated overall ... [S]he was acutely aware of the way that her colleagues were reacting to her status as a woman, a lesbian, and a transgender woman, and in her eyes one could not be separated from the other': ibid.

A survey of international equality and discrimination jurisprudence reveals a similar result. One example is the case of *Abdulaziz, Cabales and Balkandali v United Kingdom*,[86] in which the applicants, whose husbands were precluded from joining them in the United Kingdom, alleged discrimination on the grounds of both race and sex under Article 14 of the *European Convention on Human Rights*. The European Court of Human Rights approached the complaint as implying two distinct types of discrimination, despite the clear interaction of the two as the operation of the immigration rule in question relied on gendered stereotypes of immigrants of Asian descent. Only sex (and not race) discrimination was found in the case.

In the case of *Dahlab v Switzerland*,[87] a teacher who had been told to remove her Islamic headscarf complained of sex discrimination. This was dismissed as the European Court of Human Rights considered that the measure 'was not directed against her as a member of the female sex' and that the law 'could also be applied to a man who, in similar circumstances, wore clothing that clearly identified him as a member of a different faith'.[88] This legalistic abstraction appears to completely discount the specific, intersectional reality of Islamic headscarf restrictions affecting Muslim women in a particular way in a particular European context.

It is also interesting to note the older but much-praised HRC decision in *Lovelace v Canada*,[89] in which a Maliseet Indian woman had lost her status as an Indian under Canadian law due to her marriage to a non-Indian (whereas an Indian man married to a non-Indian woman would not have lost his status). The HRC chose to uphold Lovelace's rights by way of applying Article 27 of the *International Covenant on Civil and Political Rights* ('ICCPR'),[90] which protects minority rights. Interestingly, it considered that this provision was 'the one which is most directly applicable',[91] despite having the option of deciding the case under various non-discrimination and equality provisions of the ICCPR.[92] Arguably, this goes to show the difficulty of squaring intersectionality with available discrimination and equality frameworks in international human rights law.

---

[86] (1985) 7 EHRR 471.
[87] Application No 42393/98 (Unreported, European Court of Human Rights, Trial Chamber, 15 January 2001).
[88] Ibid 461.
[89] Communication No R.6/24, UN Doc A/36/40, Supp.40 166 (30 July 1981).
[90] Opened for signature 16 December 1966, 999 UNTS 171 (entered into force 23 March 1976).
[91] *Lovelace v Canada*, Communication No R.6/24, UN Doc A/36/40, Supp.40 166 (30 July 1981) [13.2].
[92] For an excellent analysis of this case, see K Knop, *Diversity and Self-Determination in International Law* (Cambridge University Press, Cambridge, 2002) 358ff.

Thus, intersectional claims may not even be able to challenge what Conaghan calls 'law's representational role'.[93] As Grabham puts it:

> Viewing intersectional analysis in the context of the genealogy of identity claims in liberal society gives us more of an understanding why it has not had the radical effects in discrimination law that we might have wished for. If single-ground rights claims are based on disciplinary identities, then intersectional rights claims (and many forms of legal intersectional analysis) are no less bound to these categories. Using more categories in legal analysis, or focusing on the intersections between legal categories, does not of itself challenge the regulatory function of liberal identity. Indeed, the precision required for intersectional perspectives can be seen to approximate the 'anatomy of detail' that goes into the production of subjects for surveillance and regulation.[94]

In sum, intersectionality has been successful at highlighting the problem of the marginalisation of certain identities and experiences in feminist politics, law and broader human rights discourse. Intersectionality feminists have had impressive influence in the international human rights arena. However, the concept's utility beyond this 'representational function' is open to question.

## 5 Conclusion

Joan Wallach Scott once wrote that the history of feminism had been 'the history of the project of reducing diversities (of class, race, sexuality, ethnicity, politics, religion, and socio-economic status) among females to a common identity of women (usually in opposition to patriarchy, a system of male domination)'.[95] This, however, is only true up to a point. It is also true that the feminist project has been for quite some time animated by another central concern, the need to conceptualise the oppression of women – as Gayle Rubin famously put it more than three decades ago – in its 'endless variety and monotonous similarity'.[96] Intersectionality purports to do exactly that as it highlights that 'pure' gender does not exist, that gender alone does not account for the complex inequalities that women worldwide persistently find themselves in.

Arguably, intersectionality is a success story of feminism on at least two counts. First, it has been a tremendously influential agenda on the global human rights arena as feminists have succeeded in integrating an intersectional gender perspective into major areas of UN human rights work. Second,

---

[93] Conaghan, above n 75, 40.
[94] Grabham, above n 63, 192.
[95] J W Scott, 'Introduction' in J W Scott (ed) *Feminism and History* (Oxford University Press, Oxford, 1996) 1, 4.
[96] G Rubin, 'The Traffic in Women' in R R Reiter (ed) *Toward an Anthropology of Women* (Monthly Press, New York, 1975) 157, 160.

it is one area in which feminist theorists and activists have worked in tandem, with theory making a difference in the 'real world'. These two successes are to be welcomed and celebrated.

More recently, however, concerns have been voiced over the limiting potential of intersectionality. It has been criticised for fragmenting subjectivity and thus colluding with the regulatory (rather than empowering) impulse of human rights. Perhaps this is an inevitable side-effect of a successful strategy. Yet if feminism is to continue to have an impact on the lives of real women, it has to take internal critique on board. This does not necessarily imply discarding intersectionality as a strategic tool. Rather, acknowledging the limitations of intersectionality means using it even more wisely and supplementing it with a range of more targeted, if less ambitious, agendas and tools.

# 9. Refugees and displaced persons: the refugee definition and 'humanitarian' protection
*Susan Kneebone**

Humanitarian: Having regard to the interests of humanity or mankind at large.[1]

The vast majority of refugees are ... unprotected under codified international law. They are 'humanitarian' refugees who seek shelter from conditions of general armed violence ... or simply bad economic conditions.[2]

[H]umanitarianism is the ideology of hegemonic states in the era of globalisation marked by the end of the Cold War and the growing North–South divide ... [T]he Northern commitment to humanitarianism coexists with a range of practices which violate its essence.[3]

## 1 Introduction

The discussion in this chapter was inspired by a talk by a distinguished Italian academic who was agonising over Italy's refugee 'crisis', which involves increased numbers of persons attempting to reach Italy by sea from North Africa and eastern Europe.[4] In this speech the academic made use of a distinction between 'refugees' and 'humanitarian entrants'. In particular, it was

---

   \* My thanks to Karen Spitz for her research assistance in connection with this chapter, and to Sarah Joseph for her helpful comments. I am responsible for any remaining misconceptions.

   [1] C T Onions (ed), *The Shorter Oxford English Dictionary On Historical Principles* (3rd ed, Clarendon Press, Oxford, 1973) 995.

   [2] K Hailbronner, 'Non-Refoulement and "Humanitarian" Refugees: Customary International Law or Wishful Legal Thinking?' (1985–86) 26 *Virginia Journal of International Law* 857.

   [3] B S Chimni, 'Globalization, Humanitarianism and the Erosion of Refugee Protection' (2000) 13 *Journal of Refugee Studies* 243.

   [4] Paola Totaro, 'Italy's island of hope to become a prison for desperate refugees', *The Age* (Australia) 7 February 2009, 15, citing UNHCR statistics that in 2008 a record 36,952 refugees landed on Italian shores (a 75 per cent increase on 2007) and that 31,000 were processed on the Italian island of Lampedusa. See S Kneebone, C McDowell and G Morrell, 'A Mediterranean Solution? Chances of Success' (2006) 18 *International Journal of Refugee Law* 492, 492–500, for a discussion of the Mediterranean 'problem'.

suggested that persons fleeing for economic reasons, or persons fleeing generalised violence, were not 'proper' refugees within the meaning of the 1951 *Convention Relating to the Status of Refugees* (the 'Refugee Convention'),[5] and that if states chose to assist them, it would be for 'humanitarian' motives. It was clear from the context of the talk that a very narrow definition of a refugee was being applied. According to the speaker, a refugee is someone who flees civil or political persecution. If this misunderstanding is widely accepted, then Italy and indeed Europe and other industrialised states do indeed have a 'refugee crisis' – a crisis of meaning.

In this chapter, I argue that the malaise of the international regime of refugee protection (as indicated by the current reluctance of Mediterranean states to process refugees arriving by boat) reflects a confused notion of 'humanitarian protection' and misunderstanding of the term 'refugee'. I suggest that industrialised states make use of a binary which they have developed between the legal definition of a refugee and the notion of humanitarian protection. When humanitarian protection is granted to refugees and asylum seekers fleeing conflict or economic disadvantage, it is associated with government 'largesse' or discretion, with the idea of extra-legal remedies.[6] The effect of this binary is to de-couple the Refugee Convention from its general humanitarian and human rights focus and to assert state border control or sovereignty in the name of 'humanitarianism'.[7] It thus strengthens the perception that there are 'genuine' and 'bogus' or 'non-genuine' refugees.

Further, as I illustrate below, the main reasons for flight today are civil wars and generalised violence, or denial of social and economic rights. Thus a restrictive reading of the Refugee Convention enables states to exclude a large portion of the world's refugees from its protection.

---

[5] *Convention Relating to the Status of Refugees*, opened for signature 28 July 1951, 1989 UNTS 137 (entered into force 22 April 1954) (the 'Refugee Convention'). In everyday parlance a 'refugee' is a person in flight, a person seeking refuge. However, in international law a 'refugee' is a person who comes within the definition in Art. 1A(2) of the Refugee Convention and the *Protocol relating to the Status of Refugees*, opened for signature on 31 January 1967, 19 UNTS 6223, 6257 (entered into force 4 October 1967).

[6] *Ruddock v Vadarlis* [2001] 1329 FCA, (2001) 110 FCR 491 [126] per Beaumont J.

[7] Guy S Goodwin-Gill and Jane McAdam, *The Refugee in International Law*, (3rd ed, Oxford University Press, Oxford, 2007) 1: 'The refugee in international law occupies a legal space characterised, on the one hand, by the principle of State sovereignty and the related principles of territorial supremacy and self-preservation and on the other competing humanitarian principles derived from general international law and from treaty.'

The argument in this chapter is essentially that restrictive approaches to refugees and to interpretation of the refugee definition reflect a confused understanding of the meaning of 'humanitarian'. As the quotations above illustrate, the word has different contextual connotations. The general term 'humanitarian' is associated historically with ethical and theological meanings and, in its 'pure' or literal sense, has the core idea of concern for humanity. In this chapter I explain how this sense of 'humanitarian' became absorbed into International Humanitarian Law after the atrocities of World War II. Subsequently, the ideas of 'humanitarian intervention' has been used to describe the basis of military intervention in certain states, and 'humanitarian assistance' has been used to describe the protection given to displaced persons. In legal terms, the roots for such intervention or assistance are very different. It is my central argument that, through conflation of ideas, 'humanitarianism' has become politicised and divorced from the original meaning of 'humanitarian'.

The argument is developed in two main sections. First, I discuss the development of the Refugee Convention definition and the mandate of the United Nations High Commissioner for Refugees (the 'UNHCR'), and the latter's mandate on the issue of internally displaced persons ('IDPs'). In that discussion I note that the UNHCR mandate covers both protection of refugees and humanitarian protection. Secondly, I will trace briefly the development of the idea of 'humanitarian protection' for displaced persons to demonstrate how this straightforward notion has lost its way.

To begin, a snapshot of the current global situation of refugees and displaced persons is provided.

## 2 The current situation: refugees and 'displaced persons'

The current regime of international refugee protection is undoubtedly under stress. Whilst the 1951 Refugee Convention contains a definition of a 'refugee'[8] which covers 11.4 million refugees, a large proportion of the world's displaced population estimated at 51 million[9] is not covered by the definition as they have not crossed an international border.[10] This cohort

---

[8] In Article 1A(2) of the Refugee Convention, a refugee is defined as a person with a 'well-founded fear of persecution' by reason of one of the five grounds set out in the article.

[9] United Nations High Commissioner for Refugees ('UNHCR'), *2007 Global Trends: Refugees, Asylum-seekers, Internally Displaced and Stateless Persons* (June 2008) 2. This figure includes 25.1 million who come under the UNHCR mandate (as explained in the text), of whom the UNHCR is providing direct assistance to 13.7 million.

[10] Such persons are known as Internally Displaced Persons ('IDPs'). Art. 1A(2) of the Refugee Convention requires a person to be 'outside the country of his nationality'.

includes 26 million affected by what the UNHCR terms as 'conflict-induced internal displacement'.[11] Conflict is also a major reason for international flight in order to seek asylum. The UNHCR's statistics on asylum seekers[12] reveal that the main countries of origin are Iraq, followed by the Russian Federation, China, Somalia, Afghanistan and Serbia.[13] After a period of decline, both the global refugee population and the total number of displaced persons are increasing.[14]

For the large part, this scenario is played out in countries far from the industrialised states that drive the policy behind international refugee protection.[15] Further, over the last two decades, those industrialised states have systematically introduced restrictive non-entrée measures and interpretations of the refugee definition which limit access to international refugee protection in those states. Of those who have left their country, 80 per cent of refugees remain in the same region, and the number of those living in 'protracted refugee situations' continues to rise.[16] Simultaneously, the number of 'urban' refugees, that is, those living in cities and recognised by the UNHCR as refugees, has increased.[17] Such persons are awaiting a 'durable solution'.[18]

---

[11]   UNHCR, above n 9, 2.

[12]   An 'asylum seeker' is a person seeking asylum from persecution who has yet to be recognised as a 'refugee' as defined in Art. 1A(2) of the Refugee Convention. But note that the UNHCR takes the view that a person who satisfies that definition is a 'refugee' without the need for a determination to that effect. This is known as the 'declaratory' theory – see UNHCR, *Handbook on Procedures and Criteria for Determining Refugee Status under the 1951 Convention and the 1967 Protocol relating to the Status of Refugees* (Geneva: 1979, re-edited 1992) ('UNHCR Handbook') [28].

[13]   UNHCR, *Asylum Levels and Trends in Industrialized Countries: First Half 2008* (17 October 2008) 6.

[14]   UNHCR, above n 9, 6.

[15]   UNHCR, *Asylum Levels and Trends in Industrialized Countries: First Half 2008: Statistical Overview of Asylum Applications Lodged in 38 European and 6 Non-European Countries* (17 October 2008) 6.

[16]   Brookings-Bern Project on Internal Displacement, *Expert Seminar on Protracted IDP Situations* (Geneva: 21–22 June 2007) – the figure quoted at p. 1 is 14.2 million. In 2005 it was calculated that the UNHCR's mandate covered 8.7 million refugees and that the total IDP population was 23.7 million. In 2006 the total IDP population had risen to 24.5 million. See ibid, Table 1 on 22. See also UNHCR, above n 9, 2: in 2007 the UNHCR figures were 11.4 million refugees and 25.1 million IDPs.

[17]   That is, they have been recognised by the UNHCR as coming within the refugee definition and are awaiting regularisation of their status as per one of the 'durable solutions' referred to below.

[18]   The three 'durable solutions' are classically stated as return (repatriation), local integration (eg through naturalisation) and resettlement. See S Kneebone, 'The Legal and Ethical Implications of Extra-territorial Processing of Asylum Seekers: the "Safe Third Country" Concept' in Jane McAdam (ed) *Moving On: Forced Migration, Human Rights and Security* (Hart Publishing, Oxford, 2008).

These trends take place within the context of a globalised world in which it is estimated that the number of people living outside their homeland stands at 200 million.[19] It has been suggested that the majority leave their place of birth because they are unable to earn a living and because there is a demand for their labour elsewhere.[20] These migrants include 'regular' (legal) and 'irregular' (illegal) migrants. The latter group includes asylum seekers. A recent UNHCR Discussion Paper has put UNHCR's role into this context with the following description:

> While the majority of people move to establish new livelihoods, improve their standard of living, join members of their family or take up educational opportunities, those of concern to UNHCR are forced to flee by human rights violations and armed conflict.[21]

This context points to a second important factor in the global refugee picture which has driven the response of the receiving industrialised states. Often the line between asylum seeker and 'illegal migrant' is fine, as many are fleeing economic disadvantage brought on by post-conflict situations or as a result of persistent discrimination. In the context of international migration, refugees are often juxtaposed with 'mere' 'economic' migrants or described as 'economic refugees'. The 'migration–asylum nexus', which is employed in this context, concentrates upon the fact that there are 'mixed flows' of asylum seekers and irregular (economic) migrants. The effect of the 'migration–asylum nexus' is to treat the protection needs of refugees as a secondary consideration to migration controls.

This is the background to the tendency of industrialised states to characterise any protection given to 'economic refugees', or those fleeing conflict, who arrive in their jurisdiction, as 'humanitarian'.[22] Such objects of 'humanitarian' protection are considered to be outside the scope of the legal refugee definition. We turn now to consider the development of the Refugee Convention definition.

---

[19] Antonio Guterres, 'UN High Commissioner for Refugees', *The Age* (Australia) 11 December 2007, 13.
[20] Ibid.
[21] *Refugee protection and durable solutions in the context of international migration*, prepared for the High Commissioner's Dialogue on Protection Challenges, UNHCR/DPC/2007/Doc.02 at [2] (19 November 2007).
[22] K Hailbronner, 'Non-Refoulement and "Humanitarian" Refugees: Customary International Law or Wishful Legal Thinking?' (1985–86) 26 *Virginia Journal of International Law* 857.

## 3 The Refugee Convention definition, the UNHCR mandate and 'humanitarian protection'

At the global level, the international system of refugee protection in the post-World War II period has mostly developed in reaction to refugee crises and mass outpourings, rather than as responses to the needs of individual refugees. As the history of the development of the Refugee Convention definition demonstrates, this means that the reality does not sit well with the legal situation. As the figures discussed above suggest, the world's refugee and displaced person population is largely out of sight of industrialised states as a result of focused policies of 'containment' or 'warehousing' of groups of refugees.

The Refugee Convention, which was negotiated in the aftermath of World War II, was intended to deal with the European problem of 1.25 million refugees arising out of the post-war chaos. In particular it was directed at the victims of Nazi and other fascist regimes. This is recognised by the refugee definition, which describes a refugee as a person with an individual 'well-founded fear of being persecuted' as a result of 'events occurring before 1 January 1951' (Article 1A(2)), with states having an option to limit their obligations to refugees from Europe under Article 1B. The *Protocol relating to the Status of Refugees* of 1967 (the 'Refugee Protocol')[23] removed these temporal and geographical limits, thus apparently indicating that the Refugee Convention applied globally.

The Refugee Convention not only provided an individualised definition of a refugee but also made it clear that it was an instrument for human rights protection. The Refugee Convention, which arose from European events and which was brokered (largely) by European nations, was a manifestation of the development of a system of international law and institutions intended to provide responses and solutions to a global problem. The importance of the establishment of the UNHCR in 1951 to administer the Refugee Convention under the United Nations General Assembly (the 'GA') should not be underestimated. This measure anticipated the development of far-reaching human rights instruments which were intended to recognise the universality of human rights. Notably, the reference in the Preamble of the Refugee Convention to the *Universal Declaration of Human Rights*[24] is relied upon to indicate the underlying human rights basis of the Refugee Convention. The view of leading refugee law scholars is reflected by Michelle Foster, who says:

---

[23] *Protocol relating to the Status of Refugees*, opened for signature on 31 January 1967, 19 UNTS 6223, 6257 (entered into force 4 October 1967) (the 'Refugee Protocol').

[24] *Universal Declaration of Human Rights*, GA Res 217(111) of 10 December 1948, UN Doc A/810 at 71 (1948) ('UDHR').

In light of the reference in the Preamble to the UDHR, it is arguable that the Refugee Convention should be placed within the context of the developing body of international human rights law.[25]

As James Hathaway has explained, the instruments[26] leading up to the 1951 Convention were inspired either by 'humanitarianism', that is 'an attempt to accommodate the reality of a largely unstoppable flow of involuntary migrants across European borders'[27] or by the need for individual human rights protection. The significance of the Refugee Convention was that it made such protection dependent upon the need to prove individual persecution rather than being applicable to categories of persons subject to human rights abuse.

Thus in this context it can be seen that the Refugee Convention is an instrument of human rights protection which was intended to implement the basic right to flee persecution and to seek and enjoy asylum, and to enshrine the right against *refoulement* or return to a place where 'life' or 'freedom' is threatened (Article 33(2)). The refugee definition in Article 1A(2) refers to a person who is outside her or his country, and who has a 'well-founded fear of being persecuted for reasons of' one of five specified grounds: namely, race, religion, nationality, membership of a particular social group or political opinion.[28] This was a significant development as previous refugee instruments had provided a generalised, descriptive refugee definition.[29] It is now regarded as well established that the Refugee Convention and the elements of the definition, including the meaning of 'persecution' and 'being persecuted', should be interpreted within a human rights framework which includes reference to the standards provided by the main human rights treaties.[30] As Hathaway has said,

---

[25] Michelle Foster, *International Refugee Law and Socio-Economic Rights: Refuge from Deprivation* (Cambridge University Press, Cambridge, 2007) 49, citations omitted. See also James C Hathaway, *The Rights of Refugees Under International Law* (Cambridge University Press, Cambridge, 2005) 8.

[26] See, eg, 1933 *Convention relating to the International Status of Refugees*, 159 LNTS No. 3663; 1938 *Convention concerning the Status of Refugees coming from Germany*, 191 LNTS No.4461. See James C Hathaway, 'The Evolution of Refugee Status in International Law: 1920–1950' (1984) 33 *International and Comparative Law Quarterly*, 348.

[27] James C Hathaway, 'A Reconsideration of the Underlying Premise of Refugee Law' (1990) 31 *Harvard International Law Journal* 129, 137.

[28] Each of these grounds has been interpreted in the light of general human rights protections.

[29] James C Hathaway, 'The Evolution of Refugee Status in International Law: 1920–1950' (1984) 33 *International and Comparative Law Quarterly*, 348.

[30] Michelle Foster, *International Refugee Law and Socio-Economic Rights: Refuge from Deprivation* (Cambridge University Press, Cambridge, 2007), Chapter 2. The role of 'soft law' and 'customary' law are less clear.

the Refugee Convention was 'rarely understood to be the primary point of reference' for refugee rights.[31]

However, in practice the elements of the definition (which are themselves undefined) have been interpreted restrictively for some categories of claims, including those which according to the UNHCR are the basis upon which most people flee, namely conflict and human rights violations.[32] In particular the Refugee Convention definition, which applies to individuals, has been interpreted to require 'targeted' persecution (through the words 'for reasons of' which have been interpreted to require a strict nexus, or causal link, between the 'predicament'[33] of the applicant for refugee status and one of the given Convention grounds). Therefore, for example, people caught up in civil war or fleeing conflict may have difficulty in bringing their claim within the Refugee Convention definition because the harm suffered by an individual is indistinguishable from that suffered by a general section of the population at large. In the context of civil war and internal conflict, a distinction has been made between laws or acts which apply to the general populace (which are prima facie not persecutory by nature) and those which single out an individual or group of individuals (and may amount to 'persecution').[34] A second restrictive technique is to interpret the Refugee Convention to cover principally abuses of civil and political rights (as did the Italian inspiration for this discussion), whereas the human rights context of the Refugee Convention makes it clear that it was intended to cover denial of or discrimination on the basis of *all* human rights, including the so-called 'second generation' social and economic rights.[35] Thus substantial numbers of refugees are excluded from protection by restrictive interpretations in receiving states.

Such restrictive interpretations reflect the history of the development of the international refugee regime. In the Cold War period, crises such as the Hungarian one of 1956 and the Czech uprising in 1968 emphasised the ideological basis of the individualised concept of refugee protection in the 1951 Refugee Convention (and thus supported a reading of the definition as focused upon civil and political rights). However, from the 1970s onwards, refugee crises in other parts of the world, largely in Africa and Asia, suggested that the

---

[31] James C Hathaway, *The Rights of Refugees Under International Law* (Cambridge University Press, Cambridge, 2005) 5.
[32] See UNHCR, above n 21, [2].
[33] See generally, Foster, above n 30, 247.
[34] *Adan v Secretary of State for the Home Department* [1999] 1 AC 293. See S Kneebone, 'Moving Beyond the State: Refugees, Accountability and Protection' in S Kneebone (ed) *The Refugee Convention 50 Years On: Globalisation and International Law* (Ashgate, Aldershot, 2003) 285–317, 297–305.
[35] Foster, above n 30.

refugee problem was not unique to Europe and that it required different approaches. As we shall see in the next section, these developments highlighted the 'humanitarian' nature of refugee protection.

The UNHCR promoted the 1967 Refugee Protocol to enable it to deal with new situations of refugees en masse, such as Chinese refugees fleeing communism and refugees from African states affected by de-colonisation, civil wars and independence movements. However, whilst the Refugee Protocol recognised the global nature of the problem, the universality of the rights of refugees, and the possibility of global solutions,[36] it did not grant the UNHCR the extra powers it wanted to deal with groups of refugees.[37] The legacy of this episode was to create a distinction between refugees who flee individualised persecution (and who can claim refugee status under the 1951 Refugee Convention) and those who flee generalised violence (who may have difficulty in proving that they are persecuted as individuals for Refugee Convention reasons). The process surrounding the creation of the Protocol also showed the tension between state interests and the UNHCR, which is dependent on the same states as donors for its operations.

## A    Development of the UNHCR mandate: refugees and humanitarian protection

The UNHCR was established by the GA in 1950 and provided with a statute to describe its role and mandate, the *Statute of the Office of the United Nations High Commissioner for Refugees* (the 'UNHCR statute').[38] It replaced the International Refugee Organisation, whose Constitution had specified categories of persons and refugees to be assisted (as mentioned above). Importantly, the UNHCR statute refers to its 'humanitarian' and 'non-political' role in the same sentence, thus endorsing the association between humanitarian ideals and neutrality. Article 2 of the UNHCR statute provided as follows:

> The work of the High Commissioner shall be of an entirely non-political character; it shall be humanitarian and social and shall relate, as a rule, to groups and categories of refugees.[39]

---

[36] Laura Barnett, 'Global Governance and the Evolution of the International Refugee Regime' (2002) 14 *International Journal of Refugee Law* 238, 248.
[37] Sara E Davies, 'Redundant or Essential? How Politics Shaped the Outcome of the 1967 Protocol' (2007) 19 *International Journal of Refugee Law* 703.
[38] UNGA res. 428(V), Annex of 14 December 1950.
[39] Ibid.

At the same time, Article 6 of the UNHCR statute adopted the Refugee Convention definition of a refugee. Thus, it has been suggested that the UNHCR statute contains an 'apparent contradiction'.[40] On the one hand it applies to groups and categories of refugees, but it also provides an individualised definition in the same terms as the 1951 Refugee Convention. It seems that no specific consideration was given to this fact. In practice the UNHCR mandate has evolved subsequently in direct response to large-scale crises to cover both refugees and other categories of displaced persons in regions of origin, asylum seekers in destination states and stateless persons, who are collectively referred to as 'persons of concern' in the UNHCR's collection of statistics.

A brief summary of the UNHCR's involvement in such crises illustrates the flexible and incremental evolution of its role and mandate. In 1957 the GA authorised the UNHCR to use its 'good offices' to intervene in the crisis of mainland Chinese in Hong Kong. The 'good offices' mandate was used again in 1959 in relation to refugees in Morocco and Tunisia.[41] Another extension of its protection mandate, which harked back to the pre-1951 period, was through the conferment of prima facie status on certain groups of refugees without the need for individual determinations.[42] Thus in this context the ideas of humanitarian and individual protection clearly ran together.

The reference to 'persons of concern' in contemporary statistical reports has it origins in the GA's use of the term 'refugees and displaced persons of concern' since the mid-1970s.[43] In particular this term was used to describe UNHCR activities in Sudan (1972) and in Vietnam (1975). At this time the term 'displaced persons' was used to refer to victims of countries split by civil war, so the legal niceties of whether they were 'refugees' was avoided. The UNHCR was reluctant to use the term 'refugee' for this category of displaced persons or to accord them prima facie status in this period.[44] It has been suggested that this category of displaced persons had its foundations in humanitarian necessity rather than legal status,[45] thus reinforcing a distinction between the legal status of 'refugee' and humanitarian status.

In particular, the UNHCR developed its mandate in the refugee crisis in Indochina in the 1970s and 1980s when up to three million people fled in the

---

[40] Goodwin-Gill and McAdam, above n 7, 23.
[41] Ibid 24–5.
[42] Ibid 27.
[43] Ibid 26.
[44] Ibid 28. See also Sara E Davies, *Legitimising Rejection: International Refugee Law in South East Asia* (Martinus Nijhoff Publishers, Leiden and Boston, 2008), Chapter 3.
[45] Goodwin-Gill and McAdam, above n 7, 27.

two decades after 1975. Always subject to critical scrutiny by donor countries and regional participants, the UNHCR experimented with various responses during this crisis. For example, 600,000 people who fled Indochina between 1975 and 1979 were initially granted prima facie status. Later the concept of temporary protection was utilised. Subsequently, the UNHCR assisted in the formulation of the Comprehensive Plan of Action (the 'CPA') for Indo-Chinese Refugees. The CPA developed in two stages. The first stage was brokered by the United Nations Secretary-General in 1979, resulting from pressure by the Association of Southeast Asian Nations (the 'ASEAN'), and involved temporary asylum to be followed by resettlement in a third country. In an attempt to deter clandestine departures it was accompanied by an Orderly Departure Programme ('ODP'). However, when the problem continued to escalate, it was followed in 1989 by the formal CPA, which had an emphasis on voluntary returns and reintegration in the country of origin. In this instance the Malaysian government requested the UNHCR to convene a second international conference, in which the ASEAN again participated. As a result, the CPA was agreed upon at a Geneva Conference held on 13–14 June 1989 by the UNHCR, the countries of first asylum and 50 resettlement countries.

The role of the UNHCR in the implementation of the CPA is nothing short of controversial.[46] The predominant features of the CPA were the emphasis on orderly departures and resettlement and consequently, although countries in the region provided initial asylum, they did not eventually sign up to the Refugee Convention. It has been suggested that the UNHCR's pragmatic approach to the problem is responsible for the current lack of commitment in the South East Asia region to refugees.[47] Further criticism arose from the fact that the UNHCR assisted with the processing of asylum seekers in countries of first asylum by producing Guidelines to encourage uniformity of practice in the region. But, as the UNHCR's role in this respect under the CPA was to 'observe and advise', individual states retained control over the selection process. Yet many critiques emerged of the processes and of the UNHCR's

---

[46] A sample of the voluminous literature on this issue includes: S A Bronée, 'The History of the Comprehensive Plan of Action' (1993) 5 *International Journal of Refugee Law* 534; W C Robinson, 'The Comprehensive Plan of Action for Indochinese Refugees, 1989–1997: Sharing the Burden and Passing the Buck' (2004) 17 *Journal of Refugee Studies* 319; Y Tran, Comment, 'The Closing of the Saga of the Vietnamese Asylum Seekers: The Implications on International Refugees and Human Rights Laws' (1995) 15 *Houston Journal of International Law* 463; UNHCR, *The State of the World's Refugees 2000: Fifty Years of Humanitarian Action* (Oxford University Press, Oxford, 2000) Chapter 4: 'Flight from Indochina'.

[47] See Davies, above n 44.

perceived failure to be more proactive in this respect.[48] The UNHCR was also criticised for its role in assisting 'voluntary' returns to Vietnam. Additionally in this period the UNHCR took on a humanitarian role which involved monitoring the situation in the country of origin for those who remained or who were returned. The UNHCR was criticised for engaging too actively with 'humanitarian' measures within Vietnam and thus breaching its 'non-political' mandate.

Altogether, the role of the UNHCR in the CPA demonstrated the complexity of its position and a flexible and pragmatic application of its mandate. Importantly, during this crisis the term 'displaced persons' was used. The CPA facilitated the incremental development of the UNHCR's role, which in the last two decades has become increasingly solution and protection oriented[49] rather than bound by legal categories. For example, UNHCR played an important role in coordinating relief in the 2004 tsunami disaster in South East Asia. It has also recently indicated its support for solutions to 'environmental refugees' who do not strictly meet the Refugee Convention refugee definition. It thus regards its humanitarian protection mandate to cover groups and persons who fall outside the legal category of 'refugee' or the strict terms of its mandate[50] in accordance with the literal meaning of the term 'humanitarian', that is, 'having regard to the interests of humanity at large'. Or, to express this in more positive terms, it perceives its mandate to refugees within the context of its broader humanitarian role.

### B   The 'internally displaced persons' issue: the UNHCR's mandate and 'humanitarianism'

The above discussion demonstrates that the legal definition of a refugee in the 1951 Refugee Convention does not cover all categories of displaced persons; but the term 'humanitarian protection' has broader application. In the 1980s, in response to mass displacements, scholars who had begun to study the phenomenon of forced migration and displaced persons pointed out the limits of the Refugee Convention definition. As David Turton expressed it, 'no sooner had the concept of refugee been confined to this legal box than it began

---

[48] See, eg, R Mushkat, 'Implementation of the CPA in Hong Kong' (1993) 5 *International Journal of Refugee Law* 562. See also Richard Towle, 'Processes and Critiques of the Indo-Chinese CPA: An Instrument of International Burden-Sharing?' (2006) 18 *International Journal of Refugee Law* (Nos 3 and 4) 537.

[49] Susan Kneebone, 'The Legal and Ethical Implications of Extra-territorial Processing of Asylum Seekers: the Safe Third Country Concept' in J McAdam (ed), *Moving On: Forced Migration and Human Rights* (Hart Publishing, Oxford, 2008) Chapter 5.

[50] Goodwin-Gill and McAdam, above n 7, 29, n 74.

jumping out'.⁵¹ Meanwhile legal academics such as Kay Hailbronner reinforced the distinction between the legal definition and humanitarian protection which is implicit in UNHCR's mandate, by focusing upon the need for particularised fear and by attacking the notion of 'humanitarian' refugees.⁵² In particular it was argued that the Refugee Convention did not apply to 'those who shelter from conditions of general armed violence', natural disaster or 'simply bad economic conditions'.⁵³

By contrast, in other regions affected by mass displacements of people, new instruments broadened the legal definition and recognised the coincidence between refugee and 'humanitarian' protection. For example, Article II(2) of the 1969 Organisation of African Unity *Convention Governing the Specific Aspects of Refugee Problems in Africa* (the 'OAU Convention')⁵⁴ states that the grant of asylum is 'a peaceful and humanitarian act'. This OAU Convention arose in the context of independence movements and massive displacements in the decolonisation period of Africa.⁵⁵ The 1969 OAU Convention was a direct inspiration for the 1984 *Cartagena Declaration on Refugees* adopted at a Colloquium held at Cartagena, Colombia, in November

---

51   David Turton, *Conceptualising Forced Migration* (October 2003) RSC Working Paper no 12, www.rsc.ox.ac.uk at 20 March 2009, 13; David Turton, *Refugee, forced resettlers and 'other forced migrants': towards a unitary study of forced migration* (September 2003) UNHCR Working Paper no 94, <http://www.unhcr.org/research/RESEARCH/3f818a4d4.pdf> at 20 March 2009; David Turton, 'Who is a forced migrant?' in Chris de Wet (ed) *Development-induced Displacement: Problems, Policies and People* (Berghahn Books, New York/Oxford, 2006) 14–37; M Cernea, 'Bridging the research divide: studying refugees and development oustees' in *In Search of Cool Ground: War, Flight & Homecoming in Northeast Africa* (United Nations Research Institute for Social Development, New York, 1996).

52   K Hailbronner, 'Non-Refoulement and "Humanitarian" Refugees: Customary International Law or Wishful Legal Thinking?' (1985–86) 26 *Virginia Journal of International Law* 857.

53   Ibid 858. See also T A Aleinikoff, 'State Centred Refugee Law: From Resettlement to Containment' (1992) 14 *Michigan Journal of International Law* 120; J Hathaway, 'A Reconsideration of the Underlying Premise of Refugee Law?' (1990) 31 *Harvard International Law Journal* 129, argued that neither a humanitarian nor a human rights approach was an adequate approach in itself to the refugee 'problem'.

54   Organisation of African Unity, *Convention Governing the Specific Aspects of Refugee Problems in Africa*, opened for signature 10 September 1969, 1001 UNTS 45 (entered into force on 20 June 1974) ('OAU Convention').

55   Between 1963 and 1966 the number of refugees in Africa rose from 300,000 to 700,000: Micah B Rankin, 'Extending the Limits or Narrowing the Scope? Deconstructing the OAU Refugee Definition Thirty Years On', UNHCR, New Issues in Refugee Research, Working Paper No. 113 (April 2005) 2.

1984 (the 'Cartagena Declaration'),[56] which relates to the 'refugee situation' in Central America. This was a response to mass refugee influxes, in this case arising from political and military instability in Central America in the 1970s and 1980s. As in the OAU Convention, the refugee definition in the Cartagena Declaration is linked to root causes[57] and confirms that the granting of asylum is 'humanitarian' in nature. The Cartagena Declaration reflected the then current experiences of refugees by expressing its 'concern' at the problem raised by military attacks on refugee camps and settlements in different parts of the world.[58] Additionally, going beyond the 'legal' refugee issue, it expressed its 'concern' at the 'situation of displaced persons within their own countries'.[59]

The term 'internally displaced person' (IDP), which came into use in the 1980s, distinguishes refugees as persons who have crossed a border, and focuses upon the fact that IDPs are 'internal refugees'. As we shall see, a different response based upon humanitarian principles and 'responsibility to protect' was formulated for IDPs. However, the UNHCR continued to play a role in the protection of IDPs in a further extension of its mandate. In so doing, the binary between legal status and humanitarian protection became entrenched.[60]

The first major international recognition of an IDP issue was the Security Council authorisation for Allied intervention in Iraq to protect the Kurds in 1991, although the issue had been acknowledged since the end of the 1980s in the context of difficulties in repatriating Cambodian and Afghan refugees. Thomas Weiss and David Korn[61] point to Resolution 1992/73[62] of the Commission on Human Rights, where the United Nations Secretary-General was requested to appoint a Special Representative on IDPs and to commission

---

[56] *Cartagena Declaration on Refugees*, OAS/Ser.L/V/II.66, doc.10, rev.1, (22 November 1984) 190–93 ('Cartagena Declaration').

[57] Art. I(2) of the OAU Convention states: 'The term "refugee" shall also apply to every person who, owing to external aggression, occupation, foreign domination or events seriously disturbing public order in either part or the whole of his country of origin or nationality, is compelled to leave his place of habitual residence in order to seek refuge in another place outside his country of origin or nationality.'

[58] Cartagena Declaration [III(7)].

[59] Cartagena Declaration [III(9)].

[60] Indeed it has been argued that the UNHCR continually sought a humanitarian role: G Loescher, 'The UNHCR and World Politics: State Interests vs Institutional Autonomy' in (2001) 35 *International Migration Review* (no 1) 33–56.

[61] Thomas G Weiss and David A Korn, *Internal Displacement – Conceptualization and Consequences* (Routledge, London, 2006), Chapter 1.

[62] UN Doc E/CN.4/1992/73 (1992).

a study of the IDP issue, as the beginning of the development of a separate 'mandate' on the issue.[63]

Throughout the 1990s, the advocates for resolution of the IDP issue sought to keep the issue out of the United Nations, whilst the UNHCR fought to retain the integrity of its protection mandate. At the same time, the UNHCR further expanded its 'good offices' mandate to provide humanitarian assistance to IDPs,[64] as for example in the Balkans crisis. In 1993, the GA authorised UNHCR involvement in IDP issues where there was a specific request from the United Nations and where the state concerned consented.[65] But this humanitarian role did not include the provision of legal protection.[66] In September 2005 the UNHCR was assigned the role of 'cluster' chair for the protection of conflict-generated IDPs in the United Nations Inter-Agency Standing Committee established to co-ordinate humanitarian protection.[67] In addition, the UNHCR chairs clusters on emergency shelter and on camp management and co-ordination under this approach.

In the debate over the role of the UNHCR in relation to IDPs there are various assumptions about the scope of its mandate. For example, it has been argued that its primary role is to determine legal status,[68] and that its role in the Balkans raised issues of conflict of interest between its 'protection' mandate to refugees and its role in 'containing' displaced persons within the country of origin.[69] Elaborating upon that point, it has been suggested that the UNHCR's role was initially conceived as 'neutral, passive and reactive'. Thus, there is continuing disagreement about the limits of the UNHCR's mandate, and about how UNHCR should perform its humanitarian role. But my argument is that there is a synergy between the legal definition of a refugee and 'humanitarianism'. In practical terms it may not be possible to draw a bright line between refugees and other groups in need of humanitarian assistance.

The IDP issue is greatest in situations where there are failed states and internal conflict (such as West Darfur, Sudan and Chad). In these situations,

---

[63] Francis Deng was the appointee. The study by Deng culminated in the Guiding Principles on Internal Displacement E/CN.4/1998/53/Add.2 of 11 February 1998.
[64] Guy S Goodwin-Gill, 'International Protection and Assistance for Refugees and the Displaced: Institutional Challenges and UN Reform', paper presented at the Refugee Studies Centre Workshop, Oxford, 24 April 2006.
[65] UNGA res. 48/116, 'Office of the United Nations High Commissioner for Refugees' of 20 December 1993 [12].
[66] Goodwin-Gill and McAdam, above n 7, 34.
[67] Established under 'Strengthening of the co-ordination of humanitarian assistance of the United Nations', GA res 46/182, of 19 December 1991 [Annex, 38].
[68] Goodwin-Gill, above n 64, 2.
[69] Goodwin-Gill and McAdam, above n 7, 49.

the distinction between IDP and refugee is fluid and technical, depending upon whether a person has managed to cross a border. Certainly IDP and protracted refugee situations often coexist on different sides of the border in Africa in particular. As the figures quoted above demonstrate, IDPs now outnumber refugees in today's world.

In light of the above discussion, it is perhaps unsurprising that a debate has developed over the UNHCR's increasingly 'solution-oriented' approach through its humanitarian work in regions of origin. One of the overarching problems which besets the international response to refugees is the tendency to 'contain' or 'warehouse' them in regions of origin.[70] The proponents of refugee rights stress the importance of the institution of asylum, and the UNHCR's role in defending it,[71] implicitly and expressly critiquing the UNHCR for putting too much focus upon regions of origin. They perceive this quest for solutions in regions of origin as fuelling the use by industrialised destination states of restrictive entry practices and restrictive interpretation of the refugee definition. This debate reflects the binary between the legal definition of a refugee and the notion of humanitarian protection – the latter is seen as the appropriate response in far-away places and the justification for refusal to grant refugee status by industrialised destination states.

## 4  IDPs and the development of humanitarian 'norms'

A plank of the argument in this chapter is that restrictive approaches to refugees reflect a confused understanding of the meaning of 'humanitarian'. As the quotations at the outset of this chapter illustrate, the word has different connotations which reflect its different uses. For example, the term 'humanitarian intervention' has been used to describe the basis of military intervention in the case of the United Nations in Iraq in 1991 (in aid of the Kurds), and subsequently by NATO in Kosovo. Often the intervention was needed in order to provide assistance to civilian populations. The term 'humanitarian assistance' has been used to describe the protection given to displaced persons, including by the UNHCR, often in the aftermath of humanitarian interventions. In legal terms, the roots for such intervention or assistance are very different. It is my central argument that, through the conflation of ideas, 'humanitarianism' has become politicised and divorced from the original meaning of 'humanitarian'. As others have said:

---

[70]  M J Gibney, 'Forced Migration, Engineered Regionalism and Justice between States' in S Kneebone and F Rawlings-Sanaei (eds), *New Regionalism and Asylum Seekers: Challenges Ahead* (Berghahn Books, Oxford, 2007), Chapter 3.

[71]  A Suhrke and K Newland, 'UNHCR: Uphill into the Future' (2001) 35 *International Migration Review* 284–302 at 292; James C Hathaway, 'Forced Migration Studies: Could We Agree Just to "Date"?' (2007) *Journal of Refugee Studies* 349.

> This contemporary debate over the purposes, principles, and politics of humanitarianism reveals a struggle to (re)define the humanitarian identity . . . The debate over the humanitarian identity reflects a search to recapture the unity and purity that is tied to its presumed universality.[72]

In this section, I provide a thumbnail sketch of the legal bases of humanitarian intervention and assistance and the debates concerning the scope of these principles. In particular I want to demonstrate how the *IDP Guiding Principles* 1998 (the 'Guiding Principles')[73] attempted to reconcile these debates and to provide a normative framework within which the rights both of displaced persons and of refugees are recognised. This is in contrast to the UNHCR mandate, which lacks an explicit normative framework. Although refugee scholars argue for the need to interpret the Refugee Convention definition broadly, in accordance with its human rights context[74] and the general framework of rights, this is not mandated.[75]

The traditional meaning of 'humanitarian law' as a branch of international law is concerned with the scope of the rules of conduct in armed conflict, now codified in the 1949 Geneva Conventions and the two Protocols of 1977. The main change in humanitarian law since World War II has been its emphasis on the shielding of the civilian population from the effects of war,[76] as well as its extension into and prescription of minimum standards of humane conduct in non-international armed conflict. It has been suggested that humanitarian law shares with human rights law, albeit on a narrower basis, 'a fundamental concern for humanity'.[77]

The International Committee of the Red Cross (the 'ICRC'), which has a unique and central role in international humanitarian law as a neutral NGO providing humanitarian assistance, maintains its own guidelines of humanitarian behaviour, albeit in a context applicable to the ICRC rather than states.

---

[72] Michael Barnett and Thomas G Weiss (eds) *Humanitarianism in Question: Politics, Power, Ethics* (Cornell University Press, Ithaca and London, 2008) 5.
[73] Report of the Representative of the Secretary-General, Mr Francis M Deng, submitted pursuant to Commission resolution 1997/39, Addendum, Guiding Principles on Internal Displacement, E/CN.4/1998/53/Add.2 (11 February 1998).
[74] This includes reference to the UDHR in the Preamble to the Refugee Convention.
[75] But note that the UNHCR Handbook recognises the human rights context and framework. However many states are reluctant to recognise its authority as other than 'mere' guidance.
[76] J-P Lavoyer, 'Forced Displacement: The Relevance of International Humanitarian Law' in Anne E Bayefsky and Joan Fitzpatrick (eds) *Human Rights and Forced Displacement* (Martinus Nijhoff Publishers, 2000), Chapter 3, 52.
[77] Rene Provost, *International Human Rights Law and Humanitarian Law* (Cambridge University Press, Cambridge, 2002) 5.

Jean Pictet famously identified seven core principles of humanitarianism for the purposes of the ICRC: humanity, impartiality, neutrality, independence, voluntary service, unity, and universality.[78]

Yet another use of the term 'humanitarian' in international law comes from the mooted doctrine of 'humanitarian intervention'. Article 2(7) of the United Nations Charter (the 'UN Charter')[79] recognises the power of the Security Council to mandate an intervention where there is a 'threat to peace' within the meaning of Chapter VII of the UN Charter (see Articles 39–42). Instances of the 'humanitarian' use by the Security Council of this power include Iraq, Somalia and Haiti, although dispute remains as to the weight accorded to humanitarian considerations in the decision to authorise intervention. There have also been arguments that states can engage in humanitarian intervention outside the auspices of the United Nations, as occurred with the NATO intervention in Kosovo.[80] Unsurprisingly, legal and policy debates around this issue have centred on the concept of state sovereignty and the politics of intervention, with some commentators pointing to inconsistencies in the use of the power to intervene in recent crises.[81]

On a broader level, the notion of humanitarian intervention has led to philosophical debates about the limits and ethics of intervention, and about the link between human rights abuse and humanitarian assistance.[82] It has

---

[78] See Jean Pictet, *The Fundamental Principles of the Red Cross* (Henry Dunant Institute, Geneva, 1979).

[79] Charter of the United Nations, available at http://www.un.org/aboutun/charter at 20 March 2009 ('UN Charter').

[80] See, generally, Chapter 1 at pp. 31–2.

[81] Klinton L Alexander, 'Ignoring the Lessons of the Past: the Crisis in Darfur and the Case for Humanitarian Intervention' (2005) 15 *Journal of Transnational Law and Policy* 1; Chimni, above n 3, 256, points out that between 1991 and 1997 the Security Council made specific reference to UNHCR assuming a humanitarian role more than 30 times in contrast to a mere 4 times prior to 1991. Barnett and Weiss, above n 72, also highlight the role of the Security Council in the internal affairs of states in the name of humanitarianism, at 27.

[82] E R McCleskey, 'Sovereignty and Humanitarian Intervention: A Conflict Between the Rights of States and Individuals' in Andrzej Bolesta (ed) *International Development and Assistance – where politics meet economy* (Leon Kozminski, Academy of Entrepreneurship and Management, Warsaw, 2004) Chapter 4; Simon Caney, '*Humanitarian Intervention, from Justice Beyond Borders: A Global Political Theory* (Oxford University Press, Oxford, 2005); K Luopajarvi, 'Is there an Obligation on States to Accept International Humanitarian Assistance to Internally Displaced Persons under International Law?' (2003) 15 *International Journal of Refugee Law* 678; J M Welsh, 'Taking Consequences Seriously: Objections to Humanitarian Intervention' in J M Welsh (ed) *Humanitarian Intervention and International Relations* (Oxford University Press, Oxford, 2004); Julie Mertus, 'Reconsidering the Legality of Humanitarian Intervention: Lessons from Kosovo' (2000) 41 *William and Mary Law Review* 1743.

been suggested that the notion of humanitarian intervention has led to a move from 'sovereignty as authority' to 'sovereignty as responsibility'.[83] For example, Abiew says that 'Humanitarian intervention is based on the notion that sovereign jurisdiction is conditional upon compliance with minimum standards of human rights.'[84] In this context there is an uneasy alliance between human rights and Western security interests in the name of humanitarianism, which potentially undermines the original sense, or 'purity', of humanitarian protection.

At the level of practical guidance, the Guiding Principles are significant in promoting the normative basis for humanitarian assistance. They focus broadly on the human rights needs of displaced persons and on the need to protect IDPs from discrimination arising from displacement generally. Importantly, the Guiding Principles are not restricted to situations of armed conflict but apply to all internally displaced persons. Moreover, the Guiding Principles are based upon existing human rights protection. The Introductory Note, paragraph 9, states quite clearly:

> The purpose of the Guiding Principles is to address the specific needs of internally displaced persons worldwide by identifying rights and guarantees relevant to their protection. The Principles reflect and are consistent with international human rights law and international humanitarian law.

They are intended to provide not only practical guidance but also to be an instrument of public policy education and consciousness-raising.[85] It is also important to note that the Guiding Principles specifically recognise the rights of asylum seekers and refugees under the Refugee Convention. Principle 15 reasserts the right of internally displaced persons to seek asylum 'in another country'.

The key principles reflect the norms of 'sovereignty as responsibility'.[86] For example, Principle 3.1 states:

> National authorities have the primary duty and responsibility to provide protection and humanitarian assistance to internally displaced persons within their jurisdiction.

---

[83] J M Welsh, 'Taking Consequences Seriously: Objections to Humanitarian Intervention' in J M Welsh (ed), *Humanitarian Intervention and International Relations* (Oxford University Press, Oxford, 2004) 52.
[84] F W Abiew, *The Evolution of the Doctrine and Practice of Humanitarian Intervention* (Kluwer, The Hague, 1999) 58.
[85] Ibid [11].
[86] Weiss and Korn, above n 61, 5.

The idea of 'sovereignty as responsibility' is a central concept of the Guiding Principles. For example, Principle 25 states as follows:

1. The primary duty and responsibility for providing humanitarian assistance to internally displaced persons lies with national authorities.
2. International humanitarian organizations and other appropriate actors have the right to offer their services in support of the internally displaced. Such an offer shall not be regarded as ... an interference in a State's internal affairs ... Consent thereto shall not be arbitrarily withheld, particularly when authorities concerned are unable or unwilling to provide the required humanitarian assistance.

Thus the Guiding Principles establish a normative framework for protection of IDPs and recognise that such may include asylum seekers. Importantly they also recognise that the causes of displacement arise from a broad range of circumstances including 'the effects of armed conflict, situations of generalised violence, violations of human rights or natural or human-made disasters'.[87] They recognise the need to protect displaced persons from discrimination 'in the enjoyment of *any* rights and freedoms' (Principle 1, emphasis added), which includes the denial of social and economic rights. The Guiding Principles contain repeated references to the need to respect human rights (Principles 5, 8, 18, 20). Principle 22 prohibits discrimination against IDPs on the basis of broad social and economic rights, including the rights to freedom of thought, conscience, religion or belief and the right to seek freely opportunities for employment and to participate in economic activities. And indeed it is because such rights are denied that IDPs flee and become asylum seekers and irregular international migrants.

As an international conference on the Ten Years of the Guiding Principles on Internal Displacement ('GP10') held in Oslo in October 2008 makes clear, although the Guiding Principles are accepted widely as spelling out the obligations of national authorities and the operational principles for protection of IDPs,[88] there are still challenges to acceptance of the normative framework of 'sovereignty as responsibility'.

Whilst the Guiding Principles recognise the 'humanitarian' needs of displaced persons, in the eyes of industrialised receiving states they are often 'economic refugees' or conflict-induced refugees who might become the objects of the exercise of humanitarian discretion. However, a proper reading

---

[87] Guiding Principles on Internal Displacement – Introduction: Scope and Purpose, E/CN.4/1998/53/Add.2 (11 February 1998) 5.

[88] In 2005, more than 190 states adopted the World Summit Outcome document, which specifically recognised the Guiding Principles. See http://www.un.org/summit2005/presskit/fact_sheet.pdf.

of the Refugee Convention definition against a human rights background would lead to recognition of their legal status as refugees in destination states and be consistent with a broad 'humanitarian' reading of the Refugee Convention.

## 5 Into the future: the UNHCR's humanitarian role and state responses

In its November 2007 Discussion Paper, the UNHCR referred to the main causes of international flight as human rights violations and armed conflict (as noted above) and said:

> Given the uneven outcomes of the globalisation process, coupled with the growing impact of climate change on the sustainability of life in many parts of the planet, it seems likely that the issue of human mobility will become increasingly complex and assume a leading role on the global policy agenda.[89]

As noted above, one of the results of such complex movements, which include 'mixed flows' of asylum seekers and irregular migrants in search of work, has been to apply restrictive entry approaches to *all* movement, because of the 'asylum–migration nexus'. Due to the negative connotations associated with that term, recently the UNHCR has determined to avoid 'asylum–migration nexus' and instead to refer to 'refugee protection and durable solutions in the context of international migration'.[90] This solution-oriented approach to international migration includes implementation of the '10 Point Plan'[91] which was conceived and drafted in the context of the Mediterranean crisis with which this chapter began. That plan arose out of UNHCR's frustration at the lack of coordinated efforts between countries and agencies in that region.[92] But the ideas behind the 10 Point Plan are intended to be applied globally.

The 10 Point Plan is intended to assist with 'durable solutions in the context of international migration'. It has a strong emphasis on practical measures, upon cooperation, and sharing of data and information between countries and agencies. Some of the language of the 10 Point Plan is reminiscent of attempts to find 'solutions' in the 1980s, as for example in the preventing of secondary

---

[89] UNHCR, above n 21 [2].
[90] Jeff Crisp, Research Paper No 155 April 2008, 'Beyond the nexus: UNHCR's evolving perspective on refugee protection and international migration'.
[91] UNHCR, above n 21 [61].
[92] See J van Selm, 'The Europeanization of Refugee Policy' in Susan Kneebone and Felicity Rawlings-Sanaei (eds) *New Regionalism and Asylum Seekers: Challenges Ahead* (Berghahn Books, Oxford, 2007), Chapter 4, 96–9, for background to this issue. See also S Kneebone, 'The Legal and Ethical Implications of Extra-territorial Processing of Asylum Seekers' <http://arts.monash.edu.au/public-history-institute/conferences/2005-asylum/kneebone.pdf> at 20 March 2009.

movement, which is linked to policies of containment in regions of origin and restrictive entry measures by receiving states. Other parts of the 10 Point Plan hark back to the CPA for Indo-Chinese Refugees by referring to 'return arrangements' and 'alternative migration options'.

But what is also interesting for the present discussion is the way in which the UNHCR refers to its 'evolving role' in this context. The UNHCR refers to its 'precise mandate'[93] and describes itself as a 'rights-based organisation'.[94] In the November 2007 Discussion Paper it was said: the 'UNHCR's mandate is to provide protection and solutions for refugees and other persons who are of concern to the Office.'[95] It was stressed that the UNHCR's 'fundamental concern is the protection of refugees'.[96] But the UNHCR simultaneously stresses that its role is to provide humanitarian assistance and to address humanitarian concerns. Thus it is clear that the UNHCR does not see its role as involving a binary between the legal status of refugee and humanitarian protection – the former is an essential aspect of its broader role.

Yet states continue to apply the term 'humanitarian protection' to their schemes for complementary and temporary protection which by their very nature recognise the extra-legal quality of protection granted to persons who are considered to fall outside the legal definition of 'refugee'. Although schemes for complementary and temporary protection are in theory based upon the prohibition against torture contained in other human rights instruments,[97] their use has the potential to undermine the Refugee Convention. Further, in many states, the use of such forms of protection far outweighs the granting of refugee status.

As Jane McAdam has pointed out, the unique feature of the Refugee Convention in comparison with other human rights instruments is that international law requires that the person be granted the status of a refugee.[98] McAdam explains that whereas the grant of Refugee Convention status enti-

---

[93] Crisp, above n 90, 1.
[94] UNHCR, above n 21 [18].
[95] Ibid [10].
[96] Ibid [13].
[97] Eg *International Covenant on Civil and Political Rights*, opened for signature 16 December 1966, 999 UNTS 171 (entered into force 23 March 1976), Art 7; *Convention Against Torture and Other Cruel, Inhuman or Degrading Treatment or Punishment*, opened for signature 10 December 1984, 1465 UNTS 85 (entered into force 26 June 1987). Art 3. See Brian Gorlick, 'The Convention and the Committee against Torture: A Complementary Protection Regime for Refugees' (1999) 11 *International Journal Of Refugee Law* 479.
[98] Jane McAdam, 'The Refugee Convention as a Rights Blueprint for Persons in Need of International Protection' in McAdam (ed) *Moving On* (2007) 267.

tles the person to a full range of rights under the Refugee Convention,[99] 'no comparable status arises from recognition of an individual's protection need under a human rights instrument'.[100] As Hathaway says: 'Refugee status is a categorical designation that reflects a unique ethical and consequential legal entitlement to make claims on the international community'.[101] Michelle Foster explains:

> Indeed, the key purpose of the Refugee Convention was not so much to define who constitutes a refugee but to provide for the rights and entitlements that follow from such recognition.[102]

In practice the Refugee Convention is bypassed in many jurisdictions, where there is an inclination to grant lesser forms of protection to recognised refugees or to deny rights due under the Refugee Convention. Increasingly, the status-conferring function of the state is used to marginalise the international system of refugee protection, and to diminish the status of refugees and asylum seekers within the community.

In some jurisdictions such as Australia and the UK there is a trend to grant what are essentially complementary forms of protection to recognised refugees. That is, such protection is treated as essentially 'humanitarian'. Australia's Temporary Protection Visa ('TPV') system, which was in place from 1999 until mid-2008,[103] is mirrored in the UK. In Australia TPV holders had less social and economic rights than other refugees.[104] In Australia there is currently no formal system of complementary protection, other than through the Minister's exercise of the so-called 'humanitarian' discretion under the *Migration Act 1958* (Cth), s. 417.[105]

---

[99] See, eg, Art 17 of the Refugee Convention: refugees lawfully staying are entitled to wage-earning employment. See S Kneebone, 'The Pacific Plan: the Provision of "Effective Protection"?' (2006) 18 *International Journal of Refugee Law* 696 at 703–5 for a summary of the entitlements under the Refugee Convention.

[100] Ibid.

[101] James C Hathaway, 'Forced Migration Studies: Could We Agree Just to "Date"?' (2007) 20 *Journal of Refugee Studies* 349, 352.

[102] Foster, above n 30, 46.

[103] In the May 2008 budget the Labor government announced its intention to abolish the TPV scheme, <http://www.minister.immi.gov.au/media/media-releases/2008/ce05-budget-08.htm> accessed 23 May 2008.

[104] See S Kneebone 'The Pacific Plan: the Provision of "Effective Protection"?' (2006) 18 *International Journal of Refugee Law* 718–20.

[105] There have been many critiques of this situation. The current government has introduced a Migration Amendment (Complementary Protection) Bill 2009 to establish a formalised system of complementary protection.

In the UK, applicants granted refugee status are given a five-year temporary residence permit, called 'limited leave to remain'. Near the end of this term applicants may apply for permanent settlement, that is, 'indefinite leave to remain' in the UK. Alternatively, an applicant may be found to be entitled to one of the two forms of complementary protection: Humanitarian Protection, which entitles the applicant to be granted leave to remain in the UK for a period of five years,[106] or Discretionary Leave, under which an applicant will be granted leave to remain for a period of no longer than three years.[107] Those applicants granted complementary protection are able to apply for indefinite leave to remain after meeting specific qualification criteria.[108]

The tendency to complementary 'humanitarian' protection is also present in the European Union asylum system. Council Directive 2004/83/EC of 29 April 2004, also known as the 'Qualification Directive', provides 'minimum standards for the qualification and status of third country nationals . . . as refugees or as persons who otherwise need international protection'. In particular the Qualification Directive lays down the criteria for 'subsidiary protection status', which is 'complementary and additional to the refugee protection enshrined in the' Refugee Convention.[109] McAdam has critiqued the Qualification Directive, saying:

> While it establishes a harmonised legal basis for complementary protection in the EU, it does so in a political environment that is suspicious of asylum-seekers, that seeks restrictive entrance policies and that is wary of large numbers of refugees.[110]

Another commentator on the Directive has said:

> European policies have changed from being primarily rooted in humanitarian considerations to becoming more focused on state interests. One of the conse-

---

[106] Immigration Rules, para. 339E, http://www.ukba.homeoffice.gov.uk/policyandlaw/immigrationlaw/immigrationrules/part11 at 20 March 2009.

[107] See Home Office, 'Asylum Policy Instructions: Discretionary Leave', 9 April 2008, <http://www.bia.homeoffice.gov.uk/sitecontent/documents/policyandlaw/asylumpolicyinstructions/> at 19 April 2008.

[108] Applicants who have completed five years' Humanitarian Protection leave will be eligible to apply for Indefinite Leave to Remain: see Home Office, 'API: Humanitarian Protection', October 2006 [9]. Applicants on Discretionary Leave are eligible to apply for Indefinite Leave to remain after completing either six or ten continuous years of Discretionary Leave (depending on the reason the applicant was granted leave): see Home Office, 'API: Discretionary Leave'.

[109] Council Directive 2004/83/EC of 29 April 2004, Preamble clause 24.

[110] Jane McAdam, 'The European Union Qualification Directive: the Creation of a Subsidiary Protection Regime' (2005) 17 *International Journal of Refugee Law* 461, 465.

quences of this change is that the human rights machinery today plays a stronger role than hitherto as an instrument to counterbalance state powers. Consequently, we are now witnessing a conflict between new refugee policies and human rights law.[111]

This statement demonstrates that one of the side effects of the binary between legal refugee status and the concept of humanitarian protection is that states use human rights instruments as their 'sword'. By relying upon the complementary protection route provided by these instruments, they undermine the Refugee Convention. As this statement recognises, humanitarian considerations morph with state interests.

## 6 Conclusion

In this chapter I have located the restrictive responses of industrialised states to refugees and asylum seekers within a binary between the legal status of a refugee (as envisaged by the Refugee Convention) and the notion of humanitarian protection as 'extra-legal'. In particular, I have referred to restrictive interpretations of the individualised Refugee Convention definition, as in the case of persons fleeing conflict or discrimination on the basis of denial of social and economic rights, to illustrate the point. I have also pointed to the tendency of industrialised states to use schemes for complementary and temporary protection as 'humanitarian protection' in place of granting refugee status as further evidence of the use of a binary.

I have pointed out that this binary appears in the UNHCR's mandate, but that the UNHCR has consistently considered refugee protection to be an aspect of its general humanitarian role. I have argued that there is a synergy between the legal definition of a refugee and 'humanitarianism', as indicated by the human rights context of the Refugee Convention. Restrictive responses to refugees and to interpretation of the refugee definition reflect a confused understanding of the meaning of 'humanitarian' and narrow readings of the Refugee Convention definition. It seems that in this context 'humanitarian' has become synonymous with state discretion and border protection, rather than with human rights protection. In other words, the use of the term 'humanitarian protection' by industrialised destination states in relation to refugees denies credence to the Refugee Convention.

In this chapter, I have put the refugee 'problem' into the broader political and international context of displaced persons. I argued, through an examination of the different uses of 'humanitarian' in the context of displaced persons,

---

[111] Morten Kjaerum, 'Refugee Protection Between State Interests and Human Rights: Where is Europe Heading?' (2002) 24 *Human Rights Quarterly* 513–36 at 513–14.

that a similar misunderstanding of the term exists at the international level. There also, the notion of humanitarian protection has become confused with state interests. This is reflected in critiques of the UNHCR's role as a humanitarian organisation. It is my central argument that, through conflation of ideas, 'humanitarianism' has become politicised and divorced from the original meaning of 'humanitarian'.

However, the IDP Guiding Principles are significant in promoting the normative basis for humanitarian assistance. Importantly, they recognise the complex causes for movement and the right to seek asylum. They should be looked to for guidance on the rights of refugees and for promoting interpretations of the Refugee Convention definition within a human rights framework.

# 10. International criminal law
## *Elies van Sliedregt and Desislava Stoitchkova*

**1 Introduction**

The term 'international criminal law' harbours various meanings. Traditionally it refers to the international aspects of national criminal law. It concerns the legal issues that arise when prosecuting cross-border crime. States conclude agreements and treaties on how to proceed when prosecuting such crimes. State sovereignty plays an important role in this type of 'internationalised' criminal law. Various designations are used to refer to it: transnational criminal law, horizontal international criminal law, or *droit pénal international*. Topics that are typically part of this type of law are: (i) extraterritorial jurisdiction, (ii) extradition, (iii) police and judicial cooperation, (iv) transfer of criminal proceedings and (v) transfer and execution of foreign judicial decisions.

Many treaties have been concluded to shape such inter-State collaboration; some extradition treaties date back to the 16th century. Criminal cooperation agreements can be bilateral or multilateral. Multilateral treaties very often are the product of cooperation within a regional or international organisation such as the Council of Europe or the United Nations (the 'UN'). In recent years, the European Union (the 'EU') has been active in setting up a cooperation regime in criminal matters for its Member States. This more informal and efficient regime replaces the classical inter-State criminal cooperation regime of the Council of Europe and is based on the principle of 'mutual recognition' of foreign judicial decisions, which limits the exercise of State sovereignty and requires States to recognise foreign judicial decisions as if they were their own. In this chapter we will refer to this branch of international criminal law as 'transnational criminal law'.

The other type of international criminal law refers to the criminal law aspects of international law. It regulates the prosecution of a small class of 'core crimes': so-called international crimes. Genocide, crimes against humanity, war crimes, and aggression are regarded as universally condemned and can be the subject of prosecution at the international level.[1] All four

---

[1] See Statute of the International Criminal Tribunal for the former Yugoslavia ('ICTY Statute'), adopted on 25 May 1993 by UN Security Council Resolution 827, Articles 2 to 5; Statute of the International Criminal Tribunal for Rwanda ('ICTR

crimes have an international pedigree in that they are defined and developed in international treaty and customary law and/or the case law of the international criminal tribunals. In contrast, torture, as defined in the *Convention Against Torture and Other Cruel, Inhuman or Degrading Treatment or Punishment* (the 'CAT'),[2] is generally not regarded as belonging to the class of international crimes. Although it has an international pedigree by being defined in an international treaty, it is not part of an international criminal statute, at least not as a self-standing crime. When committed during an armed conflict, torture can be a war crime, or, as part of a widespread or systematic attack, it can be a crime against humanity.

More and more international crimes are prosecuted at the national level, often on the basis of universal jurisdiction. This branch of international criminal law differs from transnational criminal law in that it originates from international law. Moreover, State sovereignty plays a lesser, or less prominent, role than in transnational criminal law. This follows from the applicable cooperation regime that regulates the cooperation of States with international judicial institutions such as the *ad hoc* International Criminal Tribunals for the Former Yugoslavia ('ICTY') and Rwanda ('ICTR'), and the International Criminal Court ('ICC'). This type of international criminal law has been referred to as international criminal law *per se*, supranational criminal law, vertical international criminal law, and *droit international pénal*. In this chapter we will refer to it as 'international criminal law'.

What the two branches of international criminal law have in common is that they lie on the fault line between two fields of law: international law and criminal law. These two types of law are inherently different. The subjects of international law are States, while criminal law deals with individuals. Sources of international law include unwritten, fluid rules of customary international law. Criminal law, on the other hand, requires clear written rules,[3] as stipulated by the principle of legality. The combination of these two fields may result in an unfortunate position for the individual accused, as will be illustrated below.

In Section 2, we will explore the concepts and legal instruments that make up transnational criminal law. Extradition, mutual legal assistance, and the transfer of proceedings and execution of sentences will be discussed as part of

---

Statute'), adopted on 8 November 1994 by UN Security Council Resolution 955, Articles 2 to 4; and *Rome Statute of the International Criminal Court*, opened for signature 17 June 1998, 2187 UNTS 90 (entered into force 1 July 2002) ('ICC Statute') Articles 5 to 8.

[2] Opened for signature 10 December 1984, 1465 UNTS 85 (entered into force 26 June 1987) ('CAT').

[3] While codification is becoming the norm, with regard to certain offences, defences and modes of liability, common law countries still rely on unwritten rules in the sense of legislation, although public, written judgments are given.

the traditional inter-State cooperation in criminal matters in Subsection 2A. We will then consider a new form of inter-State cooperation, the European Arrest Warrant ('EAW') in Subsection 2B. Section 3 will focus on international criminal law (*per se*). Subsection 3A contains a historical introduction to prosecution at the international level, which is followed by an overview of the international(ised) courts and tribunals that try those accused of international crimes. In Subsection 3B, substantive international criminal law will be discussed, in particular definitions of international crimes, criminal responsibility and defences. Moving from substantive law to procedural law, Subsection 3C is concerned with international criminal procedure, an emerging discipline of international criminal law. Subsection 3D deals with the cooperation between States and the international courts and tribunals. This is where the two branches of international criminal law converge. Finally, in Section 4 the position of the individual will be highlighted in both transnational criminal law and international criminal law *per se*.

## 2 Transnational criminal law

### A  *International legal cooperation*

International legal cooperation concerns those powers that a State has at its disposal to cooperate with other States in investigating, prosecuting and adjudicating cross-border crimes, crimes committed by its nationals abroad, and crimes committed by foreigners within its borders. A distinction can be made between primary legal cooperation and secondary legal cooperation.[4] Primary legal cooperation comprises those measures that provide for the transfer of an essential part of the criminal procedure, for instance, the prosecution of a crime or the enforcement of a penalty. Secondary legal cooperation encompasses various forms of assistance to another State, for instance, the extradition of a suspect or convicted person. Another distinction between legal cooperation measures can be made between cooperation measures in the phase *before* a conviction has been entered, for instance extradition of suspects or the transfer of prosecution, and cooperation measures that can be taken *after* the conviction, such as extradition of convicted persons and the transfer of sentences. In the following we will discuss the four most important legal cooperation matters.

*(i)  Extradition*  Extradition is probably the oldest form of inter-State cooperation in penal matters. It is the surrender of a person by one State to another,

---

[4]  Harman G Van der Wilt, 'Internationaal Strafrecht', in N Horbach et al (eds) *Handboek Internationaal Recht* (TMC Asser Press, The Hague, 2007) 513.

the person being accused of a crime in the requesting State or unlawfully at large after conviction.[5] Some States only extradite persons on the basis of a treaty, as required by their constitution or extradition law. While international law does not require a treaty basis for extradition, many States have concluded extradition treaties. Such treaties create legal certainty and warrant reciprocity with regard to mutual obligations. Moreover, by concluding extradition treaties, States express the trust they have in each other's criminal justice system. When an extradition treaty has been concluded, the Judge and the Executive no longer have to scrutinise the criminal system of a State to determine whether extradition to that State is opportune or even allowed.[6]

(a) Refusal grounds   Extradition treaties originate from the common interests of States in combating crimes. However, States generally still retain the power to refuse extradition requests. In fact, many States have limited their cooperation by adopting declarations, reservations and refusal grounds, so they can demand guarantees and safeguards before deciding on extradition requests. *Ne bis in idem*,[7] trials *in absentia*, prosecution of minors and extradition of nationals are all grounds upon which a refusal to cooperate can be based. This widespread practice of reservations and refusal grounds indicates that parties to an extradition treaty to a certain extent retain their sovereignty.

Many bilateral extradition treaties have been concluded between States. Multilateral extradition treaties have been signed in the context of regional and international organisations. In Europe, the most important treaties have been negotiated and endorsed under the auspices of the Council of Europe, such as the 1957 *European Extradition Convention*.[8] Since the terror attacks of 11 September 2001, there has been sufficient political support within the EU to implement a new, more efficient and expedited extradition scheme (referred to as 'surrender') by way of the EAW, discussed in subsection 2B below.

(b) Principles underlying extradition   International cooperation in criminal matters requires trust in other States' criminal justice systems. Such trust is often presumed when an extradition treaty exists. In the words of Justice

---

[5] R Cryer et al, *An Introduction to International Criminal Law and Procedure* (Cambridge University Press, Cambridge, 2007) 79.

[6] Albert H J Swart, *Nederlands Uitleveringsrecht* (WEJ Tjeenk Willink, Deventer, 1986) 56.

[7] Literally 'not twice for the same' means that no legal action can be instituted twice for the same conduct. The concept originates in Roman civil law; in common law terms it is referred to as the double jeopardy rule.

[8] *European Convention on Extradition*, opened for signature 13 December 1957, 359 UNTS 273 (entered into force 18 April 1960).

Holmes in *Glucksman v Henkel*, 'we are bound by the existence of an extradition treaty to assume that the trial will be fair'.[9] From this trust or 'good faith' principle stems the rule of non-inquiry, which prohibits a State from thoroughly scrutinising an extradition request and inquiring into the motives behind it.

On the other hand, there is no rule of international law that obliges States to trust another State blindly and to cooperate with it unconditionally, which explains the existence of refusal grounds as discussed above. Two other principles can be mentioned in this context, namely the tenet of double criminality and the rule of speciality. The principle of double criminality requires that the underlying act or omission is criminal in both the requesting and the requested State.[10] The rationale underlying this rule is primarily State sovereignty; a State should not be required to extradite a person to another State for an offence that would not amount to a crime under its own law. Some claim that the double criminality principle is closely linked to the legality precept (*nulla poena sine lege*),[11] while others hold that it serves to protect the human rights of the requested person.[12] Recently, cooperation agreements have been adopted within the EU that have abolished the double criminality requirement. The EAW, for instance, does away with double criminality for a limited number of crimes. These offences are thought to be so serious that they are considered crimes throughout the EU. We will discuss the EAW in more detail below.

The rule of speciality requires the requesting State to bring proceedings against the requested person only for the crime, or crimes, for which the person has been extradited. The rule of speciality may be waived when the requested State or the requested person consents to prosecution of, or execution of a sentence for, other offences.[13]

(c) Extradition procedure   The extradition procedure is governed by the law and practice of the requested State. Generally, a two-tier decision-making process is in place. A court considers the formal requirements and

---

[9] *Glucksman v Henkel* (1911) 221 U.S. 508.
[10] Generally see N Jareborg, *Double Criminality – Studies in International Criminal Law* (Iustus Förlag, Uppsala, 1989).
[11] R Cryer et al, above n 5, 74.
[12] M Plachta, 'The Role of Double Criminality in Penal Matters' in N Jareborg (ed) *Double Criminality – Studies in International Criminal Law* (Iustus Förlag, Uppsala, 1989) 128–9.
[13] See C Nicholls and J Knowles, *The Law of Extradition and Mutual Assistance: International Criminal Law – Practice and Procedure* (Oxford University Press, Oxford, 2007, 2nd ed) 180. See also G Gilbert, *Aspects of Extradition Law* (Martinus Nijhoff, Dordrecht, 1991) 106.

the admissibility of the extradition request, while the actual surrender is an executive decision. This 'dual key' decision-making is especially relevant with regard to refusal grounds that touch on sensitive areas, such as another State's human rights situation. The Executive is thought to be best equipped to deal with such sensitivities. As we will see below, the EAW provides for a purely judicial procedure, with the Executive having been removed to make the procedure more efficient and expeditious.

An extradition procedure is not a regular criminal procedure; it is not a 'trial' in the sense of Article 6 of the *European Convention on Human Rights* ('ECHR').[14] The trial to determine guilt or innocence will already have occurred, in the case of a convicted person being extradited to serve a sentence, or will take place in the State requesting extradition. The requested person will normally have an opportunity to be heard and an opportunity to raise objections to extradition. However, the presumption of innocence does not apply; the prosecution in the requested State does not have the onus to prove that the requested person is guilty. Rather, the burden lies on the requested person to disprove guilt. Extradition will be refused when the requested person can unequivocally demonstrate that he or she is innocent.

(d) 'Alternatives'   Extradition is a formal and rather lengthy procedure. It can take months before a person is extradited. Moreover, an extradition request does not necessarily guarantee the requested person's passage to the territory of the requesting State. After all, refusal grounds, such as the political offence exception, may pose an obstacle to extradition.[15] To circumvent ineffective extradition, or non-extradition, States have resorted to extra-judicial means to apprehend the fugitive and bring him or her before their courts.

Adolf Eichmann was abducted from Argentina by Israeli agents in order to be tried by an Israeli court for genocide.[16] Argentina, not having consented to

---

[14] *Convention for the Protection of Human Rights and Fundamental Freedoms*, opened for signature 4 November 1950, 213 UNTS 262 (entered into force 3 September 1953) ('ECHR').

[15] The political offence doctrine covers two types of crimes: 'relative' political offences, which are committed in connection with a political act or common crimes committed for political motives or in a political context, and 'pure' or 'absolute' political offences, such as treason, sedition and espionage. The latter category is covered by the exception to extradition.

[16] *Attorney-General of Israel v Eichmann* (District Court of Jerusalem, 1968) 36 ILR 5; *Attorney-General of Israel v Eichmann* (Supreme Court, 1968) 36 ILR 277; see H Silving 'In re Eichmann: A Dilemma of Law and Morality' (1961) 55 *American Journal of International Law* 307, and P O'Higgins 'Unlawful Seizure and Irregular Rendition' (1960) 36 *British Yearbook of International Law* 279.

the abduction, filed a complaint with the UN against Israel for violating its territorial sovereignty. More recently the US has relied on 'extraordinary rendition' as part of its fight against terrorism. Suspects of terrorism are captured and moved around the globe to be interrogated, and possibly tried. These 'alternatives' breach international law in terms of both State sovereignty and human rights provisions. When it comes to the human rights of the person who is subject to rendition or abduction, the rule is clear: no State may ever send a person to a place where the person is likely to be tortured, and certainly not with the intention of him or her being tortured. This has been confirmed in the *Alzery*[17] case before the Human Rights Committee and in *Agiza*[18] before the CAT committee.

The fact that extra-judicial alternatives to extradition violate international law does not mean that a court should divest itself of the power to try a person once he or she has been brought before it. The District Court of Jerusalem decided to exercise jurisdiction and try Eichmann.[19] In accordance with the maxim *male captus bene detentus*, some national courts have long been prepared to try accused persons regardless of the irregular means by which they have been apprehended.[20] In recent years the *male captus* rule has been superseded occasionally by the abuse of process doctrine, which requires a court to decline jurisdiction and stay proceedings when the defendant has been brought to court in an unlawful manner or because his human rights have been violated.[21] This doctrine has been applied by courts in New Zealand, South Africa and England.[22] The abuse of process doctrine is not recognised by the United States.

---

[17] *Alzery v Sweden*, CCPR/C/88/D/1416/2005, UN Human Rights Committee (HRC), 10 November 2006.
[18] *Agiza v Sweden*, CAT/C/34/D/233/2003, UN Committee Against Torture (CAT), 20 May 2005.
[19] *Attorney-General of Israel v Eichmann* (District Court of Jerusalem, 1968) 36 ILR 5.
[20] This has been particularly the case in the United States: see for example *Ker v Illinois* (1886) 119 US 436; *Frisbie v Collins* (1952) 342 US 519; *United States v Alvarez-Machain* (1992) 31 ILM 900. A notable exception to the *male captus* reasoning was *United States v Toscanino* (2d Cir. 1974) 500 F. 2d 267. See R Rayfuse, 'International Abduction and the United States Supreme Court: The Law of the Jungle Reigns' (1993) 42 *The International and Comparative Law Quarterly* 882.
[21] Andrew L-T Choo, 'International Kidnapping, Disguised Extradition and Abuse of Process' (1994) 57 *The Modern Law Review* 626; C Warbrick, 'Judicial Jurisdiction and Abuse of Process' (2000) 49 *The International and Comparative Law Quarterly* 489.
[22] *Regina v Hartley* (C.A. 1978) 2 NZLR 199; *State v Ebrahim* (1992) 31 ILM 888; *R v Horseferry Road Magistrates' Court, ex p. Bennet* (1993) 3 All ER.

At the ICTY, the *male captus bene detentus* rule was adhered to in the case of a Bosnian Serb who was forcibly abducted from the Republika Srpska and handed over to NATO forces, who then brought him to the Tribunal in The Hague.[23] In balancing the interest of the accused and his human rights against the interest of the international community and the legitimate expectation that those accused of international crimes would be brought to justice, the Appeals Chamber held that since there was no evidence '[t]hat the rights of the accused were egregiously violated in the process of his arrest ... the procedure adopted for his arrest did not disable the Trial Chamber exercising its jurisdiction.'[24] The *Nikolic* case demonstrates that there is an 'Eichmann exception' to the abuse of process doctrine; that is, when it comes to universally condemned offences such as genocide, crimes against humanity or war crimes, a court will not easily divest itself of jurisdiction.

*(ii) Mutual legal assistance* Another form of (secondary) legal cooperation is mutual legal assistance ('MLA'), which can be best described as providing investigative and/or prosecutorial assistance at the request of a State for the purpose of a criminal investigation or prosecution in that State. MLA may consist of the taking of witness statements, search and seizure, cross-border pursuit and observation, or the serving of documents.

Originally, MLA was regulated alongside extradition as the instrument with which a requested person's goods or articles could be seized and subsequently used as evidence. It developed into an independent instrument from the 'Letters Rogatory', a system of requests for assistance with the taking of evidence or sending delegations to another State to conduct their own investigations.

MLA is regulated in bilateral and multilateral treaties, such as the 1959 *Council of Europe Convention on Mutual Assistance in Criminal Matters*[25] and the 2000 *Convention on Mutual Assistance in Criminal Matters* between the Member States of the EU. The latter instrument simplified existing procedures and introduced new forms of cooperation.[26] In a global context, MLA

---

[23] *Prosecutor v Dragan Nikolic*, Case No. IT-94-02-AR73, T. Ch. II, ICTY (18 December 2003).
[24] Ibid [32].
[25] Opened for signature 20 April 1959, ETS No. 30 (entered into force on 12 June 1962).
[26] Such as 'joint investigation teams' where police and judicial authorities from different Member States work together in investigating and prosecuting transnational crime. See C R J Rijken and G Vermeulen, *Joint Investigation Teams in the European Union* (Cambridge University Press, Cambridge, 2006); M Plachta, 'Joint Investigation Teams' (2005) 13 *European Journal of Crime, Criminal Law and Criminal Justice* 284.

can be found in, *inter alia*, the 2003 *Corruption Convention*,[27] the 1984 *Torture Convention*,[28] and the *International Convention for the Suppression of the Financing of Terrorism*.[29]

From an individual defendant's and a State sovereignty point of view, MLA as a form of legal cooperation is less intrusive, or serious, than extradition. As a result, most legal systems provide for MLA procedures that are less formal than extradition proceedings. States may still retain the possibility to rely on refusal grounds, although the double criminality requirement is not as widely accepted a condition for MLA as it is for extradition. Moreover, in some States, MLA can be given without there being a treaty basis through informal MLA ('informal MLA').

The rule of non-inquiry also applies to MLA and this can be problematic when criminal justice systems differ with regard to certain prosecutorial and investigative powers. If, for example, the requested State has relied upon search and seizure powers that would be considered unlawful in the requesting State and the requested evidence has been produced as a result of those powers, the individual defendant cannot argue that the evidence is 'unlawful' and therefore precluded from being provided to the authorities of the requesting State (although it might still be open for the accused to argue at trial that the evidence obtained through MLA should be declared inadmissible.) MLA, like extradition, is considered an agreement between States that trust each other; the requesting State must assume that the requested State has collected the evidence in good faith and as a result it cannot be challenged in court.[30]

*(iii) Transfer of proceedings and enforcement of penalties* Transfer of proceedings and enforcement of penalties are two forms of legal cooperation that, unlike extradition and MLA, are *primary* forms of inter-State cooperation in criminal matters; a substantial part of the criminal procedure is transferred

---

[27] Opened for signature 31 October 2003, UN General Assembly Resolution 58/4 (entered into force on 14 December 2005) ('Corruption Convention').

[28] Opened for signature 10 December 1984, 1465 UNTS 85 (entered into force 26 June 1987) ('Torture Convention').

[29] Opened for signature 9 December 1999, 39 I.L.M. 270 (2000) (entered into force 10 April 2002).

[30] Consider the statement by Van Hoek and Luchtman: 'International criminal cooperation, being a part of foreign policy, is a matter that has to be dealt with by the executive ... Therefore, the courts should not – as a rule – entertain questions concerning the legitimacy of the acts of foreign authorities.' A A H van Hoek and M J J P Luchtman, 'Transnational Cooperation in Criminal Matters and the Safeguarding of Human Rights' (2005) 1 (2) *Utrecht Law Review* 2, available at <www.utrechtlawreview.org>.

from one State to another. Due to the nature of these cooperation forms, both transfer of criminal proceedings and enforcement of penalties require double criminality.

Criminal proceedings may be transferred for reasons of 'prosecutorial economy', for instance when co-accused find themselves in the requesting State, or when the requesting State has already started prosecution against the accused. Another important reason for transferring proceedings is of a humanitarian nature, that is, to facilitate reintegration into society. It makes sense to transfer a trial to the country of which the accused is a national. The trial will be conducted in his or her mother tongue and relatives can easily visit. The most well-known multilateral instrument in this area is the 1972 *European Convention on the Transfer of Proceedings in Criminal Matters* ('ECTP').[31]

Enforcement of a penalty in a jurisdiction other than where the penalty was imposed may have various justifications. Firstly, there may be humanitarian reasons, since both the transfer of proceedings and the transfer of execution of sentences aim to bring suspects and sentenced persons back to their State of nationality or residence. Secondly, agreeing to transfer the enforcement of penalties may facilitate extradition. An otherwise reluctant State may agree to extradite on condition that the requested person is returned to serve the sentence imposed.[32] Two ways of enforcing a penalty may be discerned: direct enforcement and the conversion of penalties in the administering State where the penalty is to be enforced. Both bilateral and multilateral treaties have been concluded to provide for the enforcement of penalties. The most well-known treaties are the 1970 *European Convention on the International Validity of Criminal Judgments*[33] and the 1983 *Convention on the Transfer of Sentenced Persons* ('CTSP').[34]

The ECTP provides for refusal grounds, which mainly relate to the purpose of transferring proceedings. Transfer may be refused when the accused is a non-national or does not reside in the requested State. The CTSP does not provide for a catalogue of mandatory refusal grounds and thus leaves it up to States to declare, or not, in which circumstances they refuse to cooperate.

---

[31] Opened for signature 15 May 1972, ETS No 73 (entered into force 30 March 1978).

[32] The Netherlands does not allow for the extradition and surrender of nationals, unless the penalty will be enforced in the Netherlands and converted to Dutch standards. See Section 4(2) of the *Dutch Extradition Act* ('*Extradition Act*') and the judgment of the Dutch Supreme Court, 31 March 1995, *Nederlandse Jurisprudentie* 1996, nr 382.

[33] Opened for signature 28 May 1970, ETS 070 (entered into force 26 July 1974).

[34] Opened for signature 21 March 1983, ETS 112 (entered into force 1 July 1985).

## B  New forms: the European Arrest Warrant

The Framework Decision ('Decision') establishing the EAW entered into force on 1 January 2004.[35] Since the adoption of the Italian law transposing the Decision on 22 April 2005, the EAW has been operational throughout the EU and has largely replaced traditional extradition procedures. Mutual trust, or 'a high level of confidence', has been a key notion underlying the system of cooperation in criminal matters in the EU. Mutual trust has been referred to by the Council of the European Union as the 'bedrock' of the Decision on the EAW. It provides the basis for mutual recognition, which in turn is considered to be the 'cornerstone' of EU judicial cooperation in criminal matters.

In the context of the EAW, mutual trust has been the reason for abolishing the double criminality rule for a number of crimes and for removing the Executive from the decision-making process. In October 1999 the European Council in Tampere, Finland, asserted that mutual recognition (of judicial decisions and judgments) was to be the 'cornerstone' of judicial cooperation within the EU.[36] The concept of mutual recognition and mutual trust is premised on the assumption that the EU Member States share common values and rights. However, mutual trust has not resulted in the elimination of refusal grounds. While the European Commission sought to introduce a cooperation scheme that fundamentally differed from extradition, with only a limited number of refusal grounds and no double criminality requirement for *any* of the underlying crimes, the draft proposal Framework Decision was 'watered down' in negotiations by the Council of Ministers by the insertion of concepts and refusal grounds derived from extradition law.[37] Indeed, most refusal grounds listed in the Decision establishing the EAW reflect grounds of refusal that feature in extradition treaties and national extradition statutes. In that sense there is still room for 'distrust' and sovereignty concerns.

The above may prompt us to describe the EAW as 'extradition in transition' rather than a revolutionary new form of cross-border transfer of suspects and

---

[35] *Council Framework Decision* (on the European Arrest Warrant and the Surrender Procedure between Member States, 2002/584/JHA, 13 June 2002).

[36] A programme was adopted shortly after the meeting: 'Programme of measures to implement the principle of mutual recognition of decisions in criminal matters', 2001/C12/02; *Official Journal of the European Communities*, C12/10, 15 January 2001.

[37] For instance the 'territoriality exception' whereby a State can refuse surrender in case the (alleged) crime has been committed on the territory of the executing (requested) Member State (Section 4 (7) *European Arrest Warrant Act* 2003) (the '*EAW Act*'), or where the criminal prosecution or punishment of the requested person is statute-barred according to the law of the executing (requested) Member State and the acts fall within the jurisdiction of that Member State under its own criminal law (Section 4(4) *EAW Act*).

sentenced persons.[38] There is, however, one important difference with extradition: all refusal grounds are relied upon by the courts. The EAW scheme makes judicial authorities solely responsible for surrendering individuals to other Member States – a responsibility they (used to) share with the Executive with regard to extradition.

The Decision establishing the EAW, drawn up in the aftermath of the 9/11 attacks, emphasises efficiency and expediency as a result of the desire for an informal and swift surrender procedure. Experts in and practitioners of extradition law, however, have been critical. They have held that the emphasis on efficiency is to the detriment of the requested person's (human) rights.[39] In July 2005, the German Federal Constitutional Court annulled Germany's law transposing the Decision because it did not adequately protect German citizens' fundamental rights, a condition for extraditing German nationals.[40] The Dutch Extradition Chamber was creative in inserting a humanitarian refusal ground into the *EAW Act* by analogy with section 10(2) of the *Extradition Act*. Thus it enabled refusal on 'humanitarian grounds'.[41] However, the Dutch Supreme Court quashed the ruling. It held that the legislature never intended to include a humanitarian refusal ground in the *EAW Act*. According to the Supreme Court, section 35(3) only allows for humanitarian reasons to delay surrender proceedings, not to refuse them entirely.[42]

## 3 International criminal law

### A Brief history of international prosecutions

The prosecution of international crimes finds its origins in the laws and customs of war, which have long entitled belligerent parties to put on trial nationals of the adversary for resorting to prohibited means and methods of warfare. The period following the end of the First World War was marked by several failed attempts to establish international criminal institutions for the

---

[38] E van Sliedregt, 'The European Arrest Warrant: Extradition in Transition' (2007) 3 *European Constitutional Law Review* 244–52.

[39] S Peers, 'Mutual Recognition and Criminal Law in the European Union: Has the Council got it wrong?', (2004) 41 *Common Market Law Review* 5–36. See also Chapters 11, 12 and 13 in R Blextoon and W Van Ballegooij (eds) *Handbook on the European Arrest Warrant* (Cambridge: TMC Asser Press, 2005) 167–209.

[40] 18 July 2005, 2 BvR 2236/04, available at <www.bundesverfassungsgericht.de/entscheidungen/rs20050718_2bvr223604.html> at 2 March 2009. See for a commentary C Tomuschat, 'Inconsistencies – The German Federal Constitutional Court on the European Arrest Warrant' (2006) 2 *European Constitutional Law Review* 209–26.

[41] Amsterdam District Court (2 December 2005) LJN: AU8399.

[42] Dutch Supreme Court (28 November 2006) LJN: AY6631.

prosecution of offences against the laws of nations and humanity.[43] It was not until 1945, however, that the first international tribunal was successfully established, as a reaction to the egregious crimes committed by the Nazis during the Second World War.

The Nuremberg Tribunal was set up by the Allied Powers to prosecute German military and political figures for crimes against peace, war crimes and crimes against humanity. Its jurisdiction also extended to organisations. Acknowledging the moral significance of bringing to trial not only the masterminds behind Nazi crimes but also the multitude of rank-and-file persons whose acquiescence in criminal activities ensured the smooth running of the German war machine, the Nuremberg Tribunal eventually declared the Nazi party leadership corps, the Gestapo/SD and the SS to be criminal organisations.[44] These declarations of criminality subsequently served as the basis for the prosecution of individual organisation members before the national military tribunals of the Allied Powers.

Mirroring the Nuremberg model, in 1946 the Allied Powers established the Tokyo Tribunal to prosecute crimes committed in South-East Asia between 1928 and 1945. Its subject-matter jurisdiction covered the same categories of crimes as the Nuremberg Tribunal, but there was no provision extending to organisations.[45]

Both the Nuremberg and the Tokyo Tribunals ('the Tribunals') have been heavily criticised for representing 'victors' justice'. The circumstances surrounding their set-up, the streamlined procedures and the selective prosecution of defendants cast a shadow on the impartiality and independence of the institutions. The arguably retrospective character of the Nuremberg and Tokyo Charters and the Tribunals' application of some rather unconventional legal doctrines (for example, on criminal organisations) have been viewed as unjustifiably geared towards meeting the needs of the trials and tainting the fairness of the judicial process.[46]

---

[43] See generally G Werle, *Principles of International Criminal Law* (TMC Asser Press, The Hague, 2005) 3–6.
[44] Volume 1, *Trial of the Major War Criminals Before the International Military Tribunal* 29 (Washington, 1947) 257–62.
[45] Compare Articles 9 and 10 of the Charter of the International Military Tribunal of Nuremberg (Document LX), London, 8 August 1945, *Report of Robert H. Jackson on the International Conference on Military Trials*, 420, with Article 5 of the Charter of the International Military Tribunal for the Far East, *reprinted in XV Trials of War Criminals before the Nurenberg Military Tribunals under Control Council Law No. 10* (Government Printing Office, Washington, 1950) 1218.
[46] For a general overview of such critiques see, eg, E Borgwardt, 'Re-Examining Nuremberg as a New Deal Institution: Politics, Culture and the Limits of Law in Generating Human Rights Laws' (2005) 23 (2) *Berkeley Journal of International Law*

At the same time, however, the Nuremberg and Tokyo trials set an important precedent and gave a significant impetus to the development of international criminal law. Although a multitude of defendants could have easily been imprisoned or executed without resort to complex judicial procedures, those who stood trial were given due access to law.[47] The Tribunals were cautious in imposing criminal liability. Conscious of the context in which they were operating and the legal shortcomings of the process, they made an honest effort to avoid imposing any form of strict liability or collective punishment. The trials' greatest legacy, though, lies in their endorsement of the notion of individual responsibility for international crimes and the denunciation of the acts of State and superior orders defences. Nuremberg and Tokyo set in motion a new trend in the development of international standards for legal conduct and marked the beginning of the international criminal justice system.

The political tensions caused by the Cold War precluded all immediate efforts on the part of the international community to follow up on the Nuremberg and Tokyo precedents and set up more permanent institutions for the prosecution of international crimes.[48] It was not until the early 1990s, as a response to the atrocities committed during the conflicts in Yugoslavia and Rwanda, that the UN established the first genuinely international legal mechanisms for bringing to justice individuals who had committed the most serious crimes against humankind.

The ICTY and the ICTR were established by resolutions of the Security Council under Chapter VII of the UN Charter ('UN Charter').[49] While both institutions are subsidiary organs of the UN, they are largely operationally independent.[50] The ICTY has jurisdiction over grave breaches of the Geneva Conventions of 1949, violations of the laws and customs of war, genocide and crimes against humanity perpetrated on the territory of the former Yugoslavia after 1 January 1991.[51] The subject-matter jurisdiction of the ICTR is somewhat different, reflecting the non-international nature of the Rwandan conflict. It extends to genocide, crimes against humanity, and violations of Common

---

401–62, and G Ginsburgs and V N Kudriavtsev (eds) *The Nuremberg Trial and International Law* (Kluwer Academic Publishers, Dordrecht, 1990).

[47] Borgwardt, above n 46, 457.

[48] A Cassese, *International Criminal Law* (Oxford University Press, New York, 2008) 323–4.

[49] Charter of the United Nations, 1 UNTS XVI, 24 October 1945.

[50] D McGoldrick, 'Criminal Trials Before International Tribunals: Legality and Legitimacy' in D McGoldrick, P Rowe and E Donnelly (eds) *The Permanent International Criminal Court: Legal and Policy Issues* (Hart Publishing, Portland, 2004) 24.

[51] ICTY Statute, Articles 2 to 5.

Article 3 to the Geneva Conventions and their Additional Protocol II, committed in Rwanda or by Rwandan citizens in neighbouring countries between 1 January and 31 December 1994.[52]

Both the ICTY and the ICTR have concurrent but primary jurisdiction over domestic courts.[53] Thus they may hold a retrial when national proceedings are deemed not to have been impartial, independent or diligently conducted.[54] Domestic courts are furthermore obliged to defer their competence, should the tribunals request so.[55] However, as both institutions must complete all activities by 2010, in accordance with Security Council Resolutions 1503 and 1534, no new investigations are currently being opened and low-profile cases are in fact being referred back to domestic courts.

Since their inception, the ICTY and the ICTR have been subjected to continuous criticism. While defendants have questioned their legality and legitimacy, victims and the populations of the former Yugoslavia and Rwanda have raised doubts as to the tribunals' impartiality and independence. At the same time, legal scholars and practitioners have on various occasions condemned the institutions for their perceived inefficiency, maladministration and misplaced attempts to tackle adequately contentious issues of substantive or procedural law.[56] While some of these critiques may have merit, the impact

---

[52] ICTR Statute, Articles 2 to 4.

[53] ICTY Statute, Article 9; ICTR Statute, Article 8.

[54] G Sluiter, *International Criminal Adjudication and the Collection of Evidence: Obligations of States*, (Intersentia, Antwerp, 2002) 81–8.

[55] Rule 9 of the ICTY Rules of Procedure and Evidence sets out the conditions under which a deferral may be justified. It empowers the Prosecutor to request a deferral when (i) the act investigated or prosecuted at the domestic level is characterised as an ordinary, as opposed to an international, crime, (ii) the domestic proceedings are not impartial or, alternatively, are designed to shield the accused from international criminal responsibility, or (iii) the case before the domestic court involves a factual or legal issue of significant implication to the Tribunal. The conditions attached to the Prosecutor's application for a deferral are somewhat different under the ICTR Rules of Procedure and Evidence. Rule 8 allows for a deferral to the competence of the Tribunal when the crimes subject to the domestic proceedings (i) are already being investigated by the ICTR Prosecutor, (ii) should be investigated by the ICTR Prosecutor given *inter alia* their seriousness, or (iii) are contained in an indictment already issued by the Tribunal.

[56] See, eg, E Stover, *The Witnesses. War Crimes and the Promise of Justice in the Hague* (University of Pennsylvania Press, Philadelphia, 2005); A M Danner and J S Martinez, 'Guilty Associations: Joint Criminal Enterprise, Command Responsibility, and the Development of International Criminal Law' (2005) 93 (1) *California Law Review* 75–169; A T O'Reilly, 'Command Responsibility: a Call to Realign Doctrine with Principles' (2004) 20 (1) *American University International Law Review* 71–107; P L Robinson, 'Ensuring Fair and Expeditious Trials at the ICTY' (2000) 11 (3) *European Journal of International Law*, 569–89.

of both institutions on the development of international criminal law and the current international criminal justice system cannot be denied. Along with promoting accountability, bringing justice to a multitude of victims and documenting historical truth, the jurisprudence and lessons learned from the ICTY and the ICTR have been the stepping-stone for the creation of a growing number of international courts and tribunals.

With the notable exception of the International Criminal Court ('ICC'), the myriad of institutions established by the international community for the prosecution of 'the most serious of crimes' over the past decade have been of an *ad hoc*, mixed nature. Also known as 'internationalised' courts and tribunals, these institutions are situated in the States within whose jurisdiction the crimes have been committed and comprise both international and domestic judges. Such courts and tribunals have thus far been established in Sierra Leone, Kosovo, East Timor, Cambodia and Bosnia and Herzegovina, as a result of either an agreement between the UN and post-conflict governments or a direct international intervention. The objective has generally been to bring justice closer to the victims, expedite proceedings and assist in the restoration of the domestic legal systems. Internationalised courts and tribunals are in principle viewed as less intrusive, that is, deferential to State sovereignty, but nonetheless remain governed by international criminal law standards.

The ICC, which is the only permanent legal institution in the world for the prosecution of grave international crimes, was set up by an international agreement in 1998.[57] It is an independent treaty body, whose Rome Statute ('ICC Statute') has currently been ratified by 110 States.[58] Compared with those of the *ad hoc* ICTY and ICTR and the various internationalised courts that exist at present, the jurisdiction of the ICC is considerably more expansive. Situations may be referred to the ICC for investigation by either States Parties or the Security Council acting under Chapter VII of the UN Charter, although the ICC Prosecutor may also initiate investigations *proprio motu*.[59] Its personal jurisdiction is based on the principles of nationality and territoriality.[60] The subject-matter jurisdiction of the ICC extends to the same categories of crimes as those applicable to the temporary *ad hoc* courts and tribunals,

---

[57] Opened for signature 17 June 1998, 2187 UNTS 90 (entered into force 1 July 2002) ('ICC Statute').
[58] As of 21 July 2009. For the complete list of States Parties to the Rome Statute, see the official website of the International Criminal Court at <http://www.icc-cpi.int/Menus/ASP/states+parties/> at 13 November 2009.
[59] ICC Statute, Article 15.
[60] ICC Statute, Article 12.

namely genocide, crimes against humanity and war crimes.[61] The codification of crimes against humanity and war crimes in the ICC Statute, however, is not only more detailed but also somewhat broader than the definitions adopted by its predecessors.[62] The ICC may furthermore exercise jurisdiction over the crime of aggression once a definition of the crime has been agreed upon by States Parties and the ICC Statute has been accordingly amended.[63] With regard to genocide, crimes against humanity and war crimes, the ICC's temporal jurisdiction is limited to crimes committed after 1 July 2002.[64]

Although the ICC has thus far benefited from strong support on the part of the international community, it has not been without its opponents. The principal objection raised against the ICC relates to its power to assume jurisdiction over the nationals of non-States Parties without those States' consent, particularly when the nationals concerned are military personnel.[65] The argument made largely reflects a somewhat misplaced distrust of the ICC's ability to impartially apply the principle of complementarity.[66] Being one of the most innovative and important legal features of the ICC, the principle of complementarity is intended to ensure that the ICC's jurisdiction is only secondary to domestic courts. The ICC will therefore exercise its jurisdiction only when national authorities are either unable or unwilling to genuinely investigate and prosecute the crimes committed.[67]

In order to rely on the complementarity principle, however, States must incorporate in their domestic legislation the crimes envisaged in the ICC Statute. Despite the obligation incumbent on States Parties to the Statute to do so, progress has been slow. The situation with respect to non-States Parties is even bleaker. National jurisdiction over genocide and war crimes is not a rarity. The former though has seldom been exercised, while the latter varies greatly in its scope as States differ in the type of war crimes they criminalise. With regard to crimes against humanity, only a few States have assumed jurisdiction over those as such.[68] Thus although national prosecutions of grave international crimes have been increasing in number over the past decade, they

---

[61] ICC Statute, Articles 6, 7 and 8 respectively.
[62] See below B(i), Definitions of crimes.
[63] ICC Statute, Article 5(2).
[64] ICC Statute, Article 11. For States who have become Parties to the Statute after 1 July 2002, the Court's jurisdiction extends only to crimes committed after the Statute's entry into force for those States (Article 11(2)).
[65] For an overview and critical assessment of the argument, see, eg, D Akande, 'The Jurisdiction of the International Criminal Court over Nationals of Non-Parties: Legal Basis and Limits' (2004) 1 (3) *Journal of International Criminal Justice* 618–50.
[66] Cryer et al, above n 5, 141.
[67] ICC Statute, Article 17.
[68] McGoldrick, above n 50, 12.

remain largely sporadic occurrences. Relatively few States have adopted universal jurisdiction with regard to genocide, crimes against humanity and the most serious of war crimes, even though these crimes and the obligation to prosecute them, irrespective of nationality and territoriality considerations, are generally regarded as *jus cogens*, or peremptory norms of international law.[69] With respect to such crimes though, States remain obliged to adopt legislative measures necessary for the effective prosecution of alleged perpetrators, including measures conferring jurisdiction upon the domestic judiciary. Unwillingness or inability to prosecute may be offset by adhering to the principle of *aut dedere aut judicare*; for instance, by extraditing the alleged perpetrator to a State which is capable of prosecution and which has requested that the suspect be handed over, or alternatively by the suspect's surrender to an international judicial institution like the ICC. Extradition or surrender in such circumstances, however, does not negate the overarching obligation to adopt measures enabling the national authorities to exercise jurisdiction themselves.[70]

## B  Substantive international criminal law

*(i) Definitions of crimes*  The term 'genocide' was coined in 1944 as a reaction to the Nazi crimes committed during the Second World War.[71] The Nuremberg and the Tokyo Tribunals, however, did not recognise it as a legal concept. Genocide attained the status of a separate international crime in 1946 with the adoption of UN General Assembly Resolution 96(1). In 1951, shortly after the *Convention for the Prevention and Punishment of the Crime of Genocide* ('Genocide Convention')[72] had come into force, the International Court of Justice ('ICJ') declared the prohibition on genocide to be part of customary international law.

---

[69] See, eg, C Bassiouni, 'International Crimes: *Jus Cogens* and *Obligatio Erga Omnes*' (1996) 59 (4) *Law and Contemporary Problems* 63–74.

[70] In *Guengueng et al v Senegal*, U.N. Doc. CAT/C/36/D/181/2001, 19 May 2006, a case before the CAT Committee, Senegal was held to have failed to comply with its obligations under Article 7 of the *Torture Convention* for refusing to comply with the extradition request of Belgium and for not initiating proceedings against Habré (i.e. violation of the *aut dedere aut judicare* principle).

[71] R Lemkin, *Axis Rule in Occupied Europe: Laws of Occupation, Analysis of Government, Proposals for Redress* (Washington DC: Carnegie Endowment for International Peace, 1944) 79.

[72] Opened for signature 9 December 1948, 78 UNTS 277 (entered into force 12 January 1951).

The definition of the crime of genocide set forth in Article 2 of the Genocide Convention has since been reproduced verbatim in the ICTY, ICTR and ICC Statutes. It encompasses a number of acts committed with the intent to destroy, in whole or in part, a national, ethnic, racial or religious group as such. The prohibited acts include the killing or causing of serious bodily or mental harm to members of the group, inflicting on the group conditions of life calculated to bring about its destruction, imposing measures intended to prevent births within the group or forcibly transferring children from one group to another. Although the harm suffered need not necessarily be permanent or irremediable,[73] it must be serious[74] and it may involve but not be limited to torture, starvation, sexual violence and systematic expulsion from homes.

In order to constitute genocide, the prohibited acts must be carried out with the special intent to bring about the physical or biological destruction of the group targeted. The *dolus specialis* requirement is what sets genocide apart from other international crimes. It is a crime committed against individual victims by virtue of their belonging to a national, ethnic, racial or religious group. Although the group must be objectively identifiable by reason of a common trait shared by its members, the subjective perception of the perpetrators is generally also factored in by the international criminal tribunals when determining on a case-by-case basis what constitutes a protected group.[75]

Genocide is a crime of a collective nature, committed by and against a multitude of individuals. The perpetrator must be shown to have intended or attempted the destruction of a substantial number of persons belonging to the protected group targeted.[76] The determination of the meaning of 'substantial' is a matter of judicial discretion and depends on the circumstances of each particular case. It is however generally understood to designate a part of the group whose number or significance is such that its destruction would have impacted on the survival of the group as a whole.[77] Although the existence of a plan or policy to perpetrate genocide is not a formal element of the crime and

---

[73] *Prosecutor v Akayesu*, Case No. ICTR-95-4, T. Ch. I, ICTR (2 September 1998) [502].

[74] *Prosecutor v Kayishema*, Case No. ICTR-95-1, T. Ch. II, ICTR (21 May 1999) [109].

[75] *Prosecutor v Jelisić*, Case No. IT-95-10, T. Ch. I, ICTY (14 December 1999) [69–72]; *Prosecutor v Bagilishema*, Case No. ICTR-95-1A, T. Ch. I, ICTR (7 June 2001) [65]; *Prosecutor v Semanza*, Case No. ICTR-97-20, T. Ch. III, ICTR (15 May 2003) [317].

[76] *Prosecutor v Jelisić*, Case No. IT-95-10, T. Ch. I, ICTY (14 December 1999) [82].

[77] *Prosecutor v Krštić*, Case No. IT-98-33, A. Ch., ICTY (19 April 2004) [12].

even though genocide may be committed by a single individual, the *ad hoc* tribunals and more recently the ICC have favoured an additional contextual requirement stipulating that the prohibited conduct take place in the context of a manifest pattern of similar behaviour.[78]

Until its recognition as a separate international crime in 1946, genocide was regarded as a form of crime against humanity. Even nowadays most instances of genocide would readily meet the requirements of crimes against humanity. Both categories of crimes are punishable when committed in times of war as in peace[79] and form part of customary international law. There are, however, several important differences. Unlike genocide, crimes against humanity (with the exception of persecution) do not require discriminatory intent on racial, ethnic, national or religious grounds.[80] Irrespective of their motive, certain inhumane acts constitute crimes against humanity when committed in the context of a widespread or systematic attack directed against a civilian population. The prohibited acts include *inter alia* murder, extermination, enslavement, deportation and persecution. To this list of crimes, originally codified in the *Nuremberg Charter*,[81] the ICTY and ICTR Statutes subsequently added rape, imprisonment and torture. With the adoption of the ICC Statute in 1998, enforced disappearances and apartheid were also explicitly recognised as crimes against humanity, while the list of gender crimes was expanded to also include sexual slavery, enforced prostitution, forced pregnancies and other forms of sexual violence.

To engage the criminal liability of the perpetrator for crimes against humanity, the prohibited acts must not only be committed with the requisite *mens rea* but also be directed against non-combatants in the context of a military attack or a broader mistreatment campaign. Although the perpetrator need not share in the purpose of the overall attack, he must act with knowledge of its widespread or systematic nature and its targeting of civilians. The widespread or systematic requirement is disjunctive, referring respectively to the

---

[78] *Prosecutor v Kayishema and Ruzindana*, Case No. ICTR-95-1, T. Ch. II, ICTR (21 May 1999) [94]; ICC Elements of Crimes – Article 6.

[79] Although the ICTY Statute formally requires a link to an armed conflict, in *Tadić*, the first case to be dealt with by the tribunal, the ICTY acknowledged that such a requirement with regard to crimes against humanity was inconsistent with customary international law. See *Prosecutor v Tadić*, Case No. IT-94-1, T. Ch. II, ICTY (7 May 1997) [627].

[80] The ICTR constitutes an exception in this regard. Article 3 of the ICTR Statute defines crimes against humanity as acts committed 'as part of a widespread or systematic attack against any civilian population on national, political, ethnic, racial or religious grounds'.

[81] *Charter of the International Military Tribunal*, opened for signature 8 August 1945, 82 UNTS 279 (entered into force 8 August 1945) ('*Nuremberg Charter*').

large-scale effect of the attack and its methodological organisation.[82] The threshold thus established sets crimes against humanity apart from both genocide and war crimes although the underlying acts may occasionally overlap. Although currently international criminal law remains unsettled as to the requirement of a plan or policy as a formal element, there is general agreement that isolated acts of individual criminality cannot constitute an 'attack' within the meaning of crimes against humanity.[83]

Such isolated criminal acts, however, may constitute war crimes when committed in the course of either international or internal armed conflict. War crimes are serious violations of international humanitarian law. The latter regulates the permissible means and methods of warfare with regard to combatants and further seeks to protect civilians and *hors de combat* in the course of armed conflict. The jurisdiction of the different international criminal courts and tribunals over war crimes varies according to the type of conflict that the particular legal institution has been set up to deal with and the degree of acceptance that the various norms have gained as part of customary international law at the time of the institution's establishment.

Grave breaches of the 1949 Geneva Conventions and violations of their Common Article 3 form part of *jus cogens* and constitute war crimes, irrespective of whether they are perpetrated in an international or an internal armed conflict. The situation with regard to violations of Additional Protocol II to the Geneva Conventions and other serious violations of the laws and customs of war remains unsettled and their qualifying as war crimes largely depends on the nature of the conflict in the course of which they occur.

The nexus requirement with armed conflict – international or internal – is what sets war crimes apart from crimes against humanity and other international crimes. In order to incur individual criminal responsibility, the perpetrator must have committed the prohibited act with awareness of the factual circumstances establishing the existence of the conflict. Prohibited acts fall under several broad categories, relating to violence against civilians and other protected persons, attacks on protected targets or inflicting excessive damage on civilian property, and the use of proscribed means and methods of warfare.

*(ii) Modes of individual criminal responsibility* The substantive definitions of crimes, referring to a number of physical and mental elements which need to be satisfied if the individual criminal responsibility of the offender under international law is to be engaged, provide only a preliminary jurisdictional threshold.

---

[82] *Prosecutor v Akayesu*, Case No. ICTR-95-4, T. Ch. I, ICTR (2 September 1998) [579].
[83] Cryer et al, above n 5, 195–8.

Different modes of liability, with their own conduct and *mens rea* requirements, apply across the offences falling within the jurisdiction of the international courts and tribunals. They can be clustered in several broad categories: primary liability, secondary liability, liability for omission and liability for inchoate offences. This categorisation, however, is not straightforward as there are overlaps between the different liability modes and also variations of approach among the international courts and tribunals.

Primary liability follows the commission of a crime by a person acting alone, jointly with or through another individual, or as part of a joint criminal enterprise. The joint criminal enterprise ('JCE') doctrine is the most complex and controversial liability theory recognised by contemporary international criminal law. It was first developed in the jurisprudence of the ICTY as a means to address the challenge of attributing liability in a manner which accurately describes the relative responsibility of individuals for their contribution to large-scale criminal activities of a collective nature.[84] JCE entails the criminal responsibility of individuals who participate in the perpetration of a crime as part of a group of persons acting pursuant to a common purpose.

With reference to customary international law, a rather contentious observation in itself, the ICTY has identified three different types of JCE: basic, systematic and extended.[85] Of these, extended JCE is the most contentious and far-reaching variant. It involves criminal responsibility for crimes which fall outside the common plan and which have been neither intended nor even anticipated by the JCE participant charged.[86] Thus liability is incurred for failure to reasonably foresee that, in executing the common criminal design, an offence not a part of the design but a likely consequence of its execution may be committed. The jurisprudence of the *ad hoc* tribunals grounding individual criminal responsibility on recklessness for unlawful acts physically perpetrated by others has been subjected to vigorous criticism.[87] Not only do inter-

---

[84] The concept of JCE was first used by judges and prosecutors in ICTY, *Prosecutor v Tadić*, Case No. IT-94-1, T. Ch. II, ICTY (7 May 1997). See also E van Sliedregt, *The Criminal Responsibility of Individuals for Violations of International Humanitarian Law* (TMC Asser Press, The Hague, 2003) 94–109.

[85] See *Prosecutor v Tadić*, Case No. IT-94-1, A. Ch. (15 July 1999) [195]. Basic JCE concerns cases of co-perpetration where all participants in the common criminal design share the intent to commit a particular crime (*Tadić Appeal* [196]. Systematic JCE, on the other hand, generally applies to the so-called 'concentration camp' cases. It relates to instances in which a person knowingly participates in a system of ill-treatment with the general intent to further the system (*Tadić Appeal* [202]).

[86] Ibid [204].

[87] See, eg, A Marston Danner and J S Martinez, 'Guilty Associations: Joint Criminal Enterprise, Command Responsibility and the Development of International Criminal Law' (2005) 93 (1) *California Law Review* 75–169; M J Osiel, 'Modes of Participation in Mass Atrocity' (2005) 38 (3) *Cornell International Law Journal*

*International criminal law* 263

national prosecutors rely extensively on the JCE doctrine but they also enjoy considerable discretion in defining the geographic and temporal scope of the enterprise in each particular case. The larger the JCE, the more removed from each other the participants therein and the weaker the linkage among them. Such circumstances notwithstanding, extended JCE effectively allows for the conviction of individuals for crimes unintended and by persons unknown. From the perspective of victims and the objective of international criminal law to end impunity, the JCE doctrine in its extended variant facilitates prosecution and ensures that no contribution to mass crimes goes unpunished. At the same time, from a human rights law point of view, extended JCE poses a challenge to the right of the accused to a fair trial and the overall legitimacy of the international criminal justice process. The notion of JCE has also been incorporated in the Statute of the ICC, albeit under a different name and of a somewhat dissimilar scope. Remarkably, the extended JCE variant has not been included within the scope of the 'common purpose' provision contained in Article 25(3)(d) of the Statute.[88]

Secondary liability in international criminal law encompasses several forms of criminal participation, including ordering, instigating (for example, soliciting, inducing, inciting) and aiding and abetting. Planning, preparing or attempting a grave international crime is also punishable in itself, even when the crime does not materialise in the end. Conspiracy, in the sense of the inchoate crime of agreeing to commit an offence and requiring no proof of the offence occurring, is a mode of liability applicable to genocide only. Conspiracy to commit crimes against humanity or war crimes is not subject to punishment under current international criminal law. Instigation to commit genocide is an inchoate crime in itself, giving rise to individual criminal responsibility, although it does not constitute a form of liability *stricto sensu*.

The broad range of liability modes discussed above with reference to international crimes is supplemented by the inculpatory principle of command responsibility. As a mode of criminal participation entailing individual responsibility, this principle is specific to international law and it has no corresponding paradigms in domestic legal systems. Although effectively, and somewhat contentiously, applied by the Nuremberg and Tokyo Tribunals, the concept of command responsibility was first recognised by international law as a positive

---

793–822; S Powles, 'Joint Criminal Enterprise: Criminal Liability by Prosecutorial Ingenuity or Judicial Creativity?' (2004) 2 (2) *Journal of International Criminal Justice* 606–19.

[88] See generally K Ambos, 'Individual Criminal Responsibility in International Criminal Law: A Jurisprudential Analysis – From Nuremberg to The Hague' in G K McDonald and O Swaak-Goldman (eds), *Substantive and Procedural Aspects of International Criminal Law: The Experience of International and National Courts* (Kluwer Law International, The Hague/London/Boston, 2000).

legal norm in 1977 by Additional Protocol I to the 1949 Geneva Conventions.[89] The jurisprudence of the *ad hoc* tribunals delineated its scope of application and tailored it to meet the exigencies of modern welfare. Since then, command responsibility as a mode of liability has become firmly anchored in customary international law and as such it has been incorporated in the ICC Statute. It entails the individual criminal liability of military and civilian superiors for omissions, that is, for failing to prevent and/or punish the commission of international crimes by their subordinates.[90] Notably the superiors incur responsibility not merely for dereliction of duty or inability to control their subordinates but for the actual crimes committed by the subordinates themselves. Although the substantive elements vary in interpretation among the international criminal courts and tribunals and are somewhat different for military and civilian superiors, the general requirements entail the existence of a superior–subordinate relationship, a certain degree of knowledge on the part of the superior as to the crimes contemplated by his or her subordinates, and a failure to take adequate measures in response. International jurisprudence has evidenced the lowering of the requisite knowledge threshold to recklessness and even gross negligence. Similarly to JCE, therefore, command responsibility has been criticised for failing to take due cognisance of the degree of personal culpability, particularly when individuals are prosecuted for specific intent crimes, such as genocide, contemplated and physically committed by others.[91]

The ICC Statute expressly criminalises omissions with regard to command responsibility only, although the question of whether liability for omissions is categorically excluded from the ambit of other participation modes remains largely unsettled. Prior to the adoption of the ICC Statute there was little disagreement in international criminal law on the matter and it was generally accepted that international crimes could be committed by either acts or omissions, as long as the charge related to a failure of a positive duty to act. The international *ad hoc* tribunals have long recognised omissions as part of the objective elements of a variety of liability modes, including preparation, aiding and abetting, and even direct perpetration. Given the pre-existing support in international criminal law for omissions liability, it is suggested that the ICC should interpretatively extend the scope of punishable criminal conduct to also include omissions and thus close the existing loophole, which may otherwise potentially allow for a range of wrongful conduct to go unpunished.

---

[89] Additional Protocol I to the 1949 Geneva Conventions, Article 86(2).
[90] ICC Statute, Article 28.
[91] See, eg, A T O'Reilly, 'Command Responsibility: A Call to Realign Doctrine with Principles' (2004) 20 (1) *American University International Law Review* 71–107.

*(iii) Defences* There is a certain psychological aversion towards the idea that perpetrators of grave international crimes may escape liability. In contrast to national legal systems, international criminal law pays relatively little attention to the concept of defences, many aspects of which remain unsettled. Similarly to domestic courts, though, the international criminal courts and tribunals generally differentiate between substantive and procedural defences. While the former relate to the merits of the case, the latter refer to the violation of procedural rules, which renders further substantive review of the case unwarranted. Procedural defences dealt with in international jurisprudence include, *inter alia*, statutory limitations, *ne bis in idem*, retroactivity of the law and abuse of process. By safeguarding the accused against arbitrary treatment during criminal proceedings, they form an essential component of the right to a fair trial. Substantive defences, on the other hand, encompass both justifications and excuses, although the distinction drawn between these two categories in international criminal law is less clear-cut than in domestic legal systems. Mitigating factors do not, strictly speaking, constitute defences, as they influence the sentencing rather than the criminal responsibility of the perpetrator.

Among the substantive defences applicable before the international criminal courts and tribunals and excluding the criminal responsibility of the accused are insanity, intoxication, self-defence, duress, necessity, mistake of fact or law and obedience to superior orders.[92] Diminished capacity, as opposed to mental incapacity to comprehend the nature of one's conduct, is not a defence but a mitigating factor to be taken into consideration at the sentencing stage.[93] Similarly, voluntary intoxication giving rise to diminished capacity does not exclude criminal responsibility but may mitigate the sentence.[94]

Self-defence,[95] duress and necessity apply to crimes committed under an imminent threat and are closely related to considerations of proportionality. While self-defence applies to protected persons and essential property threatened by the unlawful use of force, duress and necessity relate to threats of

---

[92] Unlike the *ad hoc* tribunals, which recognised the applicability of defences through their case law, the ICC Statute explicitly codifies the permissible defences in Articles 31, 32 and 33.

[93] *Prosecutor v Delalić, Mučić, Delić and Landžo*, Case No. IT-96-21, A. Ch., ICTY (20 February 2001) [580–90].

[94] Evidence of voluntary intoxication may raise doubts as to the existence of the requisite *mens rea* (eg premeditated intent, actual knowledge). However, in some circumstances, voluntary intoxication may be considered an aggravating rather than a mitigating factor. See, eg, *Prosecutor v Kvočka*, Case No. IT-98-30/1, T. Ch. I, ICTY (2 November 2001) [706].

[95] Self-defence as a substantive defence in international criminal law should not to be confused with collective self-defence by States provided for by Article 51 of the UN Charter.

death and serious bodily harm emanating from persons or circumstances beyond one's control. Unlike self-defence, in the case of duress or necessity there is no requirement of a relationship between the accused and the persons threatened. As with self-defence, however, the conduct forced must be proportionate to the degree of danger faced.[96] Notwithstanding, duress and necessity cannot provide a complete defence in cases of genocide as coercion does not negate the genocidal intent of the perpetrator. The *ad hoc* tribunals have also ruled these two categories of defences inapplicable to war crimes and crimes against humanity, where the underlying offences relate to the killing of innocent people.[97] The ICC Statute, however, does not expressly codify any exceptions, while duress and necessity are regarded as absolute defences.[98]

As for mistake of fact or law, liability is excluded only when the mistake serves to negate the requisite *mens rea*. Nevertheless, mistake of law cannot be pleaded with regard to genocide and crimes against humanity.[99] Considered 'manifestly unlawful', these two categories of crimes also cannot be excused when committed under superior orders.[100] When successfully coupled with a number of other defences, particularly duress and mistake of fact or law, the defence of obedience to superior orders may, however, exonerate from responsibility the perpetrators of war crimes. For the defence to apply, the accused must have been under a legal duty to obey the superior order and must be shown to have lacked knowledge as to the unlawfulness of the order.[101] Although the aforementioned requirements for the applicability of the defence have attained customary status in international law,[102] their practical application remains both difficult and controversial.

---

[96] For a description of the proportionality test, see Separate and Dissenting Opinion of Judge Cassese, *Prosecutor v Erdemović*, Case No. IT-96-22, A. Ch., ICTY (7 October 1997) [16].

[97] Ibid. See also the Joint Separate Opinion of Judge McDonald and Judge Vohrah, and the Separate and Dissenting Opinions of Judge Li and Judge Cassese to the Judgment.

[98] ICC Statute, Article 31(1)(d).

[99] Article 33(2) of the ICC Statute explicitly defines orders to commit genocide and crimes against humanity as 'manifestly unlawful'. Hence, individuals accused of having committed genocide or crimes against humanity cannot plead ignorance as to the unlawfulness of the order and, accordingly, the illegality of the act.

[100] ICC Statute, Article 33(2).

[101] ICC Statute, Article 33(1).

[102] I Bantekas, 'Defences in International Criminal Law' in D McGoldrick, P Rowe and E Donnelly (eds) *The Permanent International Criminal Court. Legal and Policy Issues* (Hart Publishing, Portland, 2004) 273.

## C  International criminal procedure

The procedural rules applicable to international criminal trials constitute a *sui generis* system, comprising elements of both the common law and the civil law tradition. While the blending of adversarial and inquisitorial facets is in part the outcome of political negotiations surrounding the establishment of the supranational justice mechanisms, it is also tailored to meet the specific needs of international trials and optimise the fairness and efficiency of proceedings. The extent to which the resulting procedural amalgam attains this objective, however, is a matter of ongoing debate.

Albeit predominantly adversarial in nature, the basic procedural framework of the *ad hoc* tribunals has been methodically supplemented in the course of the tribunals' existence with various civil law elements. Inquisitorial aspects of procedure also feature prominently in the ICC Statute. These relate, *inter alia*, to the special role of the Pre-Trial Chamber in supervising the actions of the Prosecutor, the Prosecutor's obligation to investigate equally both incriminating and exonerating circumstances, the compilation of a case file handed over to the judges before the commencement of the trial and the Court's enhanced powers of control over the proceedings (for example, the ability to call additional evidence and summon witnesses *proprio motu*).[103]

The essential underpinnings of international criminal procedure are firmly rooted in fundamental human rights standards, recognised in international treaties[104] as well as by domestic legal systems. Geared towards safeguarding the rights of the accused, these general principles of criminal process relate to the presumption of innocence, the independence and impartiality of the judicial institution, the right to fair, public and expeditious proceedings, and the prohibition on trials *in absentia*. Some of their practical manifestations, however, and in particular those pertaining to fair trial and with regard to the *ad hoc* tribunals, have not been devoid of criticism. Rules authorising mandatory pre-trial detention,[105] regulating the disclosure of evidence and acknowledging the

---

[103]  Cassese, above n 48, 386.

[104]  See, eg, the *International Covenant on Civil and Political Rights*, opened for signature 16 December 1966, 999 UNTS 171 (entered into force 23 March 1976) ('ICCPR') (Articles 9, 14 and 15), and the ECHR (Articles 5, 6 and 7). Similar provisions pertaining to the right to security of person and to fair trial are also contained in eg the *American Convention on Human Rights*, opened for signature 22 November 1969, 1144 UNTS 123 (entered into force 18 July 1978)(Articles 7, 8 and 9), and the *African Charter on Human and Peoples' Rights*, opened for signature 27 June 1981, 21 ILM 58 (entered into force 21 October 1986) (Articles 6 and 7).

[105]  In accordance with the principle of the presumption of innocence, pre-trial detention should not be mandatory. In its General Comment 8 concerning the implementation and application of Article 9 of the ICCPR the UN Committee on Civil and Political Rights has stated that 'pre-trial detention should be an exception and as short

permissibility of plea-bargaining have been among the most contentious.[106] The ICC Statute and the ICC's *Rules of Procedure and Evidence*[107] do not make significant progress in this regard as they leave many of the provisions relating to disclosure obligations subject to judicial interpretation and do not dispense categorically with the notion of plea-bargaining. On the other hand, unlike the ICTY and the ICTR, the ICC considers provisional release, provided certain specific requirements are met, as the rule rather than the exception.[108] It also enhances the role of victims, elevating their status from that of witnesses to actual participants in the proceedings, enjoying a broad range of procedural rights[109] as well as a right to reparations.[110]

### D  Cooperation regime with States

The overall effectiveness of the international judicial process ultimately depends on State cooperation. Lacking their own enforcement agencies, the international courts and tribunals must rely on domestic systems in relation to on-site investigations, summoning of witnesses, arrest and surrender of

---

as possible'. Similarly, Article 5 of the ECHR permits pre-trial detention only if the measure is considered resonably necessary to prevent an offence or to prevent flight after an offence has been committed. For a discussion of the relevant case law of the European Court of Human Rights, see eg P Van Dijk, F Van Hoof, A Van Rijn and L Zwaak (eds) *Theory and Practice of the European Convention on Human Rights* (Intersentia, Antwerpen, 2006) 471–5.

[106] S Negri, 'Equality of Arms – Guiding Light or Empty Shell?' in M Bohlander (ed) *International Criminal Justice: A Critical Analysis of Institutions and Procedures* (Cameron May Ltd, London, 2007); J Cook, 'Plea Bargaining at the Hague' (2005) 30 (2) *Yale Journal of International Law* 473–506; A-M La Rosa, 'A Tremendous Challenge for the International Criminal Tribunals: Reconciling the Requirements of International Humanitarian Law with Those of Fair Trial' (1997) 321 *International Review of the Red Cross* 635–50.

[107] ICC Rules of Procedure and Evidence, UN Doc PCNICC/2000/1/Add.1 (2000).

[108] ICC Statute, Article 60 and ICC Rules of Procedure and Evidence, UN Doc PCNICC/2000/1/Add.1 (2000) Rule 118.

[109] See ICC Appeals Chamber Decision on the Appeal of Mr Lubanga Dyilo against the Oral Decision of the Trial Chamber of 18 January 2008, ICC-01/04-01/06 OA 11, 11 July 2008; ICC Trial Chamber I Decision on Victims' Participation in the Trial, ICC-01/04-01/06, *Prosecutor v Thomas Lubanga Dyilo*, 18 January 2008; ICC Decision on the Set of Procedural Rights Attached to Procedural Status of Victim at the Pre-Trial Stage of the Case, ICC-01/04-01/07, *Prosecutor v Germain Katanga and Mathieu Ngudjolo Chui*, 13 May 2008; and ICC Decision on the Applications for Participation in the Proceedings of VPRS 1, VPRS 2, VPRS 3, VPRS 4, VPRS 5 and VPRS 6 (Public Redacted Version), ICC-01/04, *Situation in the Democratic Republic of the Congo*, 17 January 2006 (concerning the procedural rights of victims at the investigation of a situation stage).

[110] ICC Statute, Article 75.

accused, and enforcement of penalties. In contrast to inter-State cooperation, which is of a horizontal nature, cooperation between States and international jurisdictions is often described as vertical. The relationship is non-reciprocal and the prerogative to unilaterally interpret the duty of cooperation incumbent on States is vested with the international courts and tribunals.[111] The obligation to cooperate is not confined to States only; it may address international organisations and individuals as well.

The capacity of international jurisdictions to effectuate this obligation, however, is circumscribed and has given rise to many difficulties in practice.[112] In the context of the ICC, problems may arise for instance in the case of conflicting international obligations of States, as unless explicitly imposed by the Security Council acting under Chapter VII of the UN Charter, States' duty of cooperation with the Court will not automatically prevail over competing cooperation obligations.[113] Procedural requirements attached to extradition may also interfere with the surrender of suspects to the Court. Traditionally accepted formal grounds for denying inter-State legal assistance, such as the principle of double criminality, do not apply to State cooperation with the international criminal courts and tribunals. The only permissible exception relates to national security objections.[114] Nevertheless, international jurisdictions remain severely constrained in their practical ability to effectuate State cooperation. Existing mechanisms for addressing non-compliance with the duty to cooperate (for example, collective sanctions) are rarely used due to their political sensitivity and are in any case often dependent on States' willingness to implement.

## 4 Concluding observations

International criminal law consists of two main bodies of law: transnational criminal law and international criminal law (*per se*). Coming to the end of this

---

[111] Sluiter, above n 54, 82–8.
[112] See generally M Harmon and F Gaynor, 'Prosecuting Massive Crimes with Primitive Tools: Three Difficulties Encountered by Prosecutors in International Criminal Proceedings' (2004) 2 (2) *Journal of International Criminal Justice* 403–26.
[113] See, eg, ICC Statute, Article 90(7)(b). Competing cooperation obligations may arise when a State Party to the Statute receives a request from the Court to surrender an alleged perpetrator found on its territory and at the same time a request from a State not a Party to the Statute for the extradition of the same person for conduct other than the one motivating the Court's request. If the requested State has concluded an extradition agreement with the requesting State which relates to the conduct in question and is aligned with general principles of extradition law, the requested State is under no obligation to automatically give priority to the Court's request.
[114] See, eg, ICTY Rules of Procedure and Evidence UN Doc IT/32/Rev.7 (1996), Rules 54*bis* and 70; ICC Statute, Articles 72, 73 and 93(4)–(6).

chapter, the question arises as to what the relationship is between the aforementioned limbs and human rights law. This requires us to look into the position of the individual under each respective body of law.

The position of the individual in transnational criminal law is that of *object* rather than subject of law. The rule of non-inquiry and the concomitant impossibility to challenge certain evidence in court because of the inter-State 'good faith' principle and the presumption of trust illustrate this position. Transnational criminal law, consisting of procedural rules governing inter-State police and judicial cooperation, is not directly concerned with individual rights. Admittedly, human rights considerations have brought about a certain shift in the dynamics of cooperation relationships. For instance, one can think of the transfer of sentenced persons from one State to another; such transfer may be requested by individuals and granted for humanitarian reasons.[115] Still, the State-centred approach that underlies these forms of collaboration remains unaltered; it is States' right to determine the scope of their jurisdictional reach over offenders.

However, there are signs that the dominant State position is changing, for State concerns are yielding to individual concerns. One can point to the erosion of the *male captus bene detentus* rule in some jurisdictions because of human rights considerations. Moreover, human rights bodies have played an important role in setting limits to State obligations that override individual human rights. Illustrative is the landmark ruling in *Soering v United Kingdom* (*'Soering'*)[116] where the European Court of Human Rights ('ECtHR') held that the extradition of a German national to the United States to face charges of capital murder would violate Article 3 of the ECHR. The latter provision contains a ban on inhuman and degrading treatment, which would have been violated as a result of Soering's extradition since this would have meant exposing him to death row in the US. Thus, Soering's right under Article 3 ECHR, and the United Kingdom's obligation to respect that right, prevailed over the UK's obligation to extradite Soering to the US.

In international criminal law, the individual is regarded as a *subject* of law and is endowed with rights and duties. The famous quote from the Nuremberg Judgment that 'crimes against international law are committed by men, not by abstract legal entities'[117] is often cited to substantiate the existence of the prin-

---

[115] See Articles 2(2) and 5 (sentenced person may express interest/request to be transferred) of the *Convention on the Transfer of Sentenced Persons*, opened for signature 21 March 1983, ETS 112 (entered into force 1 July 1985). See further Section 2A(iii).

[116] *Soering v United Kingdom* (7 July 1989) Series A no. 161(1989), 11 EHRR 439.

[117] L Friedman, 'Trial of the Major War Criminals before the International

ciple of individual criminal responsibility. Individuals have the duty to refrain from conduct which offends the common values and norms of the international community. If they violate those norms they can be prosecuted before national or international courts for a limited class of international crimes: aggression, genocide, crimes against humanity and war crimes. States are politically bound to prosecute such crimes and in the case of war crimes even legally bound to do so.[118]

Those accused before international courts and tribunals invariably benefit from 'rights of the accused'.[119] Fair trial rights have been incorporated in the statutes of all international courts and tribunals. International judicial institutions do not consider themselves (directly) bound by human rights treaties like the ICCPR and the ECHR, as they are not Parties to such treaties. However, from ICTY and ICTR case law, it appears that human rights norms are applied as general principles of law. In ruling on issues such as *in absentia* proceedings, the right to an independent and impartial tribunal, and self-representation, the ICTY and ICTR frequently rely on case law and communications of universal and regional human rights bodies, such as the Human Rights Committee and the ECtHR. The biggest challenge facing international courts and tribunals lies in guaranteeing defendants trials 'without undue delay'.[120] Pre-trial detention at the ICTY and ICTR has proved lengthy; at the ICTR it has lasted as long as nine years.[121] Admittedly, these courts face unique difficulties – difficulties that relate to translation, protected witnesses, and proceedings conducted far removed from the scene of the crimes. Nevertheless nine years of pre-trial detention is hardly justifiable and the *ad hoc* tribunals have been rightly criticised for it. Let us hope that the ICC, once it is fully operational, will learn from past experiences and manage to keep the length of proceedings within reasonable limits.[122]

---

Military Tribunal, The Nuremberg Judgment 1945–46' (New York, 1972) II *The Law of War. A Documentary History* 940.

[118] As a result of the 'aut dedere aut judicare' clause that can be found in the Geneva Conventions (1949) and Additional Protocol I (1977) with regard to 'grave breaches' of the Conventions and API. See Articles 50, 51, 130, and 149 of the Geneva Conventions I–IV respectively, and Article 85 of Additional Protocol I.

[119] ICTR Statute, Article 20; ICTY Statute, Article 21; ICC Statute, Articles 55, 66 and 67. See further section 3.3.

[120] ICTY Statute, Article 21(4)(c); ICTR Statute, Article 20(4)(c).

[121] *Prosecutor v Bagosora, Kabiligi, Ntabakuze and Nsengiyumva*, Case No. ICTR-98-41-T, ICTR (17 November 2006).

[122] See informal expert paper, 'Measures available to the International Criminal Court to reduce the length of proceedings', available at www.icc-cpi.int/library/organs/otp/length_of_proceedings.pdf> at 2 March 2009.

# 11. The four pillars of transitional justice: a gender-sensitive analysis
*Ronli Sifris*

## 1 What is transitional justice?

### A  A general definition

The term 'transitional justice' refers to a holistic, restorative approach to justice which applies in the context of societies confronting a legacy of systematic or widespread human rights abuse. It is an approach to justice which seeks to balance the need for accountability and for recognition of victims' suffering with the desire to achieve a lasting peace and true reconciliation. The types of transitions which a society may undergo differ according to the particular context. Transitional justice has traditionally been understood as applying to countries transitioning from an authoritarian, violent past to a democratic, non-violent future. Examples of such transitions include those of many Latin American countries from military to civilian rule.[1] However, the term may also be used to refer to 'conflicted democracies'; '[i]n this context, the transition becomes one of: (a) from procedural to substantive democracy, or at least involving a deepening of substantive democracy, and (b) from violence to peace.'[2] One example of this is the Northern Ireland transition.[3]

There is no 'one size fits all' approach to transitional justice. While generalizations can be made in terms of what is necessary to institute a comprehensive transitional justice process, ultimately each society confronting a legacy of human rights abuses is different from other societies which have also had to deal with such a past. Thus while there will be common elements in the construction of a path towards justice and reconciliation, the individual nature of a society and its history will frequently determine the precise nature of the transitional justice process.

---

[1] Fionnuala Ni Aolain and Colm Campbell, 'The Paradox of Transition in Conflicted Democracies' (2005) 27 *Human Rights Quarterly* 172, 173.
[2] Ibid 179.
[3] For a detailed discussion see generally ibid.

It is often said that there are four pillars of transitional justice: prosecutions, truth commissions, reparations, and institutional reform.[4] It is commonly thought that all of these four transitional justice mechanisms must be implemented for a transitional society to confront past atrocities, deal with them, and move towards reconciliation. The core notion underpinning a comprehensive transitional justice process is that, for justice and reconciliation to be achieved, retribution alone is not enough; it must be accompanied by a thorough truth-telling exercise, damage must be repaired, and concrete changes must be made to key institutions.

Even on the assumption that retribution is the only necessary ingredient for securing justice and reconciliation, pragmatism dictates that it would be unrealistic to prosecute all perpetrators of human rights abuses in circumstances such as those which existed in Nazi Germany, the former Yugoslavia, Rwanda and Sudan. The resources simply do not exist, on a local, regional or global level, to prosecute all perpetrators. Further, it is doubtful whether a society confronting a legacy of human rights abuses would in fact benefit from a process which sought to prosecute every perpetrator irrespective of the strain on state resources and irrespective of the time-consuming nature of this exercise. Thus it is necessary, in a transitional justice context, to view justice in a holistic, restorative sense.

*B   The link between transitional justice and human rights discourse*
The field of transitional justice falls within the blurry space between international human rights and international criminal law. It overlaps with international criminal law in that prosecutions are an important component of the field of transitional justice. Thus whilst, for example, the prosecution of alleged or actual war criminals in the International Criminal Tribunal for the former Yugoslavia constitutes both the implementation and development of international criminal law, it also constitutes a key component of the transitional justice process in the former Yugoslavia. So too, whilst the internal conflict in the former Yugoslavia which took place during the 1990s gave rise to heinous violations of international human rights law, transitional justice governs the process for dealing with those violations *ex post facto*.

In a lecture on transitional justice, Louise Arbour, the then United Nations High Commissioner for Human Rights, pushed traditional boundaries in transitional justice discourse by circumventing the more prevalent focus on civil

---

[4]   Office of the High Commissioner for Human Rights (Nepal) *What is Transitional Justice?* (United Nations, Geneva, 2007). It should be noted that using the framework of 'four pillars of transitional justice' to discuss this very complex field raises the risk of oversimplification. Nevertheless, for the purpose of obtaining a useful overview, analysis of the field in terms of these core aspects is extremely helpful.

and political rights and instead concentrating her lecture on 'Economic and Social Justice for Societies in Transition'.[5] She emphasized the oft-repeated refrain that human rights are indivisible and inter-dependent and argued that, economic, social and cultural rights must therefore be addressed in the transitional justice context. She firmly rejected the view that the enforcement of economic, social and cultural rights constitutes an unjustified drain on state resources and asserted that they should be viewed as legally binding and enforceable. According to Arbour, economic, social and cultural rights should be addressed across the transitional justice framework, in contexts such as peace agreements, transitional constitutions, legislation, the judicial process, truth commissions and public sector reform. Arbour concluded her lecture by stating that:

> Transitional justice, as a dynamic and cutting edge field, could serve as [a] springboard for the systematic anchoring of economic, social and cultural rights in the political, legal and social construct of societies. By reaching beyond its criminal law-rooted mechanisms to achieve social justice, transitional justice could contribute to expand our traditional and reductive understanding of 'justice' by rendering it its full meaning.

Thus it is clear that, despite the fact that transitional justice has its initial roots in international criminal law,[6] human rights discourse is extremely relevant in the transitional justice context given that the fundamental purpose of transitional justice is to institute a process for dealing with a legacy of human rights abuse.

The (now former) High Commissioner's emphasis on expanding traditional notions of transitional justice so as to work towards the achievement of true social justice is particularly relevant when considering the field from a gendered perspective. The oft-repeated refrain that 'women's rights are human rights' takes on particular significance in the realm of transitional justice, where mechanisms have traditionally addressed the sorts of harms which are customarily suffered by men and have failed to adequately focus on the harms suffered by women. Arbour's focus on economic, social and cultural rights is

---

[5] Louise Arbour, 'Economic and Social Justice for Societies in Transition' (Speech delivered as the 2006 Annual Lecture on Transitional Justice at New York University School of Law, 25 October 2006) http://www.chrgj.org/docs/Arbour_25_October_2006.pdf at 15 December 2008.

[6] The Nuremberg and Tokyo Tribunals established in the aftermath of World War II are the first examples of non-national or multi-national institutions being established for the purpose of prosecuting or punishing crimes with an international dimension and scope: Antonio Cassese, *International Criminal Law* (Oxford University Press, Oxford, 2003) 323.

especially pertinent in this context. Transitional justice mechanisms generally prioritize addressing civil and political harms, those harms which are suffered in the public space and which, in patriarchal societies where women are frequently relegated to the private space, are ordinarily suffered by men. Transitional justice mechanisms need to evolve so as to satisfactorily address economic, social and cultural rights which tend to be violated in the private realm, the space traditionally occupied by women.

In times of conflict, women suffer various types of harm both in the public and private space, both in the civil and political realm and in the economic, social and cultural realm. Women are subjected to the same sorts of violent conduct as men, including torture and enforced disappearances. In addition, women are subjected to sexual violence as a tool of war; their lack of social standing, frequent low levels of education, and inability to protect their own property and resources often result in economic victimization; women are more likely than men to be displaced and to become refugees; women bear the brunt of the responsibility of caring for children and elderly family members, a responsibility which is an extreme burden when seeking food to cook is itself a danger.

The United Nations Secretary-General recognized the need for a gender-sensitive approach to reconstruction and rehabilitation in his 2002 report on women, peace and security.[7] He explicitly addressed the need for economic reconstruction to be informed by the specific needs of women and the importance of including women in decision-making processes. Further, when discussing social reconstruction the report specifically mentions health care, education and social services and is unambiguous in its statement that '[a]ddressing the needs and priorities of women and girls should be an integral part in the design and implementation of social healing processes'.[8]

In this chapter, the four pillars of transitional justice (prosecutions, truth commissions, reparations, and institutional reform) will now be considered in turn from a gender-sensitive perspective, culminating in a brief discussion of the broader concept of reconciliation.

## 2 Prosecutions

In his opening statement before the International Military Tribunal at Nuremburg, Justice Robert H Jackson asserted:

---

[7] Secretary-General, *Report of the Secretary-General on Women, Peace and Security*, UN Doc S/2002/1154 (16 October 2002) [54]–[60].

[8] Ibid [58].

> That four great nations, flushed with victory and stung with injury stay the hand of vengeance and voluntarily submit their captive enemies to the judgment of the law is one of the most significant tributes that Power has ever paid to Reason.[9]

Prosecutions are an extremely important component of transitional justice. They help to achieve a number of key objectives such as: holding perpetrators accountable for their actions; restoring the dignity of victims; establishing a historical record of the atrocities which were committed; providing a public forum for the society as a whole to confront, condemn and deal with the legacy of human rights abuse; re-establishing faith in the rule of law and in the State's willingness to enforce the law; and deterring future violations of human rights. As well as having these practical effects, the prosecution of those responsible for gross infringements of human rights is also significant on a symbolic level; such prosecutions mark a turning point in a society – from one devoid of respect for human rights to one where human rights form a part of the established order.[10] The courts in which perpetrators of human rights abuses are prosecuted can take a number of forms. They can be wholly international, wholly domestic, or a hybrid of the two. In light of the fact that a chapter of this book is dedicated to a discussion of international criminal law and the various courts and tribunals,[11] this section will simply provide a basic overview from a gendered perspective.

### A   International tribunals

Decades after the establishment of the Nuremberg and Tokyo tribunals following World War II, the end of the Cold War and the increased prominence of international human rights doctrine, as well as renewed atrocities, precipitated the emergence of a reinvigorated commitment to international criminal law.[12] This resulted in the establishment of the International Criminal Tribunal for the former Yugoslavia ('ICTY') and the International Criminal Tribunal for Rwanda ('ICTR') in the early 1990s. Following the establishment of these *ad*

---

[9] Robert H Jackson, *Opening Statement before the International Military Tribunal, 21 November 1945* (1945) http://www.roberthjackson.org/Man/theman2-7-8-1/ at 15 December 2009.

[10] For an interesting discussion of the nature and purpose of prosecutions in the transitional context see the debate between Diane Orentlicher and Carlos Nino: Diane Orentlicher, 'Settling Accounts: The Duty to Prosecute Human Rights Violations of a Prior Regime' (1991) 100 *Yale Law Journal* 2537; Carlos Nino, 'The Duty to Punish Past Abuses of Human Rights Put into Context: The Case of Argentina' (1991) 100 *Yale Law Journal* 2619; Diane Orentlicher, 'A Reply to Professor Nino' (1991) 100 *Yale Law Journal* 2641.

[11] See Chapter 10.

[12] Cassese, above n 6, 324–5.

*hoc* tribunals was the momentous creation of the International Criminal Court ('ICC').

## B   The ad hoc *tribunals*

The ICTY (established in 1993) and the ICTR (established in 1994) were both created by United Nations Security Council Resolutions,[13] pursuant to the Security Council's power to decide on measures necessary to maintain or restore international peace and security.[14] The ICTY and the ICTR have made significant contributions to the advancement of international criminal law. One notable area is in the prosecution of gender-based crimes. The Statutes establishing both the ICTY and the ICTR specifically include rape in the definition of 'crimes against humanity'.[15] The Statute establishing the ICTR also includes rape in its definition of 'violations of Article 3 common to the Geneva Conventions'.[16]

In a number of important decisions, the *ad hoc* tribunals have explicitly applied these significant provisions. For example, in *Prosecutor v Delalic, Mucic, Delic and Landžo*,[17] the Appeals Chamber dismissed a challenge by Delic to a number of counts of wilful killing and torture (constituted by rape and repeated incidents of forcible sexual intercourse). In *Prosecutor v Furundzija*[18] the Appeals Chamber confirmed that the appellant was guilty as an aider and abettor of outrages upon personal dignity, including rape, as a violation of the laws or customs of war. Further, the case of *Prosecutor v Kunarac, Kovac and Vukovic*[19] was the first case to be brought before an international criminal tribunal which rested solely on crimes of sexual violence against women. The ICTY has also committed resources to ensuring that prosecutions are dealt with in a gender-sensitive manner. For example, there is a legal advisor specifically for gender-related crimes, and the Rules of Procedure and Evidence also provide protection for women appearing before the tribunal in relation to gender-based crimes.[20]

---

[13]  SC Res 827, UN SCOR, 3217th mtg, UN Doc S/RES/827 (1993) (25 May 1993) and SC Res 955, UN SCOR, 3453rd mtg, UN Doc S/RES/955 (1994) (8 November 1994).
[14]  See *Charter of the United Nations* Chapter VII.
[15]  *Statute of the International Criminal Tribunal for the Former Yugoslavia*, SC Res 827, UN SCOR, 3217th mtg, UN Doc S/RES/827 (1993) (25 May 1993) Annex, Article 5(g); *Statute of the International Criminal Tribunal for Rwanda*, SC Res 955, UN SCOR, 3453rd mtg, UN Doc S/RES/955 (1994) (8 November 1994), Annex, Article 3(g).
[16]  *Statute of the International Criminal Tribunal for Rwanda* Article 4(e).
[17]  Case No IT-96-21, Judgment of 20 Feb 2001.
[18]  Case No IT-95-17/1, Judgment of 21 July 2000.
[19]  Case No IT-96-23, IT-96-23/1, Judgment of 12 June 2002.
[20]  For example Rule 96 of the *Rules of Procedure and Evidence* eliminates the

In the ground-breaking ICTR case of *Prosecutor v Akayesu*,[21] the court held Akayesu guilty of genocide, in part on the basis of his encouragement of sexual violence against Tutsi woman. However, despite this significant decision, the ICTR has been less than vigorous in its subsequent prosecution of crimes of sexual violence. Further, the tribunal has not instituted adequate structural procedures for addressing the issues that women face when appearing as victims or witnesses.[22] For example, the ICTR has gained some notoriety for not properly explaining its processes to witnesses, failing to provide translators and psychological support where necessary, and failing to provide the same medical care to witnesses as it provides to alleged perpetrators.[23] In addition, instances have been recorded of witnesses who have testified under a banner of confidentiality in the courtroom but whose identities have been leaked outside the courtroom.[24]

Notably, the Secretary-General has explicitly recognized the importance of international tribunals operating in a gender-sensitive manner. Specifically, in his 2002 report on women, peace and security the Secretary-General submitted that the Security Council should:

> Ensure that future ad hoc tribunals created by the Security Council build on existing statutes and include judges and advisers with legal expertise on specific issues, such as violations of the rights of women and girls, including gender-based and sexual violence; ensure that prosecutors of such ad hoc international tribunals respect the interests and personal circumstances of women and girls victims [sic] and witnesses and take into account the nature of crimes involving gender-based violence, sexual violence and violence against children.[25]

Despite being lauded as proof of a growing global commitment to prosecuting those responsible for fundamental human rights violations, it should be noted that serious criticism has been levelled at both the ICTY and the ICTR. For example, both tribunals have been viewed as illustrations of the global community acting too late and dispensing 'justice' to assuage the guilt of

---

need for corroboration of the victim's testimony, limits the availability of the defence of consent and prohibits evidence of the victim's prior sexual conduct.

[21] Case No ICTR-96-4-T, Judgment of 2 September 1998.

[22] Katherine M Franke, 'Gendered Subjects of Transitional Justice' (2006) 15 *Columbia Journal of Gender and Law* 813, 818.

[23] Anne Saris, *Transition for Whom? – The Involvement of Victims in International Criminal Processes: a Gender-Based Analysis* (on file with author) 38–64.

[24] Binaifer Nowrojee, 'Your Justice is Too Slow: Will the ICTR Fail Rwanda's Rape Victims?' (Occasional Paper, United Nations Institute for Social Development, 2005).

[25] Secretary-General, above n 7, [25].

having failed to prevent the commission of egregious human rights violations;[26] both tribunals have been regarded as paying inadequate attention to the rights of the accused, for example the right to a 'fair and expeditious trial';[27] and both tribunals have been accused of dispensing 'selective justice'.[28] From a gendered perspective, whilst significant improvements have been made in terms of criminalizing and prosecuting sexual violence, it is important to recognize that focusing only on sexual violence 'has had the effect of sexualizing women in ways that fail to capture both the array of manners in which women suffer gross injustice, as well as the ways in which men suffer gendered violence as well'.[29]

### C  The International Criminal Court

On 17 July 1998, after years of discussion and negotiation, the ICC was established by the Rome Statute of the International Criminal Court as a permanent, independent court 'to exercise its jurisdiction over persons for the most serious crimes of international concern' and to 'be complementary to national criminal jurisdictions'.[30] The ICC has jurisdiction over the crime of genocide, crimes against humanity, war crimes and the crime of aggression (which is as yet undefined).[31] Being such a young institution, it is unclear precisely how the ICC will operate and how it will deal with the numerous difficulties which it faces. For example, it will be interesting to observe precisely how the ICC decides which cases to prosecute; it is unclear how the ICC will approach the issue of states granting amnesty to perpetrators of human rights violations;[32] and whether it will become more of a political institution than a judicial institution is an ongoing concern.[33] This last point is based in part on the power of

---

[26]   Cassese, above n 6, 326–7.
[27]   Ibid 444.
[28]   Ibid.
[29]   Franke above n 22, 823.
[30]   *Rome Statute of the International Criminal Court*, opened for signature 17 July 1998, 2187 UNTS 90 (entered into force 1 July 2002) (*'Rome Statute'*) Article 1. The notion of an international court's jurisdiction being complementary to that of national courts was a novel idea; it is set out in Article 17 of the *Rome Statute*. For a more detailed discussion of the principle of complementarity, see Cassese, above n 6, 342–4.
[31]   *Rome Statute* Article 5.
[32]   For a discussion of the issue of the ICC's approach to national amnesty programs, see Michael P Scharf, 'The Amnesty Exception to the Jurisdiction of the International Criminal Court' (1999) 32 *Cornell International Law Journal* 447.
[33]   For a discussion of the issue of the political versus the judicial nature of the ICC, see Allison Marston Danner, 'Enhancing the Legitimacy and Accountability of Prosecutorial Discretion at the International Criminal Court' (2003) 97 *American Journal of International Law* 510.

the Security Council both to refer a case to the ICC and to suspend an investigation or prosecution. However, it is interesting to note that a core component of the United States' objections to the ICC rests on the argument that it is not sufficiently accountable to the Security Council.[34]

The *Rome Statute*, like the Statutes of the ICTY and ICTR before it, has made significant advances in the way in which various international crimes are defined. As stated above, one of the significant recent developments in international criminal law has been the increased focus on gender-based offences. Whilst the statutes of the *ad hoc* tribunals made important advances in recognizing the gravity of such offences, the *Rome Statute* expands upon the punishable sorts of gender-based offences. In its definition of 'crimes against humanity' the *Rome Statute* includes '[r]ape, sexual slavery, enforced prostitution, forced pregnancy, enforced sterilization, or any other form of sexual violence of comparable gravity'.[35] It also includes as a crime against humanity '[p]ersecution against any identifiable group or collectivity on political, racial, national, ethnic, cultural, religious, *gender* as defined in [Article 7(3)] or any other grounds that are universally recognized as impermissible under international law'.[36] In addition, the Rome Statute includes in its definition of 'war crimes' '[c]ommitting rape, sexual slavery, enforced prostitution, forced pregnancy, as defined in [Article 7(2)(f)], enforced sterilization, or any other form of sexual violence also constituting a grave breach of the Geneva Conventions or a violation of Common Article 3.'[37]

### D   Hybrid tribunals

Recent years have seen the emergence of so-called 'hybrid' tribunals – tribunals that combine aspects of international and domestic law and whose judicial body is composed of both international judges and local judges. Such tribunals have been established in Sierra Leone, East Timor, Bosnia, Kosovo and Cambodia. Hybrid tribunals differ from international tribunals in the form of their establishment and in the level of international involvement.

Cassese points out a number of advantages which a hybrid tribunal has over a purely international tribunal. It assuages the nationalistic demands of local authorities, loath to hand over the administration of justice to international

---

[34] Ronli Sifris, 'Weighing Judicial Independence against Judicial Accountability: Do the Scales of the International Criminal Court Balance?' (2008) 8 *Chicago-Kent Journal of International and Comparative Law* 88.

[35] *Rome Statute* Article 7(1)(g).

[36] *Rome Statute* Article 7(1)(h) (emphasis added). It should be noted that pursuant to Article 7(3) the term 'gender' refers to the two sexes, male and female, within the context of society.

[37] *Rome Statute* Articles 2(b)(xxii), 2(e)(vi).

bodies, and it involves persons familiar with the culture of the accused in the rendering of justice. Further, by holding trials in the territory where the crimes have been perpetrated, it exposes the local population to past atrocities, thereby publicly stigmatizing the perpetrators and providing a cathartic process for the victim. In addition, a hybrid tribunal may expedite prosecutions and trials without compromising respect for international standards and international law in general. It may also produce a significant spill-over effect in its influence on local members of the prosecution and the judiciary.[38]

Nonetheless, despite the fact that there are well-founded reasons for establishing hybrid tribunals, there are also a number of problems associated with this form of tribunal. Differences in culture and experience may cause tension between local and international members of both the prosecution and the judicial body. Funding is another never-ending source of anxiety and there are constant security concerns when tribunals are established in countries where undercurrents of social discord remain.[39]

*E   Domestic tribunals*

It should be noted that, whilst commentators on international criminal law generally focus on international tribunals, there are many instances of states conducting prosecutions for violations of human rights in the transitional context pursuant to their own domestic law in their own domestic courts. Such prosecutions have taken place in numerous countries as diverse as Mexico, Indonesia, Bosnia and Argentina. Each state has a completely different political landscape and legal system and each has faced different challenges and enjoyed different levels of prosecutorial success. Space precludes a thorough evaluation of 'domestic tribunals' as a whole. Suffice to say, there are clear advantages in having prosecutions take place at the domestic level. For example, the state and the society take ownership over their own transitional justice process; domestic prosecutions help to strengthen the domestic legal system and respect for the rule of law; aspects of local culture can be taken into account and incorporated into the judicial process; domestic prosecutions allow for easier access to witnesses and evidence than international prosecutions; and domestic tribunals do not require the same level of funding as international tribunals. However, domestic prosecutorial initiatives frequently encounter a number of problems such as lack of capacity or political will, an inadequate legal system, and lack of respect for the rule of law.[40] Further,

---

[38] Cassese, above n 6, 333–4.
[39] Ibid 334–5.
[40] Steven R Ratner and Jason S Abrams, *Accountability for Human Rights Atrocities in International Law: Beyond the Nuremberg Legacy* (Oxford University Press, Oxford, 2003) 340.

domestic tribunals may serve to invalidate the suffering of women by regarding oppression of women as a social norm rather than a criminal activity.[41]

## 3 Truth commissions

Concluding his introduction to the Report of the Chilean National Commission on Truth and Reconciliation, José Zalaquett wrote in reference to those interviewed by the Commission:

> [M]any of them asked for justice. Hardly anyone, however, showed a desire for vengeance. Most of them stressed that in the end, what really mattered to them was to know the truth, that the memory of their loved ones would not be denigrated or forgotten, and that such terrible things would never happen again.[42]

### A  Definition and purpose

Truth commissions have evolved to become a widely recognized part of the path towards reconciliation in transitioning societies. Whilst an inquiry into widespread abuses can be undertaken by bodies which are not truth commissions, truth commissions share certain characteristics: they focus on the past, investigating a pattern of abuses over a period of time, rather than a specific event; they are temporary bodies, typically in operation for six months to two years, which complete their work with the submission of a report; and they are officially sanctioned, authorized, or empowered by the state.[43] In addition, truth commissions are generally created to inquire into recent events; they generally focus on violence committed to achieve political objectives; and the abuses investigated are generally widespread as opposed to *ad hoc* instances.[44]

There are a number of reasons why a state may choose to create a truth commission as a supplement to prosecutions when confronting a legacy of human rights abuse. First, as the name suggests, perhaps the most fundamental purpose of a truth commission is to clarify and acknowledge the truth.[45]

---

[41] For an in-depth discussion of the systemic nature of discrimination against women (in both peacetime and times of conflict) and the failure to properly recognize so-called 'ordinary violence' as punishable by law, see Vasuki Nesiah et al, 'Truth Commissions and Gender: Principles, Policies, and Procedures' (Gender Justice Series Working Paper, International Center for Transitional Justice, 2006) http://www.ictj.org/static/Gender/GendHandbook.eng.pdf at 16 December 2008.

[42] José Zalaquett, 'Introduction' in National Commission on Truth and Reconciliation, *Report of the Chilean National Commission on Truth and Reconciliation* (University of Notre Dame Press, Notre Dame, Phillip E Berryman trans, 1993 ed).

[43] Priscilla B Hayner, *Unspeakable Truths: Facing the Challenges of Truth Commissions* (Routledge, New York, 2001) 14.

[44] Ibid 17.

[45] Ibid 24.

Whereas truth may be a by-product of prosecutions and a subsidiary objective, it is not the primary aim of a prosecutorial process. In contrast, truth commissions are specifically created to formulate a formal record of what abuses occurred, how they occurred, who were the perpetrators, and who were the victims.

Another purpose of a truth commission is to respond to the needs and interests of victims. The acknowledgment of suffering is an extremely important part of the healing process. Likewise, lack of knowledge of what happened to loved ones can have a stultifying effect, preventing relatives and friends of victims from being able to forgive or move forward. This is not to say that with the revelation and acknowledgment of truth automatically come forgiveness and reconciliation, but without such revelation it is extremely difficult for a society to move forward. A formal recording of the truth helps to provide closure to victims, and it is only with such closure that true reconciliation can occur. Further, in contrast to prosecutions which focus on the accused, the focus of a truth commission is on the testimony of victims. This provides victims with a public voice and results in an increasing awareness of the specific needs of victims amongst the community at large. From a more practical perspective, truth commissions also help victims by recommending reparations or by officially establishing the legal status of victims such as those who have disappeared.[46]

An additional purpose of a truth commission is to promote reconciliation and reduce tensions resulting from past violence.[47] Ultimately, all transitional justice mechanisms have as a primary objective the achievement of reconciliation, but truth commissions, perhaps more than any other transitional justice mechanism, actively seek to reduce tensions by bringing out into the open all the anger, pain and suffering which has been experienced and forcing society to confront this legacy of abuse and to deal with it.

From a gendered perspective, the fact that truth commissions provide women (who as a group have traditionally been relegated to the private realm and prevented from speaking out in public) with the opportunity to tell their stories in a public forum is validating and empowering. However, according to Vasuki Nesiah:

> Most truth commissions share the phenomenon that the vast majority of people who come forward and provide testimony are women; however the majority of those women do not speak of the violations they suffered but the harm that befell their husbands, sons, brothers and fathers – the men in their lives.[48]

---

[46] Ibid 28.
[47] Ibid 30.
[48] Vasuki Nesiah, 'Gender and Truth Commission Mandates' (International Centre for Transnational Justice) http://www.ictj.org/static/Gender/0602.GenderTRC.eng.pdf at 16 December 2008.

Even where women have testified as to their own personal experiences, the focus of truth commissions has generally been on sexual violence alone.[49] Whilst it is obviously extremely important to expose the various forms of sexual violence endured by women, such a focus unfortunately frequently results in a lack of attention to other forms of harm which are inflicted on women and reduces women to sexual beings. To once again invoke the civil and political versus the economic, social and cultural distinction – truth commissions tend to tell the truth about violations of civil and political rights whilst by-passing violations of economic, social and cultural rights. This is so despite the fact that women are disproportionately affected by violations of rights in the private sphere and despite the fact that, for women, their individual narratives of suffering will frequently include violations of both forms of rights and will not be truly capable of relegation to one specific event of sexual violence.

### B  South Africa as an example

In April 1994 South Africa held its first truly democratic election. The formerly banned African National Congress ('ANC'), led by Nelson Mandela, won the election and in July 1995 Parliament passed the *Promotion of National Unity and Reconciliation Act* ('*TRC Act*') establishing the Truth and Reconciliation Commission ('TRC'). The TRC was charged with exposing atrocities committed from 1 March 1960 onwards. It consisted of three committees: the Committee on Human Rights Violations, the Committee on Amnesty, and the Committee on Reparation and Rehabilitation.

The role of the Committee on Human Rights Violations was to gather testimony from victims and construct an accurate record of the atrocities committed during apartheid.[50] The Committee on Reparation and Rehabilitation was charged with formulating recommendations for the awarding of reparations.[51] Such recommendations included both individual as well as collective reparations and financial as well as non-financial reparations. It also made recommendations for the reform of institutions to ensure the non-repetition of abuses.[52] This is one example of the inter-relatedness of the different transitional justice mechanisms. Perhaps the most controversial aspect of the South African Truth and Reconciliation Commission concerned the Committee on

---

[49] Nesiah et al, above n 41, 8–9.
[50] *TRC Act* s 14.
[51] *TRC Act* s 25.
[52] Truth and Reconciliation Commission of South Africa, *Truth and Reconciliation Commission of South Africa Report* (2003) South African Government Information, http://www.info.gov.za/otherdocs/2003/trc/ at 16 December 2008, section 2.

Amnesty. The *TRC Act* empowered the Committee on Amnesty to grant amnesty from both prosecution and civil suit in circumstances where a person made full disclosure of acts associated with a political objective.[53] It is important to note that this was a conditional amnesty and not a 'blanket amnesty' as provided in many Latin American countries.[54]

To understand the reason for these amnesty provisions, one must understand the context of the particular transition from apartheid to democracy which took place in South Africa. The change in government in South Africa did not occur through war or coup, but was the result of decades of international condemnation and alienation as well as armed resistance by various groups. The actual transfer of power was the result of a negotiation process whereby the ruling party agreed to transfer power on the condition that amnesty would be provided in certain circumstances. Thus the choice was essentially one between a relatively peaceful transition accompanied by the granting of amnesty, on the one hand, and the continuation of armed and violent struggle against the apartheid regime, on the other. This particular issue highlights the already mentioned fact that transitional justice is context specific.

It should be noted that South Africa's decision to grant amnesty in certain circumstances was not without opposition. The case of *Azapo*[55] involved a constitutional challenge to the amnesty provisions of the *TRC Act*. The Constitutional Court declared the provisions to be constitutional on the basis of both domestic and international law. The court held that 'those who negotiated the Constitution made a deliberate choice, preferring understanding over vengeance, reparation over retaliation, ubuntu over victimisation.'[56] Further, in *Azapo* the court was of the view that amnesty was necessary in the interests of discovering and establishing the truth of what occurred during the apartheid years.[57]

The power to grant amnesty was not the only aspect of the TRC to be subjected to severe criticism. Critics have been swift to point out the lack of victim input into the structure, operation and powers of the TRC and to highlight

---

[53] *TRC Act* s 20(1).
[54] For example, in 1978 Chile handed down an amnesty decree covering human rights crimes committed between 1973 and 1978.
[55] *Azapo v President of the Republic of South Africa* [1996] 4 SA 562 (CC) ('*Azapo*').
[56] *Azapo* [1996] 4 SA 562 (CC) [2]. 'Ubuntu' has its roots in the Bantu languages of Southern Africa; it refers to 'humaneness, or an inclusive sense of community valuing everyone': Martha Minow, *Between Vengeance and Forgiveness: Facing History After Genocide and Mass Violence* (Beacon Press, Boston, 1998) 52.
[57] *Azapo* [1996] 4 SA 562 (CC) [17].

deficiencies in the psychological support provided to victims during the process.[58] There has also been criticism that the *TRC Act* defined 'victim' too narrowly, thereby further marginalizing people who had suffered under the apartheid regime.[59] Even with respect to those people who fell within the category of 'victim', concern has been expressed that not enough was done to seek and obtain all relevant testimonies and that the process of selecting only certain victims to publicly testify had the effect of alienating other victims and invalidating their suffering.[60] Further, at the conclusion of the process many victims were left with unfulfilled expectations and a sense of disillusionment.[61] Non-victim-centric critiques have also been levelled at the TRC. For example, it has been accused of prioritizing reconciliation above truth, as evidenced by its failure to subpoena certain prominent figures, such as Mangosuthu Buthelezi (President of the Inkatha Freedom Party), who were known to have been responsible for the commission of politically motivated human rights abuses.[62]

Despite the criticism, the South African TRC has been lauded as an overall success. The *TRC Act* is viewed as being essentially victim-friendly. Advocates have highlighted the extensive consultation which took place at both the political and the community level when determining the structure, powers and composition of the TRC. The actual hearings of the Committee on Human Rights Violations were generally regarded as a cathartic experience for victims and the TRC recognized the need to provide victims with psychological support as part of this process.[63] It must also be acknowledged that the Committee on Amnesty took its responsibilities seriously and carefully evaluated whether a person's application for amnesty met the criteria specified by the legislation. For example, the murderers of anti-apartheid activist Steve Biko were denied amnesty because they did not fulfil the requirements of fully disclosing a crime committed with a political objective.[64] Of significance was the decision that the TRC would 'name names'. Applicants for amnesty had their names published in both the *Government Gazette* and the TRC Report. This acted as a form of public shaming and provided victims with at least some sense that perpetrators were being held accountable for their actions, even if

---

[58] Sam Garkawe, 'The South African Truth and Reconciliation Commission: A Suitable Model to Enhance the Role and Rights of the Victims of Gross Violations of Human Rights?' (2003) 27 *Melbourne University Law Review* 334, 372.
[59] Ibid 371–2.
[60] Ibid.
[61] Ibid 334.
[62] Hayner, above n 43 (2001).
[63] Garkawe, above n 58, 334.
[64] Hayner, above n 43, 43–4.

the form of accountability was outside traditional prosecutorial means.[65] Indeed, the decision to 'name names' was extremely controversial; only a few of the truth commissions empowered to name perpetrators have actually chosen to do so. Amongst the concerns relating to identifying perpetrators are due process concerns of a substantive and procedural nature, as well as security concerns and apprehension as to the effect of such identification on the reconciliation process.[66]

From a gendered perspective, whilst the South African TRC was sensitive to gender-based concerns, by focusing on women's experiences of sexual violence it failed to communicate the full truth of women's experiences during the apartheid regime. According to Vasuki Nesiah:

> [W]omen were denied active citizenship under apartheid, and the human rights violations they suffered were often located in the private sphere or domesticated into the 'ordinary' violence that forced removals and group-area legislation deployed to segregate living and working conditions, rather than the 'extraordinary' violence of torture, killings, and disappearances. Thus, the truth commission's focus on the latter may be said to fundamentally misrepresent women's experience of apartheid and skew the truth that the commission narrated.[67]

## 4 Reparations

On 27 September 1951 West German Chancellor Konrad Adenauer declared to the Bundestag:

> The Federal government and the great majority of the German people are deeply aware of the immeasurable suffering endured by the Jews of Germany and by the Jews of the occupied territories during the period of National Socialism . . . In our name, unspeakable crimes have been committed and they demand restitution, both moral and material, for the persons and properties of the Jews who have been so seriously harmed.[68]

### A   Definition and purpose

As the name suggests, the key purpose of reparations is to repair damage caused by wrongdoing. Thus, whilst the focus of prosecutions is punishment and the focus of truth commissions is truth-telling, reparations are a victim-centric remedy focused on repairing harm. As part of the remedial process, reparations perform a dual function: they compensate victims for loss suffered

---

65   Garkawe, above n 58, 334.
66   Hayner, above n 43, 107–8.
67   Nesiah, above n 48.
68   See *FRG Background Papers: German Compensation for National Socialist Crimes*, http://www.germany-info.org/relaunch/info/archives/background/ns_crimes.html at 16 December 2008.

while at the same time reintegrating the marginalized back into society.[69] Such a remedial process is not only crucial to facilitate reconciliation; it constitutes both a moral and legal imperative. From a moral perspective, the state has a duty to acknowledge wrongdoing and to try to compensate for loss suffered as a result of such wrongdoing. From a legal perspective, international law clearly states that victims of egregious human rights abuses have a right to a remedy.[70] Reparations take different forms, depending on the type of harm suffered, the nature of the violations perpetrated and the characteristics of the society in question, as well as the resources and attitudes of the state.

A legacy of human rights abuse may leave in its trail various types of suffering at the individual, family and community levels including that which is physical, mental, emotional, financial and cultural. The mental and emotional damage caused by direct or indirect exposure to human rights violations takes numerous forms. For example, victims of human rights abuses, those who bear witness to atrocities, people who have lost loved ones and those who have been displaced by conflict all suffer from degrees of mental and emotional trauma which may in turn affect their financial status and ability to function in society. In addition, violence may result in destruction of communities and loss of culture, and may exacerbate existing problems such as those related to poverty.

As mentioned in the context of prosecutions and truth commissions, it is also important to bear in mind that the forms of harm suffered by women may be the same as those suffered by men or may be different. Further, reparations programs should be designed with the aim of not only repairing damage caused by the conflict itself but also repairing aspects of systemic discrimination which are endemic to the society. For example, reparations programs should not only provide women with appropriate medication to treat sexually transmitted diseases resulting from sexual violence during conflict; healthcare should be viewed in a more holistic sense as a means of treating afflictions,

---

[69] Naomi Roht-Arriaza, 'Reparations, Decisions and Dilemmas' (2004) 27 *Hastings International and Comparative Law Review* 157, 160.

[70] See for example *International Covenant for Civil and Political Rights*, opened for signature 16 December 1966, 999 UNTS 171 (entered into force 23 March 1976) Article 2(3); *Convention against Torture and Other Cruel, Inhuman or Degrading Treatment or Punishment*, GA Res 39/46, UN GAOR, 39th sess, 93rd plen mtg, UN Doc A/39/46 (10 December 1984) Annex, Article 14; Secretary-General, *Report of the Secretary-General on the Rule of Law and Transitional Justice in Conflict and Post-Conflict Societies*, UN Doc S/2004/616 (3 August 2004); Diane Orentlicher, *Report of Independent Expert on Principles of Impunity: Addendum: Updated Set of Principles for the Protection and Promotion of Human Rights through Action to Combat Impunity*, UN Doc E/CN.4/2005/102/Add.1 (8 February 2005).

such as malnutrition, which are the indirect result of conflict. Thus the harms which must be redressed as part of a transitional justice process are multi-faceted and too complex to comprehensively enumerate in this chapter.

After considering the types of harms which need to be remedied, logically the next issue to address is the type of remedy. Reparations are the transitional justice equivalent to damages in the domestic system. Their aim is to put the person in the position which he or she would have been in had the violation not occurred (*restitution in integrum*). In the context of human rights violations, such an aim is lofty and at times impossible to achieve. A person who has lost all of her family in a violent conflict which has resulted in her living in a refugee camp can never be properly compensated for her loss. Thus reparations for such a person will always to some extent constitute a symbolic gesture.

Reparations may be individual or collective, material or symbolic. The different forms of reparations fulfil different purposes. In the case of individual reparations, material reparations may take the form of actual financial payment, restitution of property, receipt of goods, or receipt of services such as free education or health care. When considering financial payment as a form of reparation, it is relevant to note that where such compensation is calculated on the basis of lost income which does not properly take into account the informal work sector, it will indirectly discriminate against women (who form the majority of such workers).[71] Further, it must be acknowledged that in patriarchal societies where men are the property owners, restitution of property disproportionately benefits men.[72]

Symbolic reparations may include disclosure of a loved one's disappearance or death, disclosure of the names of the perpetrators, punishment of perpetrators, acknowledgment of wrongdoing on the part of the state, and reburial of victims. Symbolic reparations provide official acknowledgment of wrongdoing and harm suffered; they are a mechanism by which the state may atone for its actions.[73]

Memorialization is a common form of symbolic reparation. Memorialization is essentially the act of establishing memorials as a mechanism for remembering the past, educating future generations, creating a historical record and publicly acknowledging the suffering of victims. Memorials

---

[71] Nesiah et al, above n 41, 36.
[72] See, for example, Heidy Rombouts, 'Women and Reparations in Rwanda: A Long Path to Travel' in R Rubio-Marín (ed) *What Happened to the Women?: Gender and Reparations for Human Rights Violations* (Social Science Research Council, Chicago, 2006) 204.
[73] Roht-Arriaza, above n 69, 159–60.

take various forms; they may be statues,[74] museums,[75] parks,[76] places of significance,[77] community-developed projects,[78] days of commemoration[79] and so on. Memorials may be established from the top down, by state institutions, or may be formed at the grass roots level by victims or others who wish to ensure that the suffering of victims is always remembered. Memorials form an important part of the process of 'repairing' a society recovering from a legacy of human rights abuse. They are a tangible way in which a state may publicly atone for its actions and pledge never to repeat them; they are a mechanism by which individuals may feel validated and victims may feel recognized; they provide a collective means to express individual pain and facilitate healing at both an individual and a societal level.

In the context of massive conflicts involving hundreds of thousands of victims, collective reparations programs are often favoured over individual reparations programs which are viewed as being impossible to implement in the presence of limited state resources. Even in the unlikely event that a state has sufficient resources to implement an individual reparations program following mass atrocities, the view has been posited that in such a situation the harm caused to the community as a whole renders collective reparations particularly appropriate.[80] Further, in the case of such conflicts, it is often extremely difficult to determine precisely who is a victim, a perpetrator and a by-stander, thereby rendering individual reparations particularly difficult to dispense.[81] Examples of collective reparations include establishing educational institutions, furnishing medical facilities, providing financial assistance to organizations whose purpose is to assist the community in question, and implementing community based development projects. Ideally, states will provide both individual and collective reparations. For example, Germany paid both individual reparations to victims of the Holocaust and collective reparations to Jewish organizations and the State of Israel.

### B  Operational aspects

When formulating a reparations program there should be widespread consultation with civil society, including with representatives of those who have

---

[74]  An example is the statue of Salvador Allende in Chile.
[75]  An example is the Terezín Memorial Museum in the Czech Republic or the District Six Museum in South Africa.
[76]  An example is the *Plaza de Mayo* in Argentina.
[77]  An example is the Tuol Sleng site in Cambodia.
[78]  An example is the Srebrenica memorial quilt.
[79]  An example is Holocaust Remembrance Day.
[80]  Roht-Arriaza, above n 69, 181.
[81]  Ibid 182.

been traditionally marginalized (such as women or particular ethnic groups). In his introduction to *The Handbook of Reparations*, Pablo de Greiff identifies seven key factors which must be considered when designing a reparations program.[82] The first is scope; the form a reparations program takes will to a large extent depend on the number of victims. The second is completeness; the completeness of a reparations program refers to its ability to adequately provide reparations to all victims. The third factor is comprehensiveness, which refers to the particular types of harms which the reparations program seeks to remedy. The fourth factor is complexity, which refers to the ways in which a reparations program seeks to provide redress. Increased types of redress and increased mechanisms for distribution of benefits result in a reparations program of greater complexity. The fifth factor is integrity or coherence; internal coherence refers to the relationship between the different types of benefits which the reparations program distributes, and external coherence refers to the relationship between the reparations program and other transitional justice mechanisms. Ideally, a reparations program should consist of an internally coherent set of 'benefits' and should be a part of a larger transitional justice process. The sixth factor is finality, namely whether the receipt of benefits from a reparations program precludes a person from pursuing other avenues of redress, such as suing the perpetrators. The final factor is munificence, which refers to the 'generosity' of the reparations program, the magnitude of the benefits distributed.

Naomi Roht-Arriaza identifies a number of additional factors which may affect the success of a reparations program. She regards the definition of who is a victim as being particularly pertinent; where 'victim' is defined too narrowly, those excluded from the definition feel that their suffering has not been recognized.[83] Women are often excluded from the definition of 'victim', either because the violence which they suffer is viewed as 'ordinary' violence (as opposed to 'extraordinary violence' such as torture), or because the harms which they suffer occur in the private sphere and are regarded as mere by-products of conflict rather than harms in need of remedy.[84]

Another issue is the extent to which claims are individualized. Whilst there are clear benefits to individualized reparations such as the recognition of degrees of suffering, such a process is time-consuming and can lead to retraumatization as victims are required to produce evidence of their suffering. A study conducted by the Chilean human rights organization CODEPU reveals that, from the perspective of victims, monetary compensation was

---

[82] Pablo de Greiff, 'Introduction' in P de Greiff (ed) *The Handbook of Reparations* (Oxford University Press, Oxford, 2006) 6–13.
[83] Roht-Arriaza, above n 69, 177–81.
[84] See Nesiah et al, above n 41.

never sufficient, as official and societal recognition of wrongdoing was deemed particularly important.[85] In addition, the evidence suggests that victims view forward-looking measures more favourably than backward-looking measures, as forward-looking measures have the potential to improve the lives of future generations.[86] Ruth Rubio-Marín points out that female victims in particular tend to express a preference for services which meet basic needs rather than monetary compensation or restitution of property; women are generally especially concerned with obtaining adequate physical and mental healthcare for themselves and their families, securing safe housing and ensuring education for their children.[87]

## 5 Institutional reform

When discussing the post-communist transitional process of the former Czechoslovakia, then-President Vaclav Havel made the following observation:

> Our society has a great need to face [the] past, to get rid of the people who had terrorized the nation and conspicuously violated human rights, to remove them from the positions that they are still holding.[88]

State-sanctioned human rights abuses occur primarily through institutions such as the army, the police, the media, and the judiciary. Consequently, when countries are engaged in a transition process whose aim is to establish respect for democratic principles such as human rights and rule of law, it is necessary to reform those institutions which are associated with that state's legacy of human rights abuse.

### A Personnel reform

Given that organizations are composed of people, and that it is individuals who must bear the responsibility for human rights violations, personnel reform is one of the most important elements of institutional reform. Other elements of institutional reform include measures designed to improve accountability, independence, representation, and responsiveness.[89]

---

[85] Roht-Arriaza, above n 69, 180.
[86] Ibid 181.
[87] Ruth Rubio-Marín, 'The Gender of Reparations: Setting the Agenda' in R Rubio-Marín (ed) *What Happened to the Women?: Gender and Reparations for Human Rights Violations* (Social Science Research Council, Chicago, 2006) 20.
[88] Adam Michnik and Vaclav Havel, 'Confronting the Past: Justice or Revenge?' (1993) 4 *Journal of Democracy* 20, 23.
[89] Roger Duthie, 'Introduction' in A Mayer-Rieckh and P de Greiff (eds) *Justice as Prevention: Vetting Public Employees in Transitional Societies* (Social Science Research Council, Chicago, 2007) 16, 31.

Vetting is a fundamental aspect of personnel reform and is therefore the focus of this discussion. The Office of the United Nations High Commissioner for Human Rights ('OHCHR') defines vetting as 'assessing integrity to determine suitability for public employment. Integrity refers to an employee's adherence to international standards of human rights and professional conduct'.[90] According to OHCHR '[v]etting processes aim at excluding from public service persons with serious integrity deficits in order to (re)-establish civic trust and (re)-legitimize public institutions.'[91] Vetting also aims 'to punish the perpetrators, and to transform institutions in order both to safeguard the democratic transition and to prevent the recurrence of human rights abuses'.[92] The extent to which vetting forms part of a larger institutional reform process to some extent depends on the specific model of institutional reform which a particular state adopts. For example, where a reappointment process is implemented it is more likely that other reforms (such as those addressing gender and ethnic imbalances) will also be implemented than if the state adopts a review process.[93]

Despite the fact that vetting programs are viewed by many as essential components of a comprehensive transitional justice process, it must be acknowledged that they raise some difficult issues. For example, it is hypocritical and counter-productive for a society which is aiming to entrench the rule of law to ignore the basic elements of due process when implementing a vetting program. Further, vetting programs which oust people on the basis of membership of a specific group (such as the Communist Party) may in some circumstances ascribe collective guilt, leading to individual injustice. In addition, vetting programs which do not distinguish between types and degrees of guilt 'tar everyone with the same brush' and may also result in individual injustice.

*B   Cultural reform*

In order to transform institutions suffering from a legacy of human rights abuse into rights-respecting institutions, it is necessary to include all voices (especially those of traditionally marginalized groups) as part of the reform process. For example, a gendered perspective must be incorporated into all core agreements following conflict (including peace agreements) and must be included in all institutional reform procedures. The United Nations Security Council recognized this imperative when it passed Resolution 1325, which

---

[90]   OHCHR, *Rule of Law Tools for Post-Conflict States – Vetting: An Operational Framework* (OHCHR, Geneva, 2006) 4.
[91]   Ibid.
[92]   Duthie, above n 89, 30.
[93]   Ibid 32.

advocates 'an increase in the participation of women at decision-making levels in conflict resolution and peace processes' and calls 'on all actors involved, when negotiating and implementing peace agreements, to adopt a gender perspective'.[94]

It is not sufficient for marginalized groups to be represented in the reform process; their concerns must actively be taken into account in order for substantive change to occur. Thus it is necessary to include women in the formulation of the reform process, ensure that women are appointed to positions within the various institutions, and implement gender sensitization training.[95] Further, concrete mechanisms must be implemented to create a rights-respecting culture. For example, in Liberia when members are recruited to the security sector they undergo mandatory training aimed at fostering a sense of unity and respect for human rights.[96] Further, the impact of legal reform must not be underestimated. Constitutional reform, enactments of new legislation, and amendments to existing legislation should prohibit discrimination and enshrine respect for fundamental human rights. Similarly, systems should be implemented to secure access to judicial (and non-judicial) institutions for disadvantaged groups, including women.[97]

## 6 Reconciliation

Archbishop Emeritus Desmond Tutu once remarked:

> As our experience in South Africa has taught us, each society must discover its own route to reconciliation. Reconciliation cannot be imposed from outside, nor can someone else's map get us to our destination: it must be our own solution. This involves a very long and painful journey, addressing the pain and suffering of the victims, understanding the motivations of offenders, bringing together estranged communities, trying to find a path to justice, truth and, ultimately, peace.[98]

---

[94] SC Res 1325, UN SCOR, 4213rd mtg, UN Doc S/RES/1325 (2000) (31 October 2000).

[95] Fionnuala Ni Aolain, *A Preliminary Audit of Identity and Representation in the context of Security Sector Reform, with Particular Emphasis on Gender* (on file with author).

[96] United States Institute of Peace ('USIP'), *Security Sector Reform in Liberia: Domestic Considerations and the Way Forward* (2007) USIP, http://www.usip.org/pubs/usipeace_briefings/2007/0403_security_liberia.html at 16 December 2008.

[97] Secretary-General, *Women, Peace and Security: Study submitted by the Secretary-General pursuant to Security Council resolution 1325 (2000)* (2002) UNICEF, http://www.unicef.org/emerg/files/WPS.pdf at 16 December 2008.

[98] D Bloomfield, T Barnes and L Huyse (eds) *Reconciliation after Violent Conflict: A Handbook* (International Institute for Democracy and Electoral Assistance, Stockholm, 2003) 4.

## A  Definition and purpose

Transitional justice mechanisms have two primary aims: the achievement of justice and the realization of a lasting peace. Reconciliation is essentially the fulfilment of both of these aims; it is the point where 'justice and peace have kissed';[99] it is the 'process through which a society moves from a divided past to a shared future'.[100] Reconciliation is an active process; it is achieved by implementing transitional justice mechanisms to deal with the past and is not achieved by simply ignoring the past. Reconciliation is not peace without justice, nor is it peace facilitated through collective amnesia. In Cambodia decades have passed since the Khmer Rouge committed unspeakable atrocities, and the recent establishment of a tribunal to prosecute perpetrators has clearly demonstrated the extent to which the notion of collective amnesia is a fiction. Reconciliation is a long-term process through which a society deals with its demons head-on and emerges with a conviction that a whole is worth more than the sum of its parts.

As well as being a long-term process, reconciliation is both a deep process in that it involves recognition of an imperfect reality and a broad process in that it involves the entire community.[101] Perpetrators may be people or institutions; they may be those who directly inflicted violence, those who knowingly accepted the benefits of oppression, or those who stood by in silence and watched the suffering of others. Victims may have suffered directly or indirectly; they may remain in the country or they may have fled elsewhere in search of a safe haven. A successful reconciliation process will involve the entire community and will not only focus on specific perpetrators or specific victims. Further, a successful reconciliation process will deal with the legacy of human rights abuse itself as well as issues such as discrimination, marginalization, intolerance and stereotyping which may have created a culture that enabled the perpetration of human rights abuses to occur in the first place. Such a process should include addressing the problem of gender-based discrimination as part of the path to securing a more just and equal society.

## B  Democracy and reconciliation

There is a powerful argument that the establishment of a democratic system is an essential component of the reconciliation process. Whilst democracy is clearly not a perfect system, and is in fact extremely problematic when

---

[99] John Paul Lederach, *Building Peace: Sustainable Reconciliation in Divided Societies* (USIP, Washington DC, 1997) 29.

[100] David Bloomfield, 'Reconciliation: An Introduction' in D Bloomfield, T Barnes and L Huyse (eds) *Reconciliation after Violent Conflict: A Handbook* (International Institute for Democracy and Electoral Assistance, Stockholm, 2003) 10.

[101] Ibid 13.

imposed from the top down, it is the best established political system from a human rights and conflict management perspective. Democracy is both a system which entrenches respect for human rights and a system which manages relationships in a way that renders recourse to violence unlikely. From a conflict management perspective, democratic systems are structured so as to manage differences of ideas in a way which does not involve resorting to violence. In a democracy, differences are dealt with through open debate and compromise; this means that even those whose ideas conflict can deal with those differences whilst still maintaining positive relationships. Consequently, the democratic form of conflict resolution is essential to the reconciliation process.[102]

From a human rights perspective, democracy entrenches human rights from both a procedural and a substantive perspective. From a procedural perspective, core democratic principles such as each person's right to vote enshrine human rights principles of liberty and equality. In his report on women, peace and security, the United Nations Secretary-General stressed the need for women to be included in the political process.[103] According to the report, quotas and training should be implemented where necessary to achieve gender equality and adequate financial support should be provided to ensure women's active participation in civil society and public life.[104]

From a substantive perspective, democratic principles enshrine respect for fundamental human rights, including of course women's rights. This conception of democracy is eloquently expressed by Aharon Barak, a survivor of the Holocaust and former President of the Supreme Court of Israel:

> Everyone agrees that a democracy requires the rule of the people, which is often effectuated through representatives in a legislative body. Therefore, frequent elections are necessary to keep these representatives accountable to their constituents. However, real or substantive democracy, as opposed to formal democracy, is not satisfied merely by these conditions. Democracy has its own internal morality, based on the dignity and equality of all human beings. Thus, in addition to formal requirements, there are also substantive requirements. These are reflected in the supremacy of such underlying democratic values and principles as human dignity, equality, and tolerance. There is no (real) democracy without recognition of basic values and principles such as morality and justice. Above all, democracy cannot exist without the protection of individual human rights – rights so essential that they must be insulated from the power of the majority.[105]

---

[102] Ibid 10–12.
[103] Secretary-General, above n 7.
[104] Ibid [56].
[105] Aharon Barak, 'Foreword: A Judge on Judging: The Role of a Supreme Court in a Democracy' (2002) 116 *Harvard Law Review* 16, 38–9.

If one adopts this understanding of democracy, it is clear that the implementation of a democratic system is fundamental to establishing a culture of respect for human rights, which in turn is instrumental in preventing the commission of future atrocities. In this way, democracy is integral to the reconciliation process.

## 7 Conclusion

Rabban Shimon ben Gamliel, a first-century Jewish sage, said that the world rests on three pillars: truth, justice and peace.[106] All transitional justice mechanisms are aimed at both achieving justice and revealing truth (though the emphasis shifts according to the mechanism) as a means of attaining a true and lasting peace. Genuine reconciliation cannot be attained if truth is revealed but justice is wanting. Similarly, justice alone is insufficient to unify a community recovering from severe pain and suffering. Accordingly, the four pillars of transitional justice must be viewed as interconnected and interdependent; all are necessary to build a peaceful and rights-respecting society which has moved on from its past trauma without forgetting it. Prosecutions result in the punishment of perpetrators and help to generate a sense of justice within the community. Truth-telling methods provide victims with a sense of closure and validation as well as ensuring that the legacy of human rights abuse is part of the country's historical record. Reparations provide public acknowledgement of wrongdoing and formal compensation for injury suffered. Institutional reform is perhaps the most forward-looking of the four transitional justice pillars; it aims to 'remove the bad apples from the cart' and to change the culture of institutions with a legacy of involvement in human rights abuse in an attempt to ensure that human rights violations are never again viewed as acceptable social conduct.

To achieve the aim of a true and lasting peace, transitional justice mechanisms must be careful not to address only the needs of the majority or the dominant class. Special attention must be paid to the needs of those who have traditionally been marginalized, such as women and certain minority groups. The only way properly to reconcile a society still licking its physical and emotional wounds is to confront not only the specific human rights violations perpetrated by the regime in question but also the broader issues of systemic discrimination and oppression which existed even before that regime came into power. To build a house properly, the foundations must be sturdy; otherwise, it will always be in danger of collapsing. This is one of the reasons why it is so important to include women in transitional decision-making processes and to ensure that all transitional mechanisms are implemented in a gender-sensitive manner.

---

[106] *Mishnah*, Avot 1, 18.

There is an African proverb which says that the world rests on three pillars: in the present there is the past; in the future there is the present and the past.[107] Societies confronting a legacy of human rights abuse will carry this with them into the future. The challenge of transitional justice is to achieve the delicate balance whereby the pain of the past is acknowledged, dealt with and remembered in a way that allows the building of a future based on respect for human rights and rule of law.

---

[107] Sekou Toure, 'Toast of the President of the Republic of Guinea' (Speech delivered at the State Dinner for the President of the Republic of Guinea, Washington DC, 26 October 1969) http://www.presidency.ucsb.edu/ws/index.php?pid=11566 at 16 December 2008.

# 12. The International Court of Justice and human rights
*Sandesh Sivakumaran*

## 1 Introduction

The International Court of Justice ('ICJ' or 'the Court') is a court of plenary jurisdiction with responsibility for general international law, yet its influence on human rights has been vast. The Court has contributed to the development of substantive human rights law, its structural framework as well as mechanisms for its enforcement. To those who do not follow the work of the Court this may come as something of a surprise. After all, the ICJ is not a human rights court; it is, rather, the principal judicial organ of the United Nations. Its judges need not have recognised competence in the field of human rights and the parties that appear before it are not individuals but states. It has limited fact-finding capabilities and its evidentiary rules are not altogether developed. There also exist multiple international and regional bodies tasked specifically with the protection of human rights and it is to these bodies that it may have been expected that disputes would be referred.

Despite these attributes or lack thereof, the Court has had occasion to engage in the consideration of human rights law. Although individuals have no standing before the Court, states may, and do, bring claims on their behalf. Human rights matters have also been the subject of many an advisory opinion. Accordingly, the subject is not infrequently before the Court, particularly in recent years. When such issues do arise, they may benefit from some judges' prior expertise as members of regional human rights courts, human rights treaty body committees, or truth commissions or as Special Rapporteurs of the Commission on Human Rights.

The contribution of the Court to the international protection of human rights is often neglected. This chapter considers the extent of the Court's contribution, focusing on four areas.[1] Section 2 ascertains the role of the Court

---

[1] For a case-by-case analysis, see S M Schwebel, 'Human Rights in the World Court' (1991) 24 *Vanderbilt Journal of Transnational Law* 945; S M Schwebel, 'The treatment of human rights and of aliens in the International Court of Justice' in V Lowe and M Fitzmaurice (eds) *Fifty Years of the International Court of Justice: Essays in Honour of Sir Robert Jennings* (Cambridge University Press, Cambridge, 1996) 327;

in the enforcement of human rights. This is gauged not only through the cases in which the Court has found a particular provision of a human rights treaty to have been violated but also through the Court's interaction with other human rights bodies and through the protection it has afforded other enforcers. The human rights treaty framework is the subject of Section 3, with analyses of the Court's jurisprudence on the application of human rights treaties, their interpretation and rules governing reservations. Section 4 moves away from the structural and towards the normative. It focuses on the Court's interpretation of the normative status of the *Universal Declaration of Human Rights* ('UDHR')[2] and the human rights clauses of the United Nations Charter. It also analyses the relative normativity of the different substantive human rights as found by the Court. Finally, Section 5 is concerned with interpretations of the substantive rights and obligations that have been subject to judicial consideration, namely the right to self-determination, the right to life and the prohibition on genocide.

## 2 Enforcement

### A *Direct enforcement*

For reasons of jurisdiction, it is not all that common for the Court to be requested to directly enforce human rights law. The contentious jurisdiction of the Court is not compulsory; the consent of the states concerned is required for the Court to entertain a case. This consent may be manifested through an optional clause declaration espousing consent for all time (until revoked) and all matters (unless reserved);[3] being party to a treaty that contains a compromissory clause that makes reference to the Court;[4] a special agreement in which the relevant states consent to a particular dispute being heard;[5] or *forum prorogatum*.[6] The Court's advisory jurisdiction requires that the request for an advisory opinion stem from the General Assembly or the Security Council, or other organs of the United Nations or specialized agencies that are authorised to request such an opinion.[7]

---

N S Rodley, 'Human Rights and Humanitarian Intervention: The Case Law of the World Court' (1989) 38 *International and Comparative Law Quarterly* 321; S R S Bedi, *The Development of Human Rights Law by the Judges of the International Court of Justice* (Hart, Oxford, 2007).

2    GA Res 217A (III), UN Doc A/810, 71 (1948).
3    *Statute of the International Court of Justice* Article 36(2) ('*ICJ Statute*').
4    *ICJ Statute* Article 36(1).
5    *ICJ Statute* Article 36(1).
6    *Rules of Court* Article 38(5).
7    *Charter of the United Nations* Article 96(1) and (2) ('*UN Charter*').

Thus, the occasions on which the Court is requested to adjudge and declare the violation of particular human rights treaty provisions are limited.[8] This is especially so given that, of the human rights treaties that contain compromissory clauses referencing the Court, some require prior resort to negotiation or arbitration,[9] others have been the subject of reservations,[10] and still others benefit from their own specialist monitoring body.[11]

This is not to say that the Court has never had the opportunity to directly enforce human rights law through the finding of violations; in three recent cases – two contentious and one advisory – the Court has done just that. In *Armed Activities on the Territory of the Congo*, the Court found Uganda to have violated provisions of the *International Covenant on Civil and Political Rights* ('ICCPR'),[12] the *Convention on the Rights of the Child* ('CRC')[13] and its *Optional Protocol on the Involvement of Children in Conflict*,[14] and the *African Charter on Human and Peoples' Rights*.[15] The Court also found Uganda to have violated provisions of international humanitarian law instruments.[16] In the *Genocide* case, the Court found that genocide had been

---

[8] Mention may be made of the *Convention on the Prevention and Punishment of the Crime of Genocide*, opened for signature 9 December 1948, 78 UNTS 277 (entered into force 12 January 1951) Article IX.

[9] See, for example, *Convention on the Elimination of All Forms of Racial Discrimination*, opened for signature 21 December 1965, 660 UNTS 195 (entered into force 4 January 1969) Article 22; *Convention on Elimination of all forms of Discrimination Against Women*, opened for signature 18 December 1979, 1249 UNTS 13 (entered into force 3 September 1981) Article 29(1) ('CEDAW'); *Convention Against Torture and Other Cruel, Inhuman or Degrading Treatment or Punishment*, opened for signature 10 December 1984, 1465 UNTS 85 (entered into force 26 June 1987) Article 30(1) ('CAT'); *Convention on the Protection of All Rights of Migrant Workers and their Families*, opened for signature 18 December 1990, 30 ILM 1517 (entered into force 1 July 2003) Article 92 ('*Migrant Workers Convention*').

[10] See, for example, the reservations of Bahrain, Chile, China, Equatorial Guinea, France, Israel, Mauritania, Morocco, Panama, Poland, Saudi Arabia, Turkey and the United States of America to Article 30(1) CAT.

[11] The seven principal UN human rights treaties currently in force all benefit from a specialist monitoring body.

[12] Opened for signature 16 December 1966, 999 UNTS 171 (entered into force 23 March 1976).

[13] Opened for signature 20 November 1989, 1577 UNTS 3 (entered into force 2 September 1990).

[14] GA Res 54/263, UN GAOR, 54th sess, 97th plen mtg, UN Doc A/Res/54/263 Annex I (25 May 2000).

[15] Opened for signature 27 June 1981, 21 ILM 58 (entered into force 21 October 1986).

[16] *Armed Activities on the Territory of the Congo (Democratic Republic of the Congo v Uganda)* [2005] ICJ Rep 116, [219] ('*Armed Activities on the Territory of the Congo*').

committed in Srebrenica and that Serbia had violated its obligation to prevent and punish genocide.[17] As these were contentious cases, the rulings are binding on the parties.[18]

In the advisory opinion on the *Legal Consequences of the Construction of a Wall in the Occupied Palestinian Territory*, the Court found Israel to have violated provisions of the ICCPR, the *International Covenant on Economic, Social and Cultural Rights* ('ICESCR')[19] and the CRC, and to have breached its obligation to respect the right of the Palestinian people to self-determination, as well as various provisions of international humanitarian law.[20] Although advisory opinions are, as their name suggests, advisory and not strictly binding, pronouncements on questions of international law contained therein are considered weighty and have wide impact, even outside the confines of the particular case in which they were made.

The indication of binding provisional measures orders is an additional means through which the Court has contributed to the enforcement of human rights obligations. In cases in which respect for human rights obligations has been the very subject matter of the dispute pending before the Court, the Court has indicated provisional measures to protect and preserve those rights pending their full consideration by the Court.[21] Thus, the *dispositif* in the provisional measures order in *Armed Activities on the Territory of the Congo* reads in relevant part: '[b]oth Parties must, forthwith, take all measures necessary to ensure full respect within the zone of conflict for fundamental human rights and for the applicable provisions of humanitarian law.'[22]

---

[17] *Application of the Convention on the Prevention and Punishment of the Crime of Genocide (Bosnia and Herzegovina v Serbia and Montenegro)* (Unreported, International Court of Justice, 26 February 2007), http://www.icj-cij.org/docket/index.php?p1=3&p2=3&k=8d&case=91&code=bhy&p3=4 at 3 February 2009, [297], [428]–[450] ('*Genocide*').
[18] *ICJ Statute* Article 59.
[19] Opened for signature 19 December 1966, 999 UNTS 3 (entered into force 3 January 1976).
[20] *Legal Consequences of the Construction of a Wall in the Occupied Palestinian Territory (Advisory Opinion)* [2004] ICJ Rep 136, [120], [122], [132], [134] ('*Wall*').
[21] The Court must also be satisfied that it has *prima facie* jurisdiction, that there is a risk of irreparable prejudice to the rights at issue and that it is a matter of some urgency.
[22] *Armed Activities on the Territory of the Congo (Democratic Republic of the Congo v Uganda) (Request for the Indication of Provisional Measures, Order of 1 July 2000)* [2000] ICJ Rep 111, [47.3]. See also *Application of the Convention on the Prevention and Punishment of the Crime of Genocide (Request for the Indication of Provisional Measures, Order of 8 April 1993)* [1993] ICJ Rep 3; *Application of the Convention on the Prevention and Punishment of the Crime of Genocide (Further*

On occasion, the Court has gone further and indicated provisional measures to protect human rights even when compliance with such obligations was not the matter strictly in dispute. For example, in certain boundary delimitation cases, the Court has indicated provisional measures, noting in *Case Concerning the Land and Maritime Boundary between Cameroon and Nigeria*, for example, that 'the events that have given rise to the request, and more especially to the killing of persons, have caused irreparable damage to the rights that the Parties may have over the Peninsula' and that 'persons in the disputed area and, as a consequence, the rights of the Parties within that area are exposed to serious risk of further irreparable damage'.[23] In so doing, the Court has recognised that 'disputes about frontiers are not just about lines on the ground but are about the safety and protection of the peoples who live there.'[24]

## B Interaction with other enforcers

The protection of international human rights by courts and tribunals is aided by the consistency of their jurisprudence. The extent to which the Court has adopted or departed from the jurisprudence of other human rights bodies thus merits consideration.

In coming to its conclusion in the *Wall* advisory opinion that the ICCPR 'is applicable in respect of acts done by a State in the exercise of its jurisdiction outside its own territory', the Court cited cases and concluding observations of the Human Rights Committee.[25] In coming to a similar conclusion in relation to the ICESCR, the Court cited the view of the Committee on Economic, Social and Cultural Rights.[26] A general comment of the Human Rights Committee was also cited in the context of discussion on derogations and limitations.[27] One expression of the weight given to the work of human rights treaty bodies comes from Judge Al-Khasawneh. After citing from a General

---

*Request for the Indication of Provisional Measures, Order of 13 September 1993)* [1993] ICJ Rep 325.

[23] *Land and Maritime Boundary between Cameroon and Nigeria (Cameroon v Nigeria) (Request for the Indication of Provisional Measures, Order of 15 March 1996)* [1996] ICJ Rep 13, [42]. See also *Case Concerning the Frontier Dispute (Burkina Faso v Mali) (Request for the Indication of Provisional Measures, Order of 10 January 1986)* [1986] ICJ Rep 3, [21].

[24] R Higgins, 'Interim Measures for the Protection of Human Rights' (1998) 36 *Columbia Journal of Transnational Law* 91, 107. For additional comment, see C Foster, 'The Role of International Courts and Tribunals in Relation to Armed Conflict' in U Dolgopol and J Gardam (eds) *The Challenge of Conflict* (Brill, Leiden, 2006) 105, 121–40.

[25] *Wall* [109], [110].
[26] *Wall* [112].
[27] *Wall* [136].

Recommendation of the Committee on the Elimination of All Forms of Discrimination against Women, Judge Al-Khasawneh stated: '[t]o be sure this clear language emanating from the human rights body charged with monitoring compliance with the Convention is not in itself determinative of the matter nor does it relieve judges of the duty of interpreting the provisions of the Convention ... Nevertheless it carries considerable weight.'[28]

Reliance has not solely been placed on the work of the treaty body committees. In *Armed Activities on the Territory of the Congo*, the Court referred *inter alia* to findings of the Special Rapporteur of the Commission on Human Rights on the situation of human rights in the Democratic Republic of the Congo ('DRC') to find that 'massive human rights violations and grave breaches of international humanitarian law were committed by the [Uganda Peoples' Defence Forces] on the territory of the DRC.'[29] Findings of the Special Rapporteur of the Commission on Human Rights on the situation of human rights in the Palestinian territories occupied by Israel since 1967, the Special Rapporteur of the Commission on Human Rights on the right to food and the Special Committee to Investigate Israeli Practices Affecting the Human Rights of the Palestinian People and Other Arabs of the Occupied Territories were used by the Court in its *Wall* opinion.[30] The Court has also placed reliance on the factual findings of non-governmental organisations, for example those contained in reports of Human Rights Watch and Amnesty International.[31]

This does not mean that the Court will always agree with the holdings of other institutions, as the case of *Avena* shows. A few years prior to the judgment of the Court in that case, the Inter-American Court of Human Rights had found Article 36 of the *Vienna Convention on Consular Relations* ('VCCR')[32] to be part of the corpus of human rights law.[33] A different view was taken by

---

[28] *Armed Activity on the Territory of the Congo (Congo v Rwanda)* (Unreported, International Court of Justice, 3 February 2006), http://www.icj-cij.org/docket/index.php?p1=3&p2=1&search="release="=&case=126&code=crw&p3=4 at 3 February 2009, [8] (Judge Al-Khasawneh) ('*Congo v Rwanda*').

[29] *Armed Activities on the Territory of the Congo* [206], [209].

[30] See, for example, *Wall* [133].

[31] *Armed Activities on the Territory of the Congo* [209]; *Genocide* [330], [341].

[32] Opened for signature 24 April 1963, 596 UNTS 261 (entered into force 19 March 1967).

[33] *The Right to Information on Consular Assistance in the Framework of the Guarantees of the Due Process of Law*, Advisory Opinion OC-16/99 (Unreported, Inter-American Court of Human Rights, 1 October 1999) ('*Right to Information on Consular Assistance*'). This finding may have been for jurisdictional reasons: see R Higgins, 'A Babel of Judicial Voices? Ruminations from the Bench' (2006) 55 *International and Comparative Law Quarterly* 791, 796.

the Court, which considered 'neither the text nor the object and purpose of the Convention, nor any indication in the travaux preparatoires' to support the view that Article 36 contained human rights.[34] No reference was made to the opinion of the Inter-American Court.[35]

That the Court has benefited from the work of the human rights bodies is clear; the benefit for human rights bodies of the work of the Court is undeniable. Human rights bodies have adopted pronouncements of the Court on matters of general international law ranging from customary international law[36] through to the bearing of costs in contentious cases.[37] They have also adopted statements of the Court on matters of human rights law, for example on the nature of the *Genocide Convention*[38] and the *erga omnes* status of certain human rights.[39] This interlocking network of adjudicatory bodies and their consistency of jurisprudence can only be of benefit to the protection of human rights.

## C  Assisting the enforcers[40]

A third way in which the Court has contributed to the enforcement of human rights is through the protections it has rendered to other enforcers. Of the

---

[34] *Avena and Other Mexican Nationals (Mexico v United States of America)* [2004] ICJ Rep 12, [61] ('*Avena*').

[35] It should be noted, however, that the Court, being of an international character, tends not to refer to the work of *regional* courts or tribunals. For further consideration of this issue, see below nn 141–5 and accompanying text.

[36] *Baena Ricardo et al (270 workers) v Panama* (2003) Inter-Am Ct HR Ser C No 104, [102]–[104] ('*Baena Ricardo*') citing *inter alia Legality of the Threat or Use of Nuclear Weapons (Advisory Opinion)* [1996] ICJ Rep 226 ('*Nuclear Weapons*') and *North Sea Continental Shelf (Federal Republic of Germany v Denmark)* [1969] ICJ Rep 3.

[37] *Loizidou v Turkey* (1998) 81 Eur Ct HR 1807, [48] citing the *Application for Review of Judgment No 158 of the United Nations Administrative Tribunal (Advisory Opinion)* [1973] ICJ Rep 166.

[38] *Baena Ricardo* [97] citing the *Reservations and Declarations to the Convention on the Prevention and Punishment of the Crime of Genocide (Advisory Opinion)* [1951] ICJ Rep 15 ('*Reservations to the Genocide Convention*').

[39] *Interpretation of the American Declaration on the Rights and Duties of Man within the Framework of Article 64 of the American Convention on Human Rights*, Advisory Opinion OC-10/89 [1989] Inter Am Ct HR 1 citing *Case Concerning the Barcelona Traction, Light and Power Company Ltd (Belgium v Spain)* [1970] ICJ Rep 3 ('*Barcelona Traction*'), *Legal Consequences for States of the Continued Presence of South Africa in Namibia (South West Africa) notwithstanding Security Council Resolution 276 (1970) (Advisory Opinion)* [1971] ICJ Rep 27 ('*Namibia*') and *United States Diplomatic and Consular Staff in Tehran (United States v Iran)* [1980] ICJ Rep 3 ('*Tehran Hostages*').

[40] The issues considered under this heading are, of course, substantive issues of international law; the Court in none of the cases mentioned framed the issue as one of 'assisting the enforcers' of human rights.

principal enforcers, the Special Rapporteurs of the Commission on Human Rights rank high. Indeed, the Court has described Special Rapporteurs thus: 'a category of persons whom the United Nations and the specialized agencies find it necessary to engage for the implementation of increasingly varied functions' and 'of importance for the whole of the United Nations system.'[41]

In its *Mazilu* opinion, the Court held that Special Rapporteurs benefit from the protection afforded by Article VI(22) of the *Convention on the Privileges and Immunities of the United Nations*,[42] the purpose of which was to enable the United Nations to entrust missions to persons who were not officials of the organisation. In the view of the Court, Article VI(22) was applicable to every expert on mission throughout its duration and irrespective of whether or not they are engaged in travel. Furthermore, the privileges and immunities may be invoked against the state of nationality or residence of the expert.[43]

Some ten years later, the Court had cause to consider Article VI(22) of the Convention once again. In the *Cumaraswamy* opinion, the Court held that it is incumbent upon the Secretary-General of the United Nations to assert the immunity of its expert on mission, to inform the particular government of his finding and request it to act accordingly, including bringing his finding to the attention of its local courts if need be.[44] In the view of the Court, '[t]hat finding, and its documentary expression, creates a presumption which can only be set aside for the most compelling reasons and is thus to be given the greatest weight by national courts'.[45] On the facts of the case, the Court also determined that the government was obliged to communicate the Court's advisory opinion to its local courts in order to satisfy its international obligations and respect the immunity of the Special Rapporteur in question.[46]

The picture is more nuanced than to simply assert that the Court will always support the enforcer of human rights. In the *Arrest Warrant* case, for example, the Court held that a sitting minister of foreign affairs enjoys immunity from

---

[41] *Applicability of Article VI Section 22 of the Convention on the Privileges and Immunities of the United Nations (Advisory Opinion)* [1989] ICJ Rep 177, [53] ('*Applicability of Article VI, Section 22*').

[42] Opened for signature 13 February 1946, 1 UNTS 15 (entered into force 17 September 1946).

[43] *Applicability of Article VI, Section 22* [45]–[55].

[44] *Difference Relating to Immunity from Legal Process of a Special Rapporteur of the Commission on Human Rights, Advisory Opinion* [1999] ICJ Rep 62, [60] ('*Immunity of a Special Rapporteur*').

[45] *Immunity of a Special Rapporteur* [61].

[46] *Immunity of a Special Rapporteur* [65]. The obligation of a government to pass on information to other internal actors was also made explicit in *LaGrand (Germany v United States of America) (Provisional Measures, Order of 3 March 1999)* [1999] ICJ Rep 9, [28], [29.1.b].

the criminal jurisdiction of domestic courts of foreign states.[47] To the chagrin of many a human rights lawyer, the Court also stated that after leaving office the former minister of foreign affairs may be tried by the domestic courts of foreign states 'in respect of acts committed prior or subsequent to his or her period of office, as well as in respect of acts committed during that period of office in a private capacity',[48] suggesting that a former minister of foreign affairs may not be tried in respect of acts committed during office in an official capacity even if such acts constituted egregious crimes.[49] However, all may not be as it first seems, for as one judge voting with the majority writes extra-judicially: 'the Court's *dictum* regarding prosecution of former foreign ministers does not affirmatively exclude' an exception for 'the most serious international crimes'.[50] The last word on the subject seems yet to be had.

From this snapshot, it may readily be seen that the Court has contributed to the enforcement of human rights in a variety of ways. However, to stop with enforcement would be to leave the picture incomplete, for the Court's real contribution lies elsewhere – in supporting the human rights treaty framework and clarifying the normative status of particular instruments and specific rights, as well as interpreting the substantive rights and obligations themselves.

## 3 The treaty framework

### A  Application of human rights treaties

In recent times, there has been some debate regarding the precise scope of application of human rights treaties, in particular whether they apply outside the territorial confines of a state[51] and whether they remain applicable in time of armed conflict. Both questions have been before the Court.

States increasingly act outside their territorial borders. The question arises as to whether in so acting they are bound by their international human rights obligations. The *European Convention on Human Rights* ('ECHR') provides in relevant part: '[t]he High Contracting Parties shall secure to everyone

---

[47] *Arrest Warrant of 11 April 2000 (DRC v Belgium)* [2002] ICJ Rep 3, [54] ('*Arrest Warrant*').
[48] *Arrest Warrant* [61].
[49] For critique, see A Cassese, 'When May Senior State Officials Be Tried for International Crimes? Some Comments on the *Congo v Belgium* Case' (2002) 13 *European Journal of International Law* 853, 867–70.
[50] V S Vereshchetin and C J Le Mon, 'Immunities of Individuals under International Law in the Jurisprudence of the International Court of Justice' (2004) 1 *Global Community Yearbook of International Law and Jurisprudence* 77, 88.
[51] See further, Chapter 3.

within their jurisdiction the rights and freedoms defined in Section I of this Convention'.[52] Similarly the ICCPR: '[e]ach State Party to the present Covenant undertakes to respect and to ensure to all individuals within its territory and subject to its jurisdiction the rights recognized in the present Covenant.'[53] Precisely what is meant by 'within their jurisdiction' or 'within its territory and subject to its jurisdiction'? In particular, is the 'and' to be read disjunctively or conjunctively? The matter is not uncontroversial with states and commentators taking different views.[54]

In its advisory opinion on the *Wall*, the Court confirmed that the jurisdiction of a state is primarily territorial but noted that 'it may sometimes be exercised outside the national territory'. In light of the object and purpose of the ICCPR, 'it would seem natural that, even when such is the case, States parties to the Covenant should be bound to comply with its provisions.'[55] After examining the practice of the Human Rights Committee and the *travaux préparatoires* of the Covenant, the Court concluded that the ICCPR 'is applicable in respect of acts done by a State in the exercise of its jurisdiction outside its own territory.'[56] The Court also considered the CRC and the ICESCR to be binding on Israel in respect of its conduct in the Occupied Palestinian Territory. In making the latter finding, the Court was strongly influenced by the fact that 'the territories occupied by Israel have for over 37 years been subject to its territorial jurisdiction as the occupying Power.'[57] The link between the extraterritorial application of the ICESCR and situations of occupation was, however, decoupled in *Armed Activities on the Territory of the Congo* with the Court interpreting its *Wall* opinion as concluding 'that international human rights instruments are applicable "in respect of acts done by a State in the exercise of its jurisdiction outside its own territory", particularly in occupied territories'.[58]

---

[52] *Convention for the Protection of Human Rights and Fundamental Freedoms*, opened for signature 4 November 1950, 213 UNTS 262 (entered into force 3 September 1953) Article 1.
[53] Article 2 ICCPR.
[54] Cf T Buergenthal, 'To Respect and to Ensure: State Obligations and Permissible Derogations' in L Henkin (ed) *The International Bill of Rights: The Covenant on Civil and Political Rights* (Columbia University Press, New York, 1981) 72, 74 with M Nowak, *UN Covenant on Civil and Political Rights* (NP Engel, Kehl, 1993) 41–3. See generally M J Dennis, 'Application of Human Rights Treaties Extraterritorially in Times of Armed Conflict and Military Occupation' (2005) 99 *American Journal of International Law* 119.
[55] *Wall* [109].
[56] *Wall* [111].
[57] *Wall* [112]–[113].
[58] *Armed Activities on the Territory of the Congo* [216].

Given the views to the contrary, these holdings are timely and important. In reality, however, they are no more than the specific application to human rights treaties of the idea also expressed by the Court that '[p]hysical control of a territory, and not its sovereignty or legitimacy of title, is the basis of State liability for acts affecting other States.'[59] Obligation and responsibility stem, then, not from sovereignty but from effective control: '[t]he responsibility of a state in international law rests largely upon a territorial basis, but behind this territorial basis lies the broader concept of control.'[60]

Another area of contention has been the extent to which the law of human rights applies in time of conflict and the relationship between that body of law and international humanitarian law. Does human rights law apply in time of conflict or is the matter governed exclusively by international humanitarian law? If it does apply in such times, what is the relationship between the two bodies? Again states and commentators disagree.[61]

In the *Nuclear Weapons* opinion, the Court stated that 'the protection of the [ICCPR] does not cease in times of war, except by operation of [Article 4 ICCPR] whereby certain provisions may be derogated from in a time of national emergency.' The Court continued, with regard to the right to life:

> In principle, the right not arbitrarily to be deprived of one's life applies also in hostilities. The test of what is an arbitrary deprivation of life, however, then falls to be determined by the applicable *lex specialis*, namely, the law applicable in armed conflict which is designed to regulate the conduct of hostilities. Thus whether a particular loss of life, through the use of a certain weapon in warfare, is to be considered an arbitrary deprivation of life contrary to [Article 6 ICCPR] can only be decided by reference to the law applicable in armed conflict and not deduced from the terms of the Covenant itself.[62]

---

[59] *Namibia* [118]. See also *Prosecutor v Mucić et al*, Case No IT-96-21-A (20 February 2001), [197].

[60] C Eagleton, 'International Organizations and the Law of Responsibility' (1950) I *Rec des Cours* 319, 386. Linked with this broader concept of control is the exercise of authority on the part of State officials of one State in another State. See, for example, *López Burgos v Uruguay*, Communication No 52/79, UN Doc A/36/40 (6 June 1979) 176.

[61] Cf the positions of the Solomon Islands (*Nuclear Weapons*, Written Observations Submitted by the Government of the Solomon Islands to the ICJ, 91–5), the United Kingdom (*Nuclear Weapons*, Statement of the Government of the United Kingdom to the ICJ, 68), available at http://www.icj-cij.org at 3 February 2009, and the United States (*Response of the United States to Request for Precautionary Measures – Detainees in Guantanamo Bay, Cuba* (2002) 41 ILM 1015, 1021). See generally R Provost, *International Human Rights and Humanitarian Law* (Cambridge University Press, Cambridge, 2002).

[62] *Nuclear Weapons* [25].

This approach was extended to other human rights treaties in the *Wall* opinion and reiterated once again in *Armed Activities on the Territory of the Congo*:

> As regards the relationship between international humanitarian law and human rights law, there are . . . three possible situations: some rights may be exclusively matters of international humanitarian law; others may be exclusively matters of human rights law; yet others may be matters of both these branches of international law.[63]

Although very much at the level of generality, the statements of the Court remain helpful in confirming the continued applicability of international human rights law in time of armed conflict. Further guidance has been provided by the Eritrea Ethiopia Claims Commission, which, after citing with approval a passage from the *Wall* advisory opinion, went on to note that human rights law in armed conflict enjoys 'particular relevance in any situations involving persons who may not be protected fully by international humanitarian law, as with a Party's acts affecting its own nationals'.[64] The application of human rights law is also considered important in the context of the international administration of territory and internal armed conflict.[65]

The Court has thus made a useful contribution to the application of human rights treaties. However, it has not always elucidated the issue. In the judgment on preliminary objections in the *Genocide* case, for example, the Court did not pronounce upon the question of whether human rights treaties were binding automatically on successor states, refraining from endorsing what has been described as this 'emerging progressive doctrine'.[66] Rather, the Court opted for noting that it did not matter whether Bosnia and Herzegovina was a party to the *Genocide Convention* automatically through its accession to independence or retroactively through its Notice of Succession; at any event it was party to the Convention at the time of filing of its Application.[67]

---

[63] *Wall* [106]; *Armed Activities on the Territory of the Congo* [216].

[64] Eritrea Ethiopia Claims Commission, *Partial Award, Civilians Claims, Ethiopia's Claim 5* (17 December 2004) [28].

[65] H Krieger, 'A Conflict of Norms: The Relationship between Humanitarian Law and Human Rights Law in the ICRC Customary Law Study' (2006) 11 *Journal of Conflict and Security Law* 265, 273–5. See also W Abresch, 'A Human Rights Law of Internal Armed Conflict: The European Court of Human Rights in Chechnya' (2005) 16 *European Journal of International Law* 741.

[66] R Higgins, 'The International Court of Justice and Human Rights' in K Wellens (ed) *International Law: Theory and Practice: Essays in Honour of Eric Suy* (Martinus Nijhoff, The Hague, 1998) 691, 694. On state succession to human rights treaties, see M T Kamminga, 'State Succession in Respect of Human Rights Treaties' 7 *European Journal of International Law* 469 (1996).

[67] *Application of the Convention on the Prevention and Punishment of the Crime of Genocide (Preliminary Objections)* [1996] ICJ Rep 595, [23].

B  Interpretation of human rights treaties
Once it is known that a treaty is applicable, it is often necessary to interpret one of its terms, such term being opaque, not altogether clear, or somewhat vague. In interpreting the particular term, a dispute may arise as to whether it should be given the meaning intended by the parties at the time of drafting or interpreted in light of the present-day conditions.

In interpreting a treaty, regard must be had to the rules of treaty interpretation found in Articles 31–2 of the *Vienna Convention on the Law of Treaties* ('VCLT'),[68] which provisions reflect customary international law.[69] In interpreting the treaty, it is important to have regard to the purpose of interpretation, namely 'to ascertain the common intentions of the parties'.[70] The issue then becomes 'what elements may properly be taken into account as indirect evidence of the parties' intentions and what weight is to be given to those elements'.[71]

On the one hand, the inter-temporal rule provides that '[a] judicial fact must be appreciated in the light of the law contemporary with it, and not of the law in force at the time such a dispute in regard to it arises or falls to be settled' and has been used by the Court on numerous occasions.[72] On the other hand, the principle of evolutionary treaty interpretation has also been used by the Court. As is well known, in its *Namibia* opinion, the Court found that certain concepts embodied in the *Covenant of the League of Nations* 'were not static, but were by definition evolutionary' and that '[t]he parties to the Covenant must consequently be deemed to have accepted them as such'. The Court continued:

> That is why, viewing the institutions of 1919, the Court must take into consideration the changes which have occurred in the supervening half-century, and its interpretation cannot remain unaffected by the subsequent development of the law, through the *Charter of the United Nations* and by way of customary law. Moreover,

---

[68] Opened for signature 23 May 1969, 1155 UNTS 331 (entered into force 27 January 1980).
[69] *Territorial Dispute (Libyan Arab Jamahiriya v Chad)* [1994] ICJ Rep 6, [41].
[70] *European Communities – Customs Classification of Certain Computer Equipment*, WTO Doc WT/DS62/AB/R, AB-1998-2 (22 June 1998) (Report of the Appellate Body) [84]. See also Eritrea-Ethiopia Boundary Commission, *Decision on Delimitation* (13 April 2002) [3.4]; *Argentine-Chile Frontier Case* (1966) 38 ILR 10, 89.
[71] R Jennings and A Watts, *Oppenheim's International Law* (Longman, London, 1992) 1271.
[72] *Island of Palmas (Netherlands v United States of America)* (1949) II RIAA 829, 845. For application by the Court, see, for example, *South West Africa (Ethiopia v South Africa; Liberia v South Africa) (Second Phase, Judgment)* [1966] ICJ Rep 6, [16].

an international instrument has to be interpreted and applied within the framework of the entire legal system prevailing at the time of the interpretation.[73]

Similarly, in the *Gabčíkovo-Nagymaros* case, the Court observed that the bilateral treaty between the parties at issue 'is not static, and is open to adapt to emerging norms of international law'.[74] In the *Aegean Sea Continental Shelf* case, the Court stated that 'it hardly seems conceivable' that terms such as 'domestic jurisdiction' and 'territorial status' contained in the *General Act for the Pacific Settlement of International Disputes*, a convention 'of the most general kind and of continuing duration', 'were intended to have a fixed content regardless of the subsequent evolution of international law'.[75] The Court's predecessor, the Permanent Court of International Justice, in the *Nationality Decrees Issued in Tunis and Morocco* opinion, observed that the interpretation of certain terms was 'an essentially relative question; it depends upon the development of international relations'.[76] The evolutionary approach to treaty interpretation has also been used by other international bodies.[77]

It is thus incumbent upon the interpreter to discover whether it was the intention of the parties to have in the treaty terms that would change over time or remain fixed. Of treaties of a constitutional nature, such as the *Charter of the United Nations*, a leading text observes that the 'general intention to secure the object and purpose of the treaty as effectively as possible in the light of the circumstances as they develop over time' should be attributed to the parties, rather than a mechanical consideration of the particular intentions of the parties on a particular provision of the treaty.[78] The same is surely true of human rights treaties. Although these statements of the Court were not made in relation to human rights treaties, they have been applied to such by international human rights tribunals,[79] providing a classic example of general state-

---

[73] *Namibia* [53].
[74] *Gabčíkovo-Nagymaros Project (Hungary v Slovakia)* [1997] ICJ Rep 7, [112].
[75] *Aegean Sea Continental Shelf (Greece v Turkey)* [1978] ICJ Rep 3, [77].
[76] *Nationality Decrees Issued in Tunis and Morocco* [1923] PCIJ Ser B No 4, 24.
[77] See, for example, *In the Arbitration Regarding the Iron Rhine Railway (Belgium v Netherlands)* (2005) 27 RIAA 127, [80]; *United States – Import Prohibition of Certain Shrimp and Shrimp Products*, WTO Doc WT/DS58/AB/R, AB-1998-4 (12 October 1998) (Report of the Appellate Body) [130].
[78] Jennings and Watts, above n 71, 1273 (FN13).
[79] See, for example, *Tyrer v United Kingdom* (1978) 26 Eur Ct HR (Ser A) 1, 15–16; *Interpretation of the American Declaration on the Rights and Duties of Man within the Framework of Article 64 of the American Convention on Human Rights*, Advisory Opinion OC-10/89 (1989) 10 Inter-Am Ct HR (Ser A) (14 July 1989). See generally R Bernhardt, 'Evolutive Treaty Interpretation, Especially of the European Convention on Human Rights' (1999) 42 *German Yearbook of International Law* 11, 16–17.

ments of international law being transposed to a particular context. Indeed, such is the acceptance of evolutionary treaty interpretation in the context of human rights treaties that their characterisation as 'living instruments' is taken for granted.

## C  Reservations to human rights treaties

A further obstacle to the enforcement of a particular treaty provision is the entry of a reservation by a state party to that provision. Reservations to human rights treaties have proven (too) popular, with 75 of 185 states entering (often multiple) reservations to the CEDAW alone and 74 of 193 to the CRC. Some states have objected to certain of these reservations – 18 in the case of reservations to CEDAW and 13 to reservations to the CRC.[80] The status of the treaty, the reservation and the relationship between reserving states and objecting and non-objecting states is thus in need of some elucidation.

The position in general international law, as found in the VCLT, is that a state may enter a reservation to a treaty provision provided that reservations in general and that type of reservation in particular are not prohibited by the treaty and provided that the purported reservation is not contrary to the object and purpose of the treaty.[81] The relationship between the reserving state and other contracting states will then depend on whether those other states accept or object to the reservation. Acceptance entails the entry into force of the treaty as between the reserving and accepting states with the provision against which the reservation was entered being modified to the extent of the reservation. Objection does not preclude the entry into force of the treaty as between the reserving and objecting states 'unless a contrary intention is definitely expressed by the objecting State'; rather, the treaty enters into force with the reserved provision 'not apply[ing] as between the two states to the extent of the reservation'.[82]

The VCLT position was heavily influenced by the *Reservations to the Genocide Convention* opinion of the Court. In that opinion, the Court was asked: (i) whether the reserving state could be regarded as a party to the Genocide Convention if other states had objected to its reservation; (ii) if the answer was in the affirmative, what the effect of the reservation was between the reserving state and those states that had (a) accepted and (b) objected to the reservation; and (iii) how the legal effect would differ if the objecting state

---

[80] See http://www.un.org/womenwatch/daw/cedaw/reservations-country.htm at 3 February 2009 (CEDAW) and http://www.unhchr.ch/pdf/report.pdf at 3 February 2009 (CRC).
[81] Article 19 VCLT.
[82] Articles 20–21 VCLT.

was (a) a signatory to the treaty but had not ratified it and (b) a non-signatory to the treaty but was entitled to sign it or accede to it.[83]

The Court noted the origin of the Convention and its special characteristics. In considering the objects of the Convention, the Court stated:

> The Convention was manifestly adopted for a purely humanitarian and civilizing purpose ... In such a convention the contracting States do not have any interests of their own; they merely have, one and all, a common interest, namely, the accomplishment of those high purposes which are the *raison d'être* of the convention. Consequently, in a convention of this type one cannot speak of individual advantages or disadvantages to States, or of the maintenance of a perfect contractual balance between rights and duties.[84]

As such, the Court stated that

> it is the compatibility of a reservation with the object and purpose of a Convention that must furnish the criteria for the attitude of a state in making the reservation on accession as well as for the appraisal by a State in objecting to the reservation.[85]

Similarly, the Court found that

> As no State can be bound by a reservation to which it has not consented, it necessarily follows that each state objecting to it will or will not, on the basis of its individual appraisal within the limits of the criteria of the object and purpose ... consider the reserving state to be a party to the Convention.[86]

The human rights bodies have – depending on the view taken – either developed the issues, considering questions that had not previously been put to the Court,[87] or departed from general international law on point. The human rights bodies have considered the legal effect of a purported reservation that offends the object and purpose of the Convention as well as pronounced on the actor competent to assess this compatibility. The Human Rights Committee,

---

[83] *Reservations to the Genocide Convention* 15, 16.

[84] *Reservations to the Genocide Convention* 23. Similar views have been put forward by the regional human rights institutions in the context of their founding instruments. See, for example, *Ireland v United Kingdom* (1980) 58 ILR 188, 291; *The Effect of Reservations on the Entry into Force of the American Convention on Human Rights*, Advisory Opinion OC-2/82 (1982) 2 Inter-Am Ct HR (Ser A) (24 September 1982) [33].

[85] *Reservations to the Genocide Convention* 24. This aspect of the Court's opinion did not find its way into the Vienna Convention.

[86] *Reservations to the Genocide Convention* 26.

[87] This is the view expressed in *Congo v Rwanda* [16] (Judges Higgins, Kooijmans, Elaraby, Simma and Owada).

for example, in *General Comment 29*, stated that '[i]t necessarily falls to the Committee to determine whether a specific reservation is compatible with the object and purpose of the Covenant' and

> The normal consequence of an unacceptable reservation is not that the Covenant will not be in effect at all for a reserving party. Rather, such a reservation will generally be severable, in the sense that the Covenant will be operative for the reserving party without benefit of the reservation.[88]

These views have provoked some consternation among states.[89] However, similar views have been put forward by the regional human rights courts.[90] The matter is currently under consideration by the International Law Commission.[91]

## 4 The normative framework

### A  *Normative status of the instruments*

Outside the treaty system, there remain a number of instruments devoted in whole or in part to the protection of human rights. Increasingly in international law, resort is had to this so-called 'soft' law; the same is no less true of human rights law. What is the normative status of these 'soft' law instruments, for example that most classic human rights document, the UDHR? Similarly, although not a human rights instrument, the *Charter of the United Nations* contains a number of provisions devoted to human rights. What force do these provisions have as a matter of positive law?

A divergence of opinion exists among scholars as to the extent to which the UDHR is binding as a matter of international law. On the one hand, it has been noted that '[t]he practical unanimity of the Members of the United Nations in stressing the importance of the Declaration was accompanied by an equally general repudiation of the idea that the Declaration imposed upon them a legal

---

[88] Human Rights Committee, *General Comment No 24: Issues relating to reservations made upon ratification or accession to the Covenant or the Optional Protocols thereto, or in relation to declarations under Article 41 of the Covenant*, UN Doc CCPR/C/21/Rev.1/Add.6 (4 November 1994) [18].

[89] See, for example, the views of the United States, (1996) 16 *Human Rights Law Journal* 422, and the United Kingdom, (1996) 16 *Human Rights Law Journal* 424. For something of a rebuttal, see R Higgins, 'Introduction' in J P Gardner (ed) *Human Rights as General Norms and a State's Right to Opt Out* (BIICL, London, 1997) xv.

[90] *Belilos v Switzerland* (1988) 132 Eur Ct HR (Ser A); *Loizidou v Turkey (Preliminary Objections)* (1995) 310 Eur Ct HR (Ser A).

[91] See the various reports of Alain Pellet, Special Rapporteur of the International Law Commission on Reservations to Treaties: http://untreaty.un.org/ilc/guide/1_8.htm at 3 February 2009.

obligation to respect the human rights and fundamental freedoms which it proclaimed'.[92] On the other hand, the view has been taken that 'the Declaration not only constitutes an authoritative interpretation of the Charter obligations but also a binding instrument in its own right'.[93]

The Court has contributed to this debate, stating in the *Tehran Hostages* case that:

> Wrongfully to deprive human beings of their freedom and to subject them to physical constraint in conditions of hardship is in itself manifestly incompatible with the principles of the Charter of the United Nations, as well as with the fundamental principles enunciated in the [UDHR].[94]

Although not commenting explicitly upon the binding nature of the UDHR, in judging conduct against the 'fundamental principles' enunciated in that instrument, the Court must have considered those fundamental principles binding on states. However, the Court did not go on to explain quite how this was so, whether through customary international law, general principles of international law or as an authoritative interpretation of Articles 55 and 56 of the *UN Charter*, which are accepted as being of paramount status.

Similarly disputed is the extent to which the human rights provisions of the Charter, such as Articles 55 and 56, constitute binding obligations. Some take the view that the Charter merely 'sets out a program of action', while others that it lays down a 'legal obligation'.[95] The *Namibia* opinion lends support to the argument that the human rights provisions of the Charter constitute obligations on the part of member states:

> Under the *Charter of the United Nations*, the former Mandatory had pledged itself to observe and respect, in a territory having an international status, human rights and fundamental freedoms for all without distinction as to race. To establish instead, and to enforce, distinctions, exclusions, restrictions and limitations exclusively based on grounds of race, colour, descent or national or ethnic origin which constitute a denial of fundamental human rights is a flagrant violation of the purposes and principles of the Charter.[96]

---

[92] H Lauterpacht, *International Law and Human Rights* (Stevens and Sons, London, 1950) 397.
[93] L Sohn, 'The Human Rights Law of the Charter' (1977) 12 *Texas International Law Journal* 129, 133.
[94] *Tehran Hostages* [91].
[95] See M O Hudson, 'Integrity of International Instruments' (1948) 42 *American Journal of International Law* 107 and Lauterpacht, above n 92, 147–9, respectively.
[96] *Namibia* [131].

This leaves little room for doubt that, in the Court's view, the Charter imposes legal obligations on members of the United Nations in matters of human rights.[97]

## B  Normative status of human rights principles

Instruments alone are not enough to protect human rights: a state may not be party to the relevant treaty; it may not have incorporated it into its domestic law; or it may have reserved its position in relation to a particular provision. Some human rights treaty provisions may also seemingly be trumped by other non-human rights treaty provisions.[98] 'Soft' law instruments may be trumped by those of a harder nature, or they may be considered merely hortatory.

The Court's pronouncements on the status of certain rights and obligations outside their instrumental framework are thus valuable. In its very first case, the Court spoke of certain 'general and well-recognized principles, namely: elementary considerations of humanity, even more exacting in peace than in war'.[99] It has also found that a great many rules of international humanitarian law constitute 'intransgressible principles of international customary law',[100] and observed that the principles underlying the *Genocide Convention* are 'recognized by civilized nations as binding on States, even without any conventional obligation', with the Convention itself confirming and endorsing 'the most elementary principles of morality'.[101]

The Court has also recognised the existence of obligations *erga omnes*. In *Barcelona Traction*, providing the antidote to its earlier judgment in the *South West Africa* cases in which it held that Liberia and Ethiopia did not have standing to challenge the conduct of South Africa, acting as Mandatory in South West Africa, the Court took the view that:

> [A]n essential distinction should be drawn between the obligations of a State towards the international community as a whole, and those arising *vis-à-vis* another State in the field of diplomatic protection. By their very nature the former are the concern of all states. In view of the importance of the rights involved, all States can be held to have a legal interest in their protection; they are obligations *erga omnes*.

---

[97] The content of those obligations remains uncertain. For further comment, see E Schwelb, 'The International Court of Justice and the Human Rights Clauses of the Charter' (1972) 66 *American Journal of International Law* 337, 348.

[98] See, for example, *Kadi v Council and Commission*, Case No T-315/01 [2005] ECR II-3649, [181] ('*Kadi*') and *Yusuf and Al Barakaat International Foundation v Council and Commission*, Case No T-306/01 [2005] ECR II-2387, [213] ('*Yusuf*') where obligations under the *UN Charter* were considered to supersede obligations under the ECHR. These decisions were however reversed by the Grand Chamber in Cases C-402/05 and C-415/05 P, Judgment of the European Court of Justice (Grand Chamber), 3 September 2008.

[99] *Corfu Channel (United Kingdom v Albania)* [1949] ICJ Rep 4, 22.

[100] *Nuclear Weapons* [79].

[101] *Reservations to the Genocide Convention* 23.

Such obligations derive, for example, in contemporary international law, from the outlawing of acts of aggression, and of genocide, as also from the principles and rules concerning the basic rights of the human person, including protection from slavery and racial discrimination.[102]

To this list the right to self-determination may now be added.[103] More recently, the Court has explicitly added its weight behind the existence of *jus cogens* norms, stating that the prohibition of genocide 'assuredly' has such a status.[104]

The recognition of *jus cogens* norms and obligations *erga omnes* has not had an effect on the jurisdiction of the Court. In *East Timor*, the Court stated that 'the *erga omnes* character of a norm and the rule of consent to jurisdiction are two different things.'[105] And in *Congo v Rwanda*, the Court confirmed this, adding 'the mere fact that rights and obligations *erga omnes* may be at issue in a dispute would not give the Court jurisdiction to entertain that dispute', continuing: '[t]he same applies to the relationship between peremptory norms of general international law (*jus cogens*) and the establishment of the Court's jurisdiction ... Under the Court's Statute that jurisdiction is always based on the consent of the parties'.[106] On an appropriate occasion, however, in a case in which the Court does have jurisdiction, a state may allege breach of an obligation *erga omnes* even though it did not suffer any harm as a result of the breach.[107]

Jurisdiction of the Court aside, the characterisation of a norm as a peremptory one is important for other reasons: determining as void a treaty that conflicts with it;[108] special consequences in the area of state responsibility;[109] and taking precedence over a conflicting Security Council resolution.[110]

---

[102] *Barcelona Traction* [33], [34].
[103] *Case Concerning East Timor (Portugal v Australia)* [1995] ICJ Rep 90, [29] ('*East Timor*'); *Wall* [88], [156].
[104] *Congo v Rwanda* [64].
[105] *East Timor* [29].
[106] *Congo v Rwanda* [65]. See also *Genocide* [147]. For greater consideration of the issues, see the Separate Opinion of Judge *ad hoc* Dugard in *Congo v Rwanda*.
[107] The point was tantalisingly raised but, in light of other findings of the Court, did not need to be considered in the *Genocide* case [185].
[108] Articles 53 and 64 VCLT.
[109] International Law Commission, *Articles on Responsibility of States for Internationally Wrongful Acts* (2001) UN, http://untreaty.un.org/ilc/texts/instruments/english/draft%20articles/9_6_2001.pdf at 3 February 2009, Articles 40 and 41. In particular, '[n]o State shall recognize as lawful a situation created by a serious breach' of an obligation arising under a peremptory norm nor shall any State 'render aid or assistance in maintaining that situation.'
[110] *Genocide (Provisional Measures Order of 13 September 1993)* [1993] ICJ Rep 3, [100] (Judge *ad hoc* Lauterpacht).

## 5  Substantive rights and obligations

Of the substantive human rights to be found in the annals of the Court's jurisprudence, this section considers those that have had a tendency to recur. Somewhat unsurprisingly, these feature among the most important, namely the prohibition of genocide, the right to self-determination and the right to life.

### A  Genocide

The Court has had numerous occasions on which to pronounce on various aspects of the definition of genocide. It will be recalled that Article II of the *Genocide Convention* reads in relevant part: 'genocide means any of the following acts committed with intent to destroy, in whole or in part, a national, ethnical, racial or religious group, as such'.[111] The 'intended destruction' of the relevant group is considered by the Court to be the 'essential characteristic' of the definition.[112] As its essential characteristic, the Court has interpreted it in a strict but orthodox manner. The Court has confirmed that 'the threat or use of force against a state cannot in itself constitute an act of genocide',[113] and that a large number of deaths of individuals of a particular protected group would not by itself amount to genocide without the presence of specific intent.[114] The Court has also stressed the need to distinguish intent from motive, specific intent from discriminatory intent and intent to forcibly displace from intent to destroy.[115] In the view of the Court '[g]reat care must be taken in finding in the facts a sufficiently clear manifestation of that intent';[116] it is not to be found lightly.

The Court has also contributed to the interpretation of the *actus reus* of genocide, opining that the destruction of the historical, religious and cultural heritage of the protected group fell outside the Convention, while reserving its position as to whether encirclement, shelling and starvation, and deportation and expulsion fell within it.[117] As to the relationship between ethnic cleansing and genocide, the Court has confirmed the distinct nature of the two and that, at least in terms of the Convention, ethnic cleansing has 'no legal significance of its own'.[118] This is welcome in light of the term 'ethnic cleansing' taking on a life of its own.[119]

---

[111] *Genocide Convention* Article II.
[112] *Genocide (Provisional Measures Order of 13 September 1993)* [42].
[113] *Legality of Use of Force (Yugoslavia v Belgium) (Provisional Measures, Order of 2 June 1999)* [1999] ICJ Rep 124, [40].
[114] *Nuclear Weapons* [26].
[115] *Genocide* [187]–[190].
[116] *Genocide* [189].
[117] *Genocide* [328], [334], [344].
[118] *Genocide* [190].
[119] It ranks alongside genocide, crimes against humanity and war crimes in the

As to the group which is the subject of the Convention protections, in the view of the Court it is to be defined in a positive rather than a negative manner,[120] with the Court in the *Genocide* case limiting the protected group to the Bosnian Muslims and not the wider non-Serb group.[121] In considering quite what constitutes a 'part' of the group, regard should be had to the nature of the individuals targeted, any geographical limitations and most importantly the number of individuals targeted.[122]

In addition to the definition of genocide, the Court has pronounced on the responsibility of states in relation to the *Genocide Convention*. Prior to the *Genocide* case, the question of whether a state could commit genocide was a vexed issue.[123] The utility of such a finding had also been queried.[124] In the *Genocide* case, the Court not only confirmed that states are under an obligation not to commit genocide; it spoke to the complicity of a state in genocide as well as its obligation to punish genocide.[125] Usefully, the Court also gave substance to the previously vague obligation of a state to prevent genocide.[126] Although careful to limit its discussion to the *Genocide Convention*, the Court's test is likely to be applied in the wider human rights field, linked as it is with due diligence, a concept familiar to those in the area.[127]

### B  Self-determination

The Court has also made important contributions to the right to self-determination. At a time when it was by no means settled,[128] the Court

context of the 'Responsibility to Protect': *2005 World Summit Outcome*, GA Res 60/L.1, 60th sess, UN Doc A/60/L.1 (15 September 2005) [138]–[139].

[120]    This is also the view of the Appeals Chamber of the International Criminal Tribunal for the former Yugoslavia: *Prosecutor v Stakić*, Case No IT-97-24-A (22 March 2006) [14]–[28], though compare the Partly Dissenting Opinion of Judge Shahabuddeen: *Genocide* [14].

[121]    *Genocide* [196].

[122]    *Genocide* [197]–[201].

[123]    See the differing views cited in W A Schabas, *Genocide in International Law* (Cambridge University Press, Cambridge, 2000) Ch 9.

[124]    In their Joint Declaration in the Judgment on Preliminary Objections in the *Genocide* case, Judges Shi and Vereshchetin took the view that the focus should be on individual criminal responsibility and that the International Court of Justice was 'perhaps not the proper venue for the adjudication of the complaints which the Applicant had raised in the current proceedings': *Genocide* [632].

[125]    *Genocide* [155]–[179], [416]–[424], [439]–[449].

[126]    The Court made clear that the obligation is one of conduct and not of result. It stated that responsibility would attach if 'the State manifestly failed to take all measures to prevent genocide which were within its power, and which might have contributed to preventing the genocide': *Genocide* [430].

[127]    See, for example, *Velásquez-Rodríguez v Honduras* (1988) 4 Inter-Am Ct HR (Ser C) (29 July 1988) 172. See also Chapter 4.

[128]    See Higgins, above n 66, 694.

confirmed that the right to self-determination applied regardless of the precise category of the mandate: 'the subsequent development of international law in regard to non-self governing territories, as enshrined in the *Charter of the United Nations*, made the principle of self-determination applicable to all of them'.[129]

On occasion, the Court has gone out of its way to consider the right. In considering in its *Western Sahara* opinion whether Western Sahara was *terra nullius*, and if not what the legal ties were between Western Sahara and Morocco and Mauritania, the Court strictly speaking need not have considered self-determination. However, the Court, mindful of the purpose of the opinion, namely to assist the General Assembly with its decolonisation policy, stated that the legal ties the General Assembly had in mind when putting the questions to it were not limited to ties established directly with the territory but extended to the people who may be found in it.[130] After considering the evidence before it, the Court found that there were no 'legal ties of such a nature as might affect the application of . . . the principle of self-determination through the free and genuine expression of the will of the peoples of the Territory'.[131]

Similarly in *East Timor*, despite finding that it did not have jurisdiction to entertain the dispute, the Court went out of its way to state that 'Portugal's assertion that the right of peoples to self-determination, as it evolved from the Charter and from United Nations practice, has an *erga omnes* character, is irreproachable' and that it constitutes 'one of the essential principles of contemporary international law',[132] statements that were subsequently confirmed in the advisory opinion on the *Wall*.[133]

Again, this is not to suggest that the Court has always been a model of clarity on the issue. In *Case Concerning the Frontier Dispute*, a Chamber of the Court noted the 'apparent conflict' between self-determination and the principle of the respect for the stability of territorial boundaries at the time of independence (*uti possidetis juris*). However, the Court did not go on to resolve that tension, confining itself to observing: 'the maintenance of the territorial status quo in Africa is often seen as the wisest course' with the *uti possidetis juris* principle taken into account in the interpretation of the principle of self-

---

[129] *Namibia* [52]–[54].
[130] *Western Sahara (Advisory Opinion)* [1975] ICJ Rep 12, [85] ('*Western Sahara*').
[131] *Western Sahara* [162].
[132] *East Timor* [29].
[133] *Wall* [88], [155]–[156].

determination.[134] Quite how the two are to be reconciled is a matter of some conjecture.[135]

## C  Right to life

The right to life, that foremost of rights, has been protected by the Court in a number of ways; a recent and innovative approach has been through the lens of consular protection. In the *Breard, LaGrand* and *Avena* line of cases, the Court was faced with a number of foreign nationals who had been arrested in the United States and subsequently tried and sentenced to the death penalty without being notified of their consular rights under Article 36(1) VCCR. Strictly speaking, then, the case was not about the death penalty and therefore the right to life at all, though in some measure it clearly was: Mexico, for example, brought its case before the Court in respect only of those individuals who had been sentenced to death by courts in the United States.[136]

In *LaGrand*, the Court held that Article 36(1) VCCR creates individual rights in addition to the rights of states.[137] This follows an earlier holding in the *International Status of South-West Africa* advisory opinion, in which the Court determined that the inhabitants of South-West Africa had acquired under international law the right of petition, such right being created by certain resolutions of the Council of the League of Nations and upon the demise of the League by Article 80 of the *UN Charter*.[138] A similar point had been made by the Permanent Court of International Justice in *Jurisdiction of the Courts of Danzig*, a pronouncement considered 'revolutionary' at the time it was made.[139] In that case, the Permanent Court had said that it is in accordance with well-established principles that international agreements 'cannot, as such, create direct rights and obligations for private individuals'; however 'it cannot

---

[134] *Case Concerning the Frontier Dispute (Burkina Faso v Mali)* [1986] ICJ Rep 554, [25]–[26].

[135] See G J Naldi, 'The Case Concerning the Frontier Dispute (Burkina Faso v Republic of Mali): Uti Possidetis in an African Perspective' (1987) 36 *International and Comparative Law Quarterly* 893; A Cassese, 'The International Court of Justice and the right of peoples to self-determination' in V Lowe and M Fitzmaurice (eds) *Fifty Years of the International Court of Justice: Essays in Honour of Sir Robert Jennings* (Cambridge University Press, Cambridge, 1996) 351, 362.

[136] The Court was careful to avoid reference to the death penalty and spoke of individuals who had been sentenced to 'severe penalties': see, for example, *LaGrand (Germany v United States)* [2001] ICJ 466, [128.7] ('*LaGrand*').

[137] *LaGrand* [77]. The rights in question were those of consular information, notification and assistance.

[138] *International Status of South-West Africa* [1950] ICJ Rep 128, 136–8.

[139] H Lauterpacht, *The Development of International Law by the International Court* (Grotius, Cambridge, reprint, 1982) 174.

be disputed that the very object of an international agreement, according to the intention of the contracting Parties, may be the adoption of the Parties of some definite rules creating individual rights and obligations and enforceable by the national courts'.[140] These findings are important as they demonstrate that, in certain situations, individuals may be granted rights directly from international law without the interposition of national law. Thus, if the rights stem from a treaty, non-incorporation of that treaty in domestic law will not prevent the individual from enforcing their rights.

Having found in *LaGrand* that Article 36 VCCR created individual rights, the Court considered it unnecessary to consider the argument that those rights were also human rights.[141] In response to a similar argument raised in *Avena*, the Court again stated that it need not consider whether the individual rights were human rights but this time went on to note that 'neither the text nor the object and purpose of the Convention, nor any indication in the *travaux préparatoires*' supported the argument.[142] It remains to be seen whether, in time, the right will be recognised as a human right given the Inter-American Court of Human Rights' determination that the right was a human right,[143] the inclusion of a version of Article 36(1) VCCR in the *Migrant Workers Convention*,[144] and reference to consular notification appearing in other human rights instruments.[145] Regardless, the finding that access to consular information is an individual right has profound implications for enforcement of that right at the domestic level.[146]

---

[140] *Jurisdiction of the Courts of Danzig* (1928) PCIJ Ser B No 16, 17–18.

[141] *LaGrand* [78]. Sir Robert Jennings, a former President of the Court has written: 'For this wise forbearance all international lawyers should give heartfelt thanks': R Y Jennings, 'The *LaGrand* Case' (2002) 1 *Law and Practice of International Courts and Tribunals* 13, 27.

[142] *Avena* [124]. The re-raising of the argument has been criticised: see B Simma and C Hoppe, 'From *LaGrand* and *Avena* to *Medellin* – A Rocky Road to Implementation' (2005) 14 *Tulane Journal of International and Comparative Law* 7, 11–13.

[143] *Right to Information on Consular Assistance* 65.

[144] *Migrant Workers Convention* Article 16(7).

[145] See, for example, the *Declaration on the Human Rights of Individuals Who are not Nationals of the Country in which They Live*, GA Res 40/144, UN GAOR, 40th sess, 116th plen mtg, UN Doc A/Res/40/144 (13 December 1985) Article 10; Article 6(3) CAT; *Body of Principles for the Protection of All Persons under Any Form of Detention or Imprisonment*, GA Res 43/173, UN GAOR, 43rd sess, 76th plen mtg, UN Doc A/Res/43/173 (9 December 1988) Principle 16(2).

[146] Witness the ripple effect of the judgment in *Avena* in the United States, for example, *Torres v Oklahoma* (2004) 43 ILM 1227; Memorandum from President Bush to the United States Attorney-General, 28 February 2005, requiring state courts to give effect to the judgment in *Avena*; *Medellin v Dretke*, 125 S Ct 2088 (2005); *Sanchez-Llamas v Oregon* 126 S Ct 2669 (2006).

One further point warrants mentioning in this context. In *Avena*, in order to aid compliance with the individual rights that are the subject of Article 36 VCCR, the Court suggested to the United States that the right to consular information should be parallel to the reading of the 'Miranda' rights, such that when an individual is arrested they should be told that if they are a foreign national they are entitled to have their consular post contacted.[147] Although not altogether novel, as such a practice already takes place in some local jurisdictions within the United States, it is novel in that it is a suggestion from the Court to a state as to how to increase compliance with certain individual rights.

*D   Other substantive human rights*
Aside from the right to life, the right to self-determination and the prohibition of genocide, the Court has considered other human rights norms from time to time. As to discrimination, for example, the Court has stated that:

> To establish . . . and to enforce, distinctions, exclusions, restrictions and limitations exclusively based on grounds of race, colour, descent or national or ethnic origin which constitute a denial of fundamental human rights is a flagrant violation of the purposes and principles of the Charter.[148]

The Court has also made clear that the principle of sovereignty over natural resources does not pertain 'to the specific situation of looting, pillage and exploitation of certain natural resources by members of the army of a state military intervening in another state'.[149] And the Court has made numerous and important contributions to international humanitarian law.[150]

## 6  Conclusion
A review of the jurisprudence of the Court reveals that disputes relating to human rights have formed a substantial part of its work and its pronouncements on the subject have been significant. This is not to overstate its role. The ICJ is not and does not pretend to be a human rights court; it is rather a court of general international law, of which human rights law forms but part. However,

---

[147] *Avena* [64].
[148] *Namibia* [131].
[149] *Armed Activities on the Territory of the Congo* [244].
[150] See, for example, *Corfu Channel*; *Military and Paramilitary Activities in and against Nicaragua (Nicaragua v United States of America)* [1986] ICJ Rep 14; *Nuclear Weapons*; *Wall*; *Armed Activities on the Territory of the Congo*. For comment, see J Gardam, 'The Contribution of the International Court of Justice to International Humanitarian Law' (2001) 14 *Leiden Journal of International Law* 349; V Chetail, 'The contribution of the International Court of Justice to international humanitarian law' (2003) 850 *International Review of the Red Cross* 235.

rarely is the work of the Court in matters of human rights overstated. Indeed, quite the opposite, with a tendency to forget or downplay its contribution.

The Court has a very real role to play in the protection of human rights. This may not necessarily be in the area of the direct enforcement, given the existence of other bodies specifically mandated with the task[151] and the jurisdictional constraints under which the Court operates.[152] The work of the Court has been invaluable in supporting and developing the structural and normative framework of human rights protection and providing clarity to the substantive rights, which may explain why some of the great human rights controversies have been submitted to the Court for its considered opinion. Admittedly the Court has not always covered itself in glory and the position is too nuanced to say that the Court has consistently developed human rights law. However, the Court can certainly stand alongside other bodies that are tasked to uphold the protection of human rights. For one that is not a human rights court, it has done much to further their protection.

---

[151] See the concern expressed in *Wall* [26]–[27] (Judge Higgins).

[152] However, even when lacking jurisdiction, the Court often reminds the parties of their obligations under human rights and humanitarian law: see *Congo v Rwanda* [93]. This has caused concern but also praise from individual judges; compare the views expressed in Declaration of Judge Buergenthal with Declaration of Judge Koroma: *Congo v Rwanda* [12]–[16].

# 13. The Council of Europe and the protection of human rights: a system in need of reform

*Virginia Mantouvalou and Panayotis Voyatzis*[*]

## 1 Introduction

Having been founded by ten countries in 1949, the Council of Europe is the oldest regional human rights organisation in Europe.[1] Its aim at its inception was to achieve greater unity between Member States in the aftermath of the Second World War, to protect and promote their common heritage and to facilitate their socio-economic progress.[2] Today both the composition and the purposes of the organisation have changed. Membership increased greatly following the fall of communism in Central and Eastern Europe, with the organisation now comprising 47 Member States.[3]

In recognition of the expansion of membership and the changing needs of Europe, a 'source of immense hope'[4] in the words of European Heads of State, there have been three Summits to reconsider the Council's evolving aims in recent years. Several declarations and action plans have been adopted, stating the new political purposes and ways to pursue them. In 1993 the Council of

---

[*] The views expressed in this text are solely those of the co-author and do not represent those of the European Court of Human Rights or any other institution. An early draft was presented in the context of the Human Rights Lecture Series of the University of Leicester, Centre for European Law and Integration.

[1] The States that established the Council of Europe are Belgium, Denmark, France, Ireland, Italy, Luxembourg, the Netherlands, Norway, Sweden and the United Kingdom.

[2] *Statute of the Council of Europe*, opened for signature 5 May 1949, 87 UNTS 103, art 1 (entered into force 3 August 1949).

[3] These States are: Albania, Andorra, Armenia, Austria, Azerbaijan, Belgium, Bosnia and Herzegovina, Bulgaria, Croatia, Cyprus, Czech Republic, Denmark, Estonia, Finland, France, Georgia, Germany, Greece, Hungary, Iceland, Ireland, Italy, Latvia, Liechtenstein, Lithuania, Luxembourg, Malta, Moldova, Monaco, Montenegro, the Netherlands, Norway, Poland, Portugal, Romania, Russia, San Marino, Serbia, Slovakia, Slovenia, Spain, Sweden, Switzerland, the former Yugoslav Republic of Macedonia, Turkey, Ukraine, and the United Kingdom.

[4] Committee of Ministers, *Vienna Declaration* (1993) Council of Europe <https://wcd.coe.int/ViewDoc.jsp?id=621771&BackColorInternet=9999CC&BackColorIntranet=FFBB55&BackColorLogged=FFAC75> at 13 February 2009.

Europe considered its new goals in the First Summit of Heads of State of the Organisation.[5] The Second Summit in 1997 emphasised the role of human rights and democracy for stability in Europe and declared that democracy, human rights and social cohesion were among the main objectives.[6] Finally in 2005, following the Third Summit, another common action plan restated the importance of these values, and presented the primary concerns of the organisation today, which revolve around issues of security, inclusiveness and citizenship, and co-operation with other international organisations and institutions.[7]

While in various declarations and Summits of Heads of States of the Council of Europe it has been recognised that the aims of the organisation have evolved, it is still fair to say that its most influential documents are those that were adopted early on in its history: the *European Convention on Human Rights*[8] and the *European Social Charter*.[9] These two treaties are generally regarded as effective at regional level and paradigmatic at international level.[10] Are these two instruments still appropriate, in regard to their content and their monitoring, for the new needs of the Council of Europe in light, for example, of the expansion of its membership and the raising of awareness of the system's success amongst Europeans? In the present chapter we present the two major regional human rights treaties, focusing primarily on their monitoring mechanisms, and discuss some key problems and prospects.

## 2  The European Convention on Human Rights

In 1950 the founding States of the Council of Europe adopted the *Convention for the Protection of Human Rights and Fundamental Freedoms* ('the ECHR'

---

[5]  Ibid.

[6]  Committee of Ministers, *Final Declaration* (1997) Council of Europe <https://wcd.coe.int/ViewDoc.jsp?id=856263&BackColorInternet=9999CC&BackColorIntranet=FFBB55&BackColorLogged=FFAC75> at 13 February 2009.

[7]  Ministers' Deputies, *Action Plan* (2005) Council of Europe <http://www.coe.int/t/dcr/summit/20050517_plan_action_en.asp> at 13 February 2009.

[8]  *Convention for the Protection of Human Rights and Fundamental Freedoms*, opened for signature 4 November 1950, 213 UNTS 262 (entered into force 3 September 1953).

[9]  *European Social Charter*, opened for signature 18 October 1961, 529 UNTS 89 (entered into force on 26 February 1965) ('Social Charter').

[10]  L Helfer and A-M Slaughter, 'Toward a Theory of Effective Supranational Adjudication' (1997) 107 *Yale Law Journal* 298. See also D Shelton, 'The Boundaries of Human Rights Jurisdiction in Europe' (2003) 13 *Duke Journal of Comparative and International Law* 95, 147–8.

or 'the Convention').[11] The ECHR entered into force in 1953, stressing in its Preamble that the protection of human rights and fundamental freedoms is one of the ways that will promote unity in Europe, and emphasising the importance of European democratic traditions.

### A   Content and supervision

The ECHR mainly protects civil and political rights, imposing upon Member States obligations to secure these to everyone within their jurisdiction (article 1). It guarantees rights such as the right to life (article 2), the prohibition of torture and inhuman and degrading treatment (article 3), the right to a fair trial (article 6), the right to privacy (article 8) and freedom of expression (article 10). The ECHR also includes certain labour rights, such as the prohibition of slavery and forced and compulsory labour (article 4), the right to form and join a trade union for the protection of workers' interests (article 11). Finally, it protects a handful of entitlements that could be described as socio-economic in separate protocols, such as the right to property and the right to education (first additional Protocol to the ECHR). Individuals can submit an application to the European Court of Human Rights ('ECtHR' or 'the Court') alleging a violation of the ECHR. In addition, there is an inter-state procedure, which has however rarely been used due to its potential political implications.[12]

The ECHR initially established two institutions to monitor compliance with its provisions: the ECtHR and the European Commission on Human Rights ('EComHR' or 'the Commission').[13] In 1998, Protocol 11 abolished the EComHR,[14] which previously examined the admissibility of complaints and attempted to negotiate 'friendly settlements', and left the full-time ECtHR as the sole body responsible for the examination of individual and inter-state complaints under the ECHR.[15] This development made the system entirely judicial and created a single full-time Court.[16]

---

[11] *Convention for the Protection of Human Rights and Fundamental Freedoms*, opened for signature 4 November 1950, 213 UNTS 262 (entered into force 3 September 1953) ('ECHR').

[12] P van Dijk and G J H van Hoof, *Theory and Practice of the European Convention on Human Rights* (Kluwer Law International, The Hague, 1998) 43.

[13] For a detailed presentation of the former and current ECHR procedure see A Mowbray, *Cases and Materials on the European Convention on Human Rights* (Butterworths, London, 2001), Chapter 1.

[14] Protocol No. 11, ETS No. 155 ECHR.

[15] A Drzemczewski, 'The European Human Rights Convention: Protocol No. 11 – Entry into Force and First Year of Application' (2000) 21 *Human Rights Law Journal* 1.

[16] On Protocol No. 11, see also V Berger, '*La Nouvelle Cour Européenne: D'une Jurisprudence à l'autre?*' (Mélanges Pettiti, Bruylant, 1998) 129; G Cohen-Jonathan, 'Le Protocole n° 11 et la Réforme du Mécanisme International de Contrôle

The number of judges of the ECtHR is equal to the number of the Parties to the ECHR.[17] Judges are elected by the Parliamentary Assembly of the Council of Europe to sit for a period of six years with the possibility of re-election. The Court has three types of decision-making bodies: the Committees, the Chambers and the Grand Chamber. The Committees of three judges, established by article 27(1) of the ECHR, deal with clearly inadmissible cases.[18] The Court is divided into five sections and each judge is assigned to one of these sections. A Chamber of seven judges examines a case, which is brought before the Court (if not dealt with by a Committee). The Grand Chamber consists of 17 judges and includes *ex officio* the President, the two Vice Presidents of the Court, the Presidents of the Sections and the national judge. It deals with applications in two situations.[19] First, a Chamber may relinquish jurisdiction in favour of the Grand Chamber when dealing with a case raising a serious question affecting the interpretation of the ECHR or the Protocols.[20] Such cases may involve novel issues that have not already been dealt with by the Court or questions where the decision of a Chamber may contradict a judgment delivered by the Court. The second possibility concerns cases where a Chamber has already issued a judgment, and one or both parties request the referral of the case to the Grand Chamber within a period of three months from the delivery of the judgment. A panel of five judges will examine the request and may accept it if the case raises a serious question affecting the interpretation or application of the ECHR or the Protocols thereto, or a serious issue of general importance.[21] The Grand Chamber may also give advisory opinions on questions concerning the interpretation of the ECHR and its Protocols.[22] The Court deals with every case free of charge.

The ECtHR is generally considered to be one of the most effective international human rights monitoring bodies.[23] Yet the specificities pertaining to the

---

de la Convention Européenne des Droits de l'Homme' (*Europe*, Chronl, 1994) No 8; A Drzemczewsky and Meyer-Ladewig, 'Principales Caractéristiques du Nouveau Mécanisme de Contrôle Etabli par la Cour Européenne des Droits de l'Homme suite au Protocole n° 11' in *Révue Universelle des Droits de l'Homme* (1994) 83.

[17] Article 20 ECHR.
[18] Article 35 ECHR.
[19] See also Council of Europe, *Chapter VII of the Rules of Court* (2008) European Court of Human Rights <http://www.echr.coe.int/NR/rdonlyres/D1EB31A8-4194-436E-987E-65AC8864BE4F/0/RulesOfCourt.pdf> at 17 February 2009.
[20] Article 30 ECHR.
[21] Article 43(2) ECHR.
[22] Articles 47–9 ECHR.
[23] For an interesting analysis, see University of Leeds, School of Law, *Centre for International Governance – Annual Report 2007* (University of Leeds, 2007) <http://www.law.leeds.ac.uk/LeedsLaw/GenericPage.aspx?ID=250&TabID=4&MenuID=42&SubMenuID=141> at 17 February 2009.

effects of its judgments and the supervision of their execution stress the inherent limitations of the international protection of human rights that involve remedies and compliance. In principle, the judgments of the ECtHR are declaratory in nature.[24] When a violation of the ECHR is established, the victim is awarded just satisfaction that may include compensation for both pecuniary and non-pecuniary damage.[25] The Court traditionally declines to impose upon States a duty to adopt general measures of reparation, such as the amendment of the impugned legislation or judicial practice. However, during the last few years, in numerous cases where the Court has found a breach of the ECHR, it has not only declared that the ECHR was violated, but has also imposed on the respondent State an obligation of *restitutio in integrum*,[26] by indicating the general or individual measures to be taken in the domestic legal order so as to restore as far as possible the situation existing before the breach of the ECHR.[27] Moreover the Court may, in a judgment, comment on the failure of a member State to implement specific measures to amend a law or address a practice found to be contrary to the ECHR in previous judgments.[28]

The Court does not interfere with the process of execution after a judgment has been delivered. The Committee of Ministers of the Council of Europe ('Committee of Ministers'), which is a political body, supervises state compliance by way of a mechanism involving resolutions where appropriate.[29] It ensures that, following a judgment finding a violation, the respondent State will adopt individual and general measures that will lead to the effective implementation of the judgment. Individual measures primarily consist of the payment of the amount that has been awarded by way of satisfaction and, eventually, the enforcement of specific measures that will put an end to the unlawful situation that has given rise to the violation of the ECHR. General

---

[24] *Assanidze v Georgia*, Application No 71501/1 (Unreported, European Court of Human Rights, Grand Chamber, 8 April 2004) 202.
[25] Article 41 ECHR.
[26] See P Leach, *Taking a Case to the European Court of Human Rights* (Oxford University Press, Oxford, 2005) 94.
[27] See also *Scozzari and Giunta v Italy*, Application No 39221/98; 41963/98 (Unreported, European Court of Human Rights, 13 July 2000); *Menteş and others v Turkey (Article 50)*, Application No. 23186/94, (Unreported, European Court of Human Rights, 24 July 1998) 24; *Maestri v Italy*, Application No 39748/98 (Unreported, European Court of Human Rights, 17 February 2004) 47; *Görgülü v Germany*, Application No 74969/01 (Unreported, European Court of Human Rights, 26 February 2004) 64; *Ilaşcu and Others v Moldova*, Application No 48787/99 (Unreported, European Court of Human Rights, 8 July 2004) 490.
[28] *Messina v Italy No. 2*, Application No 25498/94 (Unreported, European Court of Human Rights, 28 September 2000) 81–2.
[29] Article 46 ECHR.

measures focus on the prevention of future violations of the ECHR due to the problem that led to its breach in the first place.[30] Sanctions for non-compliance cannot be imposed; political pressure, however, and further political implications that stem from non-compliance are important means of ensuring compliance with the judgments of the Court.

## B  The Court's workload and Protocol No. 14

The system of protection of human rights under the ECHR is generally considered to be paradigmatic in international human rights law: governments tend to comply with the decisions that establish a breach of the ECHR, while national and other international decision-making bodies frequently cite the case law of the ECtHR.[31] Yet, today the Court faces a constantly increasing caseload, which has set the ECHR system a challenge without precedent. Just a glance at the figures reveals the scale of the problem: between 1955 and 1982 the Court received 22,000 applications, an average of 800 cases per year. At the end of 2007 the Court's backlog was more than 100,000 cases, of which almost 80,000 were pending before a decision body. What is particularly alarming is that the Court's backlog continued to increase, despite the fact that, in 2006 and 2007, it managed to increase its output by 25 per cent compared with the number of cases disposed of in 2005.[32] Moreover, the entry into force of Protocol No. 12 in 2005,[33] containing a free-standing prohibition of discrimination,[34] may further exacerbate the Court's current predicament; it is estimated that the effective implementation of Protocol No. 12 is likely to increase the Court's caseload by 30 per cent.[35]

The gradual increase of applications, particularly from the late 1990s onwards, may be attributed to two main factors. The first and most important one is the enlargement of the Council of Europe to the East since 1989. This

---

[30]  Leach, above n 26, 101.
[31]  See G Cohen-Jonathan and J-F Flauss (eds), *Le rayonnement international de la jurisprudence de la Cour européenne des droits de l'homme* (Nemesis-Bruylant, Brussels, 2005).
[32]  1560 and 1503 in 2006 and 2007, respectively, compared to 1105 in 2005 and 718 in 2004. In addition, in 2007 the ECtHR dealt with an unprecedented number of requests for interim measures (article 39 of the Rules of the Court), over 1,000 in total. See also Council of Europe, *Statistical information by year* (2009) European Court of Human Rights <http://www.echr.coe.int/ECHR/EN/Header/Reports+and+Statistics/Statistics/Statistical+information+by+year/> at 17 February 2009.
[33]  Protocol No. 12, ECHR, ETS No 177 (entered into force on 1 April 2005).
[34]  Article 14 ECHR is not a free-standing provision, but only prohibits discrimination in the enjoyment of other ECHR rights.
[35]  L Caflisch, 'The Reform of the European Court of Human Rights: Protocol No. 14 and Beyond' (2006) 6 *Human Rights Law Review* 405.

expansion of membership doubled the number of Contracting Parties to the ECHR, with some of the former communist states overfeeding the Court with new applications. It is significant to stress that five out of the 47 current Member States of the ECHR – Russia, Romania, Turkey, Poland and Ukraine – generate more than half of the Court's caseload.[36] This may be due to the fact that the domestic legal orders of these Member States present deep structural deficiencies that generate recurring violations of the ECHR. The second factor that has led to the increase in applications is the widening awareness in 'old' Member States of the machinery of the ECHR and of the fact that Governments comply with the decisions of the Court not only by compensating the applicants, but also by amending their legislation and taking further necessary and appropriate measures, when found in breach of the Convention.[37]

Two categories of cases have contributed significantly to the increase of the caseload of the Court. The first category of cases are the so-called 'committee cases', that is, all applications that are declared inadmissible either as manifestly ill-founded or because they do not fulfil one of the conditions of admissibility prescribed by article 35 of the ECHR.[38] Committee cases represent more than 90 per cent of all applications lodged with the Court. The problem that they pose to the ECHR machinery is that they occupy much of the time of the Registry and the Court, despite their lesser importance. As a consequence, there is little time to deal adequately with 'chamber cases', that is, cases that will lead to a decision on the admissibility or a judgment.

The second category of cases are the so-called 'clone cases', a term which describes all 'cookie cutter' applications that derive from the same structural cause within the internal legal order of a Member State (for example, cases concerning length of proceedings against Italy)[39] that has already led to a judgment by the Court finding a breach of the ECHR. Again, a glimpse at the figures illustrates the problem. In 2003, some 17,000 cases were declared inadmissible by the Court, which published 700 judgments. About 60 per cent

---

[36] Drzemczewski, above n 15, 404.
[37] M A Beernaert, 'Protocol 14 and New Strasbourg Procedures: Towards Greater Efficiency? And at What Price?' (2004) 5 *European Human Rights Law Review* 544.
[38] Article 35 prescribes certain admissibility criteria for an application and defines conditions in which an application would be inadmissible: (a) all domestic remedies must have been exhausted; (b) application must be made within six months of the final decision in domestic courts; (c) application must not be anonymous and (d) application must not be substantially similar to a matter already examined by the Court or by another international investigative body.
[39] See among others *Scordino v Italy (No. 1)* [GC], Application No 36813/97 (Unreported, European Court of Human Rights, 29 March 2006).

of these judgments concerned clone cases, which indicates that, notwithstanding that one or several judgments declared a violation stemming from a structural problem, the relevant Member State concerned failed to take the appropriate measures to tackle it.

The problem created by this type of case may be addressed by taking two steps. First, the principle of subsidiarity – expressed through the rule of the exhaustion of domestic remedies – should be more effectively implemented at national level, which means that rights and freedoms enshrined in the ECHR must primarily be protected domestically. National systems should have primary responsibility to prevent and effectively redress alleged violations. In this way the domestic legal orders of Member States would alleviate the task of the Court by reducing the number of well-founded applications, and at the same time, when such applications reached the Court, the availability of well-reasoned judgments by national courts would make the adjudication procedure easier. Secondly, effective and prompt measures should be taken with regard to the effective execution of judgments, in order to reduce the number of repetitive cases and give the Court the ability to prioritise judgments that identify a structural problem capable of generating a significant number of repetitive cases.[40]

The increase in the caseload led to the adoption of Protocol No. 14,[41] which aims at enhancing the effectiveness of the ECtHR by providing it with new procedural tools that promote a degree of flexibility. At the time of writing, this Protocol is not yet in force. The changes introduced by Protocol No. 14 are aimed at maintaining the effectiveness of the judicial mechanism of the ECHR without undermining the unique character of its control system. The changes attempt to reduce the time spent by the Court on clearly inadmissible or repetitive applications, and to enable it to concentrate on cases that raise more important issues of human rights. They involve three main areas. First, regarding the filtering of manifestly ill-founded cases, a single judge – instead

---

[40] W Vandenhole, 'Execution of Judgments' in P Lemmens and W Vandenhole (eds) *Protocol No. 14 and the Reform of the European Court of Human Rights* (Intersentia, Antwerp, 2005) 114.

[41] Protocol No. 14, ECHR, ETS No 194, adopted in 13 May 2004, but not yet entered into force. On this see S Greer, 'Reforming the European Convention on Human Rights: Towards Protocol 14' (2003) *Public Law* 663, and 'Protocol 14 and the Future of the European Court of Human Rights' (2005) *Public Law* 83. For an extensive analysis of the issues by the same author, see *The European Convention on Human Rights – Achievements, Problems and Prospects* (Cambridge University Press, Cambridge, 2006) 192. See also Lord Woolf and other experts, *Review of the Working Methods of the European Court of Human Rights* (European Court of Human Rights, Strasbourg, 2005) at <http://www.echr.coe.int/ECHR/Resources/Home/LORDWOOLFREVIEWONWORKINGMETHODS.pdf> at 17 February 2009.

of the current committee composed of three judges – will be competent to declare inadmissible or strike out an individual application. The single judge will be assisted by a member of the Registry of the Court in examining the unmeritorious applications.[42] Second, regarding repetitive cases, the competence of the committee of three judges will be extended to cover clone cases. The committees will be empowered to rule in a simplified procedure not solely on the admissibility of the case but on the merits as well, when the underlying question has already been addressed in well-established case law of the Court.[43] Third, the Court is given more latitude to rule simultaneously on the admissibility and the merits of individual applications. Joint decisions therefore will become the norm, though the Court is still free to decide separately the admissibility and the merits. A further aim of the Protocol is to reinforce cooperation between the Committee of Ministers and the Court. The former may decide by a two-thirds majority to bring proceedings before the Grand Chamber against a Member State that refuses to comply with a final judgment of the Court. The Grand Chamber will then be asked to decide whether the Contracting Party has fulfilled its obligations under the ECHR. The Committee of Ministers may also, in certain circumstances, be able to request the Court to give an interpretation of a judgment.[44] Finally, friendly settlements are encouraged at any stage of the proceedings and the Committee of Ministers will supervise their execution.[45]

Probably the most important modification introduced by Protocol 14, though, and the one that has given rise to significant academic debate, is a new admissibility criterion to be inserted in article 35 of the ECHR by Article 12 of the Protocol.[46] According to this provision, the Court will be able to declare inadmissible applications where the applicant has not suffered a *significant disadvantage*. No case may be rejected on this ground, however, if the matter

---

[42] P Lemmens, 'Single-judge Formations, Committees, Chambers and Grand Chamber' in P Lemmens and W Vandenhole (eds), *Protocol No. 14 and the Reform of the European Court of Human Rights* (Intersentia, Antwerp, 2005) 31.

[43] Ibid 35.

[44] Vandenhole, above n 40, 112. The Court will be empowered to specify the obligation of a Member State, with regard to individual or general measures to be taken, following a judgment of the ECHR finding a violation of the Convention.

[45] F Ang and E Berghmans, 'Friendly Settlements and Striking out of Applications' in P Lemmens and W Vandenhole (eds), *Protocol No. 14 and the Reform of the European Court of Human Rights* (Intersentia, Antwerp, 2005) 89.

[46] See M A Beernaert, 'Protocol 14 and New Strasbourg Procedures: Towards Greater Efficiency? And at What Price?' (2004) 5 *European Human Rights Law Review* 544; X-B Ruedin, 'De *minimis non curat* the European Court of Human Rights: The Introduction of a New Admissibility Criterion Article 12 of Protocol No. 14' (2008) 1 *European Human Rights Law Review* 80.

requires an examination on the merits in terms of human rights, or if the matter has not been considered by a domestic court. These two safeguard clauses provide the guarantee that the *de minimis* clause will not be applied as a *carte blanche*.[47] The first clause guarantees that the financial subject matter of the case is not the sole ground on which the Court may reject a complaint, which means that the Court may still examine the merits of a case involving an important question on the applicability of the ECHR even if any financial loss is insignificant. The second safeguard clause reflects the principle of subsidiarity, which implies that every case should necessarily receive a judicial examination at domestic level. The *de minimis* clause is important, if considered in a prospective way: it endows the Court with some degree of flexibility in view of the caseload. As it is very likely that the number of applications will continue to increase in the future, a 'safety valve' is necessary in order to pre-empt the paralysis of the Court. The extent to which this safeguard will be used depends on the caseload, the efficiency of the execution of the judgments, the handling of repetitive cases, and the quality of the implementation of the ECHR at national level.

This new admissibility criterion provoked intense controversy during the drafting process of Protocol No. 14, primarily because it does not merely entail a procedural element but concerns fundamental issues pertaining to the primary goals and purposes of the ECtHR.[48] It restricts in principle the scope of judicial protection, and in this way involves the mission and the nature of the Court, as the fundamental rule that *every* victim of *any* violation of the ECHR can expect from the Court to obtain vindication of his or her infringed right no longer prevails. It is up to the Court to preserve in principle the right of individual petition and expand its effectiveness.[49] At this stage, it can only be said that the interpretation of this admissibility criterion will depend in reality on the vision of the nature of the Court that will prevail in the controversy between those that are proponents of the 'individual' justice model and those that are proponents of a 'constitutional' one[50] – two notions that will be discussed below.

---

[47] F Vanneste, 'A New Admissibility Ground' in P Lemmens and W Vandenhole (eds) *Protocol No. 14 and the Reform of the European Court of Human Rights* (Intersentia, Antwerp, 2005) 69, 73–5.
[48] P Sardaro, 'The Right of Individual Petition to the European Court' in P Lemmens and W Vandenhole (eds) *Protocol No. 14 and the Reform of the European Court of Human Rights* (Intersentia, Antwerp, 2005) 45, 51.
[49] Ibid 67–8.
[50] See C Hioureas, 'Behind the Scenes of Protocol No 14: Politics in Reforming the European Court of Human Rights' (2006) 24 *Berkley Journal of International Law* 755–7.

Before concluding this section, it is important to note that in May 2009 the Committee of Ministers adopted Protocol 14 bis, aiming to increase the short-term capacity of the Court to process applications, pending entry into force of Protocol 14. This new Protocol allows the immediate application of two procedural elements included in Protocol 14. First, the introduction of the single judge scheme, who will be empowered to reject manifestly inadmissible applications. Second, the extension of the three-judge committees' competence to declare applications admissible and to decide on their merits in well-founded and repetitive cases. These cases are currently dealt with by chambers composed of seven judges. Protocol 14 bis has already come into force and its provisions apply to applications pending before the Court against each of the States for which the Protocol has entered into force. On 10 July 2009, the Court made use of the single Judge procedure for the first time. A total of 146 applications against the United Kingdom, Germany, the Netherlands, Switzerland and Norway, were declared inadmissible.

## 3  The European Social Charter

Despite the recent challenges facing the system of the ECHR, it has been characterised as the 'jewel in the Council of Europe crown', while its counterpart in the area of socio-economic rights, the *European Social Charter* ('the Social Charter' or 'the ESC'), has been presented as an instrument with a 'twilight existence'.[51] The unequal protection of civil and political rights, on the one hand, and economic and social rights, on the other, is not a peculiarity of the Council of Europe framework for the protection of human rights, for the majority of international human rights treaties grant different statuses to the two groups of entitlements.[52] The former group usually enjoys a relatively effective mechanism of supervision, while the latter typically suffers from weak and rather ineffective monitoring. This probably explains why Alston described social rights as 'the poor step-sister'[53] of civil and political rights, and Hepple characterised them as 'paper tigers, fierce in appearance but missing in tooth and claw'.[54]

---

[51]  D J Harris, 'A Fresh Impetus for the European Social Charter' (1992) 41 *International and Comparative Law Quarterly* 659.

[52]  See also A Eide, 'Economic, Social and Cultural Rights as Human Rights' in Eide, Krause and Rosas (eds) *Economic, Social and Cultural Rights – A Textbook* (Martinus Nijhoff, Dordrecht, 2nd ed, 2001) 9. See also M Craven, *The International Covenant on Economic, Social and Cultural Rights – A Perspective on its Development* (Oxford University Press, Oxford, 1995).

[53]  P Alston, 'Assessing the Strengths and Weaknesses of the European Social Charter's Supervisory System' in G de Búrca and B de Witte (eds) *Social Rights in Europe* (Oxford University Press, Oxford, 2005) 45, 47.

[54]  B Hepple, 'Enforcement: The Law and Politics of Cooperation and

## A  Content and supervision

The original Social Charter was adopted in 1961, more than ten years after the ECHR, and entered into force in 1965. It acknowledged in its Preamble that, together with the protection of civil and political rights, Member States of the Council of Europe seek to improve the social well-being and living standards of their populations.[55] The Social Charter set down some key socio-economic guarantees, and a system for their monitoring.

The Social Charter protects rights such as the right to work (article 1), the right to just conditions of work (article 2), the right to organise (article 5), the right to bargain collectively (article 6), the right to protection of health (article 11), the right to social and medical assistance (article 13), the right to benefit from social welfare services (article 14) and the right of migrant workers to protection and assistance (article 19). The Social Charter was later revised to contain a number of new social rights and kept labour rights as its centrepiece. The revised text entered into force in 1999. New rights include the right to take part in the determination and improvement of working conditions and working environment (article 22), the right to protection in cases of termination of employment (article 24) and the right to protection against poverty and social exclusion (article 30). The Revised Social Charter is gradually replacing the 1961 document. Only France and Portugal have accepted all its provisions.

The Social Charter allows Contracting Parties discretion as to the rights by which they will be bound, having to accept at least five out of seven so-called 'core' articles and another ten articles or 45 numbered paragraphs (article 20). In the Revised Social Charter, States have to accept at least six out of the nine core articles and a number of other rights or paragraphs provided that the total number is at least 16 articles or 63 numbered paragraphs (Part III).

The original version of the Social Charter contained no complaints procedure, but only reporting obligations. The European Committee on Social Rights ('the ECSR' or 'the Committee') – formerly the Committee of Independent Experts – did not enjoy the status of a court adopting binding decisions, but only assessed compliance with the Social Charter in its Conclusions.[56] All Reports and Conclusions were examined by a

---

Compliance' in B Hepple (ed) *Social and Labour Rights in a Global Context* (Cambridge University Press, Cambridge, 2002) 238.

[55] *European Social Charter*, opened for signature 18 October 1961, 529 UNTS 89 (entered into force on 26 February 1965) Preamble.

[56] For a detailed account of this jurisprudence, see L Samuel, *Fundamental Social Rights – Case Law of the European Social Charter* (Council of Europe Publishing, Strasbourg, 2002). For an example of the impact of the European Social Charter at national level see K D Ewing, 'Social Rights and Human Rights: Britain and the Social Charter – The Conservative Legacy' (2000) *European Human Rights Law Review* 91.

Governmental Committee, composed of ministerial representatives and attended by representatives of international organisations of employers and employees. The Parliamentary Assembly of the Council of Europe (PACE),[57] which consists of members of Parliament and performs the functions of a deliberative body, gave an opinion, and finally the Committee of Ministers could issue recommendations with a two-thirds majority. This system of supervision was criticised, and the PACE itself stated in a Recommendation in 1986 that it was 'diverted from its original purpose', having gradually 'become a slow procedure involving a confrontation of legal arguments and interpretative theories with which the public [could not] acquaint itself'.[58]

The complexity and slowness of the system, together with the expansion of the Council of Europe after 1989, led to the adoption of the *Turin Amending Protocol* ('the Turin Protocol'),[59] a development widely welcomed by scholars.[60] The Turin Protocol has not yet entered into force, as it has to be ratified by all Member States of the original Social Charter,[61] but some of its provisions have been given effect through a decision of the Committee of Ministers.[62] Under the new system, the reporting procedure is not as slow as it used to be: the Assembly no longer examines Reports and Conclusions, while the Governmental Committee is no longer competent to assess compliance with the Social Charter. Reporting on accepted core provisions has to take place every two years (article 21) and on non-core provisions every four years.[63] The Committee of Ministers, though, maintains its role and has already issued Recommendations relating to non-compliance with the Social Charter.[64] Despite efforts to revitalise the reporting system of the Social

---

[57] *Statute of the Council of Europe*, opened for signature 5 May 1949, 87 UNTS 103, art 1 (entered into force 3 August 1949) Chapter V.

[58] Parliamentary Assembly, Recommendation 1022(1986), entitled 'European Social Charter: A Political Appraisal'.

[59] Protocol amending the European Social Charter, Turin, 21 October 1991.

[60] P Alston, 'The Importance of the Inter-play Between Economic, Social and Cultural Rights, and Civil and Political Rights' in Council of Europe Press (ed) *Human Rights at the Dawn of the 21st Century* (1993) 59, 63. For an analysis of the Protocol see also Harris, above n. 51, 660 and 676.

[61] *European Social Charter*, opened for signature 18 October 1961, 529 UNTS 89 (entered into force on 26 February 1965) Article 8.

[62] Report of the Committee of Ministers, 11 December 1991, 467th meeting.

[63] Decision of the Committee of Ministers, adopted on 24–25 November 1999, reprinted in *European Social Charter – Collected Texts* (Council of Europe Publishing, Strasbourg, 2002), 233. Article 22 provides for further reporting obligations with respect to non-accepted provisions.

[64] See L Betten, 'Committee of Ministers of the Council of Europe Call for Contracting States to Account for Violations of the European Social Charter' (1994) 10 *International Journal of Comparative Labour Law and Industrial Relations* 147.

Charter, there are still significant shortcomings. The belief that socio-economic rights differ significantly from civil and political rights has probably caused the reporting system to remain primarily political rather than judicial, a position that has raised questions about its efficacy and appropriateness as a monitoring mechanism for socio-economic rights.[65]

A further effort to revitalise the Social Charter was the *Collective Complaints Protocol* ('the CCP'),[66] which was adopted in 1995 and entered into force in 1998. The CCP does not contain a right of individual petition, but recognises a right to submit complaints for non-compliance of a contracting state with the Social Charter for some international organisations of employers and employees,[67] national representative organisations of employers and employees and some international non-governmental organisations.[68] The ECSR delivers a decision and, when it finds a violation, the Committee of Ministers issues a recommendation by a majority of two-thirds.[69] While in the system of the ECHR, then, the Committee of Ministers is unable to undermine the decisions of the Court; in the case of the ECSR it may decide to refrain from adopting a recommendation to implement a decision.

The CCP established an 'increasingly judicial' procedure, and gave the ECSR the status of a 'quasi-judicial body', as Brillat argued.[70] The quasi-judicial nature of the CCP procedure was said to be evident in four respects: the adoption of decisions, the adversarial character of the proceedings and their reduced tripartite structure, and finally the publicity of documents. As of October 2008, the ECSR has received 53 collective complaints. It has examined 42 of them on the merits, and has frequently found the respondent states in breach of their duties under the Social Charter. Interesting decisions include

---

[65] Tonia Novitz, 'Remedies for Violation of Social Rights within the Council of Europe: The Significant Absence of a Court' in Kilpatrick, Novitz and Skidmore (eds) *The Future of Remedies in Europe* (Hart Publishing, Oxford, 2000) 231.

[66] *Additional Protocol to the European Social Charter Providing for a System of Collective Complaints*, ETS No. 158 (entered into force 7 January 1998). For a detailed presentation of collective complaints under the CCP see R Churchill and U Khaliq, 'The Collective Complaints System of the European Social Charter: An Effective Mechanism for Ensuring Compliance with Economic and Social Rights?' (2004) 15 *European Journal of International Law* 417.

[67] Article 2 CCP.

[68] As of 2007, only Finland recognised a right to lodge a collective complaint to NGOs. See Council of Europe, *Monitoring of Commitments Concerning Social Rights* (2007) Parliamentary Assembly, Recommendation 1795 http://assembly.coe.int/Documents/WorkingDocs/Doc08/EDOC11635.pdf at 17 February 2009.

[69] Article 9 CCP.

[70] R Brillat, 'The Supervisory Machinery of the European Social Charter: Recent Developments and their Impact' in G de Búrca and B de Witte (eds) *Social Rights in Europe* (Oxford University Press, Oxford, 2005) 31, 34.

*European Roma Rights Centre v Italy*,[71] where the Committee concluded that Italy was in breach of the right to housing of the Roma population, together with the prohibition of discrimination, and *World Organisation Against Torture v Belgium*,[72] where the lack of effective legislation banning corporal punishment of children was held to be contrary to the protection of children.

Although there have been continuous efforts to strengthen the protection of social rights in Europe, scholars have been sceptical about the contribution of the Council of Europe, with Tonia Novitz arguing, for instance, that through its system of protection of human rights the Council of Europe not only 'took its position in the ideological battlefield of the Cold War' but also 'set an important trend in the discourse of international human rights'.[73] How can this position be explained?

First, the differences between the two major instruments of the Council of Europe, the ECHR and the Social Charter, are striking. Membership of the Council of Europe is conditional upon adherence to the ECHR and compliance with the decisions of the ECtHR, while the Social Charter does not contain any similar obligation. States enjoy a unique degree of flexibility in the obligations undertaken under the Social Charter, which allows them discretion as to the rights by which they will be bound. There is no similar flexibility under the ECHR, where, under article 1, States undertake a duty to 'secure to everyone within their jurisdiction the rights and freedoms defined in Section I of this Convention'.[74] The wording of the substantive rights of the Social Charter is weak, making its provisions appear more like aspirations, rather than fully justiciable rights. Under article 11, for instance, Contracting Parties undertake 'with a view to ensuring the effective exercise of the right to protection of health ... to take appropriate measures ... to remove as far as possible the causes of ill-health'. Part I, similarly, regards Social Charter provisions 'as the aim of their policy'. The qualified wording of these provisions starkly contrasts with article 2 of the ECHR, for example, according to which '[e]veryone's right to life shall be protected by law' or article 8, which states: '[e]veryone has the right to respect for his private and family life, his home and his correspondence.'

---

[71] *European Roma Rights Centre v Italy*, Complaint No. 27/2004 (Unreported, decision on the Merits of 7 December 2005).
[72] *World Organisation Against Torture v Belgium*, Complaint No. 21/2003 (Unreported, decision on the Merits of 26 January 2005).
[73] Novitz, above n 65, 232–5.
[74] States can make a reservation to a provision of the ECHR, in accordance with the provisions of Section II of the *Vienna Convention on the Law of Treaties*, opened for signature 23 May 1969, 1155 UNTS 331 (entered into force 27 January 1980). In addition, they can choose amongst the Protocols of the ECHR, and are not under a duty to sign and ratify them all.

In addition, the personal scope of the Social Charter is surprisingly narrow. While ECHR rights are guaranteed to *everyone* within a State's jurisdiction,[75] economic and social rights of non-nationals are minimally protected under both the original text of the Social Charter and its revised version. The Appendix to the Social Charter under the title *Scope of the Social Charter in Terms of Persons Protected* states that:

> Persons covered by Articles 1 to 17 include foreigners only insofar as they are nationals of other Contracting Parties lawfully resident or working regularly within the territory of the Contracting Party concerned, subject to the understanding that these Articles are to be interpreted in the light of the provisions of Articles 18 and 19.[76]

A similar provision is to be found in subsequent protocols and revised versions of the Social Charter. This makes most of the safeguards of the document irrelevant to all residents and lawfully employed persons who are citizens of non-European States.[77]

The CCP system is a promising development, as it reflects a belief that socio-economic entitlements are justiciable. Still, its effectiveness has been questioned for a number of reasons. First, the ECSR relies upon draft conclusions prepared by permanent staff of the organisation in the context of the reporting procedure, and the Recommendations are scrutinised by the Committee of Ministers.[78] The role of the Committee of Ministers, it has been said, 'is a strong reminder both of the fact that governments remain extremely sensitive in relation to social rights and that the autonomy accorded to the ECtHR under the Protocol 11 reforms is a far cry from the continuing second-guessing role retained by governments under the ESC system'.[79] The assumption that a system of collective complaints rather than an individual petition is more appropriate to violations of social rights, evident also through the Explanatory Report to the CCP, which states that individual situations may be declared inadmissible by the ECSR, has raised

---

[75] Article 1 ECHR.

[76] *European Social Charter*, opened for signature 18 October 1961, 529 UNTS 89 (entered into force on 26 February 1965), article 18 provides for the right to engage in gainful occupation in other Contracting States, and article 19 guarantees the right of migrant workers and their families to protection and assistance.

[77] On this see J-F Akandji-Kombe, 'The Material Impact of the Jurisprudence of the European Committee on Social Rights' in G de Búrca and B de Witte (eds), *Social Rights in Europe* (Oxford University Press, Oxford, 2005) 89, 94–9.

[78] Alston, above n 53, 59.

[79] Ibid 65. For criticism of the role of the Committee of Ministers, see also Churchill and Khaliq, above n 66, 455.

further questions and criticism.[80] These drawbacks led to the characterisation of the CCP as 'hardly radical, and the Council of Europe less than enthusiastic' in its approach to the enforcement of social rights.[81]

## 4 Future steps in the protection of human rights in Europe
The protection of civil, political, economic and social rights in Europe has set an important trend in the international and regional systems of human rights. Yet, as suggested above, both systems face challenges and shortcomings that must be addressed.

### A The ECHR: a need for further reform
The aim of Protocol 14 of the ECHR, which was presented earlier in this chapter, was to permit the ECtHR to handle the constantly increasing caseload more efficiently. Its swift implementation would seem essential in order to improve the ability of the Court to deal with the constant flood of applications so as to guarantee the effectiveness of individual petition, a mechanism that lies at the heart of the Strasbourg system. However, the amendments introduced cannot relieve the machinery of the ECHR in the long run. This is mainly due to the fact that the changes are mainly procedural and not substantive. They focus on the re-organisation of committees and chambers in order to allow the Court to speed up the processing of cases and improve in this way its overall performance. In addition, it is doubtful if and when Protocol 14 will be operational. To enter into force, all Member States must ratify it. By the end of 2008, all Member States except for the Russian Federation had ratified that Protocol. Russia's ongoing refusal to ratify the Protocol creates significant operational problems for the Court[82] and may soon render it futile. The organisational tools offered to the Court enabling it to survive in the short term may soon seem obsolete as they may be overtaken by reality.[83]

Notwithstanding the issues raised by the entry into force of Protocol 14, a larger reform containing more radical solutions will probably be necessary in

---

[80] Tonia Novitz, 'Are Social Rights Necessarily Collective Rights?' (2002) *European Human Rights Law Review* 50.
[81] H Cullen, 'The Collective Complaints Mechanism of the European Social Charter' (2000) 25 *European Law Review, Human Rights Survey* 18, 29.
[82] M O'Boyle, 'On Reforming the Operation of the European Court of Human Rights' (2008) 1 *European Human Rights Law Review* 4. See also A Mowbray, 'Faltering Steps on the Path to Reform of the Strasbourg Enforcement System' (2007) 7 *Human Rights Law Review* 610–11.
[83] The yearly input of applications constantly exceeds the Court's output of finally disposed-of cases. See also European Court of Human Rights, *Annual Report 2007* (2008) <http://www.echr.coe.int/ECHR/EN/Header/Reports+and+Statistics/Reports/Annual+Reports)> at 17 February 2009.

the near future, in order to guarantee the long-term effectiveness of the control system of the ECHR. Indeed, this question is already being discussed. Further reforms were envisaged by a Group of Wise Persons (GWP), established in May 2005 by the Heads of State and Government of the Council of Europe, a development that revealed the realisation that it was time for the Court to reflect on the need to redefine the scope and role of individual petition for the years to come.

The main idea lying behind the proposals of the GWP is that it is essential to transform the current Court into a smaller and more flexible judicial mechanism that will be better able to allocate its resources on meritorious cases and leave aside 'a whole body of litigation which places an unnecessary burden on it'.[84] The GWP report formulates key proposals that can ensure the long-term effectiveness of the Court. Indeed, some of the proposals included in the report should already serve as the basis for discussion on further changes for a new Protocol. That is all the more true if one takes into account that the proposals of the GWP relied on the assumption that Protocol 14 would have already come into force in 2007, and that the processing of cases would have already been accelerated.[85]

There are two categories of measures in the GWP report that appear necessary for the drastic improvement of the Court: first, measures aiming to introduce elements of constitutional justice into the judicial mechanism of Strasbourg, and secondly, measures focusing on the effective internalisation of the ECHR in domestic legal orders. The establishment of a smaller judicial mechanism and the possibility to deliver 'judgments of principle' may enhance the 'constitutionalisation' of the judicial mechanism. The GWP proposes to set up a judicial filtering body[86] that would deliver decisions on manifestly ill-founded and manifestly well-founded applications, namely cases that give rise to questions on which the Court has developed case law. In short, the new judicial body will deal with cases that do not raise any novel questions of law by taking over the function of the Committees of three judges and the formations of single judges, as they are established by

---

[84] Ministers' Deputies, *Report of the Group of Wise Persons to the Committee of Ministers, CM(2006)203* (2006), Note 125.

[85] Ibid, see Note 33 of the report: 'The Group expects Protocol No. 14 to be rapidly implemented. It takes this protocol as a starting point. Its proposals go further than the protocol and are designed to ensure that the Court is able to perform its specific functions fully and on a long-term basis.' See also O'Boyle, above n 82, 5. The author notes that 'the reforms envisaged by the Wise Persons group are predicated on the assumption that Protocol No. 14 will actually be in operation so that government experts and others will be in a position to make a proper assessment of the effects of the operation of the Protocol and to formulate their proposals accordingly'.

[86] Ibid, a 'Judicial Committee' as it is labelled by the GWP report.

Protocol 14.[87] The role of this body will relieve the Court of a considerable number of cases, while guaranteeing that every individual application will result in a judicial decision. This proposal does not aim to create a judicial body separate from the Court, but promotes the establishment of a filter that would function under the authority of the latter.[88] It is therefore suggested by the GWP that each application should first be examined by the Registry of the Court, before being referred to the Judicial Committee. Moreover, the latter will have the competence to refer a case to the Court if it raises particular admissibility or substantive issues. On the other hand, the Court could also refer a case to the Committee if it considers that it falls within the latter's jurisdiction.[89]

With regard to the controversial issue of the possibility for the Court to adopt 'judgments of principle',[90] the GWP attempts to reconcile the double nature of supervision: the role of providing individual and constitutional justice. The report supports the idea of establishing a system under which constitutional courts or courts of last instance in the Member States could apply to the ECtHR for an advisory opinion on the interpretation of the ECHR, and proposes that in that case the Court would be empowered to refuse to answer a request for an opinion without giving reasons for its refusal. These advisory opinions would not be binding.[91]

Redefining the ability of the Court to depart from the principle of 'declaratory judgments' and redesigning the supervisory system of the Council of Europe are two necessary steps in order to achieve an effective internalisation of the case law. The GWP report contains several proposals, such as the consolidation of 'pilot judgments' and the improvement of domestic remedies, in order to identify and tackle underlying systemic problems within the domestic legal orders.[92] The idea behind the introduction of 'pilot judgments'

---

[87] Mowbray, above n 82, 614–15.
[88] GWP report, above n 84, note 57.
[89] Ibid [59, 61–2]. The idea of a judicial body that would function as a breakwater, protecting the Court from the full impact of the applications' flood, is not novel. In fact, it is a recurring proposal that started circulating in the Court's corridors not long after Protocol 11 came into force. Thus, the evaluation group charged with considering post-Protocol 11 reforms suggested in 2001 the setting up of a new division of 'Assessors' that would function within the Court and would focus on the preliminary examination of applications. See also A Mowbray, 'Beyond Protocol 14' (2006) 6 *Human Rights Law Review*, 578–84.
[90] Mowbray, above n 82, 611–12. On this issue see also S Greer, *The European Convention on Human Rights: Achievements, Problems and Prospects* (Cambridge University Press, Cambridge, 2006) 192.
[91] GWP report, above n 84, notes 81, 82 and 135.
[92] Ibid, notes 87–93 and 100–105.

is that a significant number of cases that lead to the docket crisis are generated by the existence of structural problems in domestic legal orders. In this way the Court should be empowered to identify, in the context of one individual case, the existence of a systemic problem and indicate in the operative part of the judgment, general measures that can be taken by the Member State concerned so as to find an appropriate solution.[93] The GWP report does not make any specific proposals on this issue.[94] It declares its support for the 'pilot-judgment procedure' and expresses some concern on the need to amend the existing rules of procedure to allow this model to produce full results.[95]

In the second part of the proposals, namely measures aiming at the improvement of domestic remedies for redressing violations of the rights enshrined in the ECHR, the focus is primarily on the problem of length of proceedings in civil, criminal and administrative cases. The GWP noted that this 'is one of the main sources of litigation before the Court', as 60 per cent of judgments delivered to date concern length of judicial proceedings.[96] This category of cases originates in systemic problems in the context of the domestic legal orders that can be dealt with effectively only through the introduction of the appropriate domestic legislative measures.

That the procedural amendments brought by Protocol 14 are urgently required is beyond doubt. It is also true that the GWP report proposes key reforms essential to guarantee the long-term effectiveness of the judicial mechanism of the ECHR. Nevertheless, the ability of the Court to allocate its resources efficiently in order to manage the growing backlog of cases is not limitless. Today, more than ever, the political will of Member States to implement the changes introduced by Protocol 14 and the endorsement of the measures suggested by the GWP report are essential conditions for maintaining the quality of the Court's work. There is a consequent pressing need for Member States, first, to offer the Court the necessary resources to increase its

---

[93] O'Boyle, above n 82, 7–8.
[94] GWP report, above n 84, note 105: 'In any event, the Group encourages the Court to use the "pilot judgment" procedure as far as possible in the future.'
[95] The principle of 'pilot judgments' has been introduced by the Court without a prior amendment of the Court's procedure. See *Broniowski v Poland*, Application No 31443/96 (Unreported, European Court of Human Rights, 22 June 2004); *Hutten-Czapska v Poland*, Application No 35014/97 (Unreported, European Court of Human Rights, 22 February 2005).
[96] O'Boyle, above n 82, 6. On this issue see J L Jackson, '*Broniowski v Poland*: a Recipe for Increased Legitimacy of the European Court of Human Rights as a Supranational Constitutional Court' (2006) 39 *Connecticut Law Review* 759. See also V Colandrea, 'On the Power of the European Court of Human Rights to order Specific Non-Monetary Measures: Some Remarks in Light of the *Assanidze, Broniowski* and *Sejdovic* cases' (2007) 7 *Human Rights Law Review* 396.

efficiency in the near future, and, secondly, to deal more effectively with a larger number of applications at the domestic level. Simplifying the amendment process of the ECHR when procedural changes are involved is an additional necessary step in a future reform.[97]

An overall reconsideration of the role of human rights adjudication under the ECHR is essential. A new Protocol should not only deal with procedural issues, namely the re-organisation of the Court so as to increase its output; any future reform should also focus on the profile of the Court as an international judicial institution. The main question to be answered is whether a model of constitutional or individual justice is more appropriate for the protection of human rights in Europe. If individual application is to survive, one should accept that radical reforms will soon be needed to prevent individual petition from becoming a dead letter itself.[98] The new *de minimis* admissibility criterion, the establishment of a filtering judicial body under the authority of the Court, and the consecration of 'pilot judgments' are changes that point in the right direction. However, importantly, European States should confirm their support of the Strasbourg institutions and afford more flexibility to the Court to enable it to accomplish its mission. This is because even the most radical reform of the judicial mechanism will be futile in the long run if not accompanied by the effective implementation of the case law of the Court in domestic legal orders. The internalisation of the Court requires the bolstering of domestic remedies that will be provided to those whose rights enshrined in the Court are violated.

### B  The European Social Charter: shortcomings

While in the context of the Council of Europe civil and political rights and socio-economic rights were initially clearly demarcated and set down in sepa-

---

[97] The GWP took up this question and proposed the introduction of an amendment to the Convention authorising the Committee of Ministers to carry out reforms without an amendment of the Convention being necessary each time. It is to be noted that the procedure of amending the Convention is complex and onerous as it requires the ratification by all contracting parties. See also O'Boyle, above n 82, 6.

[98] J-P Costa, the new President of the Court, has stated in this respect, 'I personally am in favour of the right of individual petition, for which a hard battle had to be fought, and am therefore in favour of retaining it. But let us not shrink from the truth. I have laid too much emphasis in the past on the principle of reality, looking beyond appearances, not to realise now that, without far-reaching reforms – some would say radical reforms – the flood of applications reaching a drowning court threatens to kill off individual petition de facto. In that case, individual petition will become a kind of catoblepas, the animal which, according to ancient fable, used to feed on its own flesh!' (Speech by J-P Costa, on the occasion of the opening of the judicial year on 19 January 2007, quoted by Mowbray, above n 82, 614).

rate instruments, it appears that as early as 1978 discussions were taking place on the possible inclusion of economic, social and cultural rights in the ECHR. A study prepared by the Legal Affairs Committee of the Council of Europe suggested which social, economic and cultural rights might be potentially justiciable and appropriate for inclusion in the ECHR system.[99] More than twenty years later, the Parliamentary Assembly adopted a Recommendation to reaffirm its strong commitment to the effective realisation of economic and social rights and to stress the need to adopt an additional social rights Protocol to the ECHR.[100] 'Economic progress', the Assembly stressed in this context, 'is not concomitant with social progress, but there should be no economic progress without recognition of social progress and social rights.'[101] Although certain social rights are already protected by the ECHR, the Assembly further emphasised, making special mention of articles 4 (prohibition of slavery and forced labour), 8 (right to private and family life), 11 (freedom of association) and 14 (prohibition of discrimination), these guarantees were not adequate. The protection of social rights through the ECtHR was, therefore, presented as a challenge of high priority for the future of the Council of Europe. In the same spirit, in the Third Summit of the Heads of State of the Council of Europe in 2005, it was stated with reference to social cohesion:

> The Council of Europe will step up its work in the social policy field on the basis of the European Social Charter and other relevant instruments. The central task is to jointly define remedies and solutions which could be effective in fighting poverty and exclusion, ensuring equitable access to social rights and protecting vulnerable groups.[102]

Although no European Court for Social Rights has yet been created, the artificial separation between civil and political rights on the one hand and economic and social rights on the other appears to be less acute today than a few decades ago. Recent developments presented earlier in this chapter, both in terms of substantive rights and in their monitoring, show signs of progress in the protection of socio-economic entitlements in Europe. To the efforts to

---

[99] Council of Europe and Legal Affairs Committee, *Document 4213 and Parliamentary Assembly Recommendation 838(1978)*. See J G Jacobs, 'The Extension of the European Convention on Human Rights to Include Economic, Social and Cultural Rights' (1978) III(3) *Human Rights Review* 166.
[100] Council of Europe, Parliamentary Assembly, Recommendation 1415, *Additional Protocol to the European Convention on Human Rights Concerning Fundamental Social Rights* (1999).
[101] Ibid [4].
[102] Minister's Deputies, *Action Plan* (2005) Council of Europe <www.coe.int/t/dcr/summit/20050517_plan_action_en.asp.> at 17 February 2009.

enhance the protection of social rights through amendment of the Social Charter and its monitoring, it is essential to add the recent trend of increasing attention paid by the ECtHR to socio-economic claims in the course of the interpretation of the ECHR. This trend opened up the possibility to implement economic and social rights, or some of their components, through petition procedures of civil and political rights.[103] This interpretive method came to be known as the 'integrated'[104] or 'holistic'[105] approach to human rights. Scholars welcomed this development as another way to give teeth to socio-economic rights by affording them indirect legal effect.[106] In the landmark *Airey v Ireland* judgment, for instance, the Court ruled that

> Whilst the Convention sets down what are essentially civil and political rights many of them have implications of a social and economic nature . . . the mere fact that an interpretation of the Convention may extend into the sphere of social and economic rights should not be a decisive factor against such an interpretation; there is no watertight division separating that sphere from the field covered by the Convention.[107]

In addition, the adoption of the integrated approach in the interpretation of the ECHR presents particular interest in the context of labour rights. On several occasions, the ECtHR took note of the Social Charter and the jurispru-

---

[103] M Scheinin, 'Economic and Social Rights as Legal Rights', in A Eide (ed) *Economic, Social and Cultural Rights: A Textbook* (Kluwer Law International, The Hague, 2001) 29, 32.

[104] The term 'integrated approach' was used by Scheinin above n 103, 32. For an analysis of two aspects of the integrated approach see V Mantouvalou, 'Work and Private Life: *Sidabras and Dziautas v Lithuania*' (2005) 30 *European Law Review* 573. See also I E Koch, 'Social Rights as Components to Personal Liberty: Another Step Forward in the Integrated Human Rights Approach?' (2002) 20 *Netherlands Quarterly of Human Rights* 29, and E Brems, 'Indirect Protection of Socio-economic Rights by the European Court of Human Rights' in D Barak-Erez and A Gross (eds) *Exploring Social Rights* (Hart, Oxford, 2007) 135.

[105] V A Leary, 'Lessons from the Experience of the International Labour Organisation', in P Alston (ed) *The United Nations and Human Rights: A Critical Reappraisal* (Oxford University Press, Oxford 1992) 580, 590.

[106] See also H Collins, '*Employment Law*' (Clarendon Press, Oxford, 2003) 235.

[107] *Airey v Ireland*, Application No 6289/73 (Unreported, European Court of Human Rights, 9 October 1979) [26]. The case involved the alleged violation of the right to a fair trial under article 6 of the ECHR, because of the lack of free legal aid for the applicant who did not have the financial means to access the High Court for her judicial separation from her husband. Other examples of decisions that involved the socio-economic implications of the Convention include environmental cases, such as *Lopez Ostra v Spain*, Application No 16798/90 (Unreported, European Court of Human Rights, 9 December 1994); *Guerra and Others v Italy*, Application No 14967/89 (Unreported, European Court of Human Rights, 19 February 1998).

dence of the ECSR in the interpretation of the provisions when relevant issues were at stake. In *Sidabras and Dziautas v Lithuania*,[108] for instance, whilst examining International Labour Organisation and Social Charter materials that would shed light on the interpretation of the ECHR, the ECtHR stated, reiterating the *Airey* principle:

> Having regard in particular to the notions currently prevailing in democratic States, the Court considers that a far-reaching ban on taking up private sector employment does affect 'private life'. It attaches particular weight in this respect to the text of Article 1(2) of the European Social Charter and the interpretation given by the European Committee of Social Rights ... and to the texts adopted by the ILO ... It further reiterates that there is no watertight division separating the sphere of social and economic rights from the field covered by the Convention.[109]

The indirect protection of social rights insofar as they fall within the scope of some ECHR right and through the machinery of the ECtHR proves that social rights can sometimes become justiciable, in the same way as civil and political rights are already enforceable through courts.[110] However, the adoption of the integrated approach cannot substitute a substantive reform that would aim at a systematic protection of all the rights of the Social Charter, not only those that happen to fall within the scope of some ECHR provision.

Additional issues that ought to be reconsidered involve both the content of the Social Charter and its monitoring. Regarding supervision, a first essential step is the open realisation of the fundamental character of both groups of rights. Social rights are no longer the 'poor step-sister' of civil and political rights nor are they by definition non-justiciable. They are not necessarily collective, contrary to the position that the CCP seems to endorse. The fact that certain labour rights, such as the right to collective bargaining, can only be exercised collectively does not mean that their breach cannot be subject to individual petition. Violations of social rights may affect individuals who need to have access to justice and a voice to be heard, in a manner similar to those

---

[108] *Sidabras and Dziautas v Lithuania*, Application Nos 55480/00 and 59330/00 (Unreported, European Court of Human Rights, 27 July 2004). For an analysis see Mantouvalou, above n 104. See also *Wilson, National Union of Journalists and Others v UK*, Application Nos. 30668/96, 30671/96 and 30678/96 (Unreported, European Court of Human Rights, 2 July 2002). For an analysis of the case, see K.D. Ewing, 'The Implications of *Wilson and Palmer*' (2003) 32 *Industrial Law Journal* 1. A more recent example is *ASLEF v UK*, Application No 11002/05 (Unreported, European Court of Human Rights, 27 February 2007). For an analysis, see K D Ewing, 'The Implications of the *ASLEF* case' (2007) 36 *Industrial Law Journal* 425.

[109] *Sidabras*, above n 108, 47.

[110] The judicial protection of social rights has been discussed at length in academic literature, and is beyond the scope of this chapter. See, generally, Chapter 2.

who suffer violations of civil and political rights. When considering a possible right to individual application, the system of supervision of the Social Charter has no doubt important lessons to learn both from other jurisdictions where social rights have been made enforceable through courts[111] and from the experience of the ECHR, which the present chapter has attempted to present in some detail. Again, the issue of political will and availability of resources to support an effective monitoring process will be a central concern. Yet it is important to appreciate that the artificial separation of rights in categories and generations pertains to Cold War ideologies and does not suit the profile and the aims of an international organisation that promotes a coherent and influential model of justice at the regional level.

Leaving the question of individual petition for alleged violations of social rights aside, other matters that ought to be revisited include the question of the flexibility allowed to Contracting Parties, which are entitled to sign up to only some of the rights of the Social Charter and not all – a provision that is no longer justified. If Member States of the Council of Europe accept that certain socio-economic entitlements are valuable and should be protected in a treaty that contains international obligations, there seems to be no longer any obvious and sustainable reason to allow them a power to choose in an *à la carte* manner only some rights by which they will be bound. Other more traditional methods that serve to modify or limit States' international treaty obligations, such as the use of reservations,[112] may be more suitable in the case of the protection of social rights too; such alternatives will help to dispel the misconception that the protection of civil and political rights and that of economic and social rights differ by definition. One of the important advantages of using reservations, rather than the current system, will be that the monitoring body of the Social Charter will be able to examine the validity of each reservation.[113] Moreover, and more generally, the very wording of the Social Charter should probably be revised to reflect the idea that social rights are no longer

---

[111] For literature on the South African experience of constitutional economic and social rights, see C Scott and P Macklem, 'Constitutional Ropes of Sand or Justiciable Guarantees? Social Rights in a New South African Constitution' (1992–1993) 141 *University of Pennsylvania Law Review* 1. For a more recent assessment of the South African jurisprudence see M Pieterse, 'Possibilities and Pitfalls in the Domestic Enforcement of Social Rights: Contemplating the South African Experience' (2004) 26 *Human Rights Quarterly* 882.

[112] See Article 19ff *Vienna Convention on the Law of Treaties*, opened for signature 23 May 1969, 1155 UNTS 331 (entered into force 27 January 1980).

[113] For an example of the role of reservations in European human rights law, see *Belilos v Switzerland*, Application No 10328/83 (Unreported, European Court of Human Rights, 29 April 1988).

mere aspirations, but fundamental entitlements whose protection lies at the heart of the ideal of justice that the Council of Europe advocates.

Finally, the lacuna in the personal scope of the Social Charter is probably the most urgent matter to address, as it seems to contradict the very essence of human rights law. The illegitimate exclusion of persons whose country of nationality is not a party to the Social Charter contradicts the ideals of equality and dignity that are fundamental values underlying human rights law. Limiting protection to certain individuals, solely on the grounds of their nationality, starkly contrasts with a number of initiatives of the Council of Europe that promote citizenship and social cohesion.[114] This discrepancy rightly led the ECSR to the adoption of the interesting decision *International Federation of Human Rights Leagues v France*,[115] where the lack of access to healthcare for children of illegal immigrants was held to be in breach of the protection of children and young persons, because, on the reasoning of the Committee, to hold otherwise would be in opposition to human dignity, which constitutes one of the Charter's most fundamental underlying values.[116]

## 5 Conclusion

The protection of civil, political, economic and social rights in Europe is one of the key aims of the Council of Europe, as stated in its Statute and frequently reiterated in recent years. Yet for Europe to be the land of hope in terms of the promotion of human rights, as the Heads of States of the Council of Europe declared in 1993,[117] systematic efforts for reform are essential. This chapter has illustrated some of the problems facing the ECHR and the Social Charter, the two most important human rights treaties of this regional organisation, and put forward suggestions on areas that are in need of improvement. While the analysis was not comprehensive, it attempted to expose certain key shortcomings that stem either from historical circumstances or (paradoxically perhaps) from the system's own success. Regarding the ECHR, we placed our primary focus on the need to reconsider the role of the Court and the right to individual petition. As for the Social Charter, we examined the proposition that its monitoring through collective complaints rather than individual petition suits better the protection of economic and social rights. At the same time we emphasised the problems revolving around the personal scope of the Social

---

[114] For an overview of the relevant activities, see Council of Europe, *Directorate General of Social Cohesion (DG III)* (2007) Council of Europe, http://www.coe.int/T/E/Social_cohesion/ at 17 February 2009.
[115] *International Federation of Human Rights Leagues v France*, Complaint No 14/2003 (Unreported, Decision on the Merits of 3 November 2004).
[116] Ibid [30–32].
[117] See above n 4.

Charter, which excludes large groups of foreign nationals, the document's weak wording and the power it offers to states to be bound by some rather than all of the obligations that it encapsulates.

The Council of Europe, a human rights organisation that is paradigmatic at international and regional level, is in need of reform. To maintain its influential role, it is essential to reflect constantly on its evolving aims, the content of the rights that it protects, and the mechanisms by way of which it attempts to safeguard them. Only through constant reform can the system keep up with present-day conditions, maintain the central role that it has gained over the last decades in international human rights law, and further promote unity and justice in Europe and elsewhere.

# 14. The Inter-American human rights system: selected examples of its supervisory work
*Diego Rodríguez-Pinzón and Claudia Martin*

## 1 Introduction

The work of the Inter-American human rights system ('Inter-American system') extends for over 50 years. The Inter-American system emerged with the adoption of the *American Declaration on the Rights and Duties of Man*[1] in April 1948. However, the Inter-American system started, in practice, with the creation of the Inter-American Commission on Human Rights ('the Commission' or 'IACHR') in 1959. In 1969 the Inter-American system adopted the *American Convention on Human Rights* ('American Convention'),[2] and in 1979 it established the Inter-American Court on Human Rights ('the Inter-American Court').

The goal of this chapter is to describe briefly the functions of the Commission and the Inter-American Court and provide some examples on how these organs have addressed human rights violations in regard to English-speaking States. Section 2 focuses on the Commission's powers and functions and contains an overview of the work carried out in monitoring the protection of human rights in the so-called war against terrorism. Section 3 describes the scope of the Inter-American Court's powers and functions within its contentious jurisdiction, and there is a brief review of a group of emblematic human rights issues which the Inter-American Court addresses, in the context of cases arising from English-speaking Caribbean States.

## 2 The Inter-American Commission on Human Rights

### A   The functions and powers of the Inter-American Commission on Human Rights

*(i) Political dimension*   The political dimension of the Commission's

---

[1]   *American Declaration of Rights and Duties of Man*, OAS Doc OEA/Ser.L.V/II.82 Doc 6 Rev 1 at 17 (1992).
[2]   *American Convention on Human Rights*, opened for signature 22 November 1969, 1144 UNTS 123 (entered into force 18 July 1978) ('ACHR') Article 44.

functions and powers refers to its capacity to promote and protect human rights through mechanisms such as negotiation and international pressure on member States to improve human rights conditions. Between the 1960s and the 1980s, the Commission used its political mechanisms primarily to confront massive and systemic violations of human rights, such as forced disappearances of persons, arbitrary executions, and torture. The Commission also periodically used its political authority to publish general reports on human rights situations in various countries, thereby applying pressure on State authorities with poor human rights records. For this reason, individual petitions were not treated in a strict adjudicatory manner. Instead, in many cases, immediate political action served as the most effective method for protecting individuals and instigating changes in the pertinent countries. The Commission did not seek to adjudicate these cases under a strictly judicial analysis, but rather used the individual cases as records to support the demands and urgent petitions of the Commission.

Among the Commission's political mechanisms, several of the Commission's enumerated powers within the Inter-American instruments are included, such as the IACHR's *Statute* ('IACHR Statute') and *Rules of Procedure* ('IACHR Procedures'). According to these documents, the Commission has the authority to take a broad range of actions to confront human rights violations, including 'quiet diplomacy' and public denunciation through press releases and general reports.

(a) On-site visits and special reports   Among the Commission's most important powers is its capacity to conduct on-site visits to investigate or observe a member State's general human rights situation. On-site visits are authorized under Article 18(g) of the IACHR Statute and are regulated according to Articles 51 and 55 of the IACHR Procedures. Typically, the investigations during on-site visits are conducted by obtaining information from non-governmental organizations ('NGOs'), victims, public officials, and other local actors. Importantly, the on-site visits serve a key role in drawing attention to human rights issues, which otherwise might not receive the level of notoriety that is deserved. The Commission, the victims, and other actors are given the opportunity to publicly present their opinions through the media and press releases. Additionally, during the on-site visits, the Commission receives formal complaints from victims and NGOs, holds hearings, and obtains relevant evidence for the individual cases.

Moreover, the Commission also has the authority to publish special reports, perform studies, and make recommendations to the member States.[3] In each of

---

[3]   ACHR Article 41(b), (c) and (d); I/A Commission H.R. IACHR Statute, Article 18(b), (c) and (d).

its Annual Reports, which are published and presented to the General Assembly of the Organization of American States ('OAS'), the Commission includes 'General Reports', which detail the human rights conditions in various States. States are evaluated according to criteria established by the Commission, indicative of human rights situations that merit special attention.[4] The Commission also includes in its Annual Report certain 'Follow-up Reports' and various thematic reports that focus on particular relevant topics in human rights.[5]

The Commission also publishes 'Special Reports', which expose human rights situations in relevant countries and, in some cases, focus on specific human rights issues. The Special Reports differ from the General Reports in that they are separately published, more complete, and more detailed. Additionally, the Special Reports may be issued following an on-site visit and include information from the investigation undertaken during the visit.

(b) <u>Special Rapporteurships, Advisory Powers, and other functions</u>  The Commission has the authority to designate a Special Rapporteur and performs an advisory function. Typically, the Commission designates one of its seven commissioners as Special Rapporteur on a relevant human rights topic. The mandates of the Commission's current Special Rapporteurs include the Rights of Women, Freedom of Expression, and Migrant Workers and their Families, among others.

Article 18(e) of the IACHR Statute provides that member States may present enquiries to the Secretariat of the Commission on human rights issues. In turn, the Commission may provide its advisory services, though it is not mandatory. Member States, however, rarely use this prerogative, preferring to seek Advisory Opinions of the Inter-American Court, due to its greater judicial authority.[6]

Additionally, the Commission has certain powers conferred under the American Convention. These include the power to request Advisory Opinions from the Inter-American Court, the power to request that the Inter-American

---

[4] For a discussion of the criteria, see IACHR, *Annual Report of 2001*, OEA/Ser./L/V/II.114, Doc. 5 rev. (16 April 2002), Chapter IV, 697–8, available at <http://www.cidh.org/annualrep/2001eng/TOC.htm>.

[5] Topics that the Commission has reported on in the past include economic, cultural, and social rights; rights of women; rights of migrant workers; asylum and its relationship to international crimes; rights of persons with mental disabilities; rights of children in armed conflicts; and the compatibility of laws of contempt with the American Convention.

[6] The Inter-American Court has issued 19 Advisory Opinions. The Commission, however, has apparently only received two advisory requests, from Colombia and Peru.

Court take provisional measures in serious and urgent situations in individual cases, and the power to submit to the OAS General Assembly certain protocols to the American Convention in order to gradually include other protected rights in the Inter-American system.

*(ii) Judicial dimension* The judicial dimension of the Commission's functions is manifested in its ability to receive complaints or claims filed against a State. In the past, the Commission exercised its legal function infrequently. However, the consolidation of democratic regimes in the majority of OAS member States is increasingly requiring the Commission to use the individual petition process. Democratic States recognise and enforce human rights through their judicial systems. Hence, this judicial predilection has incited a 'judicialised' approach to international supervision. In effect, its legal functions currently occupy a central place among the Commission's activities.

The Commission processes a considerable and increasing number of individual cases per year, which is demonstrative of the growing demand for international human rights protection. For example, in 2007 the Commission reported that 1,456 petitions were received compared with 681 in 2000 and 718 in 2001.[7] Currently, due to the Commission's limited resources, the average number of decisions issued does not exceed 100 cases per year, and this is of great concern given the importance of this function.

These individual cases are strategically important for activist work conducted by civil society organisations. Each case has an impact that goes beyond the sphere of the case itself, affecting structurally the area of human rights that the petition deals with. Thus, a case processed before the Inter-American system offers victims the possibility of compensation, while simultaneously being the basis of change for domestic norms that are incompatible with human rights standards. These cases have not only an individual and legal effect but also a general political effect.

In accordance with the principles of subsidiarity or complementarity, the States are entrusted with the primary protection of human rights. The national courts, the executive and legislative systems and other domestic bodies are called upon to respect and guarantee the human rights of individuals. International protection (the Commission and the Inter-American Court) is activated only if States fail to protect those rights. Thus, the fundamental objective of the Inter-American system is met when the protection of an individual's human rights is achieved in the national courts.

---

[7] See IACHR, *Petition System and Individual Cases of the 2000 and 2001 Annual Reports*.

## B Brief overview of the individual complaint system before the Commission

*(i) The examination of petitions in the Commission* The mechanism of individual petitions, as mentioned, is gaining importance within the Inter-American system. The Commission examines the petitions pursuant to the procedures established in the American Convention, the IACHR Statute and the Regulations of the Commission. Pursuant to this mechanism, the Commission may publish reports on the outcome of individual cases and may submit cases to the Inter-American Court.

Petitions to the Commission must be presented in written form. The Commission may receive complaints from victims, other individuals or groups, or any NGO.[8] Petitions can also be filed against member States of the OAS that have not ratified the American Convention,[9] claiming violations of rights recognised in the American Declaration.[10] Furthermore, according to Article 45 of the American Convention, States may also file petitions against other States as long as both States expressly recognise the Commission's jurisdiction to hear and determine such cases.

Once a petition is submitted, the Commission will examine the formal admissibility requirements of the communication. If the requirements are met, the Commission will transmit the petition to the State against which the claim is brought, which may present its observations. Ultimately, the Commission will assess an ample variety of evidence in order to make a determination on the merits of the case. The Commission also has certain ancillary functions that it may use under appropriate circumstances. It may adopt preventive measures or protective precautionary measures, and it may facilitate friendly settlement of the claims. The Commission can also hold public hearings, which are broadcast live through the Internet.

*(ii) The admissibility of individual petitions* The admissibility phase is a crucial step in the Commission's proceedings. There are a number of admissibility hurdles that must be overcome before a case will be heard. Indeed, most of the petitions are rejected in this phase.

First, domestic remedies must be 'pursued and exhausted in accordance with generally recognised principles of international law'.[11] That is, attempts must be made to resolve the case under the domestic laws of the State in question before a case will be admissible. However, petitioners are not required to

---

[8] ACHR Article 44.
[9] IACHR Statute Article 20.
[10] ACHR, the US and Canada, among other countries, are subject to this individual complaint procedure.
[11] ACHR Article 46(1)(a).

comply with this rule in cases where: (1) the domestic legislation of the State concerned does not afford due process of law for the protection of alleged human rights violations; (2) the party alleging violation of rights is denied access to the remedies under domestic law or is prevented from exhausting them; or (3) there is unwarranted delay in rendering a final judgment under the aforementioned remedies.[12]

Petitions must be presented within six months following the date of notification of the decision through which domestic remedies were exhausted. If domestic remedies are not exhausted due to the existence of one of the specified exceptions, then the complaint must be presented within a reasonable period of time following the occurrence of the events denounced.

Petitions that are pending before other similar international systems or petitions that substantially reproduce other cases decided or pending before the Commission are not admissible, nor are petitions that are already decided under, or that present a similar claim to cases pending before, another international mechanism.[13]

In addition, petitions may be rejected if manifestly groundless or out of order, due, for example, to an absolute lack of evidence, other evident defects, or inadmissibility generated when new evidence arises.

Petitions must demonstrate violations of the victims' rights; abstract complaints are not permissible.[14] While a case without a victim is inadmissible, the victim does not have to be the one to submit the complaint.[15] The Commission similarly considers inadmissible petitions that allege a violation of the rights of legal entities, such as corporations and NGOs: the American Convention does not protect legal entities. However, under certain circumstances, it is possible to allege that human rights are violated when certain government measures are directed against a legal entity.[16]

Finally, the Commission has developed the 'fourth instance formula' for the purpose of considering cases decided by independent and impartial national courts. The Commission will hold cases inadmissible when there is no evidence of a violation of due process standards or non-discrimination, or

---

[12] ACHR Article 46(2).
[13] ACHR Arts. 46(c) and 47(d) and IACHR Statute Article 33.
[14] ACHR Article 47(b).
[15] Inter-American Court of Human Rights ('IACtHR'), *International Responsibility for the Promulgation and Enforcement of Laws in Violation of the Convention (Arts. 1 and 2 of the American Convention on Human Rights)*, Advisory Opinion OC-14/94 of December 9, 1994, Series A No. 14, [45].
[16] IACHR, *Carvallo Quintana v Argentina*, Annual Report 2001, Report No. 67/01, Case 11.859, Argentina, June 14, 2001, OEA/Ser./L/V/II.114, Doc. 5 rev., April 16, 2002, [56–61].

other human rights violations.[17] Therefore, the Commission may not serve as an appellate court or a 'fourth instance' to review the judgments of national courts simply because the petitioner considers the domestic judgment to be erroneous or unfair.

*(iii) Decision on the Merits: Article 50 and 51 Reports* Petitions that are declared admissible are opened and reviewed by the Commission, which requests observations from the parties for further analysis. The Commission makes a final decision on the case pursuant to Article 50 of the American Convention, which may include recommendations for the respective State. States then have a period (generally from 45 to 90 days) from the date that the Article 50 Report is received to comply with the Commission's recommendations. This report is confidential. If the State concerned does not comply with the Article 50 Report, the Commission has the power to publish its decision (an Article 51 Report) or refer the case to the Inter-American Court (if the State has accepted that body's jurisdiction). Therefore, if the State does not abide by the decision, it risks public condemnation or a judicial decision of the Inter-American Court.

*(iv) Follow-up* A new function that the Commission included in 2001 is the follow-up of compliance with the recommendations incorporated in the Article 51 Reports for each country,[18] justified on the basis of the political mandate of the OAS to improve the systems for the protection of human rights.[19]

The Commission conducts follow-up of cases in relation to the individual reports adopted since 2000. The follow-ups are carried out by methods that include the possibility of holding case hearings and publishing a list of all cases by country in the Commission's Annual Report, showing the status of implementation. To this end, the Commission categorises the level of compliance as 'total compliance', 'partial compliance' or 'pending compliance'. Moreover, the State's response regarding the level of compliance is also included in the individual report when the State concerned explicitly requests its publication.

---

[17] See IACHR *Santiago Marzioni v Argentina*, Annual Report 1996, Report No. 39/96, Case 11.673, Argentina, October 15, 1996, OEA/Ser.L/V/II.95, Doc. 7 rev., March 14, 1997.
[18] IACHR Statute revised Regulations Article 46.
[19] See also AG/Res. 1890 (XXXII-O/02), *Evaluation of the Workings of the Inter-American System for the Protection and Promotion of Human Rights with a View to its Improvement and Strengthening*, 'resolves' *[3(c)–3(d)]*, available at <http://www.oas.org/juridico/english/ga02/gen_as02.htm>.

### C Terrorism and human rights: a recurrent issue on the Commission's agenda

The Commission has dealt with a wide variety of issues throughout its history. In the case of English-speaking States such as the United States, Canada and several Caribbean countries, the Commission has dealt with abortion issues, racial discrimination, political asylum, use of force, and death penalty of minors and foreign nationals, among other issues. This subsection focuses on the most relevant aspects of the Commission's reaction to the notorious events of '9/11' related to counter-terrorism measures and the need to secure human rights.

*(i) The 2002 Special Report on Terrorism and Human Rights* As mentioned above, one mode of action for the Commission is the preparation of special and general reports. The Commission's special report produced in 2002, entitled *Report on Terrorism and Human Rights* ('the terrorism report'),[20] is of particular importance. This report was one of the first comprehensive actions taken by an intergovernmental organisation following the events of 11 September 2001. The Commission engaged in an exhaustive analysis of the subject matter and recommended anti-terrorism policies to OAS member States that ensured compliance with international human rights obligations. Currently, the terrorism report is also an essential point of reference for clarifying and restating the Inter-American system's jurisprudence and human rights standards on critical issues regarding the 'War on Terror'.

The terrorism report establishes principles that advise States to apply human rights and international humanitarian law when engaged in armed conflict.[21] Thus, the terrorism report is particularly useful for those States that are immersed in internal armed conflict. Also notable is that the application of these two fields of law has set proliferative standards in the fight against terrorism that are gaining prominence in the Inter-American system.

In addition, the terrorism report includes an analysis of the rights to life, personal liberty, and due process; the prohibition against torture and cruel,

---

[20] IACHR, *Report on Terrorism and Human Rights*, OEA/Ser.L/V/ll.116 Doc. 5 rev. 1 corr. (22 October 2002) available at <http://www.cidh.org/Terrorism/Eng/toc.htm>.

[21] According to the Commission, during armed conflict international humanitarian law must be applied with the human rights provisions of the ACHR and the American Declaration. States must comply with these international law norms even during periods of terrorist activities. The Commission holds that protecting non-derogable internationally-protected human rights is consistent with international humanitarian law and, thus, States must not violate such guarantees when dealing with counter-terrorism measures.

inhuman, and degrading treatment; the principle of non-discrimination; and, *inter alia*, the rights to freedom of expression, freedom of assembly, property, and privacy. The terrorism report further examines issues related to migrant workers, asylum and refugee law, and the rights of non-citizens, all of which the Commission identified as critical in the context of the post-September 11 fight against terrorism.

Following the adoption of the terrorism report, the Commission continued monitoring the fight against terrorism and the new and developing human rights challenges in the post-September 11 world. In 2006, the Commission released a follow-up series of recommendations intended to clarify and reinforce the 2002 terrorism report.[22] These recommendations provide, in up-to-date and concise language, a clear and schematic summary of the recommendations that the Commission presented to the States in 2002.

*(ii) Country reports* The special country reports conducted by the Commission analyse the ways that the States guarantee and uphold the standards of human rights and international humanitarian law. An important pre-9/11 example is the *Third Report on the Situation of Human Rights in Colombia*.[23] In this report, the Commission analyses the Colombian armed conflict in light of the norms regarding human rights and international humanitarian law. The report refers to the Additional Protocol II and Common Article 3 of the four Geneva Conventions, and found violations not only on the part of State agents but also on the part of illegal non-governmental armed groups. It is in the context of these special reports that the Commission has developed a more comprehensive application of international norms of armed conflict. This development allows the Commission to evaluate the conduct of State and non-State actors, as both are likely to be involved in possible terrorist actions, or human rights abuses in armed conflict.

*(iii) The Commission's reports and the situation in Guantanamo* In the context of individual petitions, the Commission has the authority to issue precautionary measures[24] against any OAS member State regarding situations

---

[22] Permanent Council of the OAS, *Recommendations for the Protection of Human Rights by OAS Member States in the Fight Against Terrorism*, OEA/Ser. G CP/doc.4117/06 (9 May 2006) available at <http://scm.oas.org/doc_public/ENGLISH/HIST_06/CP16302E06.doc>.

[23] IACHR, *Third Report on the Situation of Human Rights in Colombia*, OEA/Ser.L/V/II.102, Doc. 9 rev. 1, (26 February 1999).

[24] The Commission reaffirmed the obligation that member States have to comply with precautionary measures. See IACHR, *Annual Report 1997*, OEA/Ser.L/V/II.98 Doc. 6 rev. (13 April 1998) Chapter VII [12].

of serious and urgent character. These precautionary measures constitute vital and flexible tools used to confront, *inter alia*, certain reckless and arbitrary State reaction to terrorist activity. The Commission's authority to confront abusive reactions in the so-called 'War on Terror' is exemplified in the series of precautionary measures issued against the United States regarding the detainees held at the US naval base in Guantanamo Bay, Cuba. It is worth noting that the only international human rights body with a mandate to receive international human rights complaints against the United States is the Commission.

On 12 March 2002, the Commission granted the first precautionary measures in favour of the detainees in Guantanamo Bay.[25] The Commission specifically declared that, although the Guantanamo naval base is not located in US territory, the United States was responsible for ensuring the rights of the detainees because these individuals were clearly under its authority and control.[26] The Commission informed the Bush administration that under international human rights law the US was obliged to provide information about each detainee, clarify the detainees' legal status through a competent and independent tribunal, grant the detainees the guarantees associated with their detention and respect the minimum guarantee and non-derogable rights recognised in the Inter-American System.[27]

On 12 April 2002, the United States presented its observations on the Commission's precautionary measures and argued that the Commission lacked jurisdiction to apply norms of international humanitarian law or to issue precautionary measures against OAS members that had not ratified the American Convention.[28] The Commission rejected the objections to its jurisdiction and reiterated the precautionary measures of 12 March 2002.[29] The Commission continued to issue precautionary measures from 2003 to 2006, as well as in 2008. The released communications expressed concern over the repeated reports of the detainees' illegal status and the allegations of cruel, inhuman and degrading treatment.

---

[25] Ibid 534.
[26] Ibid 533.
[27] IACHR, *Pertinent Parts of March 12, 2002 Reiteration and Further Amplification of Precautionary Measures (Detainees in Guantanamo Bay, Cuba)*, 45 I.L.M. 532, 533–4 (2002), available at 2002 WL 974501. See also Brian D Tittemore, 'Guantanamo Bay and the Precautionary Measures of the Inter-American Commission on Human Rights: A Case for International Oversight in the Struggle Against Terrorism' (2006) 6 Human Rights Law Review 378.
[28] IACHR, *Guantanamo Bay Precautionary Measures 2002*, available at <http://www.cidh.org/medidas/2002.eng.htm> [80].
[29] Ibid.

The Commission obtained information specifying that several detainees were captured in Bosnia and Pakistan. It is unclear as to whether these detainees were part of enemy armed forces, thus generating reasonable doubts about the detainees' legal status and whether the guarantees entitled to them were given.[30] Likewise, there were reports indicating that some of the detainees were minors (under 18) and were held in facilities not in accord with international standards.[31] In response to the reports of human rights violations, the Commission reiterated previously issued requests and issued new ones in the subsequent precautionary measures. The Commission requested, *inter alia*, that the US adopt all necessary measures to conduct independent, impartial, and effective investigations of the allegations of torture, taking into account the actions of perpetrators as well as any mandated superior orders.[32] The Commission also requested that the detainees be ensured the right not to be transferred to countries that may subject them to torture or other mistreatment.[33] Additionally, the Commission requested detailed information on the status and treatment of detainees in all detention centres under US control.[34]

The Commission's capacity to respond quickly and the effectiveness of the precautionary measures are restricted when compliance is an issue. For instance, the decisions and orders of the Commission have had limited impact on US conduct. However, this organ is not alone in challenging US compliance with international norms and regulations. The International Court of Justice ('ICJ'), as illustrated by the recent *Avena et al. Case*,[35] also has difficulty attaining US compliance with its measures.

Despite this reality, the Commission's provisional measures are critical in exposing and publicly condemning States, such as the US, that are defiant in complying with their international human rights obligations. The importance of the Commission's work is best analysed through its historic role in confronting compliance issues among several OAS member State authoritarian regimes. These regimes neither complied with the Commission's decisions nor did they appear before hearings. Nevertheless, the Commission was not deterred and

---

[30] Ibid.
[31] *Convention on the Rights of the Child*, opened for signature 20 November 1989, 1577 UNTS 3 (entered into force 2 September 1990) Article 37.
[32] IACHR, *On Guantanamo Bay Precautionary Measures of July 29, 2004*, 45 I.L.M. 671, 672 (2006) available at 2006 WL 1667680.
[33] IACHR, *On Guantanamo Bay Precautionary Measures of October 28, 2005*, 45 I.L.M. 673, 678 (2006) available at 2006 WL 1667681.
[34] IACHR, *On Guantanamo Bay Precautionary Measures of March 18, 2003*, 45 I.L.M. 669, 669–70 (2006) available at 2006 WL 1667679.
[35] *Avena et al. Case (Mexico v United States of America)*, 2004 (March 31), ICJ Rep 128.

continued to develop its supervisory functions, including adjucating cases even when States neglected to cooperate with proceedings.

The Commission's persistence set the path for change within the Inter-American system. First, official international recognition of human rights violations proved effective in publicly shaming States, which often led to negative political ramifications in the international sphere. Second, publicly shaming States, in many cases, provided sufficient redress in itself for victims who had suffered years of stigmatisation from national authorities and societies. Third, many cases that were dismissed by authoritarian regimes were later adequately addressed by new democratic governments that wanted to differentiate themselves from the previous regime. Fourth, all processed cases established critical international case law that is indispensible for the development of human rights and humanitarian law.

In regard to the US, there were some noteworthy compliance developments. Two years after the Commission's 2002 precautionary measures, the US Supreme Court similarly conferred US jurisdiction over *habeas corpus* suits concerning foreign nationals detained in Guantanamo and decided that the detainees' legal status must be determined by an impartial and independent adjudicator and the detainees must be ensured their judicial guarantees.[36] The US administration responded to the *Rasul v Bush* ('*Rasul*')[37] decision by setting up a military tribunal to determine the detainees' legal status. In the 2005 precautionary measures, the Commission declared that these tribunals were neither sufficiently independent nor effective.[38] In 2006, the US Supreme Court similarly reached the conclusion that military commissions 'lack the power to proceed' since they violated both the Uniform Code of Military Justice and the Geneva Conventions.[39] In 2008, the US Supreme Court went a step further in re-establishing *habeas corpus* as a constitutional right for non-US citizens,[40] thereby making it difficult for the Bush administration to bypass its obligation to ensure the legal status of all Guantanamo detainees.

However, the continued issue of non-compliance by US administrative authorities obligated the Commission to urge the US to close Guantanamo; to remove the detainees in a manner that complied with international human rights and humanitarian law; to comply with the obligation of non-

---

[36] *Rasul v Bush*, 542 U.S. 466 (2004).
[37] Ibid.
[38] IACHR, *On Guantanamo Bay Precautionary Measures of October 28, 2005*, above n 33.
[39] *Hamdan v Rumsfeld*, 126 S.C. 2749 (2006).
[40] *Boumediene v Bush*, 128 S. Ct. 2229 (2008).

refoulement; and to investigate, prosecute, and punish any acts of torture or other cruel, inhuman, or degrading treatment.[41]

Overall, the Commission has demonstrated the flexibility and adaptability of its mandates as well as their extensive responsive capacity when challenged with the most difficult encroachments of human rights. Moreover, the coordinated uses of its political and adjudicatory powers are ascertainable mechanisms that have effectively denounced and documented human rights violations. The Commission continues to play a vital role in the Inter-American system, complemented by the judicial role of the Inter-American Court.

## 3  The Inter-American Court of Human Rights

### A  Introduction to the jurisdiction of the Court

The Inter-American Court has two specific types of jurisdiction: advisory and contentious.

The advisory jurisdiction of the Inter-American Court is governed by Article 64 of the American Convention and is the broadest of all existing international tribunals. Member States of the OAS – even those that have not yet ratified the American Convention – and selected OAS organs, including the Commission, may submit requests for advisory opinions. States may request advisory opinions on the interpretation of the American Convention and 'other treaties concerning the protection of human rights in the American States',[42] as well as on the compatibility of any domestic laws with the aforementioned international instruments. The OAS bodies, in contrast, may only request interpretations of the American Convention and other international treaties. Furthermore, the scope of their requests must be limited to their respective areas of competence.

The Inter-American Court has interpreted 'other treaties concerning the protection of human rights in the American states' to encompass all human rights treaties ratified by one or more of the OAS's members, even if non-OAS members are parties as well.[43] The Inter-American Court further concluded that it has the authority to interpret a human rights provision in a treaty whose

---

[41]  IACHR, *On Guantanamo Bay Precautionary Measures of July 28, 2006*, Resolution No. 2/06, available at <http://www.cidh.org/annualrep/2006eng/ANNEXES/Annex%205eng.htm#N%BA%202/06>.
[42]  ACHR Article 64(1).
[43]  IACtHR, *'Other treaties' subject to the advisory jurisdiction of the Court (Article 64 American Convention on Human Rights)*, Advisory Opinion OC-1/82 of September 24, 1982, Series A No. 1 [48].

main purpose is not to protect such rights.[44] For example, in Advisory Opinion 16 the Inter-American Court asserted jurisdiction to interpret Article 36 of the *Vienna Convention on Consular Relations*,[45] insofar as this provision provides a right to individuals detained in foreign States to communicate with a consular officer from their country of nationality.[46]

Additionally, the Inter-American Court has the power to adopt provisional measures in extremely serious and urgent cases where there is a risk of irreparable harm to a victim. The Inter-American Court's authority is governed by Article 63(2) of the American Convention and by provisions of the Statute and Rules of the tribunal. Though the American Convention is silent on the matter, the Inter-American Court, in practice, has asserted jurisdiction to adopt provisional measures only in regard to States that have ratified the American Convention and accepted its contentious jurisdiction.[47]

The purpose of the Inter-American Court's provisional measures is to protect the victims against potential human rights violations, particularly when there is a risk of irreparable harm.[48] Provisional measures can be requested in relation to a case pending before the Inter-American Court or a petition that is not yet submitted to its cognisance. The Inter-American Court adopts provisional measures mainly to protect individual victims.[49] Regarding groups, the Inter-American Court requires that the members of the group be identifiable and in a situation of danger that directly resulted from affiliation with that specific group.[50] For the Inter-American Court to adopt an interim measure,

---

[44] IACtHR, *The Right to Information on Consular Assistance in the Framework of the Guarantees of the Due Process of Law*, Advisory Opinion OC-16/99 of October 1, 1999, Series A No. 16 [76].

[45] *Vienna Convention on Consular Relations*, opened for signature on 24 April 1963, UNTS596 (entered into force on 19 March 1967).

[46] Ibid [87].

[47] See IACtHR, *Matter of 'Globovisión' Television Station* (Venezuela), Resolution of September 4, 2004, Series E No. 5, 'considering' [1].

[48] IACtHR, *Matter of the Mendoza Prisons* (Argentina) (*'Mendoza Prisons'*), Resolution of November 22, 2004, Series E No. 5, 'considering' [4–5].

[49] IACtHR, *Matter of Haitians and Dominicans of Haitian-origin in the Dominican Republic* (Dominican Republic), Resolution of August 18, 2000, Series E No. 5, 'considering' [8]. This case concerned an alleged mass deportation of individuals with Haitian origin to Haiti, in violation of the American Convention. The Commission requested the Court to issue precautionary measures to protect a group of unidentified victims, but the Court declared that identity, for those in danger of irreparable damage, is indispensible for the adoption of these measures.

[50] IACtHR, *Matter of Monagas Judicial Confinement Center ('La Pica')* (Venezuela), Resolution of February 9, 2006, Series E No. 5, 'considering' [8]. This case concerned detainees and their deprivation of liberty. The Court held that precautionary measures applied because not only did the group of victims (or prospective

the party petitioning the measure must demonstrate *prima facie* the existence of a reasonable presumption that the alleged facts involve a situation of extreme gravity and urgency which presents a risk of irreparable harm for the victim.[51]

## B  Contentious jurisdiction

The Inter-American Court's contentious jurisdiction refers to its power to decide cases. The cases are principally based on alleged violations of the American Convention provisions. However, the Inter-American Court may also find violations of other Inter-American human rights treaties, granting the tribunal jurisdiction to supervise compliance with the obligations contained therein. Furthermore, the cases may stem from individual petitions or inter-state petitions. The only inter-state petition on record was filed by Nicaragua against Costa Rica before the Commission in 2006. The case never made it to the Inter-American Court, because it was ultimately declared inadmissible for failure to exhaust domestic remedies.[52]

The Inter-American Court may hear a case only after all proceedings before the Commission are exhausted.[53] Moreover, for the Inter-American Court to assert jurisdiction over a claim, certain requirements with respect to person, subject matter, time, and place must be satisfied. To date, the Inter-American Court has not analysed the scope of its territorial jurisdiction.

*(i)  Jurisdiction* ratione personae  The Inter-American Court's personal jurisdiction or jurisdiction *ratione personae* involves the determination of two issues, namely: who is authorised to submit a case, and against whom the case may be submitted. In contrast to the Commission, which may receive petitions submitted by individuals, groups of persons and NGOs, Article 61(1) of the American Convention only authorises the Inter-American Court to hear cases referred by the Commission or by State Parties to the American Convention.

Most of the cases decided by or pending before the Inter-American Court have been filed by the Commission. There are only two instances where a State has submitted a case to the Inter-American Court. In *Viviana Gallardo*,[54]

---

victims) belong to an identifiable group but also the alleged violations were directly linked to the detention itself.

    51    *Mendoza Prisons*, above n 48 at 'considering' [14].

    52    IACHR, *Nicaragua v Costa Rica*, Annual Report 2007, Report No. 11/07, Interstate Case 01/06, March 8, 2007, OEA/Ser./L/V/II.130, Doc. 22 rev. 1, December 29, 2007.

    53    ACHR, Article 62.

    54    Dissenting Opinion of Judge Rodolfo E Piza, IACtHR, *Matter of Viviana Gallardo et al.* (Costa Rica), Advisory Opinion of November 13, 1983, Series A No. 10181.

the case was rejected because Costa Rica submitted the case directly to the Inter-American Court without exhausting proceedings before the Commission. In *Lori Berenson*,[55] Peru submitted a brief to the Inter-American Court[56] while the Commission simultaneously referred the case to the Inter-American Court. The Inter-American Court decided that examination of the State brief was not necessary in light of the Commission's submission of the case.[57]

The Inter-American Court's ability to hear a case requires that the defendant State ratify the American Convention and recognise, by unilateral declaration, the Inter-American Court's contentious jurisdiction. Recognition is optional and may be effectuated at the time of ratification or of accession to the American Convention, or at any other subsequent time. Article 62(2) of the American Convention authorises States to recognise jurisdiction unconditionally or 'under the condition of reciprocity.' Furthermore, in the *Ivcher Bronstein*[58] and *Constitutional Court*[59] cases, the Inter-American Court held that, in light of that provision, States may only restrict their recognition of the Inter-American Court's contentious jurisdiction for a specific period of time and/or for specific cases.[60] Moreover, once a State unconditionally recognises the Inter-American Court's contentious jurisdiction it may not withdraw its declaration of acceptance.[61] States must therefore denounce the American Convention in order to be released from the legal obligations generated by such recognition.[62] Arguably, those cases also suggest that other non-stipulated limitations are not authorised by the American Convention and are therefore invalid. Recently, however, the Inter-American Court held that the temporal limitations inserted by El Salvador and Chile, preventing it from

---

[55] IACtHR, *Lori-Berenson-Mejía v Peru*, Judgment of November 25, 2004, Series C No. 119.
[56] Brief entitled: 'Petition concerning report 36/02 of the Inter-American Commission on Human Rights'.
[57] IACtHR, *Lori-Berenson-Mejía v Peru*, Judgment of November 25, 2004, Series C No. 119. [94].
[58] IACtHR, *Ivcher-Bronstein v Peru*, Judgment of September 24, 1999, Series C No. 54.
[59] IACtHR, *Constitutional Court v Peru*, Judgment of September 24, 1999, Series C, No. 55.
[60] IACtHR, *Ivcher-Bronstein v Peru*, Judgment of September 24, 1999, Series C No. 54 [36]; IACtHR, *Constitutional Court v Peru*, Judgment of September 24, 1999, Series C, No. 55 [35].
[61] Ibid *Ivcher-Bronstein v Peru*, [39]; ibid IACtHR, *Constitutional Court v Peru* [38].
[62] Ibid *Ivcher-Bronstein v Peru*, [40]; ibid IACtHR, *Constitutional Court v Peru* [39].

hearing facts which occurred or started to occur before those States' recognition of the Inter-American Court's jurisdiction, were valid.[63]

The American Convention does not explicitly establish a role for individuals in the Inter-American Court proceedings. The American Convention has no provisions that give individuals the authority either to submit cases or to participate independently in litigation before the Inter-American Court. However, in the first cases litigated before the Inter-American Court,[64] the Commission appointed the attorneys of the victim's relatives as its advisors. As Commission representatives, these advisors examined and cross-examined witnesses and presented their final arguments jointly with the Commission's attorneys. Subsequent changes in the IACHR Procedures allowed the victim's relatives and their attorneys to participate independently at the reparations phase. Currently, following the 2001 modification of the IACHR Procedures and the Inter-American Court, victims and their representatives can participate in the decision on whether the Commission should submit a case to the Inter-American Court.[65] In addition, once the case is submitted to the Inter-American Court, the claimants are granted standing to autonomously present their requests, arguments, and evidence throughout the Inter-American Court's proceedings.[66]

The Court's Rules of Procedure, however, do not define the scope of the petition that victims and their representatives can submit before the Inter-American Court. These rules are silent on whether petitioners may claim additional facts and rights violations to those stipulated in the Commission's (or State's) petitions. In *Five Pensioners v Peru*,[67] and recently, in *Saramaka People v Suriname*,[68] the Inter-American Court held that petitioners could not allege facts that were different from those claimed by the Commission, unless there were supervening facts.[69] However, petitioners may invoke the violation

---

[63] IACtHR, *Serrano-Cruz Sisters v El Salvador*, Judgment of November 23, 2004, Series C, No. 118 [61]; IACtHR, *Almonacid-Arellano v Chile*, Judgment of September 26, 2006, Series C No. 154 [44].

[64] IACtHR, *Velasquez-Rodríguez v Honduras*, Judgment of July 29, 1988, Series C No. 4; IACtHR, *Godínez-Cruz v Honduras*, Judgment of January 20, 1989, Series C No. 5; IACtHR, *Fairén-Garbi and Solís-Corrales v Honduras*, Judgment of March 15, 1989, Series C No. 6.

[65] IACHR Rules of Procedure, *Article 43*, available at Basic Documents: <http://www.cidh.org/Basicos/English/Basic.TOC.htm>.

[66] IACtHR Rules of Procedure, Article 23, available at <http://www.corteidh.or.cr/reglamento.cfm>.

[67] *Five Pensioners v Peru*, Judgment of February 28, 2003, Series C No. 98.

[68] IACtHR, *Saramaka People v Suriname*, Judgment of November 28, 2007, Series C No. 172.

[69] IACtHR, *Five Pensioners v Peru*, Judgment of February 28, 2003, Series C

of additional rights to those asserted by the Commission, because 'they are entitled to all of the rights enshrined in the American Convention, and to not admit it would be an undue restriction of their status as subjects of international human rights law.'[70]

In addition, the IACHR Procedures authorise petitioners to file requests for provisional measures in cases that are being heard by the Inter-American Court,[71] while giving that power only to the Commission in cases not yet referred to the Inter-American Court.[72] For example, urgent measures have been requested from the Inter-American Court in several cases to protect the life and security of particular persons.[73] Also, the beneficiaries of provisional measures may submit observations to the status reports, submitted by the State to the Inter-American Court, as part of the monitoring process implemented to supervise compliance with those measures.[74]

*(ii) Jurisdiction ratione materiae* The American Convention establishes that the subject matter jurisdiction of the Inter-American Court 'shall comprise all cases concerning the interpretation and application of the provisions of [the American Convention]'.[75] In *Las Palmeras v Colombia*,[76] the Inter-American Court interpreted that phrase restrictively, holding that its contentious jurisdiction was limited to finding violations of the American Convention and not to other rules of international law, such as international humanitarian law.[77] However, the Inter-American Court makes use of other norms of international law to inform the interpretation of the American Convention's provisions.[78] In *The 'Street Children' v*

---

No. 98 [153–155]; IACtHR, *Saramaka People v Suriname*, Judgment of November 28, 2007, Series C No. 172 [27].

[70] Ibid *Five Pensioners v Peru* [155], Ibid *Saramaka People v Suriname* [27].

[71] IACtHR, *Rules of Procedure, Article 25(3)* Inter-American Court on Human Rights <www.cidh.org/basicos/english/Basic18.Rules%20of%20Procedure%20of%20the%20Commission.htm> at 26 February 2009.

[72] Ibid Article 25(2).

[73] IACtHR, *Mapiripán Massacre v Colombia*, Judgment of September 15, 2005, Series C No. 134; IACtHR, *Miguel Castro-Castro Prison v Peru*, Judgment of November 25, 2006, Series C No. 160; IACtHR, *Bueno-Alves v Argentina*, Judgment of May 11, 2007, Series C No. 164.

[74] IACtHR, *Rules of Procedure, Article 25(5)* Inter-American Court on Human Rights <www.cidh.org/basicos/english/Basic18.Rules%20of%20Procedure%20of%20the%20Commission.htm> at 26 February 2009.

[75] ACHR Article 62(3).

[76] IACtHR, *Las Palmeras v Colombia*, Judgment of February 4, 2000, Series C No. 67 [32–3].

[77] Ibid.

[78] See IACtHR, *The 'Street Children' (Villagrán-Morales et al.) v Guatemala*,

*Guatemala*[79] and *Mapiripán Massacre*[80] cases, for example, the Inter-American Court used several provisions of the *United Nations Convention on the Rights of the Child*,[81] as part of a 'comprehensive international *corpus juris'* to interpret Article 19 of the American Convention, which concerns the rights of children.[82] The Inter-American Court has also used 'soft law' to aid in the interpretation of the provisions of the American Convention. For example, in *Juan Humberto Sánchez v Honduras*,[83] the Inter-American Court used the *United Nations Model Protocol for a Legal Investigation of Extra-Legal, Arbitrary and Summary Executions*, or the *Minnesota Protocol*[84] to determine the scope of the States' obligation under the American Convention to conduct a serious, impartial and effective investigation.[85]

The Inter-American Court has also asserted its jurisdiction to find violations of other Inter-American system treaties which grant jurisdiction to the Inter-American Court, to supervise compliance with States' obligations.[86] In particular, the Inter-American Court has found violations of obligations arising out of the *Inter-American Convention to Prevent and Punish Torture*,[87] the *Inter-American Convention on Forced Disappearance of Persons*,[88] and the *Inter-American Convention on the Prevention, Punishment and Eradication of*

---

Judgment of November 19, 1999, Series C No. 63 [192]. The Court justifies this practice by reference to Article 31 of the Vienna Convention on the Law of Treaties.

[79] Ibid.

[80] IACtHR, *Mapiripán Massacre v Colombia*, Judgment of September 15, 2005, Series C No. 134.

[81] *Convention on the Rights of the Child*, above n 31.

[82] IACtHR, *The 'Street Children' (Villagrán-Morales et al.) v Guatemala*, Judgment of November 19, 1999, Series C No. 63 [194]; IACtHR, *Mapiripán Massacre v Colombia*, Judgment of September 15, 2005, Series C No. 134 [153].

[83] IACtHR, *Humberto Sánchez v Honduras*, Judgment of June 7, 2003, Series C No. 99.

[84] *United Nations Model Protocol for a Legal Investigation of Extra-Legal, Arbitrary and Summary Executions,* or the *Minnesota Protocol*, UN Doc E/ST/CSDHA/.12 (1991).

[85] IACtHR, *Humberto Sánchez v Honduras*, Judgment of June 7, 2003, Series C No. 99 [127]. See also IACtHR, *Tibi v Ecuador*, Judgment of September 7, 2004, Series C No. 114 [94–122]; IACtHR, *Acosta-Calderón v Ecuador*, Judgment of June 24, 2005, Series C No. 129 [53–62].

[86] IACtHR, *Baena-Ricardo v Panama*, Judgment of February 2, 2001, Series C No. 72 [97].

[87] See, *inter alia*, IACtHR, *The 'Street Children' (Villagrán-Morales et al.) v Guatemala*, Judgment of November 19, 1999, Series C No. 63 [247–9]; IACtHR, *Gómez-Paquiyauri Brothers v Peru*, Judgment of July 8, 2004, Series C No. 110 [114].

[88] IACtHR, *Gómez-Palomino v Peru*, Judgment of November 22, 2005, Series C No. 136 [109–10].

*Violence Against Women* ('Convention of Belém do Pará').[89] Although the Additional Protocol to the *American Convention on Human Rights in the Area of Economic, Social and Cultural Rights*[90] confers upon the Inter-American Court jurisdiction to supervise compliance with two rights protected therein,[91] the Inter-American Court has yet to find a violation of those provisions in a contentious case.

Furthermore, the Inter-American Court in *Moiwana Community v Suriname*[92] and *Bueno-Alves v Argentina*[93] held that, while it generally takes into account the American Declaration when interpreting the provisions of the American Convention, its contentious jurisdiction was limited to finding violations of the American Convention only.[94]

*(iii) Jurisdiction* ratione temporis  The Inter-American Court has discussed the scope of its jurisdiction *ratione temporis* mainly in the context of cases that presented facts which occurred prior to a State's recognition of its contentious jurisdiction.[95] The Inter-American Court has consistently declared that, in light of the long-standing international law principle of non-retroactivity of treaties,[96] it cannot hear facts that transpired before such recognition.[97] The Inter-American Court maintains this position even in regard to cases where facts occurred after a State's ratification of the American Convention but before its recognition of the Inter-American Court's jurisdiction.[98] Although

---

[89]  IACtHR, *Miguel Castro-Castro Prison v Peru*, Judgment of November 25, 2006, Series C No. 160 [408].

[90]  *International Covenant on Economic, Social and Cultural Rights*, opened for signature 19 December 1966, 999 UNTS 3 (entered into force 3 January 1976).

[91]  OAS, *Protocol of San Salvador*, Article 8 (trade union rights) and 13 (right to education), Organization of American States, <http://www.oas.org/juridico/English/Treaties/a-52.html>.

[92]  IACtHR, *Moiwana Village v Suriname*, Judgment of June 15, 2005, Series C No. 124.

[93]  Ibid; see also IACtHR, *Bueno-Alves v Argentina*, Judgment of May 11, 2007, Series C No. 164.

[94]  Ibid *Moiwana Village v Suriname* [63]; ibid *Bueno-Alves v Argentina* [55–9].

[95]  See, *inter alia*, IACtHR, *Martin del Campo v Mexico*, Judgment of September 3, 2004, Series C No. 114; ibid *Moiwana Village*; IACtHR, *Nogueira de Carvalho v Brazil*, Judgment of November 28, 2006, Series C No. 161.

[96]  See, for example, *Vienna Convention on the Law of Treaties*, opened for signature 23 May 1969, 1155 UNTS 331 (entered into force 27 January 1980), Article 28.

[97]  IACtHR, *Martin del Campo v Mexico*, Judgment of September 3, 2004, Series C No. 114 [85]; IACtHR, *Cantos v Argentina*, Judgment of September 7, 2001, Series C No. 85 [37–8].

[98]  See, *inter alia*, IACtHR, *Blake v Guatemala*, Judgment of July 2, 1996, Series C No. 28; *Serrano-Cruz Sisters v El Salvador*, Judgment of November 23, 2004, Series C No. 118. See also ibid *Martin del Campo v Mexico* [68].

the Inter-American Court found that the principle of irretroactivity applies even in the absence of a State's express temporal limitation,[99] several States have restricted recognition of the Inter-American Court's contentious jurisdiction exclusively to events or legal actions subsequent to the date of deposit of their unilateral declaration.[100]

In line with other international case law, the Inter-American Court recognises that the only exceptions to the principle of non-retroactivity of treaties are the so-called 'permanent or continuing violations'. These situations originate prior to the recognition of the Inter-American Court's jurisdiction by the relevant State, but continue to exist subsequently to those dates.[101] The Inter-American Court has deemed the following to be continuous violations: the denial of justice resulting from the lack of an effective investigation of a massacre; the forced and continuous displacement of victims from their traditional lands; and the arbitrary deprivation of nationality.[102] Though the Inter-American Court has stated on several occasions, in *dicta*, that forced disappearances constitute continuous violations, it has never decided a case where it applied this exception to assert jurisdiction.[103]

## C  The scope of reparations granted by the Inter-American Court

Pursuant to Article 63(1) of the American Convention, the Inter-American Court may award reparations to the victims of human rights violations protected by the American Convention, which may include monetary

---

[99] IACtHR, *Nogueira de Carvalho v Brazil*, Judgment of November 28, 2006, Series C No. 161 [43].

[100] See, *inter alia*, declarations from Argentina, Mexico and Guatemala. Moreover El Salvador, Chile and Nicaragua have included additional restrictions on the recognition of the Court's jurisdiction, excluding not only on facts that occurred before recognition but also on those that began before that critical date – some of which even continued afterwards. See IACHR, Basic Documents: http://www.cidh.org/Basicos/English/Basic.TOC.htm.

[101] IACtHR, *Moiwana Village v Suriname*, Judgment of June 15, 2005, Series C No. 124 [39]; IACtHR, *Serrano-Cruz Sisters v El Salvador*, Judgment of November 23, 2004, Series C No. 118 [65].

[102] Ibid *Moiwana Village v Suriname* [43]; IACtHR, *Yean and Bosico v Dominican Republic*, Judgment of September 8, 2005, Series C No. 130 [132].

[103] IACtHR, *Serrano-Cruz Sisters v El Salvador*, Judgment of November 23, 2004, Series C No. 118. The Court decided three cases of forced disappearances which occurred before recognition of the defendant States' jurisdiction but in which the States accepted international responsibility without challenging the jurisdiction *ratione temporis* of the Court. See IACtHR, *Trujillo-Oroza v Bolivia*, Judgment of January 26, 2008, Series C No. 64; IACtHR, *Molina Theissen v Guatemala*, Judgment of May 4, 2004, Series C No. 106; and IACtHR, *Goiburú et al. v Paraguay*, Judgment of September 22, 2006, Series C No. 153.

compensation to victims or their relatives for pecuniary and non-pecuniary damages. Reparations also require States to adopt other measures, such as measures of satisfaction, which vindicate the memory of the victims, and non-repetition, which ensures the cessation of possible repetitive violations. The Inter-American Court has consistently held that the purpose of reparation is to eliminate the consequences of the violations committed.[104] The type of reparation (that is, its nature and amount) is based on the gravity of the human rights violation perpetrated as well as the damage inflicted upon the victims.[105] Thus, reparations must be proportional only to the violation and cannot result in the enrichment or impoverishment of the victims or their next of kin.[106]

The Inter-American Court may order both pecuniary damages, such as the compensation of lost wages or loss of income and consequential damages, and non-pecuniary damages, such as compensation for pain and suffering. Additionally, the Inter-American Court may order the restitution of all litigation costs, international and domestic, including the fees of legal representatives, if appropriate.[107] In principle, as in domestic legal proceedings, the alleged damages must be proven. Nonetheless, the Inter-American Court may presume the mental pain and suffering undergone by victims of torture,[108] illegal and arbitrary detention,[109] and extrajudicial execution preceded by ill-treatment.[110] Likewise, the Inter-American Court presupposes the suffering of relatives whose beloved disappears or is murdered on the account of State agents.[111] Finally, the Inter-American Court presumes the anguish suffered by victims or their next of kin as a result of the State's failure to investigate and punish those responsible for gross human rights violations.[112]

---

[104] Ibid *Goiburú et al.* [143]; IACtHR *Miguel Castro-Castro Prison v Peru*, Judgment of November 25, 2006, Series C No. 160 [416]; IACtHR, *Ximenes-Lopes v Brazil*, Judgment of July 4, 2006, Series C No. 149 [210].
[105] Ibid.
[106] Ibid.
[107] IACtHR, *Bueno-Alves v Argentina*, Judgment of May 11, 2007, Series C No. 164 [219].
[108] Ibid [202].
[109] See, *inter alia*, IACtHR, *Acosta-Calderón v Ecuador*, Judgment of June 24, 2005, Series C No. 129 [159].
[110] See, *inter alia*, IACtHR, *Cantoral-Huamaní and García-Santa Cruz v Peru*, Judgment of July 10, 2007, Series C No. 167 [176].
[111] See, *inter alia*, IACtHR, *Humberto Sánchez v Honduras*, Judgment of June 7, 2003, Series C No. 99 [175]; IACtHR, *Goiburú et al. v Paraguay*, Judgment of September 22, 2006, Series C No. 153 [159].
[112] IACtHR, *Mapiripán Massacre v Colombia*, Judgment of September 15, 2005, Series C No. 134 [284]; IACtHR, *Moiwana Village v Suriname*, Judgment of June 15, 2005, Series C No. 124 [195].

The amount of compensation has varied over the years, but most recently the Inter-American Court has ordered States responsible for human rights violations to indemnify the damages with amounts that are appropriate to the seriousness of the violations set forth in the case.[113] In this vein, the Inter-American Court has declared that 'jurisprudence can serve as guidance to establish principles in this matter, although it cannot be invoked as a precise norm to follow because each case must be examined in the light of its particularities.'[114]

With respect to calculation of pecuniary damages, particularly loss of income, the amount is based on the victim's activity, so the amount awarded oscillates. There are some cases, involving grave human rights violation, where calculating pecuniary damages is problematic. For instance, the victim may not have a specific profession due to his or her deprivation of liberty during the atrocities in question, such as in the *Neira Alegría*[115] case, or the victim may be a street child, such as in *The 'Street Children'*[116] case. In those cases, the Inter-American Court established, on the basis of equity, an amount of estimated income – in some cases using the minimum monthly salary applicable in the particular country – to calculate the total amount of the indemnification.[117] The Inter-American Court also uses equity as the criterion to calculate the amount of non-pecuniary damages.[118] In reimbursement issues, the Inter-American Court takes into account the circumstances of the specific case and the nature of the international human rights jurisdiction in order to assess reimbursement of litigation costs incurred by the victims or their legal representatives.[119] Likewise, such costs and expenses are assessed

---

[113] See, *inter alia*, IACtHR, *19 Tradesmen v Colombia*, Judgment of July 5, 2004, Series C No. 109; ibid *Mapiripán Massacre*; IACtHR, *Rochela Massacre v Colombia*, Judgment of May 11, 2007, Series C No. 163.

[114] IACtHR, *Trujillo-Oroza v Bolivia*, Judgment of February 27, 2002, Series C No. 92 [82].

[115] IACtHR, *Neira-Alegría et al. v Peru*, Judgment of September 19, 1996, Series C No. 29.

[116] IACtHR, *Street Children v Guatemala*, Judgment of May 26, 2001, Series C No. 77.

[117] IACtHR, *Neira-Alegría et al. v Peru*, Judgment of September 19, 1996, Series C No. 29 [49–50]; ibid *Street Children* [79]. See also IACtHR, *Gómez-Paquiyauri Brothers v Peru*, Judgment of July 8, 2004, Series C No. 110 [206]; IACtHR, *Ituango Massacres v Colombia*, Judgment of July 1, 2006 Series C No. 148 [371–2]; among others.

[118] See, for example, IACtHR, *Chaparro Álvarez y Lapo Íñiguez v Ecuador*, Judgment of November 21, 2007, Series C No. 170 [250–52]; IACtHR, *Ximenes-Lopes v Brazil*, Compliance, Order of May 2, 2008 [235].

[119] IACtHR, *Bueno-Alves v Argentina*, Judgment of May 11, 2007, Series C No. 164 [219]; IACtHR, *La Cantuta v Peru*, Judgment of November 29, 2006, Series C No. 162 [243].

on the principle of equity, whereby the Inter-American Court considers the parties' proclaimed expenses, as long as the amounts are reasonable.[120]

The other awarded measures of reparation have different purposes, namely vindicating the memory of the victims, restoring their dignity, transmitting a message of official condemnation for the human rights violations, and securing commitment from authorities that the violations will not occur again. The scope of these reparation measures has consistently expanded throughout the years and constitutes a contribution to the development of new standards in international human rights law. For instance, a measure of reparation that the Inter-American Court has consistently adopted is to compel States to investigate acts that gave rise to the human rights violations and to punish those responsible for their perpetration.[121] Moreover, the Inter-American Court has ordered States to release the results of the investigations to the public so that society, in general, can learn the truth about the violative events and the victims involved.[122]

On the other hand, in cases of forced disappearance or extrajudicial executions, the Inter-American Court has required States to find and transport the victims' remains to an appropriate resting ground chosen in agreement with the relatives' wishes.[123] Furthermore, pursuant to Article 2 of the American Convention, States must amend their domestic laws in order to comply with the obligations set forth in the treaty. For example, in *Blanco Romero* and *Goiburú*, the Inter-American Court ordered the defendant States to amend domestic legislation on forced disappearances in light of existing international standards.[124]

In addition, as a measure of satisfaction, defendant States are required to publish the Inter-American Court's judgments – or parts of them – in the country's Official Gazette and, in some cases, in a newspaper with national circulation.[125] Furthermore, as part of those measures, the Inter-American Court

---

[120] Ibid.
[121] IACtHR, *Humberto Sánchez v Honduras*, Judgment of June 7, 2003, Series C No. 99 [186]; IACtHR, *Cantoral-Huamaní and García-Santa Cruz v Peru*, Judgment of July 10, 2007, Series C No. 167 [190–91].
[122] Ibid.
[123] See, *inter alia*, IACtHR, *Street Children v Guatemala*, Judgment of May 26, 2001, Series C No. 77 [102]; IACtHR, *Bámaca-Velásquez v Guatemala*, Judgment of February 22, 2002, Series C No. 91 [81–2]; IACtHR, *Trujillo-Oroza v Bolivia*, Judgment of February 27, 2002, Series C No. 92 [115–17]; IACtHR, *Blanco-Romero et al. v Venezuela*, Judgment of November 28, 2005, Series C No. 138 [99].
[124] Ibid *Blanco-Romero* [105]; IACtHR, *Goiburú et al. v Paraguay*, Judgment of September 22, 2006, Series C No. 153 [179].
[125] See, for example, IACtHR, *Caracazo v Venezuela*, Judgment of August 29, 2002, Series C No. 95 [128]; IACtHR, *Miguel Castro-Castro Prison v Peru*, Judgment

has required States to name a school or square after a victim;[126] hold a public act of redress to acknowledge international responsibility;[127] award a scholarship with the name of the victim;[128] provide human rights training to public officials and members of the judiciary;[129] offer psychological and medical treatment to the victims or their next of kin;[130] implement a housing plan to provide adequate housing to victims or their next of kin[131] and create a system of genetic information to help in the identification of disappeared children.[132]

### D  Compliance with the judgments of the Inter-American Court

Compliance with the Inter-American Court's judgments is mandated under Articles 67 and 68 of the American Convention. Article 67 provides that judgments of the Inter-American Court are final and not subject to appeal. Article 68 obligates States Parties to comply with the Inter-American Court's judgments when the American Convention is breached. Additionally, the Inter-American Court holds that judgment compliance is based on the *pacta sunt servanda* principle, whereby States must undertake their international obligations in good faith.[133] States that accept the Inter-American Court's contentious jurisdiction are obligated to respect its orders, including those requesting information on the status of compliance with the Inter-American Court's judgments.[134]

---

of November 25, 2006, Series C No. 160 [446]; IACtHR, *Bueno-Alves v Argentina*, Judgment of May 11, 2007, Series C No. 164 [215].

[126]  IACtHR, *Street Children v Guatemala*, Judgment of May 26, 2001, Series C No. 77 [103]; IACtHR, *Baldeón-García v Peru*, Judgment of April 06, 2006, Series C No. 147 [205].

[127]  IACtHR, *Ituango Massacres v Colombia*, Judgment of July 1, 2006 Series C No. 148 [405]; IACtHR, *Cantoral-Huamaní and García-Santa Cruz v Peru*, Judgment of July 10, 2007, Series C No. 167 [193].

[128]  IACtHR, *Myrna Mack-Chang v Guatemala*, Judgment of November 25, 2003, Series C No. 101 [285].

[129]  IACtHR, *Zambrano-Vélez et al. v Ecuador*, Judgment of July 4, 2007, Series C No. 166 [157–8].

[130]  IACtHR, *19 Tradesmen v Colombia*, Judgment of July 5, 2004, Series C No. 109 [278].

[131]  IACtHR, *Ituango Massacres v Colombia*, Judgment of July 1, 2006 Series C No. 148 [407].

[132]  IACtHR, *Serrano-Cruz Sisters v El Salvador*, Judgment of March 1, 2005, Series C No. 120 [193].

[133]  IACtHR, *Bulacio v Argentina*, Compliance, Order of November 17, 2004, 'considering' [5]; IACtHR, *Barrios Altos v Peru*, Compliance, Order of September 22, 2005, 'considering' [5]; IACtHR, *Caesar v Trinidad and Tobago*, Compliance, Order of November 21, 2007, 'considering' [6].

[134]  IACtHR, *Barrios Altos v Peru*, Compliance, Order of September 22, 2005, 'considering' [7]; IACtHR, *Baldeón-García v Peru*, Compliance, Order of February 7, 2008, 'considering' [5].

The Inter-American Court has no specific authority under the American Convention or the Inter-American Court's Statute and Rules to supervise compliance or set a monitoring procedure. Nevertheless, since the first judgments on reparations in 1989, the Inter-American Court has established a practice of requesting information from States and adopting resolutions assessing the State's compliance.[135] In *Baena Ricardo et al v Panama*,[136] the Inter-American Court articulated the legal bases in support of its practice of monitoring compliance. The Panamanian government challenged the Inter-American Court's authority to require information from States and adopt resolutions on the status of compliance with its judgments. Panama argued that the Inter-American Court exceeded the scope of its jurisdiction, because the OAS General Assembly, pursuant to Article 65 of the American Convention, was the only organ authorised to monitor States. The Inter-American Court responded by reasserting its authority to determine the scope of its own jurisdiction.[137] Second, the Inter-American Court reasoned that the surveillance of judicial compliance was an inherent part of its jurisdiction.[138] Moreover, the Inter-American Court's decisions not only are intended as declaratory acts but also denote a mechanism used to effectively protect victims and provide redress for human rights violations.[139] This goal can only be achieved if decisions are fully executed.[140] Lastly, the Inter-American Court concluded that the power to supervise compliance with its judgments was based on an interpretation of several provisions of the American Convention and its Statute, and supported by a consistent monitoring practice never challenged by States before.[141]

In practice, the Inter-American Court sends written communications to States requesting information on the measures adopted to implement the judgment. States submit reports that are referred to petitioners and the Commission for their observations. As a result of this process, the Inter-American Court issues resolutions on compliance, which are published and available at the Inter-American Court's website. The supervision process is essentially in writ-

---

[135] IACtHR, *Baena Ricardo et al v Panama*, Judgment of November 28, 2003, Series C No. 104 [107]. See also IACtHR, *Moiwana Community v Suriname*, Compliance, Order of November 21, 2007, 'considering' [6]; IACtHR, *Ximenes-Lopes v Brazil*, Compliance, Order of May 2, 2008, 'considering' [6].
[136] Ibid.
[137] Ibid [68].
[138] Ibid [72].
[139] Ibid.
[140] Ibid.
[141] Ibid [84–104]. The provisions relied upon were Articles 33, 62(1) and 20 and 65 of the ACHR and Article 30 of the IACtHR Statute.

ten form, although in recent times the Inter-American Court has convened the parties and the Commission to private hearings for compliance assessment.[142] Moreover, pursuant to Article 65 of the American Convention, the Inter-American Court may submit to the General Assembly information on States that demonstrate reluctance in complying with the Inter-American Court's judgments.[143] To date, the General Assembly has limited itself to adopting resolutions urging States to comply, in general, without taking any other steps to ensure full compliance.[144]

Even though the Inter-American Court has never produced a comprehensive report as to compliance with its judgments, the tribunal's President recently stated that only 11.57 per cent of the total cases decided by the Inter-American Court have been fully complied with by the States concerned.[145] It is worth noting that many cases remain under the Inter-American Court's supervision as a result of the States' lack of compliance with the measures ordering the investigation and punishment of perpetrators of gross human rights violations.

## E  Three issues affecting English-speaking States in the Inter-American system

This section highlights some of the recent developments in the Inter-American Court's jurisprudence regarding English-speaking Caribbean States. Until recently, the Inter-American Court's influence was clearly visible and analysed mostly in the context of the Spanish-speaking countries in the Inter-American system. Indeed, analysis of the Inter-American Court's impact on English-speaking Caribbean countries is sometimes neglected. For this reason, the following discussion centres on three key issues that arose in response to

---

[142] IACtHR, *Raxcacó-Reyes v Guatemala*, Compliance, Order of May 9, 2008, 'having seen' [7].

[143] See, for example, IACtHR, Annual Report of 2003, OEA/Ser.L/V/III.61, doc. 1 (9 February 2004) 45–6, available at <http://www1.umn.edu/humanrts/iachr/Annuals/annual-03.pdf>. (Reporting on the partial compliance of Ecuador in the *Benavides Ceballos Case* and the failure of Trinidad and Tobago to inform the Court on the status of compliance in the *Hilaire, Constatine, Benjamin, et al. Case*. In both cases, the Court requests the General Assembly of the Organization of American States to urge those States to fulfil their obligations under the American Convention.)

[144] See, for example, AG/Res. 2408 (XXXVIII-O/08), *Observations and Recommendations on the Annual Report of the Inter-American Court of Human Rights*, 4th Plenary Sess. (3 June 2008) [3], available at <http://www.oas.org/DIL/AGRES_2408.doc>.

[145] Síntesis del Informe Anual de la Corte Interamericana de Derechos Humanos correspondiente al ejercicio de 2007, que se presenta a la Comisión de Asuntos Jurídicos y Políticos de la Organización de los Estados Americanos (Washington, DC, 3 de abril de 2008) (only in Spanish), p. 9.

the Inter-American Court's judgments regarding the relevant English-speaking Caribbean States, namely the mandatory application of the death penalty, the use of corporal punishment, and the rights of tribal communities.

*(i) Death penalty* The death penalty is particularly critical in the context of the English-speaking countries, because the majority of the Spanish-speaking countries in the Americas either have completely abolished the death penalty or authorise its use only in exceptional cases or cases involving military justice. In the cases of *Hilaire, Constantine and Benjamin et al v Trinidad and Tobago* (*'Hilaire'*),[146] and *Boyce et al v Barbados* (*'Boyce'*),[147] the Inter-American Court found that the mandatory application of the death penalty violated the States' obligations under the American Convention. The Inter-American Court held that the nature of mandating the death penalty was inconsistent with the American Convention, although the death penalty *per se* is not a violation.

In *Hilaire*, 32 complainants had been convicted of murder and sentenced to death under section 4 of the Offences Against the Person Act of Trinidad and Tobago, which proscribes the death penalty as the only applicable sentence for the crime of murder. The Inter-American Court concluded that the Offences Against the Person Act prevented judicial authorities from evaluating basic circumstances for determining the degree of culpability and establishing an individualised sentence, which violated Article 4(1), which ensures the right not to be arbitrarily deprived of life. In addition, by mechanically applying the death penalty to all persons found guilty of murder without judicial review of such application, the Offences Against the Person Act violated Article 4(2) of the American Convention, which limits the imposition of this punishment to only the most serious crimes. Lastly, the Inter-American Court concluded that Trinidad and Tobago's procedure for granting mercy lacked transparency, available information, and the victims' participation. Therefore, it held that the State violated Articles 4(6) and 8 – protecting due process rights – in connection with Article 1(1) of the American Convention.

In awarding reparations, the Inter-American Court held that the State had to refrain from the future application of the mandatory death penalty. Also, in accordance with Article 2 of the American Convention, the State had to bring its laws into compliance with this treaty and international human rights norms

---

[146] IACtHR, *Hilaire, Constantine and Benjamin et al v Trinidad and Tobago*, Judgment of June 21, 2002, Series C No. 94.

[147] IACtHR, *Boyce et al v Barbados*, Judgment of November 20, 2007, Series C No. 169.

within a reasonable time, and undertake legislative reform to establish different categories of murder that accounted for the particular circumstances of the crime and the offender. In anticipation of the new legislation, the Inter-American Court also ordered sentencing retrials for the victims after reforms were implemented. In addition, the State had to resubmit the victims' cases to the authority competent to render a decision on mercy, and the cases were to be conducted in accordance with the due process guaranteed in the American Convention. Furthermore, as part of the reparations, the Inter-American Court held that, regardless of the outcome of the new trials, the State should refrain from executing the complainants.

Though the Inter-American Court in *Hilaire* conclusively determined that Trinidad and Tobago's mandatory application of the death penalty was inconsistent with the American Convention, the issue surfaced again in 2007 in a case against Barbados. In *Boyce*, the Inter-American Court found that Barbados' Offences Against the Person Act of 1994, which called for mandatory application of the death penalty in all murder cases, similarly violated the State's obligations under the American Convention.

In *Boyce*, the State argued that the mandatory application of the death penalty was not incompatible with the American Convention, because defendants in capital cases could assert a wide range of common law defences and due process procedures, including review by the Barbados Privy Council,[148] which could commute the death sentence. Despite the State's arguments, the Inter-American Court found that the mandatory application of the death penalty violated an individual's right to life. Similarly, the possibility of review by the Privy Council was insufficient, because that executive procedure was only available post-sentencing. The Inter-American Court emphasised that, during the crucial judicial sentencing phase, Barbadian courts and judges had no option but to sentence all defendants convicted of murder to the death penalty. Based on those considerations, the Inter-American Court found that the mandatory application of the death penalty provided for in Barbados' Offences Against the Person Act constituted an arbitrary deprivation of life and failed to limit the death penalty to only the most serious crimes, thus violating Articles 4(1) and 4(2) of the American Convention. Although petitioners argued that the method of execution of the death sentence by hanging constituted cruel and inhuman treatment or punishment in violation of Article 5, the Inter-American Court found that it was unnecessary to address that claim. Regarding reparations, the Inter-American Court ordered the State to

---

[148] The Privy Council in Barbados was established under section 76 of the Constitution of Barbados to advise the Governor-General on the exercise of the prerogative of mercy.

commute the death sentence of one of the complainants[149] and adopt legislative or other measures necessary to ensure that the death penalty was no longer imposed in a mandatory fashion.

*(ii) Corporal punishment* In *Caesar v Trinidad and Tobago* ('*Caesar*'),[150] the Inter-American Court examined for the first time the compatibility of corporal punishment with the American Convention. In this case, Winston Caesar was convicted by the High Court of attempted rape. He was sentenced to 20 years in prison with hard labour, in addition to 15 lashes with the cat-o-nine tails. The State's Corporal Punishment Act allowed a male delinquent over the age of 16 to be beaten with a 'cat-o-nine tails', or with any other object approved by the President, in addition to the prison sentence. The cat-o-nine tails consists of nine cords of interwoven cotton, each cord approximately 30 inches long and at least a quarter of an inch in diameter, and is discharged on the prisoner in between his shoulders and lower back. Petitioners argued, *inter alia*, that Trinidad and Tobago's Corporal Punishment Act, in itself and as applied to the victim in this case, violated the right not to be subjected to torture or other cruel, inhuman and degrading treatment as protected by Article 5 of the American Convention.

Articles 5(1) and 5(2) of the American Convention provide for a prohibition of torture or other cruel, inhuman and degrading treatment or punishment. Moreover, Article 5 provides that all persons deprived of their liberty should be treated with the proper respect inherent to human dignity. In deciding whether corporal punishment violated the preceding guarantees, the Inter-American Court took into account the international community's widespread condemnation of torture and other cruel forms of punishment as inhuman and degrading. The Inter-American Court considered the international tendency to eradicate corporal punishment, as well as the increasing recognition of a prohibition on such punishment in domestic tribunals, before declaring it to constitute cruel, inhuman, and degrading treatment. The impermissible character of corporal punishment, in times of both war and peace, implied that member States, in compliance with Articles 5(1), 5(2) and 1(1), have an *erga omnes* duty to abstain from and prevent the imposition of corporal punishment, regardless of the circumstances.

The Inter-American Court concluded that, though the domestic laws authorised judicial corporal punishment, its practice nonetheless violated the

---

[149] In regard to the other three victims, one passed away and the other two had their sentences commuted before the decision of the Court was adopted. See *Boyce et al v Barbados*, above n 147 [129].

[150] IACtHR, *Caesar v Trinidad and Tobago*, Judgment of March 11, 2005, Series C No. 123.

American Convention because it amounted to institutionalised violence. As such, the Inter-American Court held that corporal punishment by flogging constituted a form of torture and therefore a *per se* violation of the rights protected by Articles 5(1) and 5(2) of the American Convention.

Furthermore, in *Caesar*, the Inter-American Court remarked that it was reasonable to assume that the beatings, which caused severe pain and physical damage, were exacerbated by the anxiety, stress and fear the victim experienced while incarcerated and awaiting punishment. Consequently, the Inter-American Court held that Caesar's sentence was executed in a seriously humiliating manner, since, aside from the aforementioned conditions, it was done in front of at least six people. As such, the Inter-American Court concluded that the corporal punishment applied to the victim constituted a form of torture and, as a result, a violation of his right to physical, mental and moral integrity as protected under Article 5 of the American Convention.

Additionally, in light of the incompatibility between Trinidad and Tobago's Corporal Punishment Act and the American Convention, the Inter-American Court concluded that when a State ratifies the American Convention it must adapt its legislation to conform to the obligations within the agreement. Therefore, its failure to do so violated Article 2 of the American Convention in relation to Articles 5(1) and 5(2).

*(iii) Rights of tribal communities in Suriname*[151]   In recent times the Inter-American Court has issued several important decisions regarding the rights of tribal communities in Suriname, in particular *Moiwana Village v Suriname* (*'Moiwana Village'*)[152] and *Saramaka People v Suriname* (*'Saramaka People'*).[153] In these two cases the Inter-American Court reaffirmed its understanding that, to ensure an effective protection of the rights of tribal communities, the particular characteristics that distinguish these communities from the general population must be taken into account when interpreting the scope of the American Convention.

In *Moiwana Village*, the Inter-American Court addressed the rights of the N'djuka tribe of Suriname. On 29 November 1986, the Surinamese military attacked Moiwana Village, a community of N'djuka in the eastern part of the

---

[151]   For the purposes of this Article, Suriname is part of the 'English-speaking Caribbean'. The reason is that (1) English is spoken extensively in Suriname, although Dutch is its official language and (2) Dutch is not one of the four official languages of the OAS.
[152]   IACtHR, *Moiwana Village v Suriname*, Judgment of June 15, 2005, Series C No. 124.
[153]   IACtHR, *Saramaka People v Suriname*, Judgment of November 28, 2007, Series C No. 172. See also Chapter 19 at p. 504.

country, burning its property and killing at least 39 members of the community. Among the victims were men, women and children, whose remains were never recovered and their perpetrators never brought to justice by the Surinamese government. Those whose lives were spared escaped to surrounding territories, including French Guyana. As a consequence of the cultural particularities of the tribal community, the injustice that resulted from the government's inaction prevented the citizens from carrying on with their lives. The N'djuka tribe's beliefs prohibited them from returning to the abandoned village of Moiwana. The survivors and the family members of those who died claimed that, to continue living their lives unburdened, they could not return until justice put at ease the spirits of the dead and proper burial rituals were allowed.

During the period of the alleged violations, Suriname had not ratified the American Convention or accepted the Inter-American Court's contentious jurisdiction. Therefore, the Inter-American Court limited its jurisdiction to those violations that continued to exist after Suriname's 1987 ratification and recognition. The Inter-American Court found that the lack of investigation, the denial of justice, and the forceful displacement of the community from its ancestral lands, from which the members continued to suffer, were continuous violations over which the Inter-American Court could assert jurisdiction.

The Inter-American Court held that Suriname's lack of investigation and the denial of justice violated the Moiwana community's right to physical, mental, and moral integrity on several grounds. First, the Inter-American Court determined that, given the notions of justice and collective responsibility shared by the N'djuka people, and given the State's failure to return the remains of the villagers killed to allow for a burial according to N'djuka traditions, Suriname caused the Moiwana community members to endure significant emotional, psychological, spiritual, and economic hardship, which amounted to a violation of Article 5(1) of the American Convention. Secondly, the Inter-American Court found that Suriname violated the victims' right to freedom of movement, as protected by Article 22 of the American Convention, given that the lack of investigation had forcibly displaced the Moiwana community members from their ancestral lands and prevented them from moving freely within the State or choosing their place of residence. Thirdly, the Inter-American Court held that the State's failure to ensure an effective investigation also entailed a violation of the right of the community to use and enjoy their traditional lands, and, as such, deprived them of their right to property provided under Article 21 of the American Convention.[154]

---

[154] The Court applied its previous holding in *Mayagna (Sumo) Awas Tingni Community v Nicaragua*, Judgment of August 31, 2001 Series C No. 79 (recognising

As part of the reparations, the Inter-American Court compensated the victims monetarily. Moreover, the Inter-American Court ordered Suriname, *inter alia*, to investigate the events complained of, prosecute and punish those responsible, and locate and identify the deceased's remains. The State also had to adopt all necessary measures to ensure the delimitation, demarcation and collective titling of the ancestral lands of the community and refrain from actions that would affect the existence, value, use or enjoyment of that property until the rights of the community are secured. Finally, the Inter-American Court ordered the State to establish a developmental fund of US$1,200,000 to invest in health, housing and educational programs for the Moiwana community members.

In *Saramaka People*, the Inter-American Court further developed and solidified the ancestral property rights of tribal communities. In this case, Suriname issued various logging and mining concessions between the years of 1997 and 2004 within the territory of the Saramaka tribal community. The Inter-American Court found that while the American Convention, specifically the right to property in Article 21, did not entirely debar the State from granting these concessions, the State did not consult the Saramaka people prior to these operations.

The specific allegations against the State in this case included non-compliance with Article 2 (duty of State to adopt necessary measures to protect American Convention rights) and violations of Articles 3 (right to juridical personality), 21 (right to property) and 25 (right to judicial protection) of the American Convention. The first issue was whether the Saramaka people constituted a 'tribal community', entitled to special measures that ensure the full exercise of its rights based on Article 1(1) of the American Convention. The Inter-American Court held that, although the Saramaka people were not indigenous to Suriname,[155] they nevertheless constituted a tribal community entitled to protection under the American Convention, because of their dependence on the land and their 'profound' spiritual connection to their ancestral territory.

The next pressing issue was whether Article 21 of the American Convention recognised the rights of the Saramaka people to use and enjoy communal property. In this regard, the Inter-American Court found that Article 21, as interpreted in the light of Suriname's other international human rights obligations, including common Article 1 (the right to self-determination) of the

---

the right of indigenous groups to a communal right to property under Article 21 of the American Convention), to the tribal Moiwana community.

[155] The Saramakas' ancestors were African slaves forcibly taken to Suriname during the European colonisation in the 17th century, who later escaped to the interior regions of the country and established autonomous communities.

*International Covenant on Civil and Political Rights* and the *International Convenant on Economic, Social and Cultural Rights*,[156] ensured the right of the Saramaka people to use and enjoy communal property. The Inter-American Court also found that, because Suriname allowed only individuals to claim a right to property under the law, it violated Article 3 of the American Convention, which protects the right to juridical personality defined 'as the right to be legally recognised as a subject of rights and obligations'.[157]

Perhaps the most compelling aspect of this decision, however, was the Inter-American Court's determination of ownership of the natural resources found within the Saramaka territory. The Inter-American Court held that members of tribal and indigenous communities had ownership of the natural resources traditionally used within their territory, because those resources were central to the survival of these groups. Notwithstanding, the Inter-American Court noted that property rights granted under Article 21 were not absolute and that the State, under certain circumstances, could restrict those rights, including issuing concessions for the exploration and extraction of natural resources within Saramaka territory.

To assess the scope of permissible restrictions of the right to property, the Inter-American Court articulated three safety measures that the State had to utilise when granting a concession for the exploration and extraction of a natural resource in Saramaka's territory. First, the State had to consult the Saramaka people and ensure effective participation in regard to any development, exploration, or extraction plan. However, in cases of major developments or investment plans that could profoundly impact the Saramaka people's property rights and affect their traditional territory, the State also had to obtain the free, prior and informed consent of the Saramakas in accordance with their traditions and customs. Secondly, the State had to guarantee that the Saramaka people would receive a benefit from any activity that took place within their property. Thirdly, the State could not issue any concession unless it had consulted with an independent entity to assess the social and environmental impact of the requested project.

In applying these safety measures to the concessions already granted by Suriname in the Saramaka territory, especially the logging and mining concessions, the Inter-American Court found that the State failed to comply with these safeguards, which violated Articles 21 and 1(1) of the American Convention.

---

[156] *International Covenant on Civil and Political Rights*, opened for signature 16 December 1966, 999 UNTS 171 (entered into force 23 March 1976). See also n 90.

[157] IACtHR, *Saramaka People v Suriname*, Judgment of November 28, 2007, Series C No. 172 [166].

As part of the reparations, the Inter-American Court ordered the State to demarcate the Saramaka territory and grant a collective property title to the Saramaka people. Additionally, the State had to amend any legislation encroaching upon the Saramaka people's right to juridical recognition, access to legal remedies, and the use and enjoyment of their property. The State also had to ensure the right of the Saramaka people to consultation, and, if necessary, set up a process through which they could grant or withhold consent in regard to large-scale projects that might affect their territory. Moreover, the State had to ensure that the environmental and social assessments were conducted by independent and competent agencies.

## 4 Conclusion

The States of the Americas currently have a more constructive relationship with the Commission and the Inter-American Court, which includes a better understanding of the complementary role that such organs play within their national institutions. This atmosphere allows for better dialogue and coordinated action between civil society, States, the Commission and the Inter-American Court in the common goal of safeguarding human rights. Several States have recently adopted national legislation and practices that broadened effective implementation of standards and decisions.

However, the increasing growth and impact of the Inter-American system has simultaneously adversely affected it. For example, OAS Members are hesitant to allocate essential additional funds for the Commission and the Inter-American Court. Moreover, some States remain suspicious of these organs and have, on occasion, attempted to undermine the system's effectiveness through covered proposals. Noteworthy is the vital role that civil society exercises in defending the autonomy and integrity of both organs – which, to a certain extent, are the main guarantors of the effectiveness of the system.

Lastly, a pending issue that remains to be addressed is the lack of universal ratification by all of the OAS State members of the core treaties of the Inter-American system, in particular the American Convention on Human Rights. Although, as previously discussed, the Commission monitors human rights compliance in the US, Canada and a number of Caribbean States under the *American Declaration on the Rights and Duties of Man*, the effectiveness of that supervision would strengthen if those States became parties to the IACHR. Furthermore, the case law developed by the Inter-American Court demonstrates that access to this tribunal would also benefit the protection of human rights in many of the English-speaking States that have not yet accepted its contentious jurisdiction.

# 15. African human rights law in theory and practice

*Magnus Killander*

## 1 Introduction

Human rights law is developed through the findings of national and international institutions and courts. National courts, human rights commissions, regional and global treaty bodies and courts make reference to each other in reports and judgments in the continuous development of the law of human rights. The African perspective, as developed by African courts, national human rights institutions, the African Commission on Human and Peoples' Rights ('African Commission') and so forth, is often forgotten in this exchange of ideas.[1]

It is sometimes argued that human rights have been imposed on the rest of the world by Western countries. To rebut this argument, the first part of this chapter considers the history of human rights discourse in Africa and its role in the struggle against colonialism. Since independence many regional human rights instruments have been adopted, often as a response to developments in the global arena. The second part of the chapter examines this regionalization of universal human rights norms and also takes note of unique features of the African normative human rights framework and areas where Africa has taken the lead in developing an international framework. The section explores to what extent the African Union ('AU') and its predecessor the Organization of African Unity ('OAU') have responded to African challenges in devising the African regional human rights system and how the often vague provisions of the main regional human rights treaty, the *African Charter on Human and Peoples' Rights* ('ACHPR' or 'the Charter'),[2] have been interpreted by the major regional human rights body, the African Commission.

---

[1] Rachel Murray, 'International Human Rights: Neglect of Perspectives from African Institutions' (2006) 55 *International and Comparative Law Quarterly* 193. African case law can be found in the *African Human Rights Law Reports* ('AHRLR') published by Pretoria University Law Press and *International Law in Domestic Courts* ('ILDC'), an online service provided by Oxford University Press. For more information see http://www.chr.up.ac.za at 29 January 2009.

[2] *African Charter on Human and Peoples' Rights*, opened for signature 27 June 1981, 21 ILM 58 (entered into force 21 October 1986). This and other African human

The final part of this chapter considers challenges and innovations in regional monitoring of compliance with international human rights norms. The proliferation of various monitoring bodies is considered in the context of the lack of adequate response to human rights at the national level in African countries and the lack of political commitment at the regional level. Note is also taken of the fledgling developments at the sub-regional level.

Research on the AU and other African organizations is made difficult by the lack of easily available information. Most of the websites of these organizations and their organs have gradually improved but they lack a publicly available document handling system like the Official Document System ('ODS') of the UN.[3]

## 2  Historical background

Human rights discourse played an important role in the struggle against colonialism.[4] The first Pan-African Congress, held on the fringes of the Versailles Peace Conference in 1919, called for the abolition of slavery, forced labour and corporal punishment and stated that it should 'be the right of every native child to learn to read and write his own language, and the language of the trustee nation at public expense'.[5] Calls for human rights were made again at the third Pan-African Congress in Lisbon in 1923 and at the fourth Congress in New York in 1927. Nnamdi Azikiwe, who was to become the first President of Nigeria, wrote in 1937, commenting on independent Ethiopia, Haiti and Liberia, that 'there is a universal identity of interest, in that Government is based on consent of the governed through constitutional provisions.'[6] This, admittedly overly positive picture, he contrasted with the colonies where 'the black man and woman . . . are protégés, not citizens'.[7]

---

rights instruments have been reprinted in Christof Heyns and Magnus Killander, *Compendium of Key Human Rights Documents of the African Union* (Pretoria University Law Press, Pretoria, 3rd ed, 2007).

[3]   See, for example, http://www.africa-union.org at 29 January 2009 and http://www.achpr.org at 29 January 2009.

[4]   Fatsah Ouguergouz, *The African Charter on Human and Peoples' Rights: A Comprehensive Agenda for Human Rights* (Martinus Nijhoff, The Hague, 2003) 6; Chidi Anselm Odinkalu, 'Back to the Future: The Imperative of Prioritizing for the Protection of Human Rights in Africa' (2003) 47 *Journal of African Law* 1, 25; Paul Gordon Lauren, *The Evolution of International Human Rights: Visions Seen* (University of Pennsylvania Press, Philadelphia, 1998) 78.

[5]   W E Burghardt Du Bois, 'The Pan-African movement' in G Padmore (ed) *Colonial and Coloured Unity – A Programme of Action* (1963) Etext, http://www.etext.org/Politics/MIM/countries/panafrican/pac1963.pdf at 29 January 2009, 16.

[6]   Nnamdi Azikiwe, *Renascent Africa* (Frank Cass & Co Ltd, London, 1968) 170.

[7]   Ibid 171. Azikiwe also discusses the rights of labourers: ibid 265.

By the time of the Fifth Pan-African Congress in Manchester in October 1945, the focus was on political and economic self-determination of the peoples of Africa, but the Congress also reiterated calls for such individual rights as freedom of association, assembly and expression.[8] In calling for the implementation of the *Atlantic Charter* everywhere, it was not only calling for self-determination but also requesting 'that all the men in all lands may live out their lives in freedom from fear and want'.[9] In December 1958 the All African People's Conference was held in Ghana. The resolutions of the conference made many references to human rights and requested that 'independent African States ensure that fundamental human rights and universal adult franchise are fully extended to everyone within their states, as an example to imperial nations who abuse and ignore the extension of those rights to Africans'.[10]

With more and more African states gaining independence, there was less focus on human rights except as a tool in the fight against colonialism and white minority rule in southern Africa. In 1963 the OAU was created. A few token references to human rights were included, but it is clear that the human rights language that had been used in opposition was no longer of value. To the extent that any attention was given to human rights by African leaders their priority was on socio-economic rights. In the words of the Tanzanian president Julius Nyerere:[11]

> What freedom has our subsistence farmer? He scratches a bare living from the soil provided the rains do not fail; his children work at his side without schooling, medical care, or even good feeding. Certainly he has freedom to vote and to speak as he wishes. But these freedoms are much less real to him than his freedom to be exploited. Only as his poverty is reduced will his existing political freedom become properly meaningful and his right to human dignity become a fact of human dignity.

A new international economic order failed to materialize and the lot of the African farmer did not improve. Authoritarian states became the norm and the bill of rights enshrined in many African constitutions remained paper tigers. The OAU early on took an interest in some human rights issues such as

---

[8] For a collection of the resolutions adopted see Padmore, above n 5.

[9] *Atlantic Charter*, signed on 14 August 1941. See, for example, the resolution on East Africa which also calls for the principles of the Four Freedoms to be put into practice at once: Padmore, above n 5, 57.

[10] Conference Resolutions on Imperialism and Colonialism [8], reprinted (with all the resolutions of the conference) in [1959] *Current History* 41, 44.

[11] Julius Nyerere cited in Issa G Shivji, *The Concept of Human Rights in Africa* (CODESRIA, London, 1989) 26.

refugees,[12] but the main principle established was the 'non-interference in the internal affairs of states'.[13] It is clear that the OAU did not contest the universality of human rights; after all the member states reaffirmed their adherence to the *Universal Declaration on Human Rights* ('UDHR')[14] in the preamble of the *OAU Charter*. However, the 'focus [of the OAU] was on protection of the state, not the individual'.[15]

## 3  Regionalizing the universal

The ACHPR was adopted in 1981. The history of the Charter has been traced elsewhere.[16] Ouguergouz notes a 'remarkable resemblance' between the Charter and the *Universal Declaration on Human Rights* ('UDHR').[17] However, it is clear that the drafters of the Charter have been inspired by a number of international treaties including the ICCPR[18] and ICESCR[19], the *American Declaration of the Rights and Duties of Man*,[20] the *American Convention on Human Rights*[21] and the *European Convention on Human Rights*.[22]

In addition to the ACHPR, the OAU and thereafter the AU have adopted many other treaties dealing with human rights. Many of these are regional

---

[12]  Bahame Tom Mukirya Nyanduga, 'Refugee Protection under the 1969 OAU Convention Governing Specific Aspects of Refugee Problems in Africa' (2004) 47 *German Yearbook of International Law* 85. On early OAU initiatives with regard to human rights see Rachel Murray, *Human Rights in Africa – From the OAU to the African Union* (Cambridge University Press, Cambridge, 2004).

[13]  *Charter of the Organization of African Unity*, opened for signature 25 May 1963, 47 UNTS 45 (entered into force 13 September 1963) Article 3(2) ('OAU Charter').

[14]  GA Res 217A (III), UN Doc A/810, 71 (1948).

[15]  Murray, above n 12, 7.

[16]  Ouguergouz, above n 4, 19–48. See also the drafts and other documentation reprinted in Christof Heyns (ed) *Human Rights Law in Africa 1999* (Kluwer Law International, The Hague, 2002) 65–105.

[17]  Ouguergouz, above n 4, 56, 60.

[18]  International Covenant on Civil and Political Rights, opened for signature 16 December 1966, 999 UNTS 171 (entered into force 23 March 1976) ('ICCPR').

[19]  International Covenant on Economic Social and Cultural Rights, opened for signature 19 December 1966, 999 UNTS 3 (entered into force 3 January 1976) ('ICESCR').

[20]  *American Declaration of Rights and Duties of Man* (1948), OAS Doc OEA/Ser.L.V/II.82 Doc 6 Rev 1 at 17 (1992).

[21]  *American Convention on Human Rights*, opened for signature 22 November 1969, 1144 UNTS 123 (entered into force 18 July 1978).

[22]  *Convention for the Protection of Human Rights and Fundamental Freedoms*, opened for signature 4 November 1950, 213 UNTS 262 (entered into force 3 September 1953) ('ECHR').

responses to treaties adopted at the UN.[23] Some treaties such as the recently adopted *African Youth Charter*[24] and the *African Charter on Democracy, Elections and Governance*[25] have no equivalent at the global level.

This section explores how the ACHPR and other regional treaties reflect both the universal and the regional.[26] 'Africanness' in these treaties could, according to Viljoen, be measured according to, on the one hand, the degree to which the regional instruments address 'the most pressing and specific human rights violations in Africa' and, on the other hand, the degree to which they reflect African tradition.[27] In the following the provisions of the Charter and associated treaties will be analysed with regard to both their 'Africanness' and their contribution to the development of human rights law.

The African Commission has interpreted the provision in Article 1 ACHPR that states 'shall undertake . . . measures to give effect' to the provisions of the Charter to mean that 'if a state neglects to ensure the rights in the African Charter, this can constitute a violation, even if the state or its agents are not the immediate cause of the violation.'[28] Applying this principle in one of its most well-known cases, dealing with the rights of the Ogoni people in the Niger delta, the Commission held that 'the Nigerian government has given the green light to private actors, and the oil companies in particular, to devastatingly affect the well-being of the Ogonis'.[29]

Provisional measures are only provided for in the Rules of Procedure of the Commission and not in the Charter itself. In the *Saro-Wiwa* case the

---

[23] Frans Viljoen, *International Human Rights Law in Africa* (Oxford University Press, Oxford, 2007) 302. For example, the *African Charter on the Rights and Welfare of the Child*, OAU Doc CAB/LEG/24.9/49 (1990) ('*African Children's Charter*') was adopted a year after the *Convention on the Rights of the Child*, opened for signature 20 November 1989, 1577 UNTS 3 (entered into force 2 September 1990) ('CRC'). Other African treaties were adopted long after the universal instruments. The *Protocol to the African Charter on Human and Peoples' Rights on the Rights of Women in Africa*, (adopted 11 July 2003, entered into force 25 November 2005) ('*Protocol on the Rights of Women*'), can be seen as a regional response to the *Convention on Elimination of all forms of Discrimination Against Women*, opened for signature 18 December 1979, 1249 UNTS 13 (entered into force 3 September 1981).
[24] Adopted on 2 July 2006, available online at http://www.africa-union.org/root/au/Documents/Treaties/Text/African_Youth_Charter.pdf at 1 February 2009.
[25] AU Doc Assembly/AU/Dec. 147 (VIII) (30 January 2007). Reprinted in Heyns and Killander, above n 2, 108–19.
[26] For a detailed examination of the ACHPR, see Ouguergouz, above n 4.
[27] Viljoen, above n 23, 304.
[28] *Commission Nationale des Droits de l'Homme et des Libertés v Chad* (2000) AHRLR 66 (ACHPR 1995) [20].
[29] *Social and Economic Rights Action Centre (SERAC) and Another v Nigeria* (2001) AHRLR 60 (ACHPR 2001) [58] ('*Ogoniland*').

Commission held that the refusal of the Nigerian government to comply with provisional measures requesting a stay of execution constituted a violation of Article 1 ACHPR.[30]

The prohibition of discrimination in Article 2 ACHPR differs from those in the UDHR and the ICCPR and ICESCR in that it includes 'ethnic group', and refers to 'fortune' rather than 'property' as an explicit prohibited ground of discrimination. Its wording indicates that it is only applicable to discrimination with regard to rights protected in the Charter and is thus similar to Article 14 ECHR.[31] However, it should be noted that because of the wide range of rights covered by ACHPR the distinction is of little practical use and the Commission has not interpreted Article 2 restrictively in its jurisprudence.

As with other regional and global instruments, there is an open-ended prohibition of discrimination on the grounds of 'other status'. The question whether 'other status' includes sexual orientation was raised in a case which was considered by the Commission in 1994, but not decided as the complaint was withdrawn.[32] The rapporteur on the case however is reported to have stated: '[b]ecause of the deleterious nature of homosexuality, the Commission seizes the opportunity to make a pronouncement on it ... Homosexuality offends the African sense of dignity and morality and is inconsistent with positive African values'.[33] This approach of limiting equality rights on the basis of African values has rightly been criticized.[34] More recent discussions of discrimination on the basis of sexual orientation at the Commission indicate increased tolerance in that respect.[35]

Article 4 ACHPR protects not only the right to life but also the integrity of the 'inviolable' human being. This right can be seen to clash with certain tradi-

---

[30] *International Pen and Others (on behalf of Saro-Wiwa) v Nigeria* (2000) AHRLR 212 (ACHPR 1998) [122]. Cf the decisions of the UN Human Rights Committee in *Piandiong and Others v the Philippines*, UN Doc CCPR/C/70/D/869/1999 (19 October 2000) [5.2] and the International Court of Justice in *LaGrand (Germany v United States of America)* [2001] ICJ 466.

[31] In contrast, Article 26 of the ICCPR prohibits discrimination with regard to any right, rather than only the rights enumerated in the ICCPR.

[32] *Courson v Zimbabwe* (2000) AHRLR 335 (ACHPR 1995).

[33] 16th Ordinary Session 1994 quoted in Evelyn A Ankumah, *The African Commission on Human and Peoples' Rights – Practice and Procedures* (Martinus Nijhoff Publishers, The Hague, 1996) 174.

[34] Ibid 174–5.

[35] See, for example, the examination of the state report of Cameroon in May 2006, discussed in Rachel Murray and Frans Viljoen, 'Towards Non-discrimination on the Basis of Sexual Orientation: The Normative Basis and Procedural Possibilities Before the African Commission on Human and Peoples' Rights and the African Union' (2007) 29 *Human Rights Quarterly* 86, 103–4.

tional practices.³⁶ That culture cannot interfere with this important right has been further elaborated on in Article 5 of the *Protocol on the Rights of Women* and in Article 21 of the *African Children's Charter*. It is thus clear that African human rights law take precedence over harmful traditions, recognizing that cultural practices are not static. It is noteworthy that African human rights law, for example the *Protocol on the Rights of Women*, often goes further in its protection against harmful practices than equivalent instruments in other regions and at the global level. Article 5 of the Protocol, with the heading 'Elimination of harmful practices', for example, provides that states should adopt criminal legislation banning all forms of female genital mutilation.

As opposed to other human rights treaties, notably the ICCPR, the Charter does not explicitly allow for the death penalty. In *Bosch* the Commission referred to one of its resolutions in urging all states 'to take all measures to refrain from exercising the death penalty'.³⁷ However, support for the death penalty remains strong in many African states, though there is a slow trend towards abolition.³⁸

Article 5 ACHPR sets out a number of rights treated separately in other international human rights instruments: the right to dignity, recognition of legal status, prohibition of exploitation and degradation, in particular slavery, and the prohibition of torture, cruel, inhuman or degrading punishment and treatment. The right to dignity offers an opportunity for protecting rights not explicitly recognized in the Charter.³⁹ For example, the right to privacy is not explicitly recognized in the Charter, but could perhaps be recognized as within the right to dignity.

Exploitation takes many forms in Africa and includes forced labour. In a continent plagued by poverty, it is however often difficult to distinguish between poor conditions of work and forced labour.⁴⁰ Article 29(2) ACHPR provides that everyone should 'serve his national community by placing his physical and intellectual abilities at its service'. This could be seen as endorsing forced labour, but this provision should be interpreted in light of the exceptions for 'normal civil obligations' recognized in the ICCPR and

---

[36] Ouguergouz, above n 4, 102–8.
[37] *Interights and Others (on behalf of Bosch) v Botswana* (2003) AHRLR 55 (ACHPR 2003) [52].
[38] Lilian Chenwi, *Towards the Abolition of the Death Penalty in Africa – A Human Rights Perspective* (Pretoria University Law Press, Pretoria, 2007).
[39] Cf the interpretation of Article 10 of the *South African Constitution* by the Constitutional Court of South Africa in *Dawood v Minister of Home Affairs* 2000 (3) SA 936 (CC).
[40] ILO, *A Global Alliance against Forced Labour* (2005) ILO, http://www.diversite.be/diversiteit/files/File/MH_TEH/documentatie/DECLARATIONWEB.pdf at 29 January 2009, 42.

the ILO forced labour conventions.[41] Mauritania was the last country in the world to formally abolish slavery in 1980. However, a number of cases before the Commission have related to discrimination which has its origin in slavery.[42]

The prohibition of arbitrary arrest and detention in Article 6 ACHPR corresponds to Article 9(1) ICCPR. However, the Charter does not explicitly recognize the procedural safeguards recognized in Article 9(2) to 9(5) ICCPR, such as the right to be promptly informed about the reason for arrest, the right to be brought promptly before a judge, the right to *habeas corpus* and the right to compensation for unlawful detention. These rights have however been recognized in the Commission's case law and in the *Principles and Guidelines on the Right to Fair Trial and Legal Assistance in Africa* adopted by the Commission in 2003.[43] The Charter also does not include any equivalent to Article 10 ICCPR dealing with conditions of detention. The Commission has instead found violations of Article 5 ACHPR when dealing with inadequate conditions of detention.[44]

In addition to the fair trial rights set out in Article 7 ACHPR, Article 26 ACHPR provides for the independence of the judiciary. Article 7 ACHPR provides for access to courts – 'the right to have his cause heard' – and safeguards with regard to criminal trials. These provisions are less elaborate than in the ICCPR but have been extended by the Commission in its resolutions and case law.[45]

The Commission has found violations of the right to freedom of conscience in Article 8 ACHPR in a complaint against Zaire on harassment of Jehovah's Witnesses,[46] and in a complaint against Sudan on persecution of Christians.[47] In a case against South Africa, the Commission found that the prohibition of the use of cannabis for sacramental use by Rastafarians was justified by the limitation clause in Article 27(2) ACHPR.[48]

The Commission has developed the content of Article 9 in its *Declaration of Principles on Freedom of Expression in Africa*. The right to 'receive

---

[41] Ouguergouz, above n 4, 111.
[42] See, for example, *Malawi African Association and Others v Mauritania* (2000) AHRLR 149 (ACHPR 2000).
[43] Reprinted in Heyns and Killander, above n 2, 288–311.
[44] See, for example, *Huri-Laws v Nigeria* (2000) AHRLR 273 (ACHPR 2000) [40]–[41].
[45] *Principles and Guidelines on the Right to a Fair Trial and Legal Assistance in Africa*, above n 43.
[46] *Free Legal Assistance Group and Others v Zaire* (2000) AHRLR 74 (ACHPR 1995) [45].
[47] *Amnesty International and Others v Sudan* (2000) AHRLR 297 (ACHPR 1999) [76].
[48] *Prince v South Africa* (2004) AHRLR 105 (ACHPR 2004) [40]–[43].

information' in Article 9(1) ACHPR is interpreted in the Declaration to include a right to 'access information held by public bodies' and information 'held by private bodies which is necessary for the exercise or protection of any right'.[49] A number of countries in Africa have followed the international trend and adopted freedom of information legislation.

Article 12(3) ACHPR uniquely among international human rights treaties recognizes the right to 'seek and obtain asylum'. This provision should be read together with Article 2(3) of the 1969 *Convention Governing the Specific Aspects of Refugee Problems in Africa*, which provides that a person may not be returned to a country where his or her life, physical integrity or liberty might be threatened.[50] The African Refugee Convention can be seen as a response to the 1967 Protocol to the 1951 *UN Refugee Convention*,[51] which expanded the scope of the latter convention beyond the situation in post-war Europe. It is noteworthy that the African Refugee Convention includes a wider definition of refugee than the UN Convention but that the *non-refoulement* provision in Article 2(3) is limited to threats to life, physical integrity or liberty. Even with this limitation the protection is wider than in Article 33 of the UN Convention, which only prohibits *refoulement* when life or freedom is threatened on the basis of discrimination.[52]

The AU is in the process of developing a treaty on internally displaced persons in recognition of the problems faced by people who are forced to leave their homes but do not cross a border.[53]

The provision in Article 12(4) ACHPR that expulsion decisions must be 'taken in accordance with the law' must be interpreted in the light of the safeguards in Article 13 ICCPR and the provisions in the refugee conventions. The prohibition on mass expulsion in Article 12(5) ACHPR has been addressed by the Commission on numerous occasions indicating that many states do not live up to their undertaking of 'African solidarity'.[54]

---

[49] *Declaration of Principles on Freedom of Expression in Africa* (2002) African Commission on Human Rights, http://www.achpr.org/english/declarations/declaration_freedom_exp_en.html at 29 January 2009.

[50] *OAU Convention Governing the Specific Aspects of Refugee Problems in Africa*, adopted on 10 September 1969, OAU Doc CAB/LEG/24.3 (entered into force on 20 June 1974), reprinted in Heyns and Killander, above n 2, 279–83.

[51] *Convention relating to the Status of Refugees*, opened for signature 28 July 1951, 189 UNTS 150 (entered into force 22 April 1954).

[52] The *Convention Against Torture and Other Cruel, Inhuman or Degrading Treatment or Punishment*, opened for signature 10 December 1984, 1465 UNTS 85 (entered into force 26 June 1987) further protects against *refoulement* if there are reasonable grounds to believe the person will be tortured in the receiving state.

[53] Permanent Delegation of the African Union in Geneva, 'HE Mme Julia Dolly Joiner, Commissioner for Political Affairs addresses the 58th session Executive Committee of the UNHCR, Geneva' (Press Release, 2 October 2007).

[54] See, for example, *Rencontre Africaine pour la Défense des Droits de*

The right to political participation in Article 13 has been considered by the Commission in a few cases. The AU has also been active in standard-setting for democratic governance. The *African Charter on Democracy, Elections and Governance*, adopted by the AU Assembly in January 2007,[55] was preceded by a number of declarations which will continue to play an important role. These include the *Declaration on Unconstitutional Change of Government* adopted by the OAU Assembly in July 2000 and the *Declaration on the Principles Governing Democratic Elections in Africa* adopted by the Assembly in July 2002.

The question is how sincerely democracy has been endorsed. Military coups are no longer a common occurrence on the continent and sanctions, such as suspension of participation in AU organs, are imposed by the African Union for unconstitutional changes of government in accordance with the *Declaration on Unconstitutional Change of Government*. However, crises such as in Zimbabwe make it clear that these declarations are only applied selectively by African leaders in their response to violations by their peers.[56] It should be noted that some current African leaders came to power through military means.[57] In most of their countries elections have been held to legitimize their rule, though the freeness and fairness of these elections is often questionable. One way of measuring democracy is to see whether a state is viewed as a democracy by its peers: 22 African countries were invited by the Convening Group to the Fourth Ministerial Meeting of the Community of Democracies in Bamako, Mali, in November 2007.[58] None of the 11 African

---

*l'Homme v Zambia* (2000) AHRLR 321 (ACHPR 1996); *Union Interafricaine des Droits de l'Homme and Others v Angola* (2000) AHRLR 18 (ACHPR 1997).

[55] On the Charter see, for example, Solomon T Ebobrah, *The African Charter on Democracy, Elections and Governance: A new dawn for the enthronement of legitimate governance in Africa?* (2007) AFRIMap, http://www.afrimap.org/english/images/paper/ACDEG&ECOWAS_Ebobrah.pdf at 29 January 2009.

[56] On the response of the AU to unconstitutional change of government see P D Williams, 'From non-intervention to non-indifference: the origins and development of the African Union's security culture' (2007) 106 *African Affairs* 253, 271–5. On the response of the AU to the crisis in Zimbabwe following the 2008 elections see *Resolution on Zimbabwe*, AU Doc Assembly/AU/Res.1 (XI) (1 July 2008).

[57] For example Muammar al-Gaddafi of Libya (1969); Teodoro Obiang Nguema Mbasogo of Equatorial Guinea (1979); Yoweri Museveni of Uganda (1986); Blaise Compaoré of Burkina Faso (1987), Omar al Bashir of Sudan (1989); Idriss Deby of Chad (1990); Meles Zenawi of Ethiopia (1991); Yahya Jammeh of The Gambia (1994); Denis Sassou Nguesso (1997); and Francois Bozize of Central African Republic (2003). In 2008 military coups took place in Mauritania and Guinea, to which the AU responded in accordance with the *Declaration on Unconstitutional Change of Government*.

[58] They were: Benin, Botswana, Cape Verde, Ghana, Kenya, Lesotho, Liberia,

countries which have a leader who has been in power for over 20 years were invited.[59]

Article 14 ACHPR protects the right to property.[60] In *Huri-Laws v Nigeria* the Commission found that since no 'public need or community interest to justify search and seizure' of the property of an NGO had been shown, Article 14 ACHPR had been violated.[61] In another case against Nigeria the Commission held that:[62]

> The right to property necessarily includes a right to have access to one's property and the right not to have one's property invaded or encroached upon. The decrees which permitted the Newspapers premises to be sealed up and for publications to be seized cannot be said to be 'appropriate' or in the interest of the public or the community in general. The Commission finds a violation of [Article 14 ACHPR].

Considering that the Preamble of the Charter states that 'civil and political rights cannot be dissociated from economic, social and cultural rights in their conception as well as universality', it is noteworthy that only three socio-economic rights are explicitly recognized in the Charter: work, health and education. There is no reference in the Charter to the progressive realization of these rights, which pervades the obligations in the ICESCR, but the Commission has held that progressive implementation is implicit.[63] The Commission has interpreted the rights recognized in the Charter widely to

---

Madagascar, Malawi, Mali, Mauritius, Morocco, Mozambique, Namibia, Niger, Nigeria, Sao Tome and Principe, Senegal, Seychelles, South Africa, Tanzania and Zambia. Algeria, Burkina Faso, Burundi, Cameroon, DRC, Djibouti, Egypt, Guinea-Bissau, Mauritania, Nigeria, Rwanda, Sierra Leone and Uganda were invited as observers: *Statement of the Convening Group of the Community of Democracies on the Invitation Process for the Fourth Ministerial Conference to be held in Bamako, Mali, November 14–17, 2007* (2007) Demcoalition, http://www.demcoalition.org/pdf/CG%20Statement%20of%20the%20Invitation%20Process%20to%20CD%20Bamako%20Ministerial%20Conference.pdf at 20 January 2009.

[59] Those leaders were: Omar Bongo of Gabon (in power since 1967); Muammar al-Gaddafi of Libya (1969); Jose Eduardo dos Santos of Angola (1979); Teodoro Obiang Nguema Mbasogo of Equatorial Guinea (1979); Robert Mugabe of Zimbabwe (1980); Hosni Mubarak of Egypt (1981); Paul Biya of Cameroon (1982); Lansana Conte of Guinea (1984); Mswati III of Swaziland (1986); Yoweri Museveni of Uganda (1986); Zine El Abidine Ben Ali of Tunisia (1987); and Blaise Compaoré of Burkina Faso (1987).

[60] Ouguergouz, above n 4, 152–5.

[61] (2000) AHRLR 273 (ACHPR 2000) [53].

[62] *Constitutional Rights Project and Others v Nigeria* (2000) AHRLR 227 (ACHPR 1999) [54].

[63] *Purohit and Another v The Gambia* (2003) AHRLR 96 (ACHPR 2003) [84] (*'Purohit'*); see also Viljoen, above n 23, 240–41.

include also, for example, the right to food and the right to housing.⁶⁴ More detailed socio-economic rights are recognized in the *African Children's Charter*, the *Protocol on Women* and the *Youth Charter*. Cultural rights are further elaborated in the *African Cultural Charter*, which was adopted in 1976.⁶⁵

The AU Assembly has also adopted a number of declarations with regard to socio-economic rights such as the *Maputo Declaration on Malaria, HIV/AIDS, Tuberculosis, and Other Related Infectious Diseases*, the *Declaration on Agriculture and Food Security in Africa* and the *Declaration and Plan of Action for Promotion of Employment and Poverty Alleviation*.⁶⁶

Article 18(1) and (2) ACHPR provides:

1. The family shall be the natural unit and basis of society. It shall be protected by the state which shall take care of its physical and moral health.
2. The state shall have the duty to assist the family which is the custodian of morals and traditional values recognized by the community.

These vague provisions can be interpreted as providing for a right to social security when the extended family fails to fulfil this function. It could also be argued that it would act as a safeguard for traditional values, but the Commission's case law gives no indication that such traditional values prevail if they should conflict with rights recognized in the Charter.

Article 18(3) ACHPR is unique in that it provides that the state 'shall ensure the protection of the rights of the woman and the child as stipulated in international declarations and conventions'. It thus incorporates the substantive provisions of other international instruments such as CEDAW, which were adopted prior to the adoption of the ACHPR.⁶⁷ The rights of women and children are further developed in the *African Charter on the Rights and Welfare of the Child* and the *Protocol on the Rights of Women in Africa*.

The *African Children's Charter* was adopted in 1990, shortly after the CRC. It can be seen as a response to perceived marginalization of Africa in the

---

⁶⁴ See *Ogoniland* and *Resolution on Economic, Social and Cultural Rights in Africa*, adopted by the Commission in 2004 and reprinted in Heyns and Killander, above n 2, 315–22.

⁶⁵ Adopted on 5 July 1976, available at http://www.africa-union.org/root/au/Documents/Treaties/Text/Cultural_Charter_for_Africa.pdf at 1 February 2009. The *Cultural Charter* will be replaced by the *Charter for an African Cultural Renaissance*, adopted by the AU Assembly in January 2006, when this treaty enters into force.

⁶⁶ AU treaties and declarations can be found on the AU website, http://www.africa-union.org, at 30 January 2009 and on http://www.chr.up.ac.za at 30 January 2009.

⁶⁷ Viljoen, above n 23, 270–71.

negotiations on the CRC.[68] In some instances the *African Children's Charter* gives wider protection than the CRC, for example with regard to child soldiers, child marriages and internally displaced children.[69]

The *Protocol on the Rights of Women in Africa* was adopted in July 2003 as an additional protocol to the ACHPR. States that have ratified the Protocol shall report on their implementation of the Protocol in their state reports submitted to the Commission under the Charter. According to Viljoen, 'the Protocol speaks in a clearer voice about issues of particular concern to African women, locates CEDAW in African reality, and returns some casualties of quests for global consensus into its fold'.[70] An important aspect of the Protocol is its inclusion of violations in the private sphere, for example domestic violence (Article 4). The Protocol is complemented by the *Solemn Declaration on Gender Equality in Africa* adopted by the AU Assembly in July 2004.[71]

Note should also be taken of the *African Youth Charter*. This treaty was adopted by the AU Assembly in July 2006 and sets out rights of young people between the ages of 15 and 35 years.[72] The focus is on participation in decision making, education and skills development, employment and health. The *African Youth Charter* and the *Protocol on the Rights of Women* are unique among international treaties in addressing the HIV/AIDS pandemic.[73]

The 'right to special measures of protection' for the aged and the disabled in article 18(4) has received less attention. There is no African equivalent to the recently adopted *UN Convention on the Rights of Persons with Disabilities*,[74] though rights of the disabled are included in the *Women's Protocol*,[75] the *Children's Charter*[76] and the *Youth Charter*.[77] At its session in May 2007 the Commission adopted a Resolution on the rights of older persons in Africa and in November 2007 it appointed one of the Commissioners as Focal Point on the Rights of Elderly Persons in Africa.[78]

---

[68] Viljoen, above n 23, 261.
[69] Viljoen, above n 23, 262.
[70] Viljoen, above n 23, 271.
[71] Reprinted in Heyns and Killander, above n 2, 138–40.
[72] As of November 2008 the *African Youth Charter* had been ratified by 11 states out of the 15 required for it to enter into force.
[73] *Women's Protocol* Article 14(1)(d) and (e); *Youth Charter* Article 16(2)(d)–(h).
[74] *Convention on the Rights of Persons with Disabilities*, opened for signature 30 March 2007, 993 UNTS 3 (entered into force 3 May 2008).
[75] *Women's Protocol* Article 23.
[76] *Children's Charter* Article 13.
[77] *Youth Charter* Article 24.
[78] *Final communiqué of the 42nd ordinary session of the African Commission on*

One of the ostensibly unique features of the Charter is the recognition of peoples' rights.[79] The Charter sets out the right of all peoples to equality (Article 19 ACHPR), self-determination (Article 20 ACHPR), free disposal of wealth and natural resources (Article 21 ACHPR), economic, social and cultural development (Article 22 ACHPR), peace and security (Article 23 ACHPR) and 'a general satisfactory environment favourable to their development' (Article 24 ACHPR).

The rights recognized in Articles 19 to 22 ACHPR are all aspects of the right to self-determination recognized also in common Article 1 of the ICCPR and the ICESCR.[80] As noted in the historical background above, the right to self-determination 'represents one of the most important roots of modern international human rights protection'.[81] Nevertheless, the inclusion of this right in common Article 1 of the ICCPR and the ICESCR was opposed by Western states and only included at the insistence of developing countries.[82] The difference between the right in the covenants and in the ACHPR is that it is more elaborate in the ACHPR than in the covenants, while, as seen above, the opposite is true with regard to most of the individual rights set out in the Charter.

Ouguergouz argues that the term 'peoples' in the ACHPR can be interpreted in four different ways: all of the nationals of the state, all of the inhabitants of the state, populations under colonial or racial domination, or ethnic groups.[83] In the context of the two covenants, Nowak interprets peoples as referring to 'peoples living under colonial rule or comparable alien subjugation' and peoples of 'independent multinational States . . . not protected as minorities'.[84] As the Charter does not include any specific minority protection corresponding to Article 27 ICCPR it is clear that peoples' rights must also be seen to protect the rights of minorities. However, when the Commission made use of the *UN Declaration of the Rights of Persons Belonging to National or Ethnic, Religious and Linguistic Minorities*[85] it was

---

*Human and Peoples' Rights held in Brazzaville, Republic of Congo, from 14 to 28 November 2007* (2007) ACHPR, http://www.achpr.org/english/communiques/communique42_en.html at 30 January 2009.

[79] Ouguergouz, above n 4, 57.

[80] On the right to self-determination in the covenants see Human Rights Committee, *General Comment No 12: Article 1*, UN Doc HRI/GEN/1/Rev.1 at 12 (1994), and Manfred Nowak, *UN Covenant on Civil and Political Rights* (N P Engel, Kehl, 2nd rev ed, 2005) 5–26. On the free disposal of wealth and natural resources see also Article 47 ICCPR and Article 25 ICESCR.

[81] Nowak, above n 80, 6.

[82] Nowak, above n 80, 12–13.

[83] Ouguergouz, above n 4, 210–11.

[84] Nowak, above n 80, 22.

[85] GA Res 47/135, UN GAOR, 47th sess, 92nd plen mtg, UN Doc A/Res/47/135 (18 December 1992).

in the context of the non-discrimination clause in Article 2 ACHPR rather than the rights of peoples to equality in Article 19 ACHPR.[86]

The UN Human Rights Committee has held that individual communications under the Optional Protocol cannot deal with Article 1 ICCPR.[87] The ACHPR does not have such a limitation and complaints of violations of Articles 19 to 24 ACHPR have been considered in a few cases.

The Commission has linked the right to political self-determination to the right to political participation in Article 13 ACHPR.[88] A violation of the right to self-determination was also found in the context of military occupation in *DRC v Burundi, Rwanda and Uganda*.[89] In a case where a liberation movement from the Katanga province of the then Zaire argued that Katanga had a right to secede from Zaire, the Commission held:

> In the absence of concrete evidence of violations of human rights to the point that the territorial integrity of Zaire could be called into question and in the absence of evidence that the people of Katanga are denied the right to participate in government as guaranteed by [Article 13(1) ACHPR] . . . Katanga is obliged to exercise a variant of self-determination that is compatible with the sovereignty and territorial integrity of Zaire.[90]

This finding is in line with a declaration adopted by the OAU Assembly in 1964 and now included in the *AU Constitutive Act*: 'respect of borders existing on achievement of independence'.[91] However, the Commission seemingly recognized a right to secession under certain limited circumstances.

In *DRC* the Commission linked the freedom of disposal of wealth and natural resources in Article 21 ACHPR to economic, social and cultural development as protected in Article 22 ACHPR:[92]

> The deprivation of the right of the people of the Democratic Republic of Congo, in this case, to freely dispose of their wealth and natural resources, has also occasioned another violation – their right to their economic, social and cultural development

---

[86] *Malawi African Association and Others v Mauritania* (2000) AHRLR 149 (ACHPR 2000) [131].
[87] *Lubicon Lake Band v Canada*, UN Doc CCPR/C/38/D/167/1984 (26 March 1990).
[88] See, for example, *Jawara v The Gambia* (2000) AHRLR 107 (ACHPR 2000).
[89] *Democratic Republic of the Congo v Burundi, Rwanda and Uganda* (2004) AHRLR19 (ACHPR 2003) [68] ('*DRC*').
[90] *Katangese Peoples' Congress v Zaire* (2000) AHRLR 72 (ACHPR 1995) [6].
[91] *AU Constitutive Act* Article 4(b). The only way to break this principle is arguably with the consent of the country from which secession takes place, as in the case of Eritrea's independence in 1993.
[92] *DRC* [95].

In the *Ogoniland* case the Commission held that:

> [I]n all their dealings with the oil consortiums, the government did not involve the Ogoni communities in the decisions that affected the development of Ogoniland. The destructive and selfish role played by oil development in Ogoniland, along with repressive tactics of the Nigerian government, and the lack of material benefits accruing to the local population, may well be said to constitute a violation of [Article 21 ACHPR].[93]

In a case against Mauritania the Commission found that 'unprovoked attacks on villages constitute a denial of the right to live in peace and security' as guaranteed in [Article 23 ACHPR]'.[94] A violation of this article was also found in the first inter-state complaint dealt with by the Commission: *DRC v Burundi, Rwanda and Uganda*.[95] Of relevance to the right to peace and security are also the *Convention for the Elimination of Mercenarism in Africa* adopted in 1977[96] and the *Convention on the Prevention and Combating of Terrorism* of 1999[97] and its Protocol of 2004.

The Commission has only dealt with the environmental rights recognized in Article 24 ACHPR in one case. In the *Ogoniland* case the Commission held that the right to a satisfactory environment in Article 24 ACHPR

> requires the state to take reasonable . . . measures to prevent pollution and ecological degradation, to promote conservation, and to secure an ecologically sustainable development and use of natural resources.[98]

Of relevance to the protection of the environment are also the *African Convention on the Conservation of Nature and Natural Resources*[99] and the *Bamako Convention on the Ban of Import into Africa and the Control of*

---

[93] *Ogoniland* [55].
[94] *Malawi African Association and Others v Mauritania* (2000) AHRLR 149 (ACHPR 2000) [140].
[95] *DRC* [68].
[96] Opened for signature 3 July 1977, OAU Doc CM/433/Rev. L. Annex 1 (1972) (entered into force 22 April 1985).
[97] Opened for signature 14 June 1999, OAU Doc AHG/Dec. 132 (XXXV) 1999 (entered into force 6 December 2002).
[98] *Ogoniland* [52]. See also Morné van der Linde and Lirette Louw, 'Considering the interpretation and implementation of article 24 of the African Charter on Human and Peoples' Rights in light of the *SERAC* communication' (2003) 3 *African Human Rights Law Journal* 167.
[99] Opened for signature 15 September 1968, 1001 UNTS 3 (entered into force 16 June 1969). See also African Convention on the Conservation of Nature and Natural Resources (Revised Version) adopted by the AU Assembly in July 2003.

*Transboundary Movement and Management of Hazardous Waste within Africa.*[100]

The emphasis that the Charter puts on duties is sometimes seen as a distinctive African feature of the Charter. However, duties are also set out in the UDHR and the *American Declaration* and *American Convention*.[101] Indeed the interests of society at large play an important role in determining the limitations of rights everywhere.[102] Many provisions of the Charter contain 'claw back clauses', for example Article 9(2) ACHPR, which reads '[e]very individual shall have the right to express and disseminate his opinions within the law'. These could be interpreted as permitting the removal of the protection of the Charter by national law. Fortunately the Commission has instead applied Article 27(2) ACHPR as a general limitation clause when the need has arisen to balance one right against another or balance a right against a legitimate societal interest.[103] In determining what limitations to allow, it must be kept in mind that limitations of rights 'must be strictly proportionate with and absolutely necessary for the advantages which are to be obtained . . . a limitation may never have as a consequence that the right itself becomes illusory'.[104]

## 4 Monitoring implementation: African challenges and innovations

Monitoring of human rights implementation is carried out in varying degrees within the states themselves, by sub-regional bodies to which the states belong, and by the various organs and institutions established under the AU. The UN and its various agencies also play an important role.[105]

The African regional human rights system is the youngest of the regional human rights systems. It was for many years limited to the African Commission on Human and Peoples' Rights. The 11-member Commission was designed as 'a tool of African governments',[106] but has gradually asserted its independence. The composition of the Commission today is in clear

---

[100] Opened for signature 30 January 1991, 30 ILM 773 (entered into force 1 February 1996).
[101] Ouguergouz, above n 4, 58.
[102] Viljoen, above n 23, 305.
[103] Christof Heyns and Magnus Killander, 'The African regional human rights system' in F G Isa and K de Feyter (eds) *International Protection of Human Rights: Achievements and Challenges* (University of Deusto, Bilbao, 2006) 519.
[104] *Media Rights Agenda and Others v Nigeria* (2000) AHRLR 200 (ACHPR 1998).
[105] For a detailed discussion of these actors and their human rights related activities see Viljoen, above n 23.
[106] Daniel D C Don Nanjira, 'The protection of human rights in Africa: The *African Charter on Human and Peoples' Rights*' in J Symonides (ed) *Human Rights: International Protection, Monitoring, Enforcement* (Ashgate, Aldershot, 2003) 227.

contrast to the early days of the Commission when it was dominated by civil servants and ambassadors. It is also noteworthy that at the time of writing, in January 2009, 7 of the 11 Commissioners are women, including the chair and vice-chair.[107] The Commission meets twice a year in two-week sessions at which civil society organizations can participate and make statements. The Commission can hold its meetings anywhere in Africa, but they are often held in Banjul, The Gambia, where the Secretariat of the Commission is based. At the conclusion of a session the Commission adopts an Activity Report which is submitted to the next AU Summit.

State reporting to the African Commission has had limited success. Some of the limitations are similar to those of state reporting under the UN human rights treaties;[108] others have been specific to the African system, such as a lack of availability of the reports for civil society organizations to make meaningful input for the process and the lack of dissemination of the concluding observations adopted.

The Commission's system of special rapporteurs and working groups is modelled on the special procedures of the UN. However, as opposed to the UN system, a special rapporteur in the African system is always also a member of the Commission. The Commission currently has six special rapporteurs charged with investigating the following issues: prisons and conditions of detention; rights of women; freedom of expression; human rights defenders and refugees; asylum seekers, migrants and internally displaced persons; and older persons.

Thematic working groups, which include both members of the Commission and external experts, deal with indigenous populations/communities, economic, social and cultural rights, torture, and the death penalty. A working group on specific issues related to the work of the African Commission, whose mandate includes the revision of the Rules of Procedure of the Commission, was established in 2005.

The response of the Commission to the *UN Declaration on the Rights of Indigenous Peoples*[109] gives an example of the innovative work of one of the working groups. In 2003 the Commission adopted a report of the working group which discussed the concept of indigenous peoples in the context of Africa.[110] In June 2006 the UN Human Rights Council adopted the *UN*

---

[107] http://www.achpr.org/english/_info/members_achpr_en.html.
[108] See, for example, Philip Alston and James Crawford (eds) *The Future of UN Human Rights Treaty Monitoring* (Cambridge University Press, Cambridge, 2000).
[109] GA Res 61/25, UN GAOR, 61st sess, 107th plen mtg, UN Doc A/RES/61/295 (13 September 2007).
[110] *Report of the African Commission's Working Group of Experts on Indigenous Populations/Communities* adopted by the African Commission at its 28th ordinary

*Declaration on the Rights of Indigenous Peoples.* However, before the Declaration could be adopted by the General Assembly it was stalled in the Third Committee by African countries. An explanation for this can be found in a declaration adopted by the AU Assembly in January 2007 in which it expressed concern about 'the political, economic, social and constitutional implications of the Declaration on the African Continent' and affirmed that the 'vast majority of the peoples of Africa are indigenous to the African Continent.'[111] As a response the African Commission presented an advisory opinion on the UN Declaration prepared by the Working Group to the AU Assembly in July 2007.[112] The advisory opinion dealt with the issues which the Assembly had identified as the most important with regard to the future negotiations on the Declaration: the definition of indigenous peoples, self-determination, ownership of land and resources, establishment of distinct political and economic institutions, and national and territorial integrity. The advisory opinion seems to have played a role in alleviating the fear of African states with regard to the implications of the Declaration, as the General Assembly finally adopted the Declaration on 13 September 2007 with no African countries voting against.[113]

The judiciary is inaccessible to the majority of Africans and human rights monitoring in African states can therefore not focus on a judicial approach.[114] National human rights institutions ('NHRI') could play an important role.[115] Lack of access to justice at the national level is one of the factors underlying the very limited number of individual petitions which have been submitted to the African Commission, despite the wide approach to standing adopted by the Commission.[116] By December 2008, more than 20 years after its inception, the Commission had published 141 final decisions on individual communications.

---

session (2005) International Working Group on Indigenous Affairs, http://www.iwgia.org/sw8768.asp at 1 February 2009.

[111] *Decision on the United Nations Declaration on the Rights of Indigenous Peoples*, AU Doc, Assembly/AU/Dec.141 (VIII) (30 January 2007).

[112] *Advisory Opinion of the African Commission on Human and Peoples' Rights on the United Nations Declaration on the Rights of Indigenous Peoples* (2007) ACHPR, http://www.achpr.org/english/Special%20Mechanisms/Indegenous/Advisory%20opinion_eng.pdf at 30 January 2009.

[113] UN, 'General Assembly Adopts Declaration on Rights of Indigenous Peoples' (Press Release, 13 September 2007).

[114] See, for example, Odinkalu, n 4 above.

[115] On NHRIs see, for example, Rachel Murray, 'National human rights institutions: criteria and factors for assessing their effectiveness' (2007) 25 *Netherlands Quarterly of Human Rights* 189.

[116] See, for example, *Ogoniland* [49], where the Commission permitted the admissibility of complaints submitted by way of *actio popularis*. Such submissions are not, for example, allowed under the ICCPR or the ECHR.

Of these decisions 63 communications were declared inadmissible, 11 were closed after withdrawal and 4 after an amicable settlement was reached. The Commission has taken 63 decisions on the merits and found a violation of one or more articles of the ACHPR in 56 of these.[117]

Under Article 56 ACHPR, local remedies must be exhausted in respect of a complaint in order for a case to be admissible, unless such remedies are unduly prolonged. In a number of cases the complainants have argued that the alleged lack of independence of the judiciary would mean that local remedies need not be exhausted. However, the Commission has guarded against becoming a tribunal of first instance which decides questions of fact rather than law.[118] Nevertheless, the admissibility decision in *Purohit* has potentially far-reaching consequences, as the Commission decided to declare the complaint admissible even though the disputed act could be challenged under Gambian legislation, as the Commission found that the availability of such a challenge would not provide 'realistic remedies ... in the absence of legal aid services'.[119]

With regard to socio-economic rights, the exhaustion of local remedies becomes problematic with regard to the many countries which only recognize socio-economic rights in their national constitutions as non-justiciable directives of state policy.[120] In such a situation a case can sometimes be brought on the basis of national legislation rather than constitutional provisions.[121] Arguably, to make these rights non-justiciable contravenes the ACHPR and anyone who has had their case thrown out by national courts on this ground could bring a complaint to the African Commission alleging a violation of the Charter.

Lack of follow-up by the Commission and the AU political organs contributes to the perceived futility of submitting a communication to the Commission. A study on the implementation of the recommendations of the Commission found that the lack of legal reasoning in many of the Commission's decisions and the long delay in delivering decisions did not

---

[117] Magnus Killander, 'Communications before the African Commission on Human and Peoples' Rights 1988–2002' (2006) 10 *Law, Democracy and Development* 101, 102–3, updated with information from the *African Human Rights Law Reports* and the Activity Reports of the Commission.

[118] However, there seems to be an exception when the state has not responded to a complaint: see *Ogoniland* [40].

[119] *Purohit* [37].

[120] On constitutional recognition of socio-economic rights see Viljoen, above n 21, 570–84. On the recognition of rights in African constitutions see Christof Heyns and Waruguru Kaguongo, 'Constitutional human rights law in Africa' (2006) 22 *South African Journal on Human Rights* 673.

[121] Viljoen, above n 23, 570–73.

impact on a state's compliance with the decision.[122] The only 'significant link' between the Commission's work and increased compliance was effective follow-up.[123] To improve compliance with its decisions the Commission must fully implement its *Resolution on the Importance of the Implementation of the Recommendations of the African Commission on Human and Peoples' Rights by States Parties*.[124] According to the resolution the Commission will include a report on compliance with its recommendations in its Activity Reports submitted to the AU Assembly. States are further requested to indicate the measures they have taken to comply with the recommendations within 90 days of notification of the decision of the Commission. Similar follow-up should be done with regard to recommendations emanating from the state reporting process and reports of special rapporteurs. In implementing the resolution the Commission could seek inspiration from the experience of the Human Rights Committee in its follow-up on concluding observations on state reports and on communications.[125] In particular a Commissioner should be appointed as special rapporteur on follow-up.

The *Protocol to the African Charter on Human and Peoples' Rights on the Establishment of an African Court on Human and Peoples' Rights* was adopted in June 1998.[126] The Protocol entered into force in January 2004, but the 11 judges were only sworn in in July 2006. The Court has its headquarters in Arusha, Tanzania. It adopted 'interim' Rules of Procedure in June 2008. While the African Charter has been ratified by all 53 AU member states, the Protocol has only been ratified by 24 states, of which only two have made a declaration allowing for direct access for individuals to the Court.[127] The Commission will thus remain important in the individual complaints process under the African Charter as it will have the role of taking cases to the Court. The Court also has advisory jurisdiction at the request of a member state, an AU organ 'or any African organization recognized by the [AU]'.[128]

---

[122] Frans Viljoen and Lirette Louw, 'State compliance with the recommendations of the African Commission on Human and Peoples' Rights' (2007) 101 *American Journal of International Law* 1, 14–16.
[123] Ibid 32.
[124] AU Doc ACHPR/Res.97(XXXX)06 (29 November 2006).
[125] For an evaluation of the follow-up process of the UN HRC with emphasis on African countries see Viljoen, above n 23, 114–20.
[126] OAU Doc OAU/LEG/EXP/AFCHPR/PROT (III) (9 June 1998) ('*African Court Protocol*').
[127] Burkina Faso is the only state party to have deposited a declaration allowing individual access with the AU Commission. Mali has also made a declaration but it had as of January 2008 not yet been deposited with the AU Commission: Email from Michel Ndayikengurukiye (African Court on Human and Peoples' Rights) to Magnus Killander, 4 February 2008.
[128] *African Court Protocol* Article 4(1).

An African Court of Justice and Human Rights will replace the current court when the *Protocol on the Statute of the African Court of Justice and Human Rights*,[129] adopted in July 2008, enters into force.[130] The new court will have a general affairs section and a human rights section. The main reason to have one African court instead of two as originally proposed is seemingly to save money.

Recently sub-regional courts have also handed down decisions with human rights implications, opening up a parallel system to the African Commission and the Court. In *James Katabazi and 21 Others v Secretary General of the East African Community and the Attorney General of Uganda*,[131] the East African Court of Justice held 'that the intervention by the armed security agents of Uganda to prevent the execution of a lawful Court order violated the principle of the rule of law' and thus constituted a violation of the treaty establishing the East African Community. The Tribunal of the Southern African Development Community ('SADC') delivered its first ruling in December 2007, a grant of provisional measures, followed by a judgment in November 2008. The case dealt with the land reform programme in Zimbabwe, which the Tribunal held was discriminatory.[132] The Community Court of Justice of the Economic Community of West African States ('ECOWAS') has abolished the requirement of exhaustion of local remedies, thus opening up a parallel jurisdiction to national courts.[133] The most prominent human rights judgment to date of the ECOWAS Court was handed down in October 2008 and dealt with slavery in Niger.[134]

The promotion and protection of human rights is not only a concern of the specialized human rights bodies, that is the African Commission, the Court and the Committee established under the Children's Charter. According to the *AU Constitutive Act* one of the objectives of the Union is to 'promote and protect human and peoples' rights in accordance with the [ACHPR] and other relevant instruments' (Article 3(h)). The Union shall function with 'respect for democratic principles, human rights, the rule of law and good governance'.

---

[129] Adopted on 1 July 2008, available online at http://www.unhcr.org/refworld/docid/4937f0ac2.html at 30 January 2009.

[130] The Protocol requires 15 ratifications to enter into force.

[131] (1/2007) [2007] EACJ 3.

[132] *Mike Campbell (Pvt) Limited and William Michael Campbell v The Republic of Zimbabwe* (2/2007) [2008] SADCT 2.

[133] Solomon T Ebobrah, 'A rights-protection goldmine or a waiting volcanic eruption? Competence of, and access to, the human rights jurisdiction of the ECOWAS Community Court of Justice' (2007) 7 *African Human Rights Law Journal* 307.

[134] *Dame Hadijatou Mani Koraou c La République du Niger*, arrest no ECW/CCJ/JUD/06/08, 27 October 2008.

One of the objectives of the Pan-African Parliament ('PAP') is to 'promote the principles of human rights and democracy in Africa'.[135] PAP, which only has consultative powers, has so far achieved little.[136] The Economic, Social and Cultural Council ('ECOSOCC') is intended to provide a voice for civil society organizations ('CSOs') in the work of the AU.[137] Human rights also fall within the ambit of the Peace and Security Council ('PSC'). However, the close cooperation between the African Commission and the PSC foreseen in the Protocol establishing the PSC has not yet materialized. The AU Commission based in Addis Ababa, Ethiopia, is the Secretariat of the Union, and will be responsible for monitoring implementation of the *African Youth Charter* and the *Charter on Democracy, Elections and Governance* when these instruments enter into force.

The African Peer Review Mechanism ('APRM') is a voluntary review process covering four governance areas: democracy and political governance, economic governance and management, corporate governance and socio-economic development. By January 2009, 29 of the 53 AU member states had signed up to undergo the APRM review, which consists of a self-assessment which should be conducted through a participatory national process leading to a national programme of action to address identified shortcomings. A Panel of African 'eminent persons' oversees the process. A member of this panel leads a review mission to the participating country when the self-assessment has been completed to ensure that the process has been conducted in a participatory and transparent manner. The report of the Panel together with the programme of action is presented to the APRM Forum of Heads of State and Government, which convenes on the fringes of the AU Summit which is held twice a year. Participating countries should submit regular follow-up reports to the Forum which should set out the measures taken to implement the programme of action and the recommendations included in the country review report. By January 2009, nine reviews had been concluded and discussed at the Forum: Ghana, Rwanda, Kenya, Algeria, South Africa, Benin, Burkina Faso, Nigeria and Uganda.[138]

---

[135] *Protocol to the Treaty Establishing the African Economic Community relating to the Pan-African Parliament* Article 3(2), available online at http://www.african-review.org/docs/civsoc/pap.pdf at 1 February 2009.

[136] Viljoen, above n 23, 186–9.

[137] AfriMAP, AFRODAD and Oxfam UK, *Towards a People-driven African Union: Current Obstacles and New Opportunities* (AfriMAP, Johannesburg, 2007) 33–7.

[138] On the APRM and its relevance for human rights see Magnus Killander, 'The African Peer Review Mechanism and human rights: the first reviews and the way forward' (2008) 30 *Human Rights Quarterly* 41.

Lack of funding and human resources have been major constraints on the work of the Commission. However, with recent massive increases in its budget financial constraints will hopefully be a thing of the past.[139]

## 5 Conclusion

The universality of human rights was reaffirmed by African leaders in the *Final Declaration of the Regional Meeting for Africa*, ahead of the 1993 Vienna World Conference on Human Rights, which held that: '[t]he universal nature of human rights is beyond question; their protection and promotion are the duty of all States, regardless of their political, economic or cultural systems.'[140] This statement could at first glance be seen as contradicting the statement further down in the same declaration that 'no ready-made model can be prescribed at the universal level since the historical and cultural realities of each nation and the traditions, standards and values of each people cannot be disregarded.'[141] However, this should not be seen as an argument for cultural relativism, but rather that individual rights often need to be balanced against other individual rights or collective interests. In the European human rights system this principle is known as the margin of appreciation. In the first case in which South Africa was taken before the African Commission, the South African government argued that this principle gave the government discretion to implement the African Charter in the way it saw fit. However, the Commission found that the margin of appreciation doctrine does 'not deny the African Commission's mandate to guide, assist, supervise and insist upon member states on better promotion and protection standards should it find domestic practices wanting.'[142]

The ACHPR is the main human rights instrument in Africa. Some observers have argued that because the text of the Charter does not explicitly include all rights and does not properly reflect its interpretation by the Commission, the Charter needs to be revised.[143] In my view the Commission's

---

[139] The budget allocated to the African Commission from the AU increased from US$1.2 million in 2007 to US$6 million in 2008. See *Activity Report of the African Commission on Human and Peoples' Rights submitted in conformity with Article 54 of the African Charter on Human and Peoples' Rights*, AU Doc EX.CL/446 (XIII) (2008).

[140] *Final Declaration of the Regional Meeting for Africa of the World Conference on Human Rights* in *Report of the Regional Meeting for Africa of the World Conference on Human Rights, Tunis, 2–6 November 1992*, UN Doc A/CONF.157/AFRM/14 (24 November 1992) [2].

[141] Ibid [5].

[142] *Prince v South Africa* (2004) AHRLR 105 (ACHPR 2004) [53].

[143] See, for example, André Mbata M Mangu, 'The changing human rights landscape in Africa: Organisation of African Unity, African Union, New Partnership for

flexibility in interpretation makes a review of the Charter unnecessary. Furthermore, an amendment process could be used by non-progressive states to put further restraints on the Commission. A revision of the Charter would also create confusion with some states ratifying the new Charter and some being bound by the old. If revision is needed this could be accomplished by adopting additional protocols.

Odinkalu has noted with regard to the African Union that there seems to be 'a deliberative strategy to bring the notion of supra-national legality into disrepute through the creation of a multiplicity of under-resourced and deliberately ineffectual institutions.'[144] To some extent this concern has been addressed. A process known as the Conference on Security, Stability, Development and Co-operation ('CSSDCA'), which would have conducted review processes similar to the APRM, has been shelved and the CSSDCA unit in the AU Commission has been converted into the African Citizens' Directorate, dealing with contacts between the AU and civil society organizations.[145] The African Court of Justice, provided for in the *AU Constitutive Act* and in a Protocol which has not yet entered into force, is yet to be established and is set to be integrated with the African Court on Human and Peoples' Rights. Other suggested rationalizations include the proposal that the African Commission should take over the responsibilities of the African Committee on the Rights and Welfare of the Child, which has achieved little since it was established in 2002.[146]

Unfortunately, human rights abuses, including those of the most egregious kind, continue to arise across the continent, often with an inadequate response from other African countries. The disappointing performance of the African regional human rights system is linked to the failure of national judicial systems. This problem will not be solved by the establishment of the African Court on Human and Peoples' Rights. Despite the odds the Commission has been quite innovative in interpreting both the substantive and procedural provisions of the Charter widely. Hopefully the Commission will lead the way for a strengthened regional human rights system by addressing submitted complaints in a timely manner, and by referring cases to the Court when the complainant so requests.[147] Without an effective Commission the whole

---

Africa's Development and the African Court' (2005) 23 *Netherlands Quarterly of Human Rights* 379.

[144] Odinkalu, above n 4, 25.
[145] AfriMAP et al, above n 137, 29.
[146] Viljoen, above n 23, 223–4.
[147] The Commission published a draft of its revised Rules of Procedure in January 2009 for comments. A meeting was planned for later in the year for the Commission and Court to harmonize their Rules of Procedure and thereby clarify the relationship between the two bodies.

African human rights system will continue to be seriously hampered. The AU Executive Council must become more responsive to the Commission's recommendations, but it is also necessary for the Commission to actively respond to the Executive Council and other AU organs and seek active engagement with institutions such as the Peace and Security Council and the African Peer Review Mechanism.

As has been shown in this chapter, Africa has taken an active role in the development of human rights law. African reality has been recognized both in standard-setting and interpretation. In theory the African Charter is a weak human rights instrument but both its substantive and procedural shortcomings have been overcome by innovative interpretation by the African Commission. It is hoped that the African Court will continue to build on the achievements of the Commission.

# 16. The political economy and culture of human rights in East Asia

*Michael C Davis*

## 1 Introduction

East Asian experience has long featured prominently among contemporary debates concerning human rights and development. The authoritarian East Asian challenge to human rights has set human rights in opposition to Asian cultural values and related East Asian developmental needs. While several East Asian countries have defied these claims and established constitutional democracies with liberal human rights protections, several others, including China and other post-communist countries in Southeast Asia, have continued to press these Asian values and developmental arguments to justify authoritarianism and severe limits on human rights. At a time when various UN reports relate achievement of the Millennium Development Goals to human rights and good governance,[1] several newly industrialised countries in East Asia have led the world in economic development.[2] This chapter will argue that full realisation of the promise of these achievements ultimately depends on constitutional reform that embraces democracy, human rights and the rule of law.

East Asian experience has tended to demonstrate that constitutional democracy with liberal human rights protection is the regime type most capable of addressing both cultural values and developmental needs. In the first generation of rapidly developing countries in East Asia, constitutionalism ultimately worked better in constructing the conditions for coping with the diverse interests that emerged in rapidly changing societies. While an East Asian brand of

---

[1] Secretary-General, *In Larger Freedom: Towards Development, Security and Human Rights for All*, UN Doc A/59/2005 (21 March 2005) ('2005 UN Report'); Report of the Secretary-General's High-Level Panel on Threats, Challenges and Change, *A More Secure World: Our Shared Responsibility* (United Nations, New York, 2004), www.un.org/secureworld at 18 August 2007 ('2004 UN Report'). See also Kofi Annan, 'In Larger Freedom: Decision Time at the UN' (2005) 84 *Foreign Affairs* 63.

[2] See United Nations, *Millennium Development Goals Report 2007* (United Nations, New York, 2007), http://www.un.org/millenniumgoals/pdf/mdg2007.pdf at 18 August 2008.

authoritarianism, with strong commitment to good governance, worked reasonably well at managing early-stage development, liberal constitutionalism, with strong human rights and rule of law commitments, is thought to have provided better tools for consolidating these achievements at the high-end stage of economic and political development. In this analysis liberal constitutionalism is understood to include three core components: democratic elections with multiparty contestation; human rights, including freedom of expression; and the rule of law with firm adherence to principles of legality.[3] To these core components I add *indigenisation* as a fourth ingredient. Indigenisation is the local institutional embodiment that connects constitutional government to the local condition.

As a preliminary matter, it is important to note that the human rights debate in East Asia has tended to be situated in domestic constitutional debates. This defies a pattern evident in those parts of the world with multilateral regional human rights regimes. In most regions of the world, regional human rights treaties and supporting institutions have provided the tools for importing human rights standards vertically from regional transnational practice. The East Asian importation of rights, in contrast, has tended to be a process of horizontal or comparative importation of international human rights standards through domestic constitutional debates and interpretations. These human rights debates have especially engaged concerns with Asian cultural values and economic development, making the so-called 'Asian values debate' one of the pre-eminent human rights debates in the world. The cultural dimension often involves local movements to promote democratisation, human rights and the rule of law in the face of Asian cultural relativist claims. The economic dimension engages the contest between authoritarian economic development and liberal democratic reform as competing avenues to economic success.

Through these locally grounded debates, countries in East Asia engage familiar international concerns with civil and political rights and economic and social rights, but do so on distinctly local terms. An authoritarian regime might claim that it provides a more stable environment for development and better protection of local cultural and social values. Local democrats and outside critics may contest this, saying that liberal political freedom, a free press, the rule of law and democratic rights best allow a country to address these developmental and cultural issues. Arguing for civil liberties in the context of development becomes an argument not only for civil liberties but

---

[3] Michael C Davis, 'The Price of Rights: Constitutionalism and East Asian Economic Development' (1998) 20 *Human Rights Quarterly* 303; Michael C Davis, 'Constitutionalism and Political Culture: The Debate Over Human Rights and Asian Values' (1997) 11 *Harvard Human Rights Journal* 109.

also for better protection of a wide range of economic and social rights, including such familiar rights as basic education, safe working conditions, a good environment, adequate health care and the like. The human rights debate is connected to the debate over political and economic stability. While human rights specialists may be more comfortable with an approach that is centered on the international human rights regime, this approach based on domestic constitutionalism may offer more immediate dividends in developmental terms by being better connected to the local condition. I believe it is precisely this strengthening of the domestic human rights debate fostered under East Asian conditions that offers something of interest to a world trying to deal with human rights concerns in many developmental contexts.

While the East Asian debate and the region would certainly benefit from the development of regional and national human rights institutions, human rights advocacy has to date been fundamentally grounded in domestic constitutional practice.[4] This chapter considers: first, the various claims on behalf of authoritarianism made in the name of Asian cultural values; second, authoritarian and competing East Asian claims relating to economic development; and third, the role of human rights and constitutionalism in addressing these issues. The aim is to look beneath the surface of this East Asian debate to better appreciate its contribution to human rights protection.

---

[4] Efforts to reach a regional consensus on human rights have gone on for many years. Most famously, in 1993, as part of the Vienna World Conference on Human Rights process, governments across the entire Asian region reached a consensus on the Bangkok Declaration, which was rather sensitive to Asian cultural and sovereignty concerns: http://law.hku.hk/lawgovtsociety/Bangkok%20Declaration.htm at 18 August 2008. The Bangkok Declaration was not converted into an Asian regional human rights charter. More recently ASEAN members have signed an ASEAN Charter, which is essentially a constitution for the ASEAN grouping that was adopted at the 13th ASEAN Summit in November 2007: http://www.aseansec.org/ASEAN-Charter.pdf at 18 August 2008. The ASEAN Charter effectively removes the ASEAN non-interference policy and calls for the creation of an ASEAN Human Rights Body for ASEAN members only, making it the first Asian regional human rights treaty that, once fully ratified, will legally obligate members to respect human rights. While a body of experts has been set up to draft the human rights body terms of reference, the generality of the human rights provisions in the Charter (only calling for respect for human rights and the creation of a human rights body) and the lack of commitment among several member states offer little hope of a robust commitment. See Amnesty International, *The ASEAN Charter and Human Rights: Window of Opportunity or Window Dressing?* (Amnesty International, 2008) http://www.amnesty.org/en/library/asset/ASA03/003/2008/en/384b86ba-4393-11dd-a1d1-2fa8cc41ebbd/asa030032008eng.pdf at 18 August 2008.

## 2 The Asian values cultural debate

The central challenge to human rights in East Asia has come from the so-called Asian values cultural debate. It is therefore useful to consider several prominent authoritarian-based East Asian arguments made on behalf of cultural values, including: first, the specific Asian values claims on a substantive level; second, a related cultural prerequisites argument which seeks to disqualify some societies from realisation of democracy and human rights; and third, claims made on behalf of community or communitarian values in the East Asian context. In introducing these Asian values arguments I will offer a critique of each, thereby rebutting the claim that human rights and democracy are culturally unsuited to Asian soil.

First, considering Confucian political values as the dominant value system in East Asia, the main substantive claim is that Asian values are illiberal and anti-democratic, rendering a liberal democratic human rights regime unsuited to the Asian cultural condition. East Asian societies are said to favour authority over liberty, the group over the individual, duties over rights, and such values as harmony, cooperation, order and respect for hierarchy.[5] East Asian supporters of authoritarianism have therefore argued that their societies are unsuited to democracy and Western liberal human rights practices. That authoritarian leaders are usually the promoters of these Asian values claims raises suspicion and has spawned a number of challenges to the claims.

The most obvious challenge is a simple empirical one: in recent decades the most successful Asian countries have generally moved on to adopt liberal democratic human rights regimes. The rapid recent development and consolidation of democracy and human rights in several East Asian societies speaks for itself. Former authoritarian systems, including those in Japan, South Korea, Taiwan, the Philippines and Indonesia all underwent democratic transitions and human rights reform in the last decades of the twentieth century. Hong Kong, Thailand, Mongolia and Malaysia have likewise seriously engaged the democracy and human rights debates through constitutional reform, though obstacles remain. While each of these systems has continued to be plagued with the lingering residue of their authoritarian past, the reformist direction is empirically evident and is indicative of a serious attraction to democracy and human rights in East Asian societies.

Beyond the challenge offered by developments on the ground, activists and analysts have offered a direct intellectual challenge to the Asian values claim, especially attacking its historical and philosophical roots. Chinese scholars of

---

5   Samuel P Huntington, 'Democracy's Third Wave', in L Diamond and M F Platner (eds) *The Global Resurgence of Democracy* (Johns Hopkins University Press, Baltimore, 1993) 3, 15.

the Confucian classics have noted that Confucianism does not embrace unquestioning acceptance of autocratic rule; that it shares with liberalism a commitment to higher norms.[6] Confucian scholar Wejen Chang has especially pointed out the prominent position of the golden rule in Confucian ethics.[7] Chang argues that the harsh autocratic practices of traditional Chinese rulers, sometimes known as neo-Confucianism, were more a structural imperative of dynastic rule and a product of Chinese legalism than a result of traditional Confucian thought.

Other scholars have challenged the motives of those who advance the above noted stereotypes concerning Asian values. Edward Said long ago accused Western societies of 'orientalism', of offering up a conception of Asia as 'the other' in order to justify Western dominance.[8] More recently Asian scholars have noted the tendency of East Asian leaders and scholars to adopt orientalism as a self-defining discourse.[9] In this latter conception of orientalism, East Asian exceptionalism replaced Western imperialism as the aim of Asian values discourse.

A related attack on the importation of Western human rights values is to argue that Asians in the early modern period simply did not understand the liberal Western institutions they were importing. So even when they attempted to import Western human rights values, the strong pull of Asian culture led them to reinterpret such Western concepts in Asian terms, surely marking Asian culture as unsuited to such importation. Such Asian reinterpretation saw democracy and related human rights as merely good government and social welfare, comparable to the Chinese *minben* (people as a basis) tradition.[10] There is no doubt that authoritarian-minded misinterpretations did occur and that Chinese nationalists, following the May 4th Movement, would sometimes distort Western liberal concepts.[11] But recent studies of early modern Chinese

---

[6] Victoria T Hui, *War and State Formation in Ancient China and Early Modern Europe* (Cambridge University Press, Cambridge, 2005).
[7] Wejen Chang, 'The Individual and the Authorities in Traditional Chinese Legal Thought' (Paper presented for the Constitutionalism and China Workshop, Columbia University, 24 February 1995). Chang emphasised the Confucian admonition that people should treat others the way they wanted to be treated.
[8] Edward Said, *Orientalism* (Vintage Books, New York, 1979).
[9] Beng-Huat Chua, *Communitarian Ideology and Democracy in Singapore* (Routledge, London, 1995).
[10] Andrew J Nathan, 'Political Rights in Chinese Constitutions' in R R Edwards, L Henkin, and A J Nathan (eds) *Human Rights in Contemporary China* (Columbia University Press, New York, 1986) 77.
[11] The May Fourth Movement was triggered by the decision of the Versailles Conference on 4 May 1919 that the German concession in Shantung was to be transferred to Japan. This caused a political movement marked by Chinese nationalism and

writings demonstrate that Chinese intellectuals often had a good grasp of leading Western liberal thinkers.[12] Accordingly, this argument may simply exaggerate the claimed distortions and the limitations imposed by cultural values.

Much of what is done today in the name of Asian values can be explained more often than not by expediency. This expediency is often accompanied by other ideological constructs, such as Marxism, that have little to do with Asian traditions. Francis Fukuyama points out that the only neo-Confucian authoritarian system evident in recent East Asian experience was the government of pre-war Japan.[13]

A second line of Asian values argument, of more contemporary relevance, claims that societies which lack certain cultural prerequisites are not suited for democracy and human rights. These claims are rooted in earlier studies that sought to measure the degree of civic culture that existed in Western democracies.[14] This is a categorically different kind of attack than the above culture-based arguments because of its basis in social scientific democratic theory. Though such a theory did not aim to support cultural relativist arguments, it was converted into such a challenge in East Asian application. As pointed out by Elizabeth Perry, in comparative studies of political development and democratisation this hopeful line of reasoning became burdened with the pessimistic view that societies that lacked civic culture were not likely to be successful at democratisation.[15] It was as if societies had to pass a test for democracy. This lent further support for authoritarian Asian values reasoning. Did societies burdened with authoritarian Asian values offer poor soil for democracy and the concomitant values associated with human rights and the rule of law?

The tautological reasoning in this line of argument is apparent. To expect a society to develop democratic culture without democracy itself is a questionable proposition. Many societies in East Asia in fact proceeded with democratisation, with or without the allegedly required civic culture. With

---

disillusionment with both the West and Chinese tradition. The ideological struggle between socialism and liberal democracy that would later become so important was born here.

[12] Marina Svensson, *The Chinese Conception of Human Rights: The Debate on Human Rights in China, 1898–1949* (Department of East Asian Languages, Lund, 1996).

[13] Francis Fukuyama, 'Confucianism and Democracy' (1995) 6 *Journal of Democracy* 20.

[14] Gabriel A Almond and Sidney Verba, *The Civic Culture: Political Attitudes and Democracy in Five Nations* (Sage Publications, Newbury Park, 2nd ed, 1989).

[15] Elizabeth Perry, 'Introduction: Chinese Political Culture Revisited' in J Wasserstrom and E Perry (eds) *Popular Protest and Political Culture in China* (Westview Press, Boulder, 1994) 1.

democratic institutions in place the emphasis then shifted to consolidation and further constitutional development.[16] Political elites and academics in East Asia have nevertheless clung tenaciously to this claim concerning prerequisites.[17] The ongoing task of documenting civic culture in East Asia contributes to a mindset that does appear to conceive of a test for democratisation. This has spawned a persistent argument by those in some communities that the local society is not yet ready for democracy and its related liberal human rights institutions.[18]

A third more consciously intended cultural relativist argument, and one that is to some extent more credible, is the community-based thesis. This argument fails to justify the denial of democracy and human rights, but it does raise some concerns that must be addressed by societies hoping to better secure human rights. For convenience here I divide community-based arguments into three categories: romanticisation of community, civic virtue and communitarianism. Romanticisation of traditional communities is a common theme in many modernising societies. The Vietnamese village has been described as 'anchored to the soil at the dawn of History . . . behind its bamboo hedge, the anonymous and unseizable retreat where the national spirit is concentrated'; while the Russian *mir* was to save Russians from the 'abhorrent changes being wrought in the West by individualism and industrialization'.[19] One may doubt just how liberating traditional village life was. Many in East Asia have migrated to the cities when they have had the chance. Few in East Asia's diverse urban societies still have the option of pursuing a traditional village lifestyle.

The second community-based argument relates to civic virtue. In East Asia this argument has ancient roots and is most often associated with Confucianism. Authoritarian leaders and even some academics in the region argue that it is still of great contemporary relevance.[20] In this view, an emphasis on civic virtue, more than liberal institutions, is seen as the key to good government.[21] Even in the West, an emphasis on civic virtue has been a persistent theme throughout the modern period of democratisation.[22] But many

---

[16] Juan J Linz and Alfred Stepan, 'Toward Consolidated Democracies' (1996) 7 *Journal of Democracy* 14.
[17] Perry, above n 15.
[18] See Davis, above n 3 (1997).
[19] Samuel Popkin, 'The Political Economy of Peasant Society' in J Elster (ed) *Rational Choice* (Blackwell, Oxford, 1986) 197.
[20] See Daniel Bell and Chaibong Hahm (eds) *Confucianism for the Modern World* (Cambridge University Press, Cambridge, 2003).
[21] Daniel Bell (ed) *Confucian Political Ethics* (Princeton University Press, Princeton, 2007).
[22] Alexis de Tocqueville, *Democracy in America* (Vintage Books, New York, 1945).

democratic founders have not been confident of the persistence of civic virtue and have sought to craft a democracy that, in James Madison's terms, is safe for the unvirtuous.[23] The earlier founding debate in the Czech Republic between Vaclav Havel, the anti-Communist idealist who emphasised civic virtue, and Vaclav Clause, the pragmatic post-communist politician who was more concerned with interest representation, is likely to be rehearsed in post-communist and post-authoritarian East Asia.[24] As has been true in other parts of the world, civic virtue alone will probably not be enough, nor will its persistence be reliable. While Asian philosophies such as Confucianism have often emphasised virtuous rule, Asian leaders, especially in the modern era, have seldom lived up to this standard, as high levels of corruption and tyranny have often prevailed.

A third community-based claim, which I label here simply as communitarianism, offers the centrality of community as an alternative to liberal individualism. Communitarianism is the most challenging contemporary discourse about community. In simple terms, Western communitarianism has tended to emphasise the common good over liberal individual rights and to emphasise the shared values of community. In this respect, communitarianism in the West has primarily offered a critique of liberalism. It also encompasses the civic virtue ethical components already discussed. There is, however, a wide gap between Western communitarianism and the more prominent forms of East Asian communitarian practice. While Western communitarians are apt to see community as a venue for democratic discourse and liberation, the conservative brand of communitarianism officially promoted in Singapore, and to some extent in China, is hardly a venue for democracy and liberation.[25] In East Asia, communitarian rhetoric has generally come with authoritarian government. Authoritarian East Asian regimes may seek to implant a value system that emphasises passive acceptance of the regime's dictates. Western communitarians, on the other hand, have often felt the need to commit to some liberal values to preserve their discourse and overcome some less acceptable values associated with traditional communities.[26] The Asian conservative variety of communitarianism has resisted increased demands for liberalisation. Those

---

[23] Robert D Putnam, *Making Democracy Work: Civic Traditions in Modern Italy* (Princeton University Press, Princeton, 1993).
[24] Aleksander Smolar, 'From Opposition to Atomization' (1996) 7 *Journal of Democracy* 24.
[25] Beng-Huat Chua, *Communitarian Ideology and Democracy in Singapore* (Routledge, London, 1995).
[26] The so-called liberal–communitarian debate has become a central debate in contemporary political philosophy: C F Delaney (ed) *The Liberalism–Communitarianism Debate* (Rowman and Littlefield Publishers, Lanham, 1994).

committed to addressing communitarian concerns may face the need to deploy some liberal institutions in ways that are responsive to these concerns or challenges.

## 3 The East Asian 'economic miracle' and the political economy of human rights

The East Asian authoritarian developmental model has functioned as the other branch of the 'Asian values' debate. For human rights scholars, this is the part of the debate that may indirectly incorporate social and economic rights in its promise of rapid and stable economic development. Although it is really a political economy argument and not about cultural values, it has often been subsumed under the Asian values debate because of its relationship to the political strategies of authoritarian regimes in the area. As with the cultural claim, this political economy claim for authoritarian development has represented a powerful East Asian challenge to universal human rights. First chronicled in a 1992 World Bank report as the 'East Asian miracle',[27] the developmental achievement of the first generation of newly industrialised countries in East Asia was fairly evident in the rapid economic growth of the 1970s and 1980s. It has since been evident in the 1990s and the new millennium in the economic growth of the second generation of East Asian rapid developers.[28]

The East Asian authoritarian developmental model first took shape in Japan, whose development model was said to combine soft political authoritarianism with economic liberalisation in a planned capitalist economy. Under this model, economic guidance was offered by an autonomous bureaucracy led by the Japanese Ministry of International Trade and Industry ('MITI').[29] In his 1982 book, Chalmers Johnson emphasised the importance of a developmentally oriented elite, organised under a tripartite coalition composed of the dominant Liberal Democratic Party, the bureaucracy, and big business.[30]

---

[27] World Bank, *The East Asian Miracle: Economic Growth and Public Policy* (World Bank, Washington DC, 1992).

[28] See Paul Krugman, 'The Myth of Asia's Miracle' (1994) 73 *Foreign Affairs* 62.

[29] See Chalmers Johnson, *MITI and the Japanese Miracle: The Growth of Industrial Policy 1925–1975* (Stanford University Press, Stanford, 1982).

[30] Ibid 51–2. With substantial state capacity these three worked together to ensure the coherent targeting of certain industries for production of exports under a system of export led growth ('ELG'): see Chalmers Johnson, 'Political Institutions and Economic Performance: The Government–Business Relationship in Japan, South Korea, and Taiwan' in F C Deyo (ed) *The Political Economy of the New Asian Industrialism* (Cornell University Press, Ithaca, 1987) 136. ELG is distinguished from an import substitution industrialisation ('ISI') strategy, which aims to substitute local goods for imports, though both usually coexist.

Johnson differentiates between a 'market-rational' (regulatory) and a 'plan-rational' (developmental) capitalist system.[31]

The Japanese model, with varied modifications, was seized upon as the paradigm for East Asian economic development. In non-Japanese hands this model would involve much higher levels of authoritarian autocratic rule with related constraints on democracy and human rights, thus making it a central feature in the East Asian human rights debate.[32] Throughout East Asia authoritarian economic developmental success often offered an excuse for resisting liberal democratic constitutional change and international human rights standards. Such repression was deemed necessary for such regimes to stay in power and maintain their achievements.

This use of the Japanese model as a basis for denying democracy and human rights is paradoxical. For all of its soft authoritarian tendencies, Japan was actually a democracy, though a democracy with long-established one-party electoral dominance. Notwithstanding Johnson's soft authoritarianism characterisations in 1982, Japan had enjoyed for decades a degree of democracy, with a functioning electoral process, a moderately free press, multiple political parties and independent courts. As a democracy, Japan also offered a paradigm for the brand of illiberal democracy with less robust constitutional and human rights institutions that often followed the overthrow of authoritarianism in the region.

The Japanese economic crisis of the 1990s called into question Japan's developmental model. It also served to highlight the inadequacies of the Japanese brand of democracy in assertively coming to grips with Japan's continuing economic problems.[33] A system based on a tradition of bureaucratic planning appears to have difficulty producing politicians and institutions willing to take political responsibility. It has also produced a rather conservative judiciary with weak protection of human rights.[34]

---

[31] Johnson, above n 29, 19. A 'plan-rational' system will be marked by bureaucratic disputes and factional infighting while a 'market-rational' system will tend toward parliamentary contest: ibid 22–3.

[32] Atul Kohli traces the role that Japanese colonialism played in facilitating this model. Atul Kohli, 'Where do High Growth Political Economies Come From? The Japanese Lineage of Korea's "Developmental State"' in M Woo-Cumings (ed) *The Developmental State* (Cornell University Press, Ithaca, 1999) 93. See Robert Wade, *Government and the Market: Economic Theory and the Role of Government in East Asian Industrialization* (Princeton University Press, Princeton, 1990); Stephan Haggard, *Pathways from the Periphery: The Politics of Growth in the Newly Industrializing Countries* (Cornell University Press, Ithaca, 1990).

[33] William H Overholt, 'Japan's Economy, at War With Itself' (2002) 81 *Foreign Affairs* 134.

[34] Michael K Young, 'Judicial Review of Administrative Guidance:

The difficulties that other East Asian economies encountered in the late-1990s East Asian financial crisis demonstrated similar political limitations in other East Asian emergent democracies. In spite of these limitations, the authoritarian developmental model has persisted as a model for the second generation of East Asian developers, including China and the post-Communist emerging developmental states in Southeast Asia. This authoritarian model remains a major challenge to human rights in the region.

This authoritarian developmental challenge in East Asia raises the question of whether authoritarianism with suppression of opposition and low levels of human rights protection will persist as a viable model in the region. The historical experience of the first-generation developers suggests this is unlikely. With economic success the authoritarian developmental state may become its own grave-digger.[35] The circumstances that seem to have been favourable to authoritarian development are more likely to be present in the early stages of development. At an early stage, proper economic policy may sometimes be more important for achieving economic growth than regime type.[36] But, at a later stage, political challenges may arise as workers and other subordinate classes demand a greater say in public affairs through protection of civil liberties and greater security for a range of basic social and economic rights. [37]

Several tendencies may operate at once. As economic elites become globally more competitive they may become less compliant and more corrupt.

---

Governmentally Encouraged Consensual Dispute Resolution in Japan' (1984) 84 *Columbia Law Review* 923; Christopher A Ford, 'The Indigenization of Constitutionalism in the Japanese Experience' (1996) 28 *Case Western Reserve Journal of International Law* 3.

[35] See William W Grimes, *Unmaking the Japanese Miracle, Macroeconomic Politics, 1985–2000* (Cornell University Press, Ithaca, 2001); Meredith Woo-Cumings, 'The State, Democracy, and the Reform of the Corporate Sector in Korea' in T J Pempel (ed) *The Politics of the Asian Financial Crisis* (Cornell University Press, Ithaca, 1996) 116; Gregory W Noble and John Ravenhill, 'The Good, the Bad and the Ugly: Korea, Taiwan and the Asian Financial Crisis' in G W Noble and J Ravenhill, *The Asian Financial Crisis and the Architecture of Global Finance* (Cambridge University Press, New York, 2000) 80.

[36] Adam Przeworski and Fernando Limongi, 'Political Regimes and Economic Growth' (1993) 7 *Journal of Economic Perspectives* (1993) 51. They conclude 'that social scientists know surprisingly little: our guess is that political institutions do matter for growth, but thinking in terms of regimes does not seem to capture the relevant differences'.

[37] In defining economic development, in addition to the GDP, economists have paid attention to a range of social welfare indicators such as education, health, gender equality, life expectancy, working conditions, infrastructure and so forth: see Amartya Sen, 'Development: Which Way Now?' in K P Jameson and Charles K Wilbur (eds) *The Political Economy of Development and Underdevelopment* (McGraw Hill College, New York, 1996) 7; United Nations, *Human Development Report 2002.*

They may seek official assistance in insuring a compliant labour force, in securing loans and in otherwise gaining business-friendly policy. To better guard their privileges, they may resist political reform that may undercut their influence or capacity to get things done. David Kang describes the transformation of corruption under the East Asian developmental paradigm from a top-down predatory state with a weak business sector under early authoritarianism to a strong business sector with bottom-up rent-seeking *vis-à-vis* a fractured state in the early democratic period, both involving large amounts of corruption.[38] Corruption may also become a substitute for dysfunctional government institutions.

Both corruption and the overloading of government institutions tend to retard the protection of human rights. With increased wealth and education in the society, ordinary citizens may become resistant to elite monopolisation of power and demand greater transparency, participation and accountability. This requires political and legal institutional reforms, both of which are instrumental to human rights protection. Because of these developments, the trend of the 1990s in the East Asian newly industrialised countries ('NICs') was toward both political and legal reform and toward integration into world markets.

Unfortunately, as the economic crisis served to illustrate, even with democratisation or substantial reforms the problems of corruption and political overload often persisted. Post-authoritarian regimes failed to reform adequately as they attempted to maintain historical strategies of developmental success. Political reformers, such as Japan and South Korea, in the 1990s clung to developmental economic policies of interference in market decisions, even while pursuing political reform.[39] The second-generation developers have sought to exclude political reform entirely, with great implications for human rights. China's economic success without substantial political reform has spawned questions about whether China will somehow defy gravity and not follow its economic success with political reform and liberalisation.[40] China, one of the newest entries in the East Asian developmental achievement, has to date pursued policies of economic liberalisation and legal reform without

---

[38] See David C Kang, 'Bad Loans to Good Friends: Money Politics and the Developmental State in South Korea' (2002) 56 *International Organization* 177, 182. Rent-seeking is understood as 'attempts by individuals to increase their personal wealth while at the same time making a negative contribution to the net wealth of their community': Thrainn Eggertsson, *Economic Behavior and Institutions* (Cambridge University Press, New York, 1990) 279.
[39] Overholt, above n 33.
[40] Minxin Pei, *China's Trapped Transition: The Limits of Developmental Autocracy* (Harvard University Press, Cambridge, 2006).

fundamental civil and political rights.[41] This has required suppression of dissent in general and particularly harsh containment of the public protests that have arisen over the denial of basic educational, health, labour and social rights. Many post-communist Southeast Asian countries in the early stages of economic development likewise cling to similar authoritarian repressive strategies with only limited legal reforms.[42] The difficulty with arguments for authoritarianism with law or other confidence-building institutions is that maintenance of such guarantees ultimately may require the security of a liberal democratic regime that fosters transparency, public accountability and human rights.[43]

The issue is not whether the East Asian brand of authoritarian developmentalism worked – it certainly brought about rapid economic development. The question is what political and institutional change will be required as the developmental process goes forward. The state institutions that are favourable to economic development in a free market system are generally believed to be those that afford the degree of order, reliability, transparency and participation sufficient to inspire confidence and thereby encourage entrepreneurial activity and investment.[44] State institutions with a higher degree of autonomy and transparency may better resist rent-seeking demands and secure open channels for the protection of basic rights. For a democracy this requires a sufficiently stable institutional base so that there are neither too many nor too few institutional actors with sufficient power over the decision-making process to either engage in excessive rent-seeking or interfere with efficient public decisions.[45] Both fighting corruption and attracting investment appear to require an institutional base that affords a balance of public decision-making autonomy and accountability. The kinds of institutions that generally are thought to achieve

---

[41] Dali L Yang, 'China in 2001, Economic Liberalization and Its Political Discontents' (2002) 42 *Asian Survey* 14. According to a 2002 Organisation for Economic Co-operation and Development (OECD) report, China is experiencing the same economic difficulties as the earlier class of 'economic miracle' states, including high levels of corruption and large problems with bad loans, economic displacement and slow-down. OECD, *China in the World Economy: The Domestic Policy Challenges* (OECD, Paris, 2002).

[42] Andrew MacIntyre, 'Institution and Investors: The Politics of the Economic Crisis in Southeast Asia' (2002) 55 *International Organization* 81.

[43] See Jon Elster, 'Constitution-Making in Eastern Europe: Rebuilding the Boat in the Open Sea' (1993) 71 *Public Administration* 169, 199–201. Elster notes that the strength of the dictator is also his weakness: 'He is *unable* to make himself *unable* to interfere with the legal system whenever it seems expedient': ibid.

[44] See Mancur Olson, 'Dictatorship, Democracy, and Development' (1993) 87 *American Political Science Review* 567, 572.

[45] Kang, above n 38, 182; MacIntyre, above n 42.

these objectives relate to maintenance of democracy, human rights and the rule of law, the ingredients of modern constitutionalism.[46]

Theorists commonly use two approaches to connect liberal constitutional democracy and development. They may focus on the statistical correlation between democracy and development, or they may trace the causal mechanisms in the development context that lead to increased demands for democratic representation, rights and legality. The first approach may address both the survivability of democracy under various economic circumstances and the role of democracy in encouraging economic development or dealing with economic crises or shocks. The second approach is concerned with the causal mechanisms by which economic development contributes to democratisation, highlighting the ways in which such democratisation may be responsive to developmental needs.

Regarding statistical correlation, Adam Przeworski and others used worldwide statistics to gauge the survivability of democracies from 1950 to 1990.[47] Such statistics demonstrated a strong correlation between wealth and the survivability of democracy, and gave no support for using dictatorships to achieve development and democracy.[48] Gerald Scully, surveying 115 countries from 1960 to 1980, reversed the dependent variable to consider the effect of democratic institutions on the economy.[49] Scully notes that open societies with human rights, the rule of law, private property, and market allocation grew at three times the rate and were two-and-a-half times as efficient as societies in which the exercise of related rights was largely proscribed.

When it comes to the special circumstances of dealing with economic crisis or shock, Dani Rodrik finds further that democracy offers more favourable results. Rodrik argues that shock will tend to be worse in societies with deep latent conflicts and that democracy affords the ultimate institutions of conflict management.[50] This argument is supported by Donald Emmerson, who argues that, in the financial crisis, affected East Asian countries with high levels of political freedom were generally more resilient.[51] A democracy such as

---

[46] Kang, above n 38, 182.

[47] See Adam Przeworski et al, 'What Makes Democracies Endure?' (1996) 7 *Journal of Democracy* 39.

[48] Ibid 44–9.

[49] Gerald W Scully, *Constitutional Environments and Economic Growth* (Princeton University Press, Princeton, 1992) 12–14, 183–4.

[50] See Dani Rodrik, 'Democracy and Economic Performance' (Paper presented at the Conference on Democratization and Economic Reform in South Africa, 16–19 January 1998).

[51] He contrasts the relatively strong recovery of Thailand and South Korea with Indonesia: Donald Emmerson, 'Americanizing Asia? (1998) 77 *Foreign Affairs* 46, 52. See also Stephan Haggard, 'The Politics of the Asian Financial Crisis' (2000) 11

Taiwan fared better during the height of the crisis and democracies caught by the crisis, such as South Korea and Thailand, bounced back more quickly. Authoritarian China also fared much better, as its financial institutions were largely protected from global currency markets in what began as a currency crisis.

Considering the second approach, Dietrich Rueschemeyer and others argue that quantitative correlative studies reach the right conclusion, but fail to offer a reason.[52] They urge that the case for liberal democracy becomes compelling at a certain stage in the industrialisation process because industrialisation transforms society in a fashion that empowers subordinate classes and makes it difficult to exclude them politically.[53] The subordinate classes, especially the working class, have the greatest interest in democracy and its related rights protections, while the bourgeoisie have every incentive to roll back or restrict democracy.[54] Democracy affords institutions that can deal with diverse interests and the resultant conflicts that emerge.

The path to the demise of the South Korean dictatorship bears a striking resemblance to Rueschemeyer and colleagues' predictions.[55] Authoritarian leadership in South Korea was built on collusion between the military, the political leadership, and the large *chaebol* (local multinational corporations ('MNCs')).[56] The success of development policies under such a narrow coalition brought out a new class force in the 1980s under the banner of the *minjung* (the masses) movement.[57] The Park and Chun regimes' earlier policies of economic liberalisation without political liberalisation brought on the demise of the regime. At the end of 1997, after South Korea's financial collapse, the ruling party, rooted in the past authoritarian regime, was pushed out with the

---

*Journal of Democracy* 130; Mark Baird, 'An economy in the balance', *International Herald Tribune* (New York), 19 September 2002, 6.

[52] Dietrich Rueschemeyer et al, *Capitalist Development and Democracy* (University of Chicago Press, Chicago, 1992).

[53] Ibid 1.

[54] Ibid 7–8, 50, 57–8. 'Capitalist development furthers the growth of civil society – by increasing the level of urbanization, by bringing workers together in factories, by improving the means of communication and transportation, by raising the level of literacy': Ibid 6.

[55] See Hagen Koo and Eun Mee Kim, 'The Developmental State and Capital Accumulation in South Korea' in R P Appelbaum and J Henderson (eds) *State and Development in the Asian Pacific Rim* (Sage, Newbury Park, 1992) 121–49. See also Rueschemeyer, above n 52.

[56] See Koo and Kim, above n 55, 144–5. This ruling coalition was decidedly narrower in South Korea than in the post-war Japanese prototype. It did not include the larger base of a popular well-organised political party and employed much more repressive policies.

[57] Ibid 145.

election of opposition leader Kim Dae-jung as president.[58] Backroom deals within the elite ruling coalition – what was then called crony capitalism – no longer inspired confidence. As David Kang highlights, both the late authoritarian period and the early democratic period were characterised by high levels of corruption.[59] South Korea was pushed to complete the reform process, to dismantle the developmental economic model that had persisted under democratisation.[60] This required South Korea to clean up the conglomerates by instituting systems of oversight and putting loans and other financial decisions on a more sound financial footing. This was added to the earlier efforts at political reform, instituting single terms for the president, a formally acceptable system of constitutional judicial review and greater rights protection through less strict control over the media and public organisations.

Taiwan, a textbook case of the East Asian miracle, appeared to follow a similar pattern. With economic success, increasing calls for democratisation were made in the 1980s. With pressure from below, a confident regime embraced the reform process in a top-down pattern. Along with democratic elections, the previously moribund systems of the rule of law and judicial review began to take on life. Taiwan fared much better than most East Asian countries in the early phase of the economic crisis, though it later showed signs of economic and political weakness associated with continued tension with China.

China is the next great East Asian challenge. China's recent policies of economic reform resemble the earlier authoritarian South Korean policies under Park Chung Hee (1963–79) of economic liberalisation without political liberalisation, accompanied by harsh human rights policies that aim to repress dissent.[61] Like South Korea, China has reached the current developmental juncture with very large industries and substantial numbers of industrial workers at risk in the reform process. Numerous worker-based demonstrations have highlighted these failures to meet basic needs. China's entry into the WTO has

---

[58] See Kate Wiltrout, 'Kim Leads Knife-edge Korea Poll', *South China Morning Post* (Hong Kong), 19 December 1997, 1. This change of direction apparently received a further vote of confidence in late 2002, with the election of an even more liberal candidate from the same party, President Roh Moo Hyun. Weon-ho Lee and Sung-ho Baik, 'Generation 2030 Bursts Onstage', *International Herald Tribune* (New York), 30 December 2002, 7.

[59] See Kang, above n 38.

[60] Ibid; MacIntyre, above n 42.

[61] One should be cautious about this comparison. While the state-owned enterprises ('SOEs') do encompass the heavy industry sector in China, there are other reforming sectors where the trend is toward dispersal, rather than concentration, of economic activity. The historical Chinese emphasis on workers' rights may also serve as a counterweight, though workers have so far taken a bruising in the reform era.

430 *Research handbook on international human rights law*

further pushed China towards a more competitive posture. To accomplish this there was a need to reduce government interventions in the economy and develop regulatory regimes.[62] Ultimately, if the other East Asian examples are instructive, this will require constitutional reform, involving democratic reform, human rights and the rule of law, though the question of timing seems uncertain.

## 4 Human rights and constitutionalism

In the absence of regional human rights institutions, domestic constitutionalism has become the primary vehicle in East Asia for implementing human rights commitments. This may be supplemented by national human rights institutions.[63] Constitutionalism has offered a venue to respond to the various claims underlying the cultural values and developmental debates in East Asia, a response to authoritarianism. The concept of constitutionalism advanced herein, as noted above, includes the fundamental elements of democracy, human rights and the rule of law and elements of local institutional embodiment – what I call indigenisation.

In the late twentieth and early twenty-first centuries constitutionalism has become one of the primary vehicles for universalising human rights. Constitutionalism serves both as a conduit for shared international and local human rights and political values and the embodiment of those values. It provides the context in which the subordinate classes can voice their basic concerns relating to both civil and political rights and to economic and social rights. In this regard, this section emphasises two aspects of the constitutional equation in East Asia: first, the empowering role of constitutionalism, in contrast to the usual view that emphasises only constraint; and second, indigenisation of constitutionalism, as an avenue to hook it up to the local condition.

### A  *The empowering role of constitutionalism and human rights*

Theorists have worried that constitutionalists place too much emphasis on constraint, always using language of 'checking, restraining or blocking'.[64] The

---

[62] See OECD, above n 41. The OECD report points out, 'Government interference leads to poor SOE management and inefficient operations, which foster low profits and high debt; this in turn makes it more difficult to restructure to improve efficiency and prompts government interventions that spread the problem by extracting resources from stronger enterprises to prop up those that are failing': ibid 16.

[63] See Brian Burdekin, *National Human Rights Institutions in Asia* (Martinus Nijhoff Publishers, Leiden, 2007).

[64] Stephen Holmes, 'Precommitment and the Paradox of Democracy' in J Elster and R Slagstad (eds) *Constitutionalism and Democracy* (Cambridge University Press, Cambridge, 1988) 195, 226.

notion of voluntary constraint is a questionable proposition in a world where leaders frequently override constraint in the interest of expediency.[65] This may result in what Guillermo O'Donnell calls 'a caesaristic plebiscitarian executive that once elected sees itself as empowered to govern the country as it deems fit'.[66] Such an executive may effectively become an elected dictator and become more concerned about retaining power than protecting human rights.

Too much emphasis on constraint may cause constitutionalists to overlook the important empowering aspects of constitutionalism. The notion of constraint under constitutional government takes on meaning and force only through popular empowerment. Under constitutional government the processes of empowerment extend beyond the institutions of electoral politics to include the institutions of human rights and the rule of law. It is the integration of political and legal institutions in the processes of constitutional government that allows both empowerment and constraint to work.

East Asia has in recent years experienced the phenomenon of the powerful state and the hazard of unconstrained government, elected or otherwise. The most notorious East Asian examples where elected leaders used their mandate to pervert the constitutional order were some of the early South Korean experiments with democracy and the Marcos regime in the Philippines.[67] As noted above, theorists have responded with two nearly opposing alternatives, often applied paradoxically to the same regimes. Some have advocated instituting the rule of law and rights protection along with authoritarianism.[68] The difficulty with this option is in inducing such authoritarian leaders to consistently accept such constraint and respect human rights. There have been some aspirations toward this notion in Singapore, Malaysia and (until recently) Indonesia.

---

[65] Jon Elster, 'Forces and Mechanisms in the Constitution-Making Process' (1995) 45 *Duke Law Journal* 364; Linz and Stepan, above n 16, 19.

[66] Guillermo O'Donnell, 'Illusions About Consolidation' (1996) 7 *Journal of Democracy* 34, 44.

[67] Jang Jip Choi, 'Political Cleavages in South Korea' in Hagen Koo (ed) *State and Society in Contemporary Korea* (Cornell University Press, Ithaca, 1993) 13; S Guingona, 'The Constitution of the Philippines: An Overview' (1989) 65 *New Zealand Law Journal* 419.

[68] Shuhe Li and Peng Lian, 'On Market Preserving Authoritarianism: An Institutional Analysis of Growth Miracles' (Conference paper presented at the Chinese University of Hong Kong, Hong Kong, 8 March 1996). This argument picks up some general support in Giovanni Sartori's proposition that 'demo-protection' (protection from tyranny or constitutional constraint) travels better than 'demo-power' (implementation of popular rule) – 'nobody wants to be imprisoned, tortured or killed': Giovanni Sartori, 'How Far Can Free Government Travel?' (1995) 6 *Journal of Democracy* 101, 101–4. Sartori would not advocate that the absence of demo-power be accepted as a long-term solution.

Alternatively, some may advocate instituting democracy but replacing liberal constraints with alleged East Asian cultural constraints and communitarian processes of bargaining to establish a so-called illiberal democracy.[69] Paradoxically this approach may be the aspirational basis of the claims to democracy made by the same regimes in Singapore, Malaysia and Suharto's Indonesia. But an alleged democracy that prohibits or suppresses opposition without core constitutional constraints does not appear to be democracy at all. A system that places emphasis on social connections and networking may lead to particularism and clientelism.[70] This situation is difficult to distinguish from authoritarianism when it comes to the potential for abuse of power and neglect of human rights.

Extra-constitutional action should more properly be understood as not just overriding constraint but as overriding democracy and its concomitant guarantees of human rights and the rule of law. Such extra-constitutional action does not just 'get the job done' but, in fact, deprives the people of democratic power. To deprive people of freedom of speech does not just serve to eliminate meddlesome critics and achieve order but may, in fact, disempower the people in securing basic human rights, both political and economic. Constitutionalists should seek to engender discourse and empowerment. The legal and human rights institutions of constitutional government are enfranchising in nature; they work to engage the citizens in a political conversation about popular concerns and values. Contrary to the Asian values claim, in a modern complex society this is the contemporary venue for values and development discourse. This is what has inspired the Asian movement to constitutionalism. If constitutionalism is openly accepted as the venue for political choice, rather than merely constraint, then the ensuing discourse within this venue may engender respect for its important constraints and processes.

To better understand this claim we must consider the constitutive process. This process can be considered at two levels: constitution-making and constitutional implementation. Constitution-making is where the explicit constitutional conversation begins. A constitutional assembly is a powerful venue for

---

[69] Some scholars have advocated an Asian model of democracy along these lines, characterising it as illiberal democracy: see, for example, Daniel A Bell, David Brown, Kanishky Jayasuriya and David Martin Jones, *Towards Illiberal Democracy in Pacific Asia* (Macmillan Press, London, 1995); Fareed Zakaria, 'The Rise of Illiberal Democracy' (1997) 76 *Foreign Affairs* 22.

[70] In East Asia such clientelism has spawned economic and political systems that are particularly noted for problems of cronyism and corruption, problems that are frequently associated with East Asia's leading countries, for example, Indonesia, South Korea, China and Japan: Richard H Mitchell, *Political Bribery in Japan* (University of Hawaii Press, Honolulu, 1996).

discourse about basic political and human rights values. This is especially true because such assemblies are usually called on the heels of a national crisis, which is inherently engaging. In recent decades the East Asian landscape has been riddled with constitution-making exercises. In the 1980s and 1990s constitution-making in the Philippines and Hong Kong offered prominent, seemingly successful examples.[71] In such constitution-making processes Jon Elster describes a venue where passion, interest and reason operate.[72] There are both upstream and downstream constraints, as well as processes for consensus-building and broadening bases of support.[73] Upstream constraints consider political settlements and may also protect members of the former regime. For the Hong Kong Basic Law, as with the post-war Japanese Constitution, the upstream constraints were dictated by outside powers.[74] Downstream constraints look to ratification or acceptance. In the Philippines, after the 'People Power' revolution, downstream acceptance was the substantial constraint.

After a constitutional founding, successful implementation of constitutional government depends on appreciation of the discursive architecture embodied in the notion of checks and balances. Most appreciated in this regard is the positive discursive machinery of constitutional judicial review, the power whereby courts review laws enacted by the elected branches of government for conformity to constitutional requirements. Constitutional judicial review has become the premier institution for securing human rights in East Asia.[75] Constitutional judicial review serves as the engine for the basic constitutional conversation about political values and commitments.[76] This constitutional conversation proceeds as legislatures pass laws and courts respond and legislatures pass new laws.[77] While much of East Asia has adopted Western civil and common law legal systems, only the democratic or quasi-democratic countries of the region

---

[71] See Guingona, above n 67; Michael C Davis, 'Constitutionalism and the Rule of Law in Hong Kong' (2006) 3 *Loyola University of Chicago International Law Review* 165.

[72] See Elster, above n 65, 377–86.

[73] Ibid 374.

[74] See Ford, above n 34; Michael C Davis, 'Human Rights and the Founding of the Hong Kong Special Administrative Region: A Framework for Analysis' (1996) 34 *Columbia Journal of Transnational Law* 301.

[75] Mauro Cappelletti, 'The "Mighty Problem" of Judicial Review and the Contribution of Comparative Analysis' (1980) 53 *Southern California Law Review* 401.

[76] Alexander M Bickel, *The Least Dangerous Branch: The Supreme Court at the Bar of Politics* (Yale University Press, New Haven, 2nd ed, 1986).

[77] A court can use various avoidance and interpretation doctrines, what Bickel calls 'passive virtues', to carry on a complex dialogue with the elected branches of government and the people: Bickel, above n 76, 23, 65–70, 117.

have fully functioning systems of constitutional judicial review.[78] These countries include Japan, the Philippines and Hong Kong, with such power vested in the ordinary courts, and Taiwan, South Korea, Mongolia, Indonesia, and Thailand, where civil law special constitutional courts are employed.[79] For the authoritarian regimes of the region, little or no judicial review power is the norm. In an authoritarian environment it is unlikely that judges can be counted on to carry out such role assertively. Using a rational choice model, in the context of democratic constitution-making and implementation, Tom Ginsburg has traced the reasoning of both constitutional drafters and courts in creating or developing constitutional judicial review.[80] While one may question whether a narrow rational choice model can fully account for the decisions of actors whose interests and identity are mutually constituted as the process unfolds, it is clear that authoritarian regimes will have little commitment to such constitutional practices.[81]

Constitutional judicial review of legislative enactments is not the sole discursive engine for crafting state-based solutions to broader societal concerns. At moments of crisis – what Stephen Krasner calls 'punctuated equilibrium' – the entire people may be mobilised to civic action or intense reflection on political value concerns of fundamental importance.[82] In normal times

---

[78] As a general proposition the structure of constitutional judicial review is divided into those systems with a central constitutional court deciding issues on referral from ordinary courts or other branches of government (usually civil law systems) and those decentralised systems where ordinary courts exercise this power in actual cases (usually common law systems): Mauro Cappelletti, above n 75, 401. Japan is the East Asian exception where a decentralised system exists in a civil law country. Hong Kong has both systems operating at once: a decentralised system for matters within local autonomy and a centralised review process by the National People's Congress ('NPC') Standing Committee in Beijing (advised by a Basic Law Committee) on matters of central authority or involving local central relations. *Hong Kong Basic Law*, Arts 17 and 158. See Randall Peerenboom (ed) *Asian Discourses of Rule of Law: Theories and Implementation of Rule of Law in Twelve Asian Countries, France and the U.S.* (Routledge, New York, 2004).

[79] See Ford, above n 34; Davis, above n 74; C Neal Tate, 'The Judicialization of Politics in the Philippines and Southeast Asia' (1994) 15 *International Political Science Review* 187.

[80] Tom Ginsburg, *Judicial Review in New Democracies, Constitutional Courts in Asian Cases* (Cambridge University Press, Cambridge, 2003). The rational choice model Ginsburg employs assumes that judges, public officials and constitution drafters will act in their narrow self-interest, typically in ways that aim to advance their power within the system.

[81] Michael C Davis, 'Constitutionalism and New Democracies' (2004) 36 *George Washington International Law Review* 681.

[82] Stephen D Krasner, 'Approaches to the State: Alternative Conceptions and Historical Dynamics' (1984) 26 *Comparative Politics* 223.

the people may be content with representation and constitutional judicial review, while they largely focus on private affairs; while at times of what Bruce Ackerman calls constitutional politics, the level of civic action may become extraordinary.[83] There is evidence of such mobilisation in the recent South Korean and Japanese constitutional politics of reform and resistance to corruption. Considerable civic action also accompanied the post-1987 constitutional reforms in Taiwan and the financial crisis and the overthrow of Suharto in Indonesia.[84]

## B  Indigenisation of constitutionalism and human rights

With a firm commitment to the constitutional fundamentals in place, a premier concern is that constitutionalism, with its democracy, human rights and rule of law ingredients, should plant its roots firmly in the local soil. Aung Sang Suu Kyi argues that as long as there is a genuine commitment to modern democratic values, there is room for variation in local institutional embodiment.[85] It is through local institutional embodiment – what I call indigenisation – that constitutionalism responds to the above noted concerns with values and development. For indigenous institutions to work, however, the constitutional fundamentals of democracy, human rights and the rule of law must be in place. Otherwise, authoritarian leaders may implant a hegemonic discourse constructive of authoritarian power and destructive of genuine community values. Local institutional embodiment may include traditional organisations and practices and more contemporary institutions responsive to developmental concerns. In this subsection I consider the ways in which constitutionalism and its related human rights institutions in East Asia have responded both to the cultural concerns raised in the Asian values debate and to developmental concerns likely to arise in post-authoritarian constitutional democracies.

Constitutionalists should consider the ways in which local culture and traditions may facilitate constitutional discourse under the umbrella of the core constitutional commitments discussed above. It is in local institutional embodiment that substantive communitarian concerns can be addressed. Local grass

---

[83] Bruce Ackerman, *We The People* (The Belknap Press, Cambridge, 1991) 34–57.

[84] The 1987 lifting of martial law in Taiwan triggered popular demonstrations, a judicial review opinion ruling the failure to hold new elections for the Legislative Yuan to replace seats long held by mainlanders elected in the 1940s unconstitutional, a National Affairs Conference and ultimately full democratic elections: Jaushieh (Joseph) Wu, *Taiwan's Democratization: Forces Behind the New Momentum* (Oxford University Press, Oxford, 1995) 125–37. Indonesia experienced high levels of civic action and fundamental constitutional reform: see MacIntyre, above n 42.

[85] Aung San Suu Kyi, 'Transcending the Clash of Cultures: Freedom, Development and Human Worth' (1995) 6 *Journal of Democracy* 11, 13.

roots and minority representation may be achieved through contemporary institutions which secure autonomy or minority rights, or through recognition of traditional ethnic or religious groups. The aim is for a realistic discourse that is anchored in the community but responsive to the contemporary urban and industrial or post-industrial conditions.

Locally sensitive representation may include attention to the usual geographic political institutional options such as federalism or autonomy, as well as consideration of various electoral models that seem likely to increase representation of minorities. Other forms of representation may include substantive or symbolic recognition of distinct ethnic, religious or linguistic communities in which traditional leaders assume leadership roles. This may include a continuing role, symbolic or substantive, for traditional monarchs, such as is evident in contemporary Malaysia, Japan and Thailand.[86] Special minority group rights may be combined with individual rights; in East Asia there are many traditional indigenous groups or distinctive communities who are promised varied degrees of autonomy in the local constitutional system. However, East Asian governments, wary of outside intervention in their sovereign territory, may be reluctant to allow the type of international recognition such autonomous communities usually covet as security for the autonomy arrangement.[87] As a rare exception, China has allowed the security of internationally recognised status for Hong Kong under the Hong Kong Basic Law, as allowed under Article 31 of the Chinese Constitution.[88]

Arend Lijphart has described the effort by elites to overcome the destabilising effect of cultural fragmentation in Europe as 'consociational democracy'.[89] The democratic element is important. A bargain across cleavage lines that only includes the elite strata would be merely authoritarian oligarchy and would not be likely to secure a channel for engaging popular will. The use of various forms of local institutional embodiment, along with core constitutional

---

[86] Abdulahi An-Na'im, 'Islam, Islamic Law and the Dilemma of Cultural Legitimacy for Universal Human Rights' in C E Welch and V A Leary (eds) *Asian Perspectives on Human Rights* (Westview Press, Boulder, 1991) 31; Y Higuchi, 'The Constitution and the Emperor System: Is Revisionism Alive?' (1990) 53 *Law and Contemporary Problems* 51; C E Keyes, *Thailand: Buddhist Kingdom as a Modern Nation State* (Westview Press, Boulder, 1987).

[87] Robert H Barnes, Andrew Gray, and Benedict Kingsbury (eds) *Indigenous Peoples of Asia* (Association of Asian Studies, Ann Arbour, 1993); Michael C Davis, 'Establishing a Workable Autonomy in Tibet' (2008) 30 *Human Rights Quarterly* 227.

[88] See Davis, above n 71. This has allowed Hong Kong to secure a fairly robust system of human rights and the rule of law, though it still lacks full democratic development. Similar Chinese solicitude has not been extended to minority nationalities in Tibet and Xinjiang.

[89] Arend Lijphart, 'Consociational Democracy' (1968) 21 *World Politics* 207.

commitments, may engender more confidence in the system, encourage local connectedness to the constitutional order and facilitate genuine values discourse.

Beyond political representation, legal structures may also address important indigenous human rights concerns. This may include the application of religious or tribal laws and the provision for genuine autonomy for national or ethnic minority groups. For such autonomy arrangements to work, democratic commitments and basic rights must be emphasised. Traditional practices can be renovated or new institutions invented to sustain important indigenous rights while maintaining core constitutional commitments. For example, in societies with long traditions of citizen petition of leaders, a mechanism for petitioning elected officials could be employed or, perhaps, a modern version thereof, the ombudsman.[90] Even a traditional monarch, who may retain symbolic and ceremonial functions, may take on an ombudsman-like role in a post-monarchical democratic society.[91] Such tradition-bound institutions may open better avenues of communication and protection in ways consistent with historical experience. Even when contemporary institutions are employed, in practice they may be expected to take on indigenous characteristics. Contemporary institutions such as human rights tribunals or commissions, election commissions or corruption-fighting bodies may be employed to address those contemporary problems that neither the core constitutional nor traditional institutions adequately respond to. The goal in all cases is orderly processes of discursive engagement or empowerment.

Hegemonic claims of adherence to Asian values without a commitment to the core constitutional and human rights fundamentals are unlikely to engender a healthy values discourse or contribute to long-term public trust. One might contrast the constitutional paths of modern Japan and China.[92] While these countries bear comparison due to similar traditional values, striking differences are in many ways explainable structurally by their contrasting post-war constitutional paths. While post-war Japan has taken a liberal constitutional path, there has been substantial indigenisation in practice. Indigenisation has even transformed the practice of constitutional judicial review, as the courts are noted for a conservative system of constitutional

---

[90] Hong Kong stands out as a system that makes use of an official ombudsman as an avenue of public complaint. This ombudsman role and a similar role played by legislative counsellors in the Hong Kong system appear to be valued for consistency to traditional Chinese systems of complaint – Chinese citizens to this day still travel to Beijing to file petitions over perceived injustices.

[91] This oversight role for a traditional monarch is still evident in contemporary Thailand and Japan.

[92] Davis, above n 3 (1997).

guidance.[93] Though conservative, this system has afforded increased rights protection and does seem to take constitutionalism seriously.[94] Even efforts at reforming the system of one-party dominance have been cautious, engendering renewed public concern with corruption.[95]

Without liberal constitutional fundamentals, China has advanced a hegemonic view concerning the constitutional fundamentals of democracy, human rights and the rule of law, which people challenge at their peril.[96] Constitutional judicial review is not allowed. Minority rights are poorly protected in a top-down system of control. The constitution provides for top-down legislative supervision by people's congresses, which are themselves not subject to competitive elections and are dominated by the central government. Even greater central control is achieved through the Chinese Communist Party. If review occurs at all it is either through informal guidance or through committee or party oversight in the passage of laws.[97] A collectivist notion of rights subjecting the rights of the individual to the interests of the state appears to undermine local rights protections.[98] The Public Security Bureau and the military take a central role in providing public security, often at the expense of basic rights.

China's economic reforms have engendered increased diversification of interests for which inadequate representation is secured. This neglect is especially pronounced for minority groups, some of which are looked upon with great suspicion. Commitments to legality, under the theory of rule by law, are shaky at best, encouraging increased corruption as the economic reform process goes forward. This has produced a values-vacuum, which the society is hard placed to deal with. Efforts to open up democratic and legal channels for representation of diverse and minority interests are often met by government indifference. Opening up appropriate legal and democratic channels will not automatically solve the current problems but such moves may offer hope for crafting orderly solutions in the future.

---

[93] Young, above n 34, 970; Ford, above n 34, 25–9, 49–55.

[94] Ford, above n 34, 29–36.

[95] Richard H Mitchell, *Political Bribery in Japan* (University of Hawaii Press, Honolulu, 1996) 121–32.

[96] Owen M Fiss, 'Two Constitutions' (1986) *Yale Journal of International Law* 492, 501.

[97] *Constitution of the People's Republic of China* (1982) Article 67; Andrew J Nathan, 'Political Rights in Chinese Constitutions' in R Randle Edwards, Louis Henkin, Andrew J Nathan (eds) *Human Rights in Contemporary China* (Columbia University Press, New York, 1986) 77.

[98] *Constitution of the People's Republic of China* (1982) Article 51; R Randle Edwards, 'Civil and Social Rights: Theory and Practice in Chinese Law' in R Randle Edwards, Louis Henkin, Andrew J Nathan (eds) *Human Rights in Contemporary China* (Columbia University Press, New York, 1986) 41.

Many of the same indigenisation arguments addressed in relation to cultural values have obvious connections, as well, to economic developmental concerns. Recognition of distinct cultural groups clearly has market and developmental implications, as such groups address their distinct developmental problems and attract investment in various resources.[99] Beyond multiculturalism, economic developmental concerns implicate a wide range of local social and economic rights.

## 5 Conclusion

This argument has emphasised several points: first, that the Asian values and other cultural arguments do not justify the choice of authoritarianism and the neglect of democracy and human rights; second, that under East Asia's current condition of substantial economic development, an authoritarian regime can no longer be adequately responsive to diverse developmental concerns; third, the positive role of constitutionalism in constructing empowering conversations in modern democratic development and as a venue for values and developmental discourse; and fourth, the importance, especially in cross-cultural and developmental contexts, of indigenisation of constitutionalism through local institutional embodiment. In the absence of the development of regional human rights institutions, in East Asia it has been the linkage of these points that has connected the constitutional regime of a given state or similar territorial community to the international processes of human rights and has established the importance of domestic human rights practices.

---

[99] Amy Chua, 'The Privatization–Nationalization Cycle: The Link Between Markets and Ethnicity in Developing Countries (1995) 95 *Columbia Law Review* 223.

# 17. Islam and the realization of human rights in the Muslim world*
*Mashood A Baderin*

## 1 Islam and human rights in the Muslim world

The discourse about the relationship between Islam and human rights in the Muslim world has been diverse and ongoing for some time.[1] The discourse is not only theoretically relevant to the universalization of human rights generally, but also specifically relevant to the practical realization of human rights in the Muslim world. This is due to the evident role that Islam has generally

---

\* This is a revised and expanded version of a paper presented by the author at the Conference on 'Reframing Islam: Politics into Law' at the Irish Centre for Human Rights, National University of Ireland, Galway held on 10–11 September 2005 and published previously as 'Islam and the Realization of Human Rights in the Muslim World: A Reflection on Two Essential Approaches and Two Divergent Perspectives' (2007) 4 *Muslim World Journal of Human Rights* Article 5. I thank Anthony Chase, Sarah Joseph and Adam McBeth for reading through the draft and for their kind comments. Responsibility for the views expressed herein is, however, mine alone.

[1] There is a wide range of literature on this subject. See, for example, A A An-Na'im, *Towards an Islamic Reformation: Civil Liberties, Human Rights and International Law* (Syracuse University Press, New York, 1990); M Monshipouri, *Islamism, Secularism and Human Rights in the Middle East* (L Rienner Publishers, Boulder, 1998); M A Baderin, *International Human Rights and Islamic Law* (Oxford University Press, Oxford, 2003); A A Mayer, *Islam and Human Rights: Tradition and Politics* (Westview Press, Boulder, 4th ed, 2006); D Arzt, 'The Application of International Human Rights Law in Islamic States' (1990) 12 *Human Rights Quarterly* 202; S A Abu-Sahlieh, 'Human Rights Conflicts between Islam and the West' (1990) *Third World Legal Studies* 257; A Sajoo, 'Islam and Human Rights: Congruence or Dichotomy' (1990) 4 *Temple International and Comparative Law Journal* 23; B Tibi, 'Islamic Law/*Shari'a*, Human Rights, Universal Morality and International Relations' (1994) 16 *Human Rights Quarterly* 277; F Halliday, 'Relativism and Universalism in Human Rights: The Case of the Islamic Middle East' (1995) 43 *Political Studies* 152; H Bielefeldt, 'Muslim Voices in the Human Rights Debate' (1995) 17 *Human Rights Quarterly* 587; J Morgan-Foster, 'A New Perspective on the Universality Debate: Reverse Moderate Relativism in the Islamic Context' (2003) 10 *ILSA Journal of International and Comparative Law* 35; A Chase, 'The Tail and the Dog: Constructing Islam and Human Rights in Political Context' in A Chase and A Hamzawy (eds) *Human Rights in the Arab World* (University of Pennsylvania Press, Philadelphia, 2006) 21.

played and continues to play in the social, cultural, political and legal affairs of many predominantly Muslim States and societies. Although some commentators do argue that Islam is, essentially, neither the solution nor the source *per se* of political and social problems in the Muslim world,[2] a careful purview of current social, cultural, political and legal developments in Muslim States such as Saudi Arabia, Iran, Iraq, Egypt, Morocco, Sudan, Nigeria, Pakistan, Indonesia, Malaysia, Palestine, and even secular Turkey,[3] among others, reveals different degrees of Islamic influence in both the private and public spheres of those States, which directly or indirectly affects human rights issues.

For example, Bielefeldt has observed that 'traditional sha'ria [sic] norms continue to mark family structures all over the Islamic world' and that 'the sha'ria [sic] criminal law is [still] applied ... in a few Islamic countries today'.[4] Buskens too has noted that: '[i]n most Muslim societies it is impossible to speak about family law except in terms of Islam',[5] which, on the one hand, denotes the cultural and legal influence of Islam in that regard, but, on the other hand, has significant impact on the application of human rights law, especially in relation to women's rights, in most Muslim States. Modirzadeh has thus observed the need to take Islamic law seriously and engage with it one way or the other in relation to the promotion and protection of human rights in the Muslim world.[6] This domestic influence of Islam is formally reflected in

---

[2] See, for example, D Brumberg, 'Islam is not the Solution (or the Problem)' (2005–06) 29 *The Washington Quarterly* 97 (argues, *inter alia,* in relation to democracy in the Muslim world, that 'naming Islam as the solution exaggerates the extent to which Islam shapes Muslims' political identity'); A Chase, 'Liberal Islam and "Islam and Human Rights": A Sceptics View' (2006) 1 *Religion and Human Rights* 145; A Chase, above n 1, 21 (argues for a contextualized understanding of the relationship between Islam and human rights in the Arab world, and notes that 'It is political, social, and economic context that explains the status of human rights, for better for worse: Islam is neither responsible for rights violations nor the core basis for advancing rights').

[3] See, for example, T W Smith, 'Between Allah and Ataturk: Liberal Islam in Turkey' (2005) 9 *The International Journal of Human Rights* 307.

[4] H Bielefeldt, 'Muslim Voices in the Human Rights Debate' (1995) 17 *Human Rights Quarterly* 587, 612 (this situation, observed by Bielefeldt in 1995, remains significantly correct today).

[5] L Buskens, 'Recent Debates on Family Law Reform in Morocco: Islamic Law as Politics in an Emerging Public Sphere' (2003) 10 *Islamic Law and Society* 70, 71.

[6] N K Modirzadeh, 'Taking Islamic Law Seriously: INGOs and the Battle for Muslim Hearts and Minds' (2006) 19 *Harvard Human Rights Journal* 192, 192 (observes, *inter alia*, that despite the increasing sophistication in the work of human rights organizations in the Muslim world, they 'remain unsure of how to address questions of Islamic law when it conflicts with international human rights law' and argues

the constitutions of some Muslim States that declare Islam as the religion of the State[7], recognize Islamic law as part of State law[8] or provide for the establishment of State courts that apply Islamic law.[9]

Apart from the domestic influence of Islam in individual Muslim States, Muslim States have also adopted regional instruments such as the *Arab Charter on Human Rights*,[10] the *Charter of the Organisation of the Islamic Conference* ('OIC'),[11] the *OIC Cairo Declaration on Human Rights in Islam*[12] and the *OIC Covenant on the Rights of the Child in Islam*,[13] all of which respectively make references to Islam as a relevant factor in the human rights discourse in the Muslim world. Also at the United Nations ('UN') level, the OIC has, for example, made submissions on behalf of Muslim States regarding proposed reforms of the UN Security Council, stating that 'any reform proposal, which neglects the adequate representation of the Islamic Ummah in any category of members in an expanded Security Council will not be acceptable to the Islamic countries'.[14] With regard to international human rights, the Organisation

---

that international non-governmental organizations need to take Islamic law more seriously and engage with it in one way or the other); see also Netherlands Scientific Council for Government Policy ('WRR'), *Dynamism in Islamic Activism: Reference Points for Democratization and Human Rights* (Amsterdam University Press, Amsterdam, 2006) (notes that 'Since the 1970s, Islam has become an increasingly important political factor' particularly in the Muslim world).

[7]   See, for example, T Stahnke and R C Blitt, 'The Religion–State Relationship and the Right to Freedom of Religion or Belief: A Comparative Textual Analysis of the Constitutions of Predominantly Muslim Countries' (2005) 36 *Georgetown Journal of International Law* 7, http://papers.ssrn.com/sol3/papers.cfm?abstract_id=761746 at 25 November 2008.

[8]   Ibid; see also WRR, above n 6, 232–3.

[9]   See, for example, the *Constitution of the Federal Republic of Nigeria* ss 260–64. 275–9; the *Constitution of the Islamic Republic of Pakistan* Article 203.

[10]   Adopted by the League of Arab States on 15 September 1994; reprinted in (1997) 18 *Human Rights Law Journal* 151. The revised version adopted on 22 May 2004 and which entered into force on 15 March 2008 is available online: http://www1.umn.edu/humanrts/instree/loas2005.html at 25 November 2008.

[11]   Opened for signature 4 March 1972, 914 UNTS 111 (entered into force 1 February 1974); recently replaced by the instrument adopted at Dakar on 14 March 2008: http://www.oic-oci.org/oicnew/is11/english/Charter-en.pdf at 25 November 2008.

[12]   UN Doc A/45/5/21797 (5 August 1990) 199.

[13]   Adopted by the 32nd Islamic Conference of Foreign Ministers in Sana'a, Yemen, in June 2005: http://timelessfaith.org/BOOKS_pdf/child-rights.pdf at 25 November 2005.

[14]   UN Doc A/59/425/S/2004/808 (11 October 2004) [56].

Expressed its determination to vigorously pursue the promotion and protection of human rights and fundamental freedoms and encouraged greater transparency, cooperation, mutual tolerance and respect for religious values and cultural diversity in the field of universal promotion and protection of human rights.[15]

Furthermore, within international human rights forums, questions regarding the relationship and impact of Islam generally, and Islamic law specifically, on the application of human rights law in Muslim States have been raised before the Human Rights Committee under the UN human rights system,[16] before the European Court of Human Rights under the European regional human rights system[17] and before the African Commission on Human and Peoples' Rights under the African regional human rights system.[18] All these, no doubt, reflect the relevance of Islam to international human rights discourse generally, but particularly its impact and role in relation to Muslim States.

Pragmatically therefore, efforts for the promotion and protection of human rights in the Muslim world must necessarily take the impact and role of Islam into account, be it positively or negatively. Islam generally, and Islamic law specifically, cannot simply be disregarded as irrelevant in any of such endeavours. An-Na'im has observed in that regard that '[t]he implementation of international human rights norms in any society requires thoughtful and well-informed engagement with religion (broadly defined) because of its strong influence on human belief systems and behaviour' and that 'religious considerations are too important for the majority of people for human rights scholars and advocates to continue to dismiss them simply as irrelevant, insignificant, or problematic'.[19] That candid observation is particularly significant in relation to Islam and human rights due to Islam's significant societal role and influence in the Muslim world generally. In her article examining the human rights reports of international non-governmental organizations ('INGOs') in Muslim States, Modirzadeh observed that '[h]uman rights discourse and Islamic legal discourse are powerful forces in the Muslim world

---

[15] Ibid [57].

[16] See, for example, Human Rights Committee, *Concluding Observations of the Human Rights Committee on The Sudan*, UN Doc CCPR/C/79/Add.85 (19 November 1997) [22]; *Concluding Observations of the Human Rights Committee on the Islamic Republic of Iran*, UN Doc CCPR/C/79/Add/25 (3 August 1993) [13].

[17] See, for example, *Refah Partisi (The Welfare Party) v Turkey* (2003) 37 European Human Rights Reports 1 ('*Refah Partisi*').

[18] See *Curtis Francis Doebbler v Sudan* (2004) 11 *International Human Rights Review* 252.

[19] A A An-Na'im, 'Islam and Human Rights: Beyond the Universality Debate' (2000) 94 *ASIL Proceedings* 95, 95.

today' but noted 'a long simmering dilemma within the Western-based human rights movement' concerning 'how the human rights movement should deal with Islamic law'[20] and thus proposed 'three possible solutions for INGOs to consider in shaping their work on Islamic law' in relation to human rights in relevant Muslim States.[21] Many other commentators have also suggested different possible solutions to the problem of realizing human rights in the Muslim world.

Against the backdrop above, this chapter presents a pragmatic and constructive argument based on two evident facts. The first fact is that Muslim States are amongst the countries with the poorest human rights records in the world today. It has been observed, in that regard, that there is a 'growing sense in the West that *something must be done* about human rights in the Muslim world'.[22] The second fact is that at least half of the predominantly Muslim States have constitutionally proclaimed Islam as the official State religion, and also 'recognize some constitutional role for Islamic law, principles, or jurisprudence'.[23] Although Stahnke and Blitt have observed that the practical ramifications of both the constitutional declaration of Islam as State religion and the constitutional recognition of Islamic law vary respectively from State to State,[24] there is no doubt that the former theoretically reflects the general religious and moral role of Islam in the respective States, while the latter means that Islamic law (as part of domestic law) can impact on the application of human rights in the respective States. This chapter, therefore, argues that while Islam may not be the sole factor for ensuring the realization of human rights in Muslim States, it is certainly a significant factor that can be constructively employed as a vehicle for improving the poor human rights situation in, at least, predominantly Muslim States that recognize Islam as State religion or apply Islamic law or Islamic principles as part of State law.

But, what is the best approach to adopt in that regard to achieve the best possible outcome? This question will be addressed in the light of what I consider to be the two essential approaches (the 'socio-cultural approach' and the 'politico-legal approach') for promoting and protecting human rights generally. After analysing those two essential human rights approaches, the chapter will then examine the two divergent perspectives (the 'adversarial perspective' and the 'harmonistic perspective') on the discourse on Islam and

---

[20] Modirzadeh, above n 6, 192.
[21] Ibid 231.
[22] Ibid 192 (emphasis original).
[23] See Stahnke and Blitt, above n 7, 6–11, which records that 22 of 44 listed predominantly Muslim States have constitutionally declared Islam as the religion of the State and have some constitutional roles for Islamic law.
[24] Ibid 6.

human rights. The chapter will advance the view that the harmonistic perspective would be most helpful for employing Islam as a vehicle for the realization of human rights in the Muslim world within the context of the socio-cultural and politico-legal approaches for promoting and protecting human rights generally. Relevant academic and policy-oriented examples, especially in relation to promoting women's rights in the Muslim world, will be cited to support this position. It is important to note that this chapter does not argue that it is only through Islam or Islamic law that human rights can be realized in the Muslim world, but rather that Islam can, within the context of the socio-cultural and politico-legal approaches to human rights analysed herein, play a significant positive role towards the realization of human rights in the Muslim world instead of the negative role often simplistically attributed to it in that regard.

## 2 The two essential approaches for promoting and protecting human rights

For their effective realization generally, human rights, in my view, must be pursued through two essential complementary approaches, which, although not usually made explicit in human rights literature, are implicit in the processes of promoting and protecting human rights universally. They are what I refer to as the 'socio-cultural approach' and the 'politico-legal approach' for promoting and protecting human rights. These two approaches relate to the moral and justificatory attributes and the legal and executive attributes of human rights respectively. The socio-cultural approach is a bottom-to-top approach while the politico-legal approach is a top-to-bottom approach. These approaches are complementary and must be simultaneously pursued for the robust and effective realization of human rights globally.

Owing to the traditional state-centric and positivist nature of international law generally, international human rights discourse and advocacy have often concentrated more on politico-legal imperatives, placing emphasis on the human rights obligations of the State, but with less attention paid to the socio-cultural imperatives necessary for the promotion and protection of international human rights norms from the grassroots within communities. Yet, as early as 1958, the first chairperson of the UN Commission on Human Rights, Eleanor Roosevelt, declared as follows:

> Where, after all, do universal human rights begin? In small places, close to home – so close and so small that they cannot be seen on any map of the world. Yet they *are* the world of the individual person: the neighborhood he [or she] lives in; the school or college he [or she] attends; the factory, farm or office where he [or she] works. Such are the places where every man, woman, and child seeks equal justice, equal opportunity, equal dignity without discrimination. Unless these rights have meaning there, they have little meaning anywhere. Without concerted citizen action

to uphold them close to home, we shall look in vain for progress in the larger world. Thus we believe that the destiny of human rights is in the hands of all our citizens in all our communities.[25]

This statement acknowledges that an effective socio-cultural approach is as essential as the politico-legal approach for the global realization of human rights generally. In my view, this is even more particularly so with respect to the developing world, of which most Muslim States are part.

### A The socio-cultural approach

The socio-cultural approach to human rights relates to education, information, orientation and empowerment of the populace through the promotion of a local understanding of international human rights norms and principles. Through the socio-cultural approach, positive social change and a cultural link to human rights can be advocated, with which negative cultural relativist arguments used by some States to justify their human rights violations can be challenged by the populace themselves from within the relevant norms of respective societies.

It is important to note that the socio-cultural approach to promoting and protecting human rights is different from the traditional concept of cultural relativism in human rights discourse. While the traditional cultural relativist argument is often advanced by States to justify their human rights violations, the socio-cultural approach to promoting and protecting human rights is a positive means for realizing human rights through relevant social and cultural norms that already exist within different societies and communities. The socio-cultural approach to human rights encourages and facilitates the localization of international human rights norms.[26] According to Acharya,

> localization describes a complex process and outcome by which norm-takers build congruence between transnational norms (including norms previously institutionalized in a region) and local beliefs and practices. In this process, foreign norms, which may not initially cohere with the latter, are incorporated into local norms.

---

[25] Eleanor Roosevelt, remarks at the presentation of *IN YOUR HANDS: A Guide for Community Action for the Tenth Anniversary of the Universal Declaration of Human Rights* to the UN Commission on Human Rights (27 March 1958): http://www.udhr.org/history/inyour.htm at 25 November 2008.

[26] See, for example, K De Feyter, 'Localizing Human Rights' (Discussion Paper 2006/02, University of Antwerp, 2006): http://www2.warwick.ac.uk/fac/soc/law/events/past/2006/rightsandjustice/participants/papers/de_feyter.pdf at 25 November 2008 (the author argues that: 'International human rights lawyers tend to focus on establishing the universality of human rights rather than on improving the usefulness of human rights in addressing local problems' and thus he 'draws attention to the need to make human rights more locally relevant').

The success of norm diffusion strategies and processes depends on the extent to which they provide opportunities for localization.[27]

In that regard, the socio-cultural approach to human rights aims principally at the populace, especially at the grassroots, and can help in empowering them with the positive understanding of human rights in their own language and within their own social and cultural contexts. It links human rights positively to relevant socio-cultural values of different societies and communities and thus enables a better appreciation of the concept by the local populace, which helps to establish the moral and justificatory attribute of human rights locally. Nelson Mandela is quoted to have once said: 'If you talk to a man in a language he understands, that goes to his head. If you talk to him in his own language, that goes to his heart.'[28] One could add that if you talk to a man in a language he does not understand, that actually goes nowhere. Thus, the socio-cultural approach to human rights facilitates bringing human rights to the grassroots populace of every society in their own 'language'[29] so that it goes to their hearts. Where the socio-cultural approach to human rights is effectively pursued, the politico-legal approach to human rights will also become much easier to achieve and be more purposeful.

To be effective, the socio-cultural approach to human rights requires a search within different societies and cultures for relevant accommodating models to help realize international human rights norms. It ensures that the local communities understand human rights as part of their own human heritage and thus push the human rights idea from the bottom to the top, which, where effectively achieved, becomes a powerful politico-legal tool for the populace, the State, and for human rights advocates generally. De Feyter has rightly observed in that regard that '[i]f the experience of local communities is to inspire the further development of human rights, community-based organizations will have to be the starting point.'[30] Thus, local non-governmental organizations ('NGOs'), civil groups, cultural groups, religious groups, educational institutions and other local associations have important roles to play in the bottom-to-top orientation of the socio-cultural approach to human rights.

---

[27] A Acharya, 'How Ideas Spread: Whose Norms Matter? Norm Localization and Institutional Change in Asian Regionalism' (2004) 58 *International Organization* 239, 241.
[28] See http://www.saidwhat.co.uk/quotes/political/nelson_mandela/if_you_talk_to_a_man_9870 at 25 November 2008.
[29] 'Language' is used here figuratively and in a broad sense, not just literally to mean 'verbal conversation'.
[30] De Feyter, above n 26, 13.

This idea of a socio-cultural approach for promoting and protecting human rights is inferable from international human rights instruments such as the *Declaration on the Right and Responsibility of Individuals, Groups and Organs of Society to Promote and Protect Universally Recognized Human Rights and Fundamental Freedoms* adopted by the UN General Assembly in 1998,[31] which recognizes, *inter alia*, 'the right and the responsibility of individuals, groups and associations to promote respect for and foster knowledge of human rights and fundamental freedoms at the national and international levels'.[32] Its importance has been emphasized mostly by human rights scholars and advocates from developing States who appreciate the need for such an approach especially in the developing world. For example, De Feyter cites the argument of Makau Mutua in that regard that '[o]nly by locating the basis for the cultural legitimacy of certain human rights and mobilizing social forces on that score can respect for universal standards be forged'.[33] Thus, in seeking to remedy the poor human rights situations in Muslim States, as part of the developing world, the socio-cultural approach to human rights is very relevant in relation to Islam.

*B  The politico-legal approach*
On the other hand, the politico-legal approach to human rights is a top-to-bottom approach that relates more to human rights responsibility and accountability on the part of the State and its organs. This approach aims principally at ensuring respect for human rights by the State through relevant political and legal policies and through the establishment of relevant public institutions for the promotion and protection of human rights. As noted earlier, much emphasis has often been placed on the politico-legal approach to human rights, whereby the focus is normally on urging States to fulfil their international, regional or constitutional human rights obligations. State practice, however, shows that developed States are often more responsive to the politico-legal approach than developing States. The guarantee of human rights under this approach depends largely on the positive political will of the government in power, which is often lacking in States of the developing world, including Muslim States. It is, thus, in the context of the politico-legal approach to human rights that States are often lobbied, internally and externally, to ratify relevant human rights treaties and pacifically pressured, where necessary, to fulfil their obligations under such treaties.

---

[31]  GA Res 53/144, UN GAOR, 53rd sess, 85th plen mtg, UN Doc A/Res/53/144 (9 December 1998) Annex.
[32]  Ibid [Preambular 8] ('GA Res 53/144').
[33]  M Mutua, *Human Rights: A Political and Cultural Critique* (Philadelphia University Press, Philadelphia, 2002) 256, cited in De Feyter, above n 26, 6.

This top-to-bottom approach to promoting and protecting human rights is acknowledged in many human rights instruments, which provide that States have the primary responsibility to promote, protect and implement human rights and that they must adopt all necessary administrative and legislative measures to ensure the guarantee of relevant human rights within their respective jurisdictions.[34] Thus, it is in the context of the politico-legal approach that the legal and executive attribute of human rights is ensured, and through it victims of human rights violations are able to seek legal redress for such violations personally or through the assistance of human rights NGOs. Being a top-to-bottom approach, factors such as good governance, positive political will, justice, good faith, and judicial independence are essential for its successful realization.

However, the politico-legal approach to human rights is, primarily, vertically-oriented and may therefore not effectively address horizontal human rights problems such as human rights violations that occur within family relations and in the private sphere, especially violations grounded on the 'victim's' consent, whereby victims of human rights violations justify the violations against themselves on grounds of cultural and traditional practices they blindly follow without questioning. Where the populace are themselves not informed or aware of their rights, or where they see human rights strictly as a foreign idea, they are often unable to challenge any violation of their human rights by the State or question any of such violations based on cultural or religious grounds. Thus, while the politico-legal approach to human rights is essential for ensuring necessary political and legislative guarantees that facilitate respect for human rights from top to bottom on the part of the State, a parallel bottom-to-top socio-cultural approach is necessary to ensure a robust and effective system of promoting and protecting human rights in every State.

### C  Application to the Muslim world

In relation to the Muslim world, it is submitted that Islam, owing to its general socio-cultural and politico-legal influence in many Muslim States and societies as identified above, can play a significant role in effectively pursuing both the socio-cultural and the politico-legal approaches for promoting and protecting human rights in relevant Muslim States. The relevance of Islam in both regards is reflected in the views of the WRR in its recently published policy-oriented report on Islamic activism in the Muslim world. The Council observed that '[p]rogressive improvements of human rights in many Muslim countries are simply easier to accept if they can be imbedded in the local tradition and culture',[35] which reflects the need for a socio-cultural approach to

---

34  See, for example, GA Res 53/144, above n 31, Articles 1 and 2.
35  WRR, above n 6, 10–11.

human rights on the one hand, and also that '[d]espite all the incentives and control mechanisms, they [human rights] can only go beyond the level of rights on paper when they can boast internal legitimacy, in other words, when they are viewed as "one's own law",[36] which reflects the need for a politico-legal approach to human rights on the other hand, both as argued in this chapter. The Council then pointed out notably that 'in a number of countries ... this "own law" is based on Sharia' and thus '[p]recisely because international law primarily acquires its force through national law, the EU [European Union] must recognize that the legitimizing power of the Sharia in Muslim countries can be used to realize international human rights'.[37]

However, the success of both the socio-cultural and politico-legal approaches for promoting and protecting human rights in Muslim States depends, substantially, on which of two divergent perspectives is adopted in addressing the relationship between Islam and human rights in the Muslim world, as analysed below.

## 3 The two divergent perspectives on the Islam and human rights discourse

A perusal of the literature on the subject reveals generally that there are two broad divergent perspectives on how the question of Islam and human rights in the Muslim world has been and continues to be addressed. These I refer to as the 'adversarial perspective' and the 'harmonistic perspective' on Islam and human rights. These two divergent perspectives are reflected in both human rights and Islamist arguments on Islam and human rights respectively. The adversarial perspective is a hostile one, while the harmonistic perspective is a receptive one.

### A  The adversarial perspective

Human rights arguments reflecting the adversarial perspective on Islam and human rights generally presume that Islam is inherently the main cause of all human rights violations in Muslim States and perceive Islam and Islamic law as strictly conservative and fossilized systems that cannot be in synergy with international human rights norms and principles at all. An example of this perspective is seen in the view of a human rights activist that 'Islamic Sharia law should be opposed by everyone who believes in universal human rights'.[38]

---

[36] Ibid 169–70.
[37] Ibid 170.
[38] A Kamguian, *Why Islamic Law should be opposed?* (2002) Middle East Women, http://www.middleastwomen.org/html/sharia.htm at 25 November 2008.

The adversarial perspective is also evident in a general view of the European Court of Human Rights expressed in the case of *Refah Partisi (The Welfare Party) and Others v Turkey* that '[i]t is difficult to declare one's respect for democracy and human rights while at the same time supporting a regime based on sharia'.[39] Similarly, there are adversarial Islamist arguments that perceive the promotion of international human rights as a Western, anti-Islamic agenda, which must not be encouraged to flourish in the Muslim world.[40]

The adversarial perspective on Islam and human rights is a confrontational and negative perspective that tends to place a wedge between Islam and human rights. It disregards any possible areas of common ground between the two systems and thus eliminates the possibility of realizing human rights within an Islamic dispensation, thereby suggesting that Muslims must make a choice between Islam and human rights. This perspective promotes an incompatibility or absolute conflict theory in the Islam and human rights discourse. While there is no doubt that there are some important areas of difference between some human rights principles and some traditional principles of Islam, which need to be addressed, the confrontational nature of the adversarial perspective is problematic in the context of both the socio-cultural and politico-legal approaches for promoting and protecting human rights in the Muslim world. It does not provide room for real dialogue and engagement as it confronts the 'Islam and human rights' question as a sort of competition between two value systems, which makes it a very difficult perspective for the realization of human rights in Muslim States through the socio-cultural and politico-legal approaches. I have argued against this 'discordant' perspective elsewhere by highlighting its general negativity and noted that such a perspective 'emanates from the traditional divide and stereotype of confrontation between the Occidental and Oriental civilisations, between religion and secularism and more specifically between Islamic orthodoxy and Western liberalism'.[41]

Deplorably, however, the poor human rights practices of governments in most Muslim States also nourish the adversarial approach to Islam and human rights, especially when such governments try to justify their human rights violations by reference to Islamic culture or Islamic law. Nevertheless, while

---

[39] See *Refah Partisi* and the Grand Chamber judgment: Application Nos 41340/98; 41342/98; 41343/98; 41344/9 (Unreported, European Court of Human Rights, Grand Chamber, 13 February 2003) [123], http://cmiskp.echr.coe.int/tkp197/view.asp?item=2&portal=hbkm&action=html&highlight=&sessionid=16524354&skin=hudoc-en at 25 November 2008.
[40] See M Baderin, above n 1, 13–16.
[41] M A Baderin, 'Human Rights and Islamic Law: The Myth of Discord' (2005) 2 *European Human Rights Law Review* 163, 165.

it is essential to challenge the arguments of governments that plead Islam or Islamic law to justify their violations of human rights, it actually tends to help their case to propose that their arguments and deplorable practices confirm that Islam and human rights are inherently divergent and adversarial in nature. In that regard, Entelis has observed, in relation to women's rights, that '[t]he claim that Islamic culture, as influenced by *shari'a* law, cannot accommodate modern human right doctrine is simply a means by which conservative Islamists in Government strive to preserve the patriarchal societies in place'.[42] In my view, it helps the promotion of human rights in the Muslim world better by countering such arguments with relevant evidence showing that neither Islam nor Islamic law supports human rights violations.

Commenting on an adversarial proposition in one article which 'urges that the United States government should put similar energy [to that it used in combating terrorism emerging from militants in the Muslim world] into combating the treatment of women under *Shari'a*', Modirzadeh observed, *inter alia*, that while it is true that serious human rights violations occur as a result of some Islamic rules for which solutions need to be found, 'to suggest that the solution to every violation is merely more "pressure" from the United States government, *seriously undermines the extent to which Islamic law is deeply ingrained in the legal, political, and social frameworks of many Muslim countries*'.[43] Thus, while an adversarial perspective on Islam and human rights might be convenient, for example, in naming and shaming governments of Muslim States that violate human rights on grounds of Islam or Islamic law, it is less helpful in the context of the socio-cultural and politico-legal approaches for promoting the realization of human rights in Muslim States. The observation of the WRR that '[a] climate of confrontation is hardly conducive to the creation of lasting conditions for ... increasing respect for human rights'[44] is instructive in that regard.

### B  The harmonistic perspective

Conversely, the harmonistic perspective on Islam and human rights is a responsive one that seeks to develop positive ways by which Islamic principles and international human rights norms can be harmonized as far as possible and thereby operate in synergy. Advocates of this perspective perceive Islamic law as a dynamic system that can respond to the dynamics and reali-

---

[42] J Entelis, 'International Human Rights: Islam's Friend or Foe?: Algeria as an Example of the Compatibility of International Human Rights Regarding Women's Equality and Islamic Law' (1997) 20 *Fordham International Law Journal* 1251, 1294–5.

[43] Modirzadeh, above n 6, 212–13 (emphasis added).

[44] WRR, above n 6, 209.

ties of human existence and is thus reconcilable with international human rights norms. In contrast to the adversarial perspective on Islam and human rights, the harmonistic perspective concentrates on realizing the ideals of human rights in Islam rather than perceiving the question of Islam and human rights as a competition between values. The harmonistic perspective on Islam and human rights therefore encourages understanding, constructive engagement and dialogue between Islam and human rights. This perspective emphasizes and explores the possibilities offered by alternative juristic views of Islamic law that are both moderate and legitimate on relevant questions of human rights in the Muslim world and thereby promotes a congruence theory in the Islam and human rights discourse. Although the harmonistic perspective promotes dialogue and understanding, this does not mean that areas of differences and conflict are downplayed or shied away from but, rather, that they should be addressed with the aim of finding constructive resolutions of them. Contextually, this perspective is the more helpful one in relation to the sociocultural and politico-legal approaches for promoting and protecting human rights in Muslim States analysed above.

Generally, the harmonistic perspective on Islam and human rights is reflected in different ways in the works and practices of many scholars and advocates on the subject,[45] some of which will be referred to in the next section. The report of the WRR also favours this perspective as a positive approach that has much more potential for the realization of human rights in the Muslim world.[46]

Owing to the evident influence of Islam in the Muslim world as identified above, I have consistently argued that approaches which encourage harmonization of Islamic principles and human rights norms have a better chance of facilitating an effective realization of the implementation of international human rights in Muslim States than approaches that tend to place a wedge between Islam and human rights or present human rights as an alternative ideology to Islam in Muslim societies.[47] It is in that vein that I reiterate the need to advance the harmonistic perspective on Islam and human rights in

---

[45] See, for example, N A Shah, 'Women's Human Rights in the Koran: An Interpretive Approach' (2006) 28 *Human Rights Quarterly* 868, 875–84, where the author discusses some different approaches to this perspective by reference to the works of Mahmood Monshipouri, Bassam Tibi, Abdullahi An-Na'im, and Mashood Baderin, respectively.

[46] WRR, above n 6.

[47] See, for example, M A Baderin, 'Establishing Areas of Common Ground between Islamic Law and International Human Rights' (2001) 5 *The International Journal of Human Rights* 72; 'Identifying Possible Mechanisms Within Islamic Law for the Promotion and Protection of Human Rights in Muslim States' (2004) 22 *Netherlands Quarterly of Human Rights* 329; above n 41.

conjunction with the socio-cultural and politico-legal approaches to human rights in the Muslim world with relevant substantiations below.

## 4 Advancing the harmonistic perspective in the Muslim world

In his conclusion in an article on the interdependence of religion, secularism and human rights,[48] An-Na'im made the important observation that: 'peoples and individuals need make no choice among religion, secularism, and human rights' and that '[t]he three can work in synergy.' He noted, however, that 'there is a related choice that does need to be made: whether or not to attempt mediating tensions among the three paradigms' and he thus urged 'scholars and policymakers to take responsibility for that mediation rather than permit further damage to be done by belief in the incompatibility of religion with secular government and human rights'.[49] In relation to Islam and human rights in the Muslim world, the populace certainly 'need make no choice' between Islam and human rights, as demanded by the adversarial perspective on Islam and human rights; they can have both Islam and human rights working in synergy. Such synergy can be achieved using the harmonistic perspective on Islam and human rights in conjunction with the socio-cultural and politico-legal approaches for promoting and protecting human rights, as has been previously argued in this chapter.

In the context of the socio-cultural approach to human rights, it is apparent that while there is a relatively strong human rights debate developing in the Muslim world today, most of that discourse is taking place high above the grassroots in most Muslim States. There is therefore an important need for the human rights debates in the Muslim world to be brought down to the populace at the grassroots in the language they understand. In the course of that, the socio-cultural approach to human rights must address two main elements, namely, social change and cultural control.

In every society, there is a need for some element of social change for the effective realization of human rights, especially in the horizontal interaction of the populace, and this is better achieved through positive improvement in social consciousness than through forceful political or legal control. Promoting social change can, however, be problematic in almost all societies, but particularly in Muslim societies when this is perceived by the populace as being externally motivated. In a recent comment on scholarship for social change in Muslim societies, An-Na'im observed, *inter alia*, that '[e]xternal

---

[48] A A An-Na'im, 'The Interdependence of Religion, Secularism, and Human Rights' (2005) 11 *Common Knowledge* 56.
[49] Ibid 80.

interventions, whatever may be [their] motivation and objectives, [are] always likely to be regarded with suspicion and scepticism by local communities.'[50]

Most advocates of human rights at the local level in Muslim societies have probably experienced this problem of suspicion and scepticism. For example, at a conference on women's rights in Islam under the auspices of the Planned Parenthood Federation of Nigeria ('PPFN') but with international sponsorship, held in 1994 at the University of Ibadan in Nigeria, there were suggestions from almost all the local Muslim participants behind the scenes, and from many of them on the conference floor, that the conference had a hidden agenda against Islamic norms and traditions which must be resisted. The local participants perceived the programme as externally driven to undermine Islam.[51] Ten years later, in 2004, there was similar suspicion and scepticism expressed by local participants at an international conference at the University of Jos in Nigeria on comparative perspectives of *shari`a* in Nigeria organized by the University of Jos in conjunction with Bayreuth University of Germany and with international sponsorship from the Volkswagen Foundation of Germany.[52]

Similar scenarios of suspicion and scepticism are not uncommon at such meetings in other Muslim States, and this needs to be addressed through local confidence-building in the international human rights system. An element of this suspicion is also institutionally reflected in the call of the OIC to its Muslim Member States 'to continue their coordination and cooperation in the area of human rights in the relevant international fora with the view to enhance Islamic solidarity in confronting attempts to use human rights as a means to politically pressurize any of the Member States'.[53]

The socio-cultural approach to human rights would work better in addressing that problem in conjunction with the harmonistic perspective to Islam and human rights. In pursuing the socio-cultural approach to human rights here, Islam can play a very positive role. On the one hand, local Muslim communities are not generally inimical to social change, but they are often more amenable to social changes that can be justified in Islam, which, one must however acknowledge, is not always a clear-cut matter due to the different 'Islamic' views that can exist on any particular issue. In that regard, there is often the problem of how to deal with hard-line Islamist views on relevant

---

[50] A A An-Nai'm, 'Human Rights and Scholarship for Social Change in Islamic Communities' (2005) 2 *Muslim World Journal of Human Rights* 1, 1–3.

[51] This author presented a paper at and participated in the Ibadan conference.

[52] This author was not present at the Jos conference but was reliably informed by some local participants at the conference.

[53] See *Final communiqué of the annual coordination meeting of Ministers for Foreign Affairs of the States members of the Organization of the Islamic Conference*, UN Doc A/59/425/S/2004/808 (11 October 2004) [57].

human rights issues. It is submitted that, using the socio-cultural approach to human rights, such hard-line views can be engaged by constructively using relevant Islamic sources and arguments, which is more feasible through the harmonistic perspective on Islam and human rights than through the adversarial perspective. There is relevant evidence within Islamic sources to aid such a congruous socio-cultural human rights discourse to promote human rights in Muslim societies.

On the other hand, resistance to social change is usually due to the cultural control of the populace. As culture provides a sense of community for ordinary people they feel protected by it and cling to it for fear of isolation. Apart from being a religion, Islam also theoretically provides a sense of an 'Islamic culture' amongst Muslims. The religious attachment to the 'Islamic culture' gives it stronger control within Muslim societies. However, different negative local traditional cultures have crept into the 'Islamic culture' of different Muslim States and have for long become wrongly perceived as part of the 'Islamic culture', even though in contradiction with Islamic norms and principles. It has been noted that such cultural components have become so deeply rooted in most Muslim societies that 'many Muslims are no longer aware of their non-religious origins.'[54] Most of the grassroots populace in the Muslim world have become subjected to such negative cultural control unknowingly, which adversely affects their enjoyment of some basic human rights.

The issue of women's rights is perhaps the clearest example of such negative cultural control in the Muslim world, which a socio-cultural approach to human rights in conjunction with the harmonistic perspective to Islam and human rights can help to address in almost all Muslim States. One example of such adverse traditional culture that threatens and continues to violate the fundamental right to life of many Muslim women, but which has been peddled wrongly in different Muslim societies as part of an 'Islamic culture', is the so-called 'honour killing' of women that sadly occurs in some parts of the Muslim world.[55] A bottom-to-top socio-cultural approach to human rights, in conjunction with a harmonistic perspective on Islam and human rights with reference to relevant Islamic sources against this inhuman act, is an important means of dealing with this problem from the grassroots in Muslim States.

---

[54] A al-Hibri, 'Islam, Law and Custom: Refining Muslim Women's Rights (1997) 12 *American University Journal of International Law and Policy* 1, 5.

[55] The so-called 'honour killing' is the murder of a family member (often female) by another family member (often male) for allegedly bringing dishonour upon the family through unapproved marriage or divorce or for committing adultery or fornication: see, for example, L Welchman and S Hossain (eds) *'Honour' Crimes, Paradigms and Violence against Women* (Zed Books, London, 2005).

Historical evidence indicates that Islamic law has actually never been static generally; rather it has been evolutionary and has responded to changes in most Muslim societies, but mostly to the advantage of the male gender. I have stated elsewhere that 'it is hypocritical if men on the one hand acquire and enjoy many rights and liberties of today's world, often through constructive and evolutionary interpretations of the *Sharī'ah*, but on the other hand consider the rights and liberties of women to be stagnated upon the juristic views of the classical schools of Islamic law'.[56] The enhancement of women's rights is therefore very important in all Muslim States and can be achieved through the harmonistic perspective on Islam and human rights in the context of both the socio-cultural and politico-legal approaches to human rights.

The relevance of the socio-cultural approach to human rights and the harmonistic perspective on Islam and human rights in relation to women's rights in Muslim societies is very well reflected in the observation of one researcher on women's rights in Afghanistan, who stated: '[f]rom my impressions and interviews in Afghanistan ... [m]any women expressed that while they were keen to have rights, they wanted it within the framework of Islam and not as a cultural imposition from the West.'[57] The author then noted that:

> Many Afghan women believed that the Qur'an offered women enough rights for them to negotiate their rights, but it was the fundamentalist interpretations that prevented women from claiming those rights and from educating themselves. Given the strategies employed by various women's organizations in Afghanistan to empower women, it became obvious that their perceptions of culture and religion played a crucial role in their women's rights strategies.[58]

Likewise Habiba Sorabi, then the Afghanistan Minister for Women's Affairs,[59] was quoted as stating in an interview that 'Islam is here to stay and women want rights within the Islamic framework; ... Islam gave women rights to education and employment and ... her Ministry was working within that framework.'[60]

Similarly, al-Hibri reflected the positive nature of the harmonistic perspective on Islam and human rights in relation to the promotion of women's rights in Muslim States by first observing that '[i]t is important to keep in mind that most Muslim women tend to be highly religious and would not want to act in

---

[56] Baderin, above n 1, 65.
[57] H Ahmed-Ghosh, 'Voices of Afghan Women: Women's Rights, Human Rights, and Culture' (2004) 27 *Thomas Jefferson Law Review* 27, 29.
[58] Ibid 31.
[59] Habiba Sorabi is currently the Governor of the Bamyan Province of Afghanistan.
[60] Ahmed-Ghosh, above n 57, 32.

contradiction to their faith'.[61] She then narrated a personal experience, which corroborates the usefulness of the harmonistic perspective on Islam and human rights in relation to the socio-cultural approach to promoting human rights in Muslim States, as follows:

> A couple of years ago, I met some 'modern' Muslim women behind closed doors in a certain Muslim country. The object was to have frank discussions about Islam and the rights of women. The women reflected a high degree of conflict and frustration. They wanted to be good Muslims, but they wanted to have their rights as well. When we focused on the issue of greatest concern to them, the Qur'anic view of gender relations, and I provided a non-patriarchal Qur'anic interpretation on the subject, sighs of relief filled the room. The conflict created by patriarchal interpretations for Muslim women who do not have the benefit of a religious education is frightening.[62]

She then argued that '[t]he majority of Muslim women who are attached to their religion will not be liberated through the use of a secular approach imposed' on them and that the best way 'is to build a solid Muslim feminist jurisprudential basis which clearly shows that Islam not only does not deprive them of their rights, but in fact demands these rights for them'.[63]

In an article commenting on Fatima Mernissi's works on women's rights in the Muslim world, the authors observed that Mernissi's approach had evolved 'from advocating secular reconstruction of Muslim societies to a position that resembles Islamic reformism',[64] which reflects a shift from an adversarial perspective to a harmonistic perspective on Islam and human rights. The authors noted that while Mernissi had argued for a reconstructive approach to Islam in relation to women's rights in her first book, *Beyond the Veil*, published in 1975, which reflected an adversarial perspective on Islam and human rights, she seemed to argue differently 16 years later for a reformative approach, which reflected a harmonistic perspective on Islam and human rights, in her book *The Veil and the Male Elite*, published in 1991. This, according to the authors, represented 'a shift from Mernissi's earlier works, in which she argued that the establishment of women's rights in Muslim societies would necessitate going beyond the limits of Islamic discourse. In *The Veil and the Male Elite*, Mernissi reveals her preference for a reformist approach to Islam and the socio-political establishment'.[65] They concluded that

---

[61] al-Hibri, above n 54, 3.
[62] Ibid.
[63] Ibid.
[64] R Barlow and S Akbarzadeh, 'Women's Rights in the Muslim World: Reform or Reconstruction?' (2006) 27 *Third World Quarterly* 1481, 1481.
[65] Ibid 1483.

'Mernissi's early reconstructivist approach ... faced the test of relevance' in the sense that '[i]f Muslim feminist theory is separated from its subjects and not able to inspire and motivate Muslim women, then that theory is diminished in relevance and effectiveness',[66] which essentially corroborates the usefulness and relevance of the harmonistic perspective on Islam and human rights in that regard.

It was noted above that the socio-cultural approach to human rights relates to the education, information, orientation and empowerment of the populace through the promotion of a local understanding of international human rights norms and principles, and that local human rights NGOs, religious groups and institutions have an important role to play in that regard. From a harmonistic perspective on Islam and human rights, I have argued elsewhere, regarding human rights education, that there is Islamic evidence to support the promotion of human rights education and awareness in the Muslim world, and that:

> [A]n Islamic and international human rights curriculum for primary, secondary and tertiary institutions in the Muslim world is very necessary in that regard. This needs to be implemented both in private and public schools. Due to the importance and the role of religion and religious institutions in the Muslim world, human rights education should not be limited to the secular institutions but also extended to the Islamic religious institutions and centres. The provisions of the Qur'an and *Sunnah* that promote the ideals of human rights must be stressed. As there are many Qur'anic provisions that buttress most of the human rights guarantees under international human rights instruments, it is essential that the international human rights provisions be explained and illustrated through the Islamic legal tradition for a religious and cultural appreciation of those rights.[67]

I have further observed in that regard that '[t]he duty of promoting human rights through education is not restricted to States alone, non-governmental organisations and religious bodies also have an important role to play in that regard and should be encouraged by the States to do so', and consequently suggested that

> a decade of human rights education and dissemination be declared by the OIC for its Member States, and Muslim States should be encouraged to adopt national plans for human rights education in that regard. Such an approach will be a bold step towards the realisation of the ideal Islamic society in which people are aware of their rights, wherein human rights are duly respected and human beings enjoy the inherent honour (*karāmah*) which their Creator had endowed in them at creation.[68]

---

[66] Ibid 1493.
[67] M A Baderin, 'Identifying Possible Mechanisms Within Islamic Law for the Promotion and Protection of Human Rights in Muslim States' (2004) 22 *Netherlands Quarterly of Human Rights*, 329, 337.
[68] Ibid 338.

From a harmonistic perspective on Islam and human rights, the establishment of local NGOs to facilitate a socio-cultural approach to human rights in Muslim States can also be substantiated in Islam by reference to an earlier practice of Prophet Muhammad. Islamic historical accounts indicate that he had participated in an organization called *Hilf al-Fudūl* (League of Excellence)[69] in Mecca around 590CE as a young man before his call to prophethood.[70] The League undertook the task of intervening and protecting the interests of the oppressed and victims of injustice in any transaction involving the chieftains and the powerful people in Mecca at that time. Prophet Muhammed is reported to have said about the League, after his prophethood many years later, that it was a league he loved to join and if he were to be 'invited to have a hand in it even after the advent of Islam, [he] would have undoubtedly joined again'.[71] The *Hilf al-Fudūl* League has been described as the first human rights NGO in Islamic history.[72] The socio-cultural promotion of human rights education and awareness, the establishment of relevant human rights NGOs and the involvement of local groups and religious institutions in that regard can therefore be positively pursued through the harmonistic perspective on Islam and human rights in the Muslim world.

The US-based Muslim Women Lawyers for Human Rights ('KARAMAH') is an example of a women's organization whose work practically reflects the harmonistic perspective on Islam and human rights, which can be seen emulated in other relevant areas of human rights for the Muslim world. Information on the organization's website indicates that it 'is committed to research, education, and advocacy work in matters pertaining to Muslim women and human rights in Islam, as well as civil rights and other related rights under the *Constitution of the United States*'.[73] The organization is said

---

[69] Also translated variously as 'League of the Virtuous', 'League of the Righteous', 'Alliance of the Righteous', 'Alliance of Excellence', 'Pact of Excellence', 'Pact of the Virtuous', 'Pact of the Righteous'.

[70] See, for example, A S Najeebabadi, *The History of Islam: Vol 1* (Darussalam International Publishers, Riyadh, 2000) 99–101; Ch Pellat, 'Hif al-Fudul' in B Lewis, V L Ménage, Ch Pellat and J Schach (eds) *Encyclopaedia of Islam: Vol III* (Brill, Leiden, 1986).

[71] Najeebabadi, above n 70, 101.

[72] See A Zaoui, 'Islam and Human Rights' (Lecture presented as part of the Vice-Chancellor's Lecture Series, Massey University, Albany, 10 August 2005) http://www.freezaoui.org.nz/system/files/Islam+and+Human+Rights+MasseyUni+Aug2005.pdf at 29 November 2008; See also 'The Pact of the Virtuous (*Hilf al-Fudul*)' in UNDP, *Arab Human Development Report 2004: Towards Freedom in the Arab World* (UNDP, New York, 2005) 74.

[73] KARAMAH, *Building Bridges* (2004) KARAMAH, http://www.karamah.org/home.htm at 29 November 2008. The Egyptian Initiative for Personal Rights

to be 'founded upon the ideal that education, dialogue, and action can counter the dangerous and destructive effects of ignorance, silence, and prejudice' and it 'supports Muslim communities in America and abroad in the pursuit of justice'. Corroborating the importance of the socio-cultural approach to human rights, the organization has also noted that '[w]hen we talk of human rights abuses, we often direct our attention to governments and institutions. We must not forget, however, that the most basic of our rights emerges within our private and our domestic spheres'.[74]

Now we turn to the politico-legal approach to human rights, which must also address two main elements, namely, political authority and legal order. Politically, the protection of human rights is about good governance and accountability, which is lacking in most parts of the developing world, including Muslim States. As earlier observed, Islam has political influence in most parts of the Muslim world. This is evidenced by the use of Islam as a political tool by the political elites in Muslim States. Even in secular Muslim States, political leaders often unpack and play up their Islamic identity to cajole the Muslim populace to their side when the political terrain gets tough. Being a top-to-bottom approach, this element of the politico-legal approach to human rights can be used to engage governments of Muslim States to adopt welfare policies that ensure the guarantee of the human rights of the populace, as required and encouraged under Islamic political principles. Employing the harmonistic perspective on Islam and human rights, the political authority, at least in those Muslim States that have constitutionally proclaimed Islam as the religion of the State, can be persuaded with relevant evidence from within Islamic sources urging accountability and good governance on the part of those entrusted with political authority.

One political question that often creeps into the Islam and human rights discourse in relation to the politico-legal approach to human rights is the issue of secularism. In relation to international human rights law, the issue of secularism is, apparently, paradoxical. While it is often suggested, from a human rights perspective, that human rights are better guaranteed within a strictly secular political dispensation, there is no specific international human rights obligation upon States to adopt a secular political system. Stahnke and Blitt have observed in this regard that:

> Under international human rights standards, a state can adopt a particular relationship with the religion of the majority of the population, including establishing a

---

('EIPR'), an Egyptian NGO, is also said to be using the harmonistic approach to argue some of its cases: *About EIPR* (2008), http://www.eipr.org/en/info/about.htm at 29 November 2008.

[74] KARAMAH, above n 73.

state religion, provided that such a relationship does not result in violations of the civil and political rights of, or discrimination against, adherents of other religions or non-believers.[75]

Nevertheless, while predominantly Muslim States may not be in violation of international human rights rules by constitutionally declaring Islam as State religion, Muslim States definitely have an obligation under international human rights law to ensure non-discrimination against adherents of other religions and non-believers within their respective jurisdictions. The poor situation regarding respect for minority rights in Muslim States has rightly attracted the interest of many Muslim scholars, who propose a re-examination of the traditional Islamic jurisprudence on the issue of minorities (*fiqh aqaliyyāt*) under Islamic law,[76] which the political authorities in most Muslim States need to address as a possible means of positively promoting respect for minority rights in the Muslim world. Berween has argued in that regard, citing relevant Islamic sources, that Muslim States have an obligation to protect minority rights under Islamic law. He observed notably that:

> In an Islamic state, although the Muslim majority rules, it does not have the power to deprive the minorities of their basic rights or to stop them from serving their society like any other citizen. The Muslim majority must obey all Islamic laws. In many ways it is like any other majority in any civilized society, the Muslim majority has the power to act, but it must act legally, fairly, and without violating the rights and liberties of any citizen. Finally, to be legitimate the Muslim majority rule must be reasonable and it must respect and protect the rights of all minorities. That requires protection of all those freedoms that make effective opposition possible. Those freedoms must, at least, include the right to full and equal political participation; freedom of expression; freedom of the press; freedom of beliefs; an independent judiciary; freedom of peaceful assembly and petition; and, freedom of choice.[77]

The realization of this obligation can be positively enhanced through the harmonistic perspective on Islam and human rights, in conjunction with the politico-legal approach to human rights as advanced in this chapter.

On the other hand, an effective legal order is also a very important element of the politico-legal approach to human rights. Although this element is often

---

[75] See Stahnke and Blitt, above n 7, 8. See also Human Rights Committee, *General Comment No. 22: The Right to Freedom of Thought, Conscience and Religion (Art 18)*, UN Doc CCPR/C/21/Rev.1/Add.4 (30 July 1993) [9].

[76] See, for example, A Ahmad, 'Extension of Shari'ah in Northern Nigeria: Human Rights Implications for Non-Muslim Minorities' (2005) 2 *Muslim World Journal of Human Rights* Article 6.

[77] M Berween, 'Non-Muslims in the Islamic State: Majority Rule and Minority Rights' (2006) 10 *The International Journal of Human Rights* 91, 101.

seen as remedial and triggered by human rights violations, it can also serve to prevent human rights violations where relevant laws are promulgated and relevant human rights institutions and mechanisms are created by the State and well utilized in that regard. Many Muslim States today have elements of Islamic law incorporated into their domestic laws, thus the relationship between Islamic law and human rights in Muslim States has constituted an important aspect of the Islam and human rights discourse. As with the issue of secularism above, States have the sovereign autonomy to adopt a legal system of their choice, as international human rights law does not impose any specific legal system on States. The impasse on the role of Islamic law in the drafting of the Iraqi constitution,[78] however, demonstrated the general presumption in human rights circles that Islamic law or *shari`a* is inimical to civil liberties and human rights.

There is no doubt that some traditional implementations of Islamic law, which when viewed historically may be considered to have been ahead of their time, are today contradictory to human rights standards. The problem is that Islamic law has been viewed and promoted in its historical context by most commentators and scholars, and also applied mostly as such by many Muslim States. It is important to emphasize in that regard that Islamic law is not, and must not be perceived as, static and fossilized, but rather is evolutionary. Its evolutionary nature makes it complementary to human rights through the harmonistic perspective advanced in this chapter. Where Islamic legal scholarship, in response to modern human rights challenges, is re-directed at emphasizing the evolutionary nature of Islamic law rather than presenting it in a historical context and as a fossilized legal system stuck in the past, its potential as a vehicle for the realization of human rights will be better enhanced. The methods of Islamic law are quite robust and flexible to facilitate the needed progressive evolution of Islamic law in that regard.[79]

For example, in adopting a new women's rights-friendly Family Code, *the Mudawwana*, based on Islamic law and principles, in 2004, Morocco demonstrated the evolutionary nature of Islamic law and the possibility of a harmonistic perspective on Islam and human rights in relation to the politico-legal approach to human rights. It has been observed that the new Moroccan

---

[78] This refers to the initial controversy as to whether Islamic law should serve as a source of legislation in the Iraqi constitution. See, for example, International Crisis Group Report, Iraq's Constitutional Challenge (2003) ICG, http://www.icg.org//library/documents/middle_east___north_africa/19_iraq_s_constitutional_challenge.pdf at 29 November 2008, 17–18, [D].

[79] See, for example, W Hallaq, *A History of Islamic Legal Theories* (Cambridge University Press, Cambridge, new ed, 1999); M H Kamali, *Principles of Islamic Jurisprudence* (Islamic Texts Society, Cambridge, 1991); Baderin, above n 1, 32–47.

Family Code, compared with the old Code, ensures considerable enhancement of women's rights within the context of Islamic law and principles in Morocco.[80] The preamble of the new Family Code stated that the Moroccan monarch had, during its drafting, 'encouraged the use of *ijtihad* (juridical reasoning) to deduce laws and precepts, while taking into consideration the spirit of our modern era and the imperatives of development, in accordance with the Kingdom's commitment to internationally recognized human rights'.[81] The preamble further observed that the provisions of the new Family Code were

> drafted in a modern legal jurisprudential style, in conformity with Islam's tolerant rules and exemplary purposes while providing balanced, fair and pragmatic solutions resulting from enlightened open *ijtihad* (juridical reasoning). This code further stipulates that human and citizenship rights are accorded to all Moroccans, women and men equally, in respect of the holy divine religious references.[82]

While the new Moroccan Family Code may be considered in human rights circles as a modest step in relation to the protection of women's rights generally, it nevertheless demonstrates that with the right political will, governments of Muslim States can positively enhance human rights within their Islamic dispensations through a harmonistic perspective on Islam and human rights in conjunction with the politico-legal approach to human rights generally. In her comments on the new Family Code, Weingartner observed that 'the reformed code more closely aligns with modern views on women's rights and privileges in a democratizing society'.[83] The WRR also referred to the adoption of the new Moroccan Family Code as an example of the harmonistic perspective on Islam and human rights through which 'considerable improvement in women's rights has taken place under the banner of Sharia' in Morocco.[84]

Regarding the establishment of relevant political and legal institutions and mechanisms for ensuring the practical implementation of human rights under the politico-legal approach to human rights, I have argued elsewhere, for example, that the creation of National Human Rights Commissions and the

---

[80] See, for example, L A Weingartner, 'Family Law and Reform in Morocco: Modernist Islam and Women's Rights in the Code of Personal Status' (2005) 82 *University of Detroit Mercy Law Review* 687.
[81] Global Rights, *English Translation of the Moroccan Family Code (Moudawana)* (2004 ) HREA, at: http://www.hrea.org/moudawana.html at 29 November 2008, [Preambular 4].
[82] Ibid [Preambular 5].
[83] Weingartner, above n 80, 687.
[84] WRR, above n 6, 11.

establishment of human rights courts in Muslim States can be Islamically justified in line with the harmonistic perspective on Islam and human rights, and I have also emphasized the importance of regional cooperation amongst Muslim States in that regard.[85] The WRR has also noted the importance of cooperation among Muslim States in relation to the politico-legal approach to human rights in conjunction with the harmonistic perspective on Islam and human rights by stating, *inter alia*, that:

> Legal implementation is not only the result of internal pressure within Muslim countries and external pressure from multilateral institutions like the UN, but also of mutual discussions and comparison among Muslim countries themselves. It is particularly over such charged issues as gender relations, freedom of religion, and cruel punishments that mutual learning processes can often be more effective than external pressure that can be interpreted as paternalistic, uninformed, or even inimical to 'Islam'.[86]

It is clear from the above analyses and illustrations that the harmonistic perspective on Islam and human rights is a more pragmatic and constructive way to enhance the realization of human rights within the context of the socio-cultural and politico-legal approaches for promoting and protecting human rights generally, which can be adopted by advocates of human rights in Muslim States and further encouraged through both human rights and Islamic legal scholarship.

## 5 Conclusion

Apart from mere human rights standard-setting, the need for the promotion and protection of human rights is positively acknowledged under international human rights law and affirmed in many international human rights treaties. Without effective promotion and protection, human rights provisions in treaties and declarations would be mere empty rights on paper. However, effective promotion and protection requires important systematic approaches and methodologies, which need to be more seriously addressed in human rights debates and literature. This chapter has been a modest attempt in that regard. Obviously, the situation in Muslim States is more complex due to many factors, with Islam being one significant factor, as analysed in this chapter. The two essential approaches for promoting and protecting human rights, and the two divergent perspectives on the Islam and human rights discourse as analysed herein, have been offered as a pragmatic and constructive take on how best to promote the realization of human rights in Muslim States. The

---

[85] Baderin, above n 67, 338–46.
[86] WRR, above n 6, 172.

position advanced in the end is informed by the author's view that human rights are best promoted through positive engagement, moral persuasion, positive political will and due process of law.

However, in advancing the harmonistic perspective on Islam and human rights in conjunction with the socio-cultural and politico-legal approaches to human rights herein, one must acknowledge the general criticism often expressed that such an approach could be slow and indulgent, especially in the face of human rights violations that need urgent attention, such as the issue of women's rights and minority rights in most Muslim States. The WRR has observed in that regard that:

> Islamic reforms in the direction of international human rights standards often appear to Western eyes either as going too slowly or even as a step backward. However, one should not exclude the possibility that it is precisely these kinds of reforms that have a better chance of taking root than large or Western-imposed steps.[87]

The WRR further noted 'the fact that permanent improvements cannot be imposed and sometimes take a long time'.[88]

To re-emphasize the relevance of the harmonistic perspective on Islam and human rights advanced in this chapter, it is instructive to conclude with another observation by the WRR as follows:

> The argument that Islam is principally incompatible with these ideas [democracy and human rights] is simply untrue. This does not necessarily mean, however, that such a policy will achieve great success in the short term. Not only are power relations stubborn, but views do not change overnight. All kinds of developments may be of influence, such as higher education, women participating in the workforce, migration, and media consumption. For this reason, the present limited influence of positive views of democracy and human rights does not mean that their potential influence will be as limited. Changes in individual behaviour as well as changes in the political make-up can increase the need for interpretations of Islam which support democracy and human rights.[89]

---

[87] Ibid 151.
[88] Ibid 171.
[89] Ibid 56.

# 18. Religion, belief and international human rights in the twenty-first century
*Peter Cumper*

## 1 Introduction

From time immemorial human beings have sought to comprehend and celebrate the metaphysical.[1] It is thus perhaps unsurprising that, of all the human rights accorded contemporary legal recognition, freedom of religion (and equivalent belief) has been described as the one with the longest lineage.[2] That said, with organised religion seemingly in decline in the West,[3] and a relative paucity of literature in the field of religious human rights,[4] one might be tempted to assume that religious belief is of little contemporary relevance. However, any such suggestion would be false. Matters pertaining to religion or belief have, in recent years, clearly had an impact on international affairs, leading to claims that there has even been a 'desecularisation of the world'.[5]

The influence of religion in the global arena is evidenced in at least three respects. First, religious belief has increasingly played a significant role in international politics,[6] a by-product of what some refer to as the rise of 'fundamentalism'.[7] Secondly, mass immigration and demographic changes have put

---

[1] See, for example, Karen Armstrong, *A History of God* (Heinemann, London, 1993).
[2] See Paul Sieghart, *The International Law of Human Rights* (Clarendon Press, Oxford, 1983) 324.
[3] See Steve Bruce, *God is Dead: Secularism in the West* (Blackwell, Oxford, 2002).
[4] Prior to the last two decades, very little was written on religious human rights. Whilst this is still a relatively undeveloped area, key texts now include: J D van der Vyver and J Witte Jr (eds) *Religious Human Rights in Global Perspective* (Martinus Nijhoff, The Hague, 1996); Malcolm Evans, *Religious Liberty and International Law in Europe* (Cambridge University Press, Cambridge, 1997); and Rex Ahdar and Ian Leigh, *Religious Freedom in the Liberal State* (Oxford University Press, Oxford, 2005).
[5] Peter L Berger (ed), *The Desecularization of the World: Resurgent Religion and World Politics* (William B Eerdmans Publishing Co, Grand Rapids, 1999).
[6] See David Westurland (ed), *Questioning the Secular State: the Worldwide Resurgence of Religion in Politics* (Hurst, London, 1996).
[7] See Karen Armstrong, *The Battle for God: Fundamentalism in Judaism, Christianity and Islam* (Harper Collins, London, 2001).

liberal democracies increasingly under pressure to accommodate religious practices that go far beyond the Judaeo-Christian tradition.[8] And thirdly, the terrorist attacks on the US on 9/11,[9] and related concerns about 'Islamist terrorism',[10] have focused attention on the role of religion generally and Islam in particular in international affairs.

If the dominant ideological battle of the twentieth century was between capitalism and communism, there is a very real possibility that the twenty-first century will be characterised by an equivalent struggle between obdurate faiths and secular values. Long-standing tensions, once assumed to have been consigned to the dustbin of history, have resurfaced, most notably in regard to the strained relationship between Islam and the West.[11] As a consequence, even though few deny that the manifestation of one's religious beliefs is anything other than a fundamental human right, there is little consensus as to how freedom of religion or belief should be protected in practice, especially in relation to the task of reconciling (seemingly inconsistent) Islamic and secular liberal values.[12] Set against such a background, this chapter seeks to analyse the way in which religion (and equivalent belief) is guaranteed under international human rights law.

The chapter is divided into four parts. First, I critically explore the legal sources of religious human rights. Secondly, I identify a number of principles that govern freedom of religion and belief under international human rights law. Thirdly, I focus on the issue of religious dress, in an attempt to illustrate the challenge of formulating principles of international human rights law that are capable of accommodating both religious and secular values in the twenty-first century. Fourthly, I conclude by commenting briefly on the prospects for reform in relation to the protection of freedom of religion and belief.

---

[8] See, for example, T Leonon and J Goldschmidt (eds), *Religious Pluralism and Human Rights in Europe: Where to Draw the Line?* (Intersentia, Antwerp and Oxford, 2007).

[9] Asma Jahangir, the current Special Rapporteur on freedom of religion or belief, has noted that 'the events of 11 September 2001 continue to have a dramatic impact on the situation of human rights, including freedom of religion or belief': Asma Jahangir, *Report of the Special Rapporteur on freedom of religion or belief*, UN Doc E/CN.4/2005/61 (20 December 2004) [77].

[10] See D Hiro, *War Without End: The Rise of Islamist Terrorism and Global Response* (Routledge, New York, 2002).

[11] It has, for example, been argued that Islam evokes a degree of fear in the West not witnessed since the Crusades in the Middle Ages: see generally Emran Qureshi and Michael Anthony Sells, *The New Crusades: Constructing the Muslim Enemy* (Columbia University Press, Columbia, 2003).

[12] See A An-Na'im, *Islam and the Secular State: Negotiating the Future of Shari`a* (Harvard University Press, Cambridge, 2007), and Ann Elizabeth Mayer, *Islam and Human Rights: Tradition and Politics* (Westview Press, Boulder, 1998).

## 2 The legal sources of freedom of religion and belief

Few issues throughout history have generated more controversy than disputes over religion or belief. As noted by one commentator, '*homo sapiens* appears to be unique in displaying a consistent pattern of persecuting its members for their heterodox opinions or beliefs especially when these are systematically manifested in the form of a religion or philosophy'.[13] Today freedom of thought, conscience and religion is a well-established principle of international human rights law, but religious freedom continues to be denied to people in many parts of the world.[14] The sources of religious human rights, which are clearly taken more seriously by some governments than by others, are now considered.

### A *The* Universal Declaration of Human Rights

The *Universal Declaration of Human Rights*[15] has long been seen as a significant landmark in the protection of international human rights.[16] Drafted largely in response to the atrocities of the Nazis in the Second World War, it was perhaps unsurprising that it should guarantee (under Article 18 UDHR) the principle of religious freedom.[17] There are three elements to Article 18 UDHR. First, it recognises that '[e]veryone has the right to freedom of thought, conscience and religion.' Secondly, it confirms that this right includes an individual's 'freedom to change his religion or belief'. And thirdly, it guarantees that everyone is entitled, 'either alone or in community with others and in public or private, to manifest his [or her] religion or belief in teaching, practice, worship and observance'.[18]

The UDHR claims to be a 'common standard of achievement for all people and all nations' and calls on 'every individual and every organ of society ... to promote respect for these rights and freedoms'.[19] The question as to whether powerful Western nations exerted a disproportionate influence during

---

[13] Sieghart, above n 2, 324.

[14] Jahangir, above n 9, [73].

[15] *Universal Declaration of Human Rights*, GA Res 217A (III), UN Doc A/810 (10 December 1948) ('UDHR').

[16] See José A Lindgren Alves, 'The Declaration of Human Rights in Postmodernity' (2002) 22 *Human Rights Quarterly* 478; A Eide, G Alfredsson, G Melander, L Adam Rehof and A Rosas (eds) *The Universal Declaration of Human Rights: A Commentary* (Scandinavian University Press and Oxford University Press, Oxford, 2002).

[17] On the Second World War as a catalyst for the UDHR, see Johannes Morsink, *The Universal Declaration of Human Rights: Origins, Drafting, and Intent* (University of Pennsylvania Press, Philadelphia, 2000) 36–91.

[18] On the process of according rights to religious communities see ibid 258–68.

[19] Preamble to the UDHR.

its drafting continues to provoke debate,[20] but what is beyond dispute is that the UDHR has been very influential in the formulation of the principles of national and international law.[21] For example, Article 18 UDHR has often provided the template used as the basis for drafting provisions that guarantee freedom of religion in a wide range of international human rights documents.[22] In particular, the phrase used in Article 18 UDHR, '[e]veryone has the right to freedom of thought, conscience and religion', was later replicated in one of the world's most influential human rights treaties, the *International Covenant on Civil and Political Rights*.[23]

*B  The* International Covenant on Civil and Political Rights
As its title indicates, the ICCPR protects a range of civil and political rights, including Article 18(1) ICCPR, which guarantees 'freedom of thought, conscience and religion'. Article 18(1) ICCPR also provides for the right 'to have or to adopt a religion or belief' of one's choice, as well as the freedom (individually and collectively) to manifest one's 'religion or belief in worship, observance, practice and teaching'. Article 18(2) ICCPR forbids coercion in respect of the 'freedom to have or to adopt a religion or belief' of one's choice, while Article 18(3) ICCPR recognises that the right to manifest one's religion or beliefs may be limited on grounds that are 'necessary to protect public safety, order, health, or morals or the fundamental rights and freedoms of others'. Finally, Article 18(4) ICCPR stipulates that the state must respect the liberty of parents or legal guardians 'to ensure the religious and moral education of their children in conformity with their own convictions'.

---

[20] See Susan Waltz, 'Reclaiming and Rebuilding the History of the Universal Declaration of Human Rights' (2002) 23 *Third World Quarterly* 437, who challenges the traditional view that the final text of the UDHR was due primarily to the influence of a handful of powerful Western nations.

[21] For example, see *South West Africa Cases* [1966] ICJ Reports 6, 288, 293 (Tanaka J).

[22] For example, see *Convention for the Protection of Human Rights and Fundamental Freedoms*, opened for signature 4 November 1950, 213 UNTS 222 (entered into force 3 September 1953) ('ECHR') Article 9; *American Convention on Human Rights*, opened for signature 22 November 1969, 1144 UNTS 123 (entered into force 18 July 1978) ('ACHR') Article 12; *African Charter on Human and Peoples' Rights*, opened for signature 27 June 1981, 1520 UNTS 217 (21 October 1986) ('ACHPR') Article 8.

[23] *International Covenant on Civil and Political Rights*, opened for signature 16 December 1966, 999 UNTS 14668 (entered into force 23 March 1976) ('ICCPR'). This same formulation is also found in the *Declaration on the Elimination of Intolerance and Discrimination Based on Religion or Belief*, GA Res 36/55, UN GAOR, 36th sess, 73rd plen mtg, UN Doc A/Res/36/55 (25 November 1981) Article 1.

The ICCPR requires states parties to submit periodic reports to the Human Rights Committee ('HRC')[24] and, in relation to states parties that have also ratified the *Optional Protocol*, grants individuals the right to complain directly to the HRC of a breach of the ICCPR by those states.[25] As the ICCPR is 'the only global human rights treaty dealing with religion that contains measures of implementation',[26] the HRC clearly has an important role to play in relation to international standard setting in the field of religion and belief.[27] The HRC has, for example, published *General Comment 22*, which offers guidance on freedom of thought, conscience and religion,[28] while it has also ruled in specific cases on issues ranging from faith based objections to military service[29] and moral education,[30] to curbs on religious dress[31] and the use of narcotics in worship.[32]

There is much to be commended in the work of the HRC, but in the field of religion and belief (as in other areas) it has a number of shortcomings. To begin with, the HRC, which consists of 18 experts of 'high moral character and recognized competence in the field of human rights',[33] lacks the status and powers of an international court or tribunal.[34] In addition, states which have ratified the ICCPR must normally report to the HRC every five years,[35] and, because governments are responsible for compiling their own reports, this increases the risk of breaches of human rights remaining

---

[24] See Article 40 ICCPR.
[25] See Article 41 ICCPR and *Optional Protocol to the International Covenant on Civil and Political Rights*, opened for signature 16 December 1966, 999 UNTS 302 (entered into force 23 March 1976).
[26] Natan Lerner, *Religion, Secular Beliefs and Human Rights* (Martinus Nijhoff, Leiden and Boston, 2006) 26.
[27] On this generally see M Nowak, *UN Covenant on Civil and Political Rights: CCPR Commentary* (Engel, Kehl, 2005).
[28] See Human Rights Committee, *General Comment 22 on Article 18 ICCPR*, UN Doc CCPR/C/21/Rev.1/Add.4 (20 July 1993).
[29] See *LTK v Finland*, UN Doc CCPR/C/OP/2 (18 October 1984) and *Yeo-Bum Yoon and Myung-Jin Choi v Korea*, UN Doc CCPR/C/88/D/1321–1322/2004 (23 January 2007).
[30] See *Hartikainen v Finland*, UN Doc CCPR/C/12/D/40/1978 (9 April 1981), and *Leirvåg v Norway*, UN Doc CCPR/C/82/D/1155/2003 (3 November 2004).
[31] See *Singh Bhinder v Canada*, UN Doc CCPR/C/37/D/208/1986 (9 November 1989); *Hudoyberganova v Uzbekistan*, UN Doc CCPR/C/82/D/931/2000 (8 December 2004).
[32] See *MAB WAT and J-AYT v Canada*, UN Doc CCPR/C/50/D/570/1993 (8 April 1994).
[33] See Articles 28–34 ICCPR.
[34] See Chapter 1, pp. 20–21.
[35] See Article 40 ICCPR.

undetected.[36] What is more, although individuals in states that have ratified the *First Optional Protocol* retain the right to present complaints directly to the HRC, a significant number of states, especially those that have poor records in the field of protecting religion or belief, have yet to grant their citizens this right.[37] And finally, because the principle of religious freedom (Article 18 ICCPR) is enshrined in only one of 27 substantive ICCPR Articles that the HRC must consider when examining state reports, there is a risk that some HRC members may view matters pertaining to Article 18 ICCPR as being relatively low in their overall list of priorities.[38]

Notwithstanding the fact that such considerations inevitably detract from the work of the HRC, it is nonetheless important to recognise the significance of the Human Rights Committee's role in setting standards under Article 18 of the ICCPR. For example, not merely has the HRC often been less deferential to states than the European Court of Human Rights in the field of religion and belief,[39] but, in spite of some textual uncertainty,[40] it has also recognised that Article 18 ICCPR guarantees the right of religious conversion.[41] There is thus little doubt that the HRC is at the vanguard of attempts to accord protection to freedom of religion and belief in the international arena. Indeed, its role in this area is particularly important given the limitations of the only human rights document that deals specifically with matters relating to religion and belief, the *Declaration on the Elimination of All Forms of Intolerance and of Discrimination Based on Religion or Belief* ('UN Declaration (1981)').

C  UN Declaration on the Elimination of All Forms of Intolerance and of Discrimination Based on Religion or Belief

The UN Declaration (1981) was adopted by General Assembly Resolution 36/55, on 25 November 1981. It guarantees freedom of thought, conscience

---

[36] On this generally, see Ineke Boerefijn, *The Reporting Procedure under the Covenant on Civil and Political Rights: Practice and Procedures of the Human Rights Committee* (Hart Intersentia, Antwerp, 1999).

[37] On this generally see Sarah Joseph, Jenny Schultz and Melissa Castan (eds), *The International Covenant on Civil and Political Rights: Cases, Materials and Commentary* (2nd edn, Oxford University Press, Oxford, 2004) 855–8 and 867–9.

[38] Paul Taylor, *Freedom of Religion* (Cambridge University Press, Cambridge, 2005) 13.

[39] Ibid 350.

[40] The text of Article 18 ICCPR fails to guarantee the right to change one's religion or belief in express terms. It merely refers to an individual's 'freedom to have or to adopt a religion or belief of his choice', whereas Article 18 UDHR recognises, in express terms, an individual's right 'to change his religion or belief'.

[41] The HRC has typically done this in its state reports. For example, see Human Rights Committee, *Concluding Observations: Islamic Republic of Iran*, UN Doc CCPR/C/79/Add.25 (2 June 2000) [36].

and religion,[42] outlaws coercion,[43] and specifies that curbs can only be imposed on the manifestation of religion or belief in limited circumstances.[44] In addition, the UN Declaration (1981) prohibits intolerance and discrimination on the grounds of religion or belief;[45] puts states under an obligation to 'take effective measures to prevent and eliminate discrimination on the grounds of religion or belief';[46] recognises the rights of parents to 'organize the life within the family in accordance with their religion or belief';[47] asserts a child's right to be 'protected from any form of discrimination on the ground of religion or belief';[48] places governments under a duty to ensure that the rights in the UN Declaration (1981) are 'accorded in national legislation';[49] and guarantees a range of fairly uncontroversial principles, which include the rights to conduct religious worship,[50] run 'charitable or humanitarian institutions',[51] 'teach a religion or belief',[52] 'solicit and receive voluntary financial ... contributions',[53] train and select religious leaders,[54] and celebrate religious holidays or rest days.[55]

In a sense the mere existence of the UN Declaration (1981) represents a triumph for international diplomacy. After all, it should perhaps not be forgotten that while it was being drafted fears were expressed that the task of producing a document that was capable of superseding Cold War rivalries, as well as accommodating differences between the Islamic and non-Islamic worlds, might be impossible.[56] Thus, on the one hand, the UN Declaration (1981) is a worthy and laudable achievement, which is undoubtedly 'a milestone in the progressive development of human rights norms'.[57] Yet, on the other hand, the value of the Declaration is tempered by the fact that it can be criticised on several grounds.

---

[42] Article 1(1) UN Declaration (1981).
[43] Article 1(2) UN Declaration (1981).
[44] Article 1(3) UN Declaration (1981).
[45] Articles 2(1) and 3 UN Declaration (1981).
[46] Article 4(1) UN Declaration (1981).
[47] Article 5(1) UN Declaration (1981).
[48] Article 5(3) UN Declaration (1981).
[49] Article 7 UN Declaration (1981).
[50] Article 6(a) UN Declaration (1981).
[51] Article 6(b) UN Declaration (1981).
[52] Article 6(e) UN Declaration (1981).
[53] Article 6(f) UN Declaration (1981).
[54] Article 6(g) UN Declaration (1981).
[55] Article 6(h) UN Declaration (1981).
[56] See Evans, above n 4, 227–61.
[57] Donna Sullivan, 'Advancing the Freedom of Religion or Belief through the UN Declaration on the Elimination of Religious Intolerance and Discrimination' (1988) 82 *American Journal of International Law* 488.

For a start, it is phrased in general and imprecise terms, a legacy of its drafters having to take account of a range of (often contradictory) ideological and religious perspectives. Moreover, the UN Declaration (1981), unlike comparable international human rights instruments that outlaw discrimination on the grounds of race[58] and sex,[59] lacks a specialist committee to monitor state compliance with its provisions. In addition, the Declaration's legal status is questionable on account of the fact that it was adopted merely as a General Assembly Resolution, which has only the status of a recommendation and so is not automatically legally binding.[60] And lastly, the Declaration arguably fails to accord sufficient weight to the principle of individual personal autonomy,[61] because it fails to guarantee (in express terms) the right to change one's religion or belief, as a result of opposition from Muslim states in the course of its drafting.[62]

At best the UN Declaration (1981) should be celebrated as a noble affirmation of the principle of religious tolerance, but at worst it is a shabby compromise which contributes little, apart from vague platitudes, to the elimination of religious intolerance and discrimination. Perhaps the true position lies somewhere in between. The fact that such an ill-defined document as the Declaration has been described as 'the most important international instrument regarding religious rights'[63] arguably demonstrates the relative lack of attention paid to the protection of religion and belief under international human rights law. Yet, whilst the UN Declaration (1981) is clearly modest in tone, one should not ignore its influence on the international community, not least in that it is used by those holding the office of the Special Rapporteur on freedom of religion or belief to gauge the extent to which states are complying with their international obligations in the field of religion and belief.

---

[58]   See *International Convention on the Elimination of All Forms of Racial Discrimination*, opened for signature 21 December 1965, 660 UNTS 195 (entered into force 4 January 1969), Article 8 of which establishes the Committee on the Elimination of Racial Discrimination.

[59]   See *Convention on the Elimination of All Forms of Discrimination against Women*, GA Res 34/180, UN GAOR, 34th sess, 107th plen mtg, UN Doc A/Res/34/180 (18 December 1979), Article 7 of which establishes the Committee on the Elimination of Discrimination Against Women.

[60]   See Evans, above n 4, 257.

[61]   On this generally see Joseph Raz, *The Morality of Freedom* (Clarendon Press, Oxford, 1986) 398.

[62]   See Sullivan, above n 57, 495–6.

[63]   Nathan Lerner, 'Religious Human Rights under the United Nations', in J D van der Vyver and J Witte Jr (eds) *Religious Human Rights in Global Perspective: Legal Perspectives* (Martinus Nijhoff, The Hague, 1996) 114.

### D  The Special Rapporteur on freedom of religion or belief[64]

The Special Rapporteur on freedom of religion or belief is an independent expert given the task (by the HRC) of examining whether government actions are compatible with the UN Declaration (1981).[65] The Special Rapporteur can request information from governments and may also (subject to invitation) undertake fact-finding visits to states. As well as identifying problems in relation to matters concerning freedom of religion and belief, the Special Rapporteur can recommend ways of ensuring that states are acting in conformity with the UN Declaration (1981).[66] In performing these functions, the Special Rapporteur is required to submit annual reports to various UN bodies (for example, the HRC and the General Assembly) on his/her work.[67]

Whilst successive Special Rapporteurs on religion and belief have played an important role in standard setting in this area, their impact overall is limited by the fact that they are under-resourced, and their only real sanction against recalcitrant states is that of negative publicity.[68] Thus, rather than being 'an agent of enforcement', the primary role of the Special Rapporteur is to 'investigate, comment and advise' on the way in which states comply with the UN Declaration (1981).[69]

A characteristic of those holding the office of Special Rapporteur has been the different way in which they have sometimes approached areas of great controversy. A case in point is that of blasphemy, where Asma Jahangir, the current Special Rapporteur, has seemingly been less willing to endorse curbs on free speech than her predecessor, Abdelfattah Amor.[70] For example, Ms Jahangir has emphasised that 'freedom of expression is as valuable as the right

---

[64] The title of the Special Rapporteur was originally 'Special Rapporteur on religious intolerance', but in 2000 the Commission on Human Rights changed it to 'Special Rapporteur on freedom of religion or belief', a decision that has been subsequently welcomed by the UN General Assembly: *Elimination of All Forms of Religious Intolerance*, GA Res 55/97, UN GAOR, 55th sess, 81st plen mtg, UN Doc A/Res/55/97 (4 December 2000) [11].

[65] UN Doc E/CN.4/1986/L.45/Rev.1 (10 March 1986).

[66] On the mandate of the Special Rapporteur on freedom of religion or belief, see Angelo Vidal d'Almeida Ribeiro, *Implementation of the Declaration on the Elimination of All Forms of Intolerance and of Discrimination Based on Religion or Belief*, UN Doc E/CN.4/1987/35 (24 December 1986) [17]–[19].

[67] For example, the first Report of the Special Rapporteur was submitted to the UN Commission at its 43rd session: UN Doc E/CN.4/1987/35 (4 December 1986).

[68] On this generally see C Evans, 'Strengthening the Role of the Special Rapporteur on Freedom of Religion or Belief' (2006) 1 *Religion and Human Rights* 75.

[69] Evans, above n 4, 247.

[70] To date there have been three Special Rapporteurs: Angelo d'Almeida Ribeiro (Portugal), 1986–1993; Abdelfattah Amor (Tunisia), 1993–2004; and since 2004, Asma Jahangir (Pakistan).

to freedom of religion or belief',[71] whereas the 'issue of [religious] defamation' was one of Mr Amor's 'major concerns',[72] and he was especially critical of the press for what he called its 'grotesque' portrayal of religion.[73] This difference of tone, on an issue as important as that of free speech, illustrates the challenge of formulating principles of international human rights law that are acceptable to those from a broad range of religious or faith traditions. That said, some differences between successive Special Rapporteurs are perhaps inevitable due to each office holder's background and individual priorities, as well as developments in the ever-changing global political arena.

Given the myriad of challenges facing the international community in the field of religion or belief, the impact of a single office holder such as the Special Rapporteur is inevitably destined to be relatively modest. Yet every Special Rapporteur continues to perform a useful function, particularly since their reports not only provide a useful snapshot of state practice in the field of religious freedom but also demonstrate the numerous ways in which religion and belief is manifested in the twenty-first century.[74]

*E   Regional documents: the European Convention on Human Rights*
Aside from the UN, the principles of thought, conscience and religion are recognised in a number of 'regional' human rights documents in the world today.[75] Of these the most influential is the European Convention on Human Rights, which was drafted in 1950 under the auspices of the Council of Europe.[76] Article 9 ECHR guarantees 'freedom of thought, conscience and religion'.[77] It also expressly recognises the right to change one's religion or belief, as well as the right to manifest it 'in worship, teaching, practice and

---

[71]   See Jahangir, above n 9, [72]. Ms Jahangir has also pointed out that '[c]onstruing all expressions defaming religion as human-rights violations would ... give rise to religious intolerance': Human Rights Council, UN Doc A/HRC/2/SR (25 October 2006) [60].

[72]   See Abdelfattah Amor, *Report of the Special Rapporteur on freedom of religion or belief*, UN Doc E/CN.4/2004/63 (16 January 2004) [137].

[73]   See Abdelfattah Amor, *Report of the Special Rapporteur on freedom of religion or belief*, UN Doc E/CN.4/2000/65 (15 February 2000) [108]. Mr Amor even called for 'a campaign to develop awareness among the media' of such matters: ibid.

[74]   On the relationship between those holding the office of Special Rapporteur on freedom of religion or belief and the other UN Special Rapporteurs see David Weissbrodt, 'The Three "Theme" Special Rapporteurs of the UN Commission on Human Rights' (1986) 80 *The American Journal of International Law* 685.

[75]   For example, see Article 12 ACHR and Article 8 ACHPR.

[76]   On the origins and history of the ECHR see J G M Merrills and A H Robertson, *Human Rights in Europe* (Manchester University Press, Manchester, 4th ed, 2001) 1–15.

[77]   Article 9(1) ECHR.

observance',[78] subject to a number of limitations that 'are prescribed by law and are necessary in a democratic society in the interests of public safety, for the protection of public order, health or morals, or for the protection of the rights and freedoms of others'.[79]

The ECHR is interpreted by the European Court of Human Rights, which has affirmed that Article 9 ECHR is not only 'one of the most vital elements that go to make up the identity of believers', but 'also a precious asset for atheists, sceptics, and the unconcerned'.[80] Moreover, Article 9 ECHR applies not just to long-established 'world religions' (such as Christianity,[81] Islam,[82] Buddhism[83] and Sikhism)[84] but also to new religious movements (such as the Church of Scientology),[85] as well as a range of philosophical beliefs such as pacifism,[86] veganism,[87] and opposition to abortion.[88]

In the past, relatively few complaints relating to religion or belief were brought under the ECHR, and it was not until 1993 that the European Court had to give judgment in a case involving Article 9 ECHR.[89] This has now changed, and with frequent allegations of religious discrimination, and minority faith groups in an ever more religiously diverse continent campaigning for the accommodation and recognition of their religious practices, the Court's workload seems set to increase in the field of religion and belief in twenty-first century Europe.

## 3   Religion and belief: common principles under human rights law

As noted above, the sources of religious freedom are diverse and varied. However, it is also the case that there are a number of common principles that govern religion and belief under international human rights law.

First, there is a general recognition that a distinction should be drawn between the 'internal' and the 'external' practice of a religion or belief. The

---

[78]   Article 9(1) ECHR.
[79]   Article 9(2) ECHR.
[80]   *Kokkinakis v Greece* (1994) 17 EHRR 397, [31].
[81]   *Stedman v UK* (1997) 23 EHRR CD 168.
[82]   *X v UK*, Application No 8160/78 (1981) 22 DR 27.
[83]   *X v UK*, Application No 5442/72 (1975) 1 DR 41.
[84]   *X v UK*, Application No 8231/78 (1982) 28 DR 5 and *X v UK*, Application No 7992/77 (1978) 14 DR 234.
[85]   *X and the Church of Scientology v Sweden*, Application No 7805/77 (1979) 16 DR 68.
[86]   *Arrowsmith v UK*, Application No 7050/75 (1980) 19 DR 5.
[87]   *H v UK* (1993)16 EHRR CD 44.
[88]   *Knudsen v Norway* (1986) 8 EHRR 45.
[89]   *Kokkinakis v Greece* (1994) 17 EHRR 397.

former, which has been described as an 'inner freedom'[90] and typically covers private religious activities such as inner faith, prayer, and personal devotions, is absolute and beyond the remit of the state.[91] In contrast the latter, the right to express or manifest one's religion or belief, is subject to a number of restrictions that are deemed necessary to protect the interests of other members of society.[92]

A second characteristic of international human rights law has been a general unwillingness to define the word 'religion'. After all, the challenge of settling upon a definition that is flexible enough to satisfy a broad cross-section of world faiths yet is also sufficiently precise to apply in specific cases is formidable.[93] Thus, in contrast to some national courts,[94] definitions of religion have generally been avoided by international bodies such as the HRC,[95] the Special Rapporteur on religion or belief,[96] and the ECHR's organs of implementation.[97]

Thirdly, it is a well-established principle that freedom of religion or belief is 'not limited in its application to traditional religions'.[98] With new religious movements having mushroomed over the last half-century, the HRC has stated that it 'views with concern any tendency to discriminate against any religions or beliefs for any reasons, including the fact that they are newly established'.[99] The current Special Rapporteur on freedom of religion or belief has also warned that 'the legalisation of a distinction between different categories of religion is liable to pave the way for . . . discrimination on the basis of religion or belief'.[100]

Fourthly, the mere presence of an official state church is not, *per se*, incompatible with a nation's human rights obligations. This principle, which has

---

[90] René Cassin, as cited in H Kanger, *Human Rights in the UN Declaration* (Almqvist and Wiksell International, Uppsala, 1984) 119.
[91] For example, see Article 18(1) ICCPR and Article 9(1) ECHR.
[92] For example, see Article 18(3) ICCPR and Article 9(2) ECHR.
[93] 'The determination of what is a "religious" belief or practice is more often than not a difficult and delicate task': *Thomas v Review Board*, 450 US 707 (1981) 714.
[94] See *Church of the New Faith v Commissioner for Pay-Roll Tax (Vic)* (1983) 154 CLR 120, 132 (Mason ACJ and Brennan J), 173 (Wilson and Deane JJ).
[95] Human Rights Committee, above n 28, [1]–[2].
[96] E Odio Benito, *Study on the Elimination of All Forms of Intolerance and Discrimination Based on Religion or Belief*, UN Doc E.89.XIV.3 (1989).
[97] For example, see *X v United Kingdom*, Application No 7291/75 (1977) 11 DR 55, where the European Commission refrained from classifying Wicca as a religion in the case of a prisoner who claimed to be one of its adherents.
[98] Jahangir, above n 9, [8].
[99] Human Rights Committee, above n 28, [2].
[100] Jahangir, above n 9, [61].

been accepted in both Europe[101] and by the HRC,[102] has also been confirmed by a previous UN Special Rapporteur on religion or belief.[103] That said, where a religion has been accorded a special or established status, governments are prohibited from interfering directly in the affairs of a state/established church,[104] while 'discrimination against adherents to other religions or non-believers' is forbidden.[105]

Fifthly, international human rights law offers protection to *believers* (rather than *beliefs per se*) from very serious vilification, and the Special Rapporteur has criticised states that have failed to make it unlawful to incite religious hatred.[106] Given that the ICCPR prohibits any 'advocacy of ... religious hatred that constitutes incitement to discrimination, hostility or violence',[107] and the UN Declaration (1981) calls on governments to 'adopt criminal law measures against organisations that incite others to practise religious intolerance',[108] states would appear to be under a duty to place restrictions on words or actions that constitute an incitement to religious hatred.

And finally, human rights documents often expressly recognise parental rights in relation to the place of religion and belief in the upbringing of children. For example, the ICCPR provides that states must 'ensure [that] the religious and moral education' of children is in conformity with the convictions of their parents or legal guardians,[109] while the ECHR stipulates that the state must respect the 'religious and philosophical convictions' of parents in relation to education and teaching.[110] However, the duty on states to respect

---

[101] *Darby v Sweden* A 187 (1991); 13 EHRR 774.
[102] Human Rights Committee, above n 28, 9.
[103] Abdelfattah Amor, *Report on Special Rapporteur's visit to Pakistan*, UN Doc E/CN.4/1996/95Add.1 (2 January 1996) [81].
[104] Abdelfattah Amor, *Report of the Special Rapporteur on freedom of religion or belief*, UN Doc E/CN.4/1997/91 (30 December 1996) [86]. See also *Hasan and Chaush v Bulgaria* (2002) 34(6) EHRR 1339 [78].
[105] Human Rights Committee, above n 28, [9].
[106] See Asma Jahangir, *Report of the Special Rapporteur on freedom of religion or belief: Summary of cases transmitted to Governments and replies received*, UN Doc E/CN.4/2005/61/Add.1 (15 March 2005) [288].
[107] Article 20(2) ICCPR.
[108] Natan Lerner, *Religion, Secular Beliefs and Human Rights* (Martinus Nijhoff, Leiden, 2006) 35. Although a duty to outlaw incitement to religious hatred is not expressly mentioned in the UN Declaration (1981), it can be implied from Article 2 (1), which provides that no discrimination should stem from 'any State institution, group of persons or person on grounds of religion or other belief'.
[109] Article 18(4) ICCPR.
[110] See the *Convention for the Protection of Human Rights and Fundamental Freedoms, Protocol 1*, opened for signature 20 March 1952, 213 UNTS 262 (entered into force 18 May 1954).

parental rights is not absolute. For example, the European Court has held that compulsory sex education programmes are lawful if 'conveyed in an objective, critical and pluralistic manner',[111] while the Human Rights Committee has also ruled that, irrespective of parental objections, classes on the history of religion and ethics are permissible if 'given in a neutral and objective way'.[112]

## 4 Religious dress, symbols and international human rights law

### A Islamic and secular values in conflict

As noted above, a number of common principles can be identified from the rules governing religion and belief in international human rights law. Yet there are also many areas where there is little agreement. Often this is a by-product of the fact that those responsible for formulating the relevant principles of international human rights law have very different perspectives on matters of faith. Accordingly, with an increasing number of Muslims now living in the West,[113] and secular norms having replaced traditional Christian values in many parts of Europe,[114] the potential for conflict between seemingly incompatible Islamic and secular liberal traditions is obvious.

This challenge of reconciling Islamic and secular western values has already been well documented. For some there is a real risk of a 'clash of civilisations',[115] whereas for others such claims are false and based on a number of erroneous assumptions.[116] It has been argued that the tenets of Islam are compatible with the principles of international human rights,[117] yet conflicts between secular and Islamic values continue to generate acrimonious and bitter disputes. A case in point is the extent to which the state may legitimately impose restrictions on forms of Islamic dress. Although this is far from being the only area where there is disagreement,[118] it is an important issue on which I will focus for four reasons.

---

[111] *Kjeldsen, Busk Madsen and Pederson v Denmark* (1975) 1 EHRR 711 [53].
[112] *Hartikainen v Finland*, UN Doc CCPR/C/12/D/40/1978 (9 April 1981) [10.4].
[113] See generally S T Hunter (ed) *Islam, Europe's Second Religion* (Praeger and CSIS, New York, 2002).
[114] For example, see L Halman and V Draulans, 'How secular is Europe?' (2006) 57 *The British Journal of Sociology* 263.
[115] See, for example, Samuel P Huntington, 'The Clash of Civilisations' (1992–1993) 77 *Foreign Affairs* 22.
[116] See Chiara Bottici and Benoit Challand, 'Rethinking Political Myth: The Clash of Civilisations as a Self-Fulfilling Prophecy' (2006) 9 *European Journal of Social Theory* 315.
[117] See M Baderin, *International Human Rights and Islamic Law* (Oxford University Press, Oxford, 2005; A An-Na'im, above n 12; and Mayer, above n 12). See also Chapter 17.
[118] For example, the challenge of reconciling Islamic and secular liberal values is

First, in recent years, the controversy generated by Islamic dress has been termed 'truly global',[119] giving rise to conflicts between Muslims and governments as far afield as South East Asia,[120] the former USSR,[121] and Western Europe.[122] Secondly, the Islamic headscarf is an emotive topic that is even capable of provoking violence, as witnessed by the kidnapping of two French journalists by an Iraqi-based Islamist group in 2004 as a protest against the French law outlawing conspicuous religious symbols.[123] Thirdly, disputes over religious dress highlight major differences between the Islamic and secular approaches to the place of faith in public life,[124] and with Islamic dress often regarded as being integral to the identity of Muslim women, it is perhaps unsurprising that many Muslims are wary of efforts by 'secular' states to regulate what they can wear in public.[125] Fourthly, it is likely that religious symbols and garments will continue to generate controversy, not least because an increasing number of young Muslims in Europe are adopting traditional Islamic styles of dress in defiance of contemporary secular Western norms.[126]

---

demonstrated in relation to contentious areas such as jihad, and the treatment of apostates. On these issues, respectively, see Abdullahi Ahmed An-Na'im, 'Why should Muslims abandon Jihad? Human rights and the future of international law' (2006) 27 *Third World Quarterly* 785 and Hassan Saeed, *Freedom of Religion, Apostasy and Islam* (Ashgate, Aldershot, 2004).

[119] Anthony Giddens, 'Beneath the Hijab: A Woman' [2004] 2 *New Perspectives Quarterly* 9, 10.

[120] See Li-ann Thio and Jaclyn Ling-Chien Neo, 'Religious Dress in Schools: The Serban Controversy in Malaysia' (2006) 55 *International & Comparative Law Quarterly* 671.

[121] See *Hudoyberganova v Uzbekistan*, UN Doc CCPR/C/82/D/931/2000 (18 January 2005).

[122] See L Auslander, 'Bavarian Crucifixes and French Headscarves: Religious Signs and the Postmodern European State' (2000) 12 *Cultural Dynamics* 283.

[123] See D Malliard, 'The Muslims in France and the French Model of Integration' (2005) 16 *Mediterranean Quarterly* 62, 77.

[124] See Olivier Roy, *Secularism confronts Islam* (Columbia University Press, Colombia, 2007) and Elisabeth Özdalga, *The Veiling Issue, Official Secularism and Popular Islam in Modern Turkey* (Routledge, 1998).

[125] See Michael Humphreys and Andrew D. Brown, 'Dress and Identity: A Turkish Case Study' (2002) 39(7) *Journal of Management Studies*, 927–52, and Debra Reece, 'Covering and Communication: The Symbolism of Dress Among Muslim Women' (1996) 7(1) *Howard Journal of Communications*, 35–52. Moreover, in the UK, a recent opinion poll found that 76 per cent of Muslims considered that schoolchildren should be free to wear religious dress irrespective of a school's particular uniform policy, in contrast to 42 per cent of the general population: see 'Muslims in Britain: a story of mutual fear and suspicion', *The Times* (London) 5 July 2006, 6.

[126] See W Shadid and P S van Koningsveld. 'Muslim Dress in Europe: Debates on the Headscarf' (2005) 16 *Journal of Islamic Studies* 35.

This issue of religious dress will now be explored in order to demonstrate the challenge of formulating principles in the field of religious human rights law that are capable of embracing both the secular liberal and Islamic traditions.

### B  Curbs on religious dress, secularism and Europe

It is well established that there is often a clear link between the manifestation of religious beliefs and particular forms of religious dress. From Jewish yarmulkes and Sikh turbans to Muslim veils and Christian crosses, the distinctive identity of each group is maintained by what is worn or displayed. This close association between faith and dress can have negative, as well as positive, connotations. Situations where people are *compelled* to display religious symbols in public (for example, Jews forced to wear the star of David in Nazi Germany) can be contrasted with those where individuals are *forbidden* from wearing the religious dress of their choice (for example, bans on Islamic headscarves).[127] Instances of the former, identified by successive Special Rapporteurs on freedom of religion or belief as constituting a serious infringement of religious freedom,[128] are rare. Thus, for the purposes of this chapter, I focus on the latter – the extent to which international human rights law protects those who wish to wear garments or emblems signifying their association with a particular religious group.[129]

It was the introduction of a law in France four years ago, banning the display of 'conspicuous' religious symbols from the classrooms of all French state schools, which particularly focused the attention of the Western world on the topic of religious dress.[130] The French law on 'conspicuous' religious symbols has attracted criticism from many sources, including academics,[131] the European Parliament[132] and the UN Committee on the Rights of the

---

[127] For example, Asma Jahangir, *Report of the Special Rapporteur on freedom of religion or belief*, UN Doc E/CN.4/2006/5/Add.4 (8 March 2006) [36].

[128] See Abdelfattah Amor, *Report of the Special Rapporteur on freedom of religion or belief*, UN Doc E/CN.4/1998/6 (22 December 1997) [60]; Asma Jahangir, *Report of the Special Rapporteur on freedom of religion or* belief, UN Doc E/CN.4/2006/5 (9 January 2006) [36]–[68].

[129] The Special Rapporteur refers to this as 'positive freedom of religion or belief', Jahangir, above n 128, [36].

[130] Law No. 2004-228, of 15 March 2004.

[131] For example, see Dawn Lyon and Deborah Spini, 'Unveiling the Headscarf Debate' (2004) 12 *Feminist Legal Studies* 333 and Liz Kekete 'Anti-Muslim Racism and the European Security State' (2004) 46 *Race and Class* 3.

[132] For example, see European Parliament Written Declaration, 20 February, 2004, DC\524428EN.doc.

Child,[133] but it continues to remain in force. France has traditionally been less willing to accommodate religious garments and symbols in public than many of its European neighbours,[134] and the law passed in 2004 was an important reaffirmation of its commitment to secular values.[135] The rationale for this was *laïcité*, the principle that religion is fundamentally incompatible with the institutions of the secular French Republic and that the manifestation of one's beliefs should be confined to the private rather than the public sphere.[136]

In considering the *degree* of respect that should be accorded to *laïcité* and comparable secular principles, the Strasbourg human rights institutions have granted states a wide margin of appreciation.[137] It was thus perhaps no great surprise when the European Court (in 2005) rejected a challenge to a Turkish law prohibiting university students from wearing Islamic headscarves in lectures or during exams, on the basis that it was reasonable to preserve the secular nature of the university.[138]

### C  Criteria for imposing limits on religious dress or symbols

The approach of the European Court to religious dress has been widely criticised,[139] but it should not be forgotten that the right to manifest one's religion or belief in this way is not absolute. There are clearly occasions where the interests of society take precedence over those of the individual in relation to the accommodation of religious beliefs in a multi-faith liberal democracy.[140]

---

[133] See Committee on the Rights of the Child, *Concluding Observations on the Second Periodic Report of France*, UN Doc CRC/C/15/Add.240 (4 June 2004) [25]–[26].

[134] For example, see S Poulter, 'Muslim Headscarves in School: Contrasting Legal Approaches in England and France' (1997) 17 *Oxford Journal of Legal Studies* 43.

[135] See D Malliard, 'The Muslims in France and the French Model of Integration' (2005) 16 *Mediterranean Quarterly* 62.

[136] For example, see J Freeman, 'Secularism as a Barrier to Integration – the French Dilemma' (2004) 42 *International Migration* 5.

[137] *Karaduman v Turkey*, Application No 16278/90 and *Bulut v Turkey*, Application No 18783/91, (1993) 74 DR 93.

[138] *Sahin v Turkey* (2007) 44 EHRR 5. More recently in *Dogru v France*, Application No. 27058/05, 4 December 2008, the European Court rejected a complaint from two Muslim schoolgirls who had been expelled from school as a result of their refusal to remove Islamic headscarves during physical education lessons.

[139] For example, see Tom Lewis, 'What Not to Wear: Religious Rights, the European Court, and the Margin of Appreciation' (2007) 56 *International and Comparative Law Quarterly* 395–414; Jill Marshall, 'Freedom of Religious Expression and Gender Equality: *Sahin v Turkey* (2006) 69(3) *Modern Law Review* 452–461; and Anastasia Vakulenco, 'Islamic Headscarves and the European Convention on Human Rights: An Intersectional Perspective' (2007) 16(2) *Social & Legal Studies*, 183–99.

[140] However, 'the burden of justifying a limitation upon the freedom to manifest

This has been recognised by the current Special Rapporteur on religion or belief, who has acknowledged that any limitation on religious dress can only be justified 'under precise conditions'.[141] According to the Special Rapporteur any such restriction must

> be based on the grounds of public safety, order, health, or morals, or the fundamental rights and freedoms of others, it must respond to pressing public or social need, it must pursue a legitimate aim and it must be proportionate to that aim.[142]

The Special Rapporteur's guidelines are of considerable value, and are now examined in more detail.

*(i) Public health and safety* The protection of public health and safety is a well-accepted criterion under international human rights law for the imposition of limits on those wishing to manifest their faith in the form of religious dress or symbols. For example, national courts and tribunals have long recognised that Sikh males working in food factories must cover their beards in order to avoid contamination.[143] Such restrictions are compatible with the principles of international human rights law.[144] Similarly, on health grounds, the HRC[145] and the European Commission of Human Rights[146] rejected the complaints of a Sikh railway employee and a Sikh motorcyclist, both of whom challenged national laws requiring them to wear (respectively) a hard hat and a crash helmet rather than a turban.

Of course the imposition of dress restrictions in relation to matters of health and safety can, on occasion, be problematic. A case in point is that of the extent to which young Sikhs should be allowed to bring their ceremonial knives (*kirpans*) into state schools, with Courts in the United States permitting this practice,[147] in contrast to those in Canada.[148] What is clear is that, as a

---

one's religion or belief lies with the state': Asma Jahangir, *Report of the Special Rapporteur on freedom of religion or belief*, UN Doc E/CN.4/2006/5/Add.4. (8 March 2006) [104].

[141] Ibid.

[142] See Jahangir, above n 128, [53].

[143] See *Panesar v Nestle Co* [1980] IRLR 64 and *Singh v Rowntree Mackintosh* [1979] IRLR 199.

[144] For example, see Article 9(2) ECHR, Article 12(3) ACHR, and Article 18(3) ICCPR.

[145] See *K Singh Bhinder v Canada*, UN Doc CCPR/C/37/D/208/1986 (9 November 1989).

[146] See *X v UK*, Application No 7992/77 (1978) 14 DR 234.

[147] Sikh schoolboys were permitted to wear their *kirpans* in a state elementary school as long as the blades were dulled and the knife was 'sewn tightly to its sheath': *Cheema v Thompson* 67 F.3d 883 (9th Cir, 1995) 886.

[148] The Quebec Court of Appeal has outlawed the wearing of *kirpans* in its schools. See *Multani v Commission scolaire Marguerite-Bourgeoys* [2006] 1 SRC 256.

general rule, in weighing the importance of a particular religious practice against the need to protect public health, international tribunals usually accord priority to the latter. This is evident from ECHR case law, where the protection of public health took precedence over religious objections when a Dutch farmer objected to joining the state's animal health-care scheme,[149] and a Sikh prisoner claimed that his faith forbade him from sweeping the floor of his prison cell.[150]

*(ii) Public order*   A second ground on which international human rights law permits the imposition of limits on religious dress or symbols is the maintenance of public order.[151] In many parts of the world religious symbols are especially capable of provoking civil unrest or violence.[152] Thus, for example, it is inconceivable in contemporary Europe that a member of a white supremacist sect would be accorded an unfettered right to display, publicly, an offensive item (for example, a swastika) on the grounds of his/her belief.

The need to maintain public order is often seen most vividly in prisons. For example, it was the rationale for the European Commission of Human Rights refusing a Sikh prisoner's request to wear the clothes of his choice,[153] and was even the basis for a Buddhist prisoner being forbidden from growing a beard.[154] Similarly, the importance of keeping good order in educational institutions explains why curbs have been imposed in schools on the display of 'religious' symbols on the basis of their association with gang culture.[155] Indeed, the need to maintain school discipline may even justify a school's ban on a Muslim pupil from wearing a religious garment that does not conform to its uniform policy.[156]

*(iii) Public morals*   A third ground on which international human rights law permits the imposition of limits on religious dress or symbols is the need to

---

[149]   *X v Netherlands*, Application No 1068/61 (1962) 5 ECHR Yearbook 278.
[150]   *X v UK*, Application No 8231/78 (1982) 28 DR 5, 38.
[151]   For example, see Article 9(2) ECHR, Article 12(3) ACHR, and Article 18(3) ICCPR.
[152]   See *Humphries v Connor* (1864) 17 ICLR 1.
[153]   *X v UK*, Application No 8231/78 (1982) 28 DR 5, 38.
[154]   *X v Austria*, Application No 1753/63 (1965) 8 ECHR Yearbook 174. In view of the increasing recognition of prisoners' rights in recent decades, this ruling, given more than forty years ago, seems unlikely to be followed today.
[155]   See *Stephenson v Davenport Community School District*, 110 F.3d 1303 (8th Cir, 1997), where a cross tattoo, sported in contravention of a school dress code, was not protected speech under the *US Constitution*.
[156]   See *R (On the Application of Begum) v Headteacher and Governors of Denbigh High School* [2006] UKHL 15, where the House of Lords held that a school acted lawfully when it prohibited a Muslim girl from wearing a garment (jilbab) that fell outside its uniform policy.

protect public morals. Were, for example, a religious emblem to undermine public morality or offend considerations of taste and decency, curbs could be placed on it.[157] Such cases are of course rare. However, just as the state may impose restrictions on what its citizens wear on the grounds of public decency,[158] so too may similar curbs legitimately be placed on items of religious dress or related symbols.

*(iv) The fundamental rights and freedoms of others* A final (and much more common) reason for imposing restrictions on religious dress is the need to 'protect the fundamental rights and freedoms of others'.[159] This phrase, which (with the exclusion of the word 'fundamental') also appears in Article 9(2) ECHR, provides that societal interests may prevail over those of an individual or group wishing to manifest their religion or belief. As a consequence, a Muslim woman wishing to travel overseas and wearing a *niqab* that only leaves her eyes visible may be required to show her face to a (preferably female) official to proceed through passport control. Similarly, the need to accord respect to the rights of others almost certainly prohibits a Sikh male from being allowed to bring his *kirpan* with him into the cabin of an aeroplane.

Yet it is not always so easy to quantify what is meant by 'the fundamental rights and freedoms of others'. For example, in *Şahin v Turkey*, the European Court upheld curbs on a medical student wearing an Islamic headscarf at her university on the basis that it was necessary to take into account 'the impact which wearing such a symbol . . . may have on those who choose not to wear it'.[160] The need to protect 'others' in such circumstances may apply particularly to children or young people, who are often clearly susceptible to peer pressure when it comes to acting or dressing in a certain way. However, the implication of the Court's ruling in *Şahin*, that rational autonomous adult university students could be pressurised into wearing the headscarf because of the decision to do so by some of their contemporaries, is open to serious question, and appears to take the protection of 'others' criterion too far.[161]

---

[157] For example, a crucifix of a naked Christ displaying his genitalia would probably fall within this category.

[158] For example, in *Boroff v Van Wert City Board of Education* 220 F.3d 465 (6th Cir, 2000); 121 S Ct 1355 (2001), a school acted lawfully in preventing a student from wearing a Marilyn Manson T-shirt on the ground that the attire was 'vulgar, offensive and contrary to the mission of the school'.

[159] Article 18(3) ICCPR.

[160] *Şahin v Turkey* (2007) 44 EHRR 5, [115] ('*Şahin*').

[161] For example, see Lewis, above n 139.

D  *International human rights law and the challenge of Islamic dress*
The criteria listed above for imposing curbs on religious dress are seldom determinative, and the Special Rapporteur has held that situations where the State imposes restrictions on religious dress or symbols must 'be considered on a case-by-case basis [taking] into account the other human rights that may be at stake'.[162] In this context certain forms of Islamic dress raise a number of difficult issues.

First, there is little consensus amongst Muslims themselves as to what constitutes an appropriate form of dress in Islam.[163] The *Qur'an* stipulates that 'believing women' should 'guard their modesty'[164] but, because modesty is a 'relative term',[165] it is open to different interpretations. International human rights tribunals are hardly the best place for resolving such disputes, a point made by Judge Tulkens in her dissenting judgement in *Şahin* when she pointed out that '[i]t is not the court's role to make an appraisal of a religion or religious practice'.

A second problem is the association of Islamic dress with the subordination of women.[166] Whilst some insist that Muslim dress codes characterise the oppression of females,[167] others deny these claims,[168] pointing out that the original purpose of Islamic rules in this area was the protection of women from predatory males.[169] It is in this context that international human rights law, which clearly forbids discrimination or unfavourable treatment on the ground

---

[162]  See Jahangir, above n 9, [70].
[163]  For example, the views of Irshad Manji, *The Trouble with Islam Today: A Muslim's Call for Reform in Her Faith* (St Martin's Griffin, New York, 2005) can be contrasted with those of Yusuf Al-Qaradawi, *The Lawful and the Prohibited in Islam* (Al-Halal Wal Haram Fil Islam) (Islamic Book Service, 1982).
[164]  Surah XXIV, verse 31.
[165]  H Afshar, 'Gender Roles and the Moral Economy of Kin Among Pakistani Women in West Yorkshire' (1989) 15 *New Community* 211, 219.
[166]  Islamic headscarves and veils also touch on issues such as sexual equality and (where girls are concerned) the relationship between schools, parents and children. See generally Committee on the Rights of the Child, *Concluding Observations on the second periodic report of France*, UN Doc CRC/C/15/Add.240 (4 June 2004) [25], [26].
[167]  See J Entelis, 'International Human Rights: Islam's friend or foe' (1996–97) 20 *Fordham International Law Journal* 1251, 1292.
[168]  It is argued that traditional Islamic dress offers women greater (not less) freedom, in giving them the confidence to move around in public free from the gaze of men: L Abu-Odeh, 'Post-Colonial Feminism and the Veil: Considering the Differences' (1992) 26 *New England Law Review* 1527.
[169]  See R Hassan, 'Rights of Women within Islamic Communities' in J van der Vyver and J Witte Jr (eds) *Religious Rights in Global Perspective* (Martinus Nijhoff, The Hague, 1996) 361.

of one's sex, must offer guidance. Such matters are highly contentious,[170] and international courts and officer holders have increasingly found themselves being asked to consider the association of certain forms of Muslim dress with radical Islam. Thus, the Special Rapporteur on religion and belief has condemned the ill-treatment of women for being forced to 'wear what is described as Islamic dress',[171] while the European Court has expressly linked the Islamic headscarf with 'extremist political movements' and the absence of 'gender equality' in Turkey.[172] The Special Rapporteur has recently spoken of the need to 'depoliticise issues relating to religion or belief',[173] but few issues in contemporary Europe are more 'politicised' than that of Islamic dress.

Thirdly, the issue of Muslim dress tends to highlight a number of significant (and seemingly irreconcilable) differences between the Islamic and secular traditions. One such difference is the role of faith in public life. A fundamental tenet of secularism is that, in the exercise of one's religion or belief, there is an important difference between the public and the private realm.[174] As a consequence, religion in the West is typically confined to the 'private' rather than the 'public' sphere. This 'privatisation' of faith has led to claims that religious beliefs are often trivialised or regarded as akin to a 'hobby' by organs of the state.[175] Yet in Islam there is no clear distinction between the public and private aspects of a person's existence.[176] Thus international human rights bodies have the invidious task of formulating rules governing what is appropriate in the public sphere for both Muslims and non-Muslims.

A fourth problem raised by curbs on religious dress is the place of secularism in multi-faith liberal democracies. In the West secular values are generally

---

[170] For example it has been argued that the principle of sex equality should take priority over considerations of religion or belief: S Mullally, 'Beliefs that Discriminate: A Rights Based Solution?' in Conor Gearty and Adam Tomkins (eds) *Understanding Human Rights* (Mansell, London, 1996) 480.

[171] See Jahangir, above n 128, [38].

[172] *Şahin* (2007) 44 EHRR 5, [115].

[173] See Asma Jahangir, *Report of the Special Rapporteur on freedom of religion or belief*, UN Doc A/HRC/4/21 (26 December 2006) [49].

[174] On the place of religion in public life generally see Roger Trigg, *Religion in Public Life: Must Faith Be Privatised?* (Oxford University Press, Oxford, 2007); David Harte, 'Defining the Legal Boundaries of Orthodoxy for Public and Private Religion in England' in R O'Dair and A Lewis (eds) *Law and Religion* (Oxford University Press, Oxford, 2001) 471–95.

[175] See generally S Carter (1994) *The Culture of Disbelief* (Anchor, New York, 1994).

[176] See A Rahman, *Islam, Ideology and The Way of Life* (Muslim Schools Trust, London, 1980).

seen as being value neutral, in contrast to those of a partisan religious tradition.[177] Thus, Western judges often stress their 'secular' credentials in order to emphasise their commitment to 'serving a multi-cultural community of many faiths'.[178] This suggestion that secularism is synonymous with neutrality is also evident in the jurisprudence of the European Court of Human Rights. For example, in *Dahlab v Switzerland*, the European Court held that a rule prohibiting a Muslim teacher from wearing the Islamic veil in school was justified on the ground that this dress ban was necessary to guarantee religious neutrality in the classroom of a multi-faith society.[179] Yet the assumption that secular values are somehow 'neutral' has been strongly challenged.[180] Some have attacked the rise of what has been variously termed 'secular fundamentalism'[181] or 'ideological secularism'.[182] Indeed, even a senior official at the UN, in warning that 'secularism should not be used to manipulate religious freedom', has recently spoken of the need to strike a balance 'between secularism and respect for freedom of religion',[183] but the practical problems of attaining such a balance remain largely unresolved.[184]

A final challenge facing those responsible for interpreting or formulating international human rights law is the fact that freedom of religion or belief may, on occasion, impose a positive obligation on states. For example, the UN Declaration (1981) stipulates that governments must 'take effective measures to prevent and eliminate discrimination on the grounds of religion or belief',[185] but there is little agreement as to when a liberal state should be required to accommodate the religious practices of an individual or faith community.[186] Given the suspicion that Islamic dress engenders in the West,

---

[177] See M Evans, 'Religion, Law and Human Rights: Locating the Debate' in P W Edge and G Harvey (eds) *Law and Religion in Contemporary Society* (Ashgate, Aldershot, 2000) 182.
[178] *Sulaiman v Juffali* [2002] 1 FLR 479, [47].
[179] Application No 42393/98 (15 February 2001, unreported).
[180] Iain Benson, 'Notes Towards a (Re)Definition of the Secular' (1999–2000) 33 *University of British Columbia Law Review* 519.
[181] On this generally see P F Campos, 'Secular Fundamentalism' (1994) 94 *Columbia Law Review* 1814.
[182] See Tariq Modood, *Multiculturalism* (Oxford University Press, Oxford, 2007) 63–86.
[183] See HRC, UN Doc A/HRC/2/SR (25 October 2006) [57].
[184] For examples of state-sponsored secularism, see Bohdan Bocieurkiw and John Strong (eds) *Religion and Atheism in the USSR and Eastern Europe* (Macmillan, London, 1975).
[185] Article 4(1) UN Declaration (1981).
[186] For example, one can compare the views of B Parekh, *Rethinking Multiculturalism: Cultural Diversity and Political Theory* ((Macmillan, London, 2000), with those of B Barry, *Culture and Equality* (Harvard University Press, Cambridge, 2002).

it seems that relatively few European nations are likely to follow the lead of the UK's Judicial Studies Board, which recently recommended that religious items of clothing (including the *niqab*) could be permitted to be worn in the courtroom as long as they did not interfere with the interests of justice.[187]

## 5 Conclusion

The fact that age-old enmities between the Islamic and Western worlds have resurfaced in recent years significantly increases the challenges facing those responsible for formulating and interpreting principles of international human rights law in the field of religion and belief.[188] Indeed, such challenges are made all the more onerous by the fact that elements of what is commonly referred to as 'fundamentalism' can be found in many religions other than Islam, including Christianity,[189] Hinduism,[190] Judaism[191] and Sikhism.[192] Yet, notwithstanding such considerations, international human rights law still has an important role to play in the elimination of religious discrimination and intolerance in the twenty-first century. After all, it is a valuable resource in the practical resolution of international disputes, as well as being of great symbolic value in highlighting the fact that freedom of religion or belief is a fundamental right.

Of course, a strong case can be made that more needs to be done to eliminate the evils of religious discrimination and intolerance.[193] This is evidently the view of the UN Human Rights Council, which recently expressed its concern at the 'slow progress' of states in implementing the terms and provisions of the UN Declaration (1981).[194] One possible way forward would be to reformulate the UN Declaration (1981) and make it a legally binding interna-

---

[187] Judicial Studies Board, *Equal Treatment Bench Book* (2007) Ch 3.3.
[188] On the relationship between the Islamic and Western worlds see Tariq Ali, *The Clash of Fundamentalisms: Crusades, Jihads and Modernity* (Verso Books, London and New York, 2002).
[189] See Steve Brouwer, Paul Gifford and Susan D Rose, *Exporting the American Gospel: Global Christian Fundamentalism* (Routledge, New York, 1996).
[190] See Sumit Sarkar, *Beyond Nationalist Frames: Postmodernism, Hindu Fundamentalism, History* (Indiana University Press, Bloomington, 2002).
[191] See Israel Shahak and Norton Mezvinsky, *Jewish Fundamentalism in Israel* (Pluto Press, London, 2004).
[192] See H Oberoi, 'Sikh Fundamentalism: Translating History into Theory', in M Marty and R Appleby (eds) *Fundamentalisms and the State: Remaking Polities, Economies, and Militance* (University of Chicago Press, Chicago, 1993) 256.
[193] See David Hodge, 'Advocating the Forgotten Human Right: Article 18 of the Universal Declaration of Human Rights – Religious Freedom' (2006) 49 *International Social Work* 431.
[194] HRC, Elimination of all Forms of Intolerance and of Discrimination Based on Religion or Belief, UN Doc A/HRC/Res/6/37 (14 December 2007) [9(k)].

tional Convention, by modelling it on, say, the *Convention on the Elimination of All Forms of Racial Discrimination*. Such a new Convention would not merely supplement existing rules under international human rights law (such as Article 18 ICCPR), but might also lead to the creation of a new Committee (similar to the Committee on the Elimination of Racial Discrimination) that could monitor the activities of states parties in the field of religion and belief. Although a former Special Rapporteur has called for the introduction of a Convention to tackle the problem of intolerance and discrimination based on religion or belief,[195] there is little enthusiasm within the international community for reform in this area. As Malcolm Evans has pointed out, the general view is that 'the time is not yet right for a Convention' outlawing discrimination on the grounds of religion or belief.[196]

Given the formidable problems of reconciling conflicting ideologies in the field of religious human rights, it is hard to imagine when the time will be right for radical reform in this area. The UN has long called on states to eliminate religious discrimination and related intolerance.[197] Yet all too often its fine words fall on deaf ears because, as the Special Rapporteur has observed, religious freedom is still 'far from being a reality' for many people in the world today.[198]

---

[195] See Angelo Vidal d'Almeida Ribeiro, *Implementation of the Declaration on the Elimination of All Forms of Intolerance and of Discrimination Based on Religion or Belief*, UN Doc E/CN.4/1988/45 (6 January 1988) [55], [66].

[196] Evans, above n 4, 261. See also Bhiyyah G Tahzib, *Freedom of Religion or Belief: Ensuring Effective International Legal Protection* (Martinus Nijhoff, Dordrecht, 1996) 441.

[197] For example, over a decade ago 'religious intolerance' was listed alongside other social evils (such as torture, summary executions, disappearances, racism, apartheid, terrorism and discrimination against women) as constituting 'serious obstacles to the full enjoyment of all human rights': *Vienna Declaration and Programme of Action*, UN Doc A/CONF.157/23 (12 July 1993) [30].

[198] See Jahangir, above n 173, [48].

# 19. DRIP feed: the slow reconstruction of self-determination for Indigenous peoples
*Melissa Castan**

## 1 Introduction

After centuries of wavering between benign neglect and outright hostility, the international arena, and in particular the institution of the United Nations, has now turned its attention to the needs and desires of Indigenous peoples. Three decades of increasing interest in Indigenous peoples, their issues, needs and human rights, have culminated in the adoption of the *Declaration on the Rights of Indigenous Peoples* ('the Declaration' or 'DRIP') by the United Nations General Assembly in late 2007.[1] The adoption of the Declaration is seen by many as a fundamental affirmation of the identity and protection of Indigenous people, and indeed necessary to their very survival.[2] However, the adoption of the Declaration is not the conclusion of an era of focus and development of international law but, rather, the culmination of a period of dynamic change; the transition from 'object' to 'subject' of international law is complete.[3] Many outstanding areas of debate about Indigenous peoples' rights are not concluded, and some debates are still evolving, particularly on those issues revolving around the meaning of self-determination, the emerging standard requiring full prior and informed consent and the relationship between collective and individual rights.

In many respects, the ongoing tension over the obligations of states to accord full recognition of these human rights for their Indigenous people centres on the challenges presented by the different meanings attributed to the

---

\* The author would like to thank David Yarrow and Jay Tilley for their invaluable assistance in the preparation of this chapter. Thanks also for the comments and suggestions provided by the editors of this book.

[1] GA Res 61/295, UN GAOR, 61st sess, 107th plen mtg, UN Doc A/Res/61/295 (13 September 2008). The resolution was adopted in the 61st session of the United Nations General Assembly on Thursday 13 September 2008.

[2] J Gilbert, 'Indigenous Rights in the Making: The United Nations Declaration on the Rights of Indigenous Peoples' (2007) 14 *International Journal on Minority and Group Rights* 207.

[3] With apologies to R Barsh, 'Indigenous People in the 1990s: From Object to Subject of International Law' (1994) 7 *Harvard Human Rights Journal* 33.

right of self-determination, both by Indigenous communities and the settler states that have long asserted sovereign power over them.

This chapter will examine some of these issues through the vehicle of an evaluation of the process towards and the content of the recent UN General Assembly *Declaration on the Rights of Indigenous Peoples*. This framework is adopted because the Declaration is a wide-reaching, long-negotiated expression of international consensus, which seeks to address most major issues of debate in the area of recognition and protection of Indigenous peoples' rights at international law. This chapter will consider the meaning and consequences of recognising rights to self-determination and the challenge to state sovereignty (if any), the protection of land, traditional economies and cultural practices, and the emerging requirement of free prior and informed consent when dealing with development in Indigenous lands.[4] Whilst these themes are captured in the Declaration, much of the international jurisprudence and debate has developed out of the UN treaty bodies and work that predates the Declaration. These treaty bodies are fundamental to the architecture of international human rights law, and the rights of Indigenous peoples.

## 2 Background

Reviewing the entire landscape of international instruments and organs that address matters of concern to Indigenous peoples would test the reader's patience, and has been done elsewhere in many excellent reviews.[5] In short, it

---

[4] There are a plethora of other issues still under debate in this context, such as the appropriate definition of who is 'Indigenous', what are the collective rights of Indigenous people as opposed to their individual rights, and the role of other human rights concepts such as equality and non-discrimination. These issues are only dealt with in passing in this chapter, but are well ventilated in the contemporary literature on the nature of Indigenous rights at international law; see, for example, B Kingsbury, 'Five Competing Conceptual Structures of Indigenous People's Claims at International Law' (2001) 34 *New York University Journal of International Law and Politics* 189; W Kymlicka, 'Theorising Indigenous Rights' 29 (1999) *University of Toronto Law Journal* 281; D Ivison, 'The Logic of Aboriginal Rights' (2003) 3 *Ethnicities* 321; A Lokan, 'From Recognition to Reconciliation: The Functions of Aboriginal Rights Law' (1999) 23 *Melbourne University Law Review* 65.

[5] S J Anaya, *Indigenous Peoples in International Law* (Oxford University Press, Oxford, 2nd ed, 2004); S Weissner, 'Rights and Status of Indigenous Peoples: A Global, Comparative and International Legal Analysis' (1999) 12 *Harvard Human Rights Journal* 57; C Charters, 'Indigenous Peoples and International Law and Policy' (2007) 18 *Public Law Review* 22; B Morse, 'The rights of indigenous and minority peoples' in E Perakis (ed) *Rights of Minority Shareholders: XVIth Congress of the International Academy of Comparative Law* (Brisbane, 2002) General Reports; J Gilbert, 'Indigenous Rights in the Making: The United Nations Declaration on the Rights of Indigenous Peoples' (2007) 14 *International Journal on Minority and Group Rights* 207.

is worth observing that the development of most issues of international law regarding Indigenous peoples has occurred through the United Nations structures and processes,[6] which has certain mechanisms that address the particular concerns of Indigenous peoples, whether as part of general human rights law or by specifically addressing Indigenous issues. For example, the long-standing Working Group on Indigenous Populations,[7] the newer Permanent Forum on Indigenous Issues,[8] and the work of the Special Rapporteur on human rights and indigenous peoples[9] and other related Special Rapporteurs[10] and Independent Experts all contribute to the burgeoning jurisprudence on Indigenous peoples and their rights. In addition there are a number of well-known declarations and protocols which also incorporate the rights, concerns and input of Indigenous peoples.[11]

---

[6] Although it should be noted that some steps have been taken through the ILO's *Convention concerning Indigenous and Tribal Peoples in Independent Countries*, opened for signature 27 June 1989, ILO Convention No 169 (entered into force 5 September 1991) ('*ILO Convention No 169*'), which has been ratified by 20 Member States. The list of these States can be found at: http://www.ilo.org/ilolex/cgi-lex/ratifce.pl?C169 at 4 February 2009.

[7] This body addressed Indigenous issues from 1982 until the dismantling of the United Nations Commission on Human Rights in 2006, when the Working Group was disbanded. Its new manifestation is known as the 'Expert Mechanism on the Rights of Indigenous Peoples' pursuant to HRC Res 6/16, UN Doc A/HRC/Res/6/16 (28 September 2007).

[8] Established in 2000 by the United Nations Economic and Social Council ('ECOSOC') in ECOSOC Res 2000/22, UN Doc E/Res/2000/22 (28 July 2000). The Permanent Forum first convened in 2002, and meets annually.

[9] For example see the 'Country Reports' available at http://www2.ohchr.org/english/issues/indigenous/rapporteur/ at 4 February 2009.

[10] See, for example, Special Rapporteur Erica-Irene Daes, *Indigenous People's Permanent Sovereignty over Natural Resources: Final Report*, UN Doc E/CN.4/Sub.2/2004/30 (13 July 2004), and Special Rapporteur on Treaties, Agreements and Constructive Arrangements between States and Indigenous Populations, Mr Miguel Alfonso Martínez, *Study on treaties, agreements and other constructive arrangements between States and indigenous populations: Final Report*, UN Doc E/CN.4/Sub.2/1999/20 (22 June 1999).

[11] *International Covenant on Economic, Social and Cultural Rights*, opened for signature 19 December 1966, 999 UNTS 3 (entered into force 3 January 1976) ('ICESCR'); *Convention on the Rights of the Child*, opened for signature 20 November 1989, 1577 UNTS 3 (entered into force 2 September 1990); *Convention on Elimination of all forms of Discrimination Against Women*, opened for signature 18 December 1979, 1249 UNTS 13 (entered into force 3 September 1981); *Convention on the Elimination of All Forms of Racial Discrimination*, opened for signature 21 December 1965, 660 UNTS 195 (entered into force 4 January 1969) ('CERD'); *Declaration on the Rights of Members belonging to National or Ethnic, Religious and Linguistic Minorities*, GA Res 47/135, UN GAOR, 47th sess, 92nd plen mtg, UN Doc

There are, as mentioned earlier, UN human rights treaties and conventions which address the rights of all people, and within those instruments there are specific and general rights which address issues of concern to Indigenous peoples. Best known of these instruments are the *International Covenant on Civil and Political Rights* ('ICCPR'),[12] and the concomitant jurisprudence of the Human Rights Committee ('HRC'), particularly regarding Articles 1 (right of self-determination) and 27 (minority rights). The text of those articles does not address the subject of Indigenous people explicitly, but the HRC has responded to this omission by specifying that these articles have a special role to play in the protection of Indigenous peoples, particularly in *General Comment 23*, elucidating the scope of Article 27 in particular:

> The enjoyment of the rights to which article 27 relates does not prejudice the sovereignty and territorial integrity of a State party. At the same time, one or other aspect of the rights of individuals protected under that article – for example, to enjoy a particular culture – may consist in a way of life which is closely associated with territory and use of its resources. This may particularly be true of members of Indigenous communities constituting a minority.[13]

The CERD likewise applies to all people, but the CERD Committee has specified the role the Convention has for Indigenous people, both in its decisions and country comments and in its *General Recommendation 23*:

> The Committee is conscious of the fact that in many regions of the world indigenous peoples have been, and are still being, discriminated against, deprived of their human rights and fundamental freedoms and in particular that they have lost their land and resources to colonists, commercial companies and State enterprises. Consequently the preservation of their culture and their historical identity has been and still is jeopardised.[14]

---

A/Res/47/135 (18 December 1992); *Rio Declaration on Environment and Development*, UN Doc A/CONF.151/26 (Vol I) (12 August 1992); *Declaration of the World Summit on Sustainable Development*, UN Doc A/CONF.199/L.6/Rev.2 (4 September 2002); and the *Convention on Biodiversity*, opened for signature 5 June 1992, 1760 UNTS 79 (entered into force 29 December 1993), to name but a few. These are reviewed in C Charters, 'Indigenous Peoples and International Law and Policy' (2007) 18 *Public Law Review* 22, and S Pritchard and C Hednow-Dorman, 'Indigenous People and International Law: A Critical Overview' (1998) 3 *Australian Indigenous Law Review* 437.

[12] Opened for signature 16 December 1966, 999 UNTS 171 (entered into force 23 March 1976).

[13] Human Rights Committee, *General Comment 23: The Rights of Minorities*, UN Doc CCPR/C/21/Rev.1/Add.5 (8 April 1994) [3.2] (see also [7]). Note too that the Inter-American Court on Human Rights has expanded upon the rights of Indigenous peoples.

[14] Committee on the Elimination of Racial Discrimination, *General*

Although there is a surfeit of other treaties and conventions, the ICCPR and the CERD have dominated the development of international standards concerning Indigenous rights because these treaties have monitoring bodies with a high degree of credibility and wide-ranging participation from the vast majority of member states.[15] Beyond the UN are the other organisations that address Indigenous peoples' rights; the ILO via *Convention 169 on Indigenous and Tribal Peoples*, the Organization of American States (with its proposed *Declaration on Indigenous Peoples*), the Inter-American Human Rights System, the European Union, and the World Bank.

## 3  Setting the groundwork

After some twenty years development, on 13 September 2007 the United Nations General Assembly finally adopted the *Declaration on the Rights of Indigenous Peoples*, with a majority of 143 of the 158 states voting in favour of its adoption.[16] The Declaration had its origins in the work of the UN Working Group on Indigenous Populations ('WGIP'), established in 1982 under the Sub-Commission on the Prevention of Discrimination and Protection of Minorities,[17] itself a subordinate body to the Commission on Human Rights. The WGIP was the first UN body specifically mandated to deal with Indigenous issues, by reviewing developments in and international standards concerning Indigenous people and their rights.[18] At that time the only international instrument to deal specifically with the rights of Indigenous people was the ILO *Convention 107 on Indigenous and Tribal Populations*.[19] Although important historically, it was not widely accepted by Indigenous people as representing their needs or concerns, and was not broadly ratified by ILO member states.[20] The WGIP became a forum for Indigenous representa-

---

*Recommendation XXIII: Indigenous Peoples*, UN Doc A/52/18 Annex V (18 August 1997).

[15]  S Joseph, J Schultz and M Castan, *The International Covenant on Civil and Political Rights: Cases, Materials and Commentary (2nd Edition)* (Oxford University Press, Oxford, 2004) 875.

[16]  Of the 15 states that did not vote in favour of the Declaration, 11 abstained (Azerbaijan, Bangladesh, Bhutan, Burundi, Colombia, Georgia, Kenya, Nigeria, Russian Federation, Samoa and Ukraine;) and 4 cast negative votes (Australia, Canada, New Zealand and the United States of America).

[17]  This body was renamed the 'Sub-Commission on the Promotion and Protection of Human Rights' in 1999.

[18]  ECOSOC Res 1982/34, UN Doc E/Res/1982/34 (7 May 1982) sets out the mandate of the WGIP.

[19]  *Convention concerning the Protection and Integration of Indigenous and Other Tribal and Semi-Tribal Populations in Independent Countries*, opened for signature 26 June 1957, ILO Convention No 107 (entered into force 2 June 1959).

[20]  Only 18 States ratified: http://www.ilo.org/ilolex/cgi-lex/ratifce.pl?C107 at 4 February 2009. See also Anaya, above n 5.

tives who, noting the absence of international and UN principles specific to their needs or developed with their input, began work on a Declaration that reflected their participation and concerns.[21]

In 1993 the WGIP agreed on its final text for the 'Draft UN Declaration on the Rights of Indigenous Peoples' ('Draft Declaration') and it was passed up the UN hierarchy to the Sub-Commission, which adopted the draft in 1994.[22] At this point, the Draft Declaration stalled for 11 years in the hands of the Working Group on the Draft Declaration ('WGDD'), an inter-sessional group created by the Commission on Human Rights to review the draft text. Unlike the WGIP and the Sub-Commission, which were each composed of independent experts, the WGDD comprised representatives from UN member states, and these representatives baulked at most of the Articles of the Draft Declaration, particularly those that enlivened thorny issues of self-determination, land rights, and collective rights.[23] Finally, in 2006, the Chairperson-Rapporteur of the WGDD broke the impasse by proposing a compromise text, which sought to meet some of the objections of the States parties and maintain the integrity of the WGIP text.

The successor to the Commission, the Human Rights Council, adopted the revised text in June 2006, and it was anticipated that the General Assembly would adopt the declaration in the next session at the end of 2006. However, last-minute concerns expressed by the African Group of nations led to a postponement, in order to further consider issues of particular concern. Those issues coalesced under similar impediments that had arisen earlier, such as concerns about the impact of the rights to self-determination and to traditional lands and natural resources, and certain constitutional concerns about maintenance of distinct political, legal and economic institutions, whilst participating in the mainstream institutions.[24] Ultimately, some further amendments to the draft text were made and were accepted by the states that had already voted in

---

[21] Erica-Irene A Daes, 'An overview of the history of indigenous peoples: self-determination and the United Nations' (2008) 21 *Cambridge Review of International Affairs* 7.
[22] This version of the text is found in the Sub-Commission's *Annual Report 1994*, UN Doc E/CN.4/Sub.2/1994/56 (26 August 1994).
[23] Gilbert, above n 2, 213. Daes, above n 21.
[24] African Commission on Human and Peoples' Rights, *Final Communiqué of the 41st Ordinary Session held in Ghana on 16–30 May 2007* (2007) ACHPR, http://www.achpr.org/english/communiques/communique41_en.html at 4 February 2009. See also W van Genugten, *The African Move towards the Adoption of the 2007 Declaration on the Rights of Indigenous Peoples: The Substantive Arguments Behind the Procedures*, Paper prepared for the Committee on the Rights of Indigenous Peoples of the International Law Association (2008) SSRN, http://ssrn.com/abstract=1103862 at 4 February 2009.

favour of the text.[25] This development paved the way for adoption in mid-September 2007.

The main sticking point in the progress to adoption of the Declaration had always been political sensitivity over the concept of self-determination by states parties, and the challenge to territorial integrity that this right superficially appeared to present. A Declaration is not a legally binding document per se, but some parts of a Declaration may reflect customary international practice or recognition of such practice, and may thus constitute international law.[26] Although the DRIP is not a legally binding document, it captures a number of human rights obligations that States have already embraced, and so to some degree it represents general principles of international law.[27] Article 38 DRIP provides that States shall, in cooperation with Indigenous peoples, 'take the appropriate measures, including legislative measures, to achieve the ends of this Declaration'.[28] Where states abide by Article 38 DRIP, they elect to become bound by their own legislative requirements.[29]

---

[25] In essence these amendments revolved around providing explicit recognition that States could adopt different methods for meeting the standards set in the Declaration, as the situation of Indigenous peoples differs across nations and regions. Paragraph 23 of the Preamble to the Declaration addressed the concerns expressed by the African nations. The amendments can be viewed at http://www.un.org/esa/socdev/unpfii/documents/Declaration_IPs_31August.pdf at 4 February 2009.

[26] For example, a wide range of authors have suggested that the *Universal Declaration of Human Rights* GA Res 217A (III), UN Doc A/810, 71 (1948) ('UDHR') has evolved into customary law: A Eide and G Alfredsson, 'Introduction' in A Eide and G Alfredsson (eds) *The Universal Declaration of Human Rights: A Common Standard of Achievement* (Martinus Nijhoff, The Hague, 1999) xxv, xxxi–ii; Louis B. Sohn: 'The new international law: protection of the rights of individuals rather than states' (1982) 32 *American University Law Review* 1 at 15–17.

[27] S J Anaya, *Report of the Special Rapporteur on the situation of human rights and fundamental freedoms of indigenous people*, UN Doc A/HRC/9/9 (11 August 2008) [43].

[28] The Supreme Court of Belize recently referred to the Declaration as expressing general principles of international law, and of such force that the Government of Belize should not disregard it; *Aurelio Cal and Ors v Belize*, Supreme Court of Belize, No 171/2007. This was the first decision of a state court to apply the UN DRIP, just one month after its adoption by the General Assembly.

[29] The nature of the Declaration was cited by Australia and Canada as reasons for not adopting the Declaration. The specifics of their reasoning will be discussed below. See Australia's concerns as expressed by Australia's Ambassador to the UN, Robert Hill, who said that, although the Declaration 'would not be binding on Australia and other States as a matter of international law, he was aware that its aspirational contents would be relied on in setting standards by which States would be judged in their relations with Indigenous peoples': United Nations Department of Public Information, 'General Assembly Adopts Declaration on Rights of Indigenous Peoples;

## 4 The legal dimensions of the right to self-determination

The articulation of the right of self-determination is the opening Article in both the ICCPR and the ICESCR, which together with the UNDP are accepted as the primary standards of human rights principles expressed in the UN human rights system. All peoples have the right to self-determination, and Indigenous peoples are 'peoples' for that purpose.[30] The prioritising of the right of self-determination is deliberate; it is a guarantee designed to protect human dignity by protecting full and free participation in civil and political processes and upholding rights to pursue economic, social and cultural development. The right to self-determination is essential to the enjoyment of all human rights.[31]

The debate about the nature of self-determination is often presented as a matter of competing claims to the sovereignty of a territory, particularly in the context of Indigenous rights to self-determination. This false dichotomy has long been discredited, yet it was instrumental in the delay in adoption of the Declaration by the WGDD and the Group of African nations, and the negative votes of the four Anglo-settler nations, Canada, Australia, New Zealand and the United States ('CANZUS'). The threat or fear of challenges to territorial sovereignty may well be a straw man argument, as there is such a wide range of state obligations to minorities and Indigenous people, the vast majority of which fall well short of any sovereign claim.[32] Nevertheless it is an argument that is raised relentlessly, as discussed below. The short answer to these expressions of uncertainty and discomfort with the rights of Indigenous peoples' self-determination may be that the Declaration and its expressions of self-determination (and the other normative standards) are all subject to, and read in conformity with, other UN instruments and articulations of human rights. Self-determination thus is incapable of being elevated to a point that brings it into conflict with international 'hard' law on territorial integrity and state sovereignty, which are essentially the 'dominant paradigms' underpinning the United Nations system.[33]

---

"Major Step Forward" Towards Human Rights for All, Says President' (Press Release, 13 September 2007).

[30] Anaya above n 5; Gilbert, above n 2, 218; P Thornberry, *Indigenous Peoples and Human Rights* (Manchester University Press, Manchester, 2002) 420.

[31] Human Rights Committee, *General Comment 12: Article 1 (right to self-determination)*, UN Doc HRI/GEN/1/Rev.1 at 12 (13 March 1984); Committee on the Elimination of Racial Discrimination, *General Recommendation 21: The right to self-determination*, UN Doc A/51/18 Annex VIII at 125 (8 March 1996).

[32] For instance consider the concept of 'relational' self-determination, reflecting the need for Indigenous people to assert some control in the relationship with the dominant institutions of the state; for example, M Murphy, 'Representing Indigenous Self-determination' (2008) 58 *University of Toronto Law Journal* 198.

[33] Anaya, above n 5.

This deference to territorial and sovereign integrity is captured by Article 46(1) DRIP:

> Nothing in this Declaration may be interpreted as implying for any State, people, group or person any right to engage in any activity or to perform any act contrary to the *Charter of the United Nations* or construed as authorizing or encouraging any action which would dismember or impair, totally or in part, the territorial integrity or political unity of sovereign and independent States.

Article 46 DRIP would appear to mollify those states that fear a reinvigorated decolonisation process for Indigenous people. Indeed, by including the explicit limitation to the meaning of self-determination in this specific context, the General Assembly has arguably acceded to a different (or lesser) quality of self-determination due to Indigenous people, in contrast to that due to peoples generally, as most other expressions of self-determination do not come with such explicit provisos.[34]

Despite its position of prominence as Article 1 ICCPR, the HRC has foreclosed the justiciability of the right of self-determination, whether for Indigenous peoples or others. It did so on the basis that the right attaches to peoples, but the *Optional Protocol*[35] (under which states submit to the complaints procedure of the ICCPR) provides a 'recourse procedure for individuals', and thus is not available for peoples in their collective sense.[36] Concomitantly, the scope of protection accorded by other articles of the ICCPR has been elevated, perhaps in part in response to the inaccessibility of Article 1 ICCPR.

Notably the HRC has emphasised the rights Indigenous people must be accorded under Article 27 ICCPR regarding the rights of minorities to enjoy their own culture. This development manifests in a variety of forms, including the traditional, cultural and economic practices associated with land and other natural resources.[37] Although some aspects of the rights under Article 27

---

[34] This development was anticipated by Thornberry, above n 30, 420.

[35] *Optional Covenant 1 to the International Convention for Civil and Political Rights*, opened for signature 16 December 1966, 999 UNTS 302 (23 March 1976).

[36] *Kitok v Sweden*, UN Doc CCPR/C/33/D/197/1985 (27 July 1988) [6.3]; *Ominayak v Canada*, UN Doc CCPR/C/38/D/167/1984 (26 March 1990) ('*Ominayak v Canada*'); *Marshall (Mikmaq) v Canada*, UN Doc CCPR/C/43/D/205/1986 (4 November 1991); *Mahuika v New Zealand*, UN Doc CCPR/C/70/D/547/1993 (15 November 2000).

[37] See Human Rights Committee, *General Comment 23: The rights of minorities (Article 27)*, UN. Doc. CCPR/C/21/Rev.1/Add.5 (8 April 1994). *Ominayak v Canada*, *Länsman v Finland*, CCPR/C/83/D/1023/2001 (15 April 2005) and reiterated by Committee on the Elimination of Racial Discrimination, *General Recommendation 23 (Rights of indigenous peoples)*, UN Doc A/52/18, Annex V at 122 (18 August 1997) ('*General Comment 23*'). For general discussion see Joseph et al, above n 15, 779–89.

ICCPR come close to some aspects of the rights under Article 1 ICCPR (particularly on control of activities carried out on traditional lands), the HRC has warned against confusing the ambit of these Articles; Article 27 ICCPR is an individual right attaching to a person who is part of a minority (or in this case Indigenous group) whereas Article 1 ICCPR attaches to peoples.

> [3.1] The Covenant draws a distinction between the right to self-determination and the rights protected under Article 27. The former is expressed to be a right belonging to peoples and is dealt with in a separate part (Part I) of the Covenant. Self-determination is not a right cognisable under the *Optional Protocol*. Article 27, on the other hand, relates to rights conferred on individuals as such and is included, like the articles relating to other personal rights conferred on individuals, in Part III of the Covenant and is cognisable under the *Optional Protocol*.[38]

The right to participate in decisions concerning one's traditional lands and resources would thus be an aspect of self-determination,[39] but also represents part of the right to protection of a minority's culture and of cultural practices over land.[40] Perhaps the Declaration represents an engagement with Indigenous peoples as peoples rather than minorities, and so opens a wider vista of self-determination recognition without stretching to breaking point the territorial integrity of States.

## 5 Consent or consult?

A notable development out of the right of self-determination (as opposed to minority rights) is the articulation of the right to free, prior and informed consent ('FPIC'), a standard that is now expressed not only in the Declaration[41] but in a number of international sources (explored below). The Declaration appears to be relatively firm on the need for states parties to secure the consent of Indigenous communities affected by state action, such as development plans, the extinguishment of property rights, or the granting of rights to third parties.

The particular rights that Indigenous peoples have to self-determination include the right to negotiate and participate in decisions relevant to them as Indigenous peoples. Whilst this is no doubt inherent in rights of equality, or non-discrimination and political participation, it also is an expression of modern legal and constitutional concepts such as the rule of law, and

---

[38] *General Comment 23*, above n 37, [3.1]; see also [3.2] set out above.
[39] As explained by A Xanthaki, *Indigenous Rights and United Nations Standards: Self-Determination, Culture and Land* (Cambridge University Press, Cambridge, 2007); Anaya, above n 5.
[40] Xanthaki, above n 39; Joseph et al, above n 15.
[41] See particularly Articles 10, 19, 28, 29 and 32 DRIP.

democratic rights.[42] Effective participation is an aspect of self-determination (this is often referred to as the 'internal' aspect[43]) and is clearly protected in Articles 1 and 27 ICCPR, Article 5(c) CERD, Article 2(3) of the *United Nations Declaration on the Rights of Members belonging to National or Ethnic, Religious and Linguistic Minorities*,[44] and the *Declaration on Friendly Relations*.[45]

The legal principles regarding participation of and consultation with Indigenous peoples are found in the jurisprudence of human rights bodies, as well as being explicitly set out in their governing instruments. For example the CERD in its General Recommendation 23 emphasised the requirement for 'informed consent' in the context of participation in public life and decisions made concerning their interests.[46] The HRC has similarly expressed the need for 'effective participation' of Indigenous peoples in decisions that impact upon their articulation of cultural practices, including those relating to land and natural resources.[47] This requirement of informed consent arises out of the minority, language and cultural rights expressed in Article 27 ICCPR.[48]

The World Bank, as ostensibly the primary international development institution, must also abide by the requirement to observe the concerns of Indigenous people affected by any development project it finances. The World Bank's *Operational Policy and Bank Procedure 4.10 on Indigenous Peoples* states that finance for development projects can only be provided when the Bank is sure that the borrower has ensured free, prior, and informed consultation, resulting in wide support for the development project by the Indigenous peoples affected by it.[49] The objective underlying this standard was said to be

---

[42] See, for example, the discussion in Xanthaki, above n 39, 253.

[43] R McCorquodale, 'Self-Determination: A Human Rights Approach' (1994) 43 *International and Comparative Law Quarterly* 857, 864.

[44] See above n 11.

[45] *Declaration on Principles of International Law Concerning Friendly Relations and Cooperation among States in Accordance with the Charter of the United Nations*, GA Res 2625(XV), UN GAOR, 25th sess, 1883rd plen mtg, UN Doc A/8018 (24 October 1970) [7]. Further see Joseph et al, above n 15, Ch 7.

[46] See CERD General Recommendation 23, above n 37, [4], which calls on states to make certain that 'Indigenous peoples have equal rights in respect of effective participation in public life and no decisions directly relating to their rights and interests are taken without their informed consent'.

[47] UN Human Rights Committee, *General Comment No 23: The rights of minorities (Art 27)*, UN Doc CCPR/C/21/Rev.1/Add.5 (8 March 1994) [7].

[48] Joseph et al, above n 15, 782.

[49] World Bank, *Operational Directive 4.10 (Indigenous People)*, World Bank Doc OP/BP4/10 (2005) World Bank, http://web.worldbank.org/WBSITE/EXTERNAL/TOPICS/EXTSOCIALDEVELOPMENT/EXTINDPEOPLE/0,,menuPK:407808~pagePK:149018~piPK:149093~theSitePK:407802,00.html at 5 February

to 'ensure that Indigenous peoples do not suffer adverse effects during the development process, particularly from Bank-financed projects, and that they receive culturally compatible social and economic benefits'.[50] Notably this requirement fell well short of requiring Indigenous peoples' 'consent', and at best provides a requirement for negotiation; there is no implicit veto right for Indigenous peoples in the World Bank policy.

The Organization of American States, in the *Proposed American Declaration on the Rights of Indigenous Peoples* ('PADRIP'),[51] expresses the requirement of minimum standards of consultation[52] and sets out an obligation on states parties to ensure that their decisions 'regarding any plan, program or proposal affecting the rights or living conditions of Indigenous people are not made without the free and informed consent and participation of those people' unless there are exceptional circumstances.[53]

This proposed Declaration has already had an impact on the development of international law. The Inter-American Commission on Human Rights, in its decision in the Western Shoshone case, *Dann v United States*, reiterated that general international legal principles included 'the right of Indigenous peoples to legal recognition of their varied and specific forms and modalities of their control, ownership, use and enjoyment of territories and property; the recognition of their property and ownership rights with respect to lands, territories and resources they have historically occupied' and specifically pointed to a requirement of mutual consent in the change to any pre-colonial property rights:

> [W]here property and user rights of Indigenous peoples arise from rights existing prior to the creation of a state, recognition by that state of the permanent and inalienable title of Indigenous peoples relative thereto and to have such title changed only by mutual consent between the state and respective Indigenous peoples when they have full knowledge and appreciation of the nature or attributes of such property.[54]

---

2009 (OP 4/10). For discussion of the World Bank and its adherence to this requirement see S Errico, 'The World Bank and Indigenous Peoples: the Operational Policy on Indigenous Peoples (OP 4.10) Between Indigenous Peoples' Rights to Traditional Lands and to Free, Prior, and Informed Consent' (2006) 13 *International Journal on Minority and Group Rights* 367.

[50] OP 4.10 [1].

[51] *Proposed American Declaration on the Rights of Indigenous Peoples*, OAS Doc OEA/Ser/L/V/.II.95 Doc.6 (26 February 1997).

[52] See Articles XII, XV, XVII PADRIP.

[53] Article XXI(2) PADRIP.

[54] *Mary and Carrie Dann v United States*, Case 11.140, Report No 75/02, Inter-Am C HR, Report No 75/02, Doc 5, Rev.1 at 860 (2002) [130], [131]. The Western Shoshone Dann sisters refused to comply with a US grazing permit system, applicable

This decision built on the Inter-American Court's findings in the earlier *Awas Tingni* case, recognising traditional or customary communal title held by the Mayangna community, and finding a violation of their property rights by Nicaragua when a foreign commercial operation was granted felling rights over Indigenous community lands.[55]

In its recent decision of *Saramaka People v Suriname* about a non-Indigenous tribal group,[56] the Inter-American Court expanded upon the standard of 'consultation', identifying three safeguards: states must ensure effective participation of an Indigenous or Tribal group whose rights to lands are to be restricted, the group members must receive a reasonable benefit from the proposal, and an independent report on the risks and impacts of the proposal must be prepared prior to any change to property rights.[57] The Court also stated that where large-scale development projects are planned that would have major impacts on the Saramakan territory, the State will have a duty to do more than consult; it must gain their consent according to their traditions and customs.[58] The decision demonstrates this Court's attempt to balance the needs of the minority group with those of the wider majority, and its decision referred to the DRIP in support of this reconciliation of competing interests.[59]

Another international instrument, outside the UN system, that addresses the requirement for consultation is the International Labour Organisation's *Convention No 169 on Indigenous and Tribal Peoples*, which was (somewhat optimistically) described by Anaya as 'the most prominent and specific international affirmation of Indigenous cultural integrity and group identity' (prior of course to the adoption of the DRIP).[60] Article 6 sets out the requirement that

---

to traditional Western Shoshone lands. The Commission found that the US had failed to ensure that the Indigenous people's property rights had been extinguished prior to the granting of the permit in accordance with rights of equality and to property, under the proposed American Declaration. Interestingly the Commission also made reference to the standards arising from the ILO *Convention No 169*, an instrument to which the US is not a party.

[55] *Mayagna (Sumo) Awas Tingni Community v Nicaragua*, Inter-Am Ct HR (Ser C) No 79 (31 August 2001).

[56] *Case of the Saramaka People v Suriname*, Inter-Am Ct H R (Ser C) No 172 (28 November 2007) ('*Sarmaka People*').

[57] *Saramaka People* [129]–[140]; see further *Saramaka People v Suriname*, Inter-Am Ct H R (Ser C) No 172 (8 August 2008).

[58] Ibid, [34].

[59] Ibid, [131].

[60] S J Anaya, 'International Human Rights and Indigenous Peoples: the Move Towards the Multicultural State' (2004) 21 *Arizona Journal of International and Comparative Law* 13, 17.

[1] Governments shall:
(a) Consult the peoples concerned, through appropriate procedures and in particular through their representative institutions, whenever consideration is being given to legislative or administrative measures which may affect them directly;
(b) Establish means by which these peoples can freely participate, to at least the same extent as other sectors of the population, at all levels of decision-making in elective institutions and administrative and other bodies responsible for policies and programmes which concern them;
(c) Establish means for the full development of these peoples' own institutions and initiatives, and in appropriate cases provide the resources necessary for this purpose.
[2] The consultations carried out in application of this Convention shall be undertaken, in good faith and in a form appropriate to the circumstances, with the objective of achieving agreement or consent to the proposed measures.[61]

Aside from the requirement of 'consent' expressed in the proposed American Declaration, all major international standards on this issue, including the requirement of participation and consultation expressed in the CERD, the HRC, the World Bank and the ILO, fall short of requiring the full agreement of the Indigenous peoples whose territories, polity, knowledge or other domains are affected by a proposed action, by the state or other third party. Thus in international law, as derived from these international institutions, participation and consultation is not equivalent to 'consent'; only a consultative or participatory standard is required to be met.

In contrast, the Declaration appears to have set a higher standard than the prevailing 'consultative' standard as articulated at international law to require a 'free prior and informed consent' of Indigenous peoples.[62] This might even amount to a power of veto over development on lands and territories understood as belonging to Indigenous people, or similarly over the use of their traditional knowledge, whether it be biological, genetic, medicinal or horticultural in nature.[63] Certainly many Indigenous communities would no doubt

---

[61] See Part II of the Convention on standards for dealing with Indigenous people and their traditional lands, and specifically Article 15 on consultation requirements regarding mineral exploration and extraction. Although consultations are required, there is no requirement for consent as such; see M Tomei and L Swenson, *Indigenous and Tribal Peoples: A Guide to ILO Convention 169* (International Labour Organization, 1996, Geneva) [8] cited in Anaya above n 5, 37.
[62] Articles 10, 11.2, 19, 28, 29(2), 32(2) DRIP.
[63] The main areas of development or state intervention where the need for FPIC is likely to arise were considered in an International Workshop convened by ECOSOC in 2005, which identified the following areas (amongst others): Indigenous lands and territories and sacred sites (for example, exploration, such as archaeological explorations, as well as development and use), treaties, agreements and other constructive arrangements between States and Indigenous peoples, tribes and nations, extractive

assert the right to prohibit unwanted incursions into their traditional domain.[64] The consent to having one's rights diminished or extinguished can be seen readily as an expression of self-determination, equivalent to those 'acts of self-determination' that have their origin in consensual transfers of territory.[65]

However, in a workshop convened under the auspices of the UN Economic and Social Council to deliberate on the meaning of 'free, prior and informed consent', the issues were considered at length as follows:

> Consultation and participation are crucial components of a consent process. Consultation should be undertaken in good faith. The parties should establish a dialogue allowing them to find appropriate solutions in an atmosphere of mutual respect in good faith, and full and equitable participation. Consultation requires time and an effective system for communicating among interest-holders. Indigenous peoples should be able to participate through their own freely chosen representatives and customary or other institutions. The inclusion of a gender perspective and the participation of Indigenous women are essential, as well as participation of children and youth, as appropriate. This process may include the option of withholding consent. Consent to any agreement should be interpreted as Indigenous peoples have (sic) reasonably understood it.[66]

The Workshop thus reverted to the consultative standard, already established in international law, and did not embrace the higher requirement for full consent.

---

industries, conservation, hydro-development, other developments and tourism activities in Indigenous areas, natural resources including biological resources, genetic resources, traditional knowledge of Indigenous peoples, and policies or programmes that may lead to the removal of their children, or their removal, displacement or relocation from their traditional territories. See ECOSOC, *Report of the International Workshop on Methodologies regarding Free, Prior and Informed Consent and Indigenous Peoples*, UN Doc E/C.19/2005/3 (17 February 2005) [45].

[64] A Carmen, 'Indigenous Peoples, Treaties and the Right to Free, Prior and Informed Consent' (Paper presented at the Symposium on the Implementation of the United Nations Declaration on the Rights of Indigenous Peoples, Vancouver, 19–20 February 2008).

[65] The Savoy Plebiscite of 1860 is an example, but one could point to contemporary examples such as those cited by the Inter-American Court in *Saramaka People*.

[66] ECOSOC, above n 63, [46]–[48]. Other aspects of the term are defined at [45]–[46], for instance: '[f]ree should imply no coercion, intimidation or manipulation; [p]rior should imply that consent has been sought sufficiently in advance of any authorization or commencement of activities and that respect is shown for time requirements of Indigenous consultation/consensus processes.' The term 'informed' is specified to imply that information is provided that covers a series of minimum aspects listed in [46], such as the nature, size, pace, reversibility and scope of any proposed project or activity, the reasons or purpose and the duration of the activity and the localities affected, as well as a requirement to provide an economic, social, cultural and environmental impact assessment, and details about the personnel and procedures involved.

Despite the strong statements of the Inter-American Court, it is unlikely at this stage that international law demands that states gain the full consent of Indigenous communities prior to embarking on actions that extinguish, modify or interfere with their human rights, particularly to lands and natural resources.[67] If this is the case, it must be recognised that international standards, including decisions of juridical committees and monitoring bodies, do require the participation of, and consultation with, Indigenous communities when such state action is anticipated. Consultations conducted in inappropriate fora, with no attempt to gain wide-ranging understanding of the issues and consequences, or without addressing the concerns expressed by the Indigenous community, will amount to *mala fides*, and will, according to prevailing jurisprudence, be in breach of a wide range of international instruments and obligations.[68]

But ultimately the nation state still holds the balance of power, as it is not yet obliged by international human rights law to gain the consent of Indigenous people so long as it satisfactorily constructs mechanisms and processes to engage, negotiate, or consult with the affected peoples.

## 6 Colonial foundations

Of course self-determination has been a central issue in international law and policy for centuries, and is a wider concept than that applicable to Indigenous people particularly. Numerous opinions of leading jurists and international judicial and treaty bodies have given tangible meaning to the concept of self-determination. Why then have certain states baulked at the prospect of according recognition to Indigenous self-determination, and in particular in the terms expressed in the DRIP?

The reasons expressed for the lack of support for the Declaration fall into a narrow band. Australia stated it had concerns that the references to self-determination could be used to instigate a secessionist movement and were only applicable in a situation of decolonisation.[69] Canada expressed concern

---

[67] This is particularly so given the DRIP is a Declaration rather than a legally binding treaty.

[68] Xanthaki, above n 39, 256, suggests the full range of methods and endeavours to meet this standard, including, but not limited to, 'discussions or meetings with local leaders and individuals or with local organisations or communities, establishment of local advisory boards, Indigenous membership on protected area management boards'.

[69] United Nations Department of Public Information, above n 29. Note that Australia recently revisited its position on the DRIP. The Commonwealth Minister for Families, Housing, Community Services and Indigenous Affairs has publicly stated that Australia now supports the Declaration. See J. Macklin, speech at Parliament House, Canberra, 3 April 2009. It remains to be seen whether the government's statements of good intention bring about substantive recognition and protection of the rights expressed in the Declaration.

at the requirement for the concept of free, prior and informed consent, citing incompatibility with Canada's parliamentary system (Australia and New Zealand made mention of similar points).[70] The United States cited the process of developing the Declaration as 'failed' and the text 'confusing', thus risking 'endless conflicting interpretations and debate about its application'.[71]

Nation states most fear self-determination in its 'external' construction, which is the right of peoples to claim certain territory, or secede, as an expression of their right to self-determination. However, this external aspect of the right is only available under limited circumstances in international law, such as when the community in question live under colonial or neo-colonial domination, or when they are severely mistreated and their human rights comprehensively and continuously abused; the external form of self-determination is then enlivened.[72] However, the right of self-determination entails more than this external aspect, and for the most part does not involve any challenge to a state's territorial integrity. Many peoples are not able to assert the external expression of self-determination but are nevertheless able to express the 'internal' construction of that right.

Anaya suggests that self-determination has both 'constitutive' and 'ongoing' aspects. The constitutive element requires that the governing institutional order must develop with the participation and accession of the peoples governed.[73] The 'ongoing' aspect means that the governing order must be one that people can live in, and progress freely within, on an evolving basis. Anaya suggests that the decolonisation process does not require turning the clock back (and thus seeking to return governance arrangements to their previous state), but that remedies responsive to present-day aspirations of the peoples denied self-determination can be developed. Remedying the injustice typically suffered by Indigenous people denied self-determination is both retrospective and prospective in nature. It does not impose any threat to territorial integrity, nor to governmental or constitutional structures.

Murphy, writing about 'relational' self-determination, refers to the inevitable interdependence between the often small and weakened Indigenous communities and their larger, politically and economically empowered settler governments. This relationship necessitates an articulation of self-determination that embraces not only the possibility of Indigenous self-governance (as is often imagined) but also the need for a

---

[70] Ibid.
[71] Ibid.
[72] Joseph et al, above n 15, 149.
[73] Anaya, above n 5.

variety of opportunities to access political power and decision making at local, provincial and national levels.[74] A diverse permeation of Indigenous influence is a more nuanced but ultimately a more holistic approach to comprehending the true meaning of self-determination for Indigenous people.[75]

Indeed this approach is probably supported by international legal principles, which do not accommodate a rule or practice of permitting assertions of sovereign or territorial independence of Indigenous people from the state in which they are located. As is regularly overlooked, international law often authenticates illegitimate acquisitions of sovereignty, particularly where it occurred in previous centuries.

Why then did the four CANZUS nations resile from their initial support for recognition of Indigenous rights at international law, and particularly in the Declaration? All are successors to the British colonial mission and, unlike other former British colonies such as India, Pakistan and Ghana (or even South Africa, belatedly), none have experienced the internal decolonisation process. All four have histories of legal and illegal dispossession of their Indigenous peoples, and they now face similar crises in the management of policy and governance in these marginalised Indigenous communities, who represent minor proportions of the dominant settler populations. Although some recognition of inherent, aboriginal or native title to lands may be apparent in each of these CANZUS states, closer examination shows that these efforts have been less than wholeheartedly embraced, whether it be by the legislatures, judiciaries or governments, be they provincial or national.[76]

Just at the point where recognition of Indigenous rights was to launch onto the international stage (after too many dress rehearsals), these four liberal democratic and wealthy nations coalesced to work to deflect and reject the claims of Indigenous peoples, their most impoverished and marginalised peoples. Whether this coalition emerged out of a reflection of national anxieties and lack of confidence in their own historical claims to national sovereignty, or domestic electoral politics played an unseen trump card, is left for speculation.[77] Perhaps the fundamentals of international law, its history and architecture are at the core.

---

[74] Murphy, above n 32, 199.
[75] J Borrows, *Recovering Canada: The Resurgence of Indigenous Law* (University of Toronto Press, Toronto, 2002) 140.
[76] K McNeil, 'Judicial Treatment of Indigenous Land Rights in the Common Law World' in B J Richardson, S Imai and K McNeil (eds) *Indigenous Peoples and the Law: Comparative and Critical Perspectives* (Hart, Oxford, 2009).
[77] D Day, *Claiming a Continent: A New History of Australia* (Harper Collins, Sydney, 1997).

If we accept that the protection of the Westphalian concept of the nation state is probably the paramount construct in modern international law, then it becomes easier to identify the source of the resistance to claims to Indigenous self-determination, whether expressed within the Declaration or beyond it. The origins of modern international law are contiguous with the colonial project; having acquired territory by displacement of indigenous sovereignty, certain states are still unable to reconceptualise their contemporary liberal legal and political structures to accommodate indigenous claims. The fear of fracturing the narrative of settlement means that the colonial project endures.[78]

## 7  Rebuilding the architecture

Fundamentally, the *Declaration on the Rights of Indigenous Peoples* is significant in at least one very important dimension: it has reinvigorated the right to self-determination as a right with particular meaning for Indigenous people after its enforceability and indeed its meaning were undermined by the HRC decision to deny access to peoples by way of its formalistic approach to the *Optional Protocol to the ICCPR*. The diminution of the role of collective rights weakened the credibility of one of the most valuable sources of international law.

Although in some respects the Declaration does little more than restate many existing human rights principles in their application to Indigenous people, in other respects it goes further. The Declaration represents an advance in international practice in its recognition of Indigenous peoples as collectivities, rather than atomised individuals. The Declaration has particularised the human rights of Indigenous peoples, and by doing so it presents a challenge to the individualistic, liberal conception of rights belonging to people, rather than peoples. This may be an example of new state practice in the elaboration of collective rights; but inherent in this practice is still a reluctance among some nations to face the rearticulation or reconception of their settlement narrative to address the continuing displacement and denigration of their Indigenous communities. The next advance will be the development of appropriate mechanisms and processes to protect these rights; without these tools the Declaration will end up as a worthy but unenforceable statement of human rights principles.

The development of implementation mechanisms is of critical importance to Indigenous communities, because their human rights (and those of many other vulnerable and marginalised groups) are only realisable where strong

---

[78] See A Anghie, *Imperialism, Sovereignty and the Making of International Law* (Cambridge University Press, Cambridge, 2005).

mechanisms of human rights practice are available to provide enforceable sanctions when states fail in their implementation and protection. Where human rights architecture is strong, protection of rights is more effectively secured. The Declaration is re-establishing the right of self-determination as a foundation stone in international human rights law.

**Postscript**
The Human Rights Committee recently expressed the view that Article 27 ICCPR requires that states parties gain Indigenous consent to measures that substantively interfere with their traditional economies. It stated in *Poma v Peru*[79] at paragraph 7.6:

> In the Committee's view, the admissibility of measures which substantially compromise or interfere with the culturally significant economic activities of a minority or indigenous community depends on whether the members of the community in question have had the opportunity to participate in the decision-making process in relation to these measures and whether they will continue to benefit from their traditional economy. The Committee considers that participation in the decision-making process must be effective, which requires not mere consultation but the free, prior and informed consent of the members of the community. In addition, the measures must respect the principle of proportionality so as not to endanger the very survival of the community and its members.

Although no mention is made of the Declaration, its impact is implicit in this HRC decision. The expression of support for the notion of Free Prior and Informed Consent from the HRC adds significantly to the notion that meaningful consent is required where the implementation of decisions or projects is likely to cause substantive interruption or interference with traditional Indigenous means of survival.

---

[79] *Poma v Peru* CCPR/C/95/D/1457/2006 (27 March 2009).

# 20. Counter-terrorism and human rights
*Alex Conte*

The relationship between terrorism and human rights is a matter that had been reflected upon well before the events of 11 September 2001. Since 9/11, with events such as the establishment of the detention camp at Guantánamo Bay and the proliferation of security and counter-terrorist legislation throughout the world, more attention has been paid to the issue of the extent to which counter-terrorism impacts upon human rights. As noted by the UN Office of the High Commissioner for Human Rights:[1]

> Some States have engaged in torture and other ill-treatment to counter terrorism, while the legal and practical safeguards available to prevent torture, such as regular and independent monitoring of detention centres, have often been disregarded. Other States have returned persons suspected of engaging in terrorist activities to countries where they face a real risk of torture or other serious human rights abuse, thereby violating the international legal obligation of non-refoulement. The independence of the judiciary has been undermined, in some places, while the use of exceptional courts to try civilians has had an impact on the effectiveness of regular court systems. Repressive measures have been used to stifle the voices of human rights defenders, journalists, minorities, indigenous groups and civil society. Resources normally allocated to social programmes and development assistance have been diverted to the security sector, affecting the economic, social and cultural rights of many.

This chapter first considers the general obligation upon States to comply with human rights when countering terrorism, pointing to relevant international and regional documents on the subject. It then moves to explain the practicalities for achieving human rights compliance while countering terrorism, taking into account the various requirements of that body of law.

## 1 The requirement to comply with human rights while countering terrorism

In September 2006, the General Assembly adopted the United Nations Global

---

[1] Office of the High Commissioner for Human Rights, 'Human Rights, Terrorism and Counter-terrorism', Fact Sheet No 32 (United Nations, New York and Geneva, 2008), available online at http://www.ohchr.org/Documents/Publications/Factsheet32EN.pdf, p. 1.

Counter-Terrorism Strategy,[2] as recommended by Kofi Annan in his report entitled *Uniting Against Terrorism*. In this report, the then Secretary-General emphasised that effective counter-terrorism measures and the protection of human rights are not conflicting goals but complementary and mutually reinforcing ones.[3] He identified the defence of human rights as essential to the fulfilment of all aspects of an effective counter-terrorism strategy and identified human rights as having a central role in every substantive section of his report. The Secretary-General stated that 'Only by honouring and strengthening the human rights of all can the international community succeed in its efforts to fight this scourge.'[4]

These sentiments are reflected within the Global Counter-Terrorism Strategy in three ways. First, respect for human rights for all and the rule of law forms one of the four pillars of the Strategy. It is also identified as 'the fundamental basis of the fight against terrorism', thus applicable to all four pillars of the Strategy. Finally, the Strategy's recognition of the importance of respect for human rights while countering terrorism is significantly strengthened through the express assertion that a lack of the rule of law and violations of human rights amount to conditions conducive to the spread of terrorism.[5] While these are very positive steps, however, the language of the Global Strategy is very broad and it does not deal with the question of whether Chapter VII resolutions of the Security Council, including those on counter-terrorism, are capable of modifying or somehow suspending human rights obligations. It is therefore necessary to further consider the question of human rights obligations in the context of countering terrorism.

Not only are counter-terrorism and human rights protection interlinked and mutually reinforcing, but compliance with human rights has practical advantages in bringing the perpetrators of terrorist acts to justice. On a national level, the obtaining of evidence by means which are found to be in violation of human rights may be inadmissible in a prosecution. At an international level, such violations may impact upon the ability of other States to rely on

---

[2] *The United Nations Global Counter-Terrorism Strategy*, GA Res 60/288, UN GAOR, 60th sess, 99th plen mtg, UN Doc A/Res/60/288 (8 September 2006). The UN General Assembly reaffirmed the UN Global Counter-Terrorism Strategy in September 2008: see GA Res 62/272, UN GAOR, 62nd sess, 120th plen mtg, UN Doc A/Res/62/272 (5 September 2008).
[3] Report of the Secretary-General, *Uniting Against Terrorism: Recommendations for a Global Counter-terrorism Strategy*, UN Doc A/60/825 (27 April 2006) [5]. See also Part VI thereof.
[4] Ibid [118].
[5] *Global Counter-Terrorism Strategy*, above n 2, Pillar I [preambular].

such evidence through mutual legal assistance.[6] It should also be observed that fighting terrorism in a non-human-rights-compliant way can lead to a decline in a State's own moral and human rights standards and/or a progressive decline in the effectiveness of checks and balances on agencies involved in fighting terrorism. As Frederich Neitzsche wrote in 1886, 'He who fights monsters should be careful lest he thereby becomes a monster. And if thou gaze long into the abyss, the abyss will also gaze into thee.'[7]

Added to the obligation of States to protect those within their jurisdiction from acts of terrorism, an obvious point should be made about the nature of international law obligations. Not only are human rights essential to the countering of terrorism, but States are obliged by law to comply with their international human rights obligations when countering terrorism. This is due to the fact that States have human rights obligations under customary international law (applicable to all States)[8] and international treaties (applicable to States parties to such treaties).[9] This principle is based not only upon a State's international obligations, but also upon directions of the UN Security Council, the General Assembly, the Commission on Human Rights, and the Human Rights Council. It was a clear message of the 2005 World Summit Outcome on the question of respect for human rights while countering terrorism, the General Assembly concluding that[10]

> [i]nternational cooperation to fight terrorism must be conducted in conformity with international law, including the Charter and relevant international conventions and protocols. States must ensure that any measures taken to combat terrorism comply with their obligations under international law, in particular human rights law, refugee law and international humanitarian law.

Before considering applicable documents of the United Nations and others, it should be noted that the universal treaties on counter-terrorism expressly require compliance with various aspects of human rights law. In the context of

---

[6] Françoise Hampson, 'Human Lights Law and Judicial Co-operation in the Field of Counter-Terrorist Activities', a paper presented at the *Expert Workshop on Human Rights and International Co-operation in Counter-Terrorism*, 15–17 November 2006, Triesenberg, Liechtenstein.

[7] Frederich Neitzsche, *Beyond Good and Evil* (Penguin Classics, London, 1973), Chapter IV ('Apophthegms and Interludes', Section 146).

[8] *Military and Paramilitary Activities in and against Nicaragua (Nicaragua v United States of America)* (Merits) [1986] ICJ Reports, [172]–[201] (*'Military and Paramilitary Activities'*).

[9] See the *Vienna Convention on the Law of Treaties*, opened for signature 23 May 1969, 1195 UNTS 311 (entered into force 27 January 1980), Article 34.

[10] *2005 World Summit Outcome*, GA Res 60/1, UN GAOR, 60th sess, 8th plen mtg, UN Doc A/Res/60/1 (16 September 2005) [85].

the International Convention for the Suppression of the Financing of Terrorism, for example, this is illustrated in article 15 (expressly permitting States to refuse extradition or legal assistance if there are substantial grounds for believing that the requesting State intends to prosecute or punish a person on prohibited grounds of discrimination); article 17 (requiring the 'fair treatment' of any person taken into custody, including enjoyment of all rights and guarantees under applicable international human rights law); and article 21 (a catch-all provision making it clear that the Convention does not affect the other rights, obligations and responsibilities of States).[11]

## A   UN General Assembly

The UN General Assembly has adopted a series of resolutions on terrorism since 1972, initially concerning measures to eliminate international terrorism, and later addressing more directly the topic of terrorism, counter-terrorism and human rights. The second series of General Assembly resolutions began in December 1993, with the adoption of resolution 48/122, entitled *Terrorism and Human Rights*. Both sets of resolutions contain various statements about the need, when implementing counter-terrorist measures, to comply with international human rights standards. A common phrasing of this idea is seen in General Assembly resolution 50/186:

> The General Assembly, . . .
> *Mindful* of the need to protect human rights of and guarantees for the individual in accordance with the relevant international human rights principles and instruments, particularly the right to life,
> *Reaffirming* that all measures to counter terrorism must be in strict conformity with international human rights standards, . . .
> 3. *Calls upon* States to take all necessary and effective measures in accordance with international standards of human rights to prevent, combat and eliminate all acts of terrorism wherever and by whomever committed.[12]

---

[11]   International Convention for the Suppression of the Financing of Terrorism, opened for signature 10 January 2000, 2179 UNTS 232 (entered into force 10 April 1992).

[12]   *Human Rights and Terrorism*, GA Res 50/186, UN GAOR, 50th sess, 99th plen mtg, UN Doc A/Res/50/186 (22 December1995) preambular [13] and [14], and operative [3]. See also *Human Rights and Terrorism*, GA Res 52/133, UN GAOR, 52nd sess, 70th plen mtg, UN Doc A/Res/52/133 (12 December 1997) preambular [12] and [13] and operative [4]; *Human Rights and Terrorism*, GA Res 54/164, UN GAOR, 54th sess, 83rd pln mtg, UN Doc A/Res/54/164 (17 December 1999) preambular [15] and [16], and operative [4]; *Human Rights and Terrorism*, GA Res 56/160, UN GAOR, 56th sess, 88th plen mtg, UN Doc A/Res/56/160 (19 December 2001) preambular [22] and [23] and operative [5] and [6]; *Human Rights and Terrorism*, GA Res 58/174, UN GAOR, 58th sess, 77th plen mtg, UN Doc A/Res/58/174 (22 December 2003) preambular [20] and [21], and operative [7].

516  *Research handbook on international human rights law*

A slightly less robust expression of these ideas was seen in resolution 56/88 following the events of September 11, although still requiring measures to be taken consistently with human rights standards.[13] That should not, however, be taken as a signal that the General Assembly was minded to turn a blind eye to adverse impacts of counter-terrorism upon human rights. On the contrary, the issue became the subject of annual resolutions on that subject alone, entitled *Protection of human rights and fundamental freedoms while countering terrorism*.[14] The first operative paragraphs of these resolutions affirm that:

---

[13]  The preambular returned to the language of combating terrorism 'in accordance with the principles of the Charter', and operative [4] talked of combating terrorism in accordance with international law 'including international standards of human rights'. See also similar statements within *Measures to Eliminate International Terrorism*, GA Res 57/27, UN GAOR, 57th sess, 52nd plen mtg, UN Doc A/Res/57/27 (19 November 2002) preambular [8] and operative [6]; *Measures to Eliminate International Terrorism*, GA Res 58/81, UN GAOR, 58th sess, 72nd plen mtg, UN Doc A/Res/58/81 (19 December 2003) preambular [9] and operative [6]; *Strengthening international cooperation and technical assistance in promoting the implementation of the universal conventions and protocols related to terrorism within the framework of the activities of the Centre for International Crime Prevention*, GA Res 58/136, UN GAOR, 58th sess, 77th plen mtg, UN Doc A/Res/58/136 (22 December 2003) preambular [10] and operative [5]; *Measures to Eliminate International Terrorism*, GA Res 59/46, UN GAOR, 59th sess, 65th plen mtg, UN Doc A/Res/59/46 (2 December 2004) preambular [10] and operative [3].

[14]  *Protection of human rights and fundamental freedoms while countering terrorism*, GA Res 57/219, UN GAOR, 57th sess, 77th plen mtg, UN Doc A/Res/57/219 (18 December 2002); *Protection of human rights and fundamental freedoms while countering terrorism*, GA Res 58/187, UN GAOR, 58th sess, 77th plen mtg, UN Doc A/Res/58/187 (22 December 2003); *Protection of human rights and fundamental freedoms while countering terrorism*, GA Res 59/191, UN GAOR, 59th sess, 74th plen mtg, UN Doc A/Res/59/191 (20 December 2004). See also *Measures to Eliminate International Terrorism*, GA Res 59/46, UN GAOR, 59th sess, 65th plen mtg, UN Doc A/Res/59/46 (2 December 2004) preambular [10] and operative [3]; *Strengthening international cooperation and technical assistance in promoting the implementation of the universal conventions and protocols related to terrorism within the framework of the activities of the United Nations Office on Drugs and Crime*, GA Res 59/153, UN GAOR, 59th sess, 74th plen mtg, UN Doc A/Res/59/153 (20 December 2004) preambular [11] and [12]; *Human Rights and Terrorism*, GA Res 59/195, UN GAOR, 59th sess, 74th plen mtg, UN Doc A/Res/59/195 (20 December 2004) preambular [5], [23] and [24] and operative [8] and [10]; *Protection of human rights and fundamental freedoms while countering terrorism*, GA Res 60/158, UN GAOR, 60th sess, 64th plen mtg, UN Doc A/Res/60/158 (16 December 2005) preambular [2], [3] and [7] and operative [1]; *Protection of human rights and fundamental freedoms while countering terrorism*, GA Res 61/171, UN GAOR, 61st sess, 81st plen mtg, UN Doc A/Res/61/171 ( 19 December 2006) preambular [3] and [5] and operative [1]; *Protection of human rights and fundamental freedoms while countering terrorism*, GA Res 62/159, UN GAOR, 62nd sess, 76th plen mtg, UN Doc

States must ensure that any measure taken to combat terrorism complies with their obligations under international law, in particular international human rights, refugee and humanitarian law.

These directions on the part of the General Assembly are reasonably strong in the language they use. It must be recalled, however, that resolutions of the General Assembly do not hold the same weight as international conventions, or decisions of the Security Council. Indeed, Article 10 of the Charter of the United Nations specifically provides that resolutions and declarations of the General Assembly are recommendatory only. This principle is equally applicable to resolutions of the Commission on Human Rights, as a subsidiary organ of the Economic and Social Council (which is only empowered to make recommendations), and those of the Commission's replacement, the Human Rights Council (a subsidiary organ of the General Assembly). Thus, the resolutions just discussed, and those of the Commission to be discussed below, represent guiding principles and non-binding recommendations (what might be termed 'soft law'), rather than binding resolutions, treaty provisions or norms of customary international law ('hard law'). Notwithstanding this, having regard to their repeated and consistent approach, these resolutions are very influential and could be described as representative of international comity. It is also relevant to recall that resolutions may constitute evidence of customary international law, if supported by State conduct that is consistent with the content of the resolutions and with the accompanying *opinio juris* required to prove the existence of customary law.[15]

## B  UN Security Council

In general terms, Security Council resolutions concerning terrorism have confined their attention upon the threat of terrorism to international peace and security, reflecting the role of the Council as the organ of the United Nations charged with the maintenance of peace and security. That role is reflected in

---

A/Res/62/159 (18 December 2007) preambular [3], [4] and [9] and operative [1]; and GA Res 63/185, UN GAOR, 63rd sess, 70th plen mtg, UN Doc A/Res/63/185 (18 December 2008), preambular [3], [5], and [10] and operative [1].

[15]  An example of the use of resolutions of the General Assembly to determine the content of customary rules can be seen in *Military and Paramilitary Activities*, above n 8, where the International Court of Justice gave consideration to two resolutions of the Assembly as evidence of the content of the principle of non-intervention: those being the *Declaration on the Inadmissibility of Intervention in the Domestic Affairs of States*, GA Res 213 (XX), UN GAOR, 20th sess, 1408th plen mtg, UN Doc A/Res/20/213 (21 December 1965) and the *Declaration on Principles of International Law Concerning Friendly Relations and Co-Operation Among States*, GA Res 2625 (XXV), UN GAOR, 25th sess, 1883rd plen mtg, UN Doc A/Res/25/2635 (24 October 1970).

the language and scope of Security Council resolutions on terrorism, which, compared with General Assembly and Commission on Human Rights resolutions on the subject, are much narrower in focus. In general terms, the Security Council's resolutions are concerned with the adverse impacts of terrorism upon the security of States and the maintenance of peaceful relations, while the General Assembly and the Commission take a much broader approach to the subject, given their plenary roles and mandates.

Apart from two notable exceptions, the main inference that can be taken from Security Council resolutions about counter-terrorism measures and their need to comply with human rights arises from general statements that counter-terrorism is an aim that should be achieved in accordance with the Charter of the United Nations and international law.[16] This means that such measures must themselves be compliant with the principles of the Charter (which, *inter alia*, seeks to promote and maintain human rights) and international human rights law as a specialised subset of international law. Notable is the fact that members of the United Nations have undertaken, under Article 55(c) and through the preamble to the UN Charter, to observe human rights and fundamental freedoms for all without distinction as to race, language or religion.

The first more express exception mentioned is the 2003 Declaration of the Security Council meeting with Ministers of Foreign Affairs, adopted under resolution 1456. This resolution deals with the question of compliance with human rights. Paragraph 6 of the Declaration provides that:

> States must ensure that any measure [sic] taken to combat terrorism comply with all their obligations under international law, and should adopt such measures in accordance with international law, in particular international human rights, refugee, and humanitarian law.

---

[16] See, for example, SC Res 1373, UN SCOR, 4293rd mtg, UN Doc S/Res/1317 (2001) (28 September 2001) preambular [5]; SC Res 1438, UN SCOR, 4624th mtg, UN Doc S/Res/1438 (2002) (14 October 2002) preambular [2]; SC Res 1440, UN SCOR, 4632nd mtg, UN Doc S/Res/1140 (2002) (24 October 2002) preambular [2]; SC Res 1450, UN SCOR, 4667th mtg, UN Doc S/Res/1450 (2002) (13 December 2002) preambular [4]; SC Res 1455, UN SCOR, 4686th mtg, UN Doc S/Res/1455 (2003) (17 January 2003) preambular [3]; SC Res 1456, UN SCOR, 4688th mtg, UN Doc S/Res/1456 (2004) (20 January 2003) preambular [8]; SC Res 1535, UN SCOR, 4936th mtg, UN Doc S/Res/1535 (2004) (26 March 2004) preambular [4]; SC Res 1540, UN SCOR, 4956th mtg, UN Doc S/Res/1540 (2004) (24 April 2004) preambular [14]; SC Res 1566, UN SCOR, 5053rd mtg, UN Doc S/Res/1566 (2004) (8 October 2004) preambular [3] and [6]; SC Res 1611, UN SCOR, 5223rd mtg, UN Doc S/Res/1611 (2005) (7 July 2005) preambular [2]; SC Res 1618, UN SCOR, 5246th mtg, UN Doc S/Res/1618 (2005) (4 August 2005) preambular [4]; SC Res 1624, UN SCOR, 5261st mtg, UN Doc S/Res/1624 (2005) (14 September 2005) preambular [2] and operative [1] and [4].

While persuasive in its wording in this regard, the status of the Declaration should be noted. Security Council resolutions, when couched in mandatory language, are binding upon members of the United Nations. In the context of the Declaration adopted under resolution 1456, the text of the Declaration (including the mentioned paragraph 6) is preceded by the sentence: 'The Security Council therefore *calls for* the following steps to be taken.'[17] Such an expression, although influential, is exhortatory and therefore not a binding 'decision' within the contemplation of Article 25 of the Charter.[18]

The second resolution to be considered is, however, both direct and binding in its terms. Security Council resolution 1624 provides, after setting out the obligations of States to counter various aspects of terrorism, that:

> States must ensure that any measures taken to implement paragraphs 1, 2 and 3 of this resolution comply with all of their obligations under international law, in particular international human rights law, refugee law, and humanitarian law.[19]

The latter provision is not preceded by exhortatory language, but instead constitutes a clearly binding decision of the Security Council.

Remaining with the Security Council, mention should be made of the Counter-Terrorism Committee (CTC), which was established under Security Council resolution 1373 of 2001, and is charged with receiving reports from UN member States on their compliance with the counter-terrorist obligations specified within that resolution. In her report and follow-up to the 2001 World Conference on Human Rights, the then United Nations High Commissioner for Human Rights, Mary Robinson, prepared guidelines for the use of the Counter-Terrorism Committee. The Commissioner sought to have the CTC issue these guidelines to States, so that they might be directed in specific and useful terms on how to counter terrorism in a manner consistent with human rights. The Committee ultimately declined to issue the Commissioner's Guidelines, something anticipated from the remarks of the then Chair of the

---

[17] SC Res 1456, UN SCOR, 4688th mtg, UN Doc S/Res/1456 (2003) (20 January 2003) preambular (emphasis added).

[18] In the *Namibia Advisory Opinion*, the International Court of Justice took the position that a resolution couched in non-mandatory language should not be taken as imposing a legal duty upon a member State: *Legal Consequences for States of the Continued Presence of South Africa in Namibia (South-West Africa) notwithstanding Security Council Resolution 276 (1990)* (Advisory Opinion) [1971] ICJ Reports 53 ('*Nambia Advisory Opinion*').

[19] SC Res 1624, UN SCOR, 5261st mtg, UN Doc S/Res/1624 (2005) (14 September 2005) [4].

Counter-Terrorism Committee in his briefing of the Security Council in January 2002:[20]

> The Counter-Terrorism Committee is mandated to monitor the implementation of resolution 1373 (2001). Monitoring performance against other international conventions, including human rights law, is outside the scope of the Counter-Terrorism Committee's mandate. But we will remain aware of the interaction with human rights concerns, and we will keep ourselves briefed as appropriate. It is, of course, open to other organizations to study States' reports and take up their content in other forums.

Since that time, however, there has been a significant shift in the approach of the Counter-Terrorism Committee to the role of human rights in its work.[21] In its comprehensive review report of 16 December 2005, the Committee stated that States must ensure that any measure taken to combat terrorism should comply with all their obligations under international law and that they should adopt such measures in accordance with international law, in particular human rights law, refugee law and humanitarian law.[22] It also stressed that the Counter-Terrorism Committee Executive Directorate should take this into account in the course of its activities.

The same approach is found in statements contained in the CTC's 2008 survey of the implementation of Security Council resolution 1373 (2001), where the Committee stated, for example, that domestic legal frameworks on counter-terrorism should ensure due process of law in the prosecution of terrorists, and protect human rights while countering terrorism as effectively as possible.[23] It is an approach also reflected in the Committee's questions under the reporting dialogue between the CTC and UN member States. In response to New Zealand's fourth report to the CTC, for instance, the Committee asked, 'What is New Zealand doing to ensure that any measures taken to implement paragraphs 1, 2 and 3 of resolution 1624 (2005) comply

---

[20] Sir Jeremy Greenstock, *Threats to International Peace and Security Posed by Terrorism*, 18 January 2002, UN Doc S/PV.4453, 5.

[21] Recognised by the UN Secretary-General in his report entitled *United Nations Global Counter-Terrorism Strategy: Activities of the United Nations system in implementing the Strategy*, UN Doc A/62/898 (2008), para 42. The Committee's website now includes a page dedicated to the subject of human rights, at http://www.un.org/sc/ctc/rights.html.

[22] Counter-Terrorism Committee, *Report of the Counter-Terrorism Committee to the Security Council for its consideration as part of its comprehensive review of the Counter-Terrorism Committee Executive Directorate*, UN Doc S/2005/800 (2005).

[23] *Survey of the implementation of Security Council resolution 1373 (2001): Report of the Counter-Terrorism Committee*, UN Doc S/2008/379 (2008), paras 141 and 143(a).

with all of its obligations under international law, in particular international human rights law, refugee law and humanitarian law?'[24]

### C  UN Human Rights Council and the former Commission on Human Rights

Not surprisingly, the United Nations Commission on Human Rights paid considerable attention to the issue of the adverse consequences that counter-terrorism can have upon the maintenance and promotion of human rights. It did so even before the flurry of anti-terrorist legislation that followed Security Council resolution 1373 (2001). In the pre-9/11 resolutions of the Commission and its Sub-Commission on the Protection and Promotion of Human Rights, it was affirmed that all States have an obligation to promote and protect human rights and fundamental freedoms, and that all measures to counter terrorism must be in strict conformity with international law, 'including international human rights standards.'[25] Post-September 11, resolutions of the Commission became more strongly worded. Two resolutions on the subject were adopted in 2004 alone. First, the issue was addressed within the Commission's annual resolution on human rights and terrorism.[26] In a resolution later that month, the Commission again reaffirmed that States must comply with international human rights obligations when countering terrorism.[27] The Commission's resolution 2005/80, pursuant to which it appointed a Special Rapporteur on the promotion and protection of human rights and fundamental freedoms while countering terrorism, stated at paragraphs 1 and 6 that it:

> *Reaffirms* that States must ensure that any measure taken to combat terrorism complies with their obligations under international law, in particular international human rights, refugee and humanitarian law;

---

[24] New Zealand National Report to the United Nations Security Council Counter-Terrorism Committee, UN Doc S/2006/384 (2006), item 2.6. See also item 2.4 on the report, which reflects the Committee's question: 'What international efforts is New Zealand participating in or considering participating in/initiating in order to enhance dialogue and broaden understanding among civilisations in an effort to prevent the indiscriminate targeting of different religions and cultures?'
[25] *Human Rights and Terrorism*, CHR Res 2001/37, UN Doc E/CN.4/RES/2001/37 (23 March 2001) preambular [18] and [19] and operative [7] and [8]. Preambular [19] was later reflected in *Human Rights and Terrorism*, UN Sub-Commission on Human Rights Res 2001/18, UN Doc E/CN.4/SUB.2/Res/2001/18 (16 August 2001) preambular [13].
[26] *Human Rights and Terrorism*, CHR Res 2004/44, UN Doc E/CN.4/Res/2004/44 (19 April 2004) preambular [24] and operative [10], [11] and [12].
[27] *Protection of human rights and fundamental freedoms while countering terrorism*, CHR Res 2004/87, UN Doc E/CN.4/Res/2004/87 (21 April 2004) [1] and [2].

*Reaffirms* that it is imperative that all States work to uphold and protect the dignity of individuals and their fundamental freedoms, as well as democratic practices and the rule of law, while countering terrorism.

The 2005 report of the Sub-Commission on the Promotion and Protection of Human Rights Special Rapporteur on Terrorism and Human Rights also addressed the matter.[28] Although the original mandate of the Special Rapporteur was to consider the impact of terrorism on human rights,[29] she commented in her 2004 report that a State's over-reaction to terrorism can itself also impact upon human rights. The Sub-Commission Rapporteur's mandate was therefore extended to develop a set of draft principles and guidelines concerning human rights and terrorism (which are discussed further below). Of note at this point, the first-stated principle under the heading 'Duties of States Regarding Terrorist Acts and Human Rights' reads:

All States have a duty to promote and protect human rights of all persons under their political or military control in accordance with all human rights and humanitarian law norms.[30]

The report of the Sub-Commission Rapporteur on terrorism and human rights includes a reasonably basic analysis of issues relating to the protection of human rights while countering terrorism. On the question of permissible limitations, the document adopts a more absolute approach than do the other guidelines, paragraph 34 providing that:

Any exceptions or derogations in human rights law in the context of counter-terrorism measures must be in strict conformity with the rules set out in the applicable international or regional instruments. A State may not institute exceptions or derogations unless that State has been subjected to terrorist acts that would justify such measures. States shall not invoke derogation clauses to justify taking hostages or to impose collective punishments.

---

[28] Kalliopi Koufa, Report of the Special Rapporteur on Terrorism and Human Rights, *Specific Human Rights Issues: New Priorities, in Particular Terrorism and Counter-Terrorism. A Preliminary Framework Draft of Principles and Guidelines Concerning Human Rights and Terrorism*, UN Doc E/CN.4/Sub.2/2005/39 (22 June 2005).
[29] This mandate was consequent to the request of the General Assembly for the Commission to do so and through the Commission's own decision to consider the issue: see respectively *Human Rights and Terrorism*, GA Res 49/185, UN GAOR, 49th sess, 94th plen mtg, UN Doc A/Res/49/185 (23 December 1994) [6]; *Human Rights and Terrorism*, CHR Res 1994/46, UN Doc E/CN.4/Res/1994/46 (4 March 1994).
[30] Koufa, above n 28, [25].

(a) Great care should be taken to ensure that exceptions and derogations that might have been justified because of an act of terrorism meet strict time limits and do not become perpetual features of national law or action.
(b) Great care should be taken to ensure that measures taken are necessary to apprehend actual members of terrorist groups or perpetrators of terrorist acts in a way that does not unduly encroach on the lives and liberties of ordinary persons or on procedural rights of persons charged with non-terrorist crimes.
(c) Exceptions and derogations undertaken following a terrorist incident should be carefully reviewed and monitored. Such measures should be subject to effective legal challenge in the State imposing exceptions or derogations.

Appointed as an independent expert, Dr Robert Goldman of the American University completed a very useful report to the Commission on Human Rights in February 2005. This report also adopts a rights-based approach, and again emphasises the need to uphold the rule of law while confronting terrorism. Dr Goldman stated that, 'Properly viewed, the struggle against terrorism and the protection of human rights are not antithetical, but complementary responsibilities of States.'[31] Consequent to the report, the Commission established a Special Rapporteur to monitor counter-terrorism measures worldwide that might threaten human rights.[32] In September 2005, the Special Rapporteur presented his first preliminary report to the General Assembly, setting out the conceptual framework for his work.[33] His first substantive report to the Commission on Human Rights included consideration of the issue of the human rights implications of the definition of terrorism.[34]

In the year 2006, the Human Rights Council was established by the UN General Assembly under its resolution 60/251 as a subsidiary body of the General Assembly and for the purpose of replacing and enhancing the former Commission on Human Rights.[35] However, it was not until March 2008 that

---

[31] Robert Goldman, *Protection of Human Rights and Fundamental Freedoms While Countering Terrorism*, UN Doc E/CN.4/2005/103 (7 February 2005) [7].

[32] Professor Martin Scheinin of Abo Akademi University in Finland was appointed to the role of Special Rapporteur by the Chairman of the Commission on Human Rights, pursuant to *Protection of human rights and fundamental freedoms while countering terrorism*, CHR Res 2005/80, UN Doc E/CN.4/Res/2005/80 (21 April 2005).

[33] Martin Scheinin, *Report of the Special Rapporteur on the Promotion and Protection of Human Rights and Fundamental Freedoms While Countering Terrorism: Promotion and Protection of Human Rights*, UN Doc A/60/370 (21 September 2005).

[34] Martin Scheinin, *Report of the Special Rapporteur on the Promotion and Protection of Human Rights and Fundamental Freedoms While Countering Terrorism: Promotion and Protection of Human Rights*, UN Doc E/CN.4/2006/98 (28 December 2005) Part III.

[35] GA Res 60/251, UN GAOR, 60th sess, 72nd plen mtg, UN Doc A/Res/60/251 (15 March 2006). See generally on the Council, Chapter 1, pp. 9–18.

the new Human Rights Council adopted a substantive resolution on the question of human rights compliance while countering terrorism. Resolution 7/7 (2008), and its 2009 restatement, do not add anything new to the already existing statements of the General Assembly and the former Commission on Human Rights, although they assist by reaffirming the principle that any measure taken to counter terrorism must comply with international human rights law.[36]

Past and present UN High Commissioners for Human Rights have been vocal in their criticism of counter-terrorism measures that have restricted the enjoyment of rights in an unnecessary or disproportionate way. Mention has already been made of the guidelines prepared by former High Commissioner Mary Robinson, annexed to her 2002 report (the Commissioner's Guidelines).[37] Commissioner Robinson's report begins with an introduction in which she states:

> An effective international strategy to counter terrorism should use human rights as its unifying framework. The suggestion that human rights violations are permissible in certain circumstances is wrong. The essence of human rights is that human life and dignity must not be compromised and that certain acts, whether carried out by State or non-State actors, are never justified no matter what the ends. International human rights and humanitarian law define the boundaries of permissible political and military conduct. A reckless approach towards human life and liberty undermines counter-terrorism measures.

The Commissioner's Guidelines begin by making statements that go to answering an important ideological question: are the objectives of countering terrorism and maintaining human rights compatible? The Guidelines recognise the counter-terrorist obligations imposed upon States by the Security Council and reaffirm that such action must be in compliance with human rights principles contained in international law.[38] They confirm the notion that human rights law allows for a balance to be struck between the unlimited enjoyment of rights and freedoms and legitimate concerns for national security through the limitation of some rights in specific and defined circumstances.[39] At para-

---

[36] HRC Res 7/7, HRC 7th Sess, UN Doc A/HRC/Res/7/7 (20 March 2008), para 1; and HRC Res 10/L.31. HRC 10th Sess, UN Doc A/HRC/Res/10/L.31 (20 March 2009), para 1.

[37] Report of the United Nations High Commissioner for Human Rights and Follow-up to the World Conference on Human Rights, *Human Rights: A Uniting Framework*, ESCOR (58th Sess) UN Doc E/CN.4/2002/18 (2002), Annex entitled 'Proposals for "further guidance" for the submission of reports pursuant to paragraph 6 of Security Council resolution 1373 (2001)'.

[38] Ibid [1].

[39] Ibid [2].

graphs 3 and 4, the Guidelines set out some instructions on how to formulate counter-terrorist measures that might seek to limit human rights:

3. Where this is permitted, the laws authorizing restrictions:
   (a) Should use precise criteria;
   (b) May not confer an unfettered discretion on those charged with their execution.
4. For limitations of rights to be lawful they must:
   (a) Be prescribed by law;
   (b) Be necessary for public safety and public order, i.e. the protection of public health or morals and for the protection of the rights and freedoms of others, and serve a legitimate purpose;
   (c) Not impair the essence of the right;
   (d) Be interpreted strictly in favour of the rights at issue;
   (e) Be necessary in a democratic society;
   (f) Conform to the principle of proportionality;
   (g) Be appropriate to achieve their protective function, and be the least intrusive instrument amongst those which might achieve that protective function;
   (h) Be compatible with the object and purposes of human rights treaties;
   (i) Respect the principle of non-discrimination;
   (j) Not be arbitrarily applied.

Also of relevance, a digest of jurisprudence on the protection of human rights while countering terrorism was prepared by the UN Office of the High Commissioner for Human Rights in September 2003. Its declared aim was to assist policy makers and other concerned parties to develop counter-terrorist strategies that respect human rights. It begins by stating:

> No one doubts that States have legitimate and urgent reasons to take all due measures to eliminate terrorism. Acts and strategies of terrorism aim at the destruction of human rights, democracy, and the rule of law. They destabilize governments and undermine civil society. Governments therefore have not only the right, but also the duty, to protect their nationals and others against terrorist attacks and to bring the perpetrators of such acts to justice. The manner in which counter-terrorism efforts are conducted, however, can have a far-reaching effect on overall respect for human rights.[40]

The digest considers decisions of UN treaty-monitoring bodies, such as the Human Rights Committee, and those of other regional bodies, including the

---

[40] United Nations High Commissioner for Human Rights ('UNHCHR'), *Digest of Jurisprudence of the UN and Regional Organizations on the Protection of Human Rights While Countering Terrorism* (United Nations Office of the High Commissioner for Human Rights, Geneva, 2003) 3. The Office of the UNHCHR is currently working on an updated edition of the Digest.

European Court of Human Rights and the Inter-American Court of Human Rights. It looks at general considerations, states of emergency and specific rights. On the subject of general considerations, two types of jurisprudence are relevant here. The first is that which emphasises the duty of States to protect those within their territories from terrorism.[41] The second is concerned with the fact that the lawfulness of counter-terrorism measures depends upon their conformity with international human rights law.[42]

### D  Other international guidelines and documents

Numerous international guidelines and reports on the relationship between human rights and counter-terrorism have been issued since the events of September 11 and the proliferation of counter-terrorist legislative action that followed. Unlike Security Council decisions, such guidelines and reports are clearly not binding. Nor do they hold the same status as General Assembly or Commission on Human Rights resolutions, which have been adopted with the consent of State representatives. Notwithstanding this, the consistent approach of these guidelines is telling.

As part of its series of occasional papers, the International Commission of Jurists commissioned a paper on terrorism and human rights in 2002.[43] The paper concluded with a list of minimum criteria that States must observe in the administration of justice when countering terrorism, including the observance of the primacy of the rule of law and of international human rights obligations, and maintaining and guaranteeing at all times rights and freedoms that are non-derogable.[44] Moreover, at its biennial conference in August 2004, the International Commission of Jurists was instrumental in the adoption of the Berlin Declaration on Upholding Human Rights and the Rule of Law in Combating Terrorism.[45] The Berlin Declaration recognises the need to combat terrorism and the duty of States to protect those within their jurisdiction.[46] It also affirms that contemporary human rights law allows States a reasonably wide margin of flexibility to combat terrorism without contravening the essence of rights.[47]

---

[41]  Ibid 11–12. See, for example, *Delgado Paez v Colombia*, UN Doc CCPR/C/39/D/195/1985 (12 July 1990) [5.5].

[42]  UNHCHR, above n 40, 13–15.

[43]  International Commission of Jurists, *Terrorism and Human Rights* (International Commission of Jurists, Geneva, 2002).

[44]  Ibid 248–51.

[45]  International Commission of Jurists, *Berlin Declaration on Upholding Human Rights and the Rule of Law in Combating Terrorism*, International Commission of Jurists, http://www.icj.org/IMG/pdf/Berlin_Declaration.pdf at 24 June 2008.

[46]  Ibid preambular [2] and operative [1].

[47]  Ibid preambular [5].

The ICJ also established an Eminent Jurists Panel on Terrorism, Counter-terrorism and Human Rights, which was composed of eight distinguished jurists from throughout the world. The Panel undertook 16 hearings in Argentina, Australia, Belgium, Canada, Colombia, Egypt, India, Indonesia, Israel, Kenya, Morocco, Northern Ireland, Pakistan, the Russian Federation, the United Kingdom, and the United States of America. In early 2009 it released its report *Assessing Damage, Urging Action*, which draws from its hearings and considers the role of intelligence in counter-terrorism and preventive measures such as control orders.[48]

In July 2002, the Committee of Ministers to the Council of Europe issued *Guidelines on human rights and the fight against terrorism*. In the preface to the guidelines, Secretary-General Walter Schwimmer warned that, although the suppression of terrorism is an important objective, States must not use indiscriminate measures to achieve that objective.[49] For a State to react in such a way, Schwimmer said, would be to fall into the trap set by terrorists for democracy and the rule of law. He urged that situations of crisis, such as those brought about by terrorism, called for even greater vigilance in ensuring respect for human rights. Drawing from the jurisprudence of the European Court of Human Rights and the UN Human Rights Committee, the Council's guidelines set out general rules on the interaction between counter-terrorism and human rights, as well as addressing specific rights and freedoms, with commentary on each stated guideline. Five of the more specific guidelines warrant mention.

The first reflects the idea that counter-terrorism is an important objective in a free and democratic society. Guideline I accordingly talks of a positive obligation upon States to protect individuals within their territory from the scourges of terrorism, pointing to decisions of the European Court in which it recognised this duty and the particular problems associated with the prevention and suppression of terrorism.[50] In *Klass v Germany*, for example, the

---

[48] Report of the Eminent Jurists Panel on Terrorism, Counter-terrorism and Human Rights, Assessing Damage, Urging Action (International Commission of Jurists, Geneva, 2009).

[49] Council of Europe, *Guidelines on Human Rights and the Fight Against Terrorism* (Council of Europe Publishing, Strasbourg, 2002) 5.

[50] See, for example, *Ireland v The United Kingdom*, ECHR, Application No 5310/71 (18 January 1978) [11]; *Aksoy v Turkey*, ECHR, Application No 21987/93 (18 December 1996) [70] and [84]; *Zana v Turkey*, ECHR, Application No 18954/91 (25 November 1997) [59] and [60]; *Incal v Turkey*, ECHR, Application No 22678/93 (9 June 1998) [58]; *United Communist Party of Turkey and Others v Turkey*, ECHR, Application No 19392/92 (20 November 1998) [59]; *Brogan and Others v The United Kingdom*, ECHR, Application No 11209/84; 11234/84; 11266/84; 11386/85 (29 November 1999) [48].

Court agreed with the European Commission that 'some compromise between the requirements for defending democratic society and individual rights is inherent in the system of the Convention.'[51]

The second and third Guidelines of the Council are directly relevant to the question of compliance with human rights. Guideline II prohibits the arbitrary limitation of rights,[52] and Guideline III requires limiting measures to be lawful, precise, necessary and proportional:[53]

*Guideline II*
All measures taken by States to fight terrorism must respect human rights and the principle of the rule of law, while excluding any form of arbitrariness, as well as any discriminatory or racist treatment, and must be subject to appropriate supervision.

*Guideline III*
1. All measures taken by States to combat terrorism must be lawful.
2. When a measure restricts human rights, restrictions must be defined as precisely as possible and be necessary and proportionate to the aim pursued.

Further guidance on possible derogations is found in Guideline XV, concerning derogations during situations of war or states of emergency threatening the life of a nation. Finally, Guideline XVI underlines that States may never act in breach of peremptory norms of international law.

A report of the Inter-American Commission on Human Rights (IACHR) on terrorism and human rights was issued in late 2002, shortly after the adoption of the *Inter-American Convention Against Terrorism*.[54] Article 15 of the latter Convention specifically requires all States parties to comply with human rights standards:

---

[51] *Klass and Others v Germany*, ECHR, Application No 5029/71 (6 September 1978) [59].

[52] Compare Article II with [3] and [4(i)]–[4(j)] of Guidelines issued by the UNHCHR: Report of the United Nations High Commissioner for Human Rights and Follow-up to the World Conference on Human Rights, *Human Rights: A Uniting Framework*, ESCOR, 58th Sess, UN Doc E/CN.4/2002/18 (27 June 2002) Annex entitled *Proposals for 'further guidance' for the submission of reports pursuant to paragraph 6 of Security Council Resolution 1373 (2001), Compliance with international human rights standards*, I General Guidance: Criteria for the Balancing of Human Rights Protection and the Combating of Terrorism.

[53] Compare Article III with [4(a)], [4(b)], [4(e)], [4(f)], and [4(g)] of the Commissioner's Guidelines: ibid.

[54] Inter-American Commission on Human Rights, *Report on Terrorism and Human Rights* (Inter-American Commission on Human Rights, 2002), http://www.cidh.org/Terrorism/Eng/toc.htm at 6 September 2005. See also Inter-American Commission on Human Rights, Recommendations of the Inter-American Commission on Human Rights for the Protection by OAS Member States of Human Rights in the Fight Against Terrorism (Washington, 8 May 2006).

The measures carried out by the states parties under this Convention shall take place with full respect for the rule of law, human rights, and fundamental freedoms.[55]

The IACHR report undertakes a rights-based approach, focusing upon the scope and potential limitation of particular rights. It also emphasises the general need for any limitation to comply with the doctrines of necessity, proportionality and non-discrimination.[56] As one of its annexes, the report recalls resolution 1906 of the General Assembly of the Organization of American States, the first operative paragraphs resolving:

1. To reiterate that the fight against terrorism must be waged with full respect for the law, human rights, and democratic institutions, so as to preserve the rule of law, freedoms, and democratic values in the Hemisphere.
2. To reaffirm the duty of the member states to ensure that all measures taken to combat terrorism are in keeping with obligations under international law.[57]

Although outside the scope of guidelines on the specific subject of counter-terrorism and human rights, attention is also paid to two generally applicable and very useful documents on the subject of human rights limitations: the *Siracusa Principles on the Limitation and Derogation of Provisions in the International Covenant on Civil and Political Rights*;[58] and General Comment 29 of the Human Rights Committee.[59] The latter document is particularly instructive since none of the States parties to the International Covenant on Civil and Political Rights ('ICCPR') have lodged any objection to General Comment 29 under Article 40(5) ICCPR. One might argue that the document has thereby gained the status of representing subsequent practice in the application of the ICCPR, which establishes the agreement of the parties regarding its interpretation.[60]

## 2 What does human rights compliance involve?

The discussion up to this point leads to an unambiguous conclusion that States

---

[55] *Inter-American Convention against Terrorism*, opened for signature 3 June 2002, 42 ILM 19 (entered into force 10 July 2003) Article 15.
[56] Ibid [51] and [55].
[57] *Human Rights and Terrorism*, OAS General Assembly Resolution 1906, 4th plen sess, OAS Doc AG/Res 1906 (XXXII-O/02) (4 June 2002).
[58] United Nations Economic and Social Council Sub-Commission on Prevention of Discrimination and Protection of Minorities, *Siracusa Principles on the Limitation and Derogation of Provisions in the International Covenant on Civil and Political Rights*, UN Doc E/CN.4/1985/4 (1985) ('*Siracusa Principles*').
[59] Human Rights Committee, *General Comment 29/2001: States of Emergency (Article 4)*, UN Doc CCPR/C/21/Rev.1/Add.11 (31 August 2001).
[60] See *Vienna Convention on the Law of Treaties*, above n 9, Article 31(3).

must comply with their international human rights obligations when countering terrorism. The United Nations has made it clear, through resolutions of three of its principal bodies, that counter-terrorism is not a motive that justifies overriding those obligations. This position can sometimes lead to an adverse reaction on the part of counter-terrorist practitioners, claiming that counter-terrorism cannot be effectively achieved without the limitation of human rights, at which point it is important to consider what 'compliance' with human rights means. It does not mean that all human rights cannot be limited, since human rights law does contain a level of flexibility which is aimed at accommodating challenges such as those posed by counter-terrorism.

The first step in applying this in practice is to identify the nature of the right upon which a proposed, or actual, counter-terrorist provision or measure impacts. Under the international human rights framework, rights are universal and indivisible. Although there is no heirarchy of rights and freedoms, human rights norms and treaty provisions can be categorised as: (a) peremptory rights at customary international law (in respect of which no limitation is permissible); (b) non-derogable rights under human rights treaties (in respect of which no derogation is permissible); (c) rights only derogable in states of emergency (which may only be limited in times of an emergency threatening the life of the nation); or (d) other rights (which, depending on their definition, may be limited when necessary so long as this is proportionate).

### A  Peremptory rights at customary international law

In determining what human rights compliance means, the first important point to be made is that there is a distinction to be made between rights that are capable of limitation and those that are not. The isolation of particular rights into the category of peremptory norms (those in respect of which no limitation is permitted) is an issue that this chapter cannot delve into too deeply. Least controversial is the status of the prohibition against torture (the commission of which is also an international crime) as falling within this category.[61] The International Law Commission has identified this, together with the prohibition against slavery, as a norm of *jus cogens*.[62] The Committee on the Elimination of Racial Discrimination has said that the principle of non-discrimination on the grounds of race has also become a norm of *jus cogens*.[63]

---

[61] International Law Commission, 'Commentary on the *Vienna Convention on the Law of Treaties*' [1966] 2 *Yearbook of the International Law Commission* 248.
[62] Ibid.
[63] Committee on the Elimination of Racial Discrimination, 'Statement on Racial Discrimination and Measures to Combat Terrorism' in *Report of the Committee on the Elimination of Racial Discrimination*, UN Doc A/57/18 (4–22 March 2002, 5–23 August 2002) 107.

## B  Non-derogable rights under human rights treaties

The distinction between peremptory rights at customary international law and non-derogable rights under applicable human rights treaties is a fine, but important, one.[64] In the case of the ICCPR, Article 4(2) sets out a list of rights that may not be derogated from even when a public emergency is declared by a State party to the Covenant. These non-derogable rights are identified in the ICCPR as the right to life, freedom from torture or cruel, inhuman or degrading treatment or punishment, the prohibition against slavery and servitude, freedom from imprisonment for failure to fulfil a contract, freedom from retrospective penalties, the right to be recognised as a person before the law, and freedom of thought, conscience and religion.[65] Article 4(1) ICCPR requires that any derogating measures must not be inconsistent with a State's other international law obligations, and must not involve discrimination solely on the ground of race, colour, sex, language, religion or social origin.

*(i)  The list of non-derogable rights*   As just mentioned, Article 4(2) ICCPR sets out a list of rights that may not be derogated from, even during a state of emergency. This list is not, however, exhaustive. The Human Rights Committee has made the point that provisions of the ICCPR relating to procedural safeguards can never be made subject to measures that would circumvent the protection of these non-derogable rights.[66]

The Committee has also pointed out that, because Article 4(1) ICCPR specifies that any derogating measures must not be inconsistent with obligations under international law, the full complement of 'non-derogable rights' includes rights applicable as part of obligations under international human rights law, international humanitarian law, and international criminal law.[67] Expanding upon this position, the Committee identified certain rights under customary international law (applicable to all States) as being non-derogable: the right of all persons deprived of their liberty to be treated with humanity and with respect for the inherent dignity of the human person; the prohibitions against taking of hostages, abductions or unacknowledged detention; the international protection of the rights of persons belonging to minorities; the prohibition against deportation or forcible transfer of population without grounds permitted under international law; and the prohibition against propaganda for

---

[64]  See Human Rights Committee, above n 59, [11].
[65]  *International Covenant on Civil and Political Rights*, opened for signature 16 December 1966, 999 UNTS 14668 (entered into force 23 March 1976) Articles 6, 7, 8(1) and (2), 11, 15, 16, and 18 respectively.
[66]  Human Rights Committee, above n 59, [15].
[67]  Ibid [9] and [10].

war, or in advocacy of national, racial or religious hatred that would constitute incitement to discrimination, hostility or violence.[68]

*(ii) The limitation of non-derogable rights* The status of a substantive right as non-derogable does not mean that limitations or restrictions upon such a right cannot be justified. In its General Comment 29, the Human Rights Committee makes this point and gives the example of the freedom to manifest one's religion or beliefs, expressed in Article 18 ICCPR.[69] Article 18 ICCPR is listed within Article 4(2) ICCPR and therefore cannot be derogated from under the Article 4 ICCPR procedure. This listing does not, however, remove the permissible limitation upon the right expressed within Article 18(3) ICCPR (such limitations as are prescribed by law and are necessary to protect public safety, order, health, or morals or the fundamental rights and freedoms of others). Thus, whereas a peremptory right may not be the subject of any limitation at all, a non-derogable treaty right may be capable of limitation depending on the particular expression of the right. Such a limitation must, however, be proportional to the exigencies of the situation.[70]

## C  Rights derogable only in states of emergency

The third category of rights are those that are only derogable in times of emergency threatening the life of the nation.[71] By way of illustration, Article 4 ICCPR provides:

> In time of public emergency which threatens the life of the nation and the existence of which is officially proclaimed, the States Parties to the present Covenant may take measures derogating from their obligations under the present Covenant to the extent strictly required by the exigencies of the situation, provided that such measures are not inconsistent with their other obligations under international law and do not involve discrimination solely on the ground of race, colour, sex, language, religion or social origin.

Assuming that such a state of emergency exists, and that the right in question is one that can be derogated from, four requirements must be noted:

---

[68] Ibid [13].

[69] Human Rights Committee, above n 59, [7]; see also [11].

[70] See the international guidelines discussed earlier, and Human Rights Committee, above n 59, [4] and [5].

[71] See Article 4 ICCPR; *European Convention for the Protection of Human Rights and Fundamental Freedoms*, opened for signature 4 November 1950, 213 UNTS 222 (entered into force 3 September 1953) Article 15; *American Convention on Human Rights*, opened for signature 22 November 1969, 1144 UNTS 123 (entered into force 18 July 1978) Article 27(1).

*(i) Determining the existence of a public emergency* The ability to derogate under Article 4(1) ICCPR is triggered only in a 'time of public emergency which threatens the life of the nation.' The Human Rights Committee has characterised such an emergency as being of an exceptional nature.[72] Not every disturbance or catastrophe qualifies as such. The Committee has commented that, even during an armed conflict, measures derogating from the ICCPR are allowed only if and to the extent that the situation constitutes a threat to the life of the nation.[73] Whether or not terrorist acts or threats establish such a state of emergency must therefore be assessed on a case-by-case basis.

Interpreting the comparable derogation provision within the *European Convention for the Protection of Human Rights and Fundamental Freedoms*,[74] the European Court of Human Rights has spoken of four criteria to establish that any given situation amounts to a 'time of public emergency which threatens the life of the nation.'[75] First, it should be a crisis or emergency that is actual or imminent. Secondly, it must be exceptional, such that 'normal' measures are inadequate. Next, the emergency must threaten the continuance of the organised life of the community. Finally, it must affect the population of the State taking measures. On this final point, early decisions of the Court spoke of an emergency needing to affect the whole population. The Court appears to have subsequently accepted that an emergency threatening the life of the nation might only materially affect one part of the nation at the time of the emergency.[76]

Outside the immediate aftermath of a terrorist attack, or in the situation where clear intelligence exists of an imminent threat of a terrorist act, it is debatable whether a continual state of emergency caused by the threat of terrorism can exist for the purpose of these derogating provisions.[77]

---

[72] Human Rights Committee, above n 59, [2].
[73] Ibid [3].
[74] *European Convention for the Protection of Rights and Fundamental Freedoms*, opened for signature 4 November 1950, 213 UNTS 222 (entered into force 3 September 1953).
[75] See *Lawless v Ireland (No 3)*, ECHR, Application No 332/57 (1 July 1961) [28]; and *The Greek Case* [1969] 12 *Yearbook of the European Court of Human Rights* 1, [153].
[76] *Brannigan and McBride v United Kingdom*, ECHR, Application No 14553/89; 14554/89 (25 May 1993), although contrast this with the dissenting opinion of Judge Walsh, [2].
[77] See, generally, the *Siracusa Principles*, above n 58, [39]–[41]. In the context of states of emergency said to be caused by the threat of terrorism (under the framework of the ICCPR) see Human Rights Committee, *Concluding Observations of the Human Rights Committee: United Kingdom of Great Britain and Northern Ireland*, UN

Ultimately, however, this will normally involve a factual question calling for consideration of the particular circumstances at hand.

*(ii) Proclamation and notice of a state of emergency* Upon establishing that an emergency exists, a proclamation of derogation must be lodged in accordance with the requirements of the particular treaty.[78] In the case of the ICCPR a State party must, before it can implement any derogating measure(s), officially proclaim the existence within its territory of a public emergency which threatens the life of the nation.[79] Through the intermediary of the UN Secretary-General, a derogating State must also immediately inform other States parties to the ICCPR of the provisions from which it has derogated and of the reasons for which it has done so.[80] The Human Rights Committee has emphasised that notification should include full information about the measures taken and a clear explanation of the reasons for them, with full documentation attached concerning the relevant law.[81] A further communication is required on the date on which the State terminates such derogation.[82] In practice, very few States have declared a state of emergency in relation to acts of terrorism.

*(iii) Review* Linked to the first requirement that the situation within the derogating State must amount to a public emergency threatening the life of the nation, it will be important for the derogating State to continually review the situation faced by it to ensure that the derogation lasts only as long as the state of emergency exists. In the context of the ICCPR derogations provisions, the Human Rights Committee has repeatedly stated that measures under Article 4 ICCPR must be of an exceptional and temporary nature, and may only continue only as long as the life of the nation concerned is threatened.[83] The restoration of a state of normality where full respect for the ICCPR can again

---

Doc CCPR/C/79/Add.18 (1993) [25]; and *Concluding Observations of the Human Rights Committee: Israel*, UN Doc CCPR/C/79/Add.93 (1998) [11]. See also Alex Conte, 'A Clash of Wills: Counter-Terrorism and Human Rights' (2003) 20 *New Zealand Universities Law Review* 338, 350–54; and James Oraa, *Human Rights in States of Emergency in International Law* (Clarendon Press, Oxford, 1992).

[78] As an example, see Article 4(3) ICCPR. See, in that regard, Human Rights Committee, above n 59, paras 2 and 17. See also the *Siracusa Principles*, above n 58, paras [42]–[47].

[79] Article 4(1) ICCPR.

[80] Article 4(3) ICCPR.

[81] Human Rights Committee, above n 59, [5], [16] and [17].

[82] Article 4(3) ICCPR.

[83] Human Rights Committee, above n 59, [2]; and the *Siracusa Principles*, above n 58, [48]–[50].

be secured, the Human Rights Committee has said, must be the predominant objective of a State party derogating from the ICCPR.[84]

*(iv) Permissible extent of derogating measures*   Finally, the extent to which any right is derogated from must be limited 'to the extent strictly required by the exigencies of the situation.' Any derogating measure must therefore be both necessary and proportionate.[85] The General Assembly, in its 2004 and 2005 resolutions on the protection of fundamental freedoms and human rights while countering terrorism, has also reaffirmed that any derogating measures are to be of an exceptional and temporary nature.[86]

## D   Other rights

The final category of rights are those that are not peremptory, non-derogable, or subject to limitation only in states of emergency. The Human Rights Committee has acknowledged, in this regard, that the limitation of rights is allowed even in 'normal times' under various provisions of the ICCPR.[87] The permissible scope of the limitation of such rights will primarily depend upon their expression within the human rights treaty. This will give rise to two possible means of limitation: (1) by a definitional mechanism; and/or (2) by a rights-specific limitations clause.

Definitional limitations are ones that fall within the meaning of the words contained in the expression of the right itself. For example, the right to a fair and open hearing does not provide a person with the right to a hearing which favours the person in all respects. Rather, it only guarantees that a person be afforded a hearing which is both open and 'fair'.[88] A counter-terrorist measure

---

[84]   Ibid [1] and [2].
[85]   See the international guidelines discussed earlier. The Human Rights Committee has also emphasised that any derogation must be shown to be required by, and proportionate to, the exigencies of the situation: Human Rights Committee, above n 59, [4] and [5]. When considering States parties' reports the Committee has expressed concern over insufficient attention being paid to the principle of proportionality: see, for example, *Concluding Observations of the Human Rights Committee: Israel*, above n 77, [11]. See also the *Siracusa Principles*, above n 58, [51].
[86]   *Protection of human rights and fundamental freedoms while countering terrorism*, GA Res 59/191, UN GAOR, 59th sess, 74th plen mtg, UN Doc A/Res/59/191 (20 December 2004) [2]; and *Protection of human rights and fundamental freedoms while countering terrorism*, GA Res 60/158, 60th sess, 64th plen mtg, UN Doc A/Res/60/158 (16 December 2005) [3]. See also *Protection of human rights and fundamental freedoms while countering terrorism*, CHR Res 2005/80, UN Doc E/CN.4/Res/2005/80 (21 April 2005) [3].
[87]   Human Rights Committee, above n 59.
[88]   See, for example, Article 14(1) ICCPR, which provides that 'All persons shall be equal before the courts and tribunals. In the determination of any criminal charge

imposing limitations upon the disclosure of information, based upon the need to protect classified security information, might for example be 'fair' if the person's counsel (with appropriate security clearance) is permitted access to the information.[89]

Rights-specific limitations are those that are authorised by a subsequent provision concerning the circumstances in which the right in question may be limited. In the context of the ICCPR, and again using the example of the right to a fair and open hearing, the first two sentences of Article 14(1) express the substance of the right (as just discussed). The next sentence then sets out the circumstances in which it is permissible to limit the right to an 'open' hearing, allowing the exclusion of the press for reasons of morals, public order, or national security.[90]

### E  Human rights compliance

The nature of human rights compliance is fairly complex and relies on fine, but important, distinctions being made between categories of rights. What is important to note is that, other than in the case of peremptory rights at customary international law and a limited number of 'non-derogable' rights, the human rights law framework incorporates a level of flexibility which is capable of dealing with exigencies such as national security and threats of terrorism. This may be through the interpretation of terms such as 'fair' and 'reasonable', or by application of rights-specific limitation provisions. Even in the case of non-derogable rights, some of those rights are themselves expressed in ways which allow accommodation to pressing needs in a democratic society. Recourse to derogations under mechanisms such as that under Article 4 ICCPR should therefore be rarely needed, hence the tight restrictions applicable to the derogations regime.

---

against him, or of his rights and obligations in a suit at law, everyone shall be entitled to a *fair* and public hearing by a competent, independent and impartial tribunal established by law' (emphasis added).

[89]  This is the means by which classified information is protected in judicial proceedings by the United Kingdom, through its *Special Immigration Appeals Commission Act 1997* (UK). In a judgment considering a decision made using this mechanism, the House of Lords implicitly accepted the validity of such a limitation: see *Secretary of State for the Home Department v Rehman* [2001] UKHL 47, [62] (Lord Hoffmann).

[90]  The third sentence of Article 14(1) ICCPR provides: 'The press and the public may be excluded from all or part of a trial for reasons of morals, public order (ordre public) or national security in a democratic society, or when the interest of the private lives of the parties so requires, or to the extent strictly necessary in the opinion of the court in special circumstances where publicity would prejudice the interests of justice; but any judgement rendered in a criminal case or in a suit at law shall be made public except where the interest of juvenile persons otherwise requires or the proceedings concern matrimonial disputes or the guardianship of children.'

## 3 Establishing counter-terrorist measures by proper means

The second step in determining the practical compliance with human rights while countering terrorism concerns the means by which the counter-terrorist provision, or the authority for the counter-terrorist measure, is established: by a prescription of law; respecting the principle of non-discrimination; not conferring an unfettered discretion; and limited to countering terrorism.

### A  Prescription by law

It is no accident that the former Commissioner's Guidelines used the term 'prescribed by law', this having been subject to examination by both domestic and international courts and tribunals, with clear pronouncements on its meaning. The expression was considered, for example, by the European Court of Human Rights in the *Sunday Times* case of 1978 where the Court concluded that two requirements flowed from it: (1) that the law must be adequately accessible so that the citizen has an adequate indication of how the law limits his or her rights; and (2) that the law must be formulated with sufficient precision so that the citizen can regulate his or her conduct.[91] This test was later reaffirmed by the European Court in the case of *Silver v UK*.[92] The same language is found in the Commissioner's Guidelines, the guidelines of the Council of Europe and the report of the Inter-American Commission on Human Rights.[93] It is likewise reflected in the Human Rights Committee's General Comment 29 and the *Siracusa Principles*.[94] It is notable that, in the particular context of the criminalisation of conduct in pursuit of counter-terrorism, the Special Rapporteur on human rights and counter-terrorism has commented upon the proper characterisation of 'terrorism' and definitional requirements of such proscription.[95]

### B  Non-discrimination and equality before the law

Although not expressly dealt with by the European Court of Human Rights in determining what is 'prescribed by law', it should be remembered that any

---

[91]  *Sunday Times v United Kingdom* (1978) 58 ILR 491, 524–7.
[92]  *Silver v The United Kingdom*, ECHR, Application No 5947/72; 6205/73; 7052/75; 7061/75; 7107/75; 7113/75; 7136/75 (25 March 1983).
[93]  See: the Commissioner's Guidelines, above n 37, [3(a)] and [4(a)]; Council of Europe Guidelines, above n 49, Guideline III; Inter-American Commission on Human Rights report, above n 54, [53].
[94]  Human Rights Council, above n 59, [16]; *Siracusa Principles*, above n 58, [15] and [17].
[95]  For a detailed discussion of this, see Alex Conte, *Counter-Terrorism and Human Rights in New Zealand* (New Zealand Law Foundation, Wellington, 2007) Ch 16. An electronic copy of this text is available online at http://www.lawfoundation.org.nz/awards/irf/conte/index.html at 16 August 2008.

legal prescription, to comply with the rule of law, must also respect the principle of non-discrimination and equality before the law.[96] Similarly, the Commissioner's Guidelines at [4] demand that any limitation respect the principle of non-discrimination, as does General Comment 29 of the Human Rights Committee.[97] It is relevant to note that Article 4 ICCPR provides that any derogation of rights in time of emergency may not involve discrimination solely on the ground of race, colour, sex, language, religion or social origin.[98] It is also significant that recent resolutions of the General Assembly and the Commission on Human Rights have stressed that the enjoyment of rights must be without distinction upon such grounds, and that the Committee on the Elimination of Racial Discrimination has declared that the prohibition against racial discrimination is a peremptory norm of international law from which no derogation is permitted.[99]

### C Scope of the prescription

The final aspects of procedural requirements concern the scope of the prescription by which a counter-terrorism measure is established. First, one must consider the conferral of any discretion by the prescription. This in turn brings two matters into consideration. Primarily, any law authorising a restriction upon rights and freedoms must not confer an unfettered discretion on those charged with its execution. This goes for the framing of the discretion. Secondly, any discretion must not be arbitrarily applied. Both requirements call for the imposition of adequate safeguards to ensure that the discretion is capable of being checked, with appropriate mechanisms to deal with any abuse or arbitrary application of the discretion. These two restrictions on the conferral of discretions are reflected within the former Commissioner's guidelines and those of the Council of Europe, as well as the *Siracusa Principles*.[100]

---

[96] Consider Albert Venn Dicey's notion of the rule of law, requiring: (1) the regulation of government action, so that the government can only act as authorised by the law, having the consequence that one can only be punished or interfered with pursuant to the law; (2) the equality of all persons before the law (which is the context in which the rule of law is referred to in this article); and (3) the requirement of procedural and formal justice. See Albert Venn Dicey, *Introduction to the Study of the Law of the Constitution* (Macmillan, London, 1885) 175–84.

[97] Human Rights Council, above n 59, [8] and [16].

[98] Article 4(1) ICCPR. See also Article 26 ICCPR.

[99] See *Protection of human rights and fundamental freedoms while countering terrorism*, GA Res 59/191, UN GAOR, 59th sess, 74th plen mtg, UN Doc A/Res/59/191 (20 December 2004) preambular [12]; *Protection of human rights and fundamental freedoms while countering terrorism*, CHR Res 2005/80, UN Doc E/CN.4/Res/2005/80 (21 April 2005) preambular [15]; and Committee on the Elimination of Racial Discrimination, above n 63, 107.

[100] See Commissioner's Guidelines, above n 37, [3(b)] and [3(j)]; Council of

It is also necessary to consider the potential scope of application of any counter-terrorist prescription or authorising provision. The point to be made here is that the objective of countering terrorism must not be used as an excuse by the State to broaden its powers in such a way that those powers are applicable to other matters. This is something expressly dealt with by both the Commission and Sub-Commission Special Rapporteurs.[101] It is also reflected within the guidelines advocated by both the Committee of Ministers to the Council of Europe and the Inter-American Commission on Human Rights, each directing that where measures taken by States to combat terrorism restrict human rights, those restrictions must be defined as precisely as possible and be necessary for the objective of countering terrorism.[102] Application of this principle, posits the author, is relevant at both the creation and the application of the prescription. In other words, the State must ensure that legislative prescriptions enacted for the purpose of countering terrorism do just that, and no more. Secondly, such measures must only be applied for the purpose of countering terrorism, rather than being 'stretched' to fit other objectives of the State. As stated in the latest *Draft of Principles and Guidelines* within the report of the Special Rapporteur to the Sub-Commission on the Promotion and Protection of Human Rights:

> Counter-terrorism measures should directly relate to terrorism and terrorist acts, *not* actions undertaken in armed conflict situations or *acts that are ordinary crimes.*[103]

## 4 Conclusion

The era of global jihadism, together with the threat of non-conventional terrorism and the need for universal and effective implementation of the international framework on counter-terrorism, has brought with it public pressure for adequate security laws and a consequent proliferation of counter-terrorist legislation and policies. The manner in which some counter-terrorist legislation and policies have developed has in turn seen a growing concern from both non-governmental and inter-governmental agencies about the need to ensure protection of human rights when seeking to combat terrorism. The aim of this

---

Europe Guidelines, above n 49, Guideline II; *Siracusa Principles*, above n 58, [16] and [18].

[101] Special Rapporteur's report, above n 33, [47]; and Sub-Commission Rapporteur's report, above n 28, [33].

[102] See Council of Europe Guidelines, above n 49, Guideline III(2); the Inter-American Commission on Human Rights report, above n 54, [51] and [55]; *Siracusa Principles*, above n 58, [17].

[103] Koufa, above n 28, [33] (emphasis added).

chapter has been to assess the various international and regional directions and guidelines on the subject and draw from these a workable set of considerations to be taken into account when attempting to determine the balance to be struck between counter-terrorism and the unlimited enjoyment of human rights.

# 21. Human rights education: a slogan in search of a definition[1]

*Paula Gerber*

The term 'human rights education' is too often used in a way that greatly oversimplifies its connotations.[2]

## 1 Introduction

In recent times human rights education ('HRE') has become one of the hot topics in international human rights law and numerous books have been written exploring different aspects of HRE.[3] This new-found interest in HRE is no doubt due, in part, to the United Nations' endeavours to promote HRE through initiatives such as the UN Decade for Human Rights Education (1995–2004)[4] and the subsequent World Programme for Human Rights Education (2005–ongoing).[5] Despite these efforts, there is still a great deal of

---

[1] Parts of this chapter have been previously published as Chapter 3 in Paula Gerber, *From Convention to Classroom: The Long Road to Human Rights Education* (VDM Publishers, Germany, 2008). My title is a play on Hillary Clinton's infamous statement that '[c]hildren's rights' is a slogan in search of definition': Hillary Rodham, 'Children Under the Law' (1973) 43 *Harvard Educational Review* 1.

[2] Committee on the Rights of the Child, *General Comment 1: The Aims of Education*, UN Doc CRC/GC/2001/1 (17 April 2001) ('*General Comment 1*') [19].

[3] See for example Gudmundur Alfredsson, 'The Right to Human Rights Education' in A Eide, C Krause and A Rosas (eds) *Economic, Social and Cultural Rights: A Textbook* (Kluwer Law International, The Hague, 2nd rev ed, 2001) Ch 15; Amnesty International, *First Steps: A Manual for Starting Human Rights Education* (Amnesty International, London, 1997); George Andreopoulos and Richard Pierre Claude (eds) *Human Rights Education for the Twenty-First Century* (University of Pennsylvania Press, Philadelphia, 1997); Ximena Erazo, Michael Kirkwood and Frederick de Vlaming (eds) *Academic Freedom 4: Education and Human Rights* (World University Service, London, 1996); Rolf Gollob, Edward Huddleston, Peter Krapf, Maria-Helena Salema and Vedrana Spajic-Vrkaš, *Tool on Teacher Training for Education for Democratic Citizenship and Human Rights Education* (Council of Europe, Strasbourg, 2004); Anja Mihr, *Human Rights Education: Methods, Institutions, Culture and Evaluation* (Institut für Politikwissenschaft, Magdeburg, 2004).

[4] *United Nations Decade for Human Rights Education*, GA Res 49/184, UN GAOR, 49th sess, 94th plen mtg, UN Doc A/RES/49/184 (23 December 1994).

[5] *World Programme for Human Rights Education*, GA Res 19/113B, UN GAOR, 59th sess, 113th plen mtg, UN Doc A/RES/59/113B (5 August 2005).

confusion and uncertainty as to what the term 'human rights education' actually means.

The phrase 'human rights education' is infinitely more complex than one might initially think. The combination of these three words conveys different meanings to different people. Why is this so? There appear to be two main reasons. The first is that the position and background of the person interpreting the words influences how the words are understood. UN diplomats and international lawyers tend to view the phrase in political or legalistic terms, while non-government organisations ('NGOs') consider the words in the context of human rights activism. Governments tend to have a narrower focus, concentrating on issues such as democracy and the rights and responsibilities of citizens, while NGOs tend to take a broader approach that incorporates the full gamut of human rights including economic, social and cultural rights ('ESC rights'). Teachers, on the other hand, are focused on inculcating students with ideals such as respect and tolerance, and many teachers see HRE as being interchangeable with moral education or the teaching of ethics. Thus a person's understanding of HRE is very much informed by their institutional allegiances, as well as their own background, experience and bias.

The second reason behind the lack of a common understanding of the term HRE is the vagueness of the words themselves; what are human rights? How do they differ from natural rights and/or civil rights? Is there a universal understanding of what constitutes human rights or is it dependent on culture and context? What does the addition of the word 'education' to the term 'human rights' mean? Is education within schools limited to formal classroom activities? Does it require that human rights be part of the standard curriculum in all schools? Is the term 'education' broad enough to include extra-curricular activities that may be related to human rights? This chapter does not attempt to answer these questions; rather it considers how different contexts, interpretations and understandings can lead to different answers to these questions and therefore different definitions of HRE.

This chapter explores how HRE has been defined by various UN bodies, and how the term is actually understood by key stakeholders such as governments, NGOs and teachers. This analysis reveals that these three groups do not share a common understanding of HRE, and their interpretations of the term are not only different from each other, but also very different from how the UN defines HRE.

The chapter concludes that, while there is no general consensus as to exactly what HRE means, this lack of a clear definition is not fatal to HRE. Although the uncertainty can make it more difficult for those attempting to implement HRE, the absence of a constraining definition can be a liberating force that enables greater inspiration and creativity when it comes to

HRE.⁶ However, the lack of a common understanding of what HRE is can make it more difficult for researchers to evaluate the nature and extent of the HRE that is actually occurring.

## 2  How the UN defines HRE

The first attempt by the UN to address HRE was in the *Universal Declaration on Human Rights*⁷ ('UDHR'). Early drafts of the UDHR referred to a right to education but were silent as to the content of such education. However, when the NGO the World Jewish Congress saw early drafts of the article on education, it immediately noted that:

> [T]he Article on education provided a technical framework but contained nothing about the spirit governing education which was an essential element. Neglect of this principle in Germany had been the main cause of two catastrophic wars.⁸

This observation was taken on board by the drafting committee and the end result was Article 26(2) UDHR, which provides that:

> Education shall be directed to the full development of the human personality and to the strengthening of respect for human rights and fundamental freedoms. It shall promote understanding, tolerance and friendship among all nations, racial or religious groups, and shall further the activities of the United Nations for the maintenance of peace.

This article has formed the basis for HRE provisions in many human rights treaties,⁹ but the one that is the focus of this chapter is Article 29(1) of the *Convention on the Rights of the Child* ('CROC'), because it is the most widely adopted articulation of HRE, having been ratified by 193 States.¹⁰ Article 29

---

⁶  Nancy Flowers, 'What is Human Rights Education?' in *A Survey of Human Rights Education* (Bertelsmann Verlag, Gütersloh, 2003) 1.
⁷  GA Res 217A (III), UN Doc A/810, 71 (1948).
⁸  UN Doc E/CN.4/AC.2/SR.8/p.4 (December 1947).
⁹  See for example: *UNESCO Convention Against Discrimination in Education*, opened for signature 14 December 1960, 429 UNTS 93 (entered into force 22 May 1962) Article 5; *International Convention on the Elimination of All Forms of Racial Discrimination*, opened for signature 7 March 1966, 660 UNTS 195 (entered into force 4 January 1969) Article 7; *International Covenant on Economic, Social and Cultural Rights*, opened for signature 16 December 1966, 999 UNTS 3 (entered into force 3 January 1976) ('ICESCR') Article 13; *Convention on Elimination of all forms of Discrimination Against Women*, opened for signature 18 December 1979, 1249 UNTS 13 (entered into force 3 September 1981) ('CEDAW') Article 10; and the *Convention on the Rights of the Child*, opened for signature 18 December 1979, 1249 UNTS 13 (entered into force 3 September 1981) Article 29(1).
¹⁰  http://www2.ohchr.org/english/bodies/ratification/11.htm accessed at 23 November 2008.

CROC breaks down the content of education that children are to receive into five parts, namely:

(a) The development of the child's personality, talents and mental and physical abilities to their fullest potential;
(b) The development of respect for human rights and fundamental freedoms, and for the principles enshrined in the Charter of the United Nations;
(c) The development of respect for the child's parents, his or her own cultural identity, language and values, for the national values of the country in which the child is living, the country from which he or she may originate, and for civilizations different from his or her own;
(d) The preparation of the child for responsible life in a free society, in the spirit of understanding, peace, tolerance, equality of sexes, and friendship among all peoples, ethnic, national and religious groups and persons of indigenous origin;
(e) The development of respect for the natural environment.

The Committee on the Rights of the Child ('the Committee') has attempted to provide greater clarity as to exactly what this provision means by publishing *General Comment 1 on the Aims of Education*,[11] which constitutes the Committee's authoritative interpretation of the normative content of Article 29(1) CROC. As Dianne Otto has noted, although not legally binding, General Comments 'carry enormous political and moral weight'[12] and 'at the very least, they provide persuasive interpretations of the treaty provisions.'[13] Indeed, Thomas Buergenthal, now of the International Court of Justice, has referred to General Comments as having become 'distinct juridical instruments'[14] and likened them to 'advisory opinions' of international tribunals.[15] However, it should be remembered that General Comments are adopted by treaty committees and are therefore consensus documents agreed to after negotiations and compromises by committee members.[16]

*General Comment 1* stresses that the paragraphs in Article 29(1) CROC are interrelated and that they reinforce, integrate and complement the other provisions in CROC, and cannot be properly understood in isolation from them.[17]

---

[11] *General Comment 1*, above n 2.
[12] Dianne Otto '"Gender Comment": Why Does the UN Committee on Economic, Social and Cultural Rights Need a General Comment on Women?' (2002) *Canadian Journal of Women and the Law* 1, 11.
[13] Ibid 13.
[14] Thomas Buergenthal, quoted in Henry J Steiner, Philip Alston and Ryan Goodman, *International Human Rights in Context: Law, Politics, Morals* (Oxford University Press, Oxford, 3rd ed, 2008) 852–3.
[15] Ibid.
[16] Otto, above n 12.
[17] *General Comment 1*, above n 2, [6].

Thus, HRE should be interpreted in a holistic manner that incorporates principles such as non-discrimination (Article 2 CROC), the best interests of the child (Article 3 CROC), and the right to express views and have them taken into account (Article 12 CROC).[18]

Article 29(1)(b) CROC refers to education being directed at 'the development of respect for human rights'. As discussed below, there is a tendency for some governments to equate human rights with civil and political rights. *General Comment 1* makes it clear that this is not what is intended by this provision. It specifically states that 'the education to which every child has a right is one designed to provide the child with life skills, to strengthen the child's capacity to enjoy the *full range* of human rights'.[19] The absence of any discussion in *General Comment 1* about civil and political rights and ESC rights indicates that the reference to human rights in Article 29(1)(b) CROC is to *all* humans rights. Thus, Article 29(1)(b) CROC requires that children learn about human rights as universal and indivisible, in conjunction with the principles in the *Charter of the United Nations*, which promote the maintenance of international peace and security by, inter alia, observing faith in fundamental human rights and in the dignity and worth of the human person and the equal rights of men and women.[20]

Article 29(1)(c) CROC provides that education about national values and respecting different civilisations should form part of HRE. The Committee sees this obligation as fundamental to creating a culture which is infused by human rights values.[21] In many ways the elements in Article 29(1)(c) CROC have a prophylactic role, that is, they are aimed at sowing the seeds of harmonious relationships among all people and helping to prevent the outbreak of violent conflicts and related human rights violations.[22]

Article 29(1)(c) CROC is inextricably linked with Article 29(1)(d) CROC in that respecting difference is a precursor to understanding, peace, tolerance and friendship among all people. Thus, *General Comment 1* emphasises that HRE must combat prejudice, racism, discrimination and xenophobia,[23] in order to promote the ethical values which facilitate peace and harmonious relations among all people.

---

[18] Ibid.
[19] Ibid, [2] (emphasis added).
[20] *Charter of the United Nations*, Preamble.
[21] *General Comment 1*, above n 2, [7].
[22] Upendra Baxi, 'Human Rights Education: The Promise of the Third Millenium?' in G Andreopoulos and R P Claude (eds) *Human Rights Education for the Twenty-First Century* (University of Pennsylvania Press, Philadelphia, 1997) 146.
[23] See for example *General Comment 1*, above n 2, [11].

Article 29(1) CROC was augmented by the UN Decade for Human Rights Education ('Decade for HRE') from 1995 to 2004, and it is relevant to consider how HRE has been defined in this initiative, and in particular, whether the definition of HRE developed by the Office of the High Commissioner for Human Rights ('OHCHR') and endorsed by the General Assembly supports the articulation of HRE in CROC, as elaborated upon by *General Comment 1*. As part of the Decade for HRE the OHCHR prepared Guidelines for National Plans of Action for HRE ('Guidelines') and the first section is headed 'Definition of Human Rights Education'.[24] It begins by highlighting references to HRE in international human rights instruments including CROC, before stating that:

> Human rights education may be defined as training, dissemination and information efforts aimed at the building of a universal culture of human rights through the imparting of knowledge and skills and the moulding of attitudes, which are directed towards:
> (a) The strengthening of respect for human rights and fundamental freedoms;
> (b) The full development of the human personality and the sense of its dignity;
> (c) The promotion of understanding, tolerance, gender equality and friendship among all nations, indigenous peoples and racial, national, ethnic, religious and linguistic groups;
> (d) The enabling of all persons to participate effectively in a free society;
> (e) The furtherance of the activities of the United Nations for the maintenance of peace.[25]

There are many similarities between this definition of HRE and Article 29(1) CROC, as well as a few differences that are of less significance. Paragraph (a) of the Guidelines corresponds to Article 29(1)(b) CROC except that it omits the reference to the Charter of the UN. Paragraph (b) above is similar to Article 29(1)(a) CROC except that it is not specific to children. Article 29(1)(d) CROC has been broken down into three separate provisions in the UN Decade for HRE definition, namely paragraphs (c), (d) and (e). The only aspect of HRE in Article 29(1) CROC that is not included in the above definition of HRE is paragraph (c) which, to recap, provides that HRE includes:

> The development of respect for the child's parents, his or her own cultural identity, language and values, for the national values of the country in which the child is living, the country from which he or she may originate, and for civilizations different from his or her own.

---

[24] OHCHR, *Guidelines for National Plans of Action for Human Rights Education*, UN Doc A/52/469/Add.1 (20 October 1997) 5.
[25] Ibid.

The first part of this paragraph is specific to children and is therefore understandably not part of a general definition of HRE. This leaves the only substantive difference between Article 29(1) CROC and the definition of HRE developed for the Decade as the references to cultural identity, national values and different civilisations. It is unclear why this provision does not form part of the later definition of HRE. It may be that values education, while relevant to HRE, was not considered to be as important as the other aspects of HRE set out paragraphs (a)–(e) of the definition developed for the Decade. Furthermore, values are referred to in the UN Decade Guidelines in the section immediately following the definition. In particular it refers to HRE as having three dimensions, including 'the development of values, beliefs and attitudes which uphold human rights'.[26] It is suggested that this broadly encompasses the concept contained in Article 29(1)(c) CROC, and thus the definition of HRE in the Guidelines generally reinforces the articulation of HRE in Article 29(1) CROC.

There is however, one significant difference between the HRE set out in the Guidelines and HRE as set out in Article 29(1) CROC. As stated above, the Guidelines refer to HRE as having three dimensions. The third dimension is identified as being 'encouragement to take action to defend human rights and prevent human rights abuses'.[27] *General Comment 1* recommends that HRE be empowering, which is clearly not as strong a directive as taking action. There are two possible explanations for this difference. The first is that the Committee, when developing *General Comment 1*, was mindful of children's different developmental stages and evolving capacities[28] and did not consider it appropriate to encourage young persons to take action to defend and prevent human rights abuses at too early an age. The second is the different provenance of these statements; *General Comment 1* is essentially a consensus document agreed to by an expert body seeking consensus whereas the Guidelines were drafted by the OHCHR. It could be expected that the OHCHR would use stronger language than the Committee.

Overall, the definition of HRE in the UN Decade Guidelines bears a strong similarity to the articulation of HRE set out in Article 29(1) CROC. The only significant difference is not in the definition of HRE, but rather in the guidance of how such HRE should be promoted, that is, by encouraging recipients of HRE to take action, which is not something that *General Comment 1* endorses.

---

26 Ibid [12(b)].
27 Ibid [12(c)].
28 *General Comment 1*, above n 2, [1], [9], [12].

When the UN Decade for HRE came to an end in late 2004, the General Assembly decided that the efforts to promote HRE needed to continue and therefore adopted the World Programme for HRE (2005–ongoing) as the vehicle by which to continue the focus on human rights education.[29] The World Programme operates in phases, with each phase concentrating on a different aspect of HRE. The first phase was from 2005 to 2007 and was directed at HRE in primary and secondary schools. The Human Rights Council then extended the first phase for a further two years (2008 to 2009) to give States more time to implement HRE.[30] In late 2009, the Human Rights Council proclaimed that the Second Phase of the World Program will focus on HRE for higher education and on human rights training programs for teachers and educators, civil servants, law enforcement officials and military personnel at all levels, and shall be for a period of five years, from 2010 to 2014.[31]

The Plan of Action for the First Phase ('Plan of Action') was prepared by the OHCHR and transmitted by the Secretary-General to the General Assembly.[32] It includes the following definition of HRE:

> Human rights education can be defined as education, training and information aiming at building a universal culture of human rights through the sharing of knowledge, imparting of skills and moulding of attitudes directed to:
> (a) The strengthening of respect for human rights and fundamental freedoms;
> (b) The full development of the human personality and the sense of its dignity;
> (c) The promotion of understanding, tolerance, gender equality and friendship among all nations, indigenous peoples and racial, national, ethnic, religious and linguistic groups;
> (d) The enabling of all persons to participate effectively in a free and democratic society governed by the rule of law;
> (e) The building and maintenance of peace;
> (f) The promotion of people-centred sustainable development and social justice.[33]

The first three paragraphs are in every respect identical to the first three paragraphs in the definition of HRE used for the UN Decade for HRE. However, the next three paragraphs reveal a further refinement of the definition of HRE. Some of the changes are stylistic rather than substantive including, for example, the deletion of the reference to the UN in the paragraph addressing the maintenance of peace. However, two changes are significant,

---

[29] Above n 5.
[30] Human Rights Council, *World Programme for Human Rights Education*, UN Doc A/HRC/RES/6/24 (28 September 2007).
[31] Resolution A/HRC/RES/12/4, 12 October 2009.
[32] OHCHR, *Plan of Action for the First Phase (2005–2007) of the World Programme for Human Rights Education*, UN Doc A/59/525/Rev.1 (2 March 2005).
[33] Ibid, [3].

namely the addition of a reference to a 'democratic society governed by the rule of law' in paragraph (d) and the inclusion of a new provision addressing sustainable development and social justice.

The mention of the 'rule of law' is a reflection of the new importance placed on this concept. As Thomas Carothers, Director of Research at the Carnegie Endowment for International Peace, noted: '[t]he concept [the rule of law] is suddenly everywhere – a venerable part of Western political philosophy enjoying a new run as a rising imperative of the era of globalization.'[34] It was in the late 1990s that the 'rule of law' re-emerged as an important concept within the notion of a democratic society.[35] Since CROC was drafted during the 1980s, when the 'rule of law' did not enjoy such a high profile in human rights discourse, it is understandable that it did not feature in Article 29(1) CROC. Similarly, sustainable development did not become part of human rights discourse until the 1990s,[36] that is, subsequent to the drafting of Article 29(1) CROC. While the idea of 'social justice' has been around for a long time, there is no authoritative definition of it.[37] Perhaps the notion of social justice has more of a collective element to it than human rights which are vested in individuals, but the terms are clearly closely linked.[38] Thus, the addition of social justice might be seen as slightly expanding the definition of HRE. It is suggested that the changes in the description of HRE between the Decade and the World Programme amount to a refinement of the definition rather than substantive modifications.

---

[34] Thomas Carothers, 'The Rule of Law Revival' (1998) 77(2) *Foreign Affairs* 95.

[35] See for example A James McAdams (ed) *Transitional Justice and the Rule of Law in New Democracies* (University of Notre Dame Press, Notre Dame, 1997); Joseph Raz, 'The Rule of Law and Its Virtue' (1997) 93 *Law Quarterly Review 195*; Jennifer Widner, *Building the Rule of Law* (W W Norton, New York, 2001); Guillermo O'Donnell, 'Why the Rule of Law Matters' (2004) 15 *Journal of Democracy* 32.

[36] See for example *Vienna Declaration and Programme of Action of the World Conference on Human Rights*, UN Doc A/CONF.157/23 (25 June 1993), Section I [20], [27], Section II [17] and [36]; Jack Donnelly, 'Human Rights, Democracy, and Development' (1999) 21 *Human Rights Quarterly* 608; Caroline Moser and Andy Norton, 'To Claim our Rights: Livelihood Security, Human Rights and Sustainable Development' (Paper presented at the Workshop on Human Rights, Assets and Livelihood Security, and Sustainable Development, Overseas Development Institute, London, 19–20 June 2001).

[37] Michael Reisch, 'Defining Social Justice in a Socially Unjust World' (2002) 83 *Families in Society* 343.

[38] See for example Virginia Held, *Rights and Goods: Justifying Social Action* (The Free Press, New York, 1984) and Clare Ferguson, 'Global Social Policy Principles: Human Rights and Social Justice' (DFID Social Development Division, 1999), www.dfid.gov.uk/pubs/files/sdd-gsp.pdf at 23 November 2007.

Like the Guidelines for the Decade for HRE, the Plan of Action follows its definition of HRE with a statement that HRE should include encouraging people to take action to defend and promote HRE.[39] As noted above, this is not something that *General Comment 1* recommends for children's HRE.

Article 29(1) CROC read in conjunction with *General Comment 1* provides a clear definition of HRE, the core elements of which are that HRE must promote respect for all human rights as universal and indivisible standards belonging to all people. It must promote respect for others, and it must actively encourage the development of values relating to peace, tolerance, and equality in an integrated and holistic manner. The international HRE initiatives subsequent to CROC essentially affirm this articulation of HRE. The few differences are minor and stem from a broadening of the definition to suit an audience that comprises more than just children, and an evolution in the understanding of HRE that has occurred since Article 29(1) CROC was drafted in the late 1980s. In particular, the inclusion of concepts such as the 'rule of law' and 'sustainable development' in the more recent articulations of HRE represent an effort to incorporate more modern ideas about what is necessary in order to achieve a culture of human rights.[40] The main area of divergence between CROC and the two subsequent initiatives is the express acknowledgement that HRE should promote action to defend and promote human rights.[41] Overall, there appears to be general consensus at the international level as to the content of HRE, with a small amount of disparity between Article 29(1) CROC and the more recent statements regarding HRE.

## 3 How governments define HRE

Having seen how HRE has been defined and explained by relevant bodies within the UN, it is important to see how these definitions compare with the definitional attempts of domestic governments. Space does not allow for a comprehensive analysis of all governments, so the Australian Federal Government has been selected for a case study to determine whether it interprets HRE in a manner consistent with the definition of HRE developed at the international level. Its interpretation has been gleaned from an analysis of documents published by the Department of Education, Science and Training ('DEST'),[42] as well as through interviews conducted with DEST staff. This analysis suggests that the Australian Government's understanding of HRE

---

[39] OCHCR, above n 32, [4].
[40] Promoting a culture of human rights is the first objective of the World Programme for HRE, OHCHR, above n 32, [7].
[41] OCHCR, above n 24, [13(c)]; above n 32, [4(c)].
[42] DEST is now known as the Department of Education, Employment and Workplace Relations ('DEEWR').

emphasises civil and political rights, in particular, citizenship and democracy, rather than ESC rights.

Under the Australian Constitution, education is the responsibility of the state and territory governments, rather than the federal government.[43] Notwithstanding this, the Australian Federal Government has found opportunities to articulate its opinion about what constitutes HRE in its reports to the UN Committee on the Rights of the Child, which include, *inter alia*, activities in Australia pursuant to Article 29(1) CROC. The first report was submitted to the Committee in December 1995,[44] and a combined second and third report was submitted in September 2003.[45] By setting out how it thinks it is complying with Article 29(1) CROC, the Australian government reveals its understanding of its obligations under this article.

The *First Report* indicates that Australia had an understanding of HRE that in many aspects was congruent with Article 29(1) CROC, but at the same time differed in some critical areas. In a lengthy section on HRE in Australia,[46] the Government addressed the majority of issues identified in Article 29(1) CROC. The report referred to the *Hobart Declaration on Schooling in Australia*[47] which sets out ten agreed national goals of education.[48] The goals relevant to HRE include cultivating respect for others; developing a capacity to exercise judgement in matters of morality, ethics and social justice; and acquiring knowledge, skills, attitudes and values which will enable students to participate as active and informed citizens in a democratic society. The *First Report* elaborates on these issues, and specifically identifies that 'the knowledge, experience and interest of women and Aboriginal and Torres Strait Islander peoples are included by the provision of cross-curricula perspectives.'[49] It also recognised that groups with special needs must be addressed, and singled out immigrant groups, children who do not yet speak English, and students with learning disabilities as being in need of additional programs.

---

[43] *Constitution of Australia* section 51.

[44] *Australia's First Report under Article 44(1)(a) of the Convention on the Rights of the Child*, UN Doc CRC/C/8/Add.31 (1 February 1996) ('*First Report*').

[45] *Australia's Combined Second and Third Reports under the Convention on the Rights of the Child*, UN Doc CRC/C/129/Add.4 (29 December 2004) ('*Second/Third Reports*').

[46] The section of the report relating to Article 29(1) CROC is in excess of 6,000 words.

[47] The *Hobart Declaration on Schooling in Australia* is a 1989 report from the Australian Education Council (now the Ministerial Council on Education, Employment, Training and Youth Affairs), a body that is made up of all state, territory and federal Ministers of Education.

[48] The agreement on uniform education goals demonstrates the operation of cooperative federalism in the field of education.

[49] *First Report*, above n 44, [1237].

The HRE referred to in Australia's *First Report* includes anti-bullying initiatives, school violence based on gender, racism and ethnicity[50] and the cumulative social and cultural effects of colonisation.[51] With the exception of colonisation, these are all expressly identified as crucial aspects of HRE in *General Comment 1*.

The *First Report* provides a comprehensive insight into how the Australian Government of the time understood the HRE required by Article 29(1) CROC. The information provided to the Committee demonstrated a thorough and wide-ranging understanding of HRE that included most of the issues contained in Article 29(1) CROC. However, it failed to include any reference to ESC rights, and made no mention of international human rights laws, the United Nations, or the principles enshrined in its Charter.

Interestingly, the report also managed to largely avoid using the words 'human rights'. The only place they appear is in the section provided by the Australian Capital Territory ('ACT') that related specifically to HRE activities undertaken within the ACT.[52] The only mention of rights in other sections is in the context of the rights and responsibilities of citizens.[53] This suggests that the Federal Government in 1995 was uncomfortable with the term 'human rights'. The language which the Federal Government seemed to prefer was 'anti-discrimination', 'social justice', 'equality', and 'civics and citizenship', all of which are used liberally throughout the *First Report*. While all of these terms are encompassed within the concept of human rights,[54] they do not have the same force and international recognition as the term 'human rights'. The Australian Government's reluctance to expressly include the term 'human rights' in the section dealing with Article 29(1) CROC in its *First Report* to the Committee suggests that the Government either lacked an understanding of what HRE was or was deliberately attempting to obfuscate the issue.

In contrast to the *First Report*, Australia's *Second/Third Reports* are extremely brief in detailing activities pursuant to Article 29(1) CROC. They identify only three issues – anti-racism, child sexual abuse, and school discipline.[55] While anti-racism initiatives clearly fall within the definition of HRE

---

[50] Ibid [1241].
[51] Ibid [1245].
[52] Ibid [1279]–[1280].
[53] Ibid [1238].
[54] For example, 'equality' is referred to in Article 29(1)(d) CROC; 'discrimination' is the subject matter of Article 2 CROC, and *General Comment 1*, above n 2, identifies it as a core part of HRE pursuant to Article 29 CROC. Social justice is about analysing and addressing oppression based on a variety of grounds including racism, sexism, heterosexism, and ableism. See Maurianne Adams, Pat Griffin and Lee Anne Bell (eds) *Teaching for Diversity and Social Justice* (Routledge, Oxford, 1997).
[55] *Second/Third Reports*, above n 45, [373].

as set out in Article 29(1) CROC and elaborated on in *General Comment 1*,[56] the other two issues are not generally considered to form part of HRE. While preventing the sexual abuse of children is clearly an aim of CROC,[57] neither Article 29(1) CROC nor *General Comment 1* contemplate it forming part of the HRE that children receive. School discipline practices could well form part of HRE, particularly when it comes to the use of corporal punishment. However, the discipline practices referred to in Australia's *Second/Third Reports* relate to procedural fairness issues when dealing with student suspension and exclusion, and reducing class sizes as a means of managing student behavioural problems.[58] These issues may be tangentially related to the HRE mandated in Article 29(1) CROC, but they are by no means a core part of the norm.

The *Second/Third Reports* failed to comply with the recommendation of the Committee regarding reporting on Article 29(1) CROC. In *General Comment 1*, the Committee requests that State Parties in their periodic reports provide details of what they consider to be the most important priorities concerning HRE, and to outline the activities that they propose to take over the next five years to address the problems identified.[59] This was not done in Australia's *Second/Third Reports*.

The extremely brief narrative about HRE activities in Australian schools set out in the second report is open to a number of interpretations. One is that State Parties' reports to the Committee are about activities not interpretations, and so the Australian Government may recognise that HRE is broader than what it is reporting on, but has only included in the report what it believes it is doing in the field of HRE. Another explanation is that the Government has a very narrow understanding of HRE, namely anti-racism, protecting children from sexual abuse, and school discipline. A third possible explanation for the brevity of reporting on HRE may be that the Government was not willing to commit resources to preparing a comprehensive report to this UN treaty committee. There have, for several years, been tensions between Australia and the UN treaty committees that may account for the apparent lack of effort in reporting.[60] Unfortunately, there is insufficient publicly available information to determine why the most recent report by the Australian Government to the Committee was so brief with regard to Article 29(1) CROC.

---

56 *General Comment 1*, above n 2, [11].
57 See Articles 19 and 34 CROC.
58 *Second/Third Reports*, above n 45, [383].
59 *General Comment 1*, above n 2, [26].
60 Hilary Charlesworth, Madelaine Chiam, Devika Hovell and George Williams, 'Deep Anxieties: Australia and the International Legal Order' (2003) 25 *Sydney Law Review* 423.

What explanation is there for this significant difference in reporting style and substance between Australia's *First Report* and *Second/Third Reports* to the Committee? The answer appears to lie in the change of government that took place between the two reports. In March 1996 a conservative Liberal-National Government replaced the Labor Government that had been responsible for the preparation of the *First Report*. That Liberal-National administration prepared the *Second/Third Reports*. The content of the *Second/Third Reports* suggests that the conservative Government did not share the previous Government's understanding of HRE. Governments change, and it is likely that educational policies and priorities will change from one administration to the next. Thus, any government's interpretation of HRE must be understood as representing only the policy or understanding of the current political party holding office. The difference between the Australian Government's *First Report* and *Second/Third Reports* therefore appears to be due to a change of government and a commensurate change in priorities, including in particular a reduced commitment to international human rights laws.[61]

From these two Reports to the Committee, it appears that Australia has an understanding of HRE that is narrower than the definition propounded in Article 29(1) CROC and elaborated on in *General Comment 1*. Interviews with employees of DEST confirm this conclusion. One senior staff member stated in an interview that 'Human rights is a very small part of your education. It's in one sense a very small part of CCE [civics and citizenship education].'[62] This perception that HRE is part of civics and citizenship education is the reverse of the approach adopted in Article 29(1) CROC. Civic and citizenship education involves teaching students about the democratic system of government and civic life. This is merely one aspect of HRE, which encompasses much more than these limited democratic values.

In conclusion, the Australian Government's *First Report* and *Second/Third Reports* to the Committee on the implementation of CROC in Australia, and the interviews with DEST employees, point to the Australian Government having a narrow understanding of HRE that encompasses only limited aspects of Article 29(1) CROC.

## 4 How NGOs define HRE

The role that non-governmental human rights organisations play in the promotion and implementation of HRE is extremely important since it is NGOs that

---

[61] For a full discussion on the differences between the human rights commitments of Labor and Liberal governments in Australia see Hilary Charlesworth, Madelaine Chiam, Devika Hovell and George Williams, *No Country is an Island: Australia and International Law* (UNSW Press, Sydney, 2006).

[62] Interview conducted on 18 June 2004. Transcript on file with author.

are developing much of the HRE materials that are being used in schools.[63] NGOs' definitions of HRE are therefore being passed on to teachers through the literature and resources they provide to schools.

Three of the more significant NGOs working in the area of HRE have been selected for consideration below, namely Amnesty International, Human Rights Education Associates ('HREA'), and the People's Movement for Human Rights Learning ('PDHRE').[64]

## A  Amnesty International

> Human rights education is both a lens through which to observe the world and a methodology for teaching and leading others.[65]

Amnesty International began as a movement to help prisoners of conscience (with an article by Benenson in The Observer entitled 'The Forgotten Prisoners' calling for an international campaign to protest against the imprisonment of people purely for their political or religious beliefs) and gradually extended its mandate to include victims of all kinds of discrimination and abuse. Today it is one of the oldest, largest,[66] and most well-respected independent international human rights organisations. While Amnesty International is perhaps best known for its campaigns to free prisoners of conscience, it also does a significant amount of work surrounding human rights education. It defines HRE as:

> A process whereby people learn about their rights and the rights of others, within a framework of participatory and interactive learning. HRE is concerned with changing attitudes and behaviours, learning new skills, and promoting the exchange of knowledge and information. HRE is long-term, and aims to provide an understanding of the issues, and equip people with the skills to articulate their rights and communicate this knowledge to others.

---

[63] See for example Amnesty International, *First Steps: A Manual for Starting Human Rights Education* (Amnesty International Publications, London, 1997); Human Security Network, *Understanding Human Rights: Manual on Human Rights Education* (Human Security Network, Graz, 2003); People's Movement for Human Rights Education, *Passport to Dignity* (PDHRE, New York, 2001); Facing History and Ourselves, *Resource Book: Holocaust and Human Behavior* (Facing History and Ourselves, Boston, 1994); and Nancy Flowers (ed) *Human Rights Here and Now: Celebrating the Universal Declaration of Human Rights* (Human Rights Educators' Network and Amnesty International, New York, 1998).

[64] This NGO was previously called the People's Decade for Human Rights Education.

[65] See http://www.amnestyusa.org/education/about.html at 23 November 2008.

[66] It has over 2.2 million members, subscribers and regular donors in over 150 countries. See http://www.amnesty.org/en/who-we-are at 23 November 2008.

HRE . . .

- Recognises the universality and indivisibility of human rights
- Increases knowledge and understanding of human rights
- Empowers people to claim their rights
- Assists people to use the legal instruments designed to protect human rights
- Uses interactive and participatory methodology to develop attitudes of respect for human rights
- Develops the skills needed to defend human rights
- Integrates the principles of human rights into everyday life
- Creates a space for dialogue and change
- Encourages respect and tolerance.[67]

In contrast to the Australian government, considered above, Amnesty International has clearly enunciated its understanding of HRE. Its activist philosophy is very apparent in its definition of HRE. Amnesty International wants students to question, challenge and take action.[68] Its definition of HRE is normative and transformative, in that it seeks to train people to assert and defend their rights and the rights of others, in other words to become human rights activists.

The reference to the 'indivisibility of human rights' and the fact that there is no distinction made between ESC rights and civil and political rights suggest that Amnesty International understands HRE to encompass the full range of human rights. This is congruent with Article 29(1) CROC as elaborated on in *General Comment 1*. Amnesty International's definition of HRE seems to be both narrower and broader than Article 29(1) CROC. Narrower, because it does not appear to cover all the matters addressed in Article 29(1)(b)–(d) CROC. For example, there is no express reference to a child developing respect for his or her parents. This is probably because Amnesty's definition of HRE is not specifically aimed at children, as Article 29(1) CROC is. It will be recalled that the HRE definitions in the UN Decade for HRE and the World Programme for HRE are also silent about human rights education including the development of respect for parents. Thus it is clear that the inclusion of a reference to respecting parents is only relevant where the recipients of that education are children.

Amnesty International's definition of HRE is broader than Article 29(1) CROC, because the treaty provision merely refers to the 'development of respect' for human rights, whereas Amnesty International aims to empower

---

[67] Amnesty International, *Make Human Rights a Reality* (2005) Amnesty International, http://www.amnesty.org/en/library/asset/POL32/001/2005/en/dom-POL320012005en.html at 23 November 2008.

[68] Flowers, above n 6.

students to defend and claim their rights, which has more of an activist element to it. Indeed, an Amnesty International staff member responsible for student groups, who was interviewed for this research, stated that she designed 'trainings that will help them to become better human rights activists'.[69] This goes beyond the purpose and intent of Article 29(1) CROC, described in *General Comment 1* as being to enable children to 'enjoy the full range of human rights and to promote a culture which is infused by appropriate human rights values'.[70] The language in Article 29(1) CROC was drafted by State representatives, and the final text had to be agreed to by the majority of States. It is therefore not surprising that it does not encourage human rights activism, as this is not something that is generally favoured by States which support maintenance of the status quo and see activism as a challenge to their power and control.[71] However, this activist approach to HRE is consistent with the other international definitions of HRE in the Guidelines for the Decade and the Plan of Action for the World Programme, both of which refer to HRE as encouraging the taking of action to defend and promote human rights.

Amnesty International relies on the UDHR for guidance on HRE, rather than Article 29(1) CROC. This is not surprising, given that the UDHR is referred to in Amnesty International's mission statement and CROC is not,[72] and that Amnesty International's HRE work is not limited to children. Overall, Amnesty International's understanding of HRE appears to be generally consistent with Article 29(1)(b) and (d) CROC, and the matters set out in Article 29(1)(c) CROC, while not explicitly addressed, may be implicit in Amnesty International's definition of HRE.

### B  Human Rights Education Associates

Human Rights Education Associates is an international non-governmental organisation that supports human rights learning; the training of activists and professionals; the development of educational materials and programming; and community-building through on-line technologies.[73] It was established in the Netherlands in 1996, and now has offices in Amsterdam and Boston.

---

[69] Interview conducted on 4 February 2004. Transcript on file with author.

[70] *General Comment 1*, above n 2, [2].

[71] Michael Ignatieff, *Human Rights as Politics and Idolatry* (Princeton University Press, Princeton, 2001).

[72] *Statute of Amnesty International* as amended by the 27th International Council, meeting in Morelos, Mexico (2005) Amnesty International, http://www.amnesty.org/en/library/asset/POL20/001/2007/en/dom-POL200012007en.pdf at 23 November 2008.

[73] See www.hrea.org at 23 November 2008.

The Executive Director of HREA was interviewed by the author and, in response to a question asking how HREA defined HRE, stated:

> The way that we define it is that it promotes understanding and the promotion and protection of human rights. So that means that human rights education has to be not only about human rights values, but it has to be done in a way that it creates some sort of a really personal understanding and commitment to human rights.
>
> So it cannot just be purely informational, it has to move people by the ideas, and move them in terms of relating it to their own lives or feeling that they're connecting to human rights, in terms of how they're acting in the world . . .
>
> We look at human rights education in terms of the goals, and not just pure content and we feel that's very important. It's not that everyone that gets human rights education is going to become a human rights lawyer or a human rights advocate, but we think those actually should be the goals, that people feel that at the minimum that the human rights ideas are something that they own and they feel close to, and that they feel the importance of protecting and promoting human rights elsewhere and empowering others. So there's self-empowerment and there's empowering others.[74]

Thus HREA is similar to Amnesty International in requiring, as a core part of HRE, that it motivate and empower individuals to effect positive change within society. The tone, if not the specific language, is adversarial or confrontational. This NGO clearly seeks to create activists who will know and be able to claim and assert their human rights. Its understanding of HRE is expressed in significantly stronger language than that used in Article 29(1) CROC; there is a clear distinction between the goal of developing respect for human rights, as Article 29(1) CROC mandates, and the goal of producing human rights lawyers and activists, as HREA advocates.

This interviewee did not seek to define the 'human rights' part of the term: she did not feel the need to elaborate on whether human rights means just civil and political rights, or the whole range of human rights. However, from the overall tone of the interview, and from a review of the literature on HREA's web page,[75] it is clear that HREA has an inclusive understanding of the term 'human rights'. However, like Amnesty International, its focus appears to be on the matters addressed in Article 29(1)(b) and (d) CROC, and it does not explicitly address the issues set out in 29(1)(c) CROC.

### C  The People's Movement for Human Rights Learning

Founded in 1988, PDHRE is a small international NGO based in New York that works to develop and advance pedagogies for HRE relevant to people's daily lives in the context of their struggles for social and economic justice and

---

[74] Interview conducted on 2 December 2003. Transcript on file with author.
[75] See http://www.hrea.org at 26 November 2008.

democracy.[76] This NGO was one of the prime instigators of the UN Decade for Human Rights Education, and in 2003 the Executive Director, Shulamith Koenig was awarded the prestigious UN Human Rights Award[77] for her work for PDHRE in the field of HRE.

The People's Movement for Human Rights Learning perceives HRE as:

> A process of learning that evokes critical thinking and systemic analysis, with a gender perspective, with the learners ... learning to analyse their situations within a holistic framework of human rights about political, civil, economic, social and cultural concern relevant to the learners' lives ... to result in a sense of ownership of human rights ... leading to equal participation in the decisions that determine our lives and taking actions to claim them.[78]

Like the other NGOs considered in this chapter, PDHRE has a broad understanding of HRE that is inclusive of ESC rights. It also adopts an activist approach, asserting that HRE should not just be about disseminating information about human rights, but also about developing skills of analysis and critical thinking that will lead the recipients of HRE to become human rights advocates. This is consistent with the HRE articulated in the Decade and the World Programme, but not Article 29(1) CROC and *General Comment 1*.

All three NGOs understand that HRE should be about empowerment and encouraging recipients of HRE to become human rights activists. While *General Comment 1* refers to empowerment twice,[79] it is not its focus. All three NGOs embrace the full range of human rights, as recommended in *General Comment 1*, but they all fail to perceive HRE as including the entirety of matters referenced in Article 29(1) CROC. In particular these NGOs did not identify the issues set out in Article 29(1)(c) CROC as being part of their understanding of HRE. These NGOs' understanding of HRE, while generally

---

[76] See http://www.pdhre.org/about.html at 26 November 2008.

[77] The Human Rights awards were instituted by *Annex: International Year for Human Rights: further programme of measures and activities recommended by the Commission on Human Rights*, GA Res 2217(XXI), UN GAOR, 21st sess, 1498th plen mtg, UN Doc A/RES/2217(XXI) (19 December 1966). They are intended to 'honour and commend people and organizations which have made an outstanding contribution to the promotion and protection of the human rights embodied in the Universal Declaration of Human Rights and in other United Nations human rights instruments'. They were first awarded in 1968, and have been given out at five-year intervals since then.

[78] Posting by Shulamith Koenig on behalf of PDHRE on the HREA Listserv (1 January 2002): see https://hrea.org/lists/hr-education/markup/maillist.php at 25 November 2008.

[79] *General Comment 1*, above n 2, [2].

similar to how HRE has been defined in Article 29(1) CROC and *General Comment 1*, are much more congruent with the other two international definitions of HRE analysed above, namely those of the UN Decade for HRE (1995–2004) and the World Programme for HRE (2005–ongoing). This is because of their aim of provoking people to take action to protect human rights.

## 5 How teachers define HRE

Since teachers are the ones ultimately charged with teaching students about human rights, it is important to understand what they actually think HRE means. As part of a doctoral research project, a number of secondary school teachers in Melbourne, Australia, and Boston in the United States were surveyed and interviewed by the author.[80] Teachers were invited to state in their own words what they understand is meant by the term human rights education. Several themes emerged from these data, and are considered below.

### A  Use of UN documents in defining HRE

While the UN, governments and even NGOs perceive human rights in a very legalistic manner, teachers do not. Teachers see a clear distinction between 'human rights' and 'human rights law'. While the UN, governments and NGOs rely on international instruments such as the UDHR when defining HRE, teachers do not tend to do so. In schools the influence of UN documents diminishes considerably.

Of the 30 teachers in Melbourne who completed and returned the survey, ten mentioned UN instruments (most often UDHR) in their definition of HRE. In addition, a further seven teachers were interviewed who had not completed the survey and, of these, two referred to the United Nations when defining HRE. Thus 32 per cent of participating Melbourne teachers defined human rights education using a framework of international human rights law. By contrast, of 33 Boston teachers surveyed and interviewed, only three (or 9 per cent) mentioned the UN or international human rights instruments in their definition of HRE. This clearly suggests that Boston teachers' understanding of HRE is not informed by international proclamations or definitions of human rights. The idea that there is a relationship between HRE and international human rights instruments was something that was understood by Melbourne teachers to a significantly greater degree than their Boston counterparts. However, the Melbourne proportion was still not high, with less than one-third including UN documents in their definition of HRE.

---

[80] In Melbourne, 30 teachers completed and returned surveys and 20 were interviewed. In Boston, 19 completed and returned surveys and 21 were interviewed. All data were collected by the author in 2004.

## B  Use of national documents in defining HRE

While Boston teachers did not refer to international instruments when defining HRE, many did place emphasis on national instruments, in particular documents such as the US Bill of Rights and the Declaration of Independence, which are firmly embedded in American culture. It was clear from both the interviews with Boston teachers and the survey responses that domestic laws strongly influenced their understanding of HRE. Examples of this attitude are clear from the following extracts:

> *Teacher 1*:   As human beings we are entitled to certain 'unalienable' rights. Our Declaration of Independence includes among them life, liberty, and the pursuit of happiness. When we are denied these, it may be considered a violation of human rights.[81]

> *Teacher 2*:   I suppose if I was going to make it a definition, I'd have to call upon the American Declaration of Independence which says that we have the right to life, liberty and the pursuit of happiness and that rights of citizenship should be offered equally to all. That's what it says in our Fourteenth Amendment, equal protection under the law.[82]

> *Teacher 3*:   We do the Bill of Rights. When I started talking about China, I compared it to the Bill of Rights here in the United States ... I ask kids if you could only pick one [right] to keep, which one would it be? I guess in some ways we relate it more to American-oriented ideas of liberty and privilege.[83]

The impact of this focus is twofold. Firstly, the existence of a Bill of Rights stimulates teachers to have a dialogue with their students about the whole notion of rights. The Bill of Rights and the Declaration of Independence provide a focal point which teachers are comfortable with, because these domestic documents are a core part of America's history, culture and identity. They are not perceived as too political or challenging, which is something that human rights are sometimes accused of.

The second effect of this focus on domestic instruments is that it narrows the scope of HRE. The rights contained in the American Bill of Rights are in the nature of civil and political rights, and not even all the civil and political rights contained in the ICCPR. Thus Boston teachers' definitions of human rights education are much more limited than those provided by Melbourne teachers, since the latter tend not to restrict HRE to civil and political rights.

---

[81]  Survey respondent B18. Transcript on file with author.
[82]  Interviewee B19. Transcript on file with author.
[83]  Interviewee B22. Transcript on file with author.

It is not surprising that CROC did not feature in teachers' definitions of HRE, given that the United States is one of only two States not to have ratified this treaty. Until such time as CROC is legally binding in the United States, it is unlikely to inform educators' understanding of HRE.

### C  Civil rights versus human rights

Linked to this reliance by Boston teachers on domestic instruments, such as the Bill of Rights, is an equating of civil rights with human rights. For many Boston teachers, human rights and civil rights are one and the same. The following extract from an interview with a Boston teacher exemplifies this.

> *Interviewer*:  So how do you see the connection between civil rights and human rights?
> *Teacher*:  They are the same thing. If you're not respecting someone's civil rights, you're violating their human rights. If you don't allow them to vote, to practise the religion they choose, to wear the headdress that their religion calls for, you're violating their human rights.[84]

On the other hand, some teachers misconstrue the two, as demonstrated in the following statement from a Boston teacher:

> Human rights are a little more general, maybe a little more like the most basic of rights. And then civil rights are more the laws that go to back up these human rights.[85]

This confusion between civil rights and human rights resulted in Boston teachers having a narrow definition of HRE that excluded a large section of human rights, particularly ESC rights. The majority of teachers gave as examples of HRE, their lessons on Martin Luther King, free speech and slavery. This is in stark contrast to Melbourne teachers, who generally included ESC rights in their definitions of HRE and gave examples of lessons on Aboriginal reconciliation, the 'Rugmark' label,[86] and the Fairwear campaign.[87]

Those Boston teachers who did see a distinction between civil rights and human rights made an interesting distinction between the two. A number of teachers expressed views similar to that voiced by the following teacher:

---

[84]  Interviewee B30. Transcript on file with author.
[85]  Interviewee B18. Transcript on file with author.
[86]  Rugmark is a global non-profit organisation working to end illegal child labour through encouraging consumers to buy carpets with the Rugmark label, which guarantees that no child labour was used in the manufacture of the carpet.
[87]  This is an initiative that aims to end the exploitation of outworkers in the Australian clothing industry.

People know about civil rights and social justice and racism and equality, but the concept of human rights seems to be something that happens 'over there'. Something that happens in Africa or Iraq.[88]

Thus, there were a number of Boston teachers who did not perceive HRE as relating to events or circumstances within America. It is difficult to have widespread HRE across schools if the very people entrusted with delivering it do not understand one of the fundamental principles of human rights, namely that they are universal, and apply as much to people living in the United States as people living in every other part of the world.

### D  Positive versus negative definitions of HRE

Another way of analysing teachers' definitions of HRE is to classify their responses according to whether they consider HRE in negative terms – that is, violations of human rights, for example genocide, slavery, torture – or whether they viewed human rights in more positive terms – that is, empowering students to become aware of and defend human rights. The following quotes highlight this distinction.

### (i) Negative definitions

*Teacher 1*: I would consider human rights education to mean teaching people about human rights violations throughout history and throughout the world. I would define human rights violations as any instance in which a group of people are singled out and attacked (may include imprisonment, torture, killing, genocide) or just generally denied basic rights (such as freedom of religion.[89]

*Teacher 2*: I'm teaching it from a historical perspective. So looking at various times in history where human rights have been denied to people and trying to address those issues.[90]

*Teacher 3*: We have much dirtier air here than just at the town over, and because of that we have the highest asthma rates in the State. And why? Because they put the trash transfer station in our neighbourhood. Because they put the bus parking lots in this neighbourhood. It's unequal. . . . Teaching human rights is first making students aware that the situations they are living in are not by accident, that decisions were made that placed their health or their welfare in jeopardy by the government or big business, and they need to be aware of those forces.[91]

---

88  Interviewee B11. Transcript on file with author.
89  Survey respondent B13. Transcript on file with author.
90  Interviewee B5. Transcript on file with author.
91  Interviewee B20. Transcript on file with author.

### (ii) Positive definitions

> *Teacher 4*: The teaching of human rights is not confined to teaching students about documents which are supposed to give rights to individuals, but about attitudes to others at age specific times, which broaden their concepts not only of rights, but responsibilities. These ideas should be explored and discussed so that a personal philosophy of inclusiveness should be developed.[92]

> *Teacher 5*: To learn about treating people with respect and compassion on a physical and emotional level within the immediate/local and international areas.[93]

> *Teacher 6*: Human rights education to me is being able to impart a sense of responsibility towards other human beings within your community, and to me it is developing strategies that make us able to see that not everything is in black and white, that there are shades of grey and that not everybody is the same, and that we need to respect and understand those differences. So it's breaking down the barriers between different groups so that we can co-exist.[94]

Thus there was no uniformity amongst the ways teachers defined HRE. When these definitions are contrasted with Article 29(1) CROC, it is apparent that the positive definitions bear a closer resemblance to the HRE mandated in that treaty. Article 29 CROC refers to aims, such as '[t]he development of respect for human rights and fundamental freedoms'[95] and '[t]he preparation of the child for responsible life in a free society, in the spirit of understanding, peace, tolerance, equality of sexes, and friendship among all peoples'.[96] Teaching students about past human rights abuses may be a way of achieving these aims, but it is suggested that the positive definitions align more closely with the objectives of Article 29 CROC.

### E  Global versus local definitions of HRE

One area where there was a significant disparity amongst teachers was the geographical breadth of their focus on HRE. Boston teachers in particular tended to define HRE by reference to US constitutional documents and focus therefore on local issues, while the Melbourne teachers took a more global approach. The following excerpts from interviews illustrate this.

> *Melbourne Teacher*: [We] look at in Australia, and worldwide, the trend and the reasons for homelessness. And we pose a question to the students, 'where would

---

[92] Survey respondent M10. Transcript on file with author.
[93] Survey respondent M12. Transcript on file with author.
[94] Interviewee M16. Transcript on file with author.
[95] Article 29(1)(b) CROC.
[96] Article 29(1)(d) CROC.

you prefer to be homeless?' In a developing country, a third world country, or a developed country?[97]

*Boston Teacher*: Americans tend to be very, very nationalistic and see the world from the United States out. So we're concerned with issues here, and we let other people take care of things in their country.[98]

Many more examples could be cited which illustrate how Melbourne teachers tend to think more globally than their Boston counterparts. The quotes above not only ably demonstrate this point, but also illustrate the different focuses that teachers have with regard to HRE. This disparity seems to flow from the above-mentioned emphasis that Boston teachers have on domestic laws rather than international human rights instruments. Melbourne teachers, on the other hand, were more in tune with the notion of universality of rights, and, while not ignoring human rights in Australia, they had a global approach to human rights.

The stark contrast between the definitions of teachers and others may be due to the fact that teachers define HRE in the context in which they are involved, that is, in secondary schools, whereas the UN definition is intended for a much broader audience, that is, it is not necessarily limited to education in the classroom.

Overall the data collected for this research project revealed that there was no common understanding amongst teachers as to what human rights education means or entails. Teachers tended not to define HRE in a way similar to the UN, governments or NGOs, in that they did not frame HRE in legalistic terms, base their understanding on international human rights instruments, or have as their goal creating human rights activists.

## 6   Conclusion

As indicated at the outset, this chapter did not purport to provide a definitive answer to the question: 'What is HRE?' Rather, it has sought to demonstrate that there are numerous understandings of HRE, which vary widely according to the vested interests of the proponent of the definition. They range from broadly consistent definitions at the international level (in Article 29(1) CROC, the UN Decade for HRE and the World Programme for HRE) to conservative and limited proposals from governments, and from activist definitions promoted by the NGO sector to teachers' non-legal interpretations, which relate more to morals and ethics than to international human rights law.

---

[97]   Interviewee M5. Transcript on file with author.
[98]   Interviewee B17. Transcript on file with author.

Thus, the term HRE, although widely used, lacks a clear definition that is universally accepted. The relative newness of HRE as a discipline may be a contributing factor to the lack of consensus regarding what it means, and over time a more harmonious approach to what HRE entails may emerge. But, until that happens, one must ask: what are the consequences of this wide disparity in understanding of what HRE is? There are several effects. First, it provides greater freedom for those working in the field; with no widely endorsed mandate about what HRE is, organisations and individuals have extreme latitude to teach whatever they want and call it HRE. They are not constrained by some prescriptive definition.

The second consequence of the lack of a single definition of HRE is that it makes evaluation problematic. With so many different understandings of HRE it is difficult for a researcher to assess what genuine human rights education activities are taking place. Some teachers may not identify their work as HRE, and therefore choose not to participate in a study of HRE, while others may consider their work to be HRE when it does not actually fit within the definition employed by the researcher.

Finally, this lack of a common understanding of what HRE is should be of concern to the UN, which for the last ten years has made HRE one of its priorities, as evidenced by the proclamation of the Decade for Human Rights Education and the World Programme for Human Rights Education. It has devoted considerable resources to advocating HRE, and yet there remains significant confusion and misunderstanding about what HRE entails. The absence of a common understanding should also be of concern to governments, if only because their inactivity in this area is creating opportunities for NGOs to fill the void with their own more radical definitions of HRE.

This chapter has demonstrated that the term 'human rights education' is more complex than one might initially think, and open to numerous different interpretations. While the UN has repeatedly provided consistent definitions of HRE (in Article 29(1) CROC, and as part of the Decade for HRE and the World Programme for HRE), these definitions do not reflect how HRE is understood by others including governments, NGOs and teachers, who all have varied opinions about what constitutes HRE. Until such time as the UN is able to garner more widespread support for its definition of HRE, human rights education will remain a slogan in search of a definition.

# Index

*Abdulaziz, Cabales and Balkandali v United Kingdom* [1985] 212
Abiew, FW 233
Aboriginal and Torres Strait Islander Peoples 551, 562
abortion 131–2, 360, 477
Acharya, A 446–7
Accra Agenda for Action 184
Ackerman, Bruce 435
Adenauer, Konrad 287
advisory opinions
   African Court on Human and People's Rights 408–9
   Inter-American Court of Human Rights 365–6
   International Court of Justice (ICJ) 300–303, 306, 309–12, 321–2
*Aegean Sea Continental Shelf* case [1978] 312
Afghanistan 218, 228
   Islam and women's rights 457
Africa 106, 190, 321
   Group 13, 497, 499
   human rights *see* African human rights law
   refugees, internally displaced persons 222–3, 227, 230
*African Charter on Democracy, Elections and Governance* 392, 397, 410
*African Charter on Human and Peoples' Rights* (ACHPR) 91, 110, 301, 388, 407, 408, 411–13
   provisions 391–404
*African Charter on the Rights and Welfare of the Child* 399
*African Children's Charter* 394, 399–400, 409
African Commission on Human and Peoples' Rights 49, 126, 388, 411–12
   *African Charter on Human and Peoples' Rights* (ACHPR) 392–404

courts *see* African Court on Human and People's Rights
   Islam 443
   judgment, compliance with 407–8
   monitoring human rights 404–11
   petitions, judicial structure and 406–7
   promotion of human rights 409–11
   structure 404–5
African Committee on the Rights and Welfare of the Child 412
*African Convention on the Conservation of Nature and Natural Resources* 403
African Court on Human and People's Rights 408–9, 410, 412
African Court of Justice and Human Rights 409, 412
*African Cultural Charter* 399
African human rights law 388–413
   *African Charter on Human and Peoples' Rights* (ACHPR) *see* *African Charter on Human and Peoples' Rights* (ACHPR)
   African Commission *see* African Commission on Human and Peoples' Rights
   history 389–91
   monitoring implementation 404–11
   *Universal Declaration of Human Rights* (UDHR) 391, 404
African National Congress 284
African Peer Review Mechanism 410, 412–13
African Union 34
   Constitutive Act 402, 409, 412
   human rights 388, 396–7, 399–400, 404, 406–7, 410–12
*African Youth Charter* 392, 399–400, 410
*Agiza v Sweden* (2005) 247
Agreement on Technical Barriers to Trade 156

aggression, crime of 241, 257, 271, 279, 318
aid *see* international co-operation and assistance; overseas development assistance
AIDS/HIV 55–6, 157–8, 188, 399–400
  UN Joint Programme on HIV/AIDS 125
  *see also* health and healthcare; medicines, affordable
*Airey v Ireland* [1979] 348–9
*Akayesu ats Prosecutor* [1998] 278
Al-Bashir, Omar 34
Algeria 410
al-Hibri, A 457–8
Al-Khasawneh, Judge 303–4
All African People's Conference 390
Allott, Philip 111
Alston, Philip 98, 188–9, 336
*Alzery, Mohammed v Sweden* (2006) 247
*American Convention on Human Rights* 85, 91, 104, 387, 391, 404
  Inter-American Commission on Human Rights (IACHR) 353, 355–9
  Inter-American Court of Human Rights 365–74, 377–9, 381–7
*American Convention on Human Rights in Economic Social and Cultural Rights* 372
*American Declaration on the Rights and Duties of Man* 85, 353, 372, 387, 391, 404
American University 523
amnesties 284–6
Amnesty International
  human rights education (HRE) 555–7, 558
  International Court of Justice (ICJ) 304
  NGOs and human rights 118–19, 129–34, 136
Amor, Abdelfattah 475–6
Anaya, S J 504, 508
An-Na'im, A A 443, 454–5
Annan, Kofi 193, 513
apartheid 260
  General Assembly condemnation 3
  South Africa 7, 83, 131, 285–7
  UN Charter 71, 83

*Arab Charter on Human Rights* 442
Arbour, Louise 273–5
Argentina 246–7, 281, 527
*Armed Activities on the Territory of the Congo* [2005] 301, 302, 304, 308, 310
armed conflict 97, 99
  counter-terrorism 528, 531–2, 533
  emergencies 533
  International Covenant on Economic Social and Cultural Rights (ICESCR) 37, 38, 59, 66, 67, 70
  human rights applying 309–10
  internal 99, 104, 113
  laws and customs 252–3, 277
  military occupation 67
  refugees and displaced persons 215–16, 222–4, 227, 229–30, 234–5, 239
  rules of conduct 231
  women's treatment 202, 205, 206
  World War II *see* World War II
*Armando Alejandre Jr and Others v Cuba* [1999] 85
*Arrest Warrant of 11 April 2000* [2002] 307
*Articles on Responsibility for Internationally Wrongful Acts* 86–90
Asia 222
  East Asia *see* East Asia and human rights
Asian tsunami 133, 226
*Assessing Damage, Urging Action* (Eminent Jurists Panel) 527
asset freezing 29
Association of Southeast Asian Nations 225
asylum seekers 216, 218, 219, 221, 224–7, 230, 233–5, 360
  African human rights 396
  *see also* refugees and displaced persons
*Atlantic Charter* 390
Aung Sang Suu Kyi 435
Australia 62, 77, 179, 237, 527
  human rights education (HRE) 550–54, 560–62, 564–5
  Indigenous peoples 499, 507, 508

*Avena* [2004] 304–5, 322–4, 363
*Awas Tingni v Nicaragua* (2001) 504
*Azapo* [1996] 285
Azikiwe, Nnamdi 389

*Baena Ricardo et al v Panama* (2003) 378
Balkans crisis 229
Bamako Convention on Ban and Management of Hazardous Waste in Africa 403–4
Bangladesh 31
*Bankovic* case 91–2, 93
Barak, Aharon 29
*Barcelona Traction* 317–18
Beijing Platform for Action 201
Belarus 12, 16
Belgium 527
Benenson, Peter 555
Benin 187, 410
Berlin Declaration on Upholding Human Rights and the Rule of Law 526
Berween, M 462
*Beyond the Veil* (Mernissi) 458
Bielefeldt, H 441
Biko, Steve 286
bilateral donors 182–3, 189
Bill of Rights 561–2
*Blanco Romero* (2006) 376
blasphemy laws 14, 475–6
Blitt, R C 444, 461–2
Bolivia 187
Bosnia-Herzegovina 12, 89, 256, 280, 281, 310, 363
*Boyce et al v Barbados* (2007) 380–82
Brah, Avtar 198, 199
Brazil 195
*Breard case* [1998] 322
Brillat, R 339
Brown, Wendy 209, 210
Buddhism 477, 485
*Bueno-Alves v Argentina* (2007) 372
Buergenthal, Thomas 544
Bulgaria 187
Burkina Faso 410
Bush administration 362–4
Buskens, L 441
Buthelezi, Mangosuthu 286
Butler, Judith 209

*Caesar v Trinidad and Tobago* [2005] 382–3
Cambodia 32, 228, 256, 280, 295
Canada 61, 64, 126, 527
    Indigenous peoples 499, 507–8
    Sikh religious symbols 484
CANZUS countries 499, 509
capital punishment *see* death sentences
CARE 118, 183
Caribbean States 353, 360, 380–87
Carnegie Endowment for International Peace 548–9
Carothers, Thomas 548–9
*Cartagena Declaration on Refugees* (1984) 227–8
Cassese, Antonio 280–81
Catholic Church 133
Center for Women's Global Leadership 203–4, 207
Central America 228
CERD *see* International Convention on the Elimination of all forms of Racial Discrimination (CERD)
Cerone, John 14
Chad 229
Chang, Wejen 418
Chapman, A 51
*Charter of the United Nations see* UN Charter
Chechnya 20
children 3–4, 37, 44, 59, 371
    African human rights 394, 399–400, 412
    child labour 99, 130
    corporal punishment 104–5, 340, 553
    crimes 259
    discrimination *see under* discrimination
    economic, social and cultural rights 80–81
    education 292, 544–7, 553–4
    extradition 244
    healthcare 188, 292, 351
    human rights education (HRE) 544–7, 551–4, 556–7
    Islam 442
    minors 360, 363
    parents 479–80, 556
    religion and beliefs 479–80, 486
    *see also* Convention on the Rights of the Child (CRC)

Chile 282, 291–2, 368–9
China 26, 28, 31, 185, 195
    political economy and human rights
        414, 418–19, 421, 424–6,
        428–30, 436–8
    refugees 218, 223, 224
Christianity 133, 468, 477, 480, 490
    religious dress 482
civil and political rights 37, 40, 46–7,
        69, 73–4
    *European Convention on Human
        Rights* (ECHR) *see European
        Convention on Human
        Rights* (ECHR)
    human rights education (HRE) 542,
        545, 550, 556, 558–9, 561–3
    *International Covenant on Civil and
        Political Rights* (ICCPR) *see
        International Covenant
        on Civil and Political Rights*
        (ICCPR)
    NGOs 131–3
    refugees 216, 222
    transitional justice 273–5, 284
civil war *see* armed conflict
Clause, Vaclav 421
*Code of Conduct on Transnational
    Corporations* 150
CODEPU 291–2
codes of conduct 129–30, 135–6, 150
Cold War 2, 3, 115, 118, 122, 222, 254,
        276, 340, 350
    religion and beliefs 473
*Collective Complaints Protocol*
        339–40, 341–2
collective rights of Indigenous peoples
    *see under* Indigenous peoples
Colombia 361, 527
colonialism 3, 7, 205, 206
    de-colonisation *see* de-colonisation
    human rights education (HRE) 552
    Indigenous peoples 507–10
Combahee River Collective 198
command responsibility 263–4
Commission on Human Rights 1, 6–9,
        10, 26, 28, 80, 92
    counter-terrorism 514, 517, 518,
        521–4, 526, 538, 539
    country-specific mandates 7–8, 9,
        12

    criticised 9, 12–13
    development, right to 176, 186–7,
        194
    International Court of Justice (ICJ)
        299, 304, 306
    Indigenous peoples 496–7
    internally displaced persons 228–9
    multinational corporations 152–3
    NGOs 125
    socio-cultural imperatives 445–6
    Sub-Commission *see* Sub-
        commission on Promotion and
        Protection of Human Rights
Commission on the Status of Women
        204–5, 207
Committee against Torture *see under
    Convention against Torture and
    other Cruel Inhuman
    or Degrading Treatment* (CAT)
Committee of Ministers *see under*
    Council of Europe
Committee on Elimination of
    Discrimination against Women
    *see under Convention on the
    Elimination of all forms of
    Discrimination against Women*
    (CEDAW)
Committee on the Rights of the Child
    *see under Convention on the
    Rights of the Child*
    (CRC)
communitarianism 421–2
compulsory licences 157–60
Conaghan, Joanne 210, 213
Conference on Security, Stability,
    Development and Cooperation
    412
Confucianism 417, 418, 419, 420, 421
*Congo v Rwanda* [2006] 318
*Constitution of the Republic of South
    Africa* 55
*Constitution of the United States* 460
*Constitutional Court* (1999) 368
constitutionalism and human rights
    414–16, 430–39
Constructivist school 122
*Convention against Torture and other
    Cruel Inhuman or Degrading
    Treatment* (CAT) 3, 23,
    25–6, 108, 242, 249

Index    571

Committee against Torture   84, 108–9, 247
  Optional Protocol   26
  *see also* torture
*Convention for the Elimination of Mercenarism in Africa*   403
*Convention for the Protection of All Persons from Enforced Disappearance*   4, 15, 23
  *see also* disappearances, enforced
*Convention Governing Specific Aspects of Refugee Problems in Africa*   227, 228, 396
  *see also* refugees and displaced persons
*Convention on Mutual Assistance in Criminal Matters* (Council of Europe)   248
*Convention on Mutual Assistance in Criminal Matters* (European Union)   248
*Convention on the Elimination of all forms of Discrimination against Women* (CEDAW)   3, 23, 25–6, 313, 399–400
  Committee on Elimination of Discrimination against Women   45, 304
  Optional Protocol   26
  *see also* women; women *under* discrimination
*Convention on the Prevention and Combating of Terrorism*   403
  *see also* terrorism
*Convention on the Privileges and Immunities of the UN*   306
*Convention on the Prohibition of Anti-Personnel Mines and their Destruction*   122
*Convention on the Rights of the Child* (CRC)   3–4, 23, 313, 371, 399–400
  Committee on the Rights of the Child   81, 483–4, 544–7
  extraterritorial obligations   79, 80–81
  human rights education (HRE)   543–7, 549–54, 556–60, 562, 564–6
  International Court of Justice (ICJ)   301, 302, 308

non-state actors   101, 125
  *Optional Protocol on the Involvement of Children in Conflict*   301
  United States   562
  *see also* children
*Convention on the Rights of Persons with Disabilities* (CRPD)   4, 12, 15, 23, 400
  extraterritorial obligations   79, 81–2, 95
  *see also* disabled persons
*Convention on the Settlement of Investment Disputes*   146
*Convention on the Transfer of Sentenced Persons*   250
*Convention 107 on Indigenous and Tribal Populations*   496
*Convention 169 on Indigenous Peoples*   496, 504–5
*Convention Relating to Status of Refugees*   396
  definition of refugee   216–17, 219–24, 226, 231
Cooper, Davina   208, 210
corporal punishment   104–5, 340, 382–3, 553
corruption   52, 249, 424–5, 436
*Corruption Convention*   249
Costa Rica   367–8
Council of Europe   241, 244, 248, 326–52
  Committee of Ministers   330–31, 336, 338, 339
    counter-terrorism   527–8, 539
  European Committee on Social Rights   337–40, 341, 351
  *European Convention on Human Rights* (ECHR) compared   340–42
  European Convention on Human Rights (ECHR) *see* European Convention on Human Rights (ECHR)
  European Social Charter   336–42
    Collective Complaints Protocol   339–40, 341–2, 349
    original structure   337–8
    shortcomings   346
    Turin Amending Protocol   338–9

future protection of human rights 342–51
goals 326–7
guidelines 537
Parliamentary Assembly 329, 338, 347
religion and beliefs 476
Council of the European Union 251
Council of the League of Nations 322
counter-terrorism and human rights 512–40
  establishing proper counter-terrorist measures 537–9
    prescription by law 537
    scope of prescription 538–9
  human rights compliance, nature of 529–36
    derogable rights in emergencies 532–5
    non-derogable rights under human rights treaties 531–2
    other rights 535–6
    peremptory rights at customary international law 530
  requirement to comply with human rights 512–29
    General Assembly 515–17, 518
    Human Rights Council and former Commission on Human Rights 521–6
    international guidelines and documents 526–9
    Security Council 517–21
Counter-Terrorism Committee 519–21
country-specific measures 7–8, 9, 12, 15–16, 17, 18
courts
  African Court on Human and People's Rights 408–9, 410, 412
  African Court of Justice and Human Rights 409, 412
  counter-terrorism and human rights 512
  domestic 55, 281–2, 307
  European Court of Human Rights *see* European Court of Human Rights
  European Court of Justice *see* European Court of Justice
  Inter-American *see* Inter-American Court of Human Rights
  international 72, 146, 488
    criminal *see* international criminal courts and tribunals
  International Court of Justice (ICJ) *see* International Court of Justice (ICJ)
  International Criminal Court (ICC) *see* International Criminal Court (ICC)
  internationalised courts and tribunals 256, 280–81
  Islamic 442
  Permanent Court of Justice 312, 322–3
  regional *see under* regional human rights bodies
  right of access to *see* fair hearing
South Africa 55
*Covenant of the League of Nations* 311
Craven, M 40
Crenshaw, Kimberlé 200, 201, 203, 206–7
crimes against humanity 32, 34, 112, 241–2, 253–4, 257–8, 266
  definition of 260–61, 263
  sexual offences 277–80
criminal law 34, 148, 241–71, 531
  international 242, 252–69
    cooperation with States 268–9
    criminal procedure 267–8
    history of international prosecutions 252–8
    substantive law 258–66
      defences 264–6
      definition of crimes 258–61
      individual criminal responsibility 261–4
  transnational 241, 243–52
    European Arrest Warrant 251–2
    international legal cooperation 243–52
      extradition 243–8, 249, 258, 270
      mutual legal assistance 248–9
      transfer of proceedings and penalty enforcement 249–50

Index 573

see also International Criminal Court (ICC)
cruel, inhuman or degrading treatment see torture
Cuba 16, 20, 85, 362
*Cumaraswamy* [1999] 306
custody see prisoners
customary international law and norms 242, 305, 316–17
   counter-terrorism 514, 528, 530, 531, 538
   diplomatic protection 87–8
   General Assembly resolutions 6
   genocide and crimes against humanity 260
   hard law, as 517
   human rights 100
   Indigenous peoples 498
   individual criminal responsibility 262, 264
   international crimes 146, 242
   Millennium Development Goals 189
   NGOs 127
   non-derogable rights 531–2, 536
   racial discrimination 530, 538
   resolutions 517
   treaty law 311
   *Universal Declaration of Human Rights* (UDHR) 2
Cyprus 85
Czech Republic 60, 100, 421
Czechoslovakia, former 222, 292

*Dahlab v Switzerland* [2001] 212, 489
*Dann v United States* (2002) 503
Darfur 13, 34, 229
De Feyter, K 447, 448
death penalty 25, 322–4, 360, 380–82, 394
de-colonisation 223, 227, 321, 500, 507–9
   see also colonialism
debt 53, 65
   right to development 171, 177, 182, 185–6
*Declaration for Promotion of Employment and Poverty Alleviation* 399
Declaration of Independence 561

*Declaration of Principles on Freedom of Expression in Africa* 395
   see also freedom of expression
*Declaration of the Rights of Persons Belonging to National or Ethnic, Religious and Linguistic Minorities* 401–2, 502
Declaration of the Security Council meeting with Ministers of Foreign Affairs 518–19
*Declaration of the Vienna Conference on Human Rights* [1993] 170
*Declaration on Agriculture and Food Security in Africa* 399
   see also food
*Declaration on Elimination of Intolerance based on Religion or Belief* 4, 472–4, 489, 490–91
   see also religion and beliefs
*Declaration on Friendly Relations* 502
*Declaration on Granting Independence to Colonial Countries and Peoples* 3
*Declaration on Indigenous Peoples* (OAS) 496
   see also Indigenous peoples
*Declaration on Principles Governing Democratic Elections In Africa* 397
*Declaration on the Right to Development* 4, 5, 60, 169–70, 173–7
   see also development and human rights
*Declaration on Right and Responsibility of Individuals, Groups and Organs* 448
   see also minorities
*Declaration on the Rights of Indigenous Peoples* (DRIP) 4, 5, 12, 405–6
   history 492, 496–8, 504
   self-determination 499–501, 510–11
   free, prior and informed consent 501–7
   objections to recognising 507–10
   see also Indigenous peoples
*Declaration on TRIPS and Public Health* 158
*Declaration on Unconstitutional Change of Government* 397

defamation of religion 13–14, 475–6
  see also religion and beliefs
*Delalic, Mucic, Delic and Landzo ats Prosecutor* [2001] 277
democracy 295–7, 327, 397–8, 410
  counter-terrorism 525, 527–8, 529, 536
  East Asia in *see under* East Asia and human rights
  human rights education (HRE) 542, 548–9, 551
  Islam 451, 466
  religion and beliefs 476–7, 483
Democratic Republic of Congo (DRC) 13, 16, 304, 402
*Democratic Republic of Congo v Uganda* [2006] 57
*Democratic Republic of the Congo v Burundi, Rwanda and Uganda* [2003] 402–3
demographic changes, religion and 467–8
Denmark 13, 62, 182
Department for International Development, UK 183
detention *see* prisoners
developing States 4, 190
  compulsory licences 157–60
  development
    aid 60–65, 70, 95, 175
    right to 171–2, 175–6, 190–94
  least developed States 51, 159, 190
  *see also* international assistance and cooperation; overseas aid
development and human rights 4, 5, 60, 167–95
  human development, definition of 168
  international law 167–8
  poverty reduction and human rights law 178–89
    Millennium Development Goals 187–9
    poverty reduction strategies 185–7
    States' policies and UN 178–84
  right to development 60, 138, 140, 168
    definition 169–70
    legal basis 169–78

    convention, towards 177–8
    legal commitment to 172–6
    legal status 170–72
  trade and investment, human rights law and 190–94
    international trade 190–93
  welfare models 168
  *see also* Declaration on the Right to Development
development assistance *see* overseas development assistance
Development Assistance Committee 62
*Development Effectiveness in Practice* workshop 184
diplomatic sanctions 28–9
disabled persons 119
  discrimination *see under* discrimination
  *see also* Convention on the Rights of Persons with Disabilities (CRPD)
disappearances, enforced 4, 8, 260, 275, 287, 289, 371, 375
  *see also* Convention for the Protection of All Persons from Enforced Disappearance
discrimination 71, 144, 331, 340
  African human rights 393, 394, 400–402
  *American Convention on Human Rights* 91
  children 45, 47, 101, 473
  counter-terrorism 530, 531–2, 537–8
  disabled persons 4, 45, 400
  economic, social and cultural rights 38, 43, 44–5, 47, 69
  extradition 515
  free, prior and informed consent 501
  International Court of Justice (ICJ) 324
  *International Covenant on Civil and Political Rights* (ICCPR) 91
  intersectional 211–13
  minorities 45, 205, 207, 212, 401–2, 462
    minority faiths 477
  non-citizens 202–3
  non-derogable right, as 531–2

racial  2, 7, 13, 197–205, 318, 360, 530, 538
  apartheid *see* apartheid
  *see also* International Convention on the Elimination of all forms of Racial Discrimination (CERD)
  refugees, displaced persons and 219, 222, 234, 239
  religion and beliefs  4, 13–14, 395, 462, 472–4, 477–9, 490–91
  trade  160–2, 163
  women  3, 45, 47, 170, 184, 188, 197–205, 304, 487–8
  *see also* CEDAW
  *see also* gender and human rights law; transitional justice; women
disease  170
  affordable drugs *see* medicines, affordable
displaced persons *see* refugees and displaced persons
dispute settlements  162–4
*Doha TRIPS Declaration*  158
domestic courts tribunals *see under* courts
domestic violence  107
Dominican Republic  187
dowry killings  107
*Draft of Principles and Guidelines*  539
drugs *see* medicines, affordable
duty to protect  32–3

East Asia and human rights  414–39
  Asian values debate  417–22
    community based arguments 420–22
  constitutionalism and human rights 414–16, 430–39
    empowering role of  430–35
      judicial review  429, 433–4, 438
    indigenisation of  415, 435–9
  democracy 414–15, 417, 419–21, 423–4, 427–8, 430, 432
    constitutionalism and human rights  431–8
  'economic miracle', political economy and  422–30

East Timor  256, 280
*East Timor* case [1995]  318, 321
ECHR *see* European Convention on Human Rights (ECHR)
economic
  globalisation *see* globalisation and human rights
  law  141–3
  sanctions  29–30
Economic Community of West African States  409
Economic, Social and Cultural Council 410
economic, social and cultural rights 36–70, 73–4, 234, 239
  *Convention on the Rights of the Child* (CRC)  3–4, 23, 80–81
  *Convention on the Rights of Persons with Disabilities* (CRPD) 81–2
  development, right to  173
  discrimination *see under* discrimination
  ECOSOC *see* ECOSOC
  *European Social Charter see under* Council of Europe
  human rights education (HRE)  542, 556, 559
  *International Covenant on Economic Social and Cultural Rights* (ICESCR) *see* International Covenant on Economic Social and Cultural Rights (ICESCR)
  justiciability  36, 38, 45, 55–6, 69
  nature of  37, 41
  NGOs  132
  non-derogability  37–8, 66–8
  State obligations under *International Covenant on Economic Social and Cultural Rights* (ICESCR) *see under International Covenant on Economic Social and Cultural Rights* (ICESCR)
    extraterritorial application *see under International Covenant on Economic Social and Cultural Rights* (ICESCR)
  transitional justice  274–5, 284

ECOSOC 6
  Commission on Human Rights 11, 517
  free, prior and informed consent 506
  human rights 6
  NGOs 124, 136–7
Ecuador 187
education 188
  fees 50–51
  globalisation 140, 149
  human rights education (HRE) *see* human rights education (HRE)
  illiteracy 170
  *International Covenant on Economic Social and Cultural Rights* (ICESCR) 37, 41, 43, 44, 47, 48, 53, 66
  religion and beliefs 479–80, 485, 489
  women 202, 275, 292, 457
Egypt 441, 527
Eichmann, Adolf 246–7, 248
Eide, A 74
El Salvador 368–9
*Elmi v Australia* [2000] 108–9
Elster, Jon 434
emergencies 133, 227, 229, 234
  counter-terrorism 526, 527, 528, 531–5
  derogable rights, in 532–5
    determining existence of emergency 533–4
    permissible extent of derogating measures 535
    proclamation and notice of 534
    review of 534
  *International Covenant on Civil and Political Rights* (ICCPR) 532–5
  *International Covenant on Economic Social and Cultural Rights* (ICESCR) 21, 38, 66, 67–8, 70
  non-derogable rights under human rights treaties 531
Eminent Jurists Panel on Terrorism, Counter-Terrorism and Human Rights 527
Emmerson, Donald 427

enforcement of human rights 1–2, 26–34
  Commission on Human Rights 7–8
  costs 33–4
  diplomatic and economic sanctions 28–30
  military force 30–33
  naming and shaming 26–8
  state sovereignty 1–2, 35
  UN Security Council 2, 30–33
Entelis, J 452
environment 68, 117, 130, 403–4
  damage to 99, 149, 170
  development, right to 184, 188, 194
  pollution 106, 139
  World Trade Organization (WTO) 163, 164
equality *see* discrimination; gender and human rights law; women
*erga omnes* obligations 317–18, 321
Eritrea Ethiopia Claims Commission 310
Ertok, Yakin 205–6
Ethiopia 317, 389
ethnic cleansing 32, 319
Europe, religion and beliefs in 477, 479, 480, 481, 490
European Arrest Warrant 243, 244–6, 251–2
European Commission 251, 528
European Commission on Human Rights 328, 484, 485
European Committee on Social Rights *see under* Council of Europe
*European Convention on Human Rights* (ECHR) 47, 104, 246, 391
  content and supervision 328–31
  counter-terrorism 528, 533
  derogation provisions 533
  European Committee on Social Rights, compared 340–42
  European Court *see* European Court of Human Rights
  extraterritoriality 91–3, 94, 307–9
  gender 212, 270–71
  Islam 443
  origins 327–8
  reform needed 342–6
  religion and beliefs 476–7, 478, 485, 486

*European Convention on the International Validity of Criminal Judgments* 250
*European Convention on Transfer of Proceedings in Criminal Matters* 250
European Court of Human Rights 270–71, 341
  counter-terrorism 526, 527–8
  derogation provisions 533
  discrimination 212
  extraterritorial obligations 82, 85, 86, 88, 91–2, 94
  Islam 451
  judgments, compliance with 329–31
  non-state actors 104–5, 126
  prescription by law 537
  reform proposals of Group of Wise Persons 342–6
  religion and beliefs 472, 477, 480, 483, 486, 488, 489
  role and constitution 328–31
  socio-economic rights 348–9
  workload and Protocol No 14 331–6, 342–5
European Court of Justice 146
*European Extradition Convention* (1957) 244
European Parliament 482
*European Roma Rights Centre v Italy* [2005] 340
*European Social Charter see under* Council of Europe
European Union 29, 63–4
  asylum system 238–9
  cooperation in criminal matters 241, 245, 248, 251–2
  Indigenous peoples 496
  Islam 450
  non-state actors 97
  trade bans 162
Evans, Malcolm 491
expert groups *see under* NGO and human rights 120–21
expression *see* freedom of expression
extradition 243–8, 249, 251–2, 258, 270, 515
extraordinary rendition 247
  *see also* counter-terrorism and human rights

extraterritorial obligations 71–96, 307–9
  content 73–5
  current international approach 94–6
  counter-terrorism 515
  legal foundation 75–86
    *Convention on the Rights of the Child* (CRC) 79, 80–81
    *Convention on the Rights of Persons with Disabilities* (CRPD) 79, 81–2, 95
    human rights treaties 82–6
    *International Covenant on Economic Social and Cultural Rights* (ICESCR) 56–66, 70, 74–5, 79–80
    UN Charter 76–9, 95
  obstacles to recognition 86–94
    jurisdictional 90–94
    State responsibility 86–90
    States' concern about human rights development 93–5, 96
ExxonMobil 129–30

Fair Labour Association 130, 136
fair trial, right to 46–7, 85, 279, 328
  access to 47, 294
  African human rights 395
  international criminal law 245, 253, 263, 265, 267–8, 271
  limitation of 535–6
  terrorism 535–6
feminism 196–200, 213–14
  *see also* gender and human rights law; women
*Final Declaration of Regional Meeting for Africa* 411
*Five Pensioners v Peru* (2003) 369
food 75, 139, 304, 399
  hunger 170, 188
  *International Covenant on Economic Social and Cultural Rights* (ICESCR) 8, 13, 37, 42, 48, 66
Food and Agriculture Organization 49
foreign aid *see* overseas development assistance
foreign direct investment *see under* trade and investment
*Forgotten Prisoners, The* 555
Foster, Michelle 220–21, 237

578  *Research handbook on international human rights law*

Fourth World Conference on Women 196
fragmentation of international law 141–3
France 31, 61, 337
   kidnap of French journalists 481
   laws on religious dress 482–3
Frankovits, Andre 179
free, prior and informed consent 492, 501–7
freedom of expression 13–14, 328, 355, 395, 475–6, 562
freedom of information 395–6
freedom of religion *see under* religion and beliefs
Freeport McMoRan 129–30
*Frontier Dispute, Case Concerning* [1986] 321–2
Frye, Marilyn 198
Fukuyama, Francis 419
fundamentalism 467, 490
   secular 489

*Gabcikovo-Nagymaros* case [1997] 312
Gamliel, Rabban Shimon ben 297
gender and human rights law 196–214
   evolvement of intersectionality 197–201
   global ascendancy of intersectionality 201–6
   intersectionality, meaning of 196–7
   problems with intersectionality 206–13
   *see also* discrimination; transitional justice; women
gender-based offences *see* transitional justice
*General Act for the Pacific Settlement of International Disputes* 312
*General Agreement on Tariffs and Trade* 155, 160–62
*General Agreement on Trade in Services* 155
General Assembly 4, 5
   apartheid 3
   counter-terrorism 512, 513, 515–18, 523–4, 526, 535, 538
   derogating provisions 535
   development, right to 170, 173, 174
   economic, social and cultural rights 36, 38, 53, 58, 61, 67, 69, 80

   gender 197
   human rights 5–6, 32–3
   Human Rights Council 11–12
   human rights education (HRE) 546, 548
   Indigenous peoples 492, 496, 497, 500
   refugees and internally displaced persons 220, 223, 224, 229
   religion and beliefs 472, 475
*General Comment 1 on the Aims of Education* 544–7, 549–50, 554, 557, 559–60
*General Comment 28 on Equality of Rights* (HRC) 201
'general exceptions' and import restrictions (WTO) 160–62
*General Recommendation XXV on Gender Related Dimensions of Racial Discrimination* (CERD) 202
*General Recommendation XXX on Discrimination* (CERD) 202–3
genetic drugs 157–9
*Geneva Conventions* (1949) 231, 277, 364
   International Court of Justice (ICJ) 305, 319–20
   international criminal law 254–5, 261, 263
genetically modified organism 162
genocide 89–90, 206
   definition 258–61, 263, 319–20
   International Court of Justice (ICJ) 301–2, 318, 319–20
   international criminal law 241–2, 254, 257–8, 266
   *jus cogens* 145
   transitional justice and gender 278
   UN 19, 31, 32
*Genocide* case 88, 89–90, 301–2, 310, 320
*Genocide Convention* 258–9, 310, 317, 319–20
Germany 59, 252–3, 273, 287, 290, 336, 455, 543
Ghana 410, 509
Ginsberg, Tom 434
Global Compact 131, 151, 194
*Global Monitoring Report* (2007) 185

globalisation and human rights 42,
    72–3, 115, 139–66, 174
  human rights law
    economic law and fragmentation
      141–3
    position in international law
      144–6
  international economic actors
    human rights obligations 146–8
    nature of 139–41
  multinational corporations 139–41,
    146–7, 149–50
  international law 150–54
  World Trade Organization 140–43,
    154–66
    dispute settlements 162–4
    import restrictions and 'general
      exceptions' 160–62
    trade agreements as barriers:
      TRIPS and right to health
      155–60
*Glucksman v Henkel* [1911] 245
*Goiburu v Paraguay* [2006] 376
Goldman, Dr Robert 523
Grabham, Emily 210–11, 213
Greiff, Pablo de 291
Group of Eight industrialized States 62
Guantanamo Bay 20, 84, 361–5, 512
Guattari, Felix 209
*Guidelines for Multinational Enterprises*
  (1976) 150, 193
Guidelines for National Plans of Action
  for Human Rights Education
  546–8, 549, 557
*Guidelines on human rights and the fight
  against terrorism* 527–8

H&M 130
Hailbronner, Kay 227
Haiti 30, 232, 389
Hampson, Francois 18
*Handbook of Reparations* 291
Hannett, Sarah 211
Hathaway, James 221–2, 237
Havel, Vaclav 100, 292, 421
health and healthcare 74, 351
  AIDS/HIV treatment 55–6
  epidemic disease and drugs *see*
    medicines, affordable
  globalisation 139–40, 149

*International Covenant on Economic
  Social and Cultural Rights*
  (ICESCR) 37, 44, 47, 48, 53,
  66–7
trade bans 162, 163
WHO data 50
women 202, 275, 288–9, 292
*see also* AIDS/HIV; medicines,
  affordable
Heavily Indebted Poor Countries 185–6
Hepple, B 336
Higgins, R 93
*Hilaire, Constantine and Benjamin v
  Trinidad and Tobago* [2002]
  380–81
*Hilf al-Fudul* League 460
Hinduism 490
HIV *see* AIDS
*Hobart Declaration on Schooling in
  Australia* 551
Holmes, Justice 244–5
Holocaust 287, 290, 296
Honduras 88
Hong Kong 224
  political economy and human rights
  417, 433, 434, 436
honour killings 456
housing 74, 139, 292, 340, 399
  ICESCR 37, 48, 53, 66
Howse, Robert 163
human development *see* development
  and human rights
*Human Development Report* 168, 171,
  181
*Human Rights-Based Approach to
  Programming* 181
Human Rights Committee (HRC)
  20–21, 106, 402, 405–6
  counter-terrorism 525, 527, 529,
    531–2, 534–5, 537–8
  emergencies 533, 534–5
  extraterritoriality 82–4, 95, 308
  gender 201, 212
  Indigenous peoples 495, 500–502,
    505, 510
  International Court of Justice (ICJ)
    303, 308
  international criminal law 247, 271
  Islam 443
  non-derogable rights 531–2

religion and beliefs 471–2, 475,
478–80, 484
reservations 314–15
self-determination 500–501, 510
Human Rights Council 1, 6, 9–18, 20,
26, 28, 31
Advisory Committee 14–15
assessment of work 12–14, 18
complaint procedure 16
composition and status 10–12
counter-terrorism 514, 517, 523–6
country-specific measures 8, 15–16,
17, 18
development, right to 177
human rights education (HRE) 548
Optional Protocol to the International
Covenant on Economic Social
and Cultural Rights 12, 53, 69
Indigenous peoples 497
multinational corporations 152–3
NGOs 125
religion and beliefs 490–91
thematic mandates 8
special procedures 15–16, 125
universal periodic review 16–18
Human Rights Council of Australia 179
human rights education (HRE) 541–66
Government definitions 550–54
meanings of 541–3
NGOs definition 554–60
Amnesty International 555–7,
558
Human Rights Education
Associates 557–8
People's Movement for Human
Rights Learning 558–60
teachers' definition 560–66
rule of law 548–50
teachers 560–66
UN definition 543–50
Human Rights Education Associates
557–8
Human Rights Strengthening Programme
181
Human Rights Watch 118, 119, 122–3,
127, 129–30, 136
International Court of Justice (ICJ)
304
humanitarian intervention and assistance
refugees *see under* refugees and
displaced persons

unilateral 31–3, 256
humanitarian law 217, 231–2, 302,
309–10, 317, 361, 364, 531
Hungary 46, 222
hunger *see under* food
Hunt, Paul 186–7
*Huri-Laws v Nigeria* 398
hybrid tribunals *see* internationalised
tribunals

ICCPR *see* International Covenant on
Civil and Political Rights
(ICCPR)
ICESCR *see* International Covenant on
Economic Social and Cultural
Rights (ICESCR)
immigration, mass, and religion 467–8
import restrictions and 'general
exceptions' 160–62
India 31, 195, 509, 527
indigenisation 415, 435–9
Indigenous peoples 4, 5, 8, 106–7, 119,
202, 405–6
collective rights 492, 497, 500, 510
counter-terrorism and human rights
512
discrimination *see* minorities *under*
discrimination
East Asia 435–9
land and land rights 493, 495, 497,
500–505, 507, 509
self-determination 492–511
consent and consulting 501–7
*Declaration on the Rights of*
*Indigenous Peoples* (DRIP)
*see Declaration on the*
*Rights of Indigenous*
*Peoples* (DRIP)
international instruments 493–8
legal dimensions of right
499–501
meaning 492–3
objections to recognising
507–10
*see also Declaration on the Rights of*
*Indigenous Peoples* (DRIP)
individual criminal responsibility
261–4, 270–71
individuals and human rights complaints
8–9, 23–5, 471–2, 500

Indochina 224–6, 236
Indonesia 281, 527
  Islam and human rights 441
  political economy and human rights 417, 431, 432, 434, 435
Inkatha Freedom Party 286
integrated approach to human rights 348–9
intellectual property 42
  TRIPS *see* TRIPS
Inter-American Commission on Human Rights (IACHR) 82, 85, 88, 95, 353–65, 367–70, 387
  complaints system 357–9
  counter-terrorism 528–9, 537, 539
  functions and powers 353–6
    judicial dimension 356
    on-site visits and special reports 354–5
    special rapporteurships 355–6
  Indigenous peoples 503
  terrorism and human rights 360–65
*Inter-American Convention against Terrorism* 528–9
*Inter-American Convention on Forced Disappearances of Persons* 371
*Inter-American Convention to Prevent and Punish Torture* 371
*Inter-American Convention on Prevention of Violence against Women* 371–2
Inter-American Court of Human Rights 104, 126, 304–5, 323, 353, 365–87
  corporal punishment 382–3
  counter-terrorism 526
  death penalty 380–82
  Inter-American Commission on Human Rights (IACHR) 355–6, 359
  Indigenous peoples 504, 506
  judgments, compliance with 377–9
  jurisdiction 365–73
  reparations 373–7, 378
Inter-American human rights system 353–87
  Inter-American Commission on Human Rights (IACHR) *see* Inter-American Commission on Human Rights (IACHR)

Indigenous peoples 496
Inter-American Court *see* Inter-American Court of Human Rights
  origins 353
internally displaced persons *see* refugees and displaced persons
Internally Displaced Persons Guiding Principles 231–5
international assistance and cooperation, 95
  *Convention on the Rights of the Child* (CRC) 79, 80–81
  *Convention on the Rights of Persons with Disabilities* (CRPD) 81–2
  development, right to 182–3
  humanitarian *see under* refugees and displaced persons
  *International Covenant on Economic Social and Cultural Rights* (ICESCR) 39, 56–66, 69–70, 73, 80
  *see also* developing States; overseas development assistance
International Bill of Rights, The 3, 5
International Campaign to Ban Landmines 126
International Commission of Jurists 120, 526
International Committee of the Red Cross 231–2
International Conference on Financing for Development (2002) 62, 183
*International Convention for the Suppression of the Financing of Terrorism* 249, 515
*International Convention on the Elimination of all forms of Racial Discrimination* (CERD) 2–3, 21, 23, 145, 491
  Committee on Elimination of Racial Discrimination 201–3, 491, 495, 530, 538
  Indigenous peoples 495–6, 502, 505
  *see also* racial *under* discrimination
*International Convention on the Protection of the Rights of all Migrant Workers and Members of their Families* (MWC) 4, 23, 25

international co-operation 144, 176
International Court of Justice (ICJ) 41,
    57, 67, 137 258, 544
  counter-terrorism 527
  extraterritorial obligations 71, 82–3,
    84, 86, 88–90, 94
  human rights 299–325
    enforcement 300–307
      assisting the enforcers 305–7
      direct 300–303
      interaction with other
        enforcers 303–5
    normative framework 315–18
      human rights principles,
        normative status of
        317–18
      normative status of
        instruments 315–17
    substantive rights and obligations
      319–24
      genocide 319–20
      life, right to 322–4
      self-determination 320–22
    treaty framework 307–15
      application 307–10
      interpretation 311–13
      reservations 313–15
    *Universal Declaration of Human
      Rights* (UDHR) 300,
      315–16
    UN Charter 300, 311, 312,
      315–17, 321, 324
  status of international economic
    bodies 147
international courts *see* 72, 146, 488
*International Covenant on Civil and
  Political Rights* (ICCPR) 3, 20,
  37, 386, 561
  African human rights law 391,
    394–5, 401–2
  counter-terrorism 529, 531–6
  derogable rights in emergencies
    532–5, 538
  development, right to 175
  extraterritorial application 56, 83,
    91, 92–3, 95, 308–9
  gender 212, 271
  Human Rights Committee (HRC) *see*
    Human Rights Committee
    (HRC)

International Court of Justice (ICJ)
    301, 302, 303, 308–9
  Indigenous peoples 495–6,
    499–502, 510
  non-derogable rights 531–2
  non-state actors 100–101, 110, 124
  Optional Protocol 3, 23, 500–501,
    510
  religion and beliefs 470–72, 491
  self-determination 499–501
  States obligations 46–7
  *see also* civil and political rights
*International Covenant on Economic
  Social and Cultural Rights*
  (ICESCR) 3, 20, 23, 36,
  386, 391, 401
  Art 2(1) 39–56
  Committee on Economic, Social and
    Cultural Rights 20
  economic, social and cultural
    rights 36, 40, 42, 47,
    51–3, 57–64, 66–9
  extraterritorial obligations 74–5,
    80–81, 95
  development, right to 173, 174,
    175–6
  extraterritorial application 37, 38,
    56–66, 70, 74–5, 79–80, 83
  International Court of Justice (ICJ)
    57, 302, 303, 308
  intellectual property 156
  justiciability 36, 38, 45, 55–6, 69
  non-derogability 37–8, 66–8, 70
  Optional Protocol 4–5, 12, 36–7,
    38, 53–5, 58, 60–61, 69
  progressive realisation 38, 42,
    45–51, 55, 56, 58, 59,
    68–9, 398
  scope examined 41–2
  States human rights obligations
    37–8, 39–56
  taking steps by all appropriate
    means 42–5, 68–9
  utilising maximum available
    resources 51–6, 69–70
  self-determination 499
  *see also* economic, social and cultural
    rights
International Criminal Court (ICC) 34,
    242, 256–8, 259–60, 264, 268–9,
    271

jurisdiction 279
*Rules of Procedure and Evidence* 268
Statute 124, 126, 148, 256–7, 259–60, 263–4, 266–8, 279–80
transitional justice and gender 277, 279–80
*see also* criminal law
international criminal courts and tribunals 254–6, 261, 264–5, 268–9, 271
*see also* International Criminal Court (ICC); International Criminal Tribunal for Rwanda (ICTR); International Criminal Tribunal for the Former Yugoslavia (ICTY)
International Criminal Tribunal for the Former Yugoslavia (ICTY) 242, 254–6, 259, 260, 262, 268, 271
transitional justice and gender 273, 276–9, 280
*see also* Yugoslavia
International Criminal Tribunal for Rwanda (ICTR) 88, 242, 248, 254–6, 259, 260, 268, 271
transitional justice and gender 276–9, 280
*see also* Rwanda
International Development Agency, Sweden 183
international economic actors *see under* globalisation and human rights
*International Federation of Human Rights Leagues v France* [2004] 351
international financial institutions 139–43, 177
*see also* globalisation and human rights
International Labour Organisation 49, 138, 150–51, 164, 349, 394
development, right to 177, 191–2, 193–4
Indigenous peoples 496, 504, 505
international law 305, 316
criminal *see under* criminal law
corporations 150–54
customary *see* customary international law

development and human rights in 167–8
economic law 141–3
economic, social and cultural rights 36–7, 75, 82
European legal space 91–2
fragmentation 141–3
gender *see* gender and human rights law
humanitarian 217, 231–2, 302, 309–10, 317, 361, 364, 531
jurisdictional competence of States 65
law of treaties 87
non-state actors 100
peremptory norms *see jus cogens*
International Law Commission 86, 102–3, 142, 315, 530
*Articles on Responsibility for Internationally Wrongful Acts* 86–90
international legal cooperation *see under* criminal law
International Monetary Fund 95, 100, 128
development, right to 177, 185–6
globalisation 140, 141
international NGOs *see* NGOs
International Organization for Standardization 130
international organizations and NGOs 123–8
International Refugee Organisation 223
*International Status of South-West Africa* [1950] 322
international trade and investment *see* trade and investment
internationalised courts and tribunals 256, 280–81
internationally agreed development goals 178–9
intersectionality *see under* gender and human rights
investment *see* trade and investment
Iran 441
Iraq 30, 218, 228, 230, 232
Iraqi based kidnap of French journalists 481
Islam and human rights 441, 463
Ireland 20, 184

Islam and human rights  13–14, 212, 440–66, 477, 490
  adversarial perspective  450–52
  courts  442
  harmonistic perspective  452–4
    advancing in Muslim world  454–65
  Islamic and secular values  480–82
    Islamic dress  481–90
  Organisation of the Islamic Conference (OIC)  442–3, 455, 459
  politico-legal approach to  444, 445, 448–50, 453, 461–5
  religious dress  480–83, 485–90
  role of Islam  440–45
  Sharia law  441–2, 450, 451–2, 455, 457, 463–4
  socio-cultural approach to  444–50, 453–61
  women's rights  441, 445, 452, 456–8, 463–4
    religious dress  487–8
Israel  58, 83, 246–7, 527
  International Court of Justice (ICJ)  302, 304, 308
  transitional justice  290, 296
  UN and human rights  12–13, 28
Italy  215, 216, 332, 340
*Ivcher Bronstein* (1999)  368

Jackson, Justice Robert H  275–6
Jahangir, Asma  475–6
*James Katabaz v Secretary General, East African Community* [2007]  409
Japan  417, 418, 422–3, 425, 433–6, 437
Jehovah's Witnesses  395
Jewish religious dress  482
Johnson, Chalmers  422–3
Johnson, Rebecca  199
joint criminal enterprise doctrine  261–3, 264
*Juan Humberto Sanchez v Honduras* (2003)  371
Judaism  482, 490
Judicial Studies Board, UK  490
*Jurisdiction of the Courts of Danzig* (1928)  322–3

*jus cogens*  145–6, 258, 261, 318, 530

Kang, David  425, 429
Kenya  410, 527
Khmer Rouge  295
Kim Dae-jung  429
Kimberley Process  131
King, Martin Luther  562
*Klass v Germany* (1978)  527–8
Koenig, Shulamith  559
Korey, William  124
Korn, David  228
Kosovo  32, 230, 232, 256, 280
Krasner, Stephen  434
Kurds  30, 228, 230

labour rights *see* work and workers
*LaGrand* case [2001]  322, 323
*Land and Maritime Boundary between Cameroon and Nigeria* [1996]  303
land rights *see under* Indigenous peoples
Landmines Treaty  124, 126
*Las Palmeras v Colombia* [2000]  370
Latin America  11, 272, 285
League of Nations  322
least developed States *see under* developing States
  *see also* developing countries
legal aid  47
*Legality of Nuclear Weapons* [1996]  147
levels of obligations *see under* obligations
Liberia  30, 294, 317, 389
licences, compulsory  157–60
life, right to  85, 139, 156, 328, 393
  death penalty *see* death penalty
  International Court of Justice (ICJ)  309, 322–4
  non-derogable right, as  531
  trade bans  162, 163
Lijphart, Arend  436
*Limberg Principles on Implementation of the International Covenant on Economic Social and Cultural Rights*  41
*Loizidou v Turkey* [1995]  85
*Lopez Burgos v Uruguay* [1981]  83–4
*Lori Berenson* (2004)  368

*Lovelace v Canada* [1981] 212
Luxembourg 62, 182

*Maastricht Guidelines on Violations of Economic Social and Cultural Rights* 41, 74, 175
Madison, James 421
malaria 158, 188, 399
Malaysia 225
  Islam and human rights 441
  political economy and human rights 417, 431, 432, 431, 432, 436
Mali 64
Mandela, Nelson 284, 447
*Mapiripan Massacre* (2005) 371
*Maputo Declaration on Malaria, HIV/AIDS, Tuberculosis* 399
Marcos, Ferdinand 431
margins of appreciation and flexibilty 483, 526, 530, 536
*Marrakesh Agreement Establishing the World Trade Organization* 155
Marxism 419
Matua, Makau 448
Mauritania 321, 394, 403
*Mazilu* [1989] 306
McAdam, Jane 236–7, 238
McBeth, Adam 191, 194
McCall, Leslie 200–201, 206
McCorquodale, Robert 139, 148
medicines, affordable 140, 156–60
  *see also* AIDS/HIV; health and healthcare
Medecins sans Frontieres 118, 183
Mernissi, Fatima 458–9
Mertus, Julie 18–19
Mexico 281, 322
migrant workers *see under* workers
*Migrant Workers Convention see International Convention on the Protection of the Rights of all Migrant Workers and Members of their Families (MWC)*
*Migration Act (1958)* 237
military force sanctions 30–33
Millennium Challenge Account 183
Millennium Declaration 60, 170
Millennium Development Goals 414
  right to development 170–71, 173–4, 176, 184, 187–9

*Minister of Health v Treatment Action Campaign* [2002] 55–6
*Minnesota Protocol* 371
minorities
  counter-terrorism and human rights 512
  discrimination against *see under* discrimination
  Indigenous *see* Indigenous peoples
  non-derogable rights 531
  *see also Declaration of the Rights of Persons Belonging to National or Ethnic, Religious and Linguistic Minorities*
*Model Protocol for a Legal Investigation of Extra-Legal Executions* 371
Modirzadeh, N K 441, 443–4, 452
Moi, Toril 209
*Moiwana Village v Suriname* (2005) 372, 383–5
Mongolia 417, 434
Monterrey Consensus 62
Moon, Secretary-General Ban Ki 18
Morocco 224, 321, 527
  Islam and human rights 441
  Moroccan Family Code 463–4
mothers *see under* women
multinational corporations 72–3, 99, 128–31
  development, right to 190, 193–4
  foreign direct investment 193–4
  globalisation and human rights *see under* globalisation and human rights
  international law 150–54
  South Korea 428
Murphy, M 508–9
Muslim Women Lawyers for Human Rights 460–61
Muslim
  human rights *see* Islam and human rights
  religious dress 480–83, 485–90
mutual legal assistance 514
  *see also* work and workers
Myanmar 13, 27, 122, 123, 129
  sanctions 29

9/11 terrorist attacks 95, 99, 122, 252, 360–61, 468

counter-terrorism 512, 516, 521, 526
*Namibia* Opinion 83, 311–12, 316
*Nationality Decrees Issued in Tunis and Morocco* [1923] 312
NATO 32, 91, 93, 230, 232, 248
natural disasters *see* emergencies
Nazis 220, 253, 258, 273, 469, 482
*Neira Alegria* (1996) 375
Neitzsche, Frederick 514
Nesiah, Vasuki 283, 287
Netherlands 62, 182, 252, 336, 557
    Netherlands Scientific Council for Government Policy (WRR) 449–50, 452, 453, 464–5, 466
    religion and beliefs 485
New Zealand 247
    counter-terrorism 520–21
    Indigenous peoples 499, 508
NGOs and human rights 7, 17, 21, 27, 115–38, 231, 354
    accountability 133–8
    development, right to 183
    feminist 203
    healthcare data 50
    human rights education (HRE) 542, 543, 554–60, 566
    influence and activities 121–33
        NGO-corporate interaction 128–31
        NGO-international organization interaction 123–8
        NGO-NGO interaction 131–3
        NGO-State interaction 121–3
    Islam 443–4, 447, 449, 459–61
    nature of human rights NGOs 118–21
        expert groups 120–21
        service NGOs 120
    role and power 116–18
    *see also* globalisation and human rights; non-state actors
Nicaragua 88, 367
*Nicaragua* case 88–9
Nigeria 195, 389, 392, 398, 410
    Indigenous peoples 504
    Islam and human rights 441, 455
Nike 130
*Nikolic, Dragan ats Prosecutor* (2003) 248

Non-Aligned Movement countries 177
non-derogable rights under human rights treaties 531–2, 536
non-discrimination *see* discrimination
non-state actors 97–114
    activity 99–100
    concepts of human rights 109–12
    definition 97–9
    future developments 112–14
    international economic actors *see under* globalisation and human rights
    international human rights law 100–103
    development of 104–9
    NGOs and human rights *see* NGOs and human rights
Non-governmental organisations *see* NGOs and human rights
*see also* globalisation and human rights
Nordstrom 130
*Norms on the Responsibilities of Transnational Corporations* [2003] 151–3
North American Free Trade Agreement 146
North Korea 29
Northern Ireland 527
Norway 62, 182, 336
Novitz, Tonia 340
Nowak, Manfred 186–7, 401
nuclear weapons 137
*Nuclear Weapons* case [1996] 309
Nuremberg Charter 260
Nuremberg tribunals 148, 253–4, 258, 263, 270–71, 275–6
Nyerere, Julius 390

obligations
    international and transnational *see* extraterritorial obligations
    levels of 48–9, 74
    States *see under* States
Odinkalu, Chidi Anselm 412
O'Donnell, Guillermo 431
Office of the High Commissioner for Human Rights (OHCHR) 17, 18–20, 35, 164, 186–8, 204, 273–4, 293

counter–terrorism and human rights 512, 519, 524–5
human rights education (HRE) 546, 548
right to development 168–9, 173, 179–80
*see also* human rights
official development assistance *see under* overseas development assistance
*Ogoniland* (2001) 403
*OIC Cairo Declaration on Human Rights in Islam* 442
*OIC Covenant on the Rights of the Child in Islam* 442
Open-ended Working Group on the Right to Development 172
*Operational Policy and Bank Procedure 4.10 on Indigenous Peoples* 502–3
*Optional Protocol on the Involvement of Children in Conflict* 301
Organisation for Economic Co-operation and Development 62, 138, 150
  development, right to 177, 182, 184, 193
Organisation of African Unity 227, 388, 390–91, 397, 402
Organization of American States 387
  counter-terrorism 529
  Indigenous peoples 496, 503
  Inter-American Commission on Human Rights (IACHR) 355–6, 359, 360–63
  Inter-American Court of Human Rights 365, 378
*Organisation of the Islamic Conference* (OIC) 13, 442–3, 455, 459
Organisation of Women of Asian and African Descent 199
Osmani, Siddiq 187
Ottawa Process 122
Otto, Dianne 11, 544
Ouguergouz, Fatsah 391, 401
overseas development assistance 60–63, 95, 173–5, 177, 189
  counter-terrorism 512
  official development assistance 182–4
  poverty reduction and human rights law *see under* development and human rights
  *see also* developing States; international assistance and cooperation
Overseas Development Institute 184
Oxfam International 65, 118, 129–30, 133, 183

pacifism 477
Pakistan 12, 363, 441, 509, 527
Palestine 441
  Palestinian Occupied Territory 12, 57, 67, 302, 304, 308
Pan-African Congresses 389–90
Pan-African Parliament 410
Panama 378
parents 479–80, 546, 556
Paris Declaration on Aid Effectiveness 184
Park Chung Hee 428, 429
Peace and Security Council 410, 413
People's Movement for Human Rights Learning 558–60
peremptory norms *see jus cogens*
Permanent Court of Justice 312, 322–3
Permanent Forum on Indigenous Issues 494
Perry, Elizabeth 419
persecution 216, 220–23, 260, 395
  *see also* refugees and displaced persons
'persons of concern' 224, 236
Peru 368
Philippines 417, 431, 433, 434
Phoenix, Ann 198, 199
Pictet, Jean 232
Planned Parenthood Federation of Nigeria 455
Pogge, Thomas 165
Poland 81, 332
political
  asylum *see* asylum seekers
  prisoners 131
  rights *see* civil and political rights
pollution *see under* environment
population 138
Portugal 61, 187, 321, 337

poverty  42, 60, 64, 140, 170, 204, 394
  reduction strategies  185–7
  see also development and human rights
*Practice Note on Human Rights in UNDP*  181
*Principles on Right to Fair Trial and Legal Assistance in Africa*  395
prisoners  68, 131, 202, 203, 260, 395
  conscience, of  555
  contracts  531
  counter-terrorism and human rights  512, 515
  Guantanamo Bay *see* Guantanamo Bay
  pre-trial detention  267, 271
  unacknowledged  531
*Promotion of National Unity and Reconciliation Act* (1995)  284–6
*Proposed American Declaration on the Rights of Indigenous Peoples*  503, 505
prosecutions
  international *see* criminal law; transitional justice
  terrorists  529
*Prosecutor v Akayesu* [1998] 278
*Prosecutor v Furundzija* [2000]  277
*Prosecutor v Kunarac, Kovac and Vukovic* [2002]  277
*Protection of human rights and fundamental freedoms while countering terrorism*  516–17
*Protocol on the Rights of Women in Africa*  393–4, 399–400
*Protocol Relating to the Status of Refugees* (1967)  220, 223
provisional measures
  African Commission on Human and Peoples' Rights  392
  Inter-American Court of Human Rights  366–7, 370
  International Court of Justice (ICJ)  302–3
Przeworski, Adam  427
public
  debate  7–8
  health *see* health and healthcare
  morals  161, 163–4, 485–6
  officials  101–2, 107–9

*Purohit* (2003)  407

'race to the bottom'  191–2
racial discrimination and racism *see International Convention on the Elimination of all forms of Racial Discrimination* (CERD); *see under* discrimination
Rastafarians  395
*Rasul v Bush* (2004)  364
reconciliation  293–7
*Refah Partisi (The Welfare Party) and Others v Turkey* (2003)  451
refoulement  221, 396, 512
regional human rights bodies  19, 24–6, 49, 87–8, 92, 94–5, 143, 271, 299
  regional courts  25–6, 88, 94, 299, 315, 409
  see also Inter-American Court of Human Rights; European Court of Human Rights
refugees and displaced persons  215–40
  *Convention Relating to Status of Refugees*  396
  definition of refugee  216–17, 219–24, 226, 231
  current situation  217–19
  legal and illegal migrants  219, 235
  humanitarian intervention and assistance  217, 230–35
  humanitarian protection, meaning of  216–17, 226–7, 230–33, 236
  UNHCR mandate and humanitarian protection  223–6
  humanitarian role and State responses  235–9
  internally displaced persons  217, 226–30
    development of humanitarian norms  230–35
    Guiding Principles  231–5, 240
  see also UN High Commissioner for Refugees (UNHCR)
religion and beliefs  4, 132–3, 467–91
  common principles under human rights law  477–80
  defamation of  13–14, 475–6

discrimination *see under* discrimination
immigration 467–8
freedom of, legal sources of 469–77
   *Declaration on Elimination of Intolerance based on Religion or Belief* 472–4
   *European Convention on Human Rights* (ECHR) 476–7
   *International Covenant on Civil and Political Rights* (ICCPR) 470–72
   Special Rapporteur 475–6, 478–9, 482, 484, 487–8, 491
      guidelines on religious dress 484–6
   *Universal Declaration of Human Rights* (UDHR) 469–70
Islam and human rights *see* Islam and human rights
non-derogable right, as 531
religious dress, symbols and human rights law 480–90
   criteria for imposing limits on dress or symbols 483–4
   fundamental rights and freedoms of others 486
   public health and safety 484–5
   public morals 485–6
   public order 485
   curbs on religious dress, secularism and Europe 482–3
   international human rights law 487–90
   Islamic and secular values 480–82
reparations 287–92, 373–7, 378, 385, 387
*Reparations for Injuries Suffered in the Service of the United Nations* [1949] 147
Report of the Chilean National Commission on Truth and Reconciliation 282
*Report on Terrorism and Human Rights* 360–61
reservations 313–15

*Reservations to the Genocide Convention* 313–14
*Resolution on Implementation of Recommendations of African Commission* 408
retroactivity 372–3, 531
Rich, Adrienne 198
Riley, Denise 198
Ringrose, Jessica 200
Rio-Tinto 129–30
Robinson, Mary 20, 204
   Guidelines 519–20, 524–5, 537–8
Rodrik, Dani 427
Roht-Arriaza, Naomi 291
Roma 202, 240
Romania 332
*Rome Statute of International Criminal Court see* Statute *under* International Criminal Court (ICC)
Roosevelt, Eleanor 445–6
Roth, Kenneth 127
Rubin, Gayle 213
Rubio-Marin, Ruth 292
Rueschemeyer, Dietrich 428
Ruggie, John 152–3, 154, 164–5, 194, 342
Russia 20, 31, 218, 332, 527
Rwanda 19, 159, 273, 410
   International Criminal Tribunal for Rwanda (ICTR) *see* International Criminal Tribunal for Rwanda (ICTR)

*Sahin v Turkey* (2007) 486
Said, Edward 418
sanctions
   diplomatic 28–9
   economic 29–30
   military force 30–33
   smart 29–30
   travel bans 29
   UN Security Council 2, 29, 30–33, 175
*Saramaka People v Suriname* (2007) 369, 383, 385–7, 504
*Saro-Wiva* (2000) 392
Sartre, Jean-Paul 208
Saudi Arabia 441
Save the Children 133, 183

Schwimmer, Walter 527
Scientology, Church of 477
Scott, Joan Wallach 213
Scully, Gerald 427
Second World War *see* World War II
secularism 461–2, 463
   Islamic and secular values 480–90
   neutrality 488–9
Security Council
   counter-terrorism 513–14, 517–21, 524, 526
   gender 196, 278, 293–4
   human rights 2, 5
   international criminal tribunals 254, 255, 256, 269, 277–80
   non-state actors 112–13
   Organisation of the Islamic Conference (OIC) 442
   permanent members 31
   refugees 228, 230, 232
   sanctions *see under* sanctions
self-defence 32
self-determination 320–22, 385, 390, 401–2
   Indigenous peoples, for *see under* Indigenous peoples
Senegal 53
Serbia-Montenegro 30, 89–90, 218, 302
sexual orientation 119, 131–2
sexual violence *see under* women
Sharia law and norms *see under* Islam and human rights
shelter *see* housing
Shelton, Dinah 146
Shestack, Jerome 110
Shue, Henry 74
*Sidabras and Dziautas v Lithuania* [2004] 349
Sierra Leone 30, 256, 280
Sikhism 477, 485, 490
   religious dress and symbols 482, 484, 485, 486
*Silver v United Kingdom* (1983) 537
Simma, Bruno 77–8
Singapore 191–2, 421, 431, 432
*Siracusa Principles* 529, 537, 538
Skogly, Sigrun 140
slavery 118, 124, 197, 205, 260, 318, 328, 562

African human rights 389, 394–5, 409
*jus cogens* 145, 530
non-derogable right, as 531
slave labour *see under* works and workers
smart sanctions 29–30
social security and services 140, 275
   *International Covenant on Economic Social and Cultural Rights* (ICESCR) 37, 53, 59
*Soering v United Kingdom* [1989] 270
soft law 315, 317, 371, 517
Sohn, Louis 144
*Solemn Declaration on Gender Equality in Africa* 400
Somalia 30, 108–9, 218, 232
Sorabi, Habiba 457
South Africa 30, 203, 247, 294, 317
   African human rights 395, 410, 411, 509
   apartheid *see under* apartheid
   justiciability of economic, social and cultural rights 55–6
   truth commission 284–7
South East Asia 481
South Korea 12
   political economy and human rights 417, 425, 428–9, 431, 434, 435
*South West Africa* cases 317
Southern African Development Community 409
special procedures 7–9, 10, 15–16
Special Rapporteur on freedom of religion *see under* religion and beliefs
Special Rapporteur on human rights and indigenous peoples 494
Special Rapporteur on the promotion and protection of human rights 521–3, 537, 539
Stahnke, T 444, 461–2
State sovereignty 1–2, 35, 75, 324
   Indigenous peoples 495, 499–500, 508–9
   international criminal law 256
   Islam 462
   refugees and displaced persons 216, 232–4
   territorial 499–500, 508–9

transnational criminal law 241–2, 244–5, 247, 249
States
   apartheid 3
   decolonised nations in UN 3, 7
   developing *see* developing States
   development, right to 178–84, 189
   *see also* development and human rights
   economic, social and cultural rights *see* economic, social and cultural rights
   extraterritorial obligations *see* extraterritorial obligations
   genocide 320
   Group of Eight 62
   Heavily Indebted Poor Countries 185–6
   human rights 2–5, 10, 15, 19–20
      concern about development 93–5, 96
      country-specific situations 7–8, 9
      enforcement *see* enforcement of human rights
      individuals, complaints from 8–9, 23–5
      NGOs 117–18, 121–3
      treaty bodies and state reports 21–2, 61–2
      universal periodic review 16–18
   human rights education (HRE) 542, 543, 548, 550–54, 557, 560, 562, 566
   *International Covenant on Civil and Political Rights* obligations *see under International Covenant on Civil and Political Rights* (ICCPR)
   *International Covenant on Economic Social and Cultural Rights* (ICESCR) obligations *see under International Covenant on Economic Social and Cultural Rights* (ICESCR)
   Indigenous peoples 492–3, 495, 497–8, 508–10
   international legal cooperation *see under* criminal law
   jurisdictional competence 65
   Non-Aligned Movement 177

officials, public 101–2, 107–9
refugees and displaced persons 216–19, 222, 225–6, 230, 234–9
religion and beliefs 471–2, 475–6, 478–80, 489–91
sovereignty *see* State sovereignty
terrorism *see* counter-terrorism and human rights
*Statute of the International Court of Justice* 41
*Statute of the Office of the United Nations High Commissioner for Refugees* 223–4
Stiglitz, Joseph 65
*Street Children, The v Guatemala* (1999) 370–71, 375
*Strengthening the UN: An Agenda for Further Change* 179–80
Sub-Commission on Prevention of Discrimination and Protection of Minorities 496–7
Sub-Commission on the Protection and Promotion of Human Rights 151–2, 521–2, 539
sub-Saharan Africa 157
Sudan 16, 31, 129, 187, 224, 229, 273, 395
   Islam and human rights 441
   President, indictment against 34
Suharto, President 432, 435
*Sunday Times v United Kingdom* (1978) 537
Suriname 383–7
sustainable development 548–50
Sweden 62, 182, 247
   International Development Agency 183
Switzerland 336

Taiwan 417, 428–9, 434, 435
Tanzania 31, 390
tariffs 155, 160–62
*Tehran Hostages* case 315
territorial sovereignty *see under* State sovereignty
terrorism 112–13, 117, 403, 452
   counter-terrorism *see* counter-terrorism and human rights
   criminal law, and 244, 247, 249

emergency, as 533–4
Inter-American Commission on
  Human Rights (IACHR)
  360–65
9/11 see 9/11 terrorist attacks
religion and beliefs 468
*Terrorism and Human Rights* 515
Thailand 417, 428, 434, 436
*The Veil and the Male Elite* (Mernissi)
  458–9
Third High Level Forum on Aid
  Effectiveness 184
*Third Report on the Situation of Human
  Right in Colombia* 361
'threat to peace' 232
Timor-Leste 12
  see also East Timor
Tokyo tribunals 148, 253–4, 258, 263,
  276
Tomuschat, Christian 83–4
torture 26, 87–8, 149, 236, 328, 371,
  394
  counter-terrorism and human rights
    512, 530
  Guantanamo Bay see Guantanamo
    Bay
  international criminal law 242, 247,
    260
  non-derogable right, as 531
  transitional justice 275, 287, 291
  see also Convention against Torture
    and other Cruel Inhuman or
    Degrading Treatment (CAT)
trade and investment
  development, right to 167–9, 171,
    174, 176, 177
    legal regimes and human rights
      law 190–94
  dispute settlements see dispute
    settlements
  foreign direct investment 190, 191,
    193–4
  General Agreement on Tariffs and
    Trade 155, 160–62
  General Agreement on Trade in
    Services 155
  TRIPS 155–60
trade unions and members 3, 97, 106,
  138, 149, 328
transitional justice 272–98

human rights discourse 273–5
institutional reform 292–4
meaning 271
prosecutions and gender 275–82
  international tribunals 276–9
    ad hoc tribunals 277–9
    domestic tribunals 280–81
    hybrid tribunals 280–81
    ICC 279–80
  reconciliation 293–7
  reparations 287–92
    definition and purpose 287–90
    operational aspects 290–92
  truth commissions 282–7
    definition and purpose 282–4
  see also discrimination; gender and
    human rights law; women
transnational
  corporations see multinational
    corporations
  criminal law see under criminal law
  NGOs 119–20
  obligations see extraterritorial
    obligations
travel bans 29
treaties
  interpreting 39–40
  law of 87
  monitoring 1, 40
treaty bodies 1, 20–26
  complaints processes 23–5
  general comments 22–3
  miscellaneous processes 25–6
  reporting function 21–2
tribal communities, rights of 383–7
Trinidad and Tobago 380–83
*Tripartite Declaration of Principles on
  Multinational Enterprises* (1977)
  151, 193–4
TRIPS (*Agreement on Trade Related
  aspects of Intellectual Property
  Rights*) 155–60
Truth, Sojourner 197–8
Truth and Reconciliation Commission
  284–7
truth commissions 282–7, 299
tuberculosis 158, 399
Tulkens, Judge 487
Tunisia 224
Turkey 85, 332, 441

religious dress 483, 486, 487, 488
Turton, David 226–7
Tutsi women 278
Tutu, Archbishop Desmond 294

UDHR see *Universal Declaration of Human Rights* (UDHR)
Uganda 31, 301, 304, 409, 410
Ukraine 332
UN
 *Charter of the United Nations see* UN Charter
 counter-terrorism 530
 expulsion from 28
 General Assembly *see* General Assembly
 High Commissioner 13
 human rights education (HRE) *see under* human rights education (HRE)
 human rights *see under* human rights
 Indigenous peoples 492, 493–6
 judicial organ *see* ICJ
 NGOs 120, 123, 124
 non-discrimination 71
 *Organisation of the Islamic Conference* (OIC) 442
 overseas aid 62–3
 privileges and immunities 306
 purposes 144
 religion and beliefs 489, 491
 role 76, 78
 Secretary-General 8, 18
 Security Council *see* Security Council
 special rapporteurs 306
UN Charter 1, 144–6
 Art 1(3) 1, 2, 76, 144
 Art 2(7) 232
 Art 10 517
 Art 25 519
 Art 39–42 232
 Art 55 1, 2, 76–8, 173, 316, 518
 Art 56 1, 2, 76–8, 173, 316
 Art 62 6
 Art 68 6
 Art 71 124
 Art 103 145
 Charter bodies 5–19, 20
 counter-terrorism 517, 518
 criticised 76
 development, right to 173, 174, 179
 extraterritorial obligations 76–9, 95
 human rights 2, 17
  ICJ *see under* ICJ
 human rights education (HRE) 545
 Indigenous peoples 500
 internally displaced persons 229
 international criminal tribunals 254, 256, 269
 military force 30
 non-discrimination 71, 78
 universalism 71
UN Children's Fund 180, 181
*UN Common Understanding on a Human Rights Based Approach* 180–81
UN Conference on Human Settlements (1996) 125
UN Conference on Trade and Development (UNCTAD) 177, 193
UN Decade for Human Rights Education 541, 546–7, 549, 556, 559–60, 565–6
UN Development Fund for Women 180
UN Development Programme 168, 171, 173, 180, 181, 188
UN Division for Advancement of Women in Zagreb, Croatia 203, 206
UN Division of Human Rights 177
UN Educational, Scientific and Cultural Organization (UNESCO) 49
*UN Global Compact see* Global Compact
UN Global Terrorism Strategy 512–15
UN High Commissioner for Human Rights *see* Office of the High Commissioner for Human Rights (OHCHR)
UN Inter-Agency Standing Committee 229
UN Joint Programme on HIV/AIDS 125
UN Millennium Summit 170–71
*UN Norms on the Responsibilities of Transnational Corporations* [2003] 151–3
UN Population Fund 180

*UN Resolution on Integration of Human Rights of Women* (2002)   205
UN Secretary-General   8, 18, 152, 306
   counter-terrorism   513, 534
   development and human rights   179, 193–4
   human rights education (HRE)   548
   refugees and displaced persons   225, 228
   Report on Women, Peace and Security   275, 278, 296
UN Security Council *see* Security Council
unilateral humanitarian intervention   31–3
United Kingdom   31, 60, 122–3, 247, 270, 336, 527
   Department for International Development   183
   feminism and racism   198–9
   Judicial Studies Board, religious dress and   490
   refugees and displaced persons   237–8
United Nations *see* UN
United Nations High Commissioner for Refugees (UNHCR)   217–20, 222–6, 231, 235–40
   *see also* refugees and displaced persons
United States   29, 31, 77, 88–9, 93, 122, 130, 247, 527
   development, right to   183, 187
   Guantanamo Bay *see* Guantanamo Bay
   teachers and human rights education (HRE)   560–65
   Indigenous peoples   499, 508
   international courts and tribunals   270, 280, 322, 324
   Islam   452, 460–61
   9/11 *see* 9/11
   Sikh religious symbols   484
*Uniting against Terrorism*   513
Universal Declaration of Human Rights (UDHR)   109, 124
   African human rights *see under* African human rights law
   development, right to   175
   human rights education (HRE)   543, 557, 560

International Court of Justice (ICJ) *see under* International Court of Justice (ICJ)
intellectual property   156
nature of rights recognised   2, 37
non-discrimination   71
refugees   220–21
religion and beliefs, freedom of   469–70
UN and human rights   1–3, 5, 17, 18, 34
   UN Charter   144–5
universalism   71
universality of human rights   110, 144, 411, 440
   counter-terrorism   530
   extraterritorial obligations   71, 76–8, 94, 96
   gender and human rights law   220, 223
   human rights education (HRE)   545, 550
urban development   125
Uruguay Round of trade negotiations   155
USSR, former   481

veganism   477
*Velasquez Rodriguez v Honduras* [1989]   104
*Vienna Convention on Consular Relations*   304–5, 322–4, 366
*Vienna Convention on the Law of Treaties*   311, 313
*Vienna Declaration and Programme of Action* (1993)   2, 60
Vietnam   32, 224, 226, 420
Viljoen, Frans   392, 400
*Viviana Gallardo* (1983)   367–8
*Voluntary Principles on Security and Human Rights*   129–30

*Wall in Occupied Palestinian Territory, The* [2004]   57, 67, 83, 302–4, 308, 310
Wapner, Paul   119, 124
war *see* armed conflict
war crimes   32, 34, 241–2, 253, 257–8, 261, 263, 266
war on terror   95, 360–62

water, right to  61, 66–8, 139–4, 149
Weingartner, L A  464
Weiss, Thomas  228
*welfare models see under* development and human rights
Western Europe and Other Group  13
*Western Sahara* [1975]  321
Williams, Patricia  111–12
women  188, 355
  African human rights law  393–4, 399–400
  discrimination *see Convention on the Elimination of all forms of Discrimination against Women* (CEDAW); *see under* discrimination
  dowry killings  107
  education *see under* education
  gender and human rights law *see* gender and human rights law
  health *see under* health and healthcare
  honour killings  456
  human rights education (HRE)  551
  Islam *see under* Islam and human rights
  Islamic dress  481–4, 486–90
  mothers  37, 44, 188
  NGOs  119, 126, 133, 138
  transitional justice  274–5
  truth commissions  283–4, 287
  violence against  371–2
    domestic  107, 400
    sexual violence  202, 259, 260, 275, 277–80, 284, 287–8
  workers  47, 138, 202, 457
Women's Rights Convention (1851)  197–8
work and workers  37, 74, 77, 128–30
  child labour  99, 161
  development, right to  191, 192, 194
  globalisation  139
  migrant  4, 125, 323, 355
  women *see under* women
  slave and forced labour  149, 161, 328, 394
  trade unions *see* trade unions and members

  *see also International Convention on the Protection of the Rights of All Migrant Workers and Members of their Families* (MWC)
Working Group on Indigenous populations  494, 496–7
Working Group on Women and Human Rights  204–5
World Bank  65, 141, 422
  development, right to  173, 177, 185–7
  Indigenous peoples  496, 502–3, 505
  NGOs and human rights  128, 138
  non-state actors  95, 100
World Conference against Racism, Xenophobia and Related Intolerance  203–4
World Conference on Human Rights  2, 125, 185, 411, 519
World Health Organization  50, 137, 147
*World Health Report 2000*  50
World Jewish Congress  543
*World Organisation Against Torture v Belgium* [2005]  340
World Programme for Human Rights Education  541, 548, 549, 556–7, 559–60, 565–6
World Summit  32–3
World Summit Outcome  514
World Trade Organization (WTO)  100, 128, 136
  China  429–30
  development, right to  177, 190–93
  dispute settlements  162–4
  formation  155–6
  globalisation and human rights *see under* globalisation and human rights
  TRIPS *see* TRIPS
World Vision  133
World War II  217, 220, 231, 253, 258, 276, 326, 469

Yemen  187
Young, Iris Marion  208–9

Yugoslavia, former 273
　International Criminal Tribunal for
　　the Former Yugoslavia (ICTY)
　　*see* International Criminal
　　Tribunal for the Former
　　Yugoslavia (ICTY)

Yuval-Davis, Nira 204, 206–7

Zaire 395, 402
Zalaquett, Jose 282
Zeigler, Jean 75, 82
Zimbabwe 31, 397, 409